TRIED A

BUCKEYE COOKERY

AND

PRACTICAL HOUSEKEEPING.

COMPILED FROM ORIGINAL RECIPES.

" Bad dinners go hand in hand with total depravity, while a properly fed man is already half saved."

TWENTY-FIFTH THOUSAND.

APPLEWOOD BOOKS
BEDFORD, MASSACHUSETTS

Buckeye Cookery and Practical Housekeeping was
originally published by the Buckeye Publishing Company
of Minneapolis, Minnesota in 1877.

Thank you for purchasing an Applewood Book.
Applewood reprints America's lively classics—books from
the past that are still of interest to modern readers.
For a free copy of our current catalog, write to:
Applewood Books, P.O. Box 365, Bedford, MA 01730.

ISBN 978-1-55709-515-2

Library of Congress Card Number: 00-110617

Manufactured in the U.S.A.

TABLE OF CONTENTS.

(4)

PREFACE.

It is becoming fashionable in these pinching times to economize, and housekeepers are really finding it a pleasant pastime to search out and stop wastes in household expenses, and to exercise the thousand little economies which thoughtful and careful women understand so readily and practice with such grace. Somebody has said that a well-to-do French family would live on what an American household in the same condition of life wastes, and this may not be a great exaggeration. Here, the greatest source of waste is in the blunders and experiments of the inexperienced. Women are slow to learn by the experience of others. Every young housekeeper must begin at the beginning (unless her mother was wise enough to give her a careful training) and blunder into a knowledge of the practical duties of the household, wasting time, temper and money in mistakes, when such simple instructions as any skillful housewife might readily give, would be an almost perfect guide. Lately there have been attempts to gather such instructions as are needed into a book, but they have been partial failures, because the authors have been good book-makers, but poor bread-makers, or because, while practically familiar with the subjects treated, they have failed to express clearly and concisely the full processes in detail. In compiling this new candidate for favor, the one aim has been to pack between its covers the greatest possible amount of practical information of real value to all, and especially to the inexperienced. It is not a hap-hazard collection of recipes, gathered at random from doubtful sources, but has been made up without sparing time, labor, or expense, from the choicest bits of the best experience of hundreds who have long traveled the daily round of household duties, not reluctantly like drudges, but lovingly, with heart and hand fully enlisted in the work. Those housewives, especially, whose purses are not over-plethoric, will, it is believed, find its pages full of timely and helpful suggestions in their efforts to make the balance of the household ledger appear on the right side, without lessening the excellence of the table or robbing home of any comfort or attraction.

The arrangement of subjects treated, whenever practicable, has been made in the simple order of the alphabet, and for the sake of still more ready reference a very full alphabetical index has been added. The instructions which precede the recipes of each department, have been carefully made up, and are entirely trustworthy, and the recipes themselves are new to print, and well indorsed. Several suggestive articles have also been introduced, which, though not belonging strictly to cookery, bear such close relations to it that the fitness of their appearance in the connection is evident.

There has been no attempt at display or effect, the only purpose being to express ideas as clearly and concisely as possible, and to make a thoroughly simple and practical work. In the effort to avoid the mistakes of others, greater errors may have been committed; but the book is submitted just as it is to the generous judgment of those who consult it, with the hope that it may lessen their perplexities, and stimulate that just pride without which work is drudgery and great excellence impossible.

BREAD-MAKING.

---

g, "bread is the staff of life," has sound reason in it. Flour from wheat, and meal from oats and Indian corn, are rich in the waste-repairing elements, starch and albumen, and head the list of articles of food for man. Good bread makes the homeliest meal acceptable, and the coarsest fare appetizing, while the most luxurious table is not even tolerable without it. Light, crisp rolls for breakfast, spongy, sweet bread for dinner, and flaky biscuit for supper, cover a multitude of culinary sins; and there is no one thing on which the health and comfort of a family so much depends as the quality of its home-made loaves.

Bread-making seems a simple process enough, but it requires a delicate care and watchfulness, and a thorough knowledge of all the contingencies of the process, dependent on the different qualities of flour, the varying kinds and conditions of yeast, and the change of seasons; the process which raises bread successfully in winter making it sour in summer. There are many little things in bread-making which require accurate observation, and, while valuable recipes and well-defined methods in detail are invaluable aids, nothing but experience will secure the name merited by so few, though earnestly coveted by every practical, sensible housekeeper— "an excellent bread-maker." Three things are indispensable to success—good flour, good yeast, and watchful care. Good flour adheres to the hand, and, when pressed, shows the imprint of the lines of the skin. Its tint is cream white. Never buy that which has a blue-white tinge. Poor flour is not adhesive, can be blown about easily, and sometimes has a dingy look, as though mixed with ashes. Never use flour without sifting; and a large tin or wooden pail with a tight-fitting cover, kept full of sifted flour, will be found a great convenience. All kinds of flour and meal, except buckwheat and Graham, need sifting, and all except wheat flour should be bought in small quantities, as they become damp and musty by long standing.

THE SPONGE.

This is made from warm water or milk, yeast and flour (some add mashed potatoes), mixed together in proper proportions. In summer, care must be taken not to set sponge too early, at least not before eight or nine o'clock in the evening. Make up a rather thick batter of flour and tepid water or milk. (Sponge mixed with bran water, warm in winter and cold in summer, makes sweeter bread. Boil bran in the proportion of one pint to a quart of water and strain.) When milk is used, scald to prevent souring, and cool before using; add yeast, cover closely, and place to rise on the kitchen table. In very hot weather, sponge can be made with cold water. In winter, mix the batter with water or milk at blood warmth, testing it with the finger, and making it as warm as can be borne; stir in the flour, which will cool it sufficiently for the yeast; cover closely and place in a warm and even temperature. A good plan is to fold a clean blanket several times, and cover with it, providing the sponge is set in a very large crock or jar, so that there is no danger of its running over. As a general rule, one small tea-cup of yeast and three pints of "wetting" will make sponge enough for four ordinary loaves. In all sponges add the yeast last, making sure that it will not be scalded; when placed to rise, always cover closely. Many think it an improvement to beat the sponge thoroughly, like batter for a cake. All the various sponges are very nice baked on a griddle for breakfast-cakes, or, better still, in muffin-rings. When used in this way, add a little salt and make the sponge rather thick.

TO MAKE GOOD BREAD.

Always be
    "Up in the morning early, just at the peep of day,"

in summer time to prevent the sponge becoming sour by too long standing, and in winter to be getting materials warmed and in readiness for use. A large, seamless tin dish-pan with handles and a tight-fitting cover, kept for this purpose alone, is better than a wooden bowl for bread. It should be thoroughly washed and scalded every time it is used. Measure and sift the flour. It is convenient to keep two quart cups, one for dry and the other for liquid measuring. In winter, always warm the flour and also the sponge. Put the flour in a bread-pan, make a large well in the center, into which pour the sponge, adding two level tea-spoons of salt (this is the quantity for four loaves of bread); mix well, being careful not to get the dough too stiff; turn out on the bread-board, rub the pan clean, and add the "rubbings" to the bread. Knead for fully twenty minutes, or until the dough ceases to stick to either the board or hands. The process of kneading is very important. Some good bread-makers knead with the palm of the hands until the dough is a flat cake, then fold once, repeating this operation until the dough is perfectly smooth and elastic; others close the hands and press hard and quickly into the dough with the fists, dipping them into the flour when the dough sticks, or, after kneading, chop with the chopping-knife and then knead again; others still knead with a potato-masher, thinking it a great saving of strength. No exact directions can be given, but experience and practice will prove the best guides. After the bread is thoroughly kneaded, form into a round mass or large loaf, sprinkle the bread-pan well with flour, and, having placed the loaf in it, sprinkle flour lightly on the top; cover, and set to rise in a warm temperature; let it rise well this time, say from one to two hours, owing to the season of the year. Place again on the bread-board, knead lightly with elastic movements for five minutes, again form into one large loaf, return to pan, and let rise, but not so long this time. Then knead down in the pan, cut into equal parts, place one at a time on the board, mold each into a smooth, oblong loaf, not too large, and put one after another into a well-greased baking-pan, and set to rise. Loaves made in the French style, long and narrow, are about half crust, and more easily digested, the action of heat anticipating part of the digestive process. In molding, do not leave any lumps or loose flour adhering to the outside, but mold until the loaves are perfectly smooth. .No particular directions can be given in regard to the time bread should stand after it is molded and placed in the pans, because here is the point where observation and discretion are so indispensable. In hot weather, when the yeast is very good and the bread very light, it must not stand over fifteen minutes before placing to bake. If it is cold weather and the yeast is less active, or the bread not perfectly raised, it may sometimes stand an hour in the pans without injury. When it is risen so as to seam or crack, it is ready for the oven; if it stands after this it becomes sour, and even if it does not sour it loses its freshness and sweetness, and the bread becomes dry sooner after baking. Bread should undergo but two fermentations; the saccharine or sweet fermentation, and the vinous, when it smells something like foaming beer. The housewife who would have good, sweet bread, must never let it pass this change, because the third or acetous fermentation then takes place. This last can be remedied by adding soda in the proportion of one tea-spoon to each quart of wetting; or, which is the same thing, a tea-spoon to four quarts of flour; but the bread will be much less nutritious and healthful, and some of the best elements of the flour will be lost. Always add salt to all bread, biscuit, griddle cakes, etc., but *never* salt sponge. A small quantity of white sugar is an improvement to all bread dough. Bread should always be mixed as *soft as it can be handled.*

TO BAKE BREAD.

Here is the important point, for the bread may be perfect thus far and then be spoiled in baking. No definite rules can be given that apply equally well to every stove and range; but one general rule must be observed, which is to have a steady, moderate heat, such as is more minutely described in the directions for baking large cakes. The oven must be just hot enough; if too hot, a firm crust is formed before the bread has expanded enough, and it will be heavy. Many test the oven by sprinkling a little flour on the bottom; if it browns very quickly, it is too hot, but if it browns gradually, it is just right. An oven in which the hand can not be held longer than to count twenty moderately, is hot enough. When the bread is done (to test which, break apart and press gently with the finger; if elastic it is done, but if clammy, not done, and must be returned to the oven), wrap in a coarse towel or bread cloth and place each loaf on its edge until cool. If by accident or neglect the bread is baked too hard, rub the loaves over with butter, wet the towel in which they are wrapped, and cover with another dry towel. In winter, bread dough may be kept sweet several days by placing it where it will be cold without freezing, or by putting it so deep into the flour barrel as to exclude it entirely from the air. When wanted for use, make into bread, or, by adding the proper ingredients, into cake, rusk, biscuit, apple dumplings, chicken pie, etc.

GRAHAM AND CORN BREAD.

It is very desirable that every family should have a constant supply of bread made of unbolted flour, or rye and Indian corn. Most persons find it palatable, and it promotes health. For these coarse breads, always add a little brown sugar or molasses, and the amount given in the recipes may be increased according to taste. They rise quicker and in a less warm atmosphere than without sweetening. A little lard or butter improves bread or cakes made of Graham or Indian meal, rendering them light and tender. Graham rises rather more quickly than fine flour, and should not be allowed to rise quite as light. The fire should be steady and sufficient to complete the baking, and the oven hot when the bread is put in. A fresh blaze will burn the crust, while a steady fire will sweeten it. Graham bread bakes more slowly than fine-flour bread, and corn bread requires more time and a hotter oven than either. Use either yellow or white corn, ground coarse, for mush, and white, ground fine, for bread, etc. In cutting the latter while warm, hold the knife perpendicularly. Rye is said to absorb more moisture from the air than any other grain; hence, all bread from this meal needs a longer application of heat, and keeps moister after being baked than that made from other grain.

SPONGE FOR WINTER USE.

Peel and boil four or five medium-sized potatoes in two quarts of water, which will boil down to one quart when done, take out and press through a colander, or mash very fine in the crock in which the sponge is made; form a well in the center, into which put one cup of flour, and pour over it the boiling water from the potatoes; stir thoroughly and when cool add a pint of tepid water, flour enough to make a *thin* batter, and a cup of yeast. This sponge makes very moist bread.

BREAD SPONGE.

Six potatoes boiled and mashed while hot, two table-spoons of white sugar, two of butter, one quart tepid water; into this stir three cups of flour; beat to a smooth batter, add six table-spoons of the yeast, set over night, and, in the morning, knead in sufficient flour to make a stiff, spongy dough; knead vigorously for fifteen minutes, set away to rise, and, when light, knead for ten minutes, mold out into moderate-sized loaves, and let rise until they are like delicate or light sponge-cake.—*Mrs. George H. Rust, Minneapolis, Minn.*

BREAD SPONGE AND BREAD.

Five pints of warm water, five quarts of sifted flour, one coffee-cup of yeast; mix in a two-gallon stone jar, cover closely, and set in a large tin pan, so that if the sponge rises over the top of the jar, the drippings may fall into the pan. Set to rise the evening before baking. In winter be careful to set in a warm place. In the morning sift six quarts of flour into a pail, pour the sponge into the bread-pan or bowl, add two table-spoons of salt, then the flour gradually; mix and knead well, using up nearly all the flour. This first kneading is the most important, and should occupy at least twenty minutes. Make the bread in one large loaf, set away in a warm place, and cover with a cloth. It ought to rise in half an hour, when it should be kneaded thoroughly again for ten minutes. Then take enough dough for three good-sized loaves (a quart bowl of dough to each), give five minutes kneading to each loaf, and place to rise in a dripping-pan well greased with lard. The loaves will be light in five or ten minutes, and will bake in a properly heated oven in half an hour. Make a well in the center of the remaining dough and into it put one-half tea-cup of white sugar, one tea-cup of lard, and two eggs, which mix thoroughly with the dough, knead into one large loaf, set in a warm place about fifteen minutes to rise, and, when light, knead five minutes and let rise again for about ten minutes, when it should be light. Take out of pan, knead on bread-board, roll about an inch in thickness, cut out with a biscuit-cutter, and place in dripping-pan; let rise five minutes and bake twenty minutes. In winter more time must be allowed for rising. This makes three loaves and ninety biscuit.—*S. A. M.*

BREAD WITH BUTTERMILK.

The evening before baking, bring to the boiling point two quarts of buttermilk, and pour into a crock in which a scant tea-cup of sifted flour has been placed. Let stand till sufficiently cool, then add half a cup of yeast, and flour to make a thick batter; the better and longer the sponge is stirred the whiter will be the bread. In the morning sift the flour into the bread-pan, pour the sponge in the center, stir in some of the flour, and let stand until after breakfast; then mix, kneading for about half an hour, the longer the better; when light, mold into loaves, this time kneading as little as possible. The secret of good bread is having good yeast, and not baking too hard. This makes four loaves and forty biscuit.—*M. C. M.*

BREAD WITH POTATO SPONGE.

Pare and boil four or five potatoes, mash fine, and add one pint of flour; pour on the mixture first boiling water enough to moisten well, then about one quart of cold water, after which add flour enough to make a stiff batter. When cooled to "scarcely milk warm," put in one-half pint (or more will do no harm) of yeast, and let it stand in a warm place over night; in the morning add to this sponge one cup of lard, stir in flour, and knead well. The more kneading the finer and whiter the bread will be; pounding also with a potato-masher improves the bread greatly, and is rather easier than so much kneading. When quite stiff and well worked and pounded, let it rise again, and when light, make into loaves or biscuit, adding no more flour except to flour the hands and board—merely enough to prevent the bread from sticking. Let it rise again, then bake; and immediately after taking from the oven, wrap in a wet towel until partly cold, in order to soften the crust. If *yeast* and *flour* are good (*essentials* in all cases), the above process will make good bread.—*Mrs. Clara Morey.*

BREAD, IN SUMMER OR WINTER.

In summer take three pints of cold or tepid water, four table-spoons of yeast, one tea-spoon of salt; stir in flour enough to make a thick sponge (rather thicker than griddle-cakes). Let stand until morning, then add more flour, mix stiff, and knead ten minutes; place in a pan, let rise until light, knead for another ten minutes; mold into four loaves, and set to rise, but do not let it get too light; bake in a moderate oven one hour. If bread is mixed at six o'clock in the morning, the baking ought to be done by ten o'clock.

In winter take one pint of buttermilk or clabbered milk; let it scald (not boil); make a well in the center of the flour, into it turn the hot milk, add one tea-spoon of salt, enough flour and water to make sufficient sponge, and one tea-cup of yeast; let stand until morning and then prepare the bread as in summer. This is more convenient to make in winter, since a hot fire is needed to heat the milk.—*Mrs. D. Buxton.*

BREAD WITH MUSH.

Pour two quarts hot corn-meal mush, made as for eating, over two quarts flour, (wheat or Graham); when cool, add one quart sponge, half cup molasses, one tea-spoon salt, half tea-spoon of soda; mix well together; add more flour if needed, and knead thoroughly; mold into small loaves; let rise and bake in small dripping-pans, (a loaf in a pan) or pie-tins, in a moderate oven.; when done, rub over with butter and wrap in a cloth.—*Mrs. W. W. W.*

GOOD BREAD.

For four small loaves boil four large potatoes; when done, pour off the water, and when it cools add to it a yeast cake; mash the potato very fine, put through a sieve, pour boiling milk on as much flour as is needed, let stand until cool, add the potato and yeast, a large tea-spoon of salt and one table-spoon of sugar; stir very stiff, adding flour as is needed. Let stand in a warm place until light, dissolve one tea-spoon of soda in a little hot water, mix well through with the hands, mold into loaves, and let rise again. When suffi-ciently raised place in a moderately hot oven, keeping up a steady fire.—*Mrs. Governor Hardin, Missouri.*

Hop-Yeast Bread.

One tea-cup yeast, three pints warm water; make a thin sponge at tea-time, cover and let it remain two hours or until very light. By adding the water to the flour first and having the sponge quite warm, it is never necessary to put the sponge over hot water or in an oven to make it rise. Knead into a loaf before going to bed; in the morning mold into three loaves, spreading a little lard between as they are put in the pan. When light, bake one hour, having oven quite hot when the bread is put in, and very moderate when it is done. (Bread made in this way is never sour or heavy.) To have fine, light biscuit, add shortening at night, and in the morning make into biscuit and bake for breakfast. By this recipe bread is baked before the stove is cold from breakfast, and out of the way for other baking.

To cool bread there should be a board for the purpose. An oaken board, covered with heavy white flannel, is the best; over this spread a fresh linen bread-cloth, and lay the bread on it right side up, with nothing over it except a very thin cover to keep off the flies. It should be placed immediately in the fresh air or wind to cool; when cool, place immediately in a tin box or stone jar, and cover closely. Bread cooled in this way will have a soft crust, and be filled with pure air.—*Mrs. J. T. Liggett, Detroit, Michigan.*

Milk-Yeast Bread.

Put into a pail holding two quarts and a half, one pint of new milk, and one pint of boiling water; mix with this one table-spoon of sugar, one of salt, and three pints of flour; beat well together, and cover tightly. Set pail into another pail or kettle, with water enough to come nearly to the top of it; to have the water of the right temperature, let half be boiling and half cold. Be very particular to set it where it will keep about the same temperature until risen. Beat the batter as often as once in every half hour until the last hour, when it must not be disturbed: it will rise in about five hours, and when risen enough the pail will be full. Put two quarts of flour into a pan, make a well in the middle of it, dissolve a tea-spoon of soda in a little hot water, and when the batter is risen just enough, turn it into the middle of the flour, pouring the dissolved soda in with it; knead well and make into loaves. Set them where they will be warm, and let them rise forty-five minutes; bake in a quick oven. It will take nearly a pint of flour to knead the bread on the board. This bread makes the nicest dry toast and sandwiches.—*Mrs. W. A. James.*

POOR-MAN'S BREAD.

One pint buttermilk or sour milk, one level tea-spoon soda, a pinch of salt, and flour enough to make as stiff as soda-biscuit dough; cut into three pieces, handle as little as possible, roll an inch thick, place in dripping-pan, bake twenty or thirty minutes in a hot oven, and when done, wrap in a bread cloth. Eat while warm, breaking open like a biscuit. Each cake will be about the size of a pie.—*Mrs. D. B.*

YEAST BREAD.

Make a well in the middle of four quarts flour, into which turn one table-spoon sugar, one of salt, and one cup of yeast; then mix with one pint of milk which has been warmed by adding one pint of boiling water; add one table-spoon lard, knead well, and let rise over night; in the morning knead again, make into loaves, let them rise one hour, and bake fifty minutes. Water can be used instead of the pint of milk, in which case use twice as much lard.

BOSTON BROWN BREAD.

One heaping coffee-cup each of corn, rye and Graham meal. The rye meal should be as fine as the Graham, or rye flour may be used. Sift the three kinds together as closely as possible, and beat together thoroughly with two cups New Orleans or Porto Rico molasses, two cups sweet milk, one cup sour milk, one dessert-spoon soda, one tea-spoon salt; pour into a tin form, place in a kettle of cold water, put on and boil four hours. Put on to cook as soon as mixed. It may appear to be too thin, but it is not, as this recipe has never been known to fail. Serve warm, with Thanksgiving turkey. The bread should not quite fill the form, (or a tin pail with cover will answer,) as it must have room to swell. See that the water does not boil up to the top of the form; also take care it does not boil entirely away or stop boiling. To serve it, remove the lid and set it a few moments into the open oven to dry the top, and it will then turn out in perfect shape. This bread can be used as a pudding, and served with a sauce made of thick *sour* cream, well sweetened and seasoned with nutmeg; or it is good toasted the next day.—*Mrs. H. S. Stevens, Minneapolis, Minn.*

EASTERN BROWN BREAD.

One pint each of rye or Graham and Indian meal, one cup molasses, three-fourths cup sour milk, one and one-half tea-spoons soda, one and one-half pints cold water. Put on stove over cold water, steam four hours, and brown over in the oven.

BROWN BREAD.

Two and one-half cups sour milk and one-half cup molasses; into these put one heaping tea-spoon soda, two cups corn meal, one cup Graham flour and one tea-spoon salt. Use coffee-cups. Steam three hours—better steamed longer.—*Mrs. D. Bassett, Minneapolis, Minn*

BOSTON CORN BREAD.

One cup sweet milk, two cups sour milk, two-thirds cup of molasses, one cup flour, four cups corn-meal, two tea-spoons soda; steam three hours, and brown a few minutes in the oven.—*Mrs. Canby, Bellefontaine.*

MRS. B.'s CORN BREAD.

One quart sour milk, three eggs, two table-spoons lard or butter (or half and half), one table-spoon sugar, a pinch of salt, handful of wheat flour, and enough corn-meal (sifted) to make a good batter; add one heaping tea-spoon soda, stir thoroughly, and bake in long dripping-pan.

PLAIN CORN BREAD.

One pint corn meal, one of sour or buttermilk, one egg, one tea-spoon soda, one of salt; bake in dripping or gem-pans. If preferred, one heaping table-spoon of sugar may be added.

CORN CAKE.

One pint corn meal sifted, one pint flour, one pint sour milk, two eggs beaten light, one-half cup sugar, piece of butter size of an egg; add, the last thing, one tea-spoon soda in a little milk; add to the beaten egg the milk and meal alternately, then the butter and sugar. If sweet milk is used, add one tea-spoon cream tartar; bake

2

twenty minutes in a hot oven.—*Mrs. H. B. Sherman, Milwaukee, Wisconsin.*

CORN BREAD.

Take one quart buttermilk, and one heaping pint corn meal, one tea-spoon soda, one tea-spoon salt, one table-spoon sugar and three eggs; have the stove very hot, and do not bake in too deep a pan. The batter seems too thin, but bakes very nicely.—*Mrs. J. H. S.*

STEAMED CORN BREAD.

Two cups each corn meal, Graham flour, and sour milk, two-thirds cup molasses, one tea-spoon soda; steam two hours and a half.—*Mrs. Jennie Guthrie Cherry, Newark.*

GRAHAM BREAD.

Take a little over a quart of warm water, one-half cup brown sugar or molasses, one-fourth cup hop yeast, and one and a half tea-spoons salt; thicken the water with unbolted flour to a thin batter; add sugar, salt and yeast, and stir in more flour until quite stiff. In the morning add a small tea-spoon soda, and flour enough to make the batter stiff as can be stirred with a spoon; put it into pans and let rise again; then bake in even oven, not too hot at first; *keep warm while rising*; smooth over the loaves with a spoon or knife dipped in water.—*Mrs. H. B. Sherman, Plankinton House, Milwaukee, Wisconsin.*

GRAHAM BREAD.

To one and a half pints of tepid water add one heaping tea-spoon of salt and one-half cup of sugar; stir in one half pint or more of the sponge made of white flour, as in recipe for "Bread with Potato Yeast," add Graham flour until almost *too stiff to stir;* put in the baking-pan and let rise well, which will take about two hours, bake in a moderate oven, and when done, wrap in a wet towel until cool.—*Mrs. Clara Woods Morey.*

QUICK GRAHAM BREAD.

One and a half pints sour milk, half cup New Orleans molasses, a little salt, two tea-spoons soda dissolved in a little hot water, and as much Graham flour as can be stirred in with a spoon; pour in well-greased pan, put in oven as soon as mixed, and bake two hours—*Mrs. E. J. W.*

RYE AND INDIAN BREAD.

One quart of rye meal or rye flour, two quarts of Indian meal, scalded (by placing in a pan and pouring just enough *boiling* water over it, stirring constantly with a spoon, to merely wet it, but not enough to make it into a batter,) one-half tea-cup molasses, two tea-spoons salt, one tea-spoon soda, one tea-cup yeast; make as stiff as can be stirred with a spoon, mixing with warm water, and let rise all night; then put in a large pan, smooth the top with the hand dipped in cold water, let it stand a short time, and bake five or six hours. If put in the oven late in the day let it remain all night. Graham may be used instead of rye, and baked as above. In the olden time it was placed in kettle, allowed to rise, then placed on the hearth before the fire, with coals on top of lid, and baked.— *Mrs. Charles Fullington.*

RYE BREAD.

Make a sponge of one quart warm water, one tea-cup yeast, thickened with rye flour; put in warm place to rise over night; scald one pint corn meal; when cool add it to sponge, and add rye flour till thick enough to knead, *knead but little*, let rise, mold into loaves, place in deep pie-tins or small pudding-pans, let rise and bake: or, thicken the sponge with rye flour, and proceed as above. Wheat sponge may be used instead of rye.—*Mrs. Eliza T. Carson.*

BREAKFAST AND TEA CAKES.

To make biscuit, take a part of the dough left from bread-making when it is ready to mold into loaves, work in the lard and any other ingredients desired, such as butter, eggs, sugar, spice, etc., also using a little more flour; let rise once, then mix down and let rise again; turn out on the bread-board; knead a few minutes, roll, and cut out with a biscuit-cutter or mold with the hand. Place in a well-greased dripping-pan, and when light bake in a quick oven from fifteen to twenty minutes. To make them a nice color, wet the top with warm water just before placing in the oven. To glaze, brush lightly with milk and sugar, or the well-beaten yolk of an egg sweetened, and a little milk added.

Biscuit may be baked in eight minutes by making the oven as hot as can be without burning, and allowing it to cool off gradually as they bake; this makes them very light, but one has to watch closely to keep them from being scorched. Any kind of bread or pastry mixed with water requires a hotter fire than that mixed with milk.

Biscuit for tea at six must be molded two hours before, which will give ample time for rising and baking. Parker House rolls for breakfast at eight must be made ready at five. Many think it unnecessary to knead down either bread or biscuit as often as here directed; but if attention is given to the dough at the right time, and it is not suffered to become *too light*, it will be much nicer, whiter and of a finer texture if these directions are followed.

Soda biscuit must be handled as little and made as rapidly as possible; mix soda and cream tartar or baking-powder in the flour, (with sweet milk use baking-powder or soda and cream tartar, with sour milk soda alone,) so that the effervescence takes place in the mixture. One tea-spoon soda and two of cream tartar, or three tea-spoons baking-powder, to every three pints of flour, is about the right proportion. Bake in a quick oven as soon as made, and they rise more quickly if put into hot pans. Gems of all kinds require a hot oven, but the fire should be built sometime before they are put into the oven and allowed to go down by the time they are light, as the heat necessary to raise them will burn them in baking if kept up.

Soda and raised biscuit and bread or cake, when stale, can be made almost as nice as fresh by plunging for an instant into cold water, and then placing in a pan in the oven ten or fifteen minutes; thus treated they should be used immediately.

Waffle-irons should be heated, then buttered or greased with lard, and one side filled with batter, closed and laid on the fire or placed on the stove, and after a few minutes turned on the other side. They take about twice as long to bake as griddle-cakes, and are delicious with a dressing of ground cinnamon. Muffins are baked in muffin-rings. In eating them, do not cut but break them open.

The success of these recipes and all others in this book in which soda and cream tartar are used, will depend on the purity of these ingredients. Always buy the *pure* English bicarbonate of soda, and the *pure* cream tartar. They are higher-priced, but cheaper in the end, and are free from injurious substances. When not found at the grocer's, they may generally be had at the druggist's.

BAKING-POWDER.

Sixteen ounces corn starch, eight of bicarbonate of soda, five of tartaric acid; mix thoroughly.—*Mrs. Dr. Allen, Oberlin.*

BAKING-POWDER.

Eight ounces flour, eight of English bicarbonate of soda, seven of tartaric acid; mix thoroughly by passing several times through a sieve.—*Mrs. Trimble, Mt. Gilead.*

BAKING-POWDER.

Two parts pure cream of tartar, one part of bicarbonate of soda, one part corn starch; mix well.—*Mrs. B. H. Gilbert, Minneapolis, Minn.*

BREAKFAST-CAKE.

Two table-spoons sugar, two of butter, two eggs, one cup milk, one (scant) quart flour, one tea-spoon soda, two of cream tartar; bake twenty minutes in a quick oven.—*Miss Emily L. Burnham, South Norwalk, Conn.*

CINNAMON CAKE.

When yeast bread is ready to knead from the sponge, knead and roll out three-fourths of an inch thick, put thin slices of butter on the top, sprinkle with cinnamon, and then with sugar; let rise well and bake.—*Miss M. E. Wilcox, Selma, Alabama.*

BUNS.

Break one egg into a cup and fill with sweet milk; mix with it half cup yeast, half cup butter, one cup sugar, enough flour to make a soft dough; flavor with nutmeg. Let rise till very light, then mold into biscuit with a few currants. Let rise a second time in pan; bake, and when nearly done, glaze with a little molasses and milk. Use the same cup, no matter about the size, for each measure.—*Mrs. W. A. James.*

BUTTERED TOAST.

Although toast is commonly used, few know how to prepare it nicely. Take bread not too fresh, cut thin and evenly, trim off the crust-edges for the crumb-jar; first warm each side of the bread, then present the first side again to the fire until it takes on a rich, even, brown color; treat the other side in the same way; butter and serve immediately. The coals should be bright and hot. Toast properly made is very digestible, because all the moisture is extracted, and the bread has become pure farina of wheat, but when it is exposed to a hot fire and the outside charred, the inside remains as moist as ever. Butter applied to it while warm does not penetrate, but floats on the surface in the form of rancid oil. Or, beat one cup of butter and three table-spoons flour to a *cream*, pour over this one and a half pints *boiling* water; place over a kettle of *boiling* water for ten minutes, dip into it the toast, and serve hot.

Or, dip each slice of toast in boiling hot water (slightly salted), spread with butter, cover and keep hot.

BREAKFAST-TOAST.

Add to one-half pint of sweet milk, two table-spoons sugar, a little salt and a well-beaten egg; dip in this slices of bread (if dry, let it soak a minute), and fry on a buttered griddle until it is a light brown on each side. This is a good way to use dry bread.—*Mrs. Dr. Morey.*

MENNONITE-TOAST.

Beat up three eggs well, add a pint of sweet milk and a pinch of salt; cut slices an inch thick from a loaf of baker's bread, remove crust, dip slices into the eggs and milk, fry like doughnuts in very hot lard or drippings till a delicate brown, butter and sprinkle with powdered sugar, and serve hot.—*Mrs. J. P. Rea, Lancaster, Pa.*

LUCY'S POP-OVERS.

Two tea-cups sweet milk, two tea-cups sifted flour heaped a little, butter size of a walnut, two eggs, one table-spoon sugar. a little salt; bake in hot gem-pans filled half full for twenty minutes, and serve immediately.—*Mrs. W. A. James.*

POCKET-BOOKS.

Warm one quart new milk, add one cup butter or lard, four table-spoons sugar; and two well-beaten eggs; stir in flour enough to make a moderately stiff sponge, add a small cup of yeast, and set in a warm place to rise, which will take three or four hours; then mix in flour enough to make a soft dough and let rise again. When well risen, dissolve a lump of soda size of a bean in a spoon of milk, work it into the dough and roll into sheets one-half inch in thickness; spread with thin layer of butter, cut into squares, and fold over, pocket-book shape; put on tins or in pans to rise for a little while, when they will be fit for the oven. In summer the sponge can be made up in the morning, and rise in time to make for tea. In cool weather it is best to set it over night.—*Mrs. J. H. Shearer.*

RUSK.

Two tea-cups raised dough, one tea-cup sugar, half cup butter, two well-beaten eggs, flour enough to make a stiff dough; set to rise, and when light, mold into high biscuit, and let rise again; sift sugar and cinnamon over the top, and place in oven.—*Mrs. Mary Lee Gere, Champaign, Ill.*

RUSK.

One pint milk, three eggs, one cup butter, one cup sugar, and one coffee-cup potato yeast; thicken with flour, and sponge over night; in the morning stir down, let rise, and stir down again; when it rises make into a loaf, and let rise again; then roll out like soda biscuit, cut and put in pans, and, when light, bake carefully. Or, when baking take four cups dough, one-half cup butter, one cup sugar, three eggs; mix thoroughly, adding enough flour to mold easily; let rise, make into rather high and narrow biscuit, let rise again, rub the tops with a little sugar and water, then sprinkle over them dry sugar. Bake twenty minutes.

LEBANON RUSK.

One cup mashed potatoes, one of sugar, one of home-made yeast, three eggs; mix together, when raised light add half cup butter or lard, and flour to make a soft dough, and when quite light, mold into small cakes, and let them rise again before baking. If wanted for tea, set about nine A. M.—*Mrs. J. S. Stahr, Lancaster, Pa.*

SUPERIOR BISCUIT.

Three and a half cups sweet milk, one cup butter and lard mixed; add yeast and flour and let rise over night. In the morning add one beaten egg, knead thoroughly, and let rise again, then form into biscuit; when light, bake delicately.—*Mrs. B. T. Skinner.*

HARD TEA BISCUIT.

Two pounds of flour, one-fourth pound butter, one salt-spoon salt, three gills milk; cut up the butter and rub it in the flour, add the salt and milk, knead dough for half an hour, cut cakes about as large as a small tea-cup and half an inch thick, prick with a fork, and bake in a moderate oven until they are a delicate brown.— *Mrs. Denmead, Columbus.*

MARYLAND BISCUIT.

Three pounds flour, one-half cup each butter and sweet lard, a little salt, water enough to mix; work an hour, roll, cut into cakes and bake.—*Mrs. G. W. Hensel, Lancaster, Pa.*

SOUTH CAROLINA BISCUIT.

One quart sweet cream or milk, one and a half cups butter or fresh lard, two table-spoons white sugar, one good tea-spoon salt; add flour sufficient to make a stiff dough, knead *well* and mold into neat, small biscuit with the hands, as our grandmothers used to do; add one good tea-spoon cream tartar if preferred; bake well, and you have good sweet biscuit that will keep for weeks in a dry place, and are very nice for traveling lunch. They are such as we used to send to the army, and the "boys" relished them "hugely."— *Mrs. Colonel Moore, Hamilton.*

SODA BISCUIT.

Put one quart of flour, before sifting, into sieve, with one tea-spoon soda and two of cream tartar (or three of baking powder), one of salt, and one table-spoon white sugar; mix all thoroughly with the flour, run through sieve, rub in one level table-spoon of lard or butter (or half and half), wet with half pint sweet milk, roll on board about an inch thick, cut with biscuit cutter, and bake in a quick oven fifteen minutes. If you have not milk, use a little more butter, and wet with water. Handle as little and make as rapidly as possible.—*M. Parloa.*

SODA BISCUIT.

One quart sifted flour, two large tea-spoons cream yeast, one table-spoon lard, a little salt; mix thoroughly and add milk enough to stir nicely, roll out half an inch thick, cut the proper size, and bake in a hot oven.—*Mrs. Governor J. D. Bedle, New Jersey.*

SPOON-BISCUIT.

One quart sour milk or buttermilk, one tea-spoon soda, a little salt, two table-spoons melted lard, and flour enough for a stiff batter; drop in a hot gem-pan and bake in a quick oven.—*Mrs. A. B. Morey.*

SALLY LUNN.

One quart flour, two eggs, one pint sweet milk, two table-spoons sugar; piece of butter size of two eggs (large size), one-half tea-spoon salt, two tea-spoons cream tartar, one tea-spoon soda; beat butter and sugar together; add eggs well beaten. Mix soda with milk, and cream tartar with flour.—*Mrs. H. B. Sherman, Milwaukee, Wisconsin.*

TEA CAKE.

One quart flour, one cup sour milk, one tea-spoon soda, one-half pound lard, one-half pound chopped raisins or currants; roll two inches thick and bake in a quick oven; split open, butter, and eat while hot.—*Mrs. Canby, Bellefontaine.*

EGG ROLLS.

Two tea-cups of sweet milk, two eggs, a little salt, three and a half scant cups of sifted flour. Bake in hot gem-pans.—*Mrs. L. S. W., Jamestown, N. Y.*

EVERY-DAY ROLLS.

Take a piece of bread dough on baking day, when molded out the last time, about enough for a small loaf, spread out a little, add one egg, two table-spoons of sugar, and three-fourths cup of lard; add a little flour and a small tea-spoon of soda if the least bit sour;

mix well, let rise, mold into rolls or biscuit, set to rise again, and they will be ready for the oven in twenty or thirty minutes.

FRENCH ROLLS.

Peel six common-sized, mealy potatoes, boil in two quarts of water, press and drain both potatoes and water through a colander; when cool enough so as not to scald, add flour to make a thick batter, beat well, and when lukewarm, add one-half cup potato yeast. Make this sponge early in the morning, and when light turn into a bread-pan, add a tea-spoon salt, half cup lard, and flour enough for a soft dough; mix up, and set in a warm, even temperature; when risen, knead down and place again to rise, repeating this process five or six times; cut in small pieces and mold on the bread-board in rolls about one inch thick by five long; roll in melted butter or sweet lard, and place in well-greased baking-pans (nine inches long by five wide and two and a half in depth, makes a convenient-sized pan, which holds fifteen of these rolls; or, if twice the width, put in two rows); press the rolls closely together, so that they will only be about half an inch in width. Let rise a short time and bake twenty minutes in a hot oven; if the top browns too rapidly, cover with paper. These rolls, if properly made, are very white, light, and tender.

Or, make rolls larger, and just before putting them in the oven, cut deeply across each one with a sharp knife. This will make the cleft roll, so famous among French cooks.—*Mrs. J. W. R.*

MINNESOTA ROLLS.

Rub one-half table-spoon of lard into one quart of flour, make a well in the middle, put in one-half cup of baker's yeast—or one cup of home-made—two tea-spoons sugar, one half pint cold boiled milk; do not stir, but let stand over night; in the morning knead well, after dinner knead again, cut out, put in pans, and let rise until tea time. Bake in a quick oven.—*Mrs. Judge West, Bellefontaine.*

PARKER HOUSE ROLLS.

Rub one half table-spoon of butter, and one half table-spoon of lard into two quarts of sifted flour; into a well in the middle pour one pint of cold boiled milk, and add one-half cup of yeast, one half cup of sugar, and a little salt. If wanted for tea, rub the flour and butter, and boil the milk, and cool it the night before; add sugar, yeast, and salt, and turn all into the flour, but do not stir. Let stand over night; in the morning stir up, knead, and let rise till near tea-time; mold and let rise again, and bake quickly. To mold, cut with cake-cutter; put a little melted butter on one-half and lap nearly over on the other half. Place them in the pan about three-quarters of an inch apart.—*Mrs. V. G. Hush, Minneapolis, Minn.*

WEDDING SANDWICH ROLLS.

Late in the evening make a rather stiff potato sponge (see directions under "Bread-Making"), and in the morning mix in as much flour as will make a soft dough, knead well, and place to rise; when sufficiently light, knead down again, repeating the operation two or three times, remembering not to let the dough become sour by rising too light; mold into common-sized loaves, place in your dripping-pan to rise, and bake very carefully, so as to secure the very lightest brown crust possible. On taking out of the oven, roll in a cloth tightly wrung out of water, with a large bread-blanket folded and wrapped around all. Let cool three or four hours, cut lengthwise of the loaf (not using the outside piece), first spreading lightly with good sweet butter, then cutting in slices not more than a quarter of an 'inch, or just as thin as possible, using for this purpose a very thin, sharp knife; lay on cold boiled ham cut in very thin shavings (no matter if in small pieces), roll up very slowly and carefully, and place where it will not unroll. Treat each sandwich in the same manner, always spreading the bread with butter before cutting. If by chance the bread is baked with too hard a crust, cut off a thin shaving of the brownest part very smoothly before making into sandwiches. These sandwiches are truly delicious if properly made, but they require great care, experience, and good judgment. Served on an oblong platter, piled in pyramid style, row upon row, they will resemble nicely rolled dinner napkins. They must be made and served the same day.—*Mrs. James W. Robinson.*

WINTER ROLLS.

Put three quarts of flour into a large crock or jar, scald one quart of buttermilk, add one cup of lard, and pour all over the flour, beating it up well; then add one quart of cold water, stir and add one-half cup of potato yeast, or one cup of brewer's; beat in well and set in a warm place to rise over night. In the morning add salt and flour enough to make a moderately stiff dough; set in a warm place to rise, and, when risen, knead down and set to rise again. This time knead down and place in a large stone crock or bowl, covered tightly with a tin pan to prevent the surface from drying, and set away in a cool place. When needed, turn out on a bread-board, cut off a piece as large as you wish to use, roll out to the thickness of ordinary soda biscuit, cut, and put in the oven to bake immediately. Set away the rest of the dough as before, and it will keep a week in winter, and is very convenient for hot breakfast-rolls.—*Mrs. D. Buxton.*

VIENNA ROLLS.

Have ready in a bowl a table-spoon of butter or lard, made soft by warming a little, and stirring with a spoon. Add to one quart of unsifted flour two heaping tea-spoons of Royal Baking-Powder; mix and sift thoroughly together, and place in a bowl with butter. Take more or less sweet milk as may be necessary to form a dough of usual stiffness, according to the flour (about three-fourths of a pint), put into the milk half a tea-spoon salt, and then stir it into the flour, etc., with a spoon, forming the dough, which turn out on a board and knead sufficiently to make smooth. Roll out half an inch thick, and cut with a large round cutter; fold each one over to form a half round, wetting a little between the folds to make them stick together; place on buttered pans, so as not to touch, wash over on top with milk to give them a gloss, and bake immediately in a hot oven about twenty minutes. It will do them no harm to stand half an hour before baking, if it is desired.

CRUMPETS.

One quart of milk with two table-spoons yeast, and flour enough to make a stiff batter; let rise over night, and in the morning add four eggs, two table-spoons of sugar, one-half cup of butter; put them in muffin-rings, and let them rise nearly half an hour; bake quickly.—*Miss Mary Gallagher.*

MUFFINS.

Mix one tea-spoon of baking-powder and a little salt into one pint of flour; add to the beaten yolks of two eggs one tea-cup of sweet milk or cream, a piece of butter (melted) half the size of an egg, the flour with baking-powder and salt mixed, and the well-beaten whites of the two eggs. Beat well, bake immediately in gem-pans in a hot oven, and take out and send to the table immediately.—*Mrs. Gib Hillock, New Castle, Ind.*

QUICK WAFFLES.

Two pints sweet milk, one cup of butter (melted), sifted flour to make a soft batter; add the well-beaten yolks of six eggs, then the beaten whites, and lastly (just before baking) four tea-spoons baking-powder, beating very hard and fast for a few minutes. These are very good with four or five eggs, but much better with more.—*Mrs. C. W. Morey.*

OHIO WAFFLES.

Four eggs, beaten separately, one quart of sweet milk, one-fourth pound of butter, a little salt, flour to make a not very thick batter; heat and butter the irons well, and bake very quickly. If for tea, grate on a little sugar and nutmeg, or cinnamon; if for breakfast, only butter.—*Mrs. O. M. Scott.*

RAISED WAFFLES.

One quart of flour, one pint of sweet, luke-warm milk, two eggs, a table-spoon of melted butter, tea-spoon of salt, half tea-cup of good yeast.—*Mrs. L. S. Williston.*

RICE WAFFLES.

Boil half a pint of rice and let it get cold, mix with it one-fourth pound of butter and a little salt. Sift in it one and a half pints of flour, beat five eggs separately, stir the yolks together with one quart of milk, add whites beaten to a stiff froth, beat hard, and bake at once in waffle-iron.—*Mrs. S. C. Lee, Baltimore, Md.*

EGG CRACKERS.

Six eggs, twelve table-spoons of sweet milk, six table-spoons of butter, one half tea-spoon of soda; mold with flour half an hour and roll thin.—*Mrs. J. S. Robinson.*

BUCKWHEAT SHORT-CAKE.

Take one pint of sour milk, one tea-spoon of soda to sweeten, and a little salt; stir in buckwheat flour enough to make quite a stiff batter, and bake in dripping-pan. Two table-spoons of melted lard may be added for shortening, if desired. This takes the place of griddle-cakes, and is very nice to eat with meat, butter, honey, or molasses.—*Mrs. Viola Wilcox, Midland, Mich.*

CORN DODGERS.

To one quart of corn meal add a little salt and a small table-spoon of lard; scald with boiling water and beat hard for a few minutes; drop a large spoonful in a well-greased pan. The batter should be thick enough to just flatten on the bottom, leaving them quite high in the center. Bake in a hot oven.

CORN ROLLS.

One pint of corn meal, two table-spoons of sugar, one tea-spoon of salt, one pint of boiling milk; stir all together and let stand till cool. Add three eggs well beaten, and bake in gem-pans.—*Mrs. Capt. J. P. Reá, Minneapolis, Minn.*

CORN MUSH.

Put fresh water in a kettle to boil, salt to suit the taste; when it begins to boil stir in the meal, letting it sift through the fingers slowly to prevent lumps, adding it a little faster at the last, until as thick as can be conveniently stirred with one hand; set in the oven in the kettle, bake an hour, and it will be thoroughly cooked. It takes corn meal so long to cook thoroughly that it is very difficult to boil it until done without burning. When intended for frying cold, some add, while making it, about a pint of flour to three quarts of meal. Have a hard-wood paddle, two feet long, with a blade two inches wide and seven inches long, to stir with.—*Mrs. W. W. Woods.*

FRIED MUSH.

A delicious breakfast relish is made by slicing cold mush thin and frying in a little hot lard. Or, dip in beaten eggs salted to taste, then in bread or cracker crumbs, and drop in *hot* lard, like dough-nuts.—*Miss A. W. S., Nashville, Tenn.*

HOE-CAKE.

Mix corn meal with water or milk (adding a little salt) to the thickness of stiff batter; stir thoroughly, spread on the baking-board, and tip up before the fire. On southern plantations they are often baked on the broad hoes used in the fields, hence the name.

ALABAMA JOHNNY-CAKE.

Cook a pint of rice till tender, add a table-spoon of butter; when cold add two beaten eggs and one pint of meal, and when mixed spread on an oaken board and bake by tipping the board up before the fire-place. When done on one side turn over. The dough should be spread half an inch thick.

JOHNNY-CAKE.

Two-thirds tea-spoon of soda, three table-spoons of sugar, one tea-spoon of cream of tartar, one egg, one cup of sweet milk, six table-spoons of Indian meal, three table-spoons of flour, and a little salt. This makes a thin batter.

RHODE ISLAND "SPAT-OUTS."

One pint of sweet milk, four table-spoons of wheat flour, two eggs well beaten, Indian meal to make a stiff batter, and a little salt; spat into round cakes half an inch thick, fry in lard like doughnuts, split, and eat warm with butter.—*One hundred years old.*

COLD-WATER GEMS.

With very cold or ice-water and Graham flour, and a little salt, make a rather stiff batter; heat and grease the irons, and bake twenty minutes in a hot oven.—*Mrs. O. M. Scott.*

GOOD GRAHAM GEMS.

Three cups of sour milk, one tea-spoon of soda, one of salt, one table-spoon of brown sugar, one of melted lard, one beaten egg; to the egg add the milk, then the sugar and salt, then the Graham flour (with the soda mixed in), together with the lard; make a stiff batter, so that it will drop, not pour, from the spoon. Have gem pans very hot, grease, fill, and bake fifteen minutes in a hot oven. —*Mrs. J. H. S.*

MRS. BUXTON'S GRAHAM GEMS.

Take one egg and beat well, add pinch of salt, one quart of

buttermilk or sour milk, and Graham flour enough to make a stiff batter; add one heaping tea-spoon of soda and stir thoroughly with a spoon; heat and grease gem-irons, and after dipping the spoon in cold water, drop a spoonful of batter in each pan, repeating until all are filled; bake in a quick oven half an hour. This measure will make a dozen.

SWEET-MILK GEMS.

Beat one egg well, add a pint of new milk, a little salt, and Graham flour until it will drop off the spoon nicely; heat and butter the gem-pans before dropping in the dough; bake in a hot oven twenty minutes.—*Mrs. R. L. Partridge.*

GRAHAM MUFFINS.

Two cups of sour milk, two table-spoons brown sugar, a little salt, one tea-spoon soda, sufficient Graham flour to make moderately stiff. If not convenient to use sour milk, use sweet, adding cream of tartar.—*Mrs. H. B. Sherman.*

GRAHAM MUSH.

Sift meal slowly into boiling salted water, stirring briskly until it is as thick as can be stirred with one hand; serve with milk or cream and sugar, or butter and syrup. It is much improved by removing from the kettle to a pan as soon as thoroughly mixed, and steaming for three or four hours. It may also be eaten cold, or sliced and fried like corn mush.

OAT-MEAL MUSH.

To two quarts boiling water well salted add one and a half cups best oat-meal. (Buy Irish, Scotch, or Canadian.) Stir in meal by degrees, and after stirring up a few times to prevent its settling down in a mass at the bottom, léave it to cook three hours *without stirring.* Cook in a custard-kettle with water in outer kettle. (While stirring in meal put inner kettle directly on stove.) To cook for breakfast it may be put on over night, allowing it to boil an hour or two in the evening, but it is better when freshly cooked. Serve with cream and sugar. This is unsurpassed as a breakfast dish, especially for growing children, who need bone and muscle-producing food. To be wholesome it must be *well cooked*, and not the pasty, half cooked mass usually served at boarding-houses. In lieu of a custard-kettle the mush can be made in a pan, or small tin bucket, and then placed in a steamer and steamed three hours.

CRACKED WHEAT.

Two quarts salted water to two cups best white winter wheat; boil two or three hours in a custard-kettle: Or, soak over night and boil at least three-fourths of an hour: Or, put boiling water in a pan or small tin bucket, set on stove, stir in wheat, set in steamer and steam four hours: Or, make a strong sack of thick muslin or drilling, moisten wheat with cold water, add a little salt, place in sack, leaving half the space for wheat to swell in. Fit a round sheet of tin, perforated with holes half an inch in diameter, to the inside of ordinary kettle, so that it will rest two or three inches from the bottom; lay sack on the tin, put in water enough to reach tin, and boil from three to four hours, supplying water as it evaporates. Serve with butter and syrup, or cream and sugar. When cold, slice and fry; or warm with a little milk and salt in a pan greased with a little butter; or make in griddle-cakes with a batter of eggs, milk, and a little flour, and pinch of salt.

FINE WHITE HOMINY OR GRITS.

Take two cups to two quarts salted water, soak over night, and boil three quarters of an hour in a custard kettle; serve with milk and sugar, or when cold slice and fry.

FRITTERS.

Make fritters quickly and beat thoroughly. A good rule for them is two eggs, one-half pint milk, one tea-spoon salt, and two cups flour; have the lard in which to cook them nice and sweet and boiling hot; test the heat by dropping in a tea-spoon of the batter—if the temperature is right it will quickly rise in a light ball with a splutter, and soon brown; take up carefully *the moment* they are done, with a wire spoon; drain in a hot colander and sift powdered sugar over them; serve hot. Pork fritters are made by dipping

3

thin bits of breakfast-bacon or fat pork in the batter; fruit fritters by chopping any kind of fresh or canned fruit fine and mixing it with batter, or by dipping quarters or halves in batter. The fruit may be improved in flavor by sprinkling sugar and grated lemon peel over it, and allowing it to remain two or three hours, after which drain and dip as above.

APPLE FRITTERS.

Three eggs beaten very light, one quart of milk; make a thin batter, add a little salt and the grated rind of one lemon; pare, core and slice thin one quart nice tart apples, add, and drop in spoonfuls in boiling lard; serve with sauce.—*Mrs. E. L. Fay, Washington Heights, New York.*

APPLE FRITTERS.

Make a batter in proportion of one cup sweet milk to two cups flour, a heaping tea-spoon baking powder, two eggs beaten separately, one table-spoon sugar, and salt-spoon salt; heat the milk a little more than milk-warm, add slowly to the beaten yolks and sugar, then add flour and whites of eggs, stir all together, and throw in thin slices of good sour apples, dipping the batter up over them; drop in boiling lard in large spoonfuls with piece of apple in each, and fry to a light brown. Serve with maple syrup or a nice syrup made of sugar.—*Mrs. James Henderson.*

CLAM FRITTERS.

Take raw clams, chopped fine, and make a batter with juice, an equal quantity of sweet milk, four eggs to each pint of liquid, and flour sufficient to stiffen; fry like other fritters.—*Mrs. H. B. S.*

CORN OYSTERS.

To one quart grated corn add three eggs and three or four grated crackers, beat well and season with pepper and salt; have ready in skillet butter and lard or beef-drippings in equal proportions, hot but not scorching; drop in little cakes about the size of an oyster (for this purpose using a tea-spoon); when brown turn and fry on the other side, watching constantly for fear of burning. If the fat is just the right heat, the oysters will be light and delicious, but if not, heavy and "soggy." Serve hot and keep dish well covered. It is better to beat whites of eggs to a stiff froth and add just before frying.—*Mrs. V. G. Hush, Minneapolis, Minn.*

CORN OYSTERS.

Mix well together one quart grated sweet corn, two tea-cups sweet milk, one tea-cup flour, one tea-spoon butter, two eggs well beaten; season with pepper and salt, and fry in butter like griddle-cakes.—*Mrs. H. B. S.*

CREAM FRITTERS.

One and a half pints flour, one pint milk, six well-beaten eggs, one-half nutmeg, two tea-spoons salt, one pint cream; stir the whole enough to mix the cream; fry in small cakes.—*Mrs. M. K. P.*

CUCUMBER FRITTERS.

Peel four large cucumbers, cut and cook in a sauce-pan with just a little water; mash and season well with salt and pepper, add two beaten eggs and flour to make a thick batter; put a table-spoon of lard in a skillet, make hot, and fry in little cakes.—*Mrs. A. H. T., Troy, New York.*

SNOW FRITTERS.

Stir together milk, flour, and a little salt, and make a rather thick batter; add *new-fallen* snow in the proportion of a tea-cup to a pint of milk; have the fat hot before stirring in the snow, and drop the batter into it with a spoon, or bake like pan-cakes on a hot griddle.

VANITIES.

Beat two eggs, stir in a pinch of salt and a half tea-spoon of rose-water, add sifted flour till just thick enough to roll out, cut with a cake-cutter, and fry quickly in hot lard. Sift powdered sugar on them while hot, and when cool put a tea-spoon of jelly in the center of each one. Nice for tea or dessert.—*Mrs. D. C. Harrington, Westfield, N. Y.*

GRIDDLE-CAKES.

Griddle-cakes should be well beaten when first made, and are much lighter when the eggs are separated, whipping the yolks to a thick cream, and adding the whites beaten to a stiff froth just before baking. Some never stir buckwheat cakes after they have risen, but take them out carefully with a large spoon, placing the spoon when emptied in a saucer, and not back again into the batter. In baking griddle-cakes have the griddle clean, and, if the cakes stick, sprinkle on some salt and rub with a coarse cloth before greasing; or, better still, provide a soapstone griddle which needs no greasing. (It must be made very *hot*, but if greased it is spoiled.) Griddle-cakes may be made with new-fallen snow, in the proportion of a tea-cup of snow to a pint of milk. Fresh snow contains a large proportion of ammonia which renders the cakes light, but which soon evaporates, rendering old snow useless for this purpose.

BUCKWHEAT CAKES.

Buckwheat flour, when properly ground, is perfectly *free from grit*. The grain should be run through the smutter with a strong blast before grinding, and the greatest care taken through the whole process. Adulteration with rye or corn cheapens the flour, but injures the quality. The pure buckwheat is best, and is unsurpassed for griddle-cakes. To make batter, warm one pint sweet milk and one pint water, (one may be cold and the other boiling); put half this mixture in a stone crock, add five tea-cups buckwheat flour, beat *well* until smooth, add the rest of the milk and water, and last a tea-cup of yeast. Or, the same ingredients and proportions may be used except adding two table-spoons of molasses or sugar, and using one quart of water instead of one pint each of milk and water.—*Miss S. A. Melching.*

BREAD CAKES.

Take stale bread and soak over night in sour milk; in the morning rub through a colander, and to one quart add the yolks of two eggs, one tea-spoon salt, one tea-spoon soda, two table-spoons sugar, and flour enough to make a batter a little thicker than for buckwheat cakes, add last the well-beaten whites of the eggs, and bake.

CRUMB GRIDDLE-CAKES.

The night before using put some bread crumbs to soak in one quart of sour milk; in the morning rub through a sieve and add four well-beaten eggs, two tea-spoons soda dissolved in a little water, one table-spoon melted butter, and enough corn meal to make them the consistency of ordinary griddle-cakes. It is better to beat yolks and whites separately. stirring the whites lightly in just before baking.—*Mrs. W. E. Scobey, Kankakee, Ill.*

FLANNEL-CAKES.

Make hot a pint of sweet milk, and into it put two heaping table-spoons butter, let melt, then add a pint of cold milk, the well-beaten yolks of four eggs—placing the whites in a cold place—a tea-spoon of salt, four table-spoons potato yeast, and sufficient flour to make a stiff batter; set in a warm place to rise, let stand three hours or over night; before baking add the beaten whites; fry like any other griddle-cakes. Be sure to make batter just stiff enough, for flour must not be added in the morning unless it is allowed to rise again.

CORN CAKES.

One pint corn-meal, one of sour milk or buttermilk, one egg, one tea-spoon soda, one of salt. A table-spoon of flour or corn starch may be used in place of the egg; bake on a griddle.

INDIAN PANCAKES.

One pint Indian meal, one tea-spoon salt, small tea-spoon soda; pour on boiling water until a little thinner than mush; let stand until cool, add the yolks of four eggs, half a cup of flour in which is mixed two tea-spoons cream tartar; stir in as much sweet milk or water as will make the batter suitable to bake; beat the whites well, and add just before baking.—*Mrs. W. W. Woods.*

RICE GRIDDLE-CAKES.

Boil half a cup rice; when cold mix one quart sweet milk, the yolks of four eggs, and flour sufficient to make a stiff batter; beat the whites to a froth, stir in one tea-spoon soda, and two of cream tartar; add a little salt, and lastly the whites of eggs; bake on a griddle. A nice way to serve is to spread them while hot with butter, and almost any kind of preserves or jelly; roll them up neatly, cut off the ends, sprinkle them with sugar, and serve immediately. —*Mrs. Walter Mitchell, Gallipolis.*

Soft Short-cake.

One cup sour cream, one tea-spoon saleratus; stir in flour enough to make a batter a little stiffer than for griddle-cakes; bake on a griddle, split open and put on milk and butter.—*Harriet O. Backus, West Killingly, Conn.*

Tomato Batter Cakes.

Make an egg batter as for batter cakes; take and slice large, solid ripe tomatoes, cover with batter and fry on a griddle like any griddle-cakes; season with pepper and salt while frying. Tomatoes so prepared make a nice breakfast dish.—*Mrs. G. W. Collins, Urbana.*

Y E A S T ·

There are various ways of making, but the three best kinds are dry, soft hop, and potato yeast. The dry should be made in May or June for summer use, and in October for winter use. In hot and damp weather, dry yeast sometimes loses its vitality; however, many use it on account of its convenience, since there is no danger of its souring in summer or freezing in winter. Soft hop or potato yeast will keep in a cool place one or two weeks in warm weather, and in cold weather five or six weeks, care being taken that it does not freeze. Never add soda to yeast; if it becomes sour it will do to start fresh yeast, but will *never* make good bread. Potato yeast is made either by boiling and mashing the potatoes, or by grating them while raw, and adding them to the boiling hop water *immediately,* for if allowed to stand they darken, and the yeast will not be as white. A good way to prevent the potatoes from darkening is to grate them into a pan half filled with cold water. As grated the potatoes sink to the bottom; when done grating, pour off the water and add the potatoes to the boiling hop water. A stone jar with a close-fitting cover is best to keep yeast in, and should be scalded as often as emptied. In taking out for use, stir up well from the bottom.

Dry Yeast.

Boil two large potatoes and a handful of hops (the latter in a bag) in three pints water; when done, take out potatoes, mash well, add one pint flour, and pour boiling hot water over all; beat well together, adding one table-spoon salt, one of ginger, and one-half cup sugar; when luke-warm add one cup good yeast and let stand two days (or only one day, if very warm weather), stirring down frequently; add good white corn meal until thick enough to make into cakes about half an inch in thickness; place to dry in the shade where the air will pass freely so as to dry them as soon as possible; turn the cakes frequently, breaking them up somewhat so they will dry out evenly; when thoroughly dried put in a paper sack, and keep in a dry place. A small cake will make sponge sufficient to bake five or six ordinary loaves.—*Mrs. E. T. Carson.*

Hop Yeast.

Boil four potatoes and a small handful of hops tied in a bag in one gallon water; when the potatoes are done, pour the water over four table-spoons flour in a stone jar, mash and add potatoes; let stand until milk warm, then add one cup hop yeast, stir well and let remain in kitchen cupboard for twelve hours undisturbed; then add half a cup sugar, put in a stone jug, cork tightly and set in a cool place. In summer add one table-spoon ginger and three of salt; shake well and take one cup yeast to three pints water. This yeast will keep sweet for six weeks.—*Mrs. J. T. Liggett, Detroit, Michigan.*

Potato Yeast without Hops.

Four good-sized potatoes peeled, boiled and mashed, four table-spoons white sugar, one of ginger, one of salt, two cups flour; pour over this a pint of boiling water, and beat till all the lumps disappear. After it has cooled, add to it one cup good yeast and set away to rise; when risen put in glass or stone jar, cover and set away in a cool place.—*Mrs. George H. Rust, Minneapolis, Minn.*

Potato Yeast.

Boil one cup hops in a sack in two quarts water for fifteen minutes, remove sack with hops, add five good-sized Irish potatoes, peeled and grated raw, one cup white sugar, one table-spoon salt, and one of ginger; stir occasionally and cook from five to ten minutes, and it will boil up thick like starch; turn into a jar, and when just tepid in summer, or quite warm in winter, add one-half pint good yeast (always save some to start with); set jar in a large tin pan, and as often as it rises, stir down until fermentation ceases, when it will be quite thin. Cover closely, and set away in a cool place and it will keep two weeks. When yeast smells sour but does not taste sour it is still good; if it has no smell it is dead. One cup will make six good-sized loaves.—*Mrs. D. Buxton.*

To Hasten Milk Yeast.

Take one tea-cup of wheat "shorts," one tea-spoon salt, one of soda, one of ginger; add boiling water enough to make a thin bat ter. Two table-spoons or less added to common milk or salt-rising yeast will cause it to rise in an hour or two. If kept in a cool place it will be good for two weeks in winter.

Yeast.

Pare and boil four ordinary-sized potatoes, boiling at the same time in a separate vessel a good handful of hops. When the potatoes are done, mash fine and add, after straining, the water in which the hops were boiled; put into this one cup white sugar and one-half cup salt, and add sufficient water to make one gallon; when cold add one cup of good yeast, let stand in a warm place for a few hours until it will "sing" on being stirred, when it is ready for use. Keep covered in a cellar or cool place—*Mrs. C. M.*

CAKE-MAKING.

"LET all things be done decently and in order," and the first to put in order when you are going to bake is yourself. Secure the hair in a net or other covering, to prevent any from falling, and brush the shoulders and back to be sure none are lodged there that might blow off; make the hands and finger-nails clean, roll the sleeves up above the elbows, and put on a large, clean apron. Clean the kitchen table of utensils and every thing not needed, and provide every thing that will be needed until the cake is baked, not forgetting even the broom-splints previously picked off the new broom and laid away carefully in a little box. (A knitting-needle may be kept for testing cake instead of splints.) If it is warm weather place the eggs in cold water, and let stand a few minutes, as they will then make a finer froth, and be sure they are fresh, as they will not make a stiff froth with any amount of beating if old. Grease the pans with fresh lard, which is much better than butter; line the bottom with paper, using six or eight thicknesses if the cake is large, and greasing the top one well. (In some ovens, however, fewer thicknesses of paper would be needed on the bottom, and in some the sides also should be lined with one or two thicknesses.) Sift flour and sugar (if not pulverized) and measure or weigh. Firkin or very salt butter should be cut in bits and washed to freshen a little; if very hard, warm carefully, but in no case allow any of it to melt. Good butter must be used, as the heat develops any latent bad qualities. Beat the yolks of eggs thoroughly, and strain; set the whites away in a cool place until the cake is ready for them, then beat them vigorously in a cool room, till they will

(41)

remain in the dish when turned upside down. Sift a part of the measured flour with the baking-powder or soda and cream tartar through a hand-sieve (which should be among the utensils of every housekeeper), and mix thoroughly with the rest of the flour. In using new flour for either bread or cake-making, it can be "ripened" for use by placing the quantity intended for baking in the hot sun for a few hours, or before the kitchen fire. In using milk, note this: that sour milk makes a spongy, light cake; sweet milk, one that cuts like pound cake; remembering that with sour milk soda alone is used, while with sweet milk baking-powder or soda and cream tartar are to be added.

Having thus gathered the material, beat the butter to a cream, add the sugar gradually, then the milk in small quantities (never use fresh and stale milk in same cake), next the yolks of eggs, then a part of the flour, then a part of the whites, and so on until the whole is used; lastly, add the flavoring. There is great "knack" in beating cake; don't *stir*, but *beat* thoroughly, bringing the batter up from the bottom of the dish at every stroke; in this way the air is driven into the cells of the batter, instead of out of them—but the cells will be finer if beaten more slowly at the last, remembering that the motion should always be upward. In winter it is easier to beat with the hand, but in summer a wooden spoon is better. Never beat a cake in tin, but use earthen or stoneware. All cakes not made with yeast should be baked as soon as possible after they are mixed. Unskillful mixing, too rapid or unequal baking, or a sudden decrease in heat before it is quite done, will cause streaks in the cake.

FRUIT CAKE.

Most ladies think fruit cake quite incomplete without wine or brandy, but it can be made equally good on strictly temperance principles, by substituting one-third of a cup of molasses for a wine-glass of brandy. To facilitate the operation of seeding raisins, pour boiling-water on a few at a time. This will not injure the fruit or cake. To seed, clip with the scissors, or cut with a sharp knife. Do not chop too fine; if for light fruit cake, seeding is all that is necessary. Slice the citron thin, and do not have the pieces too large, or they will cause the cake to break apart in cutting. Currants should be kept prepared for use as follows: Wash in warm water, rubbing well, pour off water, and repeat until the water is clear; drain them in a sieve, spread on a cloth and rub dry; pick out bad ones, dry carefully in a cool oven, and set away for use. When the fruit is all mixed, cream the butter and sugar —this is very important in all cakes—add the spices, molasses, or liquors, then the milk (if any is used), next the eggs well beaten, adding whites with the flour as previously directed. Always beat whites and yolks separately if many eggs are used, but if only a few, it is just as well to beat both together. Next add the flour (which in making black fruit cake may be browned), prepared with baking-powder or soda and cream tartar, then the flavoring (if any is used), and lastly the fruit dredged with a *very little* flour. Some prefer to *mix* the fruit with all the flour.

In making very large cakes that require three or four hours to bake, an excellent way for lining the pan is the following: Fit three papers carefully, grease thoroughly, make a paste of equal parts Graham and fine flour wet with water just stiff enough to spread easily with a spoon, place the first paper in the pan with the greased side down, and spread the paste evenly over the paper about as thick as pie-crust. In covering the sides of the pan, use a little paste to stick a portion of the paper to the top of the pan to keep it from slipping out of place, press the second paper carefully into its place with the greased side up, and next put in the third paper as you would into any baking-pan, and pour in the cake. Earthen pans are used by some, as they do not heat so quickly, and are less liable to burn the cake.

All except layer cakes should be covered with a paper cap when first put into the oven. Take a square of brown paper large enough to cover well the cake-pan, cut off the corners, and lay a plait on four sides, fastening each with a pin so as to fit nicely over the pan. This will throw it up in the center, so that the cover will not touch the cake. Save the cap, as it can be used several times.

THE OVEN.

Too much care can not be given to the preparation of the oven, which is oftener too hot than too cool; however, an oven too cold at

first will ruin any cake.   Cakes should rise and begin to bake
before browning much, large cakes requiring a good, steady, solid
heat, about such as for baking bread; layer cakes, a brisk hot fire,
as they must be baked quickly.   A good plan is to fill the stove
with hard wood (ash is the best for baking), let it burn until there
is a good body of heat, and then turn damper so as to throw the
heat to the bottom of oven for fully ten minutes before the cake is
put in.   In this way a steady heat to start with is secured.   Generally it is better to close the hearth when the cake is put in, as this
stops the draft and makes a more regular heat.   Keep adding wood
in small quantities, for if the heat becomes slack the cake will be
heavy.   Great care must be taken, for some stoves need to have the
dampers changed every now and then, but as a rule more heat is
needed at the bottom of the oven than at the top.   Many test their
ovens in this way: if the hand can be held in from twenty to thirty-
five seconds (or while counting twenty or thirty-five), it is a quick
oven, from thirty-five to forty-five seconds is "moderate," and from
forty-five to sixty seconds is "slow."   Sixty seconds is a good oven
to begin with for large fruit cakes.   All systematic housekeepers
will hail the day when some enterprising Yankee or Buckeye girl
shall invent a stove or range with a thermometer attached to the
oven, so that the heat may be regulated accurately and intelligently.
If necessary to move the cake while baking, do it very gently.   Be
careful not to remove from the oven until done, and do not leave
oven door open.   Allow about thirty minutes for each inch of thickness in a quick oven, and more time in a slow one.   Test with a
broom-splint or knitting-needle, and if the dough does not adhere, it
is done.   Settling away from the pan a little, and stopping its
"singing," are other indications that the cake is ready to leave the
oven.   It should remain in the pan at least fifteen minutes after
taking from the oven, and it is better to leave the "cap" on until
the cake is carefully removed from the pan and set away, *always*
right side up.   A tin chest or stone jar is best to keep it in.   Coffee
cake should be put away before it is cold, and so closely wrapped
in a large napkin that the aroma will not be lost.

SPONGE-CAKE.

The good quality of all delicate cake, and especially of sponge-cake, depends very much upon its being made with fresh eggs. It must be quickly put together, beaten with rapidity, and baked in a rather quick oven. It is made "sticky" and less light by being stirred long. There is no other cake so dependent upon care and good judgment in baking as sponge-cake. In making white cake, if not convenient to use the yolks that are left, they will keep until the next day by being *thoroughly* beaten and set in a cool place. To prepare cocoa-nut, cut a hole through the meat at one of the holes in the end, draw off the milk, pound the nut well on all sides to loosen the meat, crack, take out meat, and set the pieces in the heater or in a cool, open oven over night, or for a few hours, to dry, then grate; if all is not used, sprinkle with sugar (after grating) and spread out in a cool, dry place, and it will keep for weeks. In cutting layer cakes, it is better to first make a round hole in the center, with a knife, or a tin tube, about an inch and a quarter in diameter. This prevents the edge of the cake from crumbling in cutting.

CENTENNIAL CAKE.

Two cups pulverized sugar, one of butter rubbed to a light cream with the sugar, one of sweet milk, three of flour, half cup corn starch, four eggs, half pound chopped raisins, half a grated nutmeg and two tea-spoons baking-powder.—*Mrs. A. S. Chapman.*

BUCKEYE CAKE.

One cup butter, two of white sugar, four of sifted flour, five eggs beaten separately, one cup sour milk, tea-spoon soda, pound seeded raisins chopped a little; beat the butter and sugar to a cream, add the yolks and milk, and stir in the flour with soda well mixed through it; then add the white of the eggs beaten to a stiff froth, and lastly the raisins dredged with a little flour; bake one and one-half hours. Use coffee-cups to measure. This makes a cake for a six-quart pan.—*Mrs. W. W. W.*

ALMOND, HICKORY-NUT OR COCOA-NUT CAKE.

Three-fourths pound flour, half tea-spoon salt, fourth pound butter, pound of sugar, tea-cup sour cream, four eggs, lemon flavor to taste, and a tea-spoon soda dissolved in two tea-spoons hot water; mix all thoroughly, grate in the white part of a cocoa-nut, or stir in a pint of chopped hickory-nuts, or a pint of blanched almonds pounded.—*Mrs. J. W. Grubbs, Richmond, Ind.*

BLACK CAKE.

One pound powdered white sugar, three-quarters pound butter, pound sifted flour (browned or not as preferred), twelve eggs beaten separately, two pounds raisins stoned and part of them chopped, two of currants carefully cleaned, half pound citron cut in strips, quarter ounce each of cinnamon, nutmeg and cloves mixed, wineglass wine and one of brandy; rub butter and sugar together, add yolks of eggs, part of flour, the spice and whites of eggs well beaten; then add remainder of flour, and wine and brandy; mix all thoroughly together; cover bottom and sides of a four-quart milk-pan with buttered white paper, put in a layer of the mixture, then a layer of the fruit (first dredging the fruit with flour), until pan is filled up three or four inches, and then bake four hours. A small cup of Orleans molasses makes the cake blacker and more moist, but for this it is not necessary to add more flour. Bake three and one-half or four hours in a slow oven.—*Mrs. M. M. Munsell, Delaware.*

BLACK CAKE.

One pound butter, one of brown sugar, one of flour, one of raisins, one of currants, half pound citron, table-spoon each cinnamon, allspice and cloves, ten eggs the whites and yolks beaten separately, three tea-spoons baking-powder; add just before baking a wine-glass brandy, or third cup good molasses; seed raisins, chop citron fine, and wash and dry the currants; mix butter and sugar, add the eggs, and lastly the flour in which the fruit, spices and baking-powder having been well mixed; bake in a six-quart pan four hours.—*Miss Mary Sealts, Mt. Vernon.*

BLACK CAKE.

One pound flour, one of currants, one of raisins, one of sugar, half pound citron, half pound chopped figs, three-fourths pound butter, ten eggs leaving out two whites, tea-cup molasses, one of sour cream and soda, one gill brandy or good whisky, half cup cinnamon, two table-spoons allspice and cloves, four table-spoons jam.—*Mrs. Gov. Kirkwood, Iowa.*

BLACK CAKE.

Two cups brown sugar, one and one-half cups of butter, six eggs beaten separately, three cups flour (brown the flour), two table-spoons molasses, one of cinnamon, one tea-spoon mace, one of cloves, two cups sweet milk, two pounds raisins, two of currants, a half pound citron, one tea-spoon soda, two of cream tartar. Bake three hours.—*Mrs. A. B. Morey.*

BREAKFAST CAKE.

One cup Orleans molasses, one of brown sugar, one of shortening (butter and lard mixed), one of cold coffee, four of flour, one tea-spoon soda in the coffee, one each of cloves, cinnamon and allspice, and one nutmeg. Add fruit if desired.

BUFORD CAKE.

One quart flour, one pint sugar, a cup butter, a cup sweet milk, four eggs, spices of all kinds in small quantities, tea-spoon soda, two of cream tartar, half pound raisins, half pound currants; this quantity will make two large loaves.—*Mrs. Gov. D. H. Chamberlain, South Carolina.*

BREAD CAKE.

Three coffee-cups yeast dough, light enough to bake for bread, two and two-thirds cups sugar, one cup butter, three eggs, one nutmeg; put all together and work with the hands until smooth as pound-cake. It is very important that all should be mixed very thoroughly with the light dough. Add raisins and as much fruit as desired and let rise half an hour in the pans in which you bake. The oven should be about right for bread. This is easily made and is quite as nice as common loaf-cake.—*Mrs. Chas. Fullington.*

BREAD CAKE.

Two cups light bread dough, one and one-half cups sugar, half cup butter, three table-spoons sour milk in which has been dis-

solved half tea-spoon soda, half a grated nutmeg, tea-spoon cinnamon, cup raisins chopped a little and floured; stir all well together, adding fruit lastly, let rise half an hour and bake in a
moderate oven.—*Mrs. Hartle, Massillon.*

BRIDE'S CAKE.

Whites of twelve eggs, three cups sugar, small cup butter, a
cup sweet milk, four small cups flour, half cup corn starch, two
tea-spoons baking-powder, lemon to taste.   Adding a cup citron
sliced thin and dusted with flour, makes a beautiful citron cake.
—*Mrs. Harvey Clark, Piqua.*

CREAM CAKE.

Put two cups flour in a crock and mix with two level tea-
spoons cream tartar and one of soda, make well in the center into
which put one cup sugar, one of sweet cream, one. egg and small
tea-spoon salt; mix all quickly together, flavor with tea-spoon
lemon; put in pan to bake.   Add cup raisins, or currants if you
like, and it makes a nice cake pudding to eat hot with sauce.
Sour cream can be used instead of sweet by omitting the cream
tartar and using two eggs instead of one.—*Miss Sarah Cryder.*

WHIPPED-CREAM CAKE.

One cup sugar, two eggs, two table-spoons softened butter and
four of milk; beat all well together, add a cup of flour in which
has been mixed tea-spoon cream tartar and half tea-spoon soda.
Bake in rather small square dripping-pan.   When cake is cool
have ready a half pint sweet cream whipped to a stiff froth,
sweeten and flavor to taste, spread over cake and serve while
fresh.   The cream will froth easier to be made cold by setting
on ice before whipping.—*Mrs. Wm. Brown, Massillon.*

CORN-STARCH CAKE.

Two coffee-cups pulverized sugar, three-fourths cup butter, cup
corn starch dissolved in a cup of sweet milk, two cups flour, whites
of seven eggs, two tea-spoons cream tartar, tea-spoon soda mixed
thoroughly with the flour; cream butter and sugar, add starch and
milk, then add the whites and flour gradually until all is used.
Flavor with lemon or rose.—*Mrs. W. P. Anderson.*

COFFEE CAKE.

Two cups brown sugar, one of butter, one of molasses, one of strong coffee as prepared for the table, four eggs, one tea-spoon saleratus, two of cinnamon, two of cloves, one of grated nutmeg, pound raisins, one of currants, four cups flour.—*Mrs. Wm. Skinner, Battle Creek, Mich.*

COFFEE CAKE.

One cup brown sugar, cup molasses, half cup butter, cup strong coffee, one egg or yolks of two, four even cups flour, heaping tea-spoon soda in the flour, table-spoon cinnamon, tea-spoon cloves, two pounds raisins, fourth pound citron, Soften the butter, beat with the sugar, add the egg, spices, molasses and coffee, then the flour, and lastly the fruit dredged with a little flour. Bake one hour in moderate oven or make in two small loaves which will bake in a short time.—*Mrs. D. Buxton.*

COCOA-NUT CAKE.

One cup butter, three of sugar, one of sweet milk, four and a half of flour, four eggs with whites beaten to a stiff froth, a tea-spoon soda, two of cream tartar, one grated cocoa-nut.—*Mrs. J. Holland, New Castle, Ind.*

CARAMEL CAKE.

One cup butter, two of sugar, a scant cup milk, one and a half cups flour, cup corn starch, whites of seven eggs, three tea-spoons baking-powder in the flour; bake in a long pan. Take half pound brown sugar, scant quarter pound chocolate, half cup milk, butter size of an egg, two tea-spoons vanilla; mix thoroughly and cook as syrup until stiff enough to spread; spread on cake and set in the oven to dry.—*Mrs. George Bever.*

CINCINNATI CAKE.

Pour over one pound fat pork chopped fine one pint boiling water, two cups brown sugar, one of molasses, one table-spoon each of cloves and nutmeg, and two of cinnamon, two pounds raisins, fourth pound citron, half glass brandy, tea-spoon salt, three of baking-powder, and seven cups of sifted flour. Bake slowly two and a half hours.—*Mrs. G. E. Kinney.*

4

CUP-CAKE.

One pound flour, one pound sugar, half pound butter, eight eggs
beaten separately, a nutmeg, a cup milk, two tea-spoons yeast-
powder; cream butter with half the flour; mix yeast powder with
the remaining portion of the flour, sift it into the batter, add the
sugar and eggs which have been beaten together, and put it all
into the pans.—*Mrs. Gov. Hendricks, Indiana.*

CIDER CAKE.

Six cups flour, three of sugar, one of butter, one of sour cider,
tea-spoon soda, four eggs; beat the eggs, butter and sugar to a
cream, stir in the flour, and then add the cider in which the soda
has been dissolved.—*Miss Mary A. Dugan.*

CHOCOLATE CAKE.

One cup butter, three of brown sugar, one of sweet milk, four
of flour, yolks of seven eggs, nine table-spoons grated Baker's
chocolate, three tea-spoons baking-powder. This may be baked as
a layer cake, making a white cake of the whites of the eggs, baking in layers, and putting them together with frosting, alternating
the layers.—*Mrs. Frank Woods Robinson, Kenton.*

DELICATE CAKE.

Three cups flour, two of sugar, three-fourths cup sweet milk,
whites of six eggs, half cup butter, tea-spoon cream tartar, half
tea-spoon of soda. Flavor with lemon.—*Miss Mary E. Miller.*

DELICATE CAKE.

One cup sugar, small half cup butter, half cup sweet milk,
whites of four eggs beaten to a froth, one and a half cups flour, a
tea-spoon baking-powder, two of lemon, a cup seeded raisins.
Bake slowly.—*Mrs. Hyde, Mt. Vernon.*

DELICATE CAKE.

Four cups fine white sugar, five of sifted flour, one of butter, one
and a half of sweet milk, one tea-spoon soda dissolved in the milk,
two of cream tartar, whites of sixteen eggs; stir sugar and butter
to a cream, then add whites of eggs beaten to a stiff froth, next add
flour, then the milk and soda; stir several minutes, and then add

cream tartar and flavoring. This makes a large cake.—*Mrs Mary S. Moore, Granville.*

EVERLASTING CAKE.

Beat together the yolks of six eggs and three quarters of a pint white sugar, add one and a half pints blanched and shelled almonds, half pound sliced citron well floured, and the whipped whites with one and a half pints sifted flour; pour one and a half inches thick in well-greased dripping-pans, bake in a quick oven, and, when done, cut slices one inch thick across the cake, turn each slice over on its side, return to oven and bake a short time. When cold place in a tin box. These will keep a year and a half or more, and are nice to have in store.—*Mrs. J. S. Williams, Brooklyn.*

EGGLESS CAKE.

One and a half tea-cups sugar, one of sour milk, three (level) of sifted flour, half cup butter, tea-spoon soda, half tea-spoon cinnamon, half tea-spoon grated nutmeg, tea-cup raisins chopped and well floured.—*Miss Louise Skinner.*

SALEM ELECTION CAKE.

Four pounds flour, one and a half of sugar, half pound butter, four eggs, one pint yeast, and spice.—*One hundred years old.*

OLD HARTFORD ELECTION CAKE.

Five pounds sifted flour, two of butter, two of sugar, three gills distillery yeast or twice the quantity of home brewed, four eggs, gill of wine, gill of brandy, one quart sweet milk, half an ounce of nutmeg, two pounds raisins, one of citron; rub the butter and flour together very fine, add half the sugar, then the yeast and half the milk (hot in winter, blood-warm in summer), then add the eggs, then remainder of the milk, and the wine; beat well and let rise in a warm place all night; in the morning beat a long time, adding brandy, sugar, spice, and fruit well floured, and allow to rise again very light, after which put in cake-pans and let rise ten or fifteen minutes; have the oven about as hot as for bread. This cake will keep any length of time. For raised cakes use the yeast made from Mrs. Buxton's recipe; if fresh-made, it is always a perfect success for cakes. This recipe is over one hundred years old.—*Mrs. Eliza Burnham, Milford Center.*

APPLE FRUIT CAKE.

One cup butter, two of sugar, one of milk, two eggs, tea-spoon soda, three and a half cups flour, two of raisins, three of dried apples soaked over night and then chopped fine and stewed two hours in two cups molasses; beat butter and sugar to a cream, add milk in which dissolve soda, then the beaten eggs and flour, and lastly the raisins and apples well stirred in; pour in pan and bake an hour and a half.—*Mrs. C. M. Ingman.*

FRUIT CAKE.

One cup butter, one of brown sugar, half pint molasses, two eggs, cup sour milk, tea-spoon soda, pound of flour, one of currants, one and a half pounds raisins.   Flavor to taste.—*Mrs. M. E. Nicely.*

FRUIT LOAF-CAKE.

One cup butter, two of brown sugar, one of New Orleans molasses, one of sweet milk, three eggs, five cups sifted flour, two teaspoons cream tartar in the flour, teaspoon soda in the milk, tablespoon cinnamon, one nutmeg, one pound raisins, one of currants, quarter pound citron (citron may be omitted, and half the quantity of raisins and currants will do).   Put flour in a large crock, mix well with cream tartar, make a well in the center, put in other ingredients, having warmed the butter and molasses a little; mix well together with the hands, putting in the fruit last after it has been floured; bake two hours in a moderate oven.   This will make two common-sized loaves.—*Mrs. N. S. Long.*

FRUIT CAKE.

Five cups flour, five eggs, one cup butter, one of lard, two of sugar, one of molasses, one pound raisins, one of currants, half pound citron, half tea-spoon soda, and a half tea-spoon cream tartar. —*Mrs. H. E. Roberts, Upper Alton, Ill.*

FRUIT CAKE.

Three pounds butter, three of brown sugar, beaten to a cream, three of flour, six of currants, six of raisins, after seeds are removed, one of citron sliced thin, three glasses brandy, twenty-eight eggs, one ounce cinnamon, one of grated nutmeg, three-quarters ounce cloves, half ounce mace; roll the raisins, currants, and citron in part of the flour.—*Miss H. D. Martin, N. Y. City.*

Fruit Cake.

One pound brown sugar, one of butter, one of eggs, one of flour, two of raisins, two of currants, half pound citron, a nutmeg, table-spoon cloves, one of allspice, half pint brandy, and two tea-spoons baking-powder. After baking, while yet warm, pour over cake a half pint wine. This makes the cake delicious.—*Miss Angie Skinner, Somerset.*

Excellent Fruit Cake.

One and a half pounds raisins, one and a fourth pounds currants, three-fourths pound citron, pound butter, pound sugar, one and a fourth pounds flour, ten eggs, two table-spoons lemon, two tea-spoons yeast powder, and a fourth pound flour mixed in the fruit.—*Mrs. J. W. Grubbs, Richmond, Ind.*

Scotch Fruit Cake.

A cup butter, two of white sugar, four of sifted flour, three-fourths cup sour milk, half tea-spoon soda, nine eggs beaten separately, one pound raisins, half pound currants, a fourth pound citron; cream the butter and sugar, add milk gradually, then beaten yolks of eggs, and lastly, while stirring in flour, the whites well whipped. Flavor with one tea-spoon lemon and one of vanilla extract, and have raisins chopped a little, or, better still, seeded, and citron sliced thin. Wash and dry currants before using, and flour all fruit slightly. In putting cake in pan, place first a thin layer of cake, then sprinkle in some of the three kinds of fruit, then a layer of cake and so on, always finishing off with a thin layer of cake. Bake in a moderate oven for two hours.—*Mrs. J. H. Shearer.*

Thanksgiving Fruit Cake.

Six pounds flour, three of butter, three and a half of sugar, an ounce mace, two glasses wine, two glasses brandy, four pounds raisins, half pound citron, six eggs, one pint yeast, small tea-spoon soda put in at last moment. After tea, take all the flour, (except one plate for dredging raisins), a small piece butter, and a quart or more of milk, and mix like biscuit; then mix butter and sugar, and at nine o'clock in the evening, if sufficiently light, put one-third of butter and sugar into dough; at twelve add another third, and very early in the morning the remainder; about eleven o'clock, if light enough, begin kneading, and continue for an hour, adding meanwhile all the other ingredients. This will make seven loaves. —*Mrs. Woodworth, Springfield, Mass.*

FEATHER CAKE.

Half cup butter, three of flour, two of sugar, one of milk, three eggs, a little grated lemon, two tea-spoons baking-powder.—*Mrs. E. L. C., Springfield.*

CHOICE FIG, CAKE.

A large cup butter, two and a half of sugar, one of sweet milk, three pints flour with three tea-spoons baking-powder, whites of sixteen eggs, a pound and a quarter of figs well floured and cut in strips like citron; no flavoring.—*Mrs. A. B. Morey.*

GROOM'S CAKE.

Ten eggs beaten separately, one pound butter, one of white sugar, one of flour, two of almonds blanched and chopped fine, one of seeded raisins, half pound citron, shaved fine; beat butter to a cream, add sugar gradually, then the well-beaten yolks; stir all till very light, and add the chopped almonds; beat the whites stiff and add gently with the flour; take a little more flour and sprinkle over the raisins and citron, then put in the cake-pan, first a layer of cake batter, then a layer of raisins and citron, then cake, and so on till all is used, finishing off with a layer of cake. Bake in a moderate oven two hours.—*Mary Wilcox, Dalton.*

HARD-MONEY CAKE.

Gold Part.—Yolks of eight eggs, scant cup butter, two of sugar, four of flour, one of sour milk, tea-spoon soda, table-spoon corn starch; flavor with lemon and vanilla.

Silver Part.—Two cups sugar, one of butter, four (scant) of flour, one of sour milk, tea-spoon soda, table-spoon corn starch, whites of eight eggs; flavor with almond or peach. Put in pan, alternately, one spoonful of gold and one of silver.—*Miss Emma Fisher.*

HAYES' CAKE.

One cup sugar, half cup butter, three eggs beaten well together, level tea-spoon soda stirred in half cup sour milk, two small cups flour; flavor with lemon, pour in small dripping-pan, bake half an hour, and cut in squares.—*Miss Flora Ziegler, Columbus.*

HICKORY-NUT CAKE.

Two cups sugar, one of milk, two-thirds cup butter, three of flour, three eggs, two tea-spoons baking-powder, a cup nut-kernels cut fine.—*Mrs. Judge West, Bellefontaine.*

HICKORY-NUT CAKE.

A cup butter, two of sugar, three of flour, one of sweet milk, whites of seven and yolks of two eggs, a tea-spoon soda, two of cream tartar, one pint hickory-nut meats rolled and sprinkled with flour; beat the whites to a stiff froth.—*Mrs. A. B. Morey*

IMPERIAL CAKE.

One pound butter and one of sugar beaten to a cream, one pound flour, the grated rind and juice of a lemon, nine eggs, one and a quarter pounds almonds before they are cracked, half pound citron, half pound raisins; beat the yolks light, add sugar and butter, then the whites beaten to a stiff froth, and the flour, reserving a part for the fruit, and lastly, the nuts blanched, cut fine and mixed with fruit and the rest of the flour. This is very delicious, and will keep for months.—*Mrs. E. R. May, Minneapolis, Minn.*

LADY'S CAKE.

One-half cup butter, one and a half of sugar, two of flour, nearly one of sweet milk, half tea-spoon soda, one of cream tartar, whites of four eggs well beaten; flavor with peach or almond.—*Miss M. E. W., Madison.*

YELLOW LADY'S-CAKE.

One and a half cups flour, one of sugar, half cup butter, half cup sweet milk, tea-spoon soda, two tea-spoons cream tartar, yolks of four eggs, tea-spoon vanilla.—*Olivia S. Hinman, Battle Creek, Mich.*

LEMON CAKE.

One pound flour, one of sugar, three-fourths pound butter, seven eggs, juice of one and rind of two lemons. The sugar, butter, and yolks of eggs must be beaten a long time, adding by degrees the flour, and the whites of eggs last. A tumbler and a half of sliced citron may be added. This keeps well.—*Miss M. B. Fullington.*

AUNT HETTIE'S LOAF CAKE.

Two cups sugar and one of butter beaten to a cream, three eggs, the whites beaten separately, three cups flour with one tea-spoon cream tartar stirred in, yolks of the eggs stirred well with the sugar and butter; now add three cups more flour with one tea-spoon cream tartar, one cup sweet milk and the whites of the eggs, and then stir again; add one nutmeg, one pound raisins or currants dredged with flour, one tea-spoon soda dissolved in four table-spoons of water. This makes two nice loaves, and is excellent.

FRENCH LOAF CAKE.

Five cups sugar, three of butter, two of milk, ten of flour, six eggs, three nutmegs, pound seeded raisins, a grated lemon, small tea-spoon soda, wine-glass wine, one of brandy, or, two-thirds of a cup of Orleans molasses.—*Mrs. A. S. Chapman.*

OLD-FASHIONED LOAF CAKE.

Three pounds flour, one and a fourth pounds butter, one and three-fourths pounds sugar, five gills new milk, half pint yeast, three eggs, two pounds raisins, tea-spoon soda, gill of brandy or wine, two tea-spoons cinnamon and two of nutmeg. All the butter and part of the sugar should be rubbed into the flour at night. Warm the milk, and pour the yeast into it; then mix together, and let rise until light. It is better to set the sponge over night, and in the morning add the other ingredients (flouring raisins), and let rise again. When light, fill baking-pans and let rise again. Bake in a moderate oven. This recipe makes three large loaves.—*Mrs. Gov. John J. Bagley, Michigan.*

MARBLE CAKE.

White Part.—Whites of seven eggs, three cups white sugar, one of butter, one of sour milk, four of flour, sifted and heaping, one tea-spoon soda; flavor to taste.

Dark Part.—Yolks of seven eggs, three cups brown sugar, one of butter, one of sour milk, four of flour, sifted and heaping, one table-spoon each of cinnamon, allspice, and cloves, one tea-spoon soda; put in pans a spoonful of white part and then a spoonful of dark, and so on. Bake an hour and a quarter. Use coffee-cups to measure. This will make one large and one medium cake.—*Mrs. M. E. Smith, Cleveland.*

MARBLE CAKE.

White Part.—One and a half cups white sugar, half cup butter, half cup milk, two and a half cups flour, two tea-spoons baking-powder, whites of four eggs beaten to a stiff froth; flavor to taste.

Dark Part.—Yolks of four eggs, one and a half cups brown sugar, half cup butter, half cup milk, two and a half cups flour, two tea-spoons baking-powder, tea-spoon cinnamon, tea-spoon all-spice, quarter tea-spoon black pepper, half a nutmeg; stir butter and sugar, add the milk, then the eggs, and lastly the flour in which the spices and baking-powder have been well mixed; bake one hour. Of course the white and dark parts are alternated, either by putting in a spoonful of white, then of dark, or a layer of white and then of dark part, being careful that the cake may be nicely "marbleized."—*Miss Mary Sealts, Mt. Vernon.*

MARBLED CHOCOLATE CAKE.

Make a batter as for white cake, take out one tea-cup add to it five table-spoons of grated chocolate, moisten with milk, and flavor with vanilla; pour a layer of the white batter into the baking-pan, then drop the chocolate batter with a spoon in spots, and spread the remainder of the white batter over it.—*Mrs. Sarah Phelps, Springfield.*

ONE-EGG CAKE.

One cup butter, one and a half cups sugar, three of flour, one of sweet milk, one egg, tea-spoon soda, two tea-spoons cream tartar in the flour, cup raisins chopped fine.—*Mrs. A. S. C.*

ORANGE CAKE.

Two cups sugar, four eggs, leaving out the whites of two, half cup butter, one of water, two tea-spoons baking-powder, three cups flour, juice, grated rind, and pulp of one orange; use the remaining whites for frosting the top.—*Mrs. D. Buxton.*

PLAIN CAKE.

Three eggs, one and a half cups sugar, three-fourths cup butter, or butter and lard mixed, tea-spoon soda dissolved in a cup of sour milk, tea-spoon lemon, flour enough to make it pretty stiff; bake in quick oven.—*Miss Hannah Snell.*

CITRON POUND-CAKE.

One pound sugar, one of flour, three-fourths pound butter, eight large or ten small eggs, one and a fourth pound citron finely shredded; cream, butter and sugar, add the yolks, then the flour and well-whipped whites; put layer of batter in cake-pan and sprinkle thickly with citron, then another layer of batter, etc., till pan is filled. Bake slowly one and a half to two hours.—*Mrs. J. M. Southard.*

PYRAMID POUND-CAKE.

One pound sugar, one of butter, one of flour, ten eggs; bake in a dripping-pan one inch in thickness; cut when cold into pieces three and a half inches long by two wide, and frost top and sides; form on the cake stand in pyramid before the icing is quite dry by laying, first in a circle, five pieces with some space between them; over the spaces between these lay five other pieces, gradually drawing in the column and crowning the top with a bouquet of flowers.—

SOFT POUND-CAKE.

Half pound butter, one of sugar, one of flour, cup sweet milk, five eggs, small tea-spoon soda, two of cream tartar; flavor and add fruit if desired.—*Miss Emily L. Burnham, South Norwalk, Conn.*

WHITE POUND-CAKE.

One pound sugar, one of flour, half pound butter, whites of sixteen eggs, tea-spoon baking-powder sifted thoroughly with the flour; put in cool oven with gradual increase of heat. For boiled icing for the cake, take three cups sugar boiled in one of water until clear; beat whites of three eggs to very stiff froth and pour over them the boiling liquid, beating all the time for ten minutes; frost while both cake and icing are warm.—*Mrs. Ada Estelle Bever, Cedar Rapids, Iowa.*

QUEEN VIC. CAKE.

One pound flour, one of sugar, half pound butter, four eggs, one nutmeg, lemon if desired, gill of wine, one of brandy, one of sweet cream, one pound raisins, two tea-spoons baking-powder in the flour; rub the butter, sugar and yolks of eggs to a perfect cream, beating a long time; add cream, then flour, and fruit the last thing; bake an hour and a half. This makes two three-pint pans full.— *Miss Mattie B. Fullington.*

RICE CAKE.

One pound sugar, a pound of ground rice, half pound butter, nine eggs, rose-water to taste; add a little salt, beat butter and sugar together, add rose-water, salt and eggs, lastly the rice, bake in shallow pans.—*Governor Rice, Mass.*

SPONGE-CAKE.

Six eggs, two tea-cups pulverized sugar; beat yolks and sugar to a cream, add one and a half cups of flour with two small tea-spoons baking-powder in it; then add the whites beaten to stiff froth, and stir all slowly till top is covered with bubbles. Bake in moderately-quick oven.—*Mrs. S. M. Guy, Darby Plains.*

SPONGE-CAKE.

Three eggs, one and a half cups powdered sugar, two of sifted flour, two tea-spoons cream tartar, half cup cold water, tea-spoon soda, grated rind and half the juice of one lemon; bake in dripping-pan.—*Mrs. Eliza J. Starr.*

SPONGE-CAKE.

Twelve eggs, pint pulverized sugar, one of flour, measured before sifting, small tea-spoon salt, heaping tea-spoon baking-powder, essence of lemon for flavor; beat the whites to a very stiff froth, and add sugar; beat the yolks, strain and add them to the whites and sugar, and beat the whole thoroughly; mix baking-powder and salt in the flour and add last, stirring in small quantities at a time; bake one hour in a six-quart pan in a moderate oven. This makes one very large cake. By weight use one pound pulverized sugar and three-fourths pound flour.—*Miss S. Alice Melching.*

SPONGE-CAKE.

One pound sugar, one of flour, ten eggs; stir yolks of eggs and sugar till perfectly light; beat whites of eggs and add them with the flour after beating together lightly; flavor with lemon. Three tea-spoons baking-powder in the flour will add to its lightness, but it never fails without. Bake in a moderate oven.—*Mrs. Mary Reynolds, Hamilton.*

MAINE SPONGE-CAKE.

Ten eggs, their weight in sugar and half their weight in flour; beat the yolks with the sugar and flavor with lemon; beat the whites to a stiff froth and add them to the yolks and sugar; sift the flour in and stir quickly; it must not be beaten after flour is put in; bake immediately. This will make two thick loaves in six by nine pans.—*Mrs. Governor Connor, Maine.*

WHITE SPONGE-CAKE.

Whites of ten eggs, a tumbler and a half of pulverized sugar, one of flour, heaping tea-spoon cream tartar, a pinch of salt; put all through the sieve twice, then stir in lightly the eggs beaten to a stiff froth, flavor with vanilla or rose.—*Mrs. Governor Ludington, Wisconsin.*

PHIL SHERIDAN.CAKE.

Four cups sugar, one and a half cups butter, whites of sixteen eggs, five cups flour, two tea-spoons cream tartar with the flour, one tea-spoon soda with one cup sweet milk. Flavor to taste.—*Miss Mary Sheridan, Somerset.*

SPICE CAKE.

Three pounds seedless raisins, one and a half pounds citron, one pound butter, two and a half coffee-cups sugar, two of sweet milk, six eggs, two large tea-spoons baking-powder, three tea-spoons cinnamon, two of mace, four cups flour.—*Mrs. Gov. Potts, Montana.*

SILVER CAKE.

Three-quarters pound sugar, three-quarters pound butter, whites twelve eggs, yolks of two, tea-cup sweet milk, three tea-spoons yeast powder, flour to suit; beat yolks and half the sugar till very light, add whites and rest of sugar, butter, and flour enough to make a batter rather stiffer than for pound-cake.—*Mrs. Gov. Porter, Tennessee.*

SNOW CAKE.

Half tea-cup butter, one of sugar, one and a half of flour, half cup sweet milk, whites of four eggs, tea-spoon baking-powder; flavor with lemon.—*Mrs. Wm. Patrick, Midland, Mich.*

Snow Cake.

Whites of ten eggs beaten to a stiff froth, sift lightly on this one and a half cups fine white or pulverized sugar, stir well, and add cup flour mixed with tea-spoon baking-powder; flavor with lemon or vanilla.—*Mrs. Dr. Koogler, Connersville, Ind.*

Ten-Minute Cake.

One-fourth pound butter, a little less than a pound flour, the same of sugar, six eggs beaten separately; flavor with mace and bake in muffin-rings.—*Mrs. S. C. Lee, Baltimore, Md.*

Tilden Cake.

One cup butter, two of pulverized sugar, one of sweet milk, three of flour, half cup corn starch, four eggs, two tea-spoons baking-powder, two of lemon extract.—*Mrs. T. B., Chicago, Ill.*

Tin-Wedding Cake.

Rub one cup butter and three of sugar to a cream; add one cup milk, four of flour, five eggs, one tea-spoon cream tartar, half tea-spoon soda, one-fourth pound citron. This makes two loaves.—*Mrs. J. H. Ferris, South Norwalk, Conn.*

Watermelon Cake.

White Part.—Two cups white sugar, one of butter, one of sweet milk, three and a half of flour, whites of eight eggs, two tea-spoons cream tartar, one of soda dissolved in a little warm water.

Red Part.—One cup red sugar, half cup butter, third cup sweet milk, two cups flour, whites of four eggs, tea-spoon cream tartar, half tea-spoon soda, tea-cup raisins; be careful to keep the red part around the tube of the pan and the white around the edge. It requires two persons to fill the pan.—*Mrs. Baxter.*

Wedding Cake.

One pound white sugar, one of flour, three-fourths pound butter, a dozen eggs, two pounds raisins, two of currants, half pound citron, fourth ounce nutmeg, fourth ounce cloves, half ounce cinnamon, a cup of molasses, and a level tea-spoon soda.—*Mrs. M. L. France.*

Wedding Cake.

Fifty eggs, five pounds sugar, five of flour, five of butter, fifteen of raisins, three of citron, ten of currants, pint brandy, fourth ounce cloves, ounce cinnamon, four of mace, four of nutmeg. This makes forty-three and a half pounds, and keeps twenty years. —*Mrs. C. H. D., Northampton, Mass.*

WHITE CAKE.

One cup butter, two of sugar, one of sweet milk, three of flour, whites of five eggs, two tea-spoons baking-powder.—*Mrs. Daniel Miller.*

WHITE PERFECTION CAKE.

Three cups sugar, one of butter, one of milk, three of flour, one of corn starch, whites of twelve eggs beaten to a stiff froth, two tea-spoons cream tartar in the flour, and one of soda in half the milk; dissolve the corn starch in the rest of the milk, and add it to the sugar and butter well beaten together, then the milk and soda, and the flour and whites of eggs.—*Mrs. C. Jones, Bradford, Vt.*

LAYER-CAKES.

In baking layer-cakes, it is important to thoroughly grease the tins—to make it emphatic, we will say thoroughly grease and then grease again—and after using rub off with a coarse towel, taking care that they are perfectly free from all small particles of cake, grease and fill again, thus obviating the necessity of washing every time they are filled. If jelly is used to spread between the layers, it is a good plan to beat it smoothly and spread it before the cakes are quite cool. In "building," an inverted jelly-tin furnishes a perfectly level surface on which to lay and spread the cake, and it may be allowed to remain on it until perfectly cold, when it should be set away in a tin cake-box, in a cool place.

To blanch almonds, pour boiling water over them, let stand a moment, drain and throw them into cold water, slip off the skins and pound.

ALMOND CAKE.

Two cups sugar, three-fourths cup butter, one of sweet milk, two of flour, and one of corn starch well mixed, whites of six eggs, two tea-spoons cream tartar in the flour, one tea-spoon soda in the milk; cream the butter and sugar, add milk gradually, then the whites of eggs together with the flour, and bake in jelly-tins. To put between layers, take two pounds almonds, blanch and pound fine in a mortar (or a cloth will do), beat whites and yolks of two eggs together lightly, add a cup and a half sugar, then the almonds with one table-spoon vanilla.—*Mrs. Harvey Wood.*

ALMOND CREAM CAKE.

On beaten whites of ten eggs, sift one and a half goblets pulverized sugar, and a goblet flour through which has been stirred a heaping tea-spoon cream tartar; stir very gently and do not beat it; bake in jelly-pans. For cream, take a half pint sweet cream, yolks of three eggs, table-spoon pulverized sugar, tea-spoon corn starch; dissolve starch smoothly with a little milk, beat yolks and sugar together with this, boil the cream, and stir these ingredients in as for any cream-cake filling, only make a little thicker; blanch and chop fine a half pound almonds and stir into the cream. Put together like jelly cake while icing is soft, and stick in a half pound of almonds split in two.—*Mrs. Paris Gibson, Minneapolis, Minn.*

BOSTON CREAM CAKE.

Pour half pint boiling water over a cup butter, and while hot stir in two cups flour. When the whole is very smooth and thoroughly scalded, set away to cool. When cold, break in five eggs, stir until perfectly mixed, then add one-fourth tea-spoon soda. Butter a pan, drop in the mixture, a table-spoon in a place, and bake in a quick oven. When the cakes are done they will be hollow, and the top must be sliced off, the inside filled with cream, and the top replaced.

Cream for Inside.—Pint milk, half cup flour, a cup sugar, and two eggs, stirred together and heated till of the consistency of cream; flavor with lemon.——*Mrs. Gov. Noyes, Cincinnati.*

BOSTON CREAM PUFFS.

Boil one tumbler of water, add to it scant two-thirds cup butter; while boiling stir in one and a half tumblers flour; when cold add five well-beaten eggs and a table-spoon cold water; drop a spoonful in a place on well-greased tins one and a half inches apart, bake fifteen to twenty minutes in a quick oven; when cool enough to

handle, cut a hole in side, and fill with cream made as follows: Boil
two tumblers sweet milk, add two eggs, and two-thirds coffee-cup
white sugar well beaten together, then stir in one-half coffee-cup
flour till thick and smooth, and flavor.—*Mrs. J. E. Sniffin, Pleasant-
ville, N. Y.*

BUCKEYE CREAM PUFFS.

Five eggs, whites and yolks beaten separately, one and a half cups
each of white sugar and sifted flour, two tea-spoons baking-powder in
the flour; bake in tea-cups, filling about half full. The cream is prepared by placing a small tin pail containing a pint sweet milk in a
kettle of boiling water; beat the whites and yolks of two eggs separately; stir in the milk while boiling, a half tea-cup sugar, a large
table-spoon corn starch dissolved in a little sweet milk, then the
beaten yolks, and a piece of butter the size of a large walnut; flavor
with lemon or vanilla. When done cut the cakes open, put in a
spoonful of the cream, place together again, roll in the whites, and
then in coarse granulated sugar.—*Mrs. A. S. Chapman.*

FRENCH CREAM CAKE.

Three eggs, one tea-cup granulated sugar, one and a half cups
flour, two table-spoons cold water, tea-spoon baking-powder. This
is enough for two cakes baked in pie-pans, to be split while warm,
spreading the hot custard between them, or for four cakes baked in
jelly-pans, with the hot custard spread between them, the latter
being the preferable plan. For custard, boil nearly one pint sweet
milk, mix two table-spoons corn starch with a half tea-cup sweet
milk, add two well-beaten eggs; when milk has boiled add nearly a
tea-cup sugar, and stir in slowly the corn starch and eggs; add a
half tea-cup butter stirred until dissolved, flavor with one tea-spoon
vanilla, and spread between cakes while hot. This cake can be used
as a pudding by pouring over each piece a spoonful of the custard
that is left.—*Mrs. Charles Morey.*

GOLDEN CREAM CAKE.

Cream one cup sugar and one-fourth cup butter, add half cup
sweet milk, the well-beaten whites of three eggs, one and a half cups
flour, with half a tea-spoon soda, and a tea-spoon cream-tartar sifted
with it; bake in three deep jelly-tins; beat very light the yolks of

two eggs, one cup sugar, and two table-spoons rich sweet cream. flavor with vanilla, and spread on cakes; or to yolks add one and a half table-spoons corn starch, three-quarters cup sweet milk and small lump butter; sweeten and flavor to taste, cook in a custard kottle till thick, let cool, and then spread.—*Mrs. J. M. Southard.*

ICE-CREAM CAKE.

Make good sponge-cake, bake half an inch thick in jelly-pans, and let them get perfectly cold; take a pint thickest sweet cream, beat until it looks like ice-cream, make very sweet, and flavor with vanilla; blanch and chop a pound almonds, stir into cream, and put very thick between each layer. This is the queen of all cakes.— *Miss Mattie Fullington.*

ICE-CREAM CAKE.

Two cups sugar, one of butter, three and a fourth cups flour, fourth cup sweet milk some take two cups flour, one cup corn starch, and one of sweet milk), two tea-spoons baking-powder, whites of eight eggs, flavor and bake in jelly-tins. Boil two and a half cups powdered sugar in a half tea-cup water, stirring constantly; when thick and clear, pour boiling hot over the well-whipped whites of three eggs, beat till nearly cold, flavor and spread on cakes.—*Mrs. Dr. D. H. Moore, Wesleyan College, Cincinnati.*

COCOA-NUT CAKE.

To the well-beaten yolks of six eggs, add two cups powdered white sugar, three-fourths cups butter, one of sweet milk, three and a half of flour, one level tea-spoon soda and two of cream tartar, whites of four eggs well beaten; bake in jelly-cake pans. For icing, grate one cocoa-nut, beat whites of two eggs, and add one tea-cup powdered sugar; mix thoroughly with the grated cocoa-nut, and spread evenly on the layers of cake when they are cold.—*Miss Nettie Miller, Columbus.*

COCOA-NUT CAKE.

One cup butter, two of sugar, three of flour, four eggs, one cup sweet milk, one of corn starch, (not filling cups of butter and flour very full if eggs are small,) two tea-spoons cream tartar, one of soda. Make custard as follows: One cup thick sour cream stirred thin, one

5

cup sugar, one grated cocoa-nut, one egg beaten separately; spread between layers like jelly cake.—*Mrs. Mary S. Moore, Granville.*

CARAMEL CAKE.

One and a half cups sugar, three-fourths cup butter, half cup milk, two and a fourth cups flour, three eggs, one and a half heaping tea-spoons baking-powder, or a small tea-spoon soda, and two tea-spoons cream tartar; bake in jelly-tins. Make caramel as follows: Butter size of an egg, pint brown sugar, half cup milk or water, half cake chocolate; boil twenty minutes (or until thick enough) and pour over cakes while warm, piling the layers one upon the other. For frosting for top of cake, take whites of two eggs, one and a half cups sugar, a tea-spoon vanilla, three heaping tea-spoons grated chocolate. —*Mrs. Ella Snider, Minneapolis, Minn.*

DELICIOUS CHOCOLATE CAKE.

The whites of eight eggs, two cups sugar, one of butter, three full cups flour, one of sweet milk, three tea-spoons baking-powder; beat the butter to a cream, stir in the sugar, and beat until light; add the milk, then the flour and beaten whites. When well beaten, divide into two equal parts, and into half grate a cake of sweet chocolate. Bake in layers, spread with custard, and alternate the white and dark cakes. For custard for the cake, add a table-spoon of butter to one pint of milk, and let it come to a boil; stir in two eggs beaten with one cup of sugar, add two tea-spoons of corn starch dissolved in a little milk.—*Mrs. J. M. Riddle, Bellefontaine.*

CHOCOLATE CAKE.

One cup butter, two of sugar, one of milk, five eggs, leaving out the whites of three, four cups sifted flour, two tea-spoons baking-powder, or one small tea-spoon soda and two of cream tartar in the flour; bake in three layers in deep jelly-tins. For icing, take whites of three eggs, beaten stiff, one and a half cups powdered sugar, six table-spoons grated chocolate, two tea-spoons vanilla.—*Mrs. J. H. Shearer.*

"JUST SPLENDID" CUSTARD CAKE.

Two cups sugar, two and a half cups flour, half cup milk, butter size of an egg, whites of ten eggs, two tea-spoons cream tartar, one

of soda dissolved in milk. For custard take three-fourths pint rich
s(ur cream, yolks of four eggs beaten well with two table-spoons
white sugar, whites of two of the eggs beaten with the same
quantity of sugar, two pounds almonds blanched and chopped very
fine; add the beaten yolks to the cream, and beat until as thick as
sponge-cake, then add the whites and almonds; flavor with vanilla.
Spread thick between the cakes.—*Mrs. C. Hawks, Goshen, Ind.*

CUP CAKE.

Three cups sugar, one of butter, six of flour, two-thirds pint sour
cream, seven eggs (leaving out the whites of two for icing), one
even tea-spoon soda in the cream, tea-spoon soda in the flour, one of
cream tartar, and one of lemon or vanilla. Bake in pans one inch
deep, and when done spread one with icing, and lay the other on top
of it, allowing two layers for each cake.—*Mrs. Dr. Thompson.*

FIG CAKE.

Silver Part.—Two cups sugar, two-thirds cup butter, not quite two-
thirds cup sweet milk, whites of eight eggs, three heaping tea-spoons
baking-powder thoroughly sifted, with three cups flour; stir sugar
and butter to a cream, add milk and flour, and last white of eggs.

Gold Part.—One cup sugar, three-fourths cup butter, half cup
sweet milk, one and a half tea-spoons baking-powder sifted in a little
more than one and a half cups flour, yolks of seven eggs thoroughly
beaten, and one whole egg, one tea-spoon allspice, and cinnamon
until you can taste it; bake the white in two long pie-tins. Put half
the gold in a pie-tin, and lay on one pound halved figs (previously
sifted over with flour), so that they will just touch each other,
put on the rest of the gold, and bake. Put the cakes together with
frosting while warm, the gold between the white ones, and cover
with frosting.—*Miss Tina Lay, Clyde, O.*

HARD-TIMES CAKE.

Half a cup of butter, two of sugar, one of sour cream, three of
flour, three eggs, half tea-spoon of soda; bake in layers and spread
with jelly.—*Mrs. R. M. Henderson.*

JELLY ROLL.

One cup flour, one of sugar, four table-spoons melted butter, two
table-spoons water, three eggs, two level tea-spoons cream tartar,

and one of soda sifted in the flour.　Put all the ingredients together, beat ten minutes, bake in two long sheets, spread with jelly, and roll up while hot.—*Mrs. Wm. Brown, Massillon.*

ROLLED JELLY CAKE.

Beat twelve eggs and one pound pulverized sugar together very lightly, then stir in three-fourths pound of flour, making batter as light as for sponge-cake, and thin enough to spread nicely when poured; make up as quickly as possible.　Have shallow tin-pans prepared (about twelve by eighteen inches and an inch deep) by lining with thin brown paper, using no grease on pan or paper; pour in batter, spread out with a knife as thin as possible (about half an inch thick), and bake in solid oven.　When done, remove from oven, let cool a few minutes, and while still warm, but not hot, turn out of pan upside down.　With a brush or soft cloth wet in cold water, brush over the paper and pull it off; spread cake thin with jelly and roll it up, being careful to place the outer edge of roll against something so that it will not unroll until cold. Sprinkle with powdered sugar and serve.　If baked in pans such as are described above, the recipe will make two rolls, each twelve inches long, which should be cut in two, making four rolls.　Use no baking-powder, as it makes the cake too brittle.　Many use none in sponge-cake.　The paper lining should be larger than pan, to lift out the cake by taking hold of the projecting edges.—*C. W. Cyphers, Minneapolis*

KELLEY ISLAND CAKE.

One cup butter, two of sugar, three of flour, four eggs, half cup milk, three tea-spoons baking-powder; bake in jelly-tins.　For filling stir together a grated lemon, a large grated apple, an egg, and a cup sugar, and boil four minutes.—*Miss Greeley Grubbs.*

LEMON CAKE.

One and one-half cups sugar, one of butter, two and one-half of flour, five eggs beaten separately, four tea-spoons sweet milk, tea-spoon cream tartar, half tea-spoon soda.

For Jelly.—Take coffee-cup sugar, two table-spoons butter, two eggs, and the juice of two lemons: beat all together and boil until the consistency of jelly.　For orange cake use oranges instead of lemons.—*Miss Minnie Brown.*

LADY'S-FINGERS.

One and an eighth pound of flour, one of powdered sugar, ten eggs; beat eggs and sugar as light as for sponge-cake; sift in with flour one tea-spoon baking-powder and stir slowly. Make a funnel-shaped bag of heavy ticking or strong brown paper; through the hole in the small end push a funnel-shaped tin tube, one-third inch in diameter at small end and provided with a flange at the other to prevent it from slipping quite through; tie the small end of bag firmly around the tube, and you have a funnel-shaped sack with a firm nozzle projecting slightly from the small end. Into this bag pour the batter, over which gather up the bag tightly so that none will run out, press and run the dough out quickly through the tube into a pan lined with light brown paper (not buttered), making each about a finger long, and about as thick as a lead-pencil, being careful not to get them too wide. Sprinkle with granulated sugar, bake in a quick oven, and, when cool, wet the under side of the paper with a brush, remove and stick the fingers together back to back. The bag, when made of ticking, will be useful in making macaroons and other small cakes.—*Charles W. Cyphers, Minneapolis, Minn.*

MINNEHAHA CAKE.

One and a half cups granulated sugar, half cup butter stirred to a cream, whites of six eggs, or three whole eggs, two tea-spoons cream tartar stirred in two heaping cups sifted flour, one tea-spoon soda in half cup sweet milk; bake in three layers. For filling, take a tea-cup sugar and a little water boiled together until it is brittle when dropped in cold water, remove from stove and stir quickly into the well-beaten white of one egg; add to this a cup of stoned raisins chopped fine, or a cup of chopped hickory-nut meats, and place between layers and over the top.—*Mrs. E. W Herrick, Minneapolis, Minn.*

METROPOLITAN CAKE.

Two cups sugar, one of butter, one of milk, nearly four cups flour, whites of eight eggs, three tea-spoons baking-powder, flavor with lemon. Bake a little more than three-fifths of this mixture in three jelly-tins, add to the remaining batter one table-spoon ground allspice, one and a half table-spoons cinnamon, tea-spoon cloves; fourth pound each of sliced citron and chopped raisins; bake in two jelly-tins and put together with frosting, alternating dark and light.—*Mrs. Dr. D. H. Moore, Wesleyan College, Cincinnati.*

NEAPOLITAN CAKE.

Black Part.—One cup brown sugar, two eggs, half cup butter, half cup molasses, half cup strong coffee, two and a half cups flour, one of raisins, one of currants, a tea-spoon each of soda, cinnamon, and cloves, and half tea-spoon mace.

White Part.—Two cups sugar, half cup butter, one of milk, two and a quarter of flour, one of corn starch, whites of four eggs, small tea-spoon cream tartar; make frosting of whites of two eggs to put between the layers.—*Mrs. Calista Hawks Gortner, Goshen, Ind.*

ORANGE CAKE.

One cup butter, one of water, two of sugar, four of flour, three eggs, three tea-spoons baking-powder; bake in layers. Take the juice of two large or three small oranges, coffee-cup pulverized sugar, one egg; mix yolk of egg, sugar, and juice together; beat whites to a stiff froth, stir in and spread between the layers.—*Mrs. W. B. Brown, Washington, D. C.*

ORANGE CAKE.

Four tea-cups sifted flour, three tea-spoons baking-powder stirred into the flour, five eggs with the yolks of two left out, two cups sugar, scant cup of butter, one of milk; bake in thin layers. For custard take juice and grated rind of one large orange, add the two yolks that were left out, sweeten to taste, place on stove, and stir until thick enough to spread.—*Mrs. Sarah Phelps, Springfield.*

ORANGE CAKE.

Two cups sugar, half cup butter, three and a half cups sifted flour, half cup sweet milk, three eggs beaten separately, tea-spoon baking-powder mixed in flour; bake in jelly-pans. For jelly take the juice and grated rind of two oranges, two table-spoons cold water, two cups sugar; set in a pot of boiling water, and, when scalding hot, stir in the yolks of two well-beaten eggs, and just before taking from the fire stir in the white of one egg slightly beaten, and when cold put between the layers of cake. Frost the top with the other egg.—*Miss Mardie Dolbear, Cape Girardeau.*

ORANGE CAKE.

Two-thirds cup butter, two small cups sugar, one cup milk, three tea-spoons baking-powder, the yolks of five eggs, three small cups flour; bake in jelly-tins. Whites of three eggs beaten to a stiff froth, juice and grated peel of one orange, sugar to consistency; put this between the layers with white frosting on the top.—*Mrs. Gov. Pillsbury, Minnesota.*

PEACH CAKE.

Bake three sheets of sponge-cake as for jelly cake; cut peaches in thin slices, prepare cream by whipping, sweetening and adding flavor of vanilla if desired, put layers of peaches between the sheets of cake, pour cream over each layer and over the top. This may also be made with ripe strawberries.—*Mrs. Woodworth, Springfield, Mass.*

RIBBON CAKE.

Two and a half cups sugar, one of butter, one of sweet milk, tea-spoon cream tartar, half tea-spoon soda, four cups flour, four eggs; reserve a third of this mixture, and bake the rest in two loaves of the same size. Add to third reserved, one cup raisins, fourth pound citron, a cup of currants, two table-spoons molasses, tea-spoon each of all kinds of spice; bake in a tin the same size as other loaves; put the three loaves together with a little icing or currant jelly, placing the fruit loaf in the middle; frost the top and sides.—*Miss Alice Trimble, Mt. Gilead.*

FAVORITE SNOW-CAKE.

Beat one cup butter to a cream, add one and a half cups flour and stir very thoroughly together; then add one cup corn starch, and one cup sweet milk in which three tea-spoons baking-powder have been dissolved; last, add whites of eight eggs and two cups sugar well beaten together; flavor to taste, bake in sheets, and put together with icing.—*Walter Moore, Hamilton.*

Sponge-Cake.

Four eggs, whites and yolks beaten separately, two tea-cups powdered sugar, half cup corn starch, two cups sifted flour, two tea-spoons baking-powder; mix well together the flour, corn starch, and baking-powder, and add to the eggs and sugar; pour over the whole, stirring briskly, one tea-cup boiling water; flavor as you like. Put in two pans about one inch and a half deep (like jelly-pans), then put between the two cakes when done, a layer of blackberry jam. Bake carefully in a well-heated oven.

Three-ply Cake.

One half cup butter, two cups sugar, three of flour, one of cold water, three eggs, tea-spoon baking-powder; take out about one-third in another dish and add to it one cup raisins, one of currants, a little citron, table-spoon molasses; spice to taste. Bake in three layers and join while warm either with currant jelly or white icing with the fruit layer in center.—*Mrs. G. F. Hanford, Harlem, N. Y.*

Thanksgiving Cake.

Make batter as for cocoa-nut cake (Miss Nettie Miller's). Bake five layers in jelly-tins; make frosting of whites of three eggs, three tea-spoons baking-powder, and three-fourths pound of pulverized sugar; with frosting for first layer mix rolled hickory-nut meats, with that for second layer mix fine-sliced figs, for third with hickory-nut meats, for fourth with figs, and on the top spread the plain frosting, and grate cocoa-nut over thickly.—*Mrs. J. S. Robinson.*

Velvet Sponge-Cake.

Two cups sugar, six eggs leaving out the whites of three, one cup boiling hot water, two and one half cups flour, one table-spoon baking-powder in the flour; beat the yolks a little, add the sugar and beat fifteen minutes; add the three beaten whites, and the cup of boiling water just before the flour; flavor with a tea-spoon lemon extract and bake in three layers, putting between them icing made by adding to the three whites of eggs beaten to a stiff froth, six dessert-spoons of pulverized sugar to each egg, and lemon to flavor. —*Mrs. Wm. Brown, Massillon.*

Vanity Cake.

One and a half cups sugar, half cup butter, half cup sweet milk, one and a half cups flour, half cup corn starch, tea-spoon baking-powder, whites of six eggs; bake in two cakes, putting frosting between and on top.—*Olivia S. Hinman, Battle Creek, Mich.*

White Mountain Cake.

Two cups pulverized sugar, half cup butter beaten to a cream; add half cup sweet milk, two and a half cups flour, two and a half tea-spoons baking-powder in the flour, whites of eight eggs; bake in jelly-tins and put together with icing made by boiling a half tea-cup of water and three tea-cups sugar till thick; pour it slowly over the well-beaten whites of three eggs, and beat all together till cool. Beat before putting on each layer.

Sprinkle each layer thickly with grated cocoa-nut, and a handsome cocoa-nut cake will result.--*Mrs. Dr. Stall, Union City, Ind.*

DIRECTIONS FOR FROSTING.

Beat whites of the eggs to a stiff froth add powdered sugar gradually, *beating well all the time;* or break the whites into a broad platter, and *at once* begin adding powdered and sifted sugar, keep adding gradually, beating well all the while until the icing is perfectly smooth (thirty minutes beating ought to be sufficient); lastly, add flavoring (rose, pineapple, or almond for white or delicate cake, and lemon or vanilla for dark or fruit cake). If the cake is rough or brown when baked, dust with a little flour, rub off all loose particles with a cloth, put on frosting, pouring it around the center of the cake, and smooth off as quickly as possible with a knife. If the frosting is rather stiff, dip the knife in cold water. It is better to frost while the cake is still warm. A good general rule for frosting is ten heaping tea-spoons powdered sugar to each white of an egg, and some add to this a tea-spoon of corn starch. As eggs vary in size the measurement must also vary and practice only will teach when the frosting is just stiff enough. If the flavor is lemon juice, allow more sugar for the additional liquid. It is nice, when the frosting is almost cold, to take a knife and mark the cake in slices.

ALMOND FROSTING.

Blanch half pint sweet almonds by putting them in boiling water, stripping off the skins, and spreading upon a dry cloth until cold; pound a few of them at a time in a mortar till well pulverized; mix carefully whites of three eggs and three-quarters pint powdered sugar, add almonds, flavor with a tea-spoon vanilla or lemon, and dry in a cool oven or in the open air when weather is pleasant.

BOILED FROSTING.

Whites of three eggs beaten to a stiff froth, one large cup granulated sugar moistened with four table-spoons hot water; boil sugar briskly for five minutes or until it "ropes" from the end of the spoon, turn while hot upon the beaten eggs, and stir until cold. If preferred, add half pound sweet almonds blanched and pounded to a paste, and it will be perfectly delicious. This amount will frost the top of two large cakes.—*Mrs. A. S. C.*

FROSTING.

Beat whites of two eggs to a stiff froth, add gradually half pound best pulverized sugar, beat well for at least half an hour, flavor with lemon juice (and some add tartaric acid, as both whiten the icing). To color a delicate pink, use strawberry, currant or cranberry; or the grated peeling of an orange or lemon moistened with the juice and squeezed through a thin cloth, will color a handsome yellow. This amount will frost one large cake. —*Mrs. W. W. W.*

FROSTING WITH GELATINE.

Dissolve large pinch gelatine in six table-spoons boiling water, strain and thicken with sugar and flavor with lemon. This is enough to frost two cakes.—*Mrs. W. A. J.*

FROSTING WITHOUT EGGS.

To one heaping tea-spoon Poland starch and just enough cold water to dissolve it, add a little hot water and cook in a basin set in hot water till very thick (or cook in a crock; either will prevent its burning or becoming lumpy). Should the sugar be lumpy roll it thoroughly, and stir in two and two-thirds cups while the starch is hot; flavor to taste, and spread on while the cake is a little warm. This should be made the day before using, as it takes longer to harden than when made with eggs, but it will never crumble in cutting.—*Mrs. Ola Kellogg Wilcox.*

HICKORY-NUT FROSTING.

Take one or two eggs according to size of cake, a tea-cup of sugar to an egg; chop the meats very fine, mix with frosting and spread on cake as thickly as you choose.—*Mrs. A. S. Chapman.*

ORNAMENTAL FROSTING.

Draw a small syringe full of the icing and work it in any design you fancy; wheels, Grecian borders, flowers, or borders of beading, look well.—*Mrs. M. J. W.*

YELLOW FROSTING.

The yolk of one egg to nine heaping tea-spoons pulverized sugar, and flavor with vanilla. Use the same day it is made.—*Mrs. J. S. W.*

ROSE COLORING.

Mix together one-fourth ounce each of powdered alum and cream tartar, one ounce powdered cochineal, four ounces loaf sugar, and a salt-spoon soda. Boil ten minutes in a pint pure soft water, when cool bottle and cork for use. This is used for jellies, cake, ice-cream, etc.—*Mrs. W. E. H., Minneapolis.*

CRULLERS AND DOUGHNUTS.

To cook these properly the fat should be of the right heat. When hot enough it will cease to bubble and be perfectly still; try with a bit of the batter, and if the heat is right the dough will rise in a few seconds to the top and occasion a bubbling in the fat, the cake will swell, and the under side quickly become brown. Clarified drippings of roast meat are more wholesome to fry them in than lard. If the dough is cut about half an inch thick, five to eight minutes will be time enough to cook, but it is better to break one open as a test. When done, drain well in a skimmer, and place in a colander. The use of eggs prevents the dough from absorbing the fat. Doughnuts should be watched closely while frying, and the fire must be regulated very carefully. When you have finished frying, cut a potato in slices and put in the fat to clarify it, place the kettle away until the fat "settles," strain into an earthen pot kept for this purpose, and set in a cool place. The sediment remaining in the bottom of the kettle can be used for soap-grease. Fry in an iron kettle, the common skillet being too shallow for the purpose. Do not eat doughnuts between April and November. Crullers are better the day after they are made.

CRULLERS.

Two coffee-cups sugar, one of sweet milk, three eggs, a heaping table-spoon butter, three tea-spoons baking-powder mixed with six cups flour, half a nutmeg, and a level tea-spoon cinnamon. Beat eggs, sugar and butter together, add milk, spices and flour; put another cup flour on molding-board, turn the dough out on it, and knead until stiff enough to roll out to a quarter inch thick; cut in squares, make three or four long incisions in each square, lift by taking alternate strips between the finger and thumb, drop into hot lard, and cook like doughnuts.—*Miss R. J. S.*

CRULLERS.

Six eggs, one coffee-cup sugar, six table-spoons melted butter, four of sweet milk, one tea-spoon soda in milk, two tea-spoons cream tartar in the flour, one tea-spoon ginger, half a small nutmeg (or any other seasoning), flour to roll out; fry in hot lard. If the lard is not fresh and sweet, slice a raw potato, and fry before putting in the cakes.—*Miss M. B. Fullington.*

FRIED CAKES.

One coffee-cup of not too thick sour cream, or one of sour milk and one table-spoon of butter, two eggs, a little nutmeg and salt, one tea-cup sugar, one small tea-spoon soda dissolved; mix soft.—*Mrs. S. Watson, Upper Sandusky.*

Albert's Favorite Doughnuts.

One pint sour milk, one cup sugar, two eggs, one tea-spoon soda, half cup lard, nutmeg to flavor; mix to a moderately stiff dough, roll to half inch in thickness, cut in rings or twists, drop into boiling lard, and fry to a light brown.—*Mrs. A. F. Ziegler.*

Doughnuts.

One egg, a cup rich milk, a cup sugar, flour enough to roll out, three tea-spoons baking-powder.—*Mrs. Jenks, Bellefontaine.*

Raised Doughnuts.

Warm together one pint milk and one small tea-cup lard, and add one cup yeast; stir in flour to make a batter, let rise over night; add four eggs, two and a half cups sugar, two tea-spoons cassia, half tea-spoon soda, and a tea-spoon salt; knead and let rise again; roll, cut out, and let rise fifteen minutes before frying.

Trifles.

A quart flour, a cup sugar, two table-spoons melted butter, a little salt, two tea-spoons baking-powder, one egg, and sweet milk sufficient to make rather stiff; roll out in thin sheets, cut in pieces about two by four inches; make as many cuts across the short way as possible, inserting the knife near one edge and ending the cut just before reaching the other. Pass two knitting-needles under every other strip, spread the needles as far apart as possible, and with them hold the trifles in the fat until a light brown. Only one can be fried at a time.—*Miss Ettie Dalbey, Harrisburg.*

COOKIES AND JUMBLES.

These require a quick oven. A nice "finishing touch" can be given by sprinkling them with granulated sugar and rolling over lightly with the rolling-pin, then cutting out and pressing a whole raisin in the center of each; or when done a very light brown, brush over while still hot with a soft bit of rag dipped in a thick syrup of sugar and water, sprinkle with currants and return to the oven a moment.

ADA'S SUGAR CAKES.

Three cups sugar, two of butter, three eggs well beaten, one tea-spoon soda, flour sufficient to roll out.

COOKIES.

One cup butter, two of sugar, one of cold water, half tea-spoon soda, two eggs, and just flour enough to roll.—*Mrs. Mary F. Orr.*

GOOD COOKIES.

Two cups sugar, one of butter, one of sour cream or milk, three eggs, one tea-spoon soda; mix soft, roll thin, sift granulated sugar over them. and gently roll it in.—*Mrs. Judge West.*

LEMON SNAPS.

A large cup sugar, two-thirds cup butter, half tea-spoon soda dissolved in two tea-spoons hot water, flour enough to roll thin; flavor with lemon.—*Mrs. E. L. C., Springfield.*

MOLASSES COOKIES.

Two and a half cups of sugar, half cup molasses, a cup butter, half cup sweet milk, two eggs well beaten, a level tea-spoon soda, and flour enough to roll out.—*Miss J. O. De Forest, Norwalk.*

NUTMEG COOKIES.

Two cups white sugar, three-fourths cup butter, two-thirds cup sour milk, nutmeg or caraway seed for flavor, two eggs, half tea-spoon soda, and six cups of flour or enough to roll. Roll thin, and bake in a quick oven.

PEPPER-NUTS.

One pound sugar, five eggs, half pound butter, half tea-cup milk, two tea-spoons baking-powder, flour enough to roll.—*Mrs. Emma G. Rea.*

SAND TARTS.

Two cups sugar, one of butter, three of flour, two eggs, leaving out the white of one; roll out thin and cut in square cakes with a knife; spread the white of egg on top, sprinkle with cinnamon and sugar, and press a blanched almond or raisin in the center.—*Miss Clara G. Phellis.*

COCOA-NUT JUMBLES.

Two cups sugar, one of butter, two of cocoa-nut, two eggs, small tea-spoon soda mixed with flour enough to make a stiff batter. Drop heaping tea-spoons on buttered paper in pans.—*Miss M. E. C.*

JUMBLES.

Three cups sugar, one of butter, four eggs, a tea-spoon soda, and nutmeg or vanilla to flavor. Stir in flour until it will roll; roll out, sprinkle with sugar and roll it in gently, and cut out round, with a hole in the center.—*Mrs. J. Holland, New Castle, Ind.*

JUMBLES.

One and a half cups white sugar, three-fourths cup butter, three eggs, three table-spoons sweet milk, half tea-spoon soda and one of cream tartar; mix with sufficient flour to roll; roll and sprinkle with sugar; cut out and bake.—*Mrs. Mollie Pilcher, Jackson, Mich.*

GINGER-BREAD.

If in making ginger-bread the dough becomes too stiff before it is rolled out, set it before the fire. Snaps will not be crisp if made on a rainy day. Ginger-bread and cakes require a moderate oven, snaps a quick one. If cookies or snaps become moist in keeping, put them in the oven and heat them for a few moments. Always use New Orleans or Porto Rico molasses, and never syrups. Soda is used to act on the "spirit" of the molasses. In making the old-fashioned soft, square cakes of ginger-bread, put a portion of the dough on a well-floured tin sheet, roll evenly to each side, trim off evenly around the edges, and mark off in squares with a floured knife or wheel cutter. In this way the dough may be softer than where it is necessary to pick up to remove from board after rolling and cutting.

AUNT MOLLY'S GINGER-BREAD.

Three and a half pounds flour, one of butter, one quart molasses, half pint milk, one tea-spoon soda; mix the milk, molasses, and flour together, melt, and add the butter; roll out on the sheets and bake. This recipe is one hundred years old.—*Mrs. Woodworth, Springfield, Mass.*

ALUM GINGER-BREAD.

Pint molasses, tea-cup melted lard, table-spoon ginger, table-spoon salt, tea-cup boiling water; in half the water dissolve table-spoon pulverized alum, and in the other half a heaping table-spoon soda; stir in just flour enough to knead, roll about half inch thick, cut in oblong cards, and bake in a tolerably quick oven.—*Mrs. Wm. Patrick, Midland, Mich.*

GINGER-BREAD.

One gallon molasses or strained honey, one and a quarter pounds butter, quarter pound soda stirred in a half tea-cup sweet milk, tea-spoon alum dissolved in just enough water to cover it, flour to make it stiff enough to roll out; put the molasses in a very large dish, add the soda and butter melted, then all the other ingredients; mix in the evening and set in a warm place to rise over night; in the morning knead it a long time like bread, roll into squares half an inch thick and bake in bread-pans in an oven heated about right for bread. To make it glossy, rub over the top just before putting it into the oven the following: One well-beaten egg, the same amount or a little more sweet cream, stirring cream and egg well together. This ginger-bread will keep an unlimited time. The recipe is complete without ginger, but two table-spoons may be used if preferred. —*Over fifty years old, and formerly used for general muster days.*

EXCELLENT SOFT GINGER-BREAD.

One and a half cups Orleans molasses, half cup brown sugar, half cup butter, half cup sweet milk, tea-spoon soda, tea-spoon allspice, half tea-spoon ginger; mix all together thoroughly, add three cups sifted flour and bake in shallow pans.—*Mrs. S. Watson.*

SPONGE GINGER-BREAD.

One cup sour milk, one of Orleans molasses, a half cup butter two eggs, one tea-spoon soda, one table-spoon ginger, flour to make as thick as pound-cake; put butter, molasses and ginger together, make them quite warm, add the milk, flour, eggs and soda, and bake as soon as possible.—*Mrs. M. M. Munsell.*

GINGER COOKIES.

Two cups molasses, one of lard, one of sugar, two-thirds cup sour milk, table-spoon ginger, three tea-spoons soda stirred in the flour and one in the milk, two eggs.—*Miss Tina Lay, Clyde.*

EXCELLENT GINGER COOKIES.

Put one tea-spoon saleratus in a tea-cup, pour on it three table-spoons boiling water, add four table-spoons melted shortening, fill cup with molasses, and add salt and ginger to the taste; mix as soft as can be rolled.—*Mrs. S. Annie May, Stockbridge, Mass.*

GINGER CAKES.

One quart Orleans molasses, pint lard or butter, pint buttermilk, two table-spoons soda, two table-spoons ginger, flour enough to make a stiff batter; pour the molasses and milk boiling hot into a large tin bread-pan in which have been placed the ginger and soda (the pan must be large enough to prevent running over), stir in all the flour possible, after which stir in the lard or butter; when cold mold with flour and cut in cakes. Care must be taken to follow these directions implicitly or the cakes will not be good; remember to add the lard or butter last, and buttermilk, not sour milk, must be used; boil the molasses in a skillet, and after pouring it into the pan, put the buttermilk in the same skillet, boil and pour it over the molasses, ginger and soda.—*Mrs. R. M. Henderson.*

GINGER DROP-CAKES.

Take three eggs, one cup lard, one of baking molasses, one of brown sugar, one large table-spoon ginger, one table-spoon soda dissolved in a cup of boiling water, five cups unsifted flour; drop table-spoons of this mixture into a slightly-greased dripping-pan, about three inches apart.—*Mrs. L. McAllister.*

BEST GINGER-DROPS.

Half cup sugar, a cup molasses, half cup butter, one tea-spoon each cinnamon, ginger and cloves, two tea-spoons soda in a cup boiling water, two and a half cups flour; add two well-beaten eggs the last thing before baking. Baked in gem-tins or as a common ginger-bread, and eaten warm with a sauce, they make a nice dessert.—*Mrs. C. Hawks, Goshen, Ind.*

GINGER-SNAPS.

Two cups molasses, one of lard, one table-spoon soda, one of ginger, flour to roll stiff.—*Miss Mary Gallagher.*

HOTEL GINGER-SNAPS.

One gallon molasses, two pounds brown sugar, one quart melted butter, half tea-cup ground cloves, half tea-cup mace, half tea-cup cinnamon, half tea-cup ginger, two of soda.—*Mrs. Hattie Clemmons.*

MOLASSES CAKE.

Two cups molasses, one scant cup melted butter, two tea-spoons soda in one cup hot water, two tea-spoons ginger or one tea-spoon nutmeg, flour enough to make a stiff batter.—*Mrs. S. N. Fuller, New York City.*

CREAMS AND CUSTARDS.

For creams and custards eggs should never be beaten in tin, but always in stone or earthen ware, as there is some chemical influence about tin which prevents their attaining that creamy lightness so desirable. Beat quickly and sharply right through the eggs, beating whites and yolks separately When gelatine is used for creams, it is better to soak it for an hour in a little cold water or milk, set in a warm place; when dissolved, pour into the hot custard just after removing from the stove. For custards the common rule is four eggs, one cup sugar, and one small half tea-spoon salt to each quart of milk. Bake in a baking-dish until firm in the center, taking care that the heat is moderate or the custard will turn in part to whey. The delicacy of the custard depends on its being baked *slowly*. It is much nicer to strain the yolks, after they are beaten, through a small wire strainer kept for this purpose by every good housekeeper. For boiled custards or floats the yolks alone may be used, or for economy's sake the entire eggs. Always place the milk to boil in a custard-kettle (made of iron with another iron kettle inside, the latter lined with tin), or, in a pan or pail set within a kettle of *boiling* water; when the milk reaches the boiling point, which is shown by a slight foam rising on top, add the sugar which cools it so that the eggs will not curdle when added. Or, another convenient way is to mix the beaten and strained yolks with the sugar in a bowl, then add gradually several spoonfuls of the boiling milk, until the eggs and sugar are heated through, when they may be slowly stirred into the boiling milk. Let remain a few moments, stirring constantly until it thickens a little, but not long enough to curdle, then either set the pail immediately in cold water or turn out into a cold dish, adding flavoring extracts after removing from the stove. Peach leaves or vanilla beans give a fine flavor, but must be boiled in the milk and then taken out before the other ingredients are added. Boiled custards are very difficult to make, and must have the closest attention until they are finished.

In making *charlotte-russe* it is not necessary to add gelatine. The filling may be made of well-whipped cream, flavored and sweetened. Fill the mold and set on ice to harden. If preferred, it may be made up in several small molds, one for each person. In the use of spices it is well to remember that allspice and cloves are used with meats, and nutmeg and cinnamon in combination with sugar. The white part of lemon rind is exceedingly bitter, and the outer peel only should be used for grating. A better way is to rub the rind off with hard lumps of sugar. The sugar thus saturated with the oil of the lemon is called "zest," and is used, pounded fine, for creams, etc.

BOHEMIAN CREAMS.

One quart cream, two table-spoons sugar, one ounce gelatine soaked in water until dissolved; whip half the cream (rich milk may be substituted for cream) to a stiff froth; boil the other half with the sugar and a vanilla bean until the flavor is extracted (or vanilla extract may be added just after it is removed from the fire), take off the fire, add the gelatine, and when cooled a little, stir in the well-beaten yolks of the four eggs. As soon as it begins to thicken, stir steadily until smooth, when add the whipped cream, beating it in lightly. Mold and set on ice until ready to serve.

To flavor with strawberries, strain two pounds berries through a colander, sweeten to taste, add to the dissolved gelatine, set on ice, and when it thickens stir until smooth, add the whipped cream as above, and mold.

To flavor with peach, boil a dozen and a half choice fruit, sweeten and strain through a colander; add the dissolved gelatine and a teacup of cream, set on ice, and when it thickens stir until smooth, add the whipped cream, and mold.

To flavor with a pine-apple, cut fine, boil with half a pound pulverized sugar, strain through a colander, add the dissolved gelatine, set on ice, and when it thickens stir until smooth, add the whipped cream, and mold. Canned pine-apples may be used instead of fresh. In all these, never add whipped cream until the mass is cool and begins to thicken.—*Mrs. W. R. Jones, Pittsburgh, Pa.*

CHARLOTTE-RUSSE.

One ounce gelatine, one pint sweet milk, one of cream, four eggs, sugar to taste; beat the sugar and yolks of eggs together until light, boil the gelatine in the milk and strain over the eggs and sugar; whip the cream, which must be very cold, to a nice froth and add to the above; flavor with vanilla. Line the dish you wish to serve it in with sponge-cake, and pour the mixture in, then set it on ice till wanted.—*Mrs. Gov. Osborn, Kansas.*

CHARLOTTE-RUSSE.

Cut stale sponge-cake into slices about half an inch thick and line three molds with them, leaving a space of half an inch between each slice; set the molds where they will not be disturbed until the filling is ready; take a deep tin pan and fill about one-third full of either snow or pounded ice, and into this set another pan that will hold at least four quarts. Into a deep bowl or pail (a whip-churn is better), put one and a half pints of cream (if the cream is thick take one pint of cream and a half pint of milk,) whip to a froth, and when the bowl is full, skim the froth into the pan which is standing on the ice, and repeat this until the cream is all froth; then with the spoon draw the froth to one side, and you will find that some of the cream has gone back to milk; turn this into the bowl again, and whip as before; when the cream is all whipped, stir into it two-thirds cup powdered sugar, one teaspoon vanilla, and half a box of gelatine, which has been soaked in cold water enough to cover it for one hour and then dissolved in boiling water enough to dissolve it (about half a cup-ful), stir from the bottom of the pan until it begins to grow stiff; fill the molds and set them on the ice in the pan for one hour, or until they are sent to the table. When ready to dish them, loosen lightly at the sides and turn out on a flat dish; have the cream ice-cold when you begin to whip it, and it is a good plan to put a lump of ice into the cream while whipping it.—*M. Parloa.*

CHARLOTTE-RUSSE.

One quart milk, six ounces sugar, two ounces isinglass; put all into a sauce-pan and on the stove; when dissolved, take off, strain through a sieve and put on ice until it begins to set, then add one cup of wine and flavor to taste; when it begins to set, take one quart cream, beat to a stiff froth, and stir all together. Then take charlotte-russe molds, line them with sponge-cake, with a layer of jelly at the bottom, fill with the custard, and set on ice for two hours.—*Mrs. H. B. Sherman.*

CHARLOTTE-RUSSE.

One ounce gelatine dissolved in two gills of boiling milk, whites of four eggs beaten to a stiff froth, one and a half cups white powdered sugar, one pint thick cream whipped to a froth, and rose-water or vanilla for flavoring; line a large mold with thick slices of sponge-cake, mix the gelatine, sugar, cream, and flavoring together, add lightly the frothed whites of the eggs, pour into mold, set away on ice till required for use. This is an easy and excellent mode of making this most delicate dessert.—*Mrs. V. G. Hush, Minneapolis, Minn.*

HAMBURG CREAM.

The rind and juice of two large lemons, yolks of eight eggs, one cup sugar; put all in a bucket, set in a pan of boiling water, stir for three minutes, take from the fire, add the well-beaten whites of the eggs, and serve when cold in custard-glasses.—*Mrs. C. Fullington.*

ITALIAN CREAM.

Soak one-third box gelatine half an hour in cold milk, put a quart milk on to boil, and when boiling stir in yolks of eight eggs well beaten, add one cup and a half sugar and the gelatine; when the custard begins to thicken, take it off and pour into a deep dish in which the eight whites have been beaten to a stiff froth; mix well together and flavor to taste; put in molds, and allow four hours to cool. This cream is much more easily made in winter than in summer.—*Mrs. N. P. Wiles, Ripley.*

Rock Cream.

Boil one cup rice in a custard-kettle in sweet milk until soft, add two table-spoons loaf sugar, a salt-spoon salt; pour into a dish and place on it lumps of jelly; beat the whites of five eggs and three table-spoons pulverized sugar to a stiff froth, flavor to taste, add one table-spoon rich cream, and drop the mixture on the rice.—*Miss Libbie S. Wilcox, Madison.*

Rice Cream.

Boil one pint new milk in a custard-kettle, thicken to the consistency of cream with rice flour, sweeten and flavor, set in a cool place; dissolve half an ounce gelatine in half pint cold water, set in a warm place, and when dissolved beat to a froth with an egg-beater, add the well-beaten whites of two eggs, sweeten and flavor, pour in mold and place on rice to cool; turn out on dish, and serve with the rice cream around it.—*Miss Alice Trimble.*

Spanish Cream.

One box Coxe's gelatine dissolved in a pint of cold milk; into two quarts boiling milk, stir one and a half cups sugar, and the yolks of eight eggs; pour all upon the dissolved gelatine, stirring well. When cool add half a pint wine, or flavor with lemon or vanilla, place in dishes and cover with a meringue made of the beaten whites, the juice of one lemon, and one cup sugar; brown in oven two minutes and eat ice-cold.—*Susan R. Howard, Brooklyn, New York.*

Tapioca Cream.

Soak over night two table-spoons tapioca in one-half tea-cup milk (or enough to cover); bring one quart milk to boiling point; beat well together the yolks of three eggs, half tea-cup sugar, and one tea-spoon lemon or vanilla for flavoring, add the tapioca, and stir the whole into the boiling milk, let boil once, turn into the dish, and immediately spread on the whites. Serve when *cold.*—*Mrs. R. M. Henderson.*

Whipped Cream.

Place cream over ice until thoroughly chilled, and whip with an egg-beater or whip-churn until it froths. While whipping, place froth on a sieve, and return to bowl to be re-whipped all that passes through.   When cream is difficult to whip, add to it and beat with it the white of an egg.   Sweetened and flavored this is a choice dessert alone, but it may be served in various ways.   Baked apples, and fresh or preserved berries are delicious with it.   Jelly-glasses, one-third full of jelly and filled up with cream, make a very wholesome and delicious dessert.

WHIPPED CREAM.

One and one half pints good rich cream sweetened and flavored to taste, three tea-spoons vanilla; whip to a stiff froth.   Dissolve three-fourths ounce best gelatine in small tea-cup hot water, and when cool pour into the cream ; stir thoroughly, pour in molds and set on ice, or in very cool place.—*Mrs. Emma Craig, Washington, D. C.*

SNOW FLAKE.

One package gelatine, pint cold water, quart boiling water, pint wine, three lemons, three pounds sugar, half small bottle vanilla; put this away until cold; take the whites of six eggs, beat stiff, then beat up with the jelly, and place in molds.—*Mrs. Col. Woods, Greensburg, Pa.*

APPLE CUSTARD.

One pint of mashed stewed apples, one pint sweet milk, four eggs, one cup sugar and a little nutmeg; bake slowly.—*Mrs. G. W. Hensel, Quarryville, Pa.*

APPLE SNOW.

Pare, core and bring to boil in as little water as possible six tart apples, cool and strain, beat well and add the well-whipped whites of three eggs, sweeten to taste and beat thoroughly until a dish of snow is the result, flavor with lemon or vanilla, or add the grated rind of a lemon; serve with sweetened cream.   Or make custard of yolks, sugar, and a pint milk, place in a dish, and drop the froth on it in large flakes.—*Mrs. T. J. Buxton, Minneapolis, Minn.*

BLANC-MANGE

Dissolve three heaping table-spoons corn starch and three of sugar in one pint of milk; add to this three eggs well beaten, and pour the mixture into one pint of boiling milk, stirring constantly until it boils again; just before taking from the stove flavor to suit the taste and pour into cups or small molds; when cool take out and place on a glass dish with a mold of jelly in the center. Serve a spoonful of jelly and a sauce of sweetened cream with each mold. --*Mrs. E. M. R.*

CHOCOLATE BLANC-MANGE.

Half box gelatine, soaked till dissolved in as much cold water as will cover it, four ounces sweet chocolate grated, one quart sweet milk, one cup sugar; boil milk, sugar and chocolate five minutes, add gelatine, and boil five minutes more, stirring constantly; flavor with vanilla, put in molds to cool and eat with cream. If wanted for tea, make in the morning; if for dinner, the night before. For a plain blanc-mange omit the chocolate.—*Mrs. Dr. Houston, Urbana.*

RASPBERRY BLANC-MANGE.

Stew nice fresh raspberries, strain off the juice and sweeten it to taste, place over the fire, and when it boils stir in corn starch wet in cold water, allowing two table-spoons of corn starch for each pint of juice; continue stirring until sufficiently cooked, pour into molds wet in cold water and set away to cool; eat with cream and sugar. Other fruit can be used instead of raspberries.—*Mrs. J. P. Rea, Minneapolis, Minn.*

CHOCOLATE CUSTARD.

Two sections chocolate dissolved in one quart of milk, one cup sugar, yolks of six eggs, a heaping table-spoon corn starch; beat the yolks, add the sugar and corn starch, stir all slowly in the boiling milk in which the chocolate is dissolved, add a pinch of salt, and let cook a few minutes, stirring constantly; eat cold with white cake. ---*Miss Burnie Johnson.*

CORN MEAL CUSTARD.

One-fourth pound corn meal, one pint milk, boil together fifteen minutes, add one-fourth pound butter, six eggs, rose-water, salt, and sugar to taste.—*Mrs. E. M. R.*

FLOATING ISLAND.

Make a custard of the yolks of six eggs, one quart milk, a small pinch of salt, sugar to taste; beat and strain yolks before adding to the milk; place custard in a large tin pan, and set on stove, stirring *constantly* until it boils, then remove, flavor with lemon or rose, and pour into a dish (a shallow, wide one is best), spread smoothly over the boiling hot custard the well-beaten whites, grating some loaf-sugar and coacoa-nut on the top. Set the dish in a pan of ice-water and serve cold.—*Mrs. W. W. W.*

Good Baked Custard.

Eight well-beaten eggs, leaving out two whites for the top, three pints milk; sweeten and flavor to taste; bake for two hours in a slow oven. Beat the reserved whites to stiff froth with two table-spoons sugar, spread over the top, and return to oven to brown.

Gelatine Custard.

To one-third package Coxe's gelatine, add a little less than one pint boiling water; stir until gelatine is dissolved, add the juice of one lemon, and one and a half cups sugar; strain through a jelly-strainer into dish for the table, and set in a cool place. For custard, to one and a half pints milk add the yolks of four eggs (reserving the whites), and four table-spoons sugar; cook and flavor when cool. When required for the table, cut gelatine into small squares, and over them pour the custard. Add four table-spoons powdered sugar to the whites of four eggs well beaten, and when ready for the table, place over the custard with a spoon.—*Mrs. W. A. James.*

Lemon Custard.

One pound sugar, quarter pound butter, four eggs, cup sweet milk, two crackers, two lemons; beat butter and sugar together until light, add eggs beaten light, next grated crackers, then grated rind and chopped pith of lemon, and one cup milk, the juice of lemon to be added last.—*Mrs. Gov. J. P. Cochran, Delaware.*

Lemon Custard.

Beat two yolks of eight eggs till they are white, add pint boiling water, the rinds of two lemons grated, and the juice sweetened to taste; stir this on the fire till it thickens, then add a large glass of rich wine, and one-half glass of brandy; give the whole a good boil, and put in glasses. To be eaten cold.—*Mrs. Belle R. Liggett, Detroit, Mich.*

SNOW CUSTARD.

Half a package of Coxe's gelatine, three eggs, two cups of sugar, juice of one lemon; soak the gelatine one hour in a tea-cup of cold water, add one pint boiling water, stir until thoroughly dissolved, add two-thirds of the sugar and the lemon juice; beat the whites of the eggs to a stiff froth, and when the gelatine is quite cold, whip it into the whites, a spoonful at the time, from half an hour to an hour. Whip steadily and evenly, and when all is stiff, pour in a mold, or in a dozen egg-glasses previously wet with cold water, and set in a cold place. In four or five hours turn into a glass dish. Make a custard of one and one-half pints milk, yolk of eggs, and remainder of the sugar, flavor with vanilla, and when the meringue or snow-balls are turned out of the mold, pour this around the base.—*Mrs. Gov. Thayer, Wyoming Territory.*

MOONSHINE.

This dessert combines a pretty appearance with palatable flavor, and is a convenient substitute for ice-cream. Beat the whites of six eggs in a broad plate to a very stiff froth, then add gradually six table-spoons powdered sugar, beating for not less than thirty minutes, and then beat in about one heaping table-spoon of preserved peaches cut in tiny bits (or some use one cup jelly). In serving, pour in each saucer some rich cream sweetened and flavored with vanilla, and on the cream place a liberal portion of the moonshine. This quantity is enough for seven or eight persons.—*Mrs. H. C. Meredith, Cambridge City, Ind.*

ORANGE FLOAT.

One quart water, the juice and pulp of two lemons, one coffee-cup sugar; when boiling, add four table-spoons corn starch, let boil fifteen minutes, stirring all the time; when cold pour it over four or five peeled and sliced oranges, and over the top spread the beaten whites of three eggs; sweeten and add a few drops of vanilla.—*Mrs. Wm. Skinner.*

ORANGE SOUFFLE.

Peel and slice six oranges, put in a high glass dish a layer of oranges, then one of sugar, and so on until all the orange is used, and let stand two hours; make a soft boiled custard of the yolks of three eggs, one pint of milk, sugar to taste, with grating of the orange peel for flavor, and pour over the oranges when cool enough not to break the dish; beat the whites of the eggs to a stiff froth, stir in sugar, and put over the pudding.—*Mrs. Mary A. Livermore, Melrose, Mass.*

PRUNE WHIP.

Sweeten to taste and stew three-quarters of a pound of prunes; when *perfectly cold*, add the whites of four eggs beaten stiff, stir all this together till light, put in a dish, and bake twenty minutes; when cold serve in a larger dish, and cover well with good cream. *Mrs. Belle R. Liggett, Detroit, Mich.*

CONFECTIONERY.

Dissolve four pounds white sugar in one quart water; place this in a porcelain-kettle over a slow fire for half an hour, pour into it a small quantity of gelatine and gum-arabic dissolved together; all the impurities which rise to the surface skim off at once. Instead of gelatine and gum-arabic, the white of an egg may be used as a substitute with good results. To make the clarifying process still more perfect, strain through a flannel bag. To make rock-candy, boil this syrup a few moments, allow to cool, and crystallization takes place on the sides of the vessel. To make other candies bring the syrup very carefully to such a degree of heat that the "threads," which drop from the spoon when raised into the colder air, will snap like glass. When this stage is reached, add a teaspoon of vinegar or cream tartar to prevent "graining," and pour into pans as directed in the recipes which follow. To make round stick candies, pull, and roll into shape with well-floured hands as soon as cool enough to be handled. In pulling candy, some grease the hands, others flour them slightly. Colored candies are often injurious, and sometimes even poisonous, and should be avoided.

In baking macaroons and kisses use washed butter for greasing the tins, as lard or salt butter gives an unpleasant taste. After buttering, sprinkling lightly with flour and then shaking it off, is an excellent way to prepare the pan. When powdered almonds are to be used, they should be thoroughly dried in an open oven after blanching, and they will pulverize more easily.

ALMOND MACAROONS.

Pour boiling water on half a pound almonds, take skins off and throw into cold water for a few moments, then take out and pound (adding a table-spoon essence lemon) to a smooth paste, add one pound of pulverized sugar and whites of three eggs, and work the paste well together with back of spoon; dip the hands in water and roll mixture into balls the size of a nutmeg, and lay on buttered paper an inch apart; when done, dip the hands in water and pass gently over the macaroons, making the surface smooth and shining; set in a cool oven three-quarters of an hour. If this recipe is strictly followed, the macaroons will be found equal to any made by professional confectioners.—*Miss L. S. W.*

BUCKEYE BUTTER SCOTCH.

Three pounds "coffee A" sugar, fourth pound butter, half tea-spoon cream tartar, eight drops extract of lemon; add as much cold water as will dissolve the sugar; boil without stirring till it will easily break when dropped in cold water, and when *done,* add the lemon; have a dripping-pan well buttered and pour in one-fourth inch thick, and when partly cold, mark off in squares. If pulled, when partly cold, till very white, it will be like ice-cream candy.—*Mrs. J. S. R.*

BUCKEYE KISSES.

Beat the whites of four small eggs to a high, firm froth, stir into it half a pound pulverized sugar, flavor with essence lemon or rose, continue to beat until very light; then drop half the size of an egg, and a little more than an inch apart, on well-buttered letter-paper; lay the paper on a half-inch board and place in a hot oven; watch, and as soon as they begin to look yellowish take them out; or, beat to a stiff froth the whites of two eggs, stirring into them very gradually two tea-cups powdered sugar and two table-spoons corn starch; bake on buttered tins fifteen minutes in a warm oven, or until slightly brown. Chocolate puffs are, made by adding two ounces grated chocolate mixed with the corn starch.—*Mrs. W. W. W.*

BUTTER TAFFY.

Two cups sugar, three quarters cup vinegar, one half cup butter; boil until brittle when tested in water; pour in buttered pans.—*Henrietta F. Dwight, Cambridge, Mass.*

CENTENNIAL DROPS.

White of one egg beaten to a stiff froth, quarter pound pulverized sugar, half tea-spoon baking-powder; flavor with lemon; butter tins and drop with tea-spoon about three inches apart; bake in a slow oven and serve with ice-cream. This is also a very nice recipe for icing.—*Miss Alice Trimble, Mt. Gilead.*

CHOCOLATE CARAMELS.

One cup grated chocolate, four of sugar, two of molasses, two of milk, butter size of an egg, pinch of soda and flour; boil half an hour with quick fire, stirring to keep from burning; pour in pans and mark in squares when nearly cold.—*Mrs. J. F. Wilcox, New Haven, Conn.*

CHOCOLATE CARAMELS.

One and a half cups grated chocolate, four of brown sugar, one and a half of cold water, piece of butter size of an egg, table-spoon of very sharp vinegar; flavor with two table-spoons vanilla just before removing from fire. Do not stir, but shake the vessel gently while cooking. Boil on the top of stove over a brisk fire until it becomes brittle when tried in water; pour into a well buttered and floured dripping-pan, and check off in squares while soft.—*Miss Emma Collins, Urbana.*

CHOCOLATE DROPS.

Two and a half cups pulverized or granulated sugar, one-half cup cold water; boil four minutes and beat till cold enough to make into little balls; take half a cake of Baker's chocolate, cut off fine and set where it will melt, and when balls are cool enough, roll in the chocolate. This makes eighty. Or while making into balls, mold over almond meats, roll in coarse sugar, and you have delicious "cream almonds."—*Mrs. O. M. Scott.*

COCOA-NUT CARAMELS.

One pint milk, butter size of an egg, one cocoa-nut grated fine (or dessicated cocoa-nut may be used), three pounds white sugar, two tea-spoons lemon, boil slowly until stiff (some then beat to a cream), pour into shallow pans, and when partly cold cut in squares.—*Miss Nettie Brewster, Madison.*

Cocoa-nut Drops.

One pound cocoa-nut, half pound powdered sugar, and the white of one egg; work all together and roll into little balls in the hand; bake on buttered tins.—*C. W. Cyphers, Minneapolis, Minn.*

Everton Ice-cream Candy.

Squeeze the juice of one large lemon into a cup. Boil one and one-half pounds moist white sugar, two ounces butter, one and a half tea-cups water, together with half the rind of the lemon, and when done (which may be known by its becoming quite crisp when dropped into cold water), set aside till the boiling has ceased, and then stir in the juice of the lemon, butter a dish and pour in about an inch thick. When cool take out peel (which may be dried), pull until white, draw out into sticks and check about four inches long with a knife. If you have no lemons, take two table-spoons vinegar and two tea-spoons lemon extract. The fire must be quick and the candy stirred all the time.—*Mrs. J. S. R.*

German Cakes.

One pound flour, one of white sugar, quarter pound almonds cut into small pieces, five eggs, grated rind of one lemon; drop this mixture into a large buttered pan, a tea-spoonful in a place, and bake until tinged with brown. Eggs and sugar should be beaten fifteen minutes.—*Miss Flora Partridge.*

Hickory-nut Macaroons.

Take meats of hickory-nuts, pound fine and add mixed ground spice and nutmeg; make frosting as for cakes, stir meats and spices in, putting in enough to make it convenient to handle; flour the hands and make the mixture into balls the size of marbles, lay them on buttered tins, giving room to spread, and bake in a quick oven. —*Mrs. Walter Mitchell, Gallipolis.*

Hickory-nut Cakes.

One egg, half cup flour, a cup sugar, a cup nuts sliced fine; drop on buttered tins one tea-spoonful in a place, two inches apart. Or, bake like sand tarts.—*Mrs. Lamb, Bellefontaine.*

Lemon Candy.

Take a pound loaf-sugar and a large cup water, and after cooking over a slow fire half an hour, clear with a little hot vinegar, take off the scum as it rises, testing by raising with a spoon, and when the "threads" will snap like glass pour into a tin pan, and when nearly cold mark in narrow strips with a knife. Before pouring into the pans, chopped cocoa-nut, almonds, hickory-nuts, or Brazil-nuts cut in slices, may be stirred into it.—*Mrs. V. K. W.*

MERINGUES.

One pound granulated sugar, whites of nine eggs. Whip eggs until dish can be inverted without their falling off, and then simply add the sugar, incorporating it thoroughly, but stirring as little as possible. Prepare boards three-fourths of an inch thick, to fit oven, and cover them with strips of heavy brown paper about two and a half inches wide; on these drop the mixture from the end of a dessert-spoon (or use the meringue-bag described in recipe for lady's fingers), giving the meringue the form of an egg, and dropping them about two inches apart on the paper, and bake till a light brown. Take up each strip of paper by the two ends, turn it gently on the table, and with a small spoon take out the soft part of each meringue, strew over them some sifted sugar, and return to oven bottom side up to brown. These shells may be kept for weeks. When wanted for table, fill with whipped cream, place two of them together so as to inclose the cream, and serve. To vary their appearance, finely-chopped almonds or currants may be strewn over them before the sugar is sprinkled over, and they may be garnished with any bright-colored preserve. Great expedition is necessary in making them, as, if the meringues are not put into the oven as soon as the sugar and eggs are mixed, the former melts, and the mixture runs on the paper instead of keeping its egg-shape. The sweeter the meringues are made the crisper will they be, but if there is not sufficient sugar added they will most likely be tough. If damp weather should cause the shells to soften, place them again in the oven to dry.—*Miss Sarah Gill, Columbus.*

MOLASSES CANDY.

Take equal quantities brown sugar and Orleans molasses, (or all molasses may be used), and one table-spoon sharp vinegar, and when it begins to boil skim well and strain, return to the kettle and continue boiling until it becomes brittle if dipped in cold water,

7

then pour on a greased platter. As soon as cool enough, begin to throw up the edges and work, by pulling on hook or by hand, until bright and glistening like gold; flour the hands occasionally, draw into stick size, rolling them to keep round, until all is pulled out and cold. Then with shears clip a little upon them at proper lengths for the sticks, and they will easily snap; flavor as you pour the candy out to cool.—*Sterling Robinson.*

POP-CORN BALLS.

Pop the corn and reject all that is not nicely opened; place a half bushel on a table or dripping-pan; put a little water in a suitable kettle, with one pound sugar, and boil until it becomes quite waxy in cold water; remove from fire and dip into it six or seven table-spoons of gum solution, (made as thick as molasses by pouring boiling water on gum-arabic and letting stand over night); pour mixture over the corn, putting a stick or the hands under the corn, lifting it up and mixing until it is all saturated, let stand a few moments, then flour the hands slightly and press into balls. This amount will make one hundred pop-corn balls such as the street peddlers sell, but for home eating, omit the gum solution, and use a half pint of stiff taffy made as above for one peck of popped corn. This will make twenty rich balls.—*Bert Robinson.*

AUNT TOP'S NUT-TAFFY.

Two pints maple sugar, half pint water, or just enough to dissolve sugar; boil until it becomes brittle by dropping in cold water; just before pouring out add a table-spoon vinegar; having prepared the hickory-nut meats, in halves if possible, butter well the pans, line with the meats, and pour the taffy over them.—*Estelle and Hattie Hush.*

VANITY PUFFS.

Beat five or six whites of eggs very stiff, add a pound of sugar, flavor with lemon or cardamom, cut off about egg-size with a table-spoon, put on buttered paper, and let dry in a cool oven two hours.—*Mrs. H. C. Mahncke.*

CANNING FRUITS.

Cleanse the cans thoroughly and test to see if any leak or are cracked. If tin cans leak, send them to the tinner; if discolored inside they may be lined with writing-paper just before using. In buying stoneware for canning purposes, be sure that it is well glazed, as fruits canned in jars or jugs imperfectly glazed sometimes become poisonous. Never use defective glass cans, but keep them for storing things in the pantry; and in buying them, take care that they are free from flaws and blisters, else the glass will crumble off in small particles when subjected to heat. Self-sealers are very convenient, but the heat hardens the rubber rings, which are difficult to replace, so that in a year or two they are unfit for use. For this reason many prefer those with a groove around the top for sealing with wax or putty. The latter is very convenient, as jars sealed with it can be opened readily with a strong fork or knife, and are much more easily cleaned than when wax-sealed. Putty may be bought ready for use, and is soon made soft by molding in the hand. In using it should be worked out into a small roll, and pressed firmly into the groove with a knife, care being taken to keep it well pressed down as the can cools.

Fruit should be selected carefully, and all that is imperfect rejected. Large fruits, such as peaches, pears, etc., are in the best condition to can when not quite fully ripe, and should be put up as soon as possible after picking; small fruits, such as berries, should never stand over night if it is possible to avoid it. The highest-flavored and longest-keeping fruits are best put up without paring, after having carefully removed the down with a fine but stiff brush. Use only the best sugar in the proportion of half a pound of sugar to a pound of good fruit, varying the rule, of course, with the sweetness of the fruit. Or, in canning for pies omit sugar, as the natural flavor is better preserved without it, and some prefer this method for all purposes. It is economical, and well worthy of experiment. Cans put up in this way should have a special mark so as to distinguish them from the rest. When ready to can, first place the jars (glass) in a large pan of warm water on the back of the stove, make ready the syrup in a nice clean porcelain kettle, add the fruit —it is better to prepare only enough fruit or syrup for two or three cans at a time—and by the time it is done, the water in the pan will be hot and the cans ready for use. Take them out of the water and set them on a hot platter, which answers the double purpose of preventing their contact with any cold surface like the table, and saving any fruit that may be spilled. Fill as full as possible, and set aside where no current of air will strike them—or, better, wring out a towel wet in hot water and set them on it—let stand a moment or two or until wiped off, when the fruit will have shrunk away a little; fill up again with hot syrup, or, if you have none, boiling water from the tea-kettle will do, and then seal. In canning peaches, the flavor is improved by adding two or three whole peaches, or dropping in the center of the can a few of the stones. For peaches, pears and berries, some sweeten as for eating, let stand until sugar is dissolved (using no water), place on stove in porcelain kettle and keep at boiling point long enough to heat the fruit, and then can in glass jars as directed.

There are several other ways of preparing glass cans for fruit, among them the following: Wring a towel from cold water, double and wrap closely about and under the can so as to exclude the air, and put a cold silver spoon inside and fill; or, put a towel in a steamer, set in the cans, and place over a kettle of *cold* water, boil the water, and when ready to fill, remove the cans and wrap in a towel wrung from warm water, put a table-spoon rinsed in hot water inside, and fill; or, wash the cans in tepid water, place an iron rod inside, and at once pour in the boiling fruit, but not too fast. In using glass cans with tops which screw on, be sure that the rubbers are firm and close-fitting, and throw away all that are imperfect. When the can is filled to overflowing, put on the top at once and screw down tightly, and as the fruit and cans cool, causing contraction of the glass, turn down again and again until perfectly air-tight. Wrap as soon as cold with brown wrapping-paper unless the fruit-closet is very dark. Light injures all fruit, but especially tomatoes, in which it causes the formation of citric acid which no amount of sugar will sweeten. The place where canned fruits are kept should also be dry and · cool. In canning, use a porcelain-lined kettle, silver fork or broom-splint, and wire spoon or dipper. A steel fork discolors the fruit.

Cans should be examined two or three days after filling, and if syrup leaks out from the rim, they should be unsealed, the fruit thoroughly cooked and kept for jam or jelly, as it will have lost the delicacy of color and flavor so desirable in canned fruits. Pint cans are better for berries than quart. Strawberries keep their color best in stone jars; if glass cans are used for them, they should be buried in sand.

In using self-sealing cans the rubber ring must show an even edge all round, for if it slips back out of sight at any point, air will be admitted. On opening tin cans, remember to pour *all* the fruit out into an earthen or glass dish. Wines, cider, shrubs, etc., must be bottled, well corked, sealed, and the bottles placed on their sides in a box of sand or sawdust. To can maple syrup, pour either hot or cold into cans or jugs, and seal well.

The fine display of canned fruits at the Centennial Exhibition was prepared as follows: The fruits were selected with great care, of uniform size and shape, and *all perfect.* They were carefully peeled with a thin, sharp, silver fruit-knife, which did not discolor them, and immediately plunged into cold water in an earthen or wooden vessel to prevent the air from darkening them. As soon as enough for one can was prepared, it was put up by laying the fruit piece by piece in the can, and pouring syrup, clear as crysal, over it, and then, after subjecting the whole to the usual heat, sealing up.

CANNED BERRIES.

Select those the skins of which have not been broken, or the juice will darken the syrup; fill cans compactly, set in a kettle of cold water, with a cloth beneath them, over an even heat; when sufficiently heated, pour over the berries a syrup of white sugar dissolved in boiling water (the richer the better for keeping, though not for preserving the flavor of the fruit), cover the cans closely to retain heat on the top berries. To insure full cans when cold, have extra berries heated in like manner to supply the shrinkage. If the fruit swims pour off surplus syrup, fill with hot fruit, and seal up as soon as the fruit at the top is thoroughly scalded.—*Miss L. Southwick.*

PLAIN CANNED BERRIES.

Pick out stems or hulls if any—if gathered carefully the berries will not need washing—put in porcelain kettle on the stove, adding a small tea-cup water to prevent burning at first. When they come to a boil, skim well, add sugar to taste (for pies it may be omitted), let boil five minutes, fill in glass, stone, or tin cans, and seal with putty unless self-sealers are used. This rule applies to raspberries, blackberries, currants, gooseberries, or any of the small berries.

CANNED CURRANTS.

Scald ripe currants, adding a pound sugar to every pound fruit, until the seeds are well heated; spread on plates or platters for a day or two in the sun, when they will be nicely jellied, and put into cans and seal; they will keep for years.—*Mrs. Wm. Patrick, Midland, Mich.*

GREEN GOOSEBERRIES.

Cook the berries in water until white, but not enough to break them; put into cans with as little water as possible, fill up the can with boiling water and seal; when opened pour off water and cook like fresh berries.—*Mrs. O. M. S.*

CANNED PEACHES.

Pour boiling water over one peck of large clingstone peaches to remove the fuzz; make a syrup of three pounds sugar and one pint vinegar, using a little water if required to cover the peaches; cook until pretty soft, and can as usual.—*Mrs. Frank Stahr, Lancaster, Pa.*

Canned Peaches.

Have one porcelain kettle with boiling water and another with a syrup made sweet enough with white sugar for the peaches; pare, halve, and drop them into the boiling water, let them remain until a silver fork will pierce them, lift them out with a wire spoon, fill can, pour in all the boiling syrup the can will hold, and seal immediately. Continue in this way, preparing and sealing only one can at a time, until done; boil down the water in first kettle with the syrup, if any is left; if not, add more sugar, and quite a nice marmalade will result. This manner of canning peaches has been thoroughly tested, and is pronounced by the experienced the best of all methods.—*Mrs. R. A. Sharp, Kingston.*

Canned Peaches.

To peel, place in a wire basket such as is used for popping corn, dip into boiling water for a moment, then into cold water, and strip off the skin (this saves both fruit and labor). The fruit must be at a certain stage to be prepared in this way, for if too green it will not peel, and if too ripe it will be too much softened by the hot water. After peeling, seed and place in a steamer over a kettle of boiling water, first laying a cloth in bottom of steamer; fill about half full of fruit, cover tightly, make a syrup in a porcelain kettle kept for fruit alone, let the fruit steam until it can be easily pierced with a silver fork, drop gently for a moment into the hot syrup, place in the cans, fill, cover, and seal. The above recipe is for canning a few at a time, and is equally nice for pears. —*Miss Abbie Curtis, St. Louis, Mo.*

Canned Peaches.

Pare, halve and seed; make a syrup of a pint granulated sugar to a quart water, place on stove in a porcelain kettle (enough for two quart cans). When syrup boils, drop in enough fruit for one can; watch closely, testing with a silver fork, so that the moment they are done they may be removed. When the peaches are tender, lift very gently with a wire spoon, and place in the can previously heated, according to instructions for preparing glass cans. When full of peaches pour in the hot syrup, place the cover on and seal at once; then add more peaches to the hot syrup for next can, and repeat the operation. If there are more peaches than will fill the can, place them in another can and *keep hot* until more are ready, and so on until all are canned. Skim the syrup before adding peaches, making only enough syrup at one time for two cans.—*Mrs. W. W. W.*

CANNED PEARS.

Prepare and can precisely like peaches in preceding recipe, except that they require longer cooking. When done they are easily pierced with a silver fork.

CANNED PINE-APPLE.

Peel and slice, make syrup in proportion of two and a half pounds best white granulated sugar to nearly three pints of water; boil five minutes; skim or strain; add fruit and let it boil; have cans hot; fill and seal up as soon as possible.

CANNED PLUMS.

Wash and put whole into a syrup made in the proportion of a pint of water and a pound of sugar to every two pounds fruit; boil for eight minutes, can, and seal immediately. If pricked with a fork before placing in syrup, they will be less liable to burst. Cherries are canned in the same way.

CANNED STRAWBERRIES.

Fill glass jars with fresh whole strawberries, sprinkled with sugar in the proportion of half pound sugar to a pound berries, lay covers on lightly, stand them in a wash-boiler filled with water to within an inch of tops of cans (the water must not be more than milk-warm when the cans are placed in it). When it has boiled for fifteen minutes, draw to back of stove, let steam pass off, roll the hand in a towel, lift out cans, and place on a table. If the berries are well covered with their own juice, take a table-spoon and fill up the first can to the very top of the rim from the second, wipe the neck, rub dry, and screw the top down firmly, observing carefully the general directions for canning berries. Fill another from the second can, and so on until all are finished

Canned Strawberries.

For every two boxes of *fresh* strawberries, take one coffee-cup of white sugar; add a table-spoon or two of water to the fruit if there is no juice in the bottom, to prevent burning before the heat brings out the juice. As soon as the fruit boils, add the sugar, and stir gently for a few minutes until it boils up again, and can immediately. It is better not to cook any more fruit than can be put into one glass fruit-jar. Usually a few spoonfuls of the syrup will be left with which to begin the next can. Strawberries are considered difficult to keep, but there need be no trouble if the fruit is fresh and the can is closed air-tight in glass, and kept as directed in general directions for canning fruits.—*Mrs. H. S. Huntington, Galesburg, Ill.*

Canned Corn.

Dissolve an ounce tartaric acid in half tea-cup water, and take one table-spoon to two quarts of sweet corn; cook, and while boiling hot, fill the cans, which should be tin. When used, turn into a colander, rinse with cold water, add a little soda and sugar while cooking, and season with butter, pepper and salt.—*Miss Lida Cartmell.*

Canned Sweet Corn.

Pick corn when milk-ripe, cut from the cob and scrape so as to get all the juice, place in tin cans and seal up air-tight; set them in boiling water from one to two hours according to size of can, next day punch a small hole in the top of the can to allow the gases to escape, and immediately re-seal, after which place in boiling water and let remain as long or longer than at first.—*Mrs. A. I. J.*

Canned Corn and Tomatoes.

Scald, peel, and slice tomatoes (not too ripe) in the proportion of one-third corn to two-thirds tomatoes; put on in a porcelain kettle, let boil fifteen minutes, and can immediately in tin or glass (if glass, keep in the dark). Some take equal parts of corn and tomatoes, preparing them as above. Others, after cutting the corn from the cob, cook it twenty minutes, adding a little water and stirring often, then prepare the tomatoes as above, cooking in a separate kettle five minutes, and then adding them to the corn in the proportion of one-third corn to two-thirds tomatoes, mixing well until they boil up once, and then canning immediately.—*Mrs. D. Buxton.*

STRING-BEANS.

String fresh string-beans, break in several pieces, cook in boiling water ten minutes, and can like tomatoes.—*Mrs. L. W. C., Cincinnati.*

CANNED TOMATOES.

The tomatoes must be entirely fresh and not overripe; pour over them boiling water, let stand a few minutes, drain off, remove the skins, and slice crosswise into a stone jar, cutting out all the hard or defective portions; cook for a few minutes in their own juice, skimming off the scum which rises, and stirring with a wooden spoon or paddle; have the cans on the hearth filled with hot water; empty, and fill with the hot tomatoes; wipe the moisture from the tops with a soft cloth, and put on and secure the covers. If tin cans are used, press down the covers, and pour hot sealing wax into the grooves. If put up in glass jars, set away in a dark place. Either tin, glass or stone cans may be used, and all may be sealed with putty instead of wax, it being much neater and more convenient. See general instructions for canning fruit.

CANNED WATERMELON.

Cut the melons, and after taking out the cores, peel all the green part off carefully, cut the rind into small pieces two or three inches long, and boil until tender enough to pierce with a fork; have a syrup made of white sugar, allowing half pound sugar to a pound fruit; skim out the melon and place in this syrup together with a few pieces of race ginger, let cook a few minutes, put in cans and seal hot.—*Mrs. C. T. C.*

CATSUPS AND SAUCES.

Always select perfect fruit; cook in porcelain, never in metal. In making catsup, instead of boiling, some sprinkle the tomatoes with salt and let them stand over night, then strain and add spices, etc., and a little sugar. Bottle in glass or stone, and never use tin cans; keep in a cool, dry, dark place. If, on opening, there is a leathery mold on top, carefully remove every particle of it, and the catsup will not be injured. To prevent this molding, some do not fill the bottles quite to the top with catsup, but fill up with hot vinegar. If there are white specks of mold all through the catsup it is spoiled. If on opening and using a part, there is danger that the rest may sour, scald, and, if too thick, add vinegar. Sauces should always be made with great care in a pan set in hot water, having the sauce pan *clean* if a delicate flavor is desired, especially if the sauce is drawn butter. An excellent thickening for soups, sauces, and gravies, is prepared as follows: Bring butter to the boiling point in a small stew-pan, dredge in flour, stirring together until well cooked; thin this with a part of the soup, sauce or gravy, and then add it to the whole, stirring thoroughly. The flour may be browned before using if intended for brown gravies or sauces.

CUCUMBER CATSUP.

Three dozen cucumbers and eighteen onions peeled and chopped very fine; sprinkle over them three-fourths pint table-salt, put the whole in a sieve, and let drain well over night; add a tea-cup mustard seed, half tea-cup ground black pepper, mix well, and cover with good cider vinegar.—*Mrs. Hattie Clemmons, Asheville, N. C.*

Currant Catsup.

Four pounds nice fully-ripe currants, one and a half pounds sugar, table-spoon ground cinnamon, a tea-spoon each of salt, ground cloves and pepper, pint vinegar; stew currants and sugar until quite thick, add other ingredients and bottle for use.

Cherry Catsup.

One pint cherry juice to half or three-fourths pound sugar, with cloves, cinnamon, and a very little cayenne pepper; boil to a thick syrup; bottle for use.—*Miss M. Louise Southwick.*

Gooseberry Catsup.

Nine pounds gooseberries, five pounds sugar, one quart vinegar, three table-spoons cinnamon, one and a half each allspice and cloves. The gooseberries should be nearly or quite ripe. Take off blossoms, wash and put them into a porcelain kettle, mash thoroughly, scald and put through the colander, add sugar and spices, boil fifteen minutes, and add the vinegar cold; bottle immediately before it cools. Ripe grapes prepared by same rule, make an excellent catsup.—*Mrs. Col. W. P. Reid, Delaware.*

Tomato Catsup.

Half bushel tomatoes, four ounces salt, three ounces ground black pepper, one ounce cinnamon, half ounce ground cloves, one drachm cayenne pepper, one gallon vinegar, slice the tomatoes and stew in their own liquor until soft, and rub through a sieve fine enough to retain the seeds; boil the pulp and juice down to the consistency of apple butter (very thick), stirring steadily all the time to prevent burning; then add the vinegar with which a small tea-cup sugar and the spices have been mixed, boil up twice, remove from fire, let cool and bottle. Those who like the flavor of onions may add about half a dozen medium sized ones, peeled and sliced, fifteen minutes before the vinegar and spices are put in.—*Mrs. M. M. Munsell, Delaware.*

Tomato Catsup.

One gallon peeled tomatoes, four table-spoons common salt, four of black pepper, two of allspice, three of ground mustard, tea-spoon cayenne; simmer slowly in a gallon cider vinegar to about five quarts and a half of tomatoes; strain through a sieve, and bottle while hot; cork the bottle and dip into hot sealing wax.—*Mrs. Erastus Byers, Minneapolis, Minn.*

BREAD SAUCE.

Half pint grated bread crumbs, one pint sweet milk, and one onion; boil until the sauce is smooth, take out onion and stir in two spoonfuls butter with salt and pepper; boil once and serve with roast duck or any kind of game.—*Mrs. H. C. E.*

CRANBERRY SAUCE.

After removing all soft berries, wash thoroughly, place for about two minutes in scalding water, remove, and to every pound fruit add three-quarters of a pound granulated sugar and a half pint water; stew together over a moderate but steady fire. Be careful *to cover* and *not to stir* the fruit, but occasionally shake the vessel, or apply a gentler heat if in danger of sticking or burning. If attention to these particulars be given, the berries will retain their shape to a considerable extent, which adds greatly to their appearance on the table. Boil from five to seven minutes, remove from fire, turn into a deep dish, and set aside to cool. If to be kept, they can be put up at once in air-tight jars. Or, for strained sauce, one and a half pounds of fruit should be stewed in one pint of water for ten or twelve minutes, or until quite soft, then strained through a colander or fine wire sieve, and three-quarters of a pound of sugar thoroughly stirred into the pulp thus obtained; after cooling, it is ready for use. Serve with roast turkey or game. When to be kept for a long time without sealing, more sugar may be added, but its too free use impairs the peculiar cranberry flavor. For dinner-sauce half a pound is more economical, and really preferable to three-quarters, as given above. It is better, though not necessary, to use a porcelain kettle. Some prefer not to add the sugar till the fruit is almost done, thinking this plan makes it more tender, and preserves the color better.—*C. G. & E. W. Crane, Caldwell, N. J.*

CELERY SAUCE.

Scrape the outside stalks of celery and cut in pieces an inch long, let stand in cold water half hour, then put in boiling water enough to cover, and cook until tender; drain off water and dress with butter, salt, and milk or cream, thickened with a little flour: Or, make a dressing by adding to half pint milk or cream, the well-beaten yolks of two eggs, a bit of butter, and a little salt and pepper or grated nutmeg; bring just to boiling point, pour over stewed celery and serve with roast duck.—*Mrs. A. Wilson.*

Curry Powder.

An ounce of ginger, one of mustard, one of pepper, three of coriander seed, three of tumeric, one-half ounce cardamom, quarter ounce cayenne pepper, quarter ounce cummin seed; pound all fine, sift and cork tight. One tea-spoon of powder is sufficient to season any thing. This is nice for boiled meats and stews.—*Mrs. C. Fullington.*

Chili Sauce.

Twelve large ripe tomatoes, four ripe or three green peppers, two onions, two table-spoons salt, two of sugar, one of cinnamon, three cups vinegar; peel tomatoes and onions, chop all fine, and boil one and a half hours. Bottle and it will keep any length of time. One quart of canned tomatoes may be used instead of the ripe ones.—*Mrs. E. W. Herrick, Minneapolis, Minn.*

Drawn Butter.

Rub a small cup of butter into half a table-spoon flour, beating it to a cream, adding, if needed, a little salt; pour on it half a pint boiling water, stirring it fast, and taking care not to let it *quite* boil, as boiling makes it *oily* and unfit for use. The boiling may be prevented by placing the sauce-pan containing it, in a larger one of boiling water, covering and shaking frequently until it reaches the boiling point. A great variety of sauces which are excellent to eat with fish, poultry, or boiled meats, can be made by adding different herbs, such as, parsley, mint, or sweet marjoram, to drawn butter. First throw them into boiling water, cut fine, and they are ready to be added, when serve immediately, with two hard-boiled eggs, chopped fine. This makes a nice sauce to serve with baked fish. The chopped inside of a lemon with the seeds out, to which the chicken liver has been added, makes a good sauce for boiled chicken.

Holland Sauce.

Put into a sauce-pan a tea-spoon flour, two ounces butter, two table-spoons each of vinegar and water, the beaten yolks of two eggs, and salt to taste; put over the fire and stir constantly until it thickens, but do not allow it to boil, or it will curdle and require straining through a gravy strainer; add the juice of half a lemon, and serve with baked fish.

HORSE-RADISH SAUCE.

One dessert-spoon olive oil, melted butter, or cream, one of ground or prepared mustard, two table-spoons grated horse-radish, one of vinegar, one tea-spoon sugar, and a little salt stirred and beaten together until thoroughly mixed. Serve with cold meats. When made with oil or melted butter, and not with cream, this will keep two or three days.

MINT SAUCE.

Take one table-spoon powdered sugar and half tea-cup vinegar; stir in two table-spoons of green mint, chopped *very fine.* Serve with roast lamb.—*Mrs. Allie Reid Evans, Delaware.*

OYSTER SAUCE.

Set a basin on the fire with half pint oysters, from which all bits of shell have been picked, and one pint boiling water; let boil three minutes, skim well, and then stir in half a cup butter beaten to a cream, with two table-spoons flour; let this come to a boil, and serve with boiled turkey.—*Mrs. H. C. M.*

ONION SAUCE.

Boil three or four white onions till tender, mince fine; boil half pint milk, add butter half size of an egg, salt and pepper to taste, and stir in minced onion and a table-spoon of flour which has been moistened with milk.—*E. H. W.*

ROMAN SAUCE.

Put one tea-cup water and one tea-cup milk on fire to scald, and when hot stir in a table-spoon flour, previously mixed smooth with a very little cold water, add three eggs well beaten and strained, season with salt and pepper, two table-spoons butter and a little vinegar; boil four eggs hard, slice and lay over the dish; pour over sauce, and serve with boiled fish.—*Mrs. E. T. E.*

SALAD SAUCE.

Boil two eggs three minutes; mix with them a mustard-spoon of prepared mustard, a little pepper and salt, six spoonfuls drawn

butter or salad oil, six of vinegar, one of catsup.   This is excellent
for cold meat, salad or fish.—*Mrs. A. E. Brand, Minneapolis, Minn.*

TOMATO SAUCE.

Stew ten tomatoes with three cloves, and pepper and salt, for fifteen minutes (some add a sliced onion and sprig of parsley), strain
through a sieve, put on the stove in a saucepan in which a lump of
butter the size of an egg and a level table-spoon flour have been well
mixed and cooked, stir all until smooth and serve.   Canned tomatoes may be used as a substitute.

TO PREPARE MUSTARD.

Boil one pint vinegar, stir in a quarter pound mustard while hot,
add two table-spoons sugar, tea-spoon salt, and one of white pepper;
let the mixture boil.—*Mrs. Olivia S. Hinman, Battle Creek, Mich.*

MADE MUSTARD.

Take three tea-spoons ground mustard, one of flour (two if the
mustard seems very strong), half tea-spoon of sugar; pour boiling
water on these and mix into a smooth, thick paste; when cold add
vinegar enough to make ready for use, and serve with salt.   This
resembles the French Mustard.—*Mrs. Mary Herbert Huntington.*

TO PREPARE HORSE-RADISH FOR WINTER.

In the fall, mix the quantity wanted in the following proportions:
A coffee-cup of grated horseradish, two table-spoons white sugar,
half tea-spoon salt, and a pint and a half cold vinegar; bottle and
seal.

DRINKS.

To avoid adulteration buy coffee in the grain, either raw or in small quantities freshly roasted. The best kinds are the Mocha and Java, and some prefer to mix the two, having roasted them separately. West India coffee, though of a different flavor, is often very good.

Roast coffee with the greatest care—for here lies the secret of success in coffee-making—and in small quantities, for there is a peculiar freshness of flavor when newly roasted. Pick over carefully, wash and dry in a moderate oven, increase the heat and roast quickly, either in the oven, or on top of the stove or range; in the latter case, stir *constantly*, and in the oven stir *often*, with a wooden spoon or ladle kept for this purpose. The coffee must be thoroughly and evenly roasted to a dark rich brown, not black, throughout, and must be free from any burnt grains, a few of which will ruin the flavor of a large quantity. It must be tender and brittle, to test which take a grain, place it on the table, press with the thumb and if it can be crushed, it is done. Stir in a lump of butter while the coffee is hot, or wait until about half cold and then stir in a well-beaten egg. The latter plan is very economical, as coffee so prepared needs no further clarifying. Keep in a closely-covered tin or earthen vessel. Never attempt other work while roasting coffee, but give it the entire attention. Do not grind too fine, and only in quantities as needed, for the flavor is dissipated if it is long unused after grinding, even when under cover. If properly roasted, coffee will grind into distinct, hard, and gritty particles and not into a powder.

8

MAKING COFFEE.

"One for the pot" and a heaping table-spoon of ground coffee for each person, is the usual allowance. Mix well, either with a part or the whole of an egg and enough cold water to thoroughly moisten it, place in a well-scalded coffee-boiler, pour in half the quantity of boiling water needed, allowing one pint less of water than there are table-spoons of coffee. Roll a cloth tightly and stop up the nose or spout, thus keeping in all the coffee flavor. Boil rather fast five minutes, stirring down from the top and sides as it boils up, and place on back part of stove or range where it will only simmer for ten or fifteen minutes longer. When ready to serve add the remainder of the boiling water. Coffee boiled a long time is strong, but not so well flavored or agreeable as when prepared as above.

FILTERED COFFEE.

The National Coffee-pot is so widely known as not to need description here, but the "gude wife" can improvise one equally as desirable and much simpler. Make a sack of fine flannel, or canton flannel, as long as the coffee-pot is deep, and a little larger than the top; stitch up the side seam to within an inch and a half of the top, bend a piece of small but rather stiff wire in a circle, and slip it through a hem made around the top of the sack, bringing the ends together at the opening left at the top of the side seam. Having put the coffee in the sack, lower it into the coffee-pot with the ends of the wire next the handle, spread the ends of the wire apart slightly, and push it down over the top of the pot. The top of the sack will then be turned down a little over the outside of the pot, a part of it covering the "nose," and keeping in all the aroma, the elasticity of the wire causing it to close tight around the pot, holding the sack close to its sides. Instead of a wire (which must be removed to wash the sack after using), a tape may be used by tying the ends after turning the top of sack down. When the sack, with the coffee in it is in its place, pour the boiling water over the coffee, close the lid tightly, and let simmer (not boil) fifteen minutes to half an hour. In pouring for the table raise the sack off the nose but not out of pot. This makes good coffee without eggs or any thing else to settle it.

MAKING TEA.

"Polly put the kettle on, and we'll all take Tea."

Of all "cups that cheer" there is nothing like the smoking-hot cup of tea, made with *boiling* water, in a *thoroughly scalded* tea-pot. If it is the good, old-fashioned green tea of "ye ancient time," you must put it to *draw* and not to boil; if it is genuine "English Breakfast," or *best* black tea, the water must not only be boiling hot at the very moment of pouring it on, but the tea must actually boil for at least five or ten minutes. To insure "keeping hot" while serving, make the simple contrivance known as a "bonnet" which is warranted a sure preventative against that most insipid of all drinks—a warmish cup of tea. It is merely a sack, with a loose elastic in the bottom, large enough to cover and encircle the entire tea-pot. Make it with odd pieces of silk, satin, or cashmere, lined, quilted or embroidered; draw this over the tea-pot as soon as the tea is poured into it, and it will remain piping hot for half an hour. One tea-spoon of tea and one tea-cup of hot water is the usual allowance for each person. Freshly boiled soft water is the best for either tea or coffee. Always have a water-pot of hot water on the waiter with which to weaken each cup if desired. Serve both tea and coffee with the best and richest cream, but in the absence of this luxury, a tolerable substitute is prepared as follows: Take fresh, new milk, set in a pan or pail where it will slowly simmer, but not boil or reach the boiling point, stir frequently to keep the cream from separating and rising to the top, and allow to simmer until it is rich, thick and creamy. In absence of both cream and milk, the white of an egg beaten to a froth, with a small bit of butter well mixed with it, may be used. In pouring coffee, it must be turned on gradually so as not to curdle it.

COFFEE WITH WHIPPED CREAM.

For six cups of coffee of fair size, take one cup sweet cream whipped light with a little sugar; put into each cup the desired amount of sugar and about a table-spoon boiling milk; pour the coffee over these and lay upon the surface of the hot liquid a large spoonful of the frothed cream, giving a gentle stir to each cup before serving. This is known to some as *meringued* coffee, and is an elegant French preparation of the popular drink.—*Marion Harland.*

COFFEE FOR ONE HUNDRED.

Take five pounds roasted coffee, grind and mix with six eggs; make small muslin sacks, and in each place a pint of coffee, leaving room for it to swell; put five gallons boiling water in a large coffee urn or boiler having a faucet at the bottom; put in part of the sacks and boil two hours; five or ten minutes before serving raise the lid and add one or two more sacks, and if you continue serving several times add fresh sacks at regular intervals, taking out from time to time those first put in and filling up with boiling water as needed. In this way the full strength of the coffee is secured and the fresh supplies impart that delicious flavor consequent on a few moments boiling.

To make coffee for twenty persons, use one and a half pints ground coffee and one gallon of water.—*Mrs. C. S. Ogden.*

VIENNA COFFEE.

Filter instead of boiling the coffee, allowing one table-spoon ground coffee to each person and "one for the pot;" put a quart of cream into a custard-kettle or pail set in boiling water, and put it where the water will keep boiling; beat the white of an egg to a froth, and mix well with three table-spoons cold milk. As soon as the cream is hot, remove from fire, add the mixed egg and milk, stir together briskly for a minute, and then serve.

Another method is to pour boiling water over the coffee, cover closely, boil one minute, remove to the side of the stove a few minutes to settle, and serve. Allow two heaping table-spoons coffee to a pint of water.

The less time the coffee is cooked the more coffee is required, but the finer the flavor. The late Professor Blot protested against boiling coffee at all, as in his opinion the aroma was evaporated, and only the bitter flavor left.

CHOCOLATE.

Take six table-spoons scraped chocolate, or three of chocolate and three of cocoa, dissolve in a quart of boiling water, boil hard fifteen minutes, add one quart of rich milk, let scald and serve hot;

this is enough for six persons. Cocoa can also be made after this recipe. Some boil either cocoa or chocolate only one minute and then serve, while others make it the day before using, boiling it for one hour, and when cool skimming off the oil, and when wanted for use, heat it to the boiling point and add the milk. In this way it is equally good and much more wholesome.

SPICED CHOCOLATE.

One quart milk, two squares chocolate, one stick cinnamon, a little grated nutmeg; grate chocolate, boil the milk, reserving a little cold to moisten chocolate, which must be mixed, perfectly smooth to a paste; when the milk boils put in and boil cinnamon, then stir in the chocolate and let boil quickly, pour into a pitcher, and grate in nutmeg. It is nice to add rich cream.

VIENNA CHOCOLATE.

Put into a coffee-pot set in boiling water, one quart of new milk (or a pint each of cream and milk), stir into it three heaping table-spoons grated chocolate mixed to a paste with cold milk, let it boil two or three minutes and serve at once.

CIDER.

Cider should be made from ripe apples only, and for this reason, and to prevent fermentation, it is better to make it late in the season. Use only the best-flavored grafted fruit, rejecting all that are decayed or wormy. The best mills crush, not grind, the apples. The utmost neatness is necessary throughout the process. Press and strain juice as it comes from the press through a woollen cloth into a perfectly clean barrel; let stand two or three days if cool, if warm not more than a day; rack once a week for four weeks, put in bottles and cork tightly. This will make perfect, unfermented cider. Do not put any thing in it to preserve it, as all so called preservatives are humbugs. Lay the bottles away on their sides in sawdust.—*C. T. Carson, Mt. Pleasant Farm.*

CREAM NECTAR.

Two ounces tartaric acid, two pounds white sugar, juice of one lemon, and three pints water; boil together five minutes, and when cold add the well-beaten whites of three eggs, half cup flour mixed with a little water, and a half ounce essence of wintergreen or any other flavoring; bottle and keep in a cool place. To use put one-fourth tea-spoon soda in a tumbler of water, and then add two table-spoons of this syrup.—*Mrs. J. S. Robinson.*

GRANDMOTHER'S HARVEST DRINK.

One quart of water, table-spoon sifted ginger, three heaping table-spoons sugar, half pint vinegar.

LEMONADE.

Roll six lemons well, slice thin in an earthen vessel, put over them two tea-cups white sugar; let stand fifteen minutes, add one gallon water and lumps of ice, pour into pitcher and serve. Some add soda after the glasses are filled, and stir rapidly for "sparkling lemonade."

RASPBERRY SHRUB.

Place red raspberries in a stone jar, cover them with good cider vinegar, let stand over night; next morning strain, and to one pint of juice add one pint of sugar, boil ten minutes, and bottle while hot.—*Mrs. Judge West.*

SHERBETS.

Wash ripe fruit (strawberries, currants, pine-apples, cherries, or raspberries), and pass first through a coarse sieve and then through a cloth; to every quart juice add a quart water, sweeten to taste by mixing thoroughly with powdered sugar, bottle and surround with ice, serve in wine-glasses. Pine-apples must be grated before straining. Grapes, especially the Catawba and Scuppernong, are excellent for this purpose, and even the wild fox-grape may be used. They must be mashed, and the juice washed out with water.

SODA BEER.

Two pounds white sugar, whites of two eggs, two ounces tartaric acid, two table-spoons flour, two quarts water; boil two or three minutes, and flavor to taste. When wanted for use, take a half tea-spoon soda, dissolve in half a glass of water, pour into it about two table-spoons of the acid, and it will foam to the top of the glass.—*Mrs. Geo. W. Sampson.*

LEMON SYRUP.

Take the juice of twelve lemons, grate the rind of six in it, let it stand over night, then take six pounds of white sugar, and make a thick syrup. When it is quite cool, strain the juice into it, and squeeze as much oil from the grated rind as will suit the taste. A table-spoonful in a goblet of water will make a delicious drink on a hot day, far superior to that prepared from the stuff commonly sold as lemon syrup.—*Miss Abbie G. Backus, West Killingly, Conn.*

ICED TEA.

Prepare tea in the morning, making it stronger and sweeter than usual; strain and pour into a clean stone jug or glass bottle, and set aside in the ice-chest until ready to use. Drink from goblets without cream. Serve ice broken in small pieces on a platter nicely garnished with well-washed grape-leaves. Iced tea may be prepared from either green or black alone, but it is considered an improvement to mix the two.

LEMON TEA.

Tea made like that for iced tea (or that left in the tea-pot after a meal), with sugar to taste, a slice or two of lemon, a little of the juice, and some pieces of cracked ice, makes a delightful drink. Serve in glasses.

RASPBERRY VINEGAR.

Fill a stone jar with ripe raspberries, cover with the purest and strongest vinegar, let stand for a week, pour the whole through a sieve or strainer, crushing out all the juice of the berries; to each pint of this vinegar, add one and a half pounds lump sugar and let boil long enough to dissolve, removing scum which may arise; then remove from the fire, let cool, bottle and cork tightly. Two table-spoons of this vinegar, stirred into a tumbler of iced water, makes a delicious drink, or a little soda may be added.

EGGS.

The fresher they are the better and more wholesome, though new-laid eggs require to be cooked longer than others. Eggs over a week old will do to fry, but not to boil. In boiling, they are less likely to crack if dropped in water not quite to the boiling point. Eggs will cook soft in three minutes, hard in five, *very hard* (to serve with salads, or to slice thin—seasoned well with pepper and salt—and put between thin slices of bread and butter) in ten to fifteen minutes. There is an objection to the ordinary way of boiling eggs not generally understood. The white, under three minutes rapid cooking, is toughened and becomes indigestible, and yet the yolk is left uncooked. To be wholesome, eggs should be cooked evenly to the center, and this result is best reached, by putting the eggs into a dish having a tight cover (a tin pail will do), and pouring boiling water over them in the proportion of two quarts to a dozen eggs; cover, and set away from the stove for eight to fifteen minutes. The heat of the water cooks the eggs slowly to a jelly-like consistency, and leaves the yolk harder than the white. The egg thus cooked is very nice and rich.

Put eggs in water in a vessel with a smooth level bottom, to tell good from bad; those which lie on the side are good, but reject those which stand on end as bad; or, look through each egg separately toward the sun, or toward a lamp in a darkened room; if the white looks clear, and the yolk can be easily distinguished the egg is good; if a dark spot appears in either white or yolk, it is stale; if they appear heavy and dark, or if they gurgle when shaken gently, they are " totally depraved." The best and safest plan is to break each egg in a saucer before using. For preserving eggs for winter use, always secure *fresh* ones; after packing, cover closely and keep in a cool place.

TO MAKE OMELETS.

To make an omelet, beat the yolks until thick and creamy, then add the milk, the salt, pepper, and flour if any is used, and lastly the whites beaten to a stiff froth. Have the skillet as hot as it can be without scorching the butter; put in a table-spoon of butter and pour in the omelet, which should at once begin to bubble and rise in flakes. Slip under it a thin, broad-bladed knife, and every now and then raise it up to prevent burning. As soon as the under side is hard enough to hold together, and the eggs begin to "set," fold over, shake the skillet so as to entirely free the omelet, carefully slide it on a hot platter, and serve at once. It should be cooked in from three to five minutes. To bake an omelet, place in the frying-pan on top of stove until it begins to "set" in the middle, then place in a rather hot oven; when slightly browned, fold if you like, or turn a hot dish on top of the pan, upset the latter with a quick motion, and so dish the omelet with the under side uppermost. It should be baked in from five to ten minutes. Where a large quantity of eggs are used, instead of making into one large omelet, divide and make several, sending each to the table as soon as done. Ham, chicken, and all kinds of meat omelets, are made by chopping the meat fine and placing between the folds before dishing.

For a plain, easily-made omelet, take three table-spoons milk and a pinch of salt for each egg; beat the eggs lightly for three or four minutes, pour them into a hot pan in which a piece of butter the size of a walnut has just been melted, cook three or four minutes, fold over and serve at once. Some scald a little parsley, pour off the water, chop it, and mix with the omelet just before pouring into the pan.

BOILED EGGS.

Put them on in cold water, and when it has boiled the eggs will be done, the whites being soft and digestible, as they are not when put on in boiling water.

BOILED EGGS.

Put the eggs in a dish without breaking the shells, pour boiling water over them and let them stand in it away from the fire for from five to eight mintes; this is better than boiling rapidly on the stove, as it cooks them through without hardening the whites too much.—*Mrs. A. R. Gould, Delaware.*

BAKED EGGS.

Break eight eggs into a well-buttered dish, put in pepper and salt, bits of butter, and three table-spoons cream; set in oven and bake about twenty minutes; serve very hot.

CURRIED EGGS.

Slice two onions and fry in butter, add a table-spoon curry-powder and one pint good broth or stock, stew till onions are quite tender, add a cup of cream thickened with arrowroot or rice flour, simmer a few moments, then add eight or ten hard-boiled eggs, cut in slices and heat them well, but do not boil.—*Mrs. E. L. Fay, Washington Heights.*

EGGS ON TOAST.

Cut the bread three-quarters of an inch thick, warm through on each side and brown nicely; from a dish of melted butter put a very little upon each slice with a spoon; place toast in a covered dish and set in the oven or where it will keep warm; put a sauce-pan of boiling water on the stove, break in the eggs, let remain until whites are stiff, take up carefully with a spoon and lay one on each half-slice of toast; put the toast thus crowned on a warm platter and send to table.—*Mrs. L. E. Bellus.*

FRIZZLED HAM AND EGGS.

Take bits of either boiled or fried ham, chop fine, and place in skillet prepared with butter or beef drippings; take four to six well-beaten eggs, pour over ham, and when heated through, season well with pepper and salt; stir together, cook until done brown, and turn over without stirring.

OMELET.

Seven eggs beaten separately, tea-spoon flour, tea-spoon salt, a pint of warm milk (see general directions for making an omelet). This will make one large omelet or two small ones; bake twenty minutes.

Corn Omelet.

Take six ears corn, grate or cut the kernels fine, add four eggs, a table-spoon of flour, a cup of milk; season with pepper and salt, and bake half an hour.—*Mrs. Frank Stahr, Lancaster, Pa.*

Omelet.

Beat the yolks and whites of four eggs separately, the whites to a froth; remove all crust from a large-sized slice of light white bread, pour just enough sweet milk over it to moisten it through, rub through a sieve, add it to the yolks, beating all very thoroughly; salt and pepper to taste. A little finely chopped parsley or ham may be added if desired. Melt a large table-spoon of butter in a clean frying-pan; let it "sputter" but not brown; whip the frothed whites very lightly into the yolks, bread, etc., pour the whole into the omelet pan, and shake gently and constantly, but do not stir, loosening the omelet from the edge of the pan with a blunt spoon. Four minutes is generally sufficient time to cook it. Have ready a hot platter, and before slipping the omelet out of the pan, turn one-half over the other like an old-fashioned turn-over. Serve at once.

Puff Omelet.

Stir into the yolks of six eggs, and the whites of three beaten very light, one table-spoon of flour mixed into a tea-cup of cream or milk, with salt and pepper to taste; melt a table-spoon butter in a pan, pour in the mixture and set the pan into a hot oven; when it thickens, pour over it the remaining whites of eggs well beaten, return it to the oven and let it bake a delicate brown. Slip off on large plate and eat as soon as done.—*Mrs. W. D. Hall.*

Poached Eggs.

Break the eggs in hot water and boil for two minutes, pour off the water, and beat the eggs until they are light; season with salt, pepper and butter; serve on toast, or in sauce dishes.

Another nutritious and palatable way of poaching is to drop them into boiling milk, and when done soft, pour into a sauce-dish and add a little pepper and salt. To keep them whole and round, drop them in *boiling* water, or stir with a spoon and drop the egg in the eddy thus made, and keep stirring till egg is cooked. They can be fried in boiling lard (a pint or two) in the same way.

PICKLED EGGS.

Pint strong vinegar, half pint cold water, tea-spoon each of cinnamon, allspice, and mace; boil the eggs till very hard and take off the shell; put on the spices tied in a white muslin bag, in the cold water, boil, and if the water wastes away, add enough so as to leave a half pint when done; add the vinegar, and pour over the eggs, put in as many eggs as the mixture will cover, and when they are used, the same will do for another lot.

RUMBLED EGGS.

Beat up three eggs with two ounces fresh or washed butter, add a tea-spoon of cream or fresh milk; put in a sauce-pan and keep stirring over the fire for five minutes, or till it rises; serve on toast.—*Mrs. C. C. Lyman, Harmar.*

SCALLOPED EGGS.

Mix equal parts minced ham and fine bread crumbs, season with salt, pepper, and melted butter, adding milk to moisten till quite soft; half fill buttered gem-pans or small patty-pans with this mixture, and break an egg carefully upon the top of each, dust with salt and pepper, sprinkle finely powdered crackers over all, set in the oven and bake eight minutes. Serve immediately.—*Mary Wilcox, Dalton.*

SCRAMBLED EGGS.

In a deep earthen pie-plate, warm sweet milk, allowing two table-spoons to each egg (or less, with a large number of eggs), add a bit of butter size of a walnut, and a little salt and pepper. When nearly to boiling point drop in the eggs, broken one at a time in a saucer; with a spoon or thin-bladed knife gently cut the eggs, and scrape the mixture up from the bottom of the plate as it cooks. If it begins to cook dry and fast at the bottom, move the dish back instantly, for success depends wholly on cooking gently and evenly, proportions being of secondary importance. Take from stove before it has quite all thickened, and continue turning it up from bottom of dish a moment longer. If served in another dish (it keeps warmer served in same) have it well heated. The mixture should be in large flakes of mingled white and yellow, and as delicate as baked custard.—*Mrs. L. S. Williston, Jamestown, N. Y.*

SCRAMBLED EGGS.

Beat eight eggs very light, prepare skillet with one table-spoon butter, and when hot, pour in the eggs, season with salt and pepper, stir constantly until done and serve hot.

TO KEEP EGGS.

Put a two-inch layer of salt in bottom of stone jar, then a layer of *fresh* eggs, small end down; then salt, then eggs, and so on till jar is full, with a layer of salt at top; cover and put in a cool place, but not where they will freeze. Or, dip the eggs in melted wax, or a weak solution of gum, or in flax-seed oil, each of which renders the shell impervious to air. For one's own use the latter is a good method, keeping the eggs perfectly, but it discolors the shells, and renders them unfit for market.

To prepare eggs for winter use, take a small basket, and place in it about one dozen perfectly fresh eggs; have a large pot of boiling water on the stove. Holding the basket by the handle, let it down very slowly into the water until the eggs are entirely covered by the water: let it remain in the *boiling* water an instant (while counting ten), then withdraw slowly. If the eggs strike the water too suddenly they crack. Having thus prepared all, pack them in salt, the small end down.—*Mrs. H. S. Huntington, Galesburg, Ill.*

Another method is as follows: Be very sure they are perfectly fresh. Slake a pound of stone lime in two gallons of pure water. When cold add a pint of salt, and stir the whole together thoroughly. If too strong of lime it will destroy the egg-shell and ruin the whole. When the mixture is settled quite clear take a large stone pot, keg or half-barrel, according to the quantity to be put down. Put the eggs into the vessel, small end down; pack carefully close together, taking care not to crack the shell. One broken or cracked egg will ruin the whole. This done, pour over them the clear lime-water without disturbing the sediment. Pour in carefully so as not to wash the eggs out of place. Be sure that they are more than covered, and lest, by air getting in while the liquid is poured on, they may not be thoroughly submerged, it is well to wait a few minutes till no bubbles rise to the surface, and then pour on more lime-water if necessary. Then close the jar closely, and do not disturb them till needed.—*Mrs. Henry Ward Beecher.*

FISH.

Fish are easier of digestion but less nutritious than meats, if salmon is excepted, which is extremely hearty food and should be eaten sparingly by children and those whose digestion is not strong. Fish must be fresh, the fresher the better—those being most perfect which go straight from their native element into the hands of the cook. The white kinds are least nutritious; and the oily, such as salmon, eels, herrings, etc., most difficult of digestion.

As soon as possible after fish are caught, remove all scales (these may be loosened by pouring on hot water), and scrape out entrails and every particle of blood and the white skin that lies along the backbone, being careful not to crush the fish more than is absolutely necessary in cleaning. Rinse thoroughly in cold water, using only what is necessary for perfect cleanliness, drain, wipe dry, and place on ice until ready to cook. To remove the earthy taste from fresh-water fish, sprinkle with salt, and let stand over night, or at least a few hours, before cooking; rinse off, wipe dry, and to completely absorb all the moisture, place in a folded napkin a short time. Fresh-water fish should never be soaked in water except when frozen, when they may be placed in ice-cold water to thaw, and then cooked immediately. Salt fish may be soaked over night in cold water, changing water once or twice if very salt.

Fish should always be well cooked, being both unpalatable and unwholesome when underdone. For boiling, a fish-kettle is almost indispensable, as it is very difficult to remove a large fish without breaking from an ordinary kettle. The fish-kettle is an oblong boiler, in which is suspended a perforated tin plate, with a handle at each end, on which the fish rests while boiling, and with which it is lifted out when done. From this tin it is easily slipped off to the platter on which it goes to the table. When no fish-kettle is at hand, wrap in a cloth, lay in a circle on a plate, and set in the kettle. When done the fish may be lifted out gently by the cloth and thus removed to the platter.

In frying by dipping into hot fat or drippings (or olive oil is still better), a wire basket, in which the fish is placed and lowered into the fat, is a great convenience.

One of the most essential things in serving fish, is to have every thing hot, and quickly dished, so that all may go to the table at once. Serve fresh fish with squash and green pease, salt fish with beets and carrots, salt pork and potatoes with either.

In the East there is a great variety of fish in the winter. The blue fish is excellent boiled or baked with a stuffing of bread, butter, and onions. Sea bass are boiled with egg-sauce, and garnished with parsley. Salmon are baked or boiled, and smelts are cooked by dropping into boiling fat. The sheep's-head, which requires most cooking of all fish, is always stuffed and baked.

Nearly all the larger fresh fish are boiled, the medium-sized are baked or broiled, and the small are fried. The very large ones are cut up and sold in pieces of convenient size.

In cooking fish, care must be taken not to use the same knives or spoons in the preparation of it and other food, or the latter will be tainted with the fishy flavor.

In boiling fish, allow five to ten minutes to the pound, according to thickness, after the water begins to boil. To test, pass a knife along a bone, and if done the fish will separate easily. Remove the moment it is done, or it will become "woolly" and insipid.

Fish is made firmer if a little salt and vinegar is added to the water in which it is boiled. The water should be cold when the fish is put in, except in the case of salmon, when the water should be hot, to preserve the rich color. Garnishes for fish are parsley, sliced beets, fried smelts (for turbot), lobster coral (for boiled fish). For hints on buying fish, see "Marketing."

Baked Fish.

Clean, rinse, and wipe dry a white fish, or any fish weighing three or four pounds, rub the fish inside and out with salt and pepper, fill

with a stuffing made like that for poultry, but drier; sew it up
and put in a hot pan, with some drippings and a lump of butter;
dredge with flour, and lay over the fish a few thin slices of salt
pork or bits of butter, and bake an hour and a half, basting occasionally.—*Mrs. A. Wilson, Rye, New York.*

BAKED SHAD.

Open and clean the fish, cut off its head (or not as preferred),
cut out the backbone from the head to within two inches of the
tail, and fill with the following mixture: Soak stale bread in water,
squeeze dry; cut a large onion in pieces, fry in butter, chop fine,
add the bread, two ounces of butter, salt, pepper, and a little parsley or sage; heat thoroughly, and when taken from the fire, add two
yolks of well-beaten eggs; stuff, and, when full, wind the fish several times with tape, place in baking-pan, baste slightly with butter,
and cover the bottom of pan with water; serve with the following
sauce: Reduce the yolks of two hard-boiled eggs to a smooth paste,
add two table-spoons olive-oil, half tea-spoon mustard, and pepper
and vinegar to taste.—*Miss H. D. M.*

BAKED FISH.

Open the fish so that it will lie perfectly flat; rub salt over it,
and lay in a dripping-pan (skin side next the pan), with a little
butter and water; set in a very hot oven, bake half an hour, and
when done it will be a delicate brown.

BAKED SALMON, TROUT OR PICKEREL.

Clean thoroughly, wipe carefully, and lay in a dripping-pan with
water enough to prevent scorching (a perforated tin sheet or rack
fitting loosely in the pan, or several muffin-rings may be used to
keep the fish from the bottom of the pan, and the fish may be made
to form a circle by tying head and tail together); bake slowly, basting often with butter and water. When done, have ready a cup of
sweet cream into which a few spoonfuls of hot water have been
poured, stir in two table-spoons melted butter and a little chopped
parsley, and heat in a vessel of boiling water; add the gravy from
the dish and boil up once. Place the fish in 'a hot dish, and pour
over the sauce.—*Mrs. Theo. Brown, Cape Girardeau, Mo.*

Codfish a la mode.

Tea-cup codfish picked up fine, two cups mashed potatoes, one pint cream or milk, two eggs well-beaten, half tea-cup butter, salt and pepper; mix well, bake in baking-dish from twenty to twenty-five minutes.—*Mrs. E. L Fay, New York City.*

Boiled Fish.

To boil a fish, fill with a rich dressing of rolled crackers seasoned with butter, pepper, salt and sage, wrap it in in a well-floured cloth, tie closely with twine or sew, and place in well-salted boiling water. (It may be formed in the shape of the letter S by tying a cord around the tail, passing it through the center of the body, and tying the other end around the head.) Allow from eight to ten minutes to the pound, according to size and thickness of fish, for cooking.

Boiled Codfish.

Soak over night, put in a pan of cold water, and simmer two or three hours. Serve with drawn butter, with hard-boiled eggs sliced on it. Cod-fish is also excellent broiled. After soaking sufficiently, grease the bars of the gridiron, broil, and serve with bits of butter dropped over it. This is a nice relish for tea.—*Mrs. Lewis Brown.*

Boiled Fresh Cod.

Put the fish in fish-kettle (or tie up in cloth) in water with some salt and scraped horse-radish, boil till done, place a folded napkin on a dish, turn fish upon it, and serve with drawn butter, oyster or egg-sauce. When cold, chop fine, pour over it drawn butter or egg-sauce, and add pepper to taste; warm thoroughly, stirring to prevent burning, make up in rolls or any other form, and brown before the fire.

Boiled Salt Mackerel.

After freshening wrap in a cloth and simmer for fifteen minutes; remove, lay on it two hard-boiled eggs sliced, pour over it drawn butter, and trim with parsley leaves. Boiling salt-fish hardens it.

Boiled White Fish.

Dress the fish nicely, and cover in fish-kettle with cold water seasoned well with salt; remove the scum as it rises, and boil very slowly, allowing from eight to ten minutes time to every pound;

9

when about half done, add a little vinegar or lemon juice, take out, drain, and dish carefully, pouring over it drawn butter; or garnish with sprigs of parsley, and serve with egg-sauce.—*Mrs. M. Smith, Pittsburgh*

BOILED FISH WITH VEGETABLES.

Put a whole fish in kettle, and cover with stock made as follows: Fry in a sauce-pan two onions, a carrot, a piece of celery or celery seed, a table-spoon butter and one of flour, a sprig of parsley, a tea-spoon of whole black peppers, and three cloves; add two and a half quarts water, two tea-cups vinegar, boil twenty minutes, salt and skim. Pour this over the fish and boil gently until done. Serve with egg-sauce.—*Mrs. S. D. R., Philadelphia.*

BROILED WHITE FISH.

Clean, split down the back, and let stand in salted water for several hours; wipe dry, and place on a well-greased gridiron over hot coals, sprinkling with salt and pepper. Put flesh side down at first, and when nicely browned, turn carefully on the other. Cook for twenty or thirty minutes, or until nicely browned on both sides. —*Mrs. H. Colwell, Chicago, Ill.*

BROOK TROUT.

Wash and drain in a colander a few minutes, split nearly to the tail, flour nicely, salt, and put in pan, which should be hot but not burning; throw in a little salt to prevent sticking, and do not turn until brown enough for the table. Trout are nice fried with slices of salt pork.

CODFISH BALLS.

Soak codfish cut in pieces, about an hour in lukewarm water, remove skin and bones, pick to small pieces, and return to stove in cold water. As soon as it begins to boil, change the water, and bring to a boil again. Have ready potatoes boiled tender, well mashed, and seasoned with butter. Mix thoroughly with the potatoes half the quantity of codfish while both are still hot, form into flat, thick cakes or round balls, fry in hot lard or drippings, or dip in hot fat, like doughnuts. The addition of a beaten egg before making into balls renders them lighter. Cold potatoes may be used, by reheating, adding a little cream and butter, and mixing while hot.—*Mrs. J. H. Shearer.*

CANNED SALMON.

The California canned salmon is nice served cold with any of the fish-sauces. For a breakfast dish, it may be heated, seasoned with salt and pepper, and served on slices of toast, with milk thickened with flour and butter poured over it.

CROQUETTES OF FISH.

Separate dressed fish of any kind from the bones, mince with a little seasoning, add one egg beaten with a tea-spoon of flour and one of milk, and make into balls; brush the outside with egg, dredge well with bread or cracker crumbs, and fry to a nice brown. The bones, heads, tails, an onion, and an anchovy, with a pint of water, will make the gravy.—*Mrs. H. B. S.*

FISH CHOWDER.

The best fish for chowder are haddock and striped bass, although any kind of fresh fish may be used. Cut in pieces over an inch thick and two inches square; place eight good-sized slices of salt pork in the bottom of an iron pot and fry till crisp; remove the pork, leaving the fat, chop fine, put in the pot a layer of fish, a layer of split crackers, and some of the chopped pork with black and red pepper and chopped onions, then another layer of fish, another of crackers and seasoning, and so on. Cover with water, and stew slowly till the fish is perfectly done; remove from the pot, put in dish in which you serve it and keep hot; thicken the gravy with rolled cracker or flour, boil it up once and pour over the chowder. Some add a little catsup, port wine and lemon juice to the gravy just before taking up, but I think it nicer without them.—*Mrs. Woodworth, Springfield, Mass.*

FRIED FISH.

Clean thoroughly, cut off the head, and, if large, cut out the back-bone, and slice the body crosswise into five or six pieces; dip in Indian meal or wheat flour, or in a beaten egg, and then in bread crumbs (trout and perch should never be dipped in meal), put into a thick-bottomed skillet, skin side uppermost, with hot lard or drip-

pings (never in butter, as it takes out the sweetness and gives a bad
color), fry slowly, and turn when a light brown. The roe and the
backbone, if previously removed, may be cut up and fried with the
other pieces. A better way is to dredge the pieces in the flour,
brush with beaten egg, roll in bread-crumbs, and fry in hot lard
or drippings enough to completely cover them. If the fat is *very hot,*
the fish will not absorb it, and will be delicately cooked. When
brown on one side, turn over in the fat and brown the other, and
when done let them drain. Slices of large fish may be cooked in
the same way. Serve with tomato sauce or slices of lemon.

KATY'S CODFISH.

Soak pieces of codfish several hours in cold water, pick fine, and
place in skillet with water; boil a few minutes, pour off water and
add fresh, boil again and drain off as before ; then add plenty of
sweet milk, a good-sized piece of butter, and a thickening made of
a little flour (or corn starch) mixed with cold milk until smooth
like cream. Stir well, and when done take from the fire, and add the
yolks of three well-beaten eggs; stir quickly and serve.—*Mrs. Helen
M. Stevenson.*

BAKED HERRING.

Soak salt herring over night, roll in flour and butter, and place
in a dripping-pan with a very little water over them; season with
pepper.—*Mrs. E. J. Starr.*

POTTED FRESH FISH.

Let the fish lie in salt water for several hours ; then for five pounds
fish take three ounces salt, two of ground black pepper, two of cinnamon, one of allspice, and a half ounce cloves; cut fish in slices,
and place in the jar in which it is to be cooked, first a layer of fish,
then the spices, flour and bits of butter sprinkled on, repeating till
done. Fill the jar with equal parts vinegar and water, cover closely
with a cloth well-floured on top so that no steam can escape, and
bake six hours. Let it remain in jar until cold, cut in slices, and
serve for tea.—*Mrs. L. Brown.*

PAN-FISH.

Place in pan with heads together, and fill spaces with smaller fish ;
when ready to turn, put a plate over, drain off fat, invert pan, and

the fish will be left unbroken on the plate. Put the lard back in the pan, and when *hot,* slip back the fish, and when the other side is brown, drain, turn on plate as before, and slide them on the platter to go to the table. This improves the appearance, if not the flavor. The heads should be left on, and the shape preserved as fully as possible.

STEWED FISH.

Cut a fish across in slices an inch and a half thick, and sprinkle with salt; boil two sliced onions until done, pour off water, season with pepper, add two tea-cups hot water and a little parsley, and in this simmer the fish until thoroughly done. Serve hot. Good method for any fresh-water fish.

TURBOT.

Take a white fish, steam till tender, take out bones, and sprinkle with pepper and salt. For dressing, heat a pint of milk, and thicken with a quarter pound of flour; when cool, add two eggs and a quarter pound of butter, and season with onion and parsley (very little of each); put in the baking-dish a layer of fish, then a layer of sauce, till full, cover the top with bread-crumbs, and bake half an hour.— *Mrs. Robert A. Liggett, Detroit, Mich.*

FRUITS.

The arrangement of fresh fruits for the table affords play for the most cultivated taste and not a little real inventive genius. Melons, oranges, and indeed all kind of fruits, are appropriate breakfast dishes; and a raised center-piece of mixed fruits furnishes a delicious dessert, and is an indispensable ornament to an elegant dinner-table. Melons should be kept on ice, so as to be thoroughly chilled when served. Clip the ends of water-melons, cut them across in halves, set up on the clipped ends on a platter, and serve the pulp only, removing it with a spoon: or, cut across in slices, and serve with rind. Nutmeg melons should be set on the blossom end, and cut in several equal pieces from the stem downward, leaving each alternate piece still attached; the others may then be loosened, and the seeds removed, when the melon is ready to serve. Fruit should be carefully selected. Havana and Florida oranges are the best, but do not keep well, and on the whole, the Messina are preferable. A rough yellow skin covers the sweetest oranges, the smooth being more juicy and acid; a greenish tinge indicates that they were picked unripe. The Messina lemons, "November cut," are the best, and come into market in the spring. Freestone peaches with yellow meat are the handsomest, but not always the sweetest. California pears take the lead for flavor, the Bartlett being the best. The best winter pear is the "Winter Nellis." The "Pound" pear is the largest, but is good only for cooking. Fine-grained pears are best for eating. A pyramid of grapes made up of Malagas, Delawares, and Concords, makes a showy center-piece and a delicious dessert. The Malaga leads all foreign grapes, and comes packed in cork-dust which is a non-conductor of heat and absorbent of moisture, and so is always in

(134)

good condition. Of native grapes, the Delaware keeps longest. In pine-apples the "Strawberry" is best, while the "Sugar Loaf" ranks next, but they are so perishable that to keep even for a few days they must be cooked. When served fresh they should be cut in small squares and sprinkled with sugar. Buy cocoa nut cautiously in summer, heat being likely to sour the milk. In almonds, the Princess is the best variety to buy in the shell; of the shelled, the "Jordan" is the finest, though the "Sicily" is good. For cake or confectionery, the shelled are most economical. In raisins the "Seed-less" rank first for puddings and fine cakes, but the "Valencia" are cheaper and more commonly used; for table use, loose "Muscatels" and layer raisins (of which the "London Layer" is the choicest brand) take the preference. In melons, every section has its favorite varieties, any of which make a wholesome and luscious dessert dish. Sliced fruits or berries are more attractive and pala-table sprinkled with sugar about an hour before serving, and then with pounded ice just before sending to the table. An apple-corer, a cheap tin tube, made by any tinner, is indispensable in preparing apples for cooking. They are made in two sizes, one for crab-apples and the other for larger varieties.

AMBROSIA.

Six sweet oranges, peeled and sliced (seeds and as much of the core as possible taken out), one pine-apple peeled and sliced (the canned is equally good), and one large cocoa-nut grated; alter-nate the layers of orange and pine-apple with grated cocoa-nut, and sprinkle pulverized sugar over each layer. Or, use six oranges, six lemons and two cocoa-nuts, or only oranges and cocoa-nuts, pre-pared as above.—*Mrs. Theo. Brown.*

APPLES IN JELLY.

Pare and core small-sized apples without cutting open; then put them, with some lemons, in water to cover, let boil slowly, until tender, and take out carefully, without breaking; make a syrup of half a pound white sugar to a pound of apples; cut lemons in slices and put them and the apples into syrup; boil very slowly until the apples are clear, take them out in a deep glass dish; put to the syrup an ounce of isinglass dissolved, let it boil up, lay a slice of lemon on each apple, and strain the syrup over them.

APPLE SAUCE.

Pare, core and cut in quarters apples that do not cook to pieces easily, and put on to stew in cold water with plenty of sugar. Cover close and stew an hour or more. The addition of the sugar at first preserves the pieces whole. If they are preferred finely mashed, add sugar after they are done.

BAKED APPLES.

Cut out the blossom and stem, in the stem end put some sugar, place in dish with a small quantity of water if apples are sweet; if sour the juice will be sufficient; bake till soft; serve either warm or cold. For an extra nice dish, pare and core apples, place in pan, put butter and sugar in cavity, and sprinkle cinnamon over them, and serve warm with cream or milk. Or, pare and quarter tart apples, put a layer in earthen baking-dish, add lumps of butter, and sprinkle with cinnamon, then a layer of apples, etc., till dish is full; bake till soft.

ICED APPLES.

Pare and core one dozen large apples, fill with sugar and a little butter and nutmeg; bake until nearly done, let cool, and remove to another plate, if it can be done without breaking them, (if not, pour off the juice). Ice tops and sides with cake-icing, and brown *lightly*; serve with cream.—*Mrs. R. C. Carson, Harrisburg.*

FRIED APPLES.

Quarter and core apples without paring; prepare frying-pan by heating it and putting in beef-drippings, lay the apples in the pan, skin side down, sprinkle with a little brown sugar, and when nearly done, turn and brown thoroughly.

BLACK CAPS.

Pare and core tart apples with apple-corer, fill the center with sugar, stick four cloves in the top of each, and bake in deep pie-plates, with a little water.

FRIED BANANAS.

Peel and slice lengthwise, fry in butter, sprinkle with sugar, and serve. Thus prepared they make a nice dessert. The bananas must be ripe.

Iced Currants.

Wash and drain dry, large bunches of ripe currants, dip into beaten whites of eggs, put on a sieve so they will not touch each other, sift powdered sugar thickly over them, and put in a warm place till dry. Cherries and grapes may be prepared in the same way.

Gooseberry Fool.

Stew gooseberries until soft, add sugar, and press through a colander (earthen is best), then make a boiled custard, or sweeten enough rich cream (about one gill to each quart), and stir carefully into the gooseberries just before sending to table.—*Mrs. L. S. W.*

Oranges in Jelly.

Boil the smallest-sized oranges in water until a straw will easily penetrate them, clarify half a pound of sugar for each pound of fruit, cut in halves or quarters, and put them to the syrup, set over a slow fire until the fruit is clear; then stir into it an ounce or more of dissolved isinglass, and let it boil for a short time longer. Before taking it up try the jelly, and if it is not thick enough, add more isinglass, first taking out the oranges into a deep glass dish, and then straining the jelly over them. Lemons may be prepared in the same manner.

Orange Pyramid.

Cut the peel in six or eight equal pieces, making the incisions from the stem downward; peel each piece down about half way, and bend it sharply to the right, leaving the peeled orange apparently in a cup, from which it is removed without much difficulty. Pile the oranges so prepared in a pyramid on a high fruit-dish, and you have an elegant center-piece.

Baked Pears.

Bake washed, unpeeled pears in pan with only a tea-spoon or two of water; sprinkle with the sugar, and serve with their own syrup.

Baked Pie-plant.

Cut in pieces about an inch long, put in baking-dish in layers with an equal weight of sugar, cover closely and bake.

BAKED PEACHES.

Wash peaches which are nearly or quite ripe, place in a deep dish, sprinkle with sugar, cover, and bake until tender.

STEWED PIE-PLANT.

Make a rich syrup by adding sugar to water in which long strips of orange peel have been boiled until tender, lay into it a single layer of pieces of pie-plant three inches long, and stew gently until clear. When done remove and cook another layer. This makes a handsome dessert-dish, ornamented with puff-paste cut in fanciful shapes. Use one orange to two and a half pounds pie-plant.

PEACH PYRAMID.

Cut a dozen peaches in halves, peel and take out stones, crack half the seeds, and blanch the kernels; make a clear boiling syrup of one pound of white sugar, and into it put the peaches and kernels; boil very gently for ten minutes, take out half the peaches, boil the rest for ten minutes longer, and take out all the peaches and kernels; mix with the syrup left in the kettle the strained juice of three lemons, and an ounce of isinglass dissolved in a little water and strained; boil up once, fill a mold half full of this syrup or jelly, let stand until "set," add part of the peaches and a little more jelly, and when this is "set," add the rest of the peaches, and fill up the mold with jelly. This makes an elegant ornament. —*Miss E. Orissa Dolbear, Cincinnati.*

FROZEN PEACHES.

Pare and divide large, fresh, ripe and juicy peaches, sprinkle over them granulated sugar, freeze them like ice-cream for an hour; remove them just before serving, and sprinkle with a little more sugar. Canned peaches and all kinds of berries may be prepared in the same way.—*Mrs. A. G. Wilcox, Minneapolis, Minn.*

TO KEEP PINE-APPLES.

Pare and cut out the eyes of a ripe pine-apple, strip all the pulp from the core with a silver fork, to a pint of this add a pound of granulated sugar, stir occasionally until sugar is dissolved, put in glass fruit-cans, and turn down the covers as closely as possible. This will keep a long time.

BAKED QUINCES.

Wash and core ripe quinces, fill with sugar, and bake in baking-dish with a little water.

MOCK STRAWBERRIES.

Cut ripe peaches and choice well-flavored apples, in proportion of three peaches to one apple, into quarters about the size of a strawberry, place in alternate layers, sprinkle the top thickly with sugar, and add pounded ice; let stand about two hours, mix peaches and apples thoroughly, let stand an hour longer, and serve.—*Miss C. B., Newburyport, Mass.*

SNOW FLAKES.

Grate a large cocoa-nut into a glass dish, and serve with cream, preserves, jellies, or jams.

BAKED SWEET APPLES.

The most elaborate combination of the most skillful cook, can not surpass simple sweet apples, properly baked. They are wonderfully rich and luscious. The best is the "Pound Sweeting," but the "Geere Sweet," well known in Ohio, is almost equal to it. Never core sweet apples; wash them, set in oven in baking-pan with a little water in it, and bake slowly for several hours. When done, they are of a rich, dark-brown color. If taken out too soon they are insipid.

BAKED SOUR APPLES.

Quarter and core tart apples without paring, put into baking-dish, sprinkle with sugar and bits of butter, add a little water, and bake until tender. The proportion is a gill of sugar, and butter the size of half an egg, to three pints of apples, and a gill and a half of water.

GAME.

Of game birds the woodcock out-ranks all in delicate tenderness and sweet flavor. The thigh is especially deemed a choice tidbit. The leg is the finest part of the snipe, but generally the breast is the most juicy and nutritious part of birds.

Birds should be carefully plucked or skinned, drawn, wiped clean, and all shot removed. Game should not be washed, unless absolutely necessary for cleanliness. With care in dressing, wiping will render them perfectly clean. If necessary to wash, do it quickly and use as little water as possible. The more plainly all kinds of game are cooked, the better they retain their fine flavor. They require a brisker fire than poultry, but take less time to cook. Their color, when done, should be a fine yellowish brown. Serve on toast.

Broiling is a favorite method of cooking game, and all birds are exceedingly nice roasted. To broil, split down the back, open and flatten the breast by covering with a cloth and pounding, season with pepper, and lay the inside first upon the gridiron; turn as soon as browned, and when almost done, take off, place on a platter, sprinkle with salt, and return to the gridiron. When done, place in a hot dish, butter both sides well, and serve at once. The time required is usually about twenty minutes.

To roast, season with salt and pepper, place a lump of butter inside, truss, skewer, and place in oven. The flavor is best preserved without stuffing, but a plain bread-dressing, with a piece of salt pork or ham skewered on the breast, is very nice. A delicate way of dressing is to place an oyster dipped in the well-beaten yolk of an egg or in melted butter, and then rolled in bread crumbs, inside each bird. Allow thirty minutes to roast or longer if stuffed. Wild ducks, pheasants and grouse are always best roasted.

To lard game, cut fat salt pork into thin, narrow strips, thread a larding-needle with one of the strips, run the needle under the skin and a little of the flesh of the bird, and draw the pork half way through, so that the ends of the strips exposed will be of equal length. The strips should be about one inch apart. The larding interferes with the natural flavor of the bird, but renders it more juicy. Many prefer tying a piece of bacon on the breast instead.

Pigeons should be cooked a long time as they are usually quite lean and tough, and they are better to lie in salt water half an hour, or to be parboiled in it for a few moments. They are nice roasted or made into a pie.

If the "wild flavor" of the larger birds, such as pheasants, prairie chickens, etc., is disliked, they may be soaked over night in salt water, or two or three hours in soda and water, or parboiled with an onion or two in the water, and then cooked as desired. The coarser kinds of game, such as geese, ducks, etc., may lie in salt water for several hours, or be parboiled in it with an onion inside each to absorb the rank flavor, and afterwards thoroughly rinsed in clear water, stuffed and roasted; or pare a fresh lemon without breaking the thin, white, inside skin, put inside the game for a day or two, renewing the lemon every twelve hours. This will absorb unpleasant flavors from almost all meat and game. Some lay slices of onion over game while cooking, and remove before serving. In preparing fat wild ducks, for invalids, it is a good plan to remove the skin, and keep a day or two before cooking. Squirrels should be carefully skinned and laid in salt water a short time before cooking; if old, parboil. They are delicious broiled, and are excellent cooked in any way with thin slices of bacon. Venison, as in the days of good old Isaac, is still justly considered a "savoury dish." The haunch, neck, shoulder and saddle should be roasted; roast or broil the breast, and fry or broil the steaks. Venison requires more time for cooking than beefsteak. The hams are excellent pickled, smoked and dried, but they will not keep so long as other smoked meats.

The garnishes for game are fresh or preserved barberries, currant jelly, sliced oranges, and apple sauce.

BROILED PHEASANT, OR PRAIRIE CHICKEN.

Scald and skin, cut off the breast and cut the rest up in joints, being careful to remove all shot; put in hot water all except the breast (which will be tender enough without parboiling), and boil until it can be pierced with fork, take out, rub over salt, pepper, and butter, and broil with breast over brisk fire; place a lump of butter on each piece, and set all in the oven for a few minutes. For breakfast, serve on fried mush, and for dinner on toast with a bit of currant jelly over each piece. Or it may be served with toast cut in pieces about two inches square, over which pour gravy made by thickening the liquor in which the birds were boiled, with a little butter and flour rubbed together and stirred in while boiling. Squirrels may be prepared the same way.—*Mrs. W. W. Woods.*

BROILED QUAIL.

Split through the back and broil over a hot fire, basting frequently with butter. When done place a bit of butter on each piece, and set in oven a few moments to brown. Serve on pieces of toast with currant jelly. Plovers are cooked in the same way. Pigeons should be first parboiled and then broiled.

JUGGED HARE.

Skin, cut in pieces, strew with pepper and salt, fry brown, season with two anchovies, a sprig of thyme, a little chopped parsley, nutmeg, mace, cloves, and grated lemon peel. Put a layer of the pieces with the seasoning into a jug, then a layer of bacon sliced very thin, and so on till all is used; add a scant half pint of water, cover the jug close and put in cold water, let boil three or four hours, according to the age of the hare; take the jug out of kettle, pick out the unmelted bacon and make a gravy of a little butter and flour with a little catsup. A tea-spoon of lemon peel will heighten the flavor.—*Mrs. Louise M. Lincoln.*

JUGGED PIGEONS.

Truss and season the pigeons with pepper and salt; and having stuffed them with a mixture of their own livers, shred with beef suet, bread crumbs, parsley, marjoram, and two eggs; sew them up at both ends, and put them into the jug, the breast downward, with half a pound of butter. Stop up the jug, so that no steam can get out; then set them in a pot of water to stew. They will take two hours and more in doing, and they must boil all the time. When stewed enough, take them out of the gravy, skim off the fat clean; put in a spoonful of cream, a little lemon peel, an anchovy shred, a few mushrooms; add a little white wine to the gravy, and having thickened it with butter and flour, and dished up the pigeons, pour the sauce over them. Garnish with sliced lemon.—*From "The Complete Woman Cook," published in 1796.*

PARTRIDGE PIE.

Line a deep baking-dish with veal cutlets and over them place thin slices of ham and a seasoning of pepper and salt; pluck, draw, wipe and quarter four partridges, rub each part with a seasoning of pepper, salt, minced parsley and butter; put in baking-dish, pour over them a pint of strong soup-stock, line the edges of the dish with a light puff-paste, cover with the same, brush over with the yolk of an egg, and bake one hour. If the paste is in danger of becoming too brown, cover with a thick paper.

PRAIRIE CHICKENS.

Cut out all shot, wash thoroughly but quickly, using some soda in the water, rinse and dry, fill with dressing, sew up with cotton thread, and tie down the legs and wings; place in a steamer over hot water till done, remove to a dripping-pan, cover with butter, sprinkle with salt and pepper, dredge with flour, place in the oven and baste with the melted butter until a nice brown; serve with either apple-sauce, cranberries, or currant jelly.—*Mrs. Godard.*

QUAIL ON TOAST.

Dry-pick them, singe them with paper, cut off heads, and legs at first joint, draw, split down the back, soak in salt and water for five or ten minutes, drain and dry with a cloth, lard them with bacon or butter, and rub salt over them, place on broiler and turn often, dipping two or three times into melted butter; broil about twenty minutes. Have ready as many slices of buttered toast as there are birds, and serve a bird, breast upward, on each slice.—*Mrs. Emma L. Fay.*

ROAST QUAILS.

Pluck and dress like chickens, wipe clean, and rub both inside and out with salt and pepper; stuff with any good dressing, and sew up with fine thread; spread with butter and place in an oven with a good steady heat, turning and basting often with hot water seasoned with butter, salt and pepper; bake three-quarters of an hour. When about half done add a little hot water to the pan, and it is well to place a dripping-pan over them to prevent browning too much. Add to the gravy, flour and butter rubbed together, and water if needed.

ROAST HAUNCH OF VENISON.

Wash in warm water and dry well with a cloth, butter a sheet of white paper and put over the fat, lay in a deep baking-dish with a very little boiling water, cover with a close-fitting lid or with a coarse paste one-half inch thick. If the latter is used, a thickness or two of coarse paper should be laid over the paste. Cook in a moderately hot oven for from three to four hours, according to the size of the haunch, and about twenty minutes before it is done, quicken the fire, remove the paste and paper or dish-cover, dredge the joint with flour and baste well with butter until it is nicely frothed and of a delicate brown color; garnish the knuckle-bone with a frill of white paper, and serve with a gravy made from its own dripping, having first removed the fat. Have the dishes on which the venison is served and the plates very hot. Always serve with currant jelly.

ROAST GOOSE.

The goose should not be more than eight months old, and the fatter the more tender and juicy the meat. A "green" goose (four months old) is the choicest. Kill at least twenty-four hours before cooking; cut the neck close to the back, beat the breast-bone flat with a rolling-pin, tie the wings and legs securely, and stuff with the following mixture: three pints bread crumbs, six ounces butter or part butter and part salt pork, two chopped onions, one tea-spoon each of sage, black pepper and salt. Do not stuff very full, and stitch openings firmly together to keep flavor in and fat out. If the goose is not fat, lard it with salt pork, or tie a slice on the breast. Place in baking-pan with a little water, and baste frequently with salt and water (some add onion and some vinegar), turning often so that the sides and back may all be nicely browned. When nearly done baste with butter and a little flour. Bake two hours, or more if old; when done take from the pan, pour off the fat, and to the brown gravy left add the chopped giblets which have previously been stewed till tender, together with the water they were boiled in; thicken with a little flour and butter rubbed together, bring to a boil, and serve with currant jelly. Apple sauce and onion sauce are proper accompaniments to roast goose.—*Mrs. J. H. Shearer.*

ROAST DUCK.

Ducks are dressed and stuffed in the same manner as above, or a stuffing of mashed potatoes and onions in equal proportions, seasoned with butter, pepper, sage and salt, may be used. Young ducks should roast from twenty-five to thirty minutes; full-grown for an hour or more with frequent basting. Some prefer them underdone, served very hot, but thorough cooking will prove more generally palatable. Serve with currant jelly, apple sauce, and green pease. If old, parboil before roasting.

Place the remains of a cold roast duck in a stew-pan with a pint of gravy and a little sage, cover closely, and let it simmer for half an hour; add a pint of boiled green pease, stew a few minutes, remove to a dish, and pour over it the gravy and pease.

BOILED DUCK.

Dress and rub well inside with salt and pepper, truss and tie in shape, drawing the legs in to the body, in which put one or two sage leaves, a little finely-chopped onion, and a little jellied stock or gravy; rub over with salt and pepper; make a paste in the proportion of one-half pound butter to one pound flour, in which enclose the duck, tie a cloth around all, and boil two hours or until quite tender, keeping it well covered with boiling water. Serve by pour-

10

ing round it brown gravy made as follows: Put a lump of butter of the size of an egg, in a sauce-pan with a little minced onion; cook until slightly brown, then adding a small table-spoon of flour, stir well, and when quite brown, add a half pint stock or water; let cook a few minutes, strain, and add to the chopped giblets, previously stewed till tender.—*Mrs. L. S. Williston.*

REED BIRDS.

Roasting by suspending on the little wire which accompanies the roaster, is the best method; turn and baste frequently, or wash and peel with as thin a paring as possible large potatoes of equal size, cut a deep slice off one end of each, and scoop out a part of the potato; drop a piece of butter into each bird, pepper and salt, and put it in the hollows made in the potatoes; put on as covers the pieces cut off, and clip the other end for them to stand on. Set in a baking pan upright, with a little water to prevent burning, bake slowly, and serve in the dish in which they were baked.

Or, boil in a crust like dumplings.

RABBITS.

Rabbits, which are in the best condition in midwinter, may be fricasseed like chicken in white or brown sauce. To make a pie, first stew till tender, and make like chicken-pie. To roast, stuff with a dressing made of bread-crumbs, chopped salt pork, thyme, onion, and pepper and salt, sew up, rub over with a little butter, or pin on it a few slices of salt pork, add a little water in the pan, and baste often. Serve with mashed potatoes and currant jelly.

SNIPE.

Snipe are best roasted with a piece of pork tied to the breast, or they may be stuffed and baked.—*Mrs. M. R.*

FRIED WOODCOCK.

Dress, wipe clean, tie the legs, skin the head and neck, turn the beak under the wing and tie it; tie a piece of bacon over it, and immerse in hot fat for two or three minutes. Serve on toast.

Another favorite way is to split them through the back and broil, basting with butter, and serving on toast. They may also be roasted whole before the fire for fifteen or twenty minutes.

ICES AND ICE-CREAM.

Perfectly fresh sweet cream makes the most delicious ice-cream. A substitute is a preparation of boiled milk, etc., made late in the evening if for dinner, in the morning if for tea, and placed on ice. One mixture is a custard made as follows: Take two quarts milk, put on three pints to boil in a custard-kettle, or a pail set within a kettle of boiling water, beat yolks and whites of eight eggs separately, mix the yolks with the remaining pint and stir *slowly* into the boiling milk, boil two minutes, remove from the stove, *immediately* add one and a half pounds sugar, let it dissolve, strain while *hot* through a crash towel, cool, add one quart rich cream and two table-spoons vanilla, (or season to taste, remembering that the strength of the flavoring and also the sweetness is very much diminished by the freezing). Set the custard and also the whites (not beaten) in a cool place until needed, and about three hours before serving begin the preparations for freezing. Put the ice in a coarse coffee-sack, pound with an ax or mallet until the lumps are no larger than a small hickory-nut; see that the freezer is properly set in the tub, the beater in and the cover secure; place around it a layer of ice about three inches thick, then a layer of coarse salt—rock salt is best—then ice again, then salt, and so on until packed full, with a layer of ice last. The proportion should be about three-fourths ice and one-fourth salt. Pack very solid, pounding with a broom-handle or stick, then remove the cover and pour the custard to which you have just added the well-whipped whites into the freezer, filling two-thirds full to give room for expansion; replace the cover and begin turning the freezer; after ten minutes pack the ice down again, drain off most of the water, add more ice and turn again, repeat-

ing this operation several times until the cream is well frozen,
and you can no longer turn the beater. (The above quantity ought
to freeze in half an hour, but the more pure cream used the longer
it takes to freeze). Brush the ice and salt from and remove the
cover, take out the beater, scrape the cream down from the sides
of freezer, beat well several minutes with a wooden paddle, replace
the cover, fill the hole with a cork, pour off all the water, pack
again with ice, (using salt at the bottom, but none at the top of
tub), heap the ice on the cover, spread over it a piece of carpet or
a thick woollen blanket, and set away in a cool place until needed;
or, if molds are used, fill them when you remove the beater, packing the cream in very tightly, and place in ice and salt for two
hours. To remove the cream, dip the molds for an instant in warm
water. When cream is used in making ice-cream, it is better to
whip a part of it, and add just as the cream is beginning to set.

Coffee ice-cream should be thickened with arrowroot; the flavoring for almond cream should be prepared by pounding the kernels
to a paste with rose-water, using arrowroot for thickening. For
cocoa-nut cream, grate cocoa-nut and add to the cream and sugar
just before freezing. The milk should never be heated for pine-
apple, strawberry, or raspberry cream. Berry flavors are made
best by allowing whole berries to stand for awhile well-sprinkled
with sugar, mashing, straining the juice, adding sugar to it, and
stirring it into the cream. For a quart of cream, allow a quart
of fruit and a pound of sugar. In addition to this, add whipped
cream and sweetened whole berries, just as the cream is beginning
to set, in the proportion of a cup of berries and a pint of whipped
cream to three pints of the frozen mixture. Canned berries may
be used in the same way. A pint of berries or peaches, cut fine,
added to a quart of ordinary ice-cream, while in process of freezing, makes a delicious fruit ice-cream.

Freeze ice-cream in a warm place (the more rapid the melting
of the ice the quicker the cream freezes), always being careful that
no salt or water gets within the freezer. If cream begins to melt
while serving, beat up well from the bottom with a long wooden
paddle. Water-ices are made from the juices of fruits, mixed with
water, sweetened, and frozen like cream. In making them, if they

are not well mixed before freezing, the sugar will sink to the bottom, and the mixture will have a sharp, unpleasant taste. It is a better plan to make a syrup of the sugar and water, by boiling and skimming when necessary, and, when cold, add the juice of the fruit.

The following directions for making "self-freezing ice-cream" are from "Common Sense in the Household." After preparing the freezer as above, but leaving out the beater, remove the lid carefully, and with a long wooden ladle or flat stick beat the custard as you would batter steadily for five or six minutes. Replace the lid, pack the ice and salt over it, covering it with about two inches of the mixture; spread above all several folds of blanket or carpet, and leave it untouched for an hour; at the end of that time remove the ice from above the freezer-lid, wipe off carefully and open the freezer. Its sides will be lined with a thick layer of frozen cream. Displace this with the ladle or a long knife, working every part of it loose; beat up the custard again firmly and vigorously, until it is all smooth, half-congealed paste. The perfection of the ice-cream depends upon the thoroughness of the beating at this point. Put on the cover again, pack in more ice and salt, turn off the brine, cover the freezer entirely with the ice, and spread over all, the carpet. At the end of two or three hours more, again turn off the brine and add fresh ice and salt, but do not open the freezer for two hours more. At that time take the freezer from the ice, open it, wrap a towel wet in hot water about the lower part, and turn out a solid column of ice-cream, close grained, firm, delicious. Any of the recipes for custard ice-cream may be frozen in this way.

Ice-creams may be formed into fanciful shapes by the use of molds. After the cream is frozen, place in mold, and set in pounded ice and salt until ready to serve. Cream may be frozen without a patent freezer, by simply placing it in a covered tin pail, and setting the latter in an ordinary wooden bucket, packing into the space between them, very firmly, a mixture of one part salt to two parts of snow or pounded ice. When the space is full to within an inch of the top, remove cover, and stir with a wooden spoon or paddle, keeping the freezing cream detached from the sides, until the whole is stiff;

replace the cover, pour off the water, repack, cover the whole with a blanket or carpet, and set away in a cool place.

The juice of the poke or scoke berry gives a very beautiful color to creams and ices. The large dark-purple clusters of berries are gathered when ripe, and boiled slowly. in a porcelain kettle until the skins break, strained, sugar added in the proportion of one pound to a pint of juice, and, after a few minutes more of boiling, bottled and sealed. To color, add a tea-spoonful to each pint of cream, deepening the color by adding more, if desired.

Brown Ice-cream.

Melt one and a half pounds brown sugar in an iron frying-pan, stirring it to dissolve thoroughly and prevent burning, pour it into one pint boiling milk, let cool, pour into three quarts cream, and freeze.—*Miss C. P. S., Warren.*

Chocolate Ice-cream.

Scald one pint new milk, add by degrees three quarters of a pound sugar, two eggs, and five table-spoons chocolate, rub smooth in a little milk. Beat well for a moment or two, place over the fire and heat until it thickens well, stirring constantly, set off, add a table-spoon of thin, dissolved gelatine, and when cold, place in freezer; when it begins to set, add a quart of rich cream, half of it well whipped.

To make a mold of chocolate and vanilla, freeze in separate freezers, divide a mold through the center with card-board, fill each division with a different cream, and set mold in ice and salt for an hour or more.

To make chocolate fruit ice-cream, when almost frozen, add a coffee-cup of preserved peaches, or any other preserves, cut in fine pieces.

Eggless Ice-cream.

A scant tea-cup flour to two quarts new milk; put three pints on to boil (in tin pail set in a kettle of boiling water), mix the flour with the other pint till smooth, then stir it in the boiling milk; let it boil ten or fifteen minutes, and, just before taking it from the fire, stir in one and a half pounds pulverized sugar (any good white sugar will do). Care must be taken to stir all the time after putting in the sugar, only letting it remain a moment, or just long enough to dissolve it; take from stove, and strain at once through a crash towel. When cold add one quart cream. Flavor with vanilla, in the proportion of a table-spoon to a gallon.—*Mrs. Libbie Dolbear.*

EGGLESS ICE-CREAM.

Two quarts milk, one pound sugar, three heaping table-spoons corn starch; wet the starch with a little cold milk, scald the milk by putting it in a tin pail and setting it in a pot of boiling water, let boil and stir in the sugar and starch, strain, let cool, flavor and freeze.—*Miss Louise Skinner, Battle Creek, Mich.*

FRUIT FRAPPEES.

Line a mold with vanilla ice-cream, fill the center with fresh berries, or fruit cut in slices, cover with ice-cream, cover closely, and set in freezer for half an hour, with salt and ice well packed around it. The fruit must be chilled, but not frozen. Strawberries and ripe peaches are delicious thus prepared.—*Mrs. J. C. P., Stockbridge, Mass.*

ICE-CREAM.

Three pints sweet cream, quart new milk, pint powdered sugar, the whites of two eggs beaten light, table-spoon vanilla; put in freezer till thoroughly chilled through, and then freeze.—*Mrs. Cogswell, New York.*

ICE-CREAM.

One quart milk, two eggs, two table-spoons corn starch; heat the milk in a dish set in hot water, then stir in the corn starch mixed smooth in a little cold water; let it boil for one or two minutes, then remove from stove and cool, and stir in the eggs and a half pound sugar. If to be extra nice, add a pint of rich cream, and one-fourth pound sugar, strain the mixture, and when cool add the flavoring, and freeze as follows: Prepare freezer in the usual manner, turn the crank one hundred times, then pour upon the ice and salt a quart boiling water from the tea-kettle. Fill up again with ice and salt, turn the crank fifty times one way and twenty-five the other (which serves to scrape the cream from sides of freezer); by this time it will turn very hard, indicating that the cream is frozen sufficiently.—*Mrs. Wm. Herrick, Minneapolis, Minn.*

LEMON ICE-CREAM.

Squeeze a dozen lemons, make the juice quite thick with white sugar, stir into it very slowly three quarts of cream, and freeze. Orange ice-cream is prepared in the same way, using less sugar.

PINE-APPLE ICE-CREAM.

Three pints cream, two large ripe pine-apples, two pounds powdered sugar; slice the pine-apples thin, scatter the sugar between the slices, cover and let the fruit stand three hours, cut or chop it up in the syrup, and strain through a hair sieve or double bag of coarse lace; beat gradually into the cream, and freeze as rapidly as possible; reserve a few pieces of pine-apple unsugared, cut into square bits, and stir through cream when half frozen, first a pint of well-whipped cream, and then the fruit. Peach ice-cream may be made in the same way.—*Mrs. L. M. T., New York City.*

STRAWBERRY ICE-CREAM.

Prepare milk as for any ice-cream, omitting the flavoring; sweeten berries as for the table, mash, and add to the milk one quart berries to each gallon of milk, stir all together, strain through a close wire strainer, and freeze.

MRS. WATSON'S ICE-CREAM.

Boil a half pint arrowroot mixed smooth with milk, and two quarts milk; when cold add two quarts cream, whites of six eggs, table-spoon of flavoring and two pounds of sugar. Freeze as above.

FROZEN PUDDING.

Make a half gallon rich boiled custard, sweeten to taste, add two table-spoons gelatine, or a heaping table-spoon of sea-moss farine dissolved in a half tea-cup cold milk; let the custard cool, put it in freezer, and as soon as it begins to freeze, add one pound raisins, one pint strawberry preserves, one quart whipped cream; stir and beat well like ice-cream. Blanched almonds or grated cocoa-nut are additions Some prefer currants to raisins, and some also add citron chopped fine.—*Mrs. Gov. J. B. McCreary, Kentucky.*

APPLE ICE.

Grate, sweeten and freeze well-flavored apples, pears, peaches or quinces. Canned fruit may be mashed and prepared in the same way.

CURRANT ICE.

Boil down three pints of water and a pound and a half sugar to one quart, skim, add two cups of currant juice, and when partly frozen, add the whites of five eggs.

LEMON ICE.

One gallon water, four pounds sugar, juice of twelve lemons, well-beaten whites of twelve eggs; to the water and sugar (if boiled, when cold) add the juice and the sliced rind of half the lemons; let stand an hour or two, then strain, freeze, and when half frozen add the whites.—*Mrs. Gov. Silas Garber, Nebraska.*

ORANGE ICE.

Boil three-quarters of a pound of sugar in one quart of water; when cool add the juice of six oranges; steep the rinds in a little water, strain, and flavor to taste with it. The juice and rind of one or two lemons added to the orange is a great improvement. Freeze like ice-cream.

TEA ICE-CREAM.

Pour over four table-spoons of Old Hyson tea, a pint of cream, scald in a custard-kettle, or by placing the dish containing it in a kettle of boiling water, remove from fire, and let stand five minutes; strain it into a pint of cold cream, put on to scald again, and when hot, mix with it four eggs and three-fourths pound sugar, well beaten together; let cool and freeze.—*Miss A. C. L., Pittsfield, Mass.*

WATER ICE.

To a quart of water, add one pound of sugar, flavor to taste, and freeze.

JELLIES AND JAMS.

Always make jellies in a porcelain kettle if possible, but brass may be used if scoured very bright and the fruit is removed immediately on taking from the fire. Use the best refined or granulated sugar, and do not have the fruit, especially currants and grapes, overripe.

To extract the juice, place fruit in kettle with just enough water to keep from burning, stir often, and let remain on the fire until thoroughly scalded; or a better but rather slower method is to place it in a stone jar set within a kettle of tepid water, boil until the fruit is well softened, stirring frequently, and then strain a small quantity at a time through a strong coarse flannel or cotton bag wrung out of hot water, after which let it drain, and squeeze it with the hands as it cools, emptying the bag and rinsing it off each time it is used. The larger fruits, such as apples and quinces, should be cut in pieces, cores removed if at all defective, water added to just cover them, boiled gently until tender, turned into bag and placed to drain for three or four hours, or over night. Make not over two or three pints of jelly at a time, as larger quantities require longer boiling. As a general rule allow equal measures juice and sugar. Boil juice rapidly ten minutes from the first moment of boiling, skim, add sugar, and boil ten minutes longer; or spread the sugar in a large dripping-pan, set in the oven, stir often to prevent burning, boil the juice just twenty minutes, add the hot sugar, let boil up once, and pour into jelly-glasses. To test jelly, drop a little in a glass of very cold water, and if it immediately falls to the bottom it is done; or drop in a saucer, and set on ice or in a cool place; if it does not spread, but remains rounded, it is finished.

(154)

Some strain through the bag into the glasses, but this involves waste, and if skimming is carefully done is not necessary. If jelly is not very firm, let it stand in the sun covered with bits of window glass or pieces of mosquito netting, for a few days. Never attempt to make jellies in damp or cloudy weather if firmness and clearness are desired. Currants and berries should be made up as soon as picked; never let them stand over night. When ready to put away, cover with pieces of tissue or writing-paper cut to fit and pressed closely upon the jelly, and put on the lid or cover with thick paper, brushed over on the inside with the white of an egg, and turned down on outside of glass.

APPLE OR BLACKBERRY JELLY.

Prepare nice, tart, juicy apples as in general directions, using three quarters of a pint of sugar to a pint of juice. Prepare blackberry jelly according to general directions for berries.

CALF'S-FOOT JELLY.

Boil three or four pounds of calf's feet slowly in four quarts of water, until one half the water has evaporated, strain through a cloth and set away for several hours; then remove all the fat, and to one quart of clear jelly add a pint of wine, a pound of sugar, the whites (slightly beaten) and the crushed shells of four eggs, and four lemons with the outside peel removed. Boil fifteen minutes without stirring, skim off carefully all the scum that arises, throw in a cup of cold water, let boil three minutes, skim and strain, pour into molds wet with cold water, and set in a refrigerator.

CURRANT JELLY.

Do not pick from the stem, but carefully remove all leaves and imperfect fruit, place in a stone jar, and follow general directions; or place one pint currants, picked off the stem, and one pint sugar, in the kettle on the stove, scald well, skim out currants, and dry on plates; or make into jam with one-third currants and two-thirds raspberries, straining juice after sweetening, and cooking until it "jellies." After currants are dried put them in stone jars and cover closely.—*Mrs. A. B. M.*

CRANBERRY JELLY.

Prepare juice as in general directions, add one pound sugar to every pint, boil and skim, test by dropping a little into cold water (when it does not mingle with the water it is done), rinse glasses in cold water before pouring in the jelly to prevent sticking. The pulp may be sweetened and used for sauce.—*C. G. & E. W. Crane, Caldwell, N. J.*

CRAB APPLE JELLY.

Wash and quarter large Siberian crabs, but do not core, cover to the depth of an inch or two with cold water, and cook to a mush; pour into a coarse cotton bag or strainer, and when cool enough, press or squeeze hard, to extract all the juice. Take a piece of fine Swiss muslin or crinoline, wring out of water, spread over a colander placed over a crock, and with a cup dip the juice slowly in, allowing plenty of time to run through; repeat this process twice, rinsing out the muslin frequently. Allow the strained juice of four lemons to a peck of apples, and three quarters of a pound of sugar to each pint of juice. Boil the juice from ten to twenty minutes, while boiling sift in the sugar slowly, stirring constantly, and boil five minutes longer. This is generally sufficient, but it is always safer to "try it," and ascertain whether it will "jelly." This makes a very clear, sparkling jelly.—*Mrs. Carol Gaytes, Riverside, Ill.*

COFFEE JELLY.

Half box Coxe's gelatine soaked half an hour in a half tea-cup cold water (as little water as possible), one quart strong coffee, made as if for the table and sweetened to taste; add the dissolved gelatine to the hot coffee, stir well, strain into a mold rinsed with cold water just before using, set on ice or in a very cool place, and serve with whipped cream. This jelly is very pretty, formed in a circular mold with tube in center; when turned out fill the space in center with whipped cream heaped up a little.—*Mrs. A. Wilson, Rye, N. Y.*

EASTER JELLY.

Color calf's-foot jelly a bright yellow by steeping a small quantity of dried saffron leaves in the water. Pare lemons in long strips about the width of a straw, boil in water until tender, throw them into a rich syrup, and boil until clear. Make a blanc-mange of cream, color one-third pink with poke-berry syrup, one-third green with spinach, and leave the other white. Pour out eggs from a hole a half inch in diameter in the large end, wash and drain the shells carefully, set them in a basin of salt to fill, and pour in the blanc-mange slowly through a funnel, and place the dish in a refrigerator for several hours. When ready to serve, select a round, shallow dish about as large as a hen's nest, form the jelly in it as a lining, scatter the strips of lemon peel over the edge like straws, remove the egg-shells carefully from the blanc-mange, and fill the nest with them.—*Mrs. C. M. Coates, Philadelphia.*

GRAPE JELLY.

Prepare fruit and rub through a sieve; to every pound of pulp add a pound of sugar, stir well together, boil slowly twenty minutes, then follow general directions; or, prepare the juice, boil twenty minutes, and add one pound of sugar to one pound of juice after it is reduced by boiling; then boil ten or fifteen minutes. Or put on grapes just beginning to turn, boil, place in jelly-bag and let drain; to one pint juice add one pint sugar, boil twenty minutes, and just before it is done add one tea-spoon dissolved gum-arabic.

ISINGLASS JELLY.

Two ounces isinglass, five pints of water, one and a half pounds sugar, the whites of three eggs well beaten; season highly with cinnamon, orange peel, mace and good brandy; after dissolving isinglass and adding spices, let it boil fifteen minutes, strain through flannel bag, and when nearly cool add the brandy.—*Mrs. Gov. J. B. McCreary, Kentucky.*

LEMON JELLY.

Three good-sized lemons sliced, half a pound white sugar, two ounces isinglass or gelatine dissolved in two quarts of cold water, a stick of cinnamon, and a little grated nutmeg. Beat the whites of three or four eggs, and when the gelatine is all dissolved stir them well with the other ingredients; boil five minutes, strain through a flannel jelly-bag into molds and set on ice; or the eggs, cinnamon and nutmeg may be omitted.—*Miss Ella L. Starr.*

ORANGE JELLY.

Two quarts water, four ounces gelatine, nine oranges and three lemons, a pound sugar, whites of three eggs; soak gelatine in a pint of water, boil the three pints water and sugar together, skim well, add dissolved gelatine, orange and lemon juice, and beaten whites; let come to a boil, skim off carefully all scum, boil until it jellies, and pour jelly into mold. Strain scum and add to mold.

QUINCE JELLY

Rub the quinces with a cloth until perfectly smooth, cut in small pieces, pack tight in kettle, pour on cold water until level with the fruit, boil until very soft; make a three-cornered flannel bag, pour in fruit and hang up to drain, occasionally pressing on the top and sides to make the juice run more freely, taking care not to press hard enough to expel the pulp. There is not so much need of pressing a bag made in this shape, as the weight of the fruit in the larger part causes the juice to flow freely at the point. To a pint of juice add a pint of sugar and boil fifteen minutes, or until it is jelly; pour into tumblers, or bowls, and finish according to general directions. If quinces are scarce, the parings and cores of quinces with good tart apples, boiled and strained as above, make excellent jelly, and the quinces are saved for preserves.—*Mrs. M. J. W.*

WILD CRAB-APPLE JELLY.

Cook the crab-apples until the skins will peel off, after which remove, punch out the cores with a goose-quill, and to each gallon add one gallon of cold water, allowing all to soak together for two or three days, after which take out the apples, and add to the liquid half as much water as there is liquid; to every two pints of this, add one and a fourth pints of sugar, and boil until it is jelly. By making a syrup, the apples can be used afterward for preserves, if desired.—*Mrs. Samuel Woods, Milford Center.*

WILD PLUM JELLY.

Wash clean, put in porcelain kettle, add water till it comes just to the top of plums (not to cover), boil till soft, pour into a colander, drain well but do not squeeze, strain the juice through a flannel bag, to each pint add a pint of sugar, boil juice ten to fifteen minutes, then add sugar and boil till it "jellies." To make marmalade, rub the plums through the colander, add a pint of sugar to a pint of pulp, and boil half an hour, stirring all the time; put in small jars and cover as directed for jelly. Any variety of crab-apples may be prepared as above, adding to the marmalade a small piece of ginger-root, broken in bits: Or, add one-third pint sugar to one pint pulp, boil three-quarters of an hour, seal in fruit jars and use for pies, adding milk, egg, and sugar, as for pumpkin or squash pies.

WINE JELLY.

Dissolve one box Coxe's gelatine in one pint of cold water, with the juice and rind of two lemons, and half an ounce of stick-cinnamon if you wish; soak three-quarters of an hour, pour upon it three pints boiling water, and one pint sherry, add four coffee-cups sugar, and strain through flannel into molds.—*Mrs. J. A. Rea, Minneapolis.*

JAMS.

In making jams, the fruit should be carefully cleaned and *thoroughly* bruised, as mashing it before cooking prevents it from becoming hard. Boil fifteen or twenty minutes before adding the sugar, as the flavor of the fruit is thus better preserved (usually allowing three-quarters of a pound of sugar to a pound of fruit), and then boil half an hour longer. Jams require almost constant stirring, and every house-keeper should be provided with a small paddle with handle at right angles with the blade (similar to an apple-butter "stirrer," only smaller), to be used in making jams and marmalades.

To tell when any jam or marmalade is sufficiently cooked, take out some of it on a plate and let it cool. If no juice or moisture gathers about it, and it looks dry and glistening, it is done thoroughly. Put up in glass or small stone jars, and seal or secure like jellies. Keep jellies and jams in a cool, dry, and dark place.

CURRANT JAM.

Pick from stems and wash thoroughly with the hands, put into a preserving kettle and boil fifteen or twenty minutes, stirring often and skimming off any scum that may arise; then add sugar in the proportion of three-fourths pound sugar to one pound fruit, or, by measure, one coffee-cup of sugar to one pint mashed fruit; boil thirty minutes longer, stirring almost constantly. When done, pour in small jars or glasses, and either seal, or secure like jelly, by first pressing paper, cut to fit the glasses, down close on the fruit, and then larger papers, brushed on the inside with white of eggs, with the edges turned down over the outside of the glass.

GOOSEBERRY JAM.

Stew the berries in a little water, press through a coarse sieve, and return to the kettle, add three-fourths pound sugar to each pound of the pulped gooseberry; boil three-quarters of an hour, stirring constantly; pour in jars or bowls, and cover as directed for currant jams.

GRAPE OR PLUM JAM.

Stew in a little water, and press the fruit through a colander or coarse sieve, adding a little water to plums to get all the pulp through; add sugar, and finish as in other jams.

RASPBERRY JAM.

Make by itself, or, better, combined with currants in the proportion of one-third currants to two-thirds raspberries; mash the fruit well, and proceed as in currant jam.

Make blackberry jam like raspberry, except that it should not be mixed with currants.

Strawberry jam is made exactly like blackberry.

MEATS.

Inattention to the temperature of the water and too early application of salt cause great waste in boiling meats. To make fresh meat rich and nutritious it should be placed in a kettle of *boiling* water (pure soft water is best), skimmed well as soon as it begins to boil again, and placed where it will slowly but constantly simmer. The meat should be occasionally turned and kept well under the water, and fresh hot water supplied as it evaporates in boiling. The hot water hardens the fibrine on the outside, encasing and retaining the rich juices—and the whole theory of correct cooking in a nut-shell, is to retain as much as possible of the nutriment of food. No salt should be added until the meat is nearly done, as it extracts the juices of the meat if added too soon. Boil gently, as rapid boiling hardens the fibrine and renders the meat hard, tasteless, and scarcely more nutritious than leather, without really hastening the process of cooking, every degree of heat beyond the boiling point being worse than wasted. Salt meat should be put on in cold water so that it may freshen in cooking. Allow twenty minutes to the pound for fresh, and thirty-five for salt meats, the time to be modified, of course, by the quality of the meat. A pod of red pepper in the water will prevent the unpleasant odor of boiling from filling the house.

Roasting is almost unknown in these days of stoves and ranges—baking, a much inferior process, having taken its place. In roasting proper, the joint is placed close to a brisk fire, turned so as to expose every part to the heat, and then moved back to finish in a more moderate heat. The roast should be basted frequently with the drippings, and when half cooked, with salt and water. In prepar-

11   (161)

ing roasts, dash them over with cold water, wash quickly and wipe
dry. English cooks never wash beef, but wipe with a towel wrung
out of cold water. To bake, place in the dripping-pan with bony side
up, flour well, put one pint hot water in pan, adding more when
needed, and set in a rather brisk oven, afterward graduated to a
moderate heat. Baste frequently, turning the pan often so that the
parts may roast equally, and when about half done add pieces of
carrot, onion, and a few sprigs of parsley, flour again, salt, turn
over and flour the other side, seasoning with salt and pepper
about half an hour before serving. Many roast meat on a grate
placed in the dripping-pan, adding but little water at a time (when
there is too much the meat is steamed instead of roasting, and the
gravy will not become brown). In roasting all meats, success depends upon flouring thoroughly, basting frequently, turning often
so as to prevent burning, and carefully regulating the heat of the
oven. Allow fifteen to twenty-five minutes to the pound in roasting, according as it is to be rare or well done, taking into consideration the quality of the meat. Roasts prepared with dressing
require more time. In roasting meats many think it better not to
add any water until the meat has been in the oven about half an
hour, or until it begins to brown.

Broiling is a far more wholesome method of cooking meats than
frying. Tough steak is made more tender by pounding or hacking
with a dull knife, but some of the juices are lost by the operation;
cutting it across in small squares with a *sharp* knife on both sides
is better than either. Trim off all superfluous fat, but never wash
a freshly-cut steak. Place the steak on a hot, well-greased gridiron, turn often so that the outside may be seared at once; when
done, which will require from five to ten minutes, dish on a hot
platter, season with salt and pepper and bits of butter, cover with
a hot platter and serve at once. A small pair of tongs are best to
turn steaks, as piercing with a fork frees the juices. If fat drips on
the coals below, the blaze may be extinguished by sprinkling with
salt, always withdrawing the gridiron to prevent the steak from ac-
quiring a smoky flavor. Always have a brisk fire, whether you
cook in a patent broiler directly over the fire, or on a gridiron over
a bed of live coals. Broiling steak is the very last thing to be done

in getting breakfast or dinner; every other dish should be ready for the table, so that this may have the cook's undivided attention. A steel gridiron with slender bars is best, as the common, broad, flat, iron bars fry and scorch the meat, imparting a disagreeable flavor. Never season with salt while cooking.

Frying is properly cooking in fat enough to cover the article, and when the fat is hot, and properly managed, the food is crisped at the surface, and does not absorb the fat. The process of cooking in just enough fat to prevent sticking has not yet been named in English, and is *sautéing*, but is popularly known as frying.

To thaw frozen meat, place in a warm room over night, or lay it for a few hours in cold water—the latter plan being the best. The ice which forms on the surface as it thaws is easily removed. If cooked before it is entirely thawed it will be tough. Meat once frozen should not be allowed to thaw until just before cooking.

Beef in boiling loses rather more than one-quarter; in roasting it loses one-third; legs of mutton lose one-fifth in boiling, and one-third in roasting, and a loin of mutton in roasting loses rather more than a third.

Beef suet may be kept a long time in a cool place without freezing, or by burying it deep in the flour barrel so as to entirely exclude the air.

The garnishes for meats are parsley, slices of lemon, sliced carrot, sliced beets, and currant jelly.

For hints on buying meats, see "Marketing."

Broiled Beefsteak.

Lay a thick tender steak upon a gridiron well greased with butter or beef suet, over hot coals; when done on one side have ready the warmed platter with a little butter on it, lay the steak, without pressing it, upon the platter with the cooked side down so that the juices which have gathered may run on the platter, quickly place it again on gridiron, and cook the other side. When done to liking, put on platter again, spread lightly with butter, season with salt and pepper, and place where it will keep warm (over boiling steam is best) for a few moments, but do not let butter become oily.

Serve on hot plates. Many prefer to *sear* on one side, turn immediately and sear the other, and finish cooking, turning often; garnish with fried sliced potatoes, or with browned potato balls the size of a marble, piled at each end of platter.—*Mrs. W. W. W.*

FRIED BEEFSTEAK.

When the means to broil are not at hand, the next best method is to heat the frying-pan very hot, put in steak previously hacked, let remain a few moments, loosen with a knife and turn quickly several times; repeat this, and when done transfer to a hot platter, salt, pepper, and put over it bits of butter; pile the steaks one on top of another, and cover with a hot platter. This way of frying is both healthful and delicate. Or, heat the skillet, trim off the fat from the steak, cut it in small bits and set on to fry; meanwhile pound steak, then draw the bits of suet to one side and put in the steak, turn quickly over several times so as to sear the outside, take out on a hot platter previously prepared with salt and pepper, dredge well, return to skillet, repeating the operation until the steak is done; dish on a hot platter, covering with another platter, and place where it will keep hot while making the gravy. Place a table-spoon dry flour in the skillet, being sure to have the fat boiling hot, stir until brown and free from lumps (the bits of suet may be left in, drawing them to one side until the flour is browned), pour in about half a pint boiling water (milk or cream is better), stir well, season with pepper and salt, and serve in a gravy tureen. Spread bits of butter over steak and send to table at once. This is more economical, but not so wholesome as broiling.

BEEFSTEAK TOAST.

Chop cold steak very fine, cook in a little water, put in cream or milk, thicken, season with butter, salt, and pepper, and pour it over slices of toast. Prepare boiled ham in the same way, adding the yolk of an egg.—*Mrs. John Gortner, Goshen, Ind.*

BEEFSTEAK SMOTHERED IN ONIONS.

Slice the onions thin and drop in cold water: put steak in pan with a little suet. Skim out onions and add to steak, season with pepper and salt, cover tightly, and put over the fire. When the juice of the onions has dried up, and the meat has browned on one side, remove onions, turn steak, replace onions, and fry till done, being careful not to burn.

BOILED CORNED BEEF.

Soak over night if very salt, but if beef is young and properly corned this is not necessary; pour over it cold water enough to cover it well, after washing off the salt. The rule for boiling meats is twenty-five minutes to a pound, but corned beef should be placed on a part of the stove or range where it will simmer, not boil, uninterruptedly from four to six hours, according to the size of the piece. If to be served cold, some let the meat remain in the liquor until cold, and some let tough beef remain in the liquor until the next day, and bring it to the boiling point just before serving. Simmer a brisket or plate-piece until the bones are easily removed, fold over, forming a square or oblong piece, place sufficient weight on top to press the parts closely together, and set where it will become cold. This gives a firm, solid piece to cut in slices, and is a delightful relish. Boil liquor down, remove the fat, season with pepper or sweet herbs, and save it to pour over finely minced scraps and pieces of beef; press the meat firmly into a mold, pour over it the liquor, and place over it a close cover with a weight upon it. When turned from the mold, garnish with sprigs of parsley or celery, and serve with fancy pickles or French mustard.—*Mrs. S. H. J.*

BEEF OMELET.

Three pounds beef chopped fine, three eggs beaten together, six crackers rolled fine, one table-spoon salt, one tea-spoon pepper, one table-spoon melted butter, sage to taste. Mix well and make like a loaf of bread; put a little water and bits of butter into the pan, invert a pan over it, baste occasionally, bake an hour and a quarter, and when cold slice very thin.—*Mrs. John W. Grubbs, Richmond, Ind.*

BEEF A LA MODE.

Take about six pounds of the round of beef, gash it through at intervals of an inch to receive strips of salt pork half an inch wide, tie it securely by winding a string around and lengthwise; put it into a large pot with a plate in the bottom to prevent adhering, pour in a quart of water in which are salt, pepper, cloves, cinnamon, and allspice; keep the pot closed, and when beef is taken out, add a little water and flour to make a gravy.—*Mrs. Wm. Lee.*

BOILED BEEF TONGUE.

Wash clean, put in the pot with water to cover it, a pint of salt, and a small pod of red pepper; if the water boils away, add more so as to keep the tongue nearly covered until done; boil until it can be pierced easily with a fork, take out, and if needed for present use, take off the skin and set away to cool; if to be kept some days, do not peel until wanted for table. The same amount of salt will do for three tongues if the pot is large enough to hold them, always remembering to keep sufficient water in the kettle to cover all while boiling. Soak salt tongue over night, and cook in same way, omitting the salt. Or, after peeling, place the tongue in sauce-pan with one cup water, one-half cup vinegar, four tablespoons sugar, and cook till liquor is evaporated.—*M. J. W.*

RAGOUT OF BEEF.

For six pounds of the round, take half dozen ripe tomatoes, cut up with two or three onions in a vessel with a tight cover, add half a dozen cloves, a stick of cinnamon, and a little whole black pepper; cut gashes in the meat, and stuff them with half pound of fat salt pork, cut into square bits; place the meat on the other ingredients, and pour over them half a cup of vinegar and a cup of water; cover tightly, and bake in a moderate oven; cook slowly four or five hours, and, when about half done, salt to taste. When done, take out the meat, strain the gravy through a colander and thicken with flour.— *Mrs. D. W. R., Washington City.*

ROAST MEAT WITH PUDDING.

Never wash the meat, but if necessary wipe with a damp cloth, sprinkle with salt, pepper, and flour; if not fat, put three or four pieces of butter the size of a hickory-nut on it; put in the dripping-pan without water, letting it rest on a wire frame or some small sticks to keep it from the pan; baste and turn often, baking from fifteen to twenty minutes for every pound. Make a Yorkshire pudding, to eat like vegetables with the roast, as follows: For every pint of milk take three eggs, three cups of flour, and a pinch of salt; stir to a smooth batter, and pour into the dripping-pan under the meat, half an hour before it is done.—*Mrs. C. T. Carson.*

BEEF AFTER THE FRENCH MODE.

Four pounds round of beef, half pound fat salt pork; cut pork into strips half an inch thick, roll strips in the following mixture: Half tea-spoon each powdered sage, black pepper, and celery salt, quarter tea-spoon summer savory, and half tea-cup best vinegar; let the pork soak in mixture twenty minutes, remove bone from center of beef, and with a sharp knife pierce beef through with holes an inch apart; draw into these holes the seasoned pork, press down smoothly, fill up opening from which the bone was taken with the seasoned pork, draw a band of cloth around the beef, and pin it securely; then lay in bottom of an earthen dish some veal or beef bones, place the meat on the bones, and pour slowly over, two table-spoons vinegar so that it may sink into the meat; lay over top a thin slice of fat pork, add a cup of water, cut up an onion, a carrot, a few blades of celery and a bunch of sweet herbs tied up in a muslin bag, and add all to meat; cover tightly and bake in a moderate oven for four hours. For the last hour, baste the meat often with drippings from the dish.

A BROWN STEW.

Put on stove a rather thick piece of beef with little bone and some fat (any poor piece will do), four hours before needed, pour on just *boiling* water enough to cover, cover with a close-fitting lid, add a little salt, and as the water boils away, add only just enough from time to time to keep from burning, so that when the meat is tender, the water may all be boiled away, as the fat will allow the meat to brown without burning; brown over a slow fire, and make a gravy of the drippings, or cut down cold for supper.—*Mrs. G. W. Collins.*

BREAKFAST KIDNEYS.

Cut all the good parts into small pieces, lay them into salt and water half an hour, wash well, and put on to boil in clean water.

After fifteen minutes boiling, pour off water, put on again with clean, adding a chopped onion, butter, pepper and salt, and let simmer slowly all the evening. In the morning warm over, and thicken the gravy to serve with them, if desired.

BREAKFAST STEW.

Cut three-fourths of a pound of cold roast beef into small pieces, heat slowly with half a pint cold water, one table-spoon Chili sauce, a tea-spoon salt, and half a tea-spoon pepper. Rub two table-spoons flour with some butter and a little of the hot gravy, add to the beef, let cook until the flour is done, and then serve with bits of dry toast.

BEEF TONGUE.

Wash tongue, cover with cold water, and soak over night; next day put it in a kettle, cover with cold water, boil till tender, remove skin, trim carefully, and serve with rice boiled dry, or with mashed potatoes, heaped around it. If the tongue is to be eaten cold, leave it to cool in the water in which it was cooked.

SPICED BEEF TONGUE.

Rub into the tongue a mixture of half a pint of sugar, a piece of saltpeter the size of a pea, and a table-spoon of ground cloves; immerse it in a brine made of three-fourths pound salt to two quarts water, taking care that it is kept covered; let lie two weeks, take out, wash well, and dry with a cloth; roll out a thin paste made of flour and water, wrap the tongue in it, and put it in pan to bake; bake slowly, basting well with lard and water; when done, remove paste and skin, and serve.

FRIZZLED BEEF.

Slice dried beef thin, pour on boiling water to freshen, pour off water, frizzle beef in butter, dredge with a little flour, add from a half pint to a pint new milk in proportion to quantity of beef. Stir well while cooking, and just before removing add the yolk of an egg, let boil, stirring well all the time, and serve. Cold boiled or baked beef may be sliced and cooked in the same way.

When ends or thin pieces of dried beef become too dry and hard, put in cold water and boil slowly six or eight hours, and slice when cold; or, soak over night in cold water, and boil three or four hours. Many think all dried beef is improved by this method.

BROILED LIVER.

Cut beef's or calf's liver in thin slices, wash, and soak in salt and water for half an hour; wash it again, season with pepper and salt, and broil, basting with butter, or fry to a nice brown.

CHOPPED LIVER.

Fry liver cut in small pieces with slices of pork; cut both into square bits, nearly cover with water, add a little lemon juice and pepper, thicken the gravy with fine bread-crumbs, or browned flour, and serve.

FRIED LIVER.

Cut in thin slices and place on a platter, pour on boiling water and immediately pour it off (sealing the outside, taking away the unpleasant flavor and making it much more palatable); have ready in skillet on the stove, some hot lard or beef drippings, or both together, dredge the liver with rolled crackers or dried bread-crumbs rolled fine and nicely seasoned with pepper and salt, put in skillet, placing the tin cover on, fry slowly until both sides are dark-brown, when the liver will be thoroughly cooked. The time required is about a quarter of an hour.

LARDED LIVER.

Lard a calf's liver with bacon or ham, season with salt and pepper, tie a cord around the liver to keep in shape, put in a kettle with one quart of cold water, a quarter of a pound of bacon, one onion chopped fine, and one tea-spoon sweet marjoram; let simmer slowly for two hours, pour off gravy into gravy-dish, and brown liver in kettle. Serve with the gravy.—*Mrs. E. L. Fay, Washington Heights, New York City.*

STEW WITH TOMATOES.

Cut up three pounds lean beef, veal, or pork; put into a stew-pan with two quarts of tomatoes, peeled, sliced, and seasoned with pepper and salt; cover close, but watch carefully, and when tomatoes are dissolved, add three table-spoons fresh butter rolled in flour, and stew fifteen minutes longer, or until the meat is thoroughly done. Serve hot with dry toast.

BROILED TRIPE.

Drain, dredge in flour, broil on a greased gridiron for ten minutes; season with salt, pepper and butter, and serve on very hot dishes. In buying tripe, get the "honey-comb," as it is the best.

FRIED TRIPE.

Dredge with flour, or dip in egg and cracker crumbs, fry in hot butter, or other fat, until a delicate brown on both sides, lay it on a dish, add vinegar to the gravy, and pour over the tripe (or the vinegar may be omitted, and the gravy added, or the tripe may be served without vinegar or gravy). Or make a batter by mixing gradually one cup of flour with one of sweet milk, then add an egg well beaten and a little salt; drain the tripe, dip in batter, and fry in hot drippings or lard. Salt pork and pig's feet may be cooked by the same rule.

FRICASSEED TRIPE.

Cut tripe in narrow strips, add water or milk to it, and a good bit of butter rolled in flour, season with pepper and a little salt, let simmer slowly for some time, and serve hot garnished with parsley.

SOUSED TRIPE.

After preparing it according to directions in "How to cut and cure meats," place in a stone jar in layers, seasoning every layer with pepper and salt, and pour over boiling vinegar, in which, if desired, a few whole cloves, a sprinkle of mace, and a stick of cinnamon have been boiled; or cover with the jelly or liquor in which the tripe was boiled. When wanted for table, take out of jar, scrape off the liquid, and either broil, fricassee, fry in batter, or fry plain.—*Mrs. Eliza T. Carson, Mt. Pleasant Farm.*

TOAD-IN-THE-HOLE.

Make a batter of one pint flour, one egg wet with milk, and a little salt; grease dish well with butter, put in lamb chops, add a little water with pepper and salt, pour batter over it and bake for one hour.

Boiled Mutton with Caper Sauce.

Have ready a pot of boiling water, and throw in a handful of salt; wash a leg of mutton and rub salt through it. If it is to be rare, cook about two hours, if well done, three hours or longer, according to size. Boil a pint of milk, thicken with flour well blended, add butter, salt, pepper and two table-spoons of capers, or mint sauce if preferred.—*Mrs. E. L. F.*

Lamb Stewed with Pease.

Cut the neck or breast in pieces, put it in a stew-pan with some salt pork sliced thin, and enough water to cover it; cover close and let stew until the meat is tender, then skim free from scum, add a quart of green pease shelled, and more hot water, if necessary; cover till the pease are done tender, then add a bit of butter rolled in flour, and pepper to taste; let simmer for a few minutes and serve.

Lamb Chops.

Trim neatly, broil over a clear fire, season with pepper and salt, and serve with green pease. The chops may be arranged on the platter in the form of an oval with the bones lapping one over another.

Mutton Chops.

Season with salt and pepper, put in skillet, cover closely, and fry five minutes, turning over once; dip each chop in beaten egg, than in cracker or bread-crumbs, and fry till tender or nicely browned on each side; or put in oven in a dripping-pan, with a little water, salt and pepper; baste frequently and bake until brown.

Winter Hotch-potch.

This can be made of beef or mutton (or for those who are partial to Scotch cookery, of a sheep's head and feet), one pound of old green pease steeped all night, one large turnip, three carrots, four leeks, a little parsley (all cut small with the exception of one carrot, which should be grated), sweet herbs, pepper and salt. The pease require two hours cooking, the vegetables two hours, the head three hours, and the feet four hours.—*Mrs. E. L. Fay, New York City.*

Mutton Pie and Tomatoes.

Spread the bottom of a baking-dish with bread-crumbs, and fill with alternate layers of cold roast mutton, cut in thin slices, and tomatoes, peeled and sliced; season each layer with pepper, salt and bits of butter. The last layer should be of tomatoes spread with bread-crumbs. Bake three-quarters of an hour, and serve immediately.

Leg of Mutton a la Venison.

Remove all rough fat from a leg of mutton, lay in a deep earthen dish, and rub into the meat very thoroughly the following mixture: One table-spoon salt, one each of celery, salt, brown sugar, black pepper, made mustard, allspice, and sweet herbs mixed and powdered. After these have been rubbed into all parts of meat, pour over it slowly a tea-cup good vinegar, cover tightly and set in a cool place for four or five days, turning ham, and basting it with the liquid three or four times a day. To cook, leave in a clean kettle a quart boiling water, have in kettle an inverted tin-pan or rack made for the purpose; on it lay ham just as taken out of pickle; cover kettle tightly, and stew for four hours. Do not allow the water to touch the meat. Add a tea-cup of hot water to the pickle, and baste the ham with it. When ready to serve, thicken the liquid in the kettle with flour, strain through a fine strainer, and serve the meat with it and a relish of currant jelly.

Frogs.

Frogs may be broiled, or made into a fricassee seasoned with tomato catsup. The hind legs alone are eaten, and are a great delicacy.

Fricatelli.

Chop raw fresh pork very fine, add a little salt, plenty of pepper, and two small onions chopped fine, half as much bread as there is meat, soaked until soft, two eggs; mix well together, make into oblong patties, and fry like oysters. These are nice for breakfast; if used for supper, serve with sliced lemon.—*Mrs. W. F. W.*

BONED HAM.

Having soaked a well-cured ham in tepid water over night, boil it till perfectly tender, putting it on in warm water; take up in a wooden tray, let cool, remove bone carefully, press the ham again into shape, return to boiling liquor, remove pot from fire, and let the ham remain in it till cold. Cut across and serve cold.—*Miss L. L., Richmond.*

BOILED HAM.

Pour boiling water over it and let stand until cool enough to wash, scrape clean (some have a coarse hair-brush on purpose for cleaning hams), put in a thoroughly cleansed boiler with cold water enough to cover; boil steadily for five hours (if the ham weighs twelve pounds), take up and put into a baking-pan to skin; dip the hands in cold water, take the skin between the fingers and peel as you would an orange; set in a moderate oven, placing the lean side of the ham downward, and if you like, sift over pounded or rolled crackers; bake one hour. The baking brings out a great quantity of fat, leaving the meat much more delicate, and in warm weather it will keep in a dry, cool place a long time; if there is a tendency to mold, set it a little while into the oven again. Or, after the ham is boiled and peeled, cover with the white of a raw egg, and sprinkle sugar or bread-crumbs over it, place in the oven and brown; or cover with a regular cake-icing and brown; or, quarter two onions, stick whole allspice and black pepper in the quarters, with a knife make slits in the outside of the ham in which put the onions, place in dripping-pan, lay parsley around, and bake till nicely browned. The nicest portion of a boiled ham may be served in slices, and the ragged parts and odds and ends chopped fine for sandwiches, or by adding three eggs to one pint of chopped ham, a delicious omelet may be made. If the ham is very salt, it should lie in water over night.

BROILED HAM.

Cut the ham in slices of medium thickness, place on a hot grid-iron, and broil until the fat readily flows out and the meat is slightly browned, take from the gridiron with a knife and fork, drop into a pan of cold water, then return again to the gridiron, repeat several times, and the ham is done; place in a hot platter, add a few lumps of butter and serve at once. If too fat trim off a part; it is almost impossible to broil the fat part without burning, but this does not impair the taste. Pickled pork and breakfast bacon may be broiled in the same way.—*Mrs. A. E. Brand, Minneapolis, Minn.*

BROILED HAM.

Cut the slices thin, trim carefully, freshen by covering with water and heating gradually nearly to the boiling point; test by the taste, and if still too salt, change the water and heat again; dry with a cloth, broil over a clear fire, and season with pepper and a little butter. The ham should not be old.—*Mrs. J. S. W.*

DELICIOUS FRIED HAM.

Place the slices in boiling water and cook till tender; put in frying-pan and brown, and dish on a platter; fry some eggs by dripping gravy over them till done, instead of turning; take up carefully and lay them on the slices of ham. This is a tempting dish, and if nicely prepared, quite ornamental.—*Mrs. J. F. Woods, Milford Center.*

HAM BALLS.

Chop fine cold, cooked ham; add an egg for each person, and a little flour; beat together, make into balls, and fry brown in hot butter.—*Mrs. Howard Evans, Delaware.*

MIXED SANDWICHES.

Chop fine, cold ham, tongue and chicken; mix with one pint of the meat half a cup melted butter, one table-spoon salad oil, one of mustard if desired, the yolk of a beaten egg, and a little pepper; spread on bread cut thin and buttered. Ham alone may be prepared in this way.—*Mrs. E. Byers, Minneapolis, Minn.*

TO ROAST A PIG.

Fill a six-weeks pig with a stuffing made of bread and butter moistened with milk and water, and seasoned with pepper, salt, and herbs if liked, and sew it up, or tie a string around it; then put it to the fire, dredge it well with a little flour, baste it well with a little butter and hot water (the fire must be hotter at each end than in the middle), saving all the gravy that runs from it. When the pig is done enough, stir up the fire; take a coarse cloth, with about a quarter of a pound of butter in it, and rub the pig all over until the crackling is crisp; then take it up. It may be served whole if small, or lay it in a dish, cut off the head, then split the body in two before drawing out the spit; cut off the ears from the head, and lay them at each end, lay the two halves of the body close together in the middle of the dish, split the head and lay at each side with the ears. Take the gravy which has run from the meat, chop the liver, brains, and heart small, and put them to it (boil them before chopping, till tender), and put in a stew-pan with some bits of butter, dredge in flour, and give it one boil, and serve in a gravy-boat. The pig may be prepared in the same way and baked in an oven; or half or a quarter may be baked at a time, basting with water and vinegar in equal proportions, seasoned with salt and cayenne pepper.—*Robert Paine, Center Hill. Miss.*

SPARE-RIB POT-PIE.

Cut the spare-ribs once across and then in strips three or four inches wide, put on in kettle with hot water enough to cover, stew until tender, season with salt and pepper, and turn out of kettle;

place a layer of spare-ribs in the bottom, add a layer of peeled potatoes (quartered if large), some bits of butter, some small squares of baking-powder dough rolled quite thin, season again, then another layer of spare ribs, and so on until the kettle is two-thirds full, leaving the squares of crust for the last layer; then add the liquor in which the spare-ribs were boiled, and hot water if needed, cover, boil half to three-quarters of an hour, being careful to add hot water so as not to let it boil dry. The crust can be made of light biscuit dough, without egg or sugar, as follows: Roll thin, cut out, let rise, and use for pie, remembering to have plenty of water in the kettle, so that when the pie is made and the cover on, it need not be removed until dished. To warm over pot-pie, set it in a dripping-pan in the oven, and more squares of dough may be laid on the top.—*Mrs. W. W. W.*

PIGS'-FEET SOUSE.

Take off the horny parts of feet and toes, scrape, clean, and wash thoroughly, singe off the stray hairs, place in a kettle with plenty of water, boil, skim, pour off water and add fresh, and boil until the bones will pull out easily; do not bone, but pack in a stone jar with pepper and salt sprinkled between each layer; mix some good cider vinegar with the liquor in which feet were boiled, using two-thirds vinegar to one-third liquor, and fill up jar. When wanted for the table, take out a sufficient quantity, put in a hot skillet, add more vinegar, salt and pepper if needed, boil until thoroughly heated, stir in a smooth thickening of flour and water, and boil until flour is cooked; serve hot as a nice breakfast dish. Or when the feet have boiled until perfectly tender, remove the bones and pack in stone jar as above; slice down cold when wanted for use.

BARBECUED SHEEP.

Dig a hole in ground, in it build a wood fire, and drive four stakes or posts just far enough away so they will not burn; on these build a rack of poles to support the carcass. These should be of a kind of wood that will not flavor the meat. When the wood in the pit has burned to coals, lay sheep on rack, have a bent stick with a large sponge tied on one end, and the other fastened on one corner of the rack, and turn so that it will hang over the mutton; make a mixture of ground mustard and vinegar, salt and pepper, add sufficient water to fill the sponge the necessary number of times, and let it drip over the meat until done; have another fire burning near from which to add coals as they are needed.—*Mrs. Ella Turner.*

PIG'S HEAD CHEESE.

Having thoroughly cleaned a hog's or pig's head, split it in two, take out the eyes and the brain; clean the ears, throw scalding water over the head and ears, then scrape them well; when very clean, put in a kettle with water to cover it, and set it over a rather quick fire; skim it as any scum rises; when boiled so that the flesh leaves the bones, take it from the water with a skimmer into a large wooden bowl or tray; then take out every particle of bone, chop the meat fine, season to taste with salt and pepper (a little pounded sage may be added), spread a cloth over the colander, put the meat in, fold cloth closely over it, lay a weight on it so that it may press the whole surface equally, (if to be lean use a heavy weight, if fat, a lighter one); when cold take off weight, remove from colander, and place in crock. Some add vinegar in proportion of one pint to a gallon crock. Clarify the fat from the cloth, colander, and liquor of the pot, and use for frying.

FRIED PORKSTEAKS.

Fry like beefsteaks, with pepper and salt; or sprinkle with dry powdered sage if the sausage flavor is liked.—*Mrs. B. A. Fay.*

FRIED SALT PORK.

Cut in rather thin slices, and freshen by letting lie an hour or two in cold water or milk and water, roll in flour and fry till crisp (if you are in a hurry, pour boiling water on the slices, let stand a few minutes, drain, roll in flour and fry as before); drain off most of the grease from frying-pan, stir in while hot one or two table-spoons of flour, about half a pint of new milk, a little pepper, and salt if not salt enough already from the meat; let boil and pour into gravy dish. This makes a nice white gravy when properly made.

YANKEE PORK AND BEANS.

Pick over carefully a quart of beans and let them soak over night; in the morning wash and drain in another water, put on to boil in cold water with half a tea-spoon of soda, boil thirty minutes, drain and put them in an earthen pot with two table-spoons of molasses. When half the beans are in the pot, put in the dish half or three-fourths of a pound of well-washed salt pork with the rind cut in slices; cover all with hot water and bake six hours or longer in a moderate oven; they can not be baked too long. Keep covered so that they will not burn on the top. Serve in the dish in which they are cooked, and always have enough left to know the luxury of cold beans, or baked beans warmed over. If salt pork is too robust for the appetites to be served, season delicately with salt, pepper, and a little butter, and roast a fresh spare-rib to serve with them.

LARDED SWEETBREAD.

Lard five sweetbreads with strips of salt pork, letting them project evenly about half an inch on the upper side, put them on the fire with a half pint water and let them stew slowly for half an hour, take them out and put them in a small dripping-pan with a little butter and a sprinkle of flour; brown them slightly, add half

12

a gill of mingled milk and water, and season with pepper; heat a half pint of cream and stir it in the gravy in the pan. Have pease ready boiled and seasoned, place the sweetbreads in the center of the dish, pour the gravy over them, and put the pease around them —*In the Kitchen.*

Sweetbreads with Tomatoes.

Slice two quarts of ripe tomatoes, and stew until they break; strain through a sieve into a sauce-pan, and add four or five sweetbreads that have been well trimmed and soaked in warm water; stir in two or three ounces of butter rolled in flour, with salt and cayenne pepper to taste; just before serving, add the beaten yolks of two eggs. Serve in a deep dish, with the tomatoes poured over the sweetbread.

Canned Sausage or Tenderloin.

Make the sausage in small cakes and fry until done, fill the can up with the cooked cakes, pour boiling lard over the top and seal the same as fruit. Cut the tenderloin in squares, fry till done and can the same way.

Fried Veal Cutlets.

Make a batter of half pint of milk, a well-beaten egg, and flour; fry the veal brown in sweet lard or beef-drippings, dip it in the batter and fry again till brown; drop some spoonfuls of batter in the hot lard after the veal is taken up, and serve them on top of the meat; put a little flour paste in the gravy with salt and pepper, let it come to a boil and pour it over the whole. The veal should be cut thin and cooked nearly an hour. Cracker crumbs and egg may be used instead of batter, but the skillet should then be kept covered, and the veal cooked slowly for half an hour over a moderate fire.

Paté de Veau.

Three and a half pounds leg of veal, fat and lean chopped fine, six or eight small crackers rolled fine, two eggs, piece of butter size of an egg, one table-spoon salt, one of pepper, one nutmeg, a slice of salt pork chopped fine, or if preferred, a little more salt or butter; work all together in the form of a loaf, put bits of butter on top, grate bread-crumbs over it, put into dripping-pan and baste often; bake two hours and slice when cold.—*Mrs. General Mitchell, Columbus.*

VEAL LOAF.

Chop fine a leg or loin of veal, roll one dozen crackers, put half of them in the veal with two eggs, pepper, salt, and butter size of an egg; mix all together and make into a solid form; then take the crackers that are left and spread smoothly over the outside; bake three-quarters of an hour, and eat cold.—*Gov. Tilden, N. Y.*

PRESSED VEAL.

To three pounds veal take one pound salt pork; remove all lean parts and the rind from pork, and chop both veal and pork together very fine, season with pepper, and a tea-spoon of chopped onion or summer savory; press firmly into a deep baking-dish, and bake two hours; serve cold.—*Mrs. Harvey C. Young, Indianapolis.*

ROAST LOIN OF VEAL.

Wash and rub thoroughly with salt and pepper, leaving in the kidney, around which put plenty of salt; roll up, let stand two hours; in the meantime make dressing of bread-crumbs, salt, pepper, and chopped parsley or thyme moistened with a little hot water and butter—some prefer chopped salt pork—also add an egg. Unroll the veal, put the dressing well around the kidney, fold, and secure well with several yards white cotton twine, covering the meat in all directions; place in the dripping-pan with the thick side down, put to bake in a rather hot oven, graduating it to moderate heat afterward; in half an hour add a little hot water to the pan, baste often; in an other half hour turn over the roast, and when nearly done, dredge lightly with flour, and baste with melted butter. Before serving, carefully remove the twine. A four-pound roast thus prepared will bake thoroughly tender in about two hours. To make the gravy, skim off fat if there is too much in the drippings, dredge some flour in the pan, stir until it browns, add some hot water if necessary, boil a few moments and serve in gravy boat. This roast is very nice to slice down cold for Sunday dinners. Serve with green pease and lemon jelly.—*Mrs. W. G. Hillock.*

STEWED KIDNEY.

.Boil kidneys the night before till very tender, turn meat and gravy into a dish and cover over. In the morning, boil for a few moments, thicken with flour and water, add part of an onion chopped very fine, pepper, salt, and a lump of butter, and pour over toasted bread well buttered.—*Mrs. E. L. F.*

VEAL STEW.

Boil two and a half pounds of the breast of veal one hour in water enough to cover, add a dozen potatoes, and cook half an hour; before taking off the stove, add one pint of milk and flour enough to thicken; season to taste. If preferred make a crust as for chicken-pie, bake in two pie-pans, place one of the crusts on the platter, pour over the stew, and place the other on top.—*Kate Thompson, Millersburg, Ky.*

VEAL SWEETBREAD.

Sweetbreads should be soaked in cold water for an hour as soon as they come from market, as they do not keep well; cut through each, draw a piece of salt pork through the incision, and put on to boil in salt water or soup-stock until thoroughly done; take off, place in cold water for a few minutes, remove the little pipes and skin, and put away in a cold place until ready to cook for the table. When wanted season with salt and pepper, roll in bread-crumbs, and fry in a frying-pan, or, like doughnuts, in hot fat. Serve with green pease, or with a gravy made by pouring a cup of milk thickened with flour into the frying-pan.

Or prepare for frying as above, and bake with pieces of salt pork, carrot, celery, and parsley, for about twenty minutes, and serve with fried bread and pease, or tomato-sauce.

Or prepare as for frying, slice thin, sprinkle over grated nutmeg and chopped parsley, dip into a batter made of one cup milk, one egg, one cup of flour, a pinch of salt, and a half tea-spoon baking-powder, and fry like fritters.—*Mrs. V. G. Hush.*

VEAL WITH OYSTERS.

Two pounds of tender veal cut in thin bits, dredge with flour, and fry in sufficient hot lard to prevent sticking; when nearly done add one and a half pints of fine oysters, thicken with a little flour, season with salt and pepper, and cook until both are done. Serve very hot in a covered dish.—*In the Kitchen.*

PASTRY.

Butter or lard for pastry should be sweet, fresh, and solid. When freshly-made butter can not be had, work well two or three times in cool, fresh water.

A very nice paste for family use may be made by reducing the quantity of shortening to even so little as a half pound to a quart of flour, especially when children or dyspeptics are to be considered. With the exception of mince-pies, which are warmed over before serving, pastry should be eaten the day it is made. In warm weather, when not ready to bake immediately after making up paste, keep it in the ice-chest till wanted, several days if necessary, and, in any event, it is better to let it thus remain for one or two hours.

To prevent the juice of pies from soaking into the under crust, beat an egg well, and with a bit of cloth dipped into the egg, rub over the crust before filling the pies.

For a more wholesome pie-crust shortening, boil beans or potatoes until soft, make into a broth, work through a colander, mix as much into the flour as can be done and preserve sufficient tenacity in the dough. Knead moderately stiff, and roll a little thicker than crust shortened with lard. It is a good plan to make a puff-paste for the top crust, and for the under crust use less shortening. Many practice this, adding a little soda and cream tartar to the under crust—one half as much soda as cream tartar, which is always the rule when these ingredients are used in biscuit, cake, etc.

When using green currants, pie-plant, gooseberries, or other fruits which require the juice to be thickened, fill the lower crust, sprinkle corn starch evenly over, and put on the upper crust. This prevents the juice from running over, and, when cold, forms a

nice jelly.   Meringue, for pies or puddings, is made in the proportion of one table-spoon sugar to white of one egg, with flavoring added.   Never fill pies until just before putting them in the
oven.   Always use tin pie-pans, since, in earthen pans, the under
crust is not likely to be well baked.   Just before putting on the
upper crust, wet the rim of the lower *with a thick paste of flour and
water*, or egg and flour, and press the two crusts firmly together;
this will prevent that bane of all pastry cooks—a burst pie.   Bake
fruit pies in a moderate oven, having a better heat at the bottom
than at the top of the oven, or the lower crust will be clammy
and raw.   When done, the crust will separate from the pan, so
that the pie may be easily removed.   Remove at once from the
tins, or the crust will become "soggy."

The vices of the mince-pie have served to point many a hygienic
moral, but while it is quite true that it is not strictly hygienic, it
is not an every-day dish.   The mince-pie is one of the few articles
of food that have come down to us from a remote period, and it
still has the flavor of old associations and the solid respectability
which belongs to centuries of history and tradition.   It is less to be
feared than many apparently simple forms of highly concentrated
food, such as butter and sugar, and often a piece of common pound-
cake will produce a bigger "nightmare" than a piece of the richest
mince-pie.   Mince-pie, if not rich, is not the real thing, and it is
its deterioration, and the fact that it is left nowadays, like almost
every thing else, to servants, who do not even know how to properly
boil a piece of beef, that have brought it into disrepute.   Its preparation should be confined to no careless or unworthy hands, but
every ingredient should be thoughtfully provided and delicately
prepared, and the whole put together and blended with the skill
of an artist, and the precision of a mechanic.   Tact, wisdom, judgment, knowledge, and experience all go into the proper construction of a genuine mince-pie, to say nothing of kindness of heart
and liberality of disposition.

Aunty Phelps' Pie Crust.

To one pint of sifted flour, add one even tea-spoon baking powder,
and sweet cream enough to wet the flour, leaving crust a little stiff.
This is enough for two pies.

Good Common Paste.

One coffee-cup lard, three of sifted flour, and a little salt. In winter, soften the lard a little (but not in summer), cut it well into the flour with a knife, then mix with cold water quickly into a moderately stiff dough, handling as little as possible. This makes four common-sized covered pies. Take a new slice of paste each time for top crust, using the trimmings, etc., for under crust.—*Miss Katy Rupp.*

Graham Paste.

Mix lightly half a pound Graham flour, half a pint sweet cream, half a tea-spoon salt, roll, and bake like other pastry.

Puff-Paste.

One heaping pound superfine sifted flour, one of butter; place the flour on board (or marble slab is better), make a well in center, squeeze in juice of half a lemon, and add yolk of one egg, beaten with a little ice-water; stir with one hand and drop in ice-water with the other, until the paste is as hard as the butter; roll paste out in a smooth square an inch thick, smooth sides with a rolling-pin, spread the butter over half the paste; lay the other half over like an old-fashioned turn-over, leave it for fifteen minutes in a cold place, then roll out in a long strip, keeping the edges smooth, and double it in three parts, as follows: Fold one-third over on the middle third, roll it down, then fold over the other outside third, roll out in a long strip and repeat the folding process; let it lie for fifteen minutes, and repeat this six times, allowing fifteen minutes between each rolling, and the paste is ready for use. Handle as little as possible through the whole process. All the flour used must be of the very best quality, and thoroughly sifted. The quantity of water depends on the capacity of the flour to absorb it, which is quite variable. Too little makes the paste tough, and too much makes it thin, and prevents the flakiness so desirable. Rich paste requires a quick oven.—*Mrs. V. G. Hush, Minneapolis, Minnesota.*

Puff-Paste.

One quart flour, three-quarters pound butter or lard, yolks of two eggs, a tea-spoon salt, and a table-spoon powdered sugar; mix with cold or ice-water in a cool temperature. Place the flour on a board, sprinkle over the salt and sugar, add gradually the yolks of eggs beaten up with a little ice-water, pouring them in with one hand and mixing with the tips of the fingers of the other, until it becomes a smooth dough, as soft as can be readily handled. Roll out as described in preceding recipe.

PASTE WITH DRIPPINGS.

Rub three-fourths pound beef-drippings to a fine powder through one pound flour; add half a tea-spoon salt, make a well in center, pour in half a pint ice-water, mix, flour board and hands, roll out paste, fold, roll out and fold again, and repeat, and it is ready for use.—*Mrs. M. E. S.*

PASTE WITH SUET.

Roll a pound of the best suet, with very little membrane running through it, on a board for several minutes, removing all the skin and fibers that appear when rolling; the suet will be a pure and sweet shortening, looking like butter. Rub this into the flour, salt, and mix it with ice-water; roll out for the plates, and put on a little butter in flakes, rolling it in as usual.

APPLE PIE.

Line pan with crust; pare and quarter three or four nice tart apples and spread on crust, sprinkle with two table-spoons sugar and small bits of butter; mix one table-spoon flour, one tea-spoon essence of lemon, two table-spoons sugar, and three or four of water together, pour over the apples and bake till they are thoroughly cooked; serve warm with sweetened milk or cream. Or, half a tea-spoon cinnamon, nutmeg, or allspice, may be used in place of essence of lemon, sprinkling it on just before baking. Or, after putting in apples, pour over them a custard made of two eggs and a pint of milk, sweetened to taste.—*Miss S. A. Melching.*

APPLE MERINGUE PIE.

Pare, slice, stew and sweeten ripe, tart and juicy apples, mash and season with nutmeg, (or stew lemon peel with them for flavor), fill crust and bake till done; spread over the apple a thick meringue. made by whipping to froth whites of three eggs for each pie, sweet

ening with three table-spoons powdered sugar; flavor with vanilla,
beat until it will stand alone, and cover pie three-quarters of an
inch thick; if two thin add a little corn starch. Set back in a
quick oven till well "set," and eat cold. In their season, substitute peaches for apples.

APPLE CUSTARD PIE.

Peel sour apples and stew until soft, and not much water is left in
them, and rub through a colander. Beat three eggs for each pie.
Put in at the rate of one cup butter, and one of sugar for three
pies. Season with nutmeg.—*Mrs. D. G. Cross.*

DRIED-APPLE PIE.

Put apples in warm water and soak over night; in the morning
chop up, stew a few moments in a small amount of water, add a
sliced lemon, and sugar to taste; cook half an hour, make into
pies and bake.

SLICED-APPLE PIE.

Line pie-pan with crust, sprinkle with sugar, fill with tart apples
sliced very thin, sprinkle sugar and a very little cinnamon over
them, and add a few small bits of butter, and a table-spoon water;
dredge in flour, cover with the top crust, and bake half to three-
quarters of an hour; allow four or five table-spoons sugar to one
pie. Or, line pans with crust, fill with sliced apples, put on top
crust and bake; take off top crust, put in sugar, bits of butter and
seasoning, replace crust and serve warm. It is delicious with sweetened cream.— *Mrs. D. Buxton.*

CRAB-APPLE PIE.

Follow above recipe, and if made of " Transcendents," the pies
will fully equal those made of larger varieties of the apple.

BANANA PIE.

Slice raw bananas, add butter, sugar, allspice and vinegar, or
boiled cider, or diluted jelly; bake with two crusts. Cold-boiled
sweet potatoes may be used instead of bananas, and are very nice.
—*Mrs. Ella Turner, Selma, Alabama.*

BUTTERMILK PIE.

Beat together a heaping cup sugar and four eggs; add half cup butter, beat thoroughly, and add one and a half pints buttermilk; line the pie-tins with crust, slice an apple thin, and lay in each pie, fill the crust with the mixture, and bake with no upper crust.

CORN STARCH PIES.

One quart milk, yolks of two eggs, two table-spoons corn starch, three cups sugar; mix starch in a little milk, boil the rest of the milk to a thick cream, beat the yolks and add starch, put in the boiled milk and add sugar; bake with an under crust, beat whites with two table-spoons sugar, and put on top of pies, and when done, return to oven and brown.—*Mrs. J. W. Grubbs, Richmond, Indiana.*

CREAM PIE.

Take one pint sweet milk, three eggs, small tea-cup of sugar, two table-spoons corn starch; beat yolks, sugar and starch together; let the milk come to a boil, and stir in the mixture, adding a tea-spoon of butter and a pinch of salt. Bake crust, fill with the custard, bake, spread on whites (previously beaten to a stiff froth with two table-spoons sugar), and brown in a quick oven.—*Mrs. J. F. Woods, Milford Centre.*

CREAM PIE.

Beat thoroughly together the white of one egg, half tea-cup sugar, and table-spoon of flour; then add tea-cup rich milk (some use part cream), bake with a bottom crust, and grate nutmeg on top.—*Mrs. Luther Liggett.*

CREAM PIE.

Pour a pint cream upon a cup and a half powdered sugar; let stand until the whites of three eggs have been beaten to a stiff froth; add this to the cream, and beat up thoroughly, grate a little nutmeg over the mixture, and bake in two pies without upper crusts.—*Mrs. Henry C. Meredith, Cambridge City, Ind.*

WHIPPED-CREAM PIE.

Sweeten with white sugar one tea-cup very thick sweet cream, made as cold as possible without freezing, and flavor it with lemon or vanilla to taste; beat until as light as eggs for frosting, and keep cool until the crust is ready; make crust moderately rich, prick well with a fork to prevent blistering, bake, spread on the cream, and to add finish, put bits of jelly over the top. The above will make two pies.—*Mrs. A. M. Alexander, Harrisburg.*

CRUMB PIE.

Soak one tea-cup bread-crumbs half an hour, add three table-spoons sugar, half a tea-spoon butter, half a cup of water, a little vinegar, and nutmeg to suit the taste; bake with two crusts, made the same as for other pies.—*Miss Sylvia J. Courter.*

COCOA-NUT PIE.

One pint milk, a cocoa-nut, tea-cup sugar, three eggs; grate cocoa-nut, mix with the yolks of the eggs and sugar, stir in the milk, filling the pan even full, and bake. Beat whites of eggs to a froth, stirring in three table-spoons pulverized sugar, pour over pie and bake to a light brown. If prepared cocoa-nut is used, one heaping tea-cup is required.—*Miss N. B. Brown, Washington City.*

COMBINATION PIE.

Fill a bottom crust with ripe grapes or cranberries, sweeten well and dredge over it a little flour; when baked, pour over it a sponge-batter made as follows: Three eggs, one cup sugar, one cup flour, two table-spoons water, two tea-spoons baking-powder; return to oven and brown slightly. This is sufficient for two pies.—*Miss Mary Collins, Urbana.*

CUSTARD PIE.

For a large pie, take three eggs, one pint of milk, and half table-spoon of corn starch, half cup sugar, and flavor.—*Mrs. N. S. Long.*

CHESS PIE.

Three eggs, two-thirds cup sugar, half cup butter (half cup milk may be added if not wanted so rich); beat butter to a cream, then add yolks and sugar beaten to a froth with the flavoring; stir all together rapidly, and bake in a nice crust. When done, spread with the beaten whites, and three table-spoons sugar and a little flavoring. Return to oven and brown slightly. This makes one pie, which should be served immediately.—*Miss J. Carson, Glendale.*

GREEN CURRANT PIE.

Line an inch pie-dish with good pie-crust, sprinkle over the bottom two heaping table-spoons sugar and two of flour (or one of corn starch) mixed; then pour in one pint green currants washed clean, and two table-spoons currant jelly; sprinkle with four heaping table-spoons sugar, and add two table-spoons cold water; cover and bake fifteen or twenty minutes.—*Miss S. Alice Melching.*

RIPE CURRANT PIE.

One cup mashed ripe currants, one of sugar, two table-spoons water, one of flour beaten with the yolks of two eggs; bake, frost the top with the beaten whites of the eggs and two table-spoons powdered sugar, and brown in oven.—*Mrs. W. E. H., Minneapolis.*

LEMON PIE.

One lemon grated, one cup sugar, the yolks of three eggs, small piece butter, three table-spoons milk, one tea-spoon corn starch; beat all together and bake in a rich crust; beat the whites with three table-spoons sugar, place on the pie when done, and then brown in the oven.—*Mrs. W. E. Scobey.*

LEMON PIE.

A cup white sugar, a lemon, table-spoon corn starch, two eggs, yolks and whites beaten separately, tea-spoon butter, cup boiling water; beat corn starch with yolks of eggs, stir it into the scalding water, add the sugar and juice and grated rind of a large lemon, and stir in the butter. Have ready a pie-dish lined with rich paste, pour in mixture and bake until crust is delicately browned. Beat the whites to a stiff froth with two table-spoons powdered sugar, spread over the top and return to oven till a pale brown.—*Mrs. Wm. Brown, Massillon.*

LEMON PIE.

Four eggs, one and a half cups sugar, two-thirds cup water, two table-spoons flour, one lemon. Beat the yolks of eggs until very smooth (beat the yolks a long time and whip the whites well), add the grated peel of lemon and the sugar, beat well, stir in the flour, and add the lemon juice (if lemons are small two may be necessary), and lastly the water; stir well, and pour in pie-pans lined with paste. When baked, take from oven, and spread over them the whites of the eggs beaten dry and smooth with four table-spoons pulverized sugar; return to oven and brown slightly. The above recipe is for two pies.—*Mrs. Virginia C. Meredith.*

MINCE-MEAT.

Take five or six pounds scraggy beef—a neck piece will do—and put to boil in water enough to cover it; take off the scum that rises when it reaches the boiling point, add hot water from time to time until it is tender, then remove the lid from the pot, salt, let boil till almost dry, turning the meat over occasionally in the liquor, take from the fire, and let stand over night to get thoroughly cold; pick bones, gristle, or stringy bits from the meat, chop very fine, mincing at the same time three pounds of nice beef suet; seed and cut four pounds raisins, wash and dry four pounds currants, slice thin a pound of citron, chop fine four quarts good-cooking tart apples; put into a large pan together, add two ounces cinnamon, one of cloves, one of ginger, four nutmegs, the juice and grated rinds of two lemons, one table-spoon salt, one tea-spoon pepper, and two pounds sugar. Put in a porcelain kettle one quart boiled cider, or, better still, one quart currant or grape juice (canned when grapes are turning from green to purple), one quart nice molasses or syrup, and, if you have any syrup left from sweet pickles, add some of that, also a good lump of butter; let it come to boiling point, and pour over the ingredients in the pan after having first mixed them well, then mix again thoroughly. Pack in jars and put in a cool place, and, when cold, pour molasses over the top an eighth of an inch in thickness, and cover tightly. This will keep two months. For baking, take some out of a jar, if not moist enough add a little hot water, and strew a few whole raisins over each pie. Instead of boiled beef, a beef's-heart or roast meat may be used; and a good proportion for a few pies is one-third chopped meat and two-thirds apples, with a little suet, raisins, spices, butter, and salt.

The above is a good formula to use, but, of course, may be varied to suit different tastes or the material at hand. If too rich, add more chopped apples; in lieu of cider, vinegar and water in equal proportions may be used; good preserves, marmalades, spiced pickles, currant, or grape jelly, canned fruit, dried cherries, etc., may take the place of raisins, currants, and citrons. Wine or brandy is considered by many a great improvement, but if "it causeth thy brother to offend" do not use it. Lemon and vanilla extracts are often used, also preserved lemon or orange peel. The mince-meat is better to stand over night, or several days, before baking into pies, as the materials will be more thoroughly incorporated. Many prefer to freeze their pies after baking, heating them as needed.

MINCE-MEAT.

Two bowls chopped apples, one of chopped meat, with one-fourth pound suet, grated rind and juice of one lemon, two tea-cups molasses, one large tea-spoon each of cinnamon and cloves, one nutmeg, one pound raisins, half pound currants, one-fourth pound citron cut fine, one quart cider, and sugar and salt to taste.—*Mrs. J. R. Wilcox, New Haven, Connecticut.*

MOCK MINCE-PIE.

Twelve crackers rolled fine, one cup hot water, half cup vinegar, one cup molasses, one of sugar, one of currants, one of raisins, spice to taste; measure with a tea-cup. Some use one cup dried bread-crumbs, and also add a small cup butter. This is for four pies.— *Mrs. Annie E. Gillespie, Indianapolis, Ind.*

ORANGE PIE.

Grated rind and juice of two oranges, four eggs, four table-spoons sugar, and one of butter; cream the butter and sugar, add the beaten eggs, then the rind and juice of the oranges, and, lastly, the whites beaten to a froth, and mixed in lightly. Bake with an under crust.—*Gov. Stearns, Florida.*

PIE-PLANT PIE.

Mix half tea-cup white sugar and one heaping tea-spoon flour together, sprinkle over the bottom crust, then add the pie-plant cut up fine; sprinkle over this another half tea-cup sugar and heaping tea-spoon flour; bake fully three-quarters of an hour in a slow oven. Or, stew the pie-plant, sweeten, add grated rind and juice of a lemon and yolks of two eggs, and bake and frost like lemon pie.—*Mrs. D. Buxton.*

DRIED-PEACH PIE.

Stew peaches until perfectly soft, mash fine, and add, for two pies, half tea-cup sweet cream, and one tea-cup sugar; bake with two crusts. Or, omit cream, and add half tea-cup boiling water, and butter size of a hickory-nut.

POTATO PIE.

A common-sized tea-cup of grated raw potato, a quart sweet milk; let milk boil and stir in grated potato; when cool add two or three eggs well beaten, sugar and nutmeg to taste; bake without upper crust; eat the day it is baked. This recipe is for two pies.—*Miss Sarah Thompson, Delaware.*

POTATO PIE.

Boil either Irish or sweet potatoes until well done, mash and rub through a sieve; to a pint of pulp, add three pints sweet milk, table-spoon melted butter, tea-cup sugar, three eggs, pinch of salt, and nutmeg or lemon to flavor. Use rich paste for under crust.—*Mrs. R. C. Carson, Harrisburg.*

PUMPKIN PIE.

Stew pumpkin cut into small pieces, in a half pint water; and, when soft, mash with potato-masher very fine, let the water dry away, watching closely to prevent burning or scorching; for each pie take one egg, half cup sugar, two table-spoons pumpkin, half pint rich milk (a little cream will improve it), a little salt; stir well together, and season with cinnamon or nutmeg; bake with under crust in a hot oven.—*Mrs. A. B. Morey.*

DELICIOUS PUMPKIN PIE.

Cut a pumpkin into thin slices, and boil until tender in as little water as possible, watching carefully that it does not scorch; set the stew-kettle on top of stove, mash the pumpkin fine, heaping it against the sides of the kettle so that the water may drain from it and dry away; repeat this process until the water has all evaporated, and the pumpkin is quite dry. This will require from half an hour to an hour. Mash and rub through a sieve, adding, while warm, a good-sized lump of butter; to every quart of pumpkin, after it is mashed, add two quarts of milk and six eggs, the yolks and whites beaten separately, sugar to taste, one tea-spoon salt, table-spoon ground cinnamon, one grated nutmeg, tea-spoon ginger; bake in a hot oven until well set and a nice brown. It is as well to heat the batter scalding-hot, stirring constantly until it is poured into the pie-dishes.—*Mrs. Gov. Irwin, California.*

PINE-APPLE PIE.

A cup sugar, a half cup butter, one of sweet cream, five eggs, one pine-apple grated; beat butter and sugar to a cream, add beaten yolks of eggs, then the pine-apple and cream, and, lastly, the beaten whites whipped in lightly. Bake with under crust only.—*Mrs. Wm. Smith, Jacksonville, Florida.*

PRESERVE PUFFS.

Roll out puff-paste very thin, cut into round pieces, and lay jam on each, fold over the paste, wet edges with white of an egg, and close them; lay them on a baking sheet, ice them, and bake about fifteen minutes.—*Mrs. H. A. E.*

PLUM COBBLER.

Take one quart of flour, four table-spoons melted lard, half tea-spoon salt, two tea-spoons baking-powder; mix as for biscuit, with either sweet milk or water, roll thin, and line a pudding-dish or dripping-pan, nine by eighteen inches; mix three table-spoons flour and two of sugar together, and sprinkle over the crust; then pour in three pints canned damson plums, and sprinkle over them one coffee-cup sugar; wet the edges with a little flour and water mixed, put on upper crust, press the edges together, make two openings by cutting two incisions at right angles an inch in length, and bake in a quick oven half an hour. Peaches, apples, or any kind of fresh or canned fruit, can be made in the same way.—*Miss S. Alice Melching.*

SOUTHERN TOMATO PIE.

Stew sliced green tomatoes (not peeled) in a small quantity of water; for one pie, add one table-spoon butter, two of sugar, and flavor with nutmeg; bake with two crusts.

Vinegar Pie.

One egg, one heaping table-spoon flour, one tea-cup sugar; beat all well together and add one table-spoon sharp vinegar, and one tea-cup cold water; flavor with nutmeg and bake with two crusts.— *Mrs. B. A. Fay.*

Bina's Strawberry Shortcake.

Two heaping tea-spoons baking-powder sifted into one quart flour, scant half tea-cup butter, two table-spoons sugar, a little salt, enough sweet milk (or water) to make a soft dough; roll out almost as thin as pie-crust, place one layer in a baking-pan, and spread with a very little butter, upon which sprinkle some flour, then add another layer of crust and spread as before, and so on until crust is all used. This makes four layers in a pan fourteen inches by seven. Bake about fifteen minutes in a quick oven, turn out upside down, take off the top layer (the bottom when baking), place on a dish, spread plentifully with strawberries (not mashed) previously sweetened with pulverized sugar, place layer upon layer, treating each one in the same way, and when done you will have a handsome cake, to be served warm with sugar and cream. The secret of having light dough is to handle it as little and mix it as quickly as possible. Shortcake is delicious served with charlotte-russe or whipped cream. Raspberry and peach shortcakes may be made in the same way.

Orange Shortcake.

One quart flour, two table-spoons butter, two tea-spoons baking-powder thoroughly mixed with the flour; mix (not very stiff) with cold water, work as little as possible, bake, split open, and lay sliced oranges between; cut in squares and serve with pudding sauce.—*Mrs. Canby, Bellefontaine.*

Apple Tarts.

Pare, quarter, core, and boil in a half tea-cup of water until very soft, ten large tart apples; beat till *very* smooth, then add the yolks of six eggs or three whole eggs, juice and grated rind of two lemons, half cup butter, one and a half cups sugar, or more if not sweet enough; beat all thoroughly, line little tart-tins with puff-paste, and fill with the mixture, bake five minutes in a hot oven.

13

If wanted very nice, take the whites of the six eggs (when the yolks of six are used), mix with six table-spoons pulverized sugar, spread on the top of the tarts, return to oven and brown slightly. *Mrs. L. J. T., Memphis.*

ALMOND TARTS.

Beat to a cream the yolks of three eggs and quarter of a pound of sugar, add half a pound of shelled almonds pounded slightly, put in tart-tins lined with puff-paste, bake eight minutes; take the whites mixed with three table-spoons powdered sugar, spread on top of tarts, return to oven and brown delicately.—*Mrs. Davis, Montreal.*

COCOA-NUT TARTS.

Dissolve half pound sugar in quarter of a pint water, add half a grated cocoa-nut, let this boil slowly for a few minutes, and when cold, add the well-beaten yolks of three eggs, and the white of one; beat all well together, and pour into patty-pans lined with a rich crust; bake a few minutes, cover with the whites of the two eggs mixed with two table-spoons sugar, and put in oven till a delicate brown.—*Mrs. Johnson, San Francisco.*

CREAM TARTS.

Mix a pound flour, a salt-spoon salt, a quarter pound each sugar and butter, one egg, and half tea-spoon soda or baking-powder dissolved in a spoonful of water; wet up with cold water, and line small patty-pans; bake in a quick oven, fill with mock cream, as in recipe for Boston Cream Cakes, sprinkle over with sugar, and brown in oven. Or, fill shells with jelly and cover with a meringue (table-spoon sugar to white of one egg), and brown in oven.

TART SHELLS.

Roll out thin a nice puff-paste, cut out with a glass or biscuit cutter, with a wine-glass or smaller cup cut out the center of two out of three of these, lay the rings thus made on the third, and bake immediately. If the paste is light the shells will be fine and may be used for tarts or oyster patties.

PUDDINGS AND SAUCES.

In making puddings always beat the eggs separately, straining the yolks and adding the whites the last thing. If boiled milk is used, let it cool somewhat before adding the eggs; when fruit is added, stir it in at the last. Raisins are better to lie in hot water for one or two minutes until they are plumped. Puddings are either baked, boiled or steamed; rice, bread, custard, and fruit puddings require a moderate heat; batter and corn starch, a rather quick oven. Always bake them as soon as mixed.

For boiled puddings, use either a tin mold, muslin bag, or bowl with cloth tied over it; grease the former well on the inside with lard or butter, and in boiling do not let the water reach quite to the top. If a bag is used, make it of firm drilling, tapering from top to bottom, and rounded on the corners; stitch and fell the seams, which should be outside when in use, and sew a tape to the seam about three inches from top. Wring the bag out of hot water, flour the inside well, pour in the pudding, tie securely leaving room to swell (especially when made of Indian meal, bread, rice, or crackers), and place in a kettle with a saucer at the bottom to prevent burning; pour in enough boiling water to entirely cover the bag, which must be turned several times, keep it boiling constantly, filling up from the tea-kettle when needed. If the pudding is boiled in a bowl, grease, fill, and cover with a square of drilling wrung out of hot water, floured and tied on. To use a pan, tie a cloth tightly over the rim, bringing the ends back together, and pinning them over the top of the pan; the pudding may then be lifted out easily by a strong fork put through the ends or corners of the cloth. For plum puddings, invert the pan when put in the kettle,

(195)

and the pudding will not become water-soaked. When the pudding is done, give whatever it is boiled in, a quick plunge into cold water, and turn out at once, serving immediately. As a general rule, boiled puddings require double the time required for baked. Steaming is safer than either boiling or baking, as the pudding is sure to be light and wholesome. In making sauces, do not boil after the butter is added. In place of wine or brandy, flavor with juice of the grape, or any other fruit prepared for this purpose in its season by boiling and bottling and sealing while hot. Pudding cloths, however coarse, should never be washed with soap, but in clear, clean water, dried as quickly as possible, and kept dry and out of dust in a drawer or cupboard free from smell. Dates are an excellent substitute for sugar in Graham or any other pudding.

APPLE ROLEY POLEY.

Peel, quarter and core sour apples, make rich soda-biscuit dough, (or raised-biscuit dough may be used if rolled thinner), roll to half an inch thick, slice the quarters, and lay on the prepared paste or crust, roll up, tuck ends in, prick deeply with a fork, lay in a steamer and place over a kettle of boiling water, cook an hour and three-quarters. Or, wrap in a cloth, tie up the ends and baste up sides, put in kettle of boiling water, and boil an hour and a half or more, keeping the water boiling constantly. Cut across, and eat with sweetened cream or butter and sugar. Cherries, dried fruit, any kind of berries, jelly, or apple-butter (with the two last raisins may be added), can be used.—*Mrs. T. B. J.*

BOILED APPLE DUMPLINGS.

Add to two cups sour milk one tea-spoon soda, and one of salt, half cup lard, flour enough to make dough a little stiffer than for biscuit; peel, halve and core apples, put two halves with a little sugar in the cavity in each dumpling (it is nice to tie a cloth around each one), put into kettle of boiling water slightly salted, boil half an hour, taking care that the water covers the dumplings. They are also very nice steamed. To bake, make in same way, using a soft dough, place in a shallow pan, bake in a hot oven, and serve with cream and sugar. Fresh or canned peaches may be made in the same way.—*Mrs. G. E. Kinney.*

Rolled Apple-Dumplings.

Peel and chop fine tart apples, make a crust of one cup rich buttermilk, one tea-spoon soda, and flour enough to roll; roll half an inch thick, spread with the apple, sprinkle well with sugar and cinnamon, cut in strips two inches wide, roll up like jelly-cake, set up the rolls in a dripping-pan, putting a tea-spoon butter on each, put in a moderate oven, and baste them often with the juice.

Bird's-nest Pudding.

Pare and core without quartering enough quick-cooking tart apples to fill a pudding-pan; make a custard of one quart milk and the yolks of six eggs; sweeten, spice, pour over apples, and bake; when done, use the whites of eggs beaten stiff with six table-spoons white sugar; spread the custard on, brown lightly, and serve either hot or cold.

Brown Betty.

Put a layer of sweetened apple sauce in a buttered dish, add a few lumps butter, then a layer of cracker crumbs sprinkled with a little cinnamon, then layer of sauce, etc., making the last layer of crumbs; bake in oven, and eat hot with cold, sweetened cream.—*Mrs. T. J. Buxton, Minneapolis.*

Rice Apples.

Boil half a pound rice in custard-kettle till tender in one quart milk, sweetened with half tea-cup sugar; pare and core with apple-corer seven or eight good-cooking apples, place in slightly buttered baking-dish, put a tea-spoon of jam or jelly into each cavity, and fill with rich cream; put the rice in around apples, leaving top uncovered; bake thirty minutes, then cover with the whites of two eggs, sift on sugar, and return to the oven for ten minutes. Serve with sweetened cream.—*Mrs. S. M. Guy, Mechanicsburg.*

Bread Pudding.

One quart sweet milk, quart bread-crumbs, four eggs, four table-spoons sugar; soak bread in half the milk until soft; mash fine, add the rest of milk, the well-beaten eggs and sugar, and a tea-cup raisins; bake one hour, serve warm with warm sauce.—*Mrs. French Reynolds, Allegheny City, Pa.*

BLACK PUDDING.

Half pint molasses, fourth cup butter, fourth cup sugar, one and a half cups flour, fourth cup sweet milk, three eggs, half tea-spoon ground cloves, half tea-spoon soda, half tea-spoon cinnamon ; steam one hour in a buttered pan. Avoid lifting the lid of the steamer while cooking, as it will render the pudding heavy. Serve with a sauce made of two-thirds cup butter, third cup sugar, and half cup boiling water ; thicken with tea-spoon flour stirred in a little cold water until smooth ; let boil two or three minutes, stirring all the time, and flavor to taste with vinegar, rose-water, or nutmeg.—*Miss Ida Nörton, Delaware.*

BLACKBERRY MUSH.

To two quarts ripe berries add one and a half pints boiling water, and one pound sugar; cook a few moments, then stir in a pint of wheat flour, boil a few moments longer, put in greased mold to cool, and serve with cream or hard sauce.—*Miss H. D. Martin, New York City.*

CORN-STARCH PUDDING.

One pint sweet milk, whites of three eggs, two table-spoons corn starch, three of sugar, and a little salt. Put the milk in a pan or small bucket set in a kettle of hot water on the stove, and when it reaches the boiling point add the sugar, then the starch dissolved in a little cold milk, and lastly the whites of eggs whipped to a stiff froth; beat it, and let cook a few minutes, then pour into tea-cups, filling about half full, and set in cool place. For sauce, make a boiled custard as follows: Bring to boiling point one pint of milk, add three table-spoons sugar, then the beaten yolks thinned by adding one table-spoon milk, stirring all the time till it thickens; flavor with two tea-spoons lemon or two of vanilla, and set to cool. In serving, put one of the molds in a sauce-dish for each person, and pour over it some of the boiled custard. Or the pudding may be made in one large mold.

To make a chocolate pudding, flavor the above pudding with vanilla, remove two-thirds of it, and add half a cake of chocolate softened, mashed, and dissolved in a little milk. Put a layer of half the white pudding into the mold, then the chocolate, then the rest of the white; or two layers of chocolate may be used with a white between; or the center may be cocoa (made by adding half a cocoa-nut grated fine), and the outside chocolate; or pine-apple chopped fine (if first cooked in a little water, the latter makes a nice dressing), or strawberries, may be used.—*Mrs. D. Buxton.*

CREAM PUDDING.

Stir together a half pint of cream, an ounce and a half sugar, the yolks of three eggs, and a little grated nutmeg; add the well-beaten whites, stirring lightly, and pour into a buttered pie-plate on which has been sprinkled the crumbs of stale bread to about the thickness of an ordinary crust; sprinkle over the top a layer of bread-crumbs and bake.

COTTAGE PUDDING.

One cup sugar, half cup butter, one egg, cup sweet milk, tea-spoon soda dissolved in the milk, two tea-spoons cream tartar in the flour, three cups flour, half tea-spoon extract of lemon. Sprinkle a little sugar over the top just before putting in the oven, bake in a small bread-pan, and when done cut in squares, and serve with sauce made of two table-spoons butter, cup sugar, table-spoon flour wet with a little cold water and stirred until like cream; add a pint boiling water, let boil two or three minutes, stirring all the time. After taking from the fire, add half tea-spoon extract of lemon. Nutmeg may be used in place of lemon. What is left of the pudding and sauce may be served cold for tea.—*Mrs. Howard Vosbury.*

CHOCOLATE PUDDING.

One quart sweet milk, three ounces grated chocolate, one cup sugar, yolks of five eggs; scald milk and chocolate together, and when cool add sugar and eggs, and bake. When done, put beaten whites and five table-spoons sugar on top, and set in oven to brown. Or boil one pint milk, add half cup butter, one of sugar, and three ounces grated chocolate; pour this over two slices of bread soaked in water; when cool, add the well-beaten yolks of four eggs, bake, and when done, spread over the whites beaten with sugar, and brown in oven. Serve hot or cold.—*Miss Greeley Grubbs, Richmond, Indiana.*

COCOA-NUT PUDDING.

Grate one cocoa-nut, saving the milk if perfectly sweet, boil a quart of milk, and pour upon it, adding five eggs beaten with one cup of sugar and one table-spoon butter, add a little salt, two tea-spoons vanilla extract, and milk from nut, and bake in a pudding-dish lined with rich paste. This is excellent baked like pie with under crust only.—*Mrs. T. B. Johnson, Lagrange, Tenn.*

ENGLISH CARROT PUDDING.

One pound grated carrots, three-fourths pound chopped suet, half pound each raisins and currants, four table-spoons sugar, eight table-spoons flour, and spices to suit the taste. Boil four hours, place in the oven for twenty minutes, and serve with wine-sauce.—*Mrs. E. A. W., Washington, D. C.*

DELMONICO PUDDING.

A quart milk, three table-spoons corn starch dissolved in cold milk, the yolks of five eggs beaten well, six table-spoons sugar. Boil three or four minutes, pour into a pudding-dish and bake about half an hour; beat whites of eggs with six table-spoons sugar, put over top, and return pudding to oven until it is a delicate brown.—*Mrs. J. Holland, New Castle, Ind.*

ESTELLE PUDDING.

Three eggs well beaten, two and a half table-spoons sugar, two of butter, three-fourths cup sweet milk, one of raisins chopped fine, one table-spoon baking-powder, flour to make it the consistency of cake batter; steam thirty-five minutes, and serve with cream-sauce. —*Mrs. Andrew Wilson, Rye, N. Y.*

FANNIE'S PUDDING.

One quart sweet milk, a little salt, two table-spoons corn starch dissolved in part of the milk, yolks of four eggs, half a cup sugar; scald milk, add starch and sugar, and then the beaten yolks; flavor to taste, pour in dish, cover with whites beaten, with four table-spoons sugar, and brown in oven.—*Mrs. W. E. Davidson, Boston.*

FRUIT PUDDING.

One cup molasses, one of sweet milk, one of suet chopped fine, or half a cup melted butter, one of raisins, half cup currants, two and a half cups flour, half tea-spoon soda; mix well, salt and spice to taste, and steam two hours.—*Mrs. S. W. Case, Minneapolis, Minn.*

SIMPLE FRUIT PUDDINGS.

Stew currants, or any small fruits, fresh or dried, with sugar to taste, and pour hot over thin slices of baker's-bread with crust cut off, making alternate layers of fruit and bread, and leaving a thick layer of fruit for the last. Put a plate on top, and when cool set on ice; serve with sifted sugar, or cream and sugar.

This pudding is delicious made with Boston or milk crackers, split open and stewed apricots or peaches, with plenty of juice, arranged as above. Or another way is to toast and butter slices of bread, pour over it hot stewed fruit in alternate layers, and serve warm with rich hot sauce.—*Mrs. L. S. W.*

FIG PUDDING.

Half pound figs, quarter pound grated bread, two and a half ounces powdered sugar, three ounces butter, two eggs, one tea-cup milk; chop figs fine and mix with butter, and by degrees add the other ingredients; butter and sprinkle a mold with bread-crumbs, pour in pudding, cover closely, and boil for three hours.—*Florence Woods Hush.*

HALF-HOUR PUDDING.

Beat four table-spoons butter to a cream with half a pint powdered sugar; add the yolks of three eggs, beating them in thoroughly, then a rounded half pint of corn meal, and the whites of the eggs beaten to a stiff froth. Mix well and bake in a pudding-dish, well buttered. Serve hot with sauce.

BOILED INDIAN PUDDING.

Warm a pint of molasses and pint of milk, stir well togther, beat four eggs and stir gradually into molasses and milk, add a pound of beef suet chopped fine, and Indian meal sufficient to make a thick batter; add a tea-spoon pulverized cinnamon, nutmeg and a little grated lemon-peel, and stir all together thoroughly; dip cloth into boiling water, shake, flour a little, turn in the mixture, tie up leaving room for the pudding to swell, and boil three hours; serve hot with sauce made of drawn butter, wine, and nutmeg.—*Mrs. A. E. Brand, Minneapolis, Minn.*

PLAIN BOILED INDIAN PUDDING.

Scald one and a half pints Indian meal with half pint boiling water; add four table-spoons Graham flour, one pint milk (either sweet or sour), two table-spoons molasses, half tea-spoon ginger, a little salt and one level tea-spoon soda, (or a little more if sour milk is used); two table-spoons chopped suet will make it more light and tender, but may be omitted. Put into a well-greased pudding-boiler (two-quart), leaving room to swell, and boil three or four hours in a kettle of water. Or it may be tied in a pudding-cloth, leaving room to swell; or steamed in a small tin pail for same length of time.—*Mrs. L. S. W.*

BAKED INDIAN PUDDING.

A quart sweet milk, an ounce butter, four well-beaten eggs, tea-cup corn meal, half pound raisins, fourth pound sugar; sca... milk and stir in meal while boiling; let stand until blood warm, stir all well together; bake one and a half hours, and serve with sauce.—*Mrs. Carrier.*

PLAIN BAKED INDIAN PUDDING.

Scald two quarts sweet milk, into which stir ten rounded table-spoons Indian meal, seven table-spoons molasses, one tea-spoon ginger, and a little salt. Put in moderate oven to bake, and in half an hour stir in half cup of cold milk; bake in a very slow oven four hours, and a longer time will not injure it. Serve with cream or hot sauce.

KISS PUDDING.

Boil one quart sweet milk in custard-kettle, stir into it four heaping table-spoons sugar and four table-spoons corn starch, dissolved in a little cold water or milk, and added to the well-beaten and strained yolks of four eggs. Have the whites of eggs beaten to a stiff froth with tea-cup pulverized sugar and one tea-spoon essence of vanilla, spread on top of pudding, set in a quick oven, and brown; take out, sprinkle with grated cocoa-nut, and set dish away in a cool place; serve cold after three or four hours. The sweet liquor which settles to the bottom in cooling, serves as a sauce.—*Mrs. W. E. Baxter.*

LEMON PUDDING.

Stir into yolks of six eggs one cup sugar, half a cup water, and the grated yellow rind and juice of two lemons; soften in warm water six crackers or some slices of cake, lay in bottom of a baking-dish, pour custard over them, bake till firm; beat whites of eggs to a froth, add six table-spoons sugar and beat well; when custard is done, pour frosting over it, return to the oven and brown. Eat either warm or cold.—*Mrs. Walter Mitchell, Gallipolis.*

DELICIOUS LEMON PUDDING.

The juice and grated rind of one lemon, cup sugar, yolks of two eggs, three table-spoons flour, and milk enough to fill the dish; line dish with paste, pour in custard, and bake till done; beat whites of two eggs, add four table-spoons sugar, spread on top, and brown.—*Mrs. M. J. Woods, Greensburg, Pa.*

MARCH PUDDING.

One cup dried apples, cup molasses, one and one-fourth cups flour, fourth cup butter, one egg, one tea-spoon each of soda and cinnamon, half tea-spoon cloves; wash and soak apples over night, cut fine and mix with water in which they were soaked, add molasses and spice; mix egg, butter and flour together; stir soda with apples and molasses; add and bake immediately; serve hot with sauce made of half cup butter and one cup sugar, beaten smooth and flavored with nutmeg, lemon or vanilla.—*Miss Lizzie March.*

MINUTE PUDDING.

Take sweet milk, or half water and milk, a pinch of salt, let boil, stir in wheat flour, as in making corn-meal mush, until of same thickness as mush; remove from fire, and serve at once with sweetened cream flavored with nutmeg. Some think it improved by adding blackberries, raspberries or cherries, either canned or fresh, just after taking from stove.—*Yankee Girl.*

MOLASSES PUDDING.

Three cups of flour, one each of molasses, melted butter, and hot water; one tea-spoon soda; steam three hours; serve with a sauce of butter and sugar worked to a cream, with hot water added to make it the proper consistency, and flavored with vanilla.—*Mrs. Jenks, Bellefontaine.*

ONE-TWO-THREE-FOUR PUDDING.

One cup butter, two of sugar, three of flour, four eggs (beaten separately), one cup sweet milk, and two tea-spoons baking-powder;

flavor with nutmeg and bake in pudding or cake mold; leave in mold till next day, when steam for three-quarters of an hour over a kettle of boiling water and serve with hot sauce.—*Mrs. C. A. Malin.*

CHRISTMAS PLUM PUDDING.

One quart seeded raisins, pint currants, half pint citron cut up, quart of apples peeled and chopped, a quart of fresh and nicely chopped beef-suet, a heaping quart of stale bread-crumbs, eight eggs beaten separately, pint sugar, grated nutmeg, tea-spoon salt; flour fruit thoroughly from a quart of flour, then mix remainder as follows: In a large bowl or tray put the eggs with sugar, nutmeg and milk, stir in the fruit, bread-crumbs and suet, one after the other until all are used, adding enough flour to make the fruit stick together, which will take about all the quart; dip pudding-cloth in boiling water, dredge on inside a thick coating of flour, put in pudding and tie tightly, allowing room to swell, and boil from two to three hours in a good-sized pot with plenty of hot water, replenishing as needed from tea-kettle. When done, turn in a large flat dish and send to table with a sprig of holly, or any bit of evergreen with bright berries, stuck in the top. Serve with any pudding-sauce. This recipe furnishes enough for twenty people, but if the family is small, one-half the quantity may be prepared, or it is equally good warmed over by steaming. For sauce, cream a half pound sweet butter, stir in three-quarters pound brown sugar, and the beaten yolk of an egg; simmer for a few moments over a slow fire, stirring almost constantly; when near boiling add a half pint bottled grape-juice, and serve after grating a little nutmeg on the surface.—*Mrs. Gov. Coke, Texas.*

ENGLISH PLUM PUDDING.

Beat six yolks and four whites of eggs very light, and add to them a tumbler of sweet milk; stir in gradually one-fourth pound grated or chopped stale bread, a pound flour, three-quarters pound sugar, and a pound each of beef-suet chopped very fine, currants nicely washed and dried, and stoned raisins, well floured; stir well, then add two nutmegs, a table-spoon mace, one of cinnamon or cloves, a wine-glass brandy, a tea-spoon salt, and finally another tumbler of milk. Boil in bowls or molds five hours, and serve with sauce

made of drawn butter, wine, sugar, and nutmeg. These will keep
for months; when wanted, boil one hour before using. A pound of
citron or blanched sweet almonds adds to the richness of the pudding, but may be omitted.—*Mrs. Collier, Bellefontaine.*

Eggless Plum Pudding.

Heaping cup bread-crumbs, two cups flour, one of suet chopped
fine, one of raisins, one of molasses, one of sweet milk, table-spoon
soda, tea-spoon salt, one of cloves, and one of cinnamon; boil two
and a half hours in a two-quart pail, set in a kettle of boiling water,
or steam for the same time. For sauce take one cup white sugar,
butter size of an egg, grated rind of one lemon, and white of an
egg.—*Mrs. Mary Lee Gere.*

Half-batch Plum Pudding.

Three eggs, half pound each of flour and sugar, fourth pound
bread-crumbs soaked in one pint milk, half table-spoon each mace,
cloves and cinnamon, half gill molasses, half gill of wine or brandy,
half pound each of raisins and currants, and fourth pound citron
well floured. Bake or steam.—*Mrs. E. L. Hanford, Harlem, N. Y.*

Iced Plum Pudding.

Take two dozen sweet and half a dozen bitter almonds; blanch
in scalding water, throw into a bowl of cold water; pound one at
a time in a mortar, till they become a smooth paste free from the
smallest lumps; add frequently a few drops of rose-water or lemon
juice to make them light and prevent "oiling." Seed and cut a
quarter pound of the best bloom raisins; mix with them a quarter
pound of Zante currants, picked, washed and dried, and three
ounces of chopped citron; dredge well with flour. Take a half
pint of very rich milk, split a vanilla bean, cut it into pieces two
or three inches long, and boil it in the milk till the flavor of the
vanilla is well extracted, then strain it out and mix the vanilla
milk with a pint of rich cream, and stir in gradually a half pound
of powdered loaf-sugar and a nutmeg grated. Then add the
pounded almonds, and a large wine-glass of either maraschino,
noyau, curacoa or the very best brandy. Beat in a shallow pan
the yolks of eight eggs till very light, thick and smooth, and stir

them gradually into the mixture. Simmer over the fire (stirring all the time), but take off just before it boils, otherwise it will curdle. At once stir in the fruit, set to cool, and then add a large tea-cup preserved strawberries or raspberries, half a dozen preserved apricots or peaches, half a dozen preserved green limes, and any other very nice and delicate sweatmeats; add a pint whipped cream lightly to the mixture; put the whole into a large melon-mold that opens in the middle, and freeze four hours in the usual way. Turn out when wanted and serve on a glass dish.— *Mrs. Gov. Grover, Oregon.*

PRAIRIE PLUM PUDDING.

Stew together a tea-cup raisins and half tea-cup citron; prepare dish with butter, put in a layer of sponge-cake (any kind of cake will do, or Boston crackers, sliced and buttered may be used, or even stale Graham bread-crumbs), then a layer of fruit, and so on, with cake or bread for last layer; pour over it custard made of a quart of milk and yolks of four eggs, sweetened to taste; bake until on inserting a knife the milk has become water. Make a frosting of the whites of four eggs and four table-spoons pulverized sugar, spread on pudding, brown in oven, and serve with sauce made of one tea-cup white sugar, two-thirds pint water, one table-spoon butter, one tea-spoon corn starch mixed smoothly with a little cold milk; let sugar and water boil, add the rest and allow to boil a few moments, then add the white of one well-beaten egg with one tea-spoon vanilla essence.—*Mrs. M. E. Godard.*

PLUM PUDDING.

Beat together half cup sugar, two eggs and one tea-spoon butter, add three pints sweet milk, a little salt, six crackers rolled fine, one cup raisins, and half sheet gelatine dissolved in a little water; season with nutmeg or cinnamon. Bake in a pudding-dish.— *Mrs. Dr. Stall, Union City.*

POOR MAN'S PUDDING.

A quart of milk, half tea-cup rice, salt to taste, and one tea-cup sugar; place in the oven while cold, stirring occasionally while the rice is swelling. It is better to bake quite slowly about two hours.

It should be cream-like when done. To vary this, a small cup raisins and a tea-spoon lemon or vanilla may be added.—*Mrs. Louise Lincoln, New Rutland, Ill.*

PINE-APPLE PUDDING.

Butter a pudding-dish, and line the bottom and sides with slices of stale cake (sponge-cake is best), pare and slice thin a large pine-apple, place in the dish first a layer of pine-apple, then strew with sugar, then more pine-apple, and so on until all is used, pour over a small tea-cup water, and cover with slices of cake which have been dipped in cold water; cover the whole with a buttered plate, and bake slowly for two hours.—*Mrs. Wm. Smith, Jacksonville, Fla.*

POTATO PUDDING.

Boil six good mealy potatoes, mash very fine, beat well with the yolks of five eggs, half pound white sugar, quarter pound butter; beat whites of eggs to stiff froth, add the grated rind and juice of one lemon, stir well, and add a little salt and a pint of good milk or cream; bake an hour and a half; reserve some of the whites of eggs, mix with sugar and ice the top.—*Mrs. Gov. Ingersoll, Conn.*

PRUNE PUDDING.

Scald one pound French prunes, let them swell in the hot water till soft, drain and extract the stones, spread on a dish and dredge with flour; take a gill milk from a quart, stir into it gradually eight table-spoons sifted flour; beat six eggs very light and stir by degrees into the remainder of quart of milk, alternating with the batter; add prunes, one at a time, stir the whole very hard, boil two hours, and serve with wine-sauce or cream.—*Mrs. Emma L. Fay.*

PUFF PUDDING.

One and one-half cups flour, one of milk, two eggs, and a little salt; bake in hot oven twenty minutes in patty-pans, serve with sauce.—*Mrs. L. N. Fuller.*

QUICK PUFF PUDDING.

Stir one pint flour, two tea-spoons baking-powder, and a little salt into milk until very soft; place in steamer well-greased cups, put in each a spoonful of batter, then one of berries, steamed apples, or any sauce convenient, cover with another spoonful of batter and steam twenty minutes. This pudding is delicious made with fresh strawberries, and eaten with a sauce made of two eggs, half cup butter and cup of sugar, beaten thoroughly with a cup boiling milk and one of strawberries.—*Mrs. B. T. Skinner, Battle Creek, Michigan.*

QUEEN OF PUDDINGS.

One pint fine sifted bread-crumbs, one quart milk, one cup sugar, yolks of four eggs, a piece of butter the size of an egg, (some add grated rind of lemon); bake until done—but do not allow to become watery—and spread with a layer of jelly. Whip whites of eggs to a stiff froth with five table-spoons sugar, and juice of one lemon, spread on the top and brown. Good with or without sauce, and very good cold. Make a hard sauce for it as follows: One cup very light brown sugar, half cup butter, half grated rind and the juice of one lemon; beat until very light. Vanilla may be used instead of the lemon.

Or, for cocoa-nut pudding, soak half cup dessicated cocoa-nut in boiling hot milk for half an hour or more, and add to the pudding, baking and finishing as above; or for orange pudding add a half dozen grated oranges.—*Mrs. Prof. R. P. Kidder, Cape Girardeau, Mo.*

RICE PUDDING.

To a cup of rice boiled in a custard-kettle in a pint of water (seasoned well with salt) until dry, add a pint of milk in which a little corn starch has been dissolved, and boil again; add the yolks of two eggs beaten with half a cup of sugar, stir well together, and lastly add the juice and grated rind of one lemon. Place in a dish, and bake slowly in the oven ; when done, spread over the top the whites beaten with two table-spoons sugar, and brown in oven. A cup of raisins may be added just before baking. Or, after boiling the rice with the milk, eggs, and sugar, add a lump of butter and place a layer of the rice, about an inch thick, in a buttered dish sprinkled with bread-crumbs, then a layer of peaches (either fresh or canned), repeating until dish is full, leaving rice for the last layer; bake slowly for half an hour, and when done, cover with the beaten whites, as above. Or, after preparing the rice as above, add pine-apple, chopped fine, or oranges, or dried cherries; mix thoroughly, and bake and finish as above.—*Mrs. J. R. W., Madison, Wisconsin.*

RICE SNOW BALLS.

Boil one pint rice until soft in two quarts water with a tea-spoon salt; put in small cups, and when perfectly cold place in a dish. Make a boiled custard of the yolks of three eggs, one pint sweet milk, and one tea-spoon corn starch; flavor with lemon. When cold, pour over the rice-balls half an hour before serving. This is a very simple but nice dessert.—*Miss Louise Skinner.*

SAGO AND APPLE PUDDING.

Pare six apples and punch out the cores, fill holes with cinnamon and sugar, using two tea-spoons cinnamon to a cup of sugar; take one table-spoon sago to each apple, wash thoroughly and let soak an hour in water enough to cover the apples, pour water and sago over the apples, and bake an hour and a half.

APPLE TAPIOCA PUDDING.

Pare and core tart apples, fill openings with butter and sugar, put into a pan a heaping tea-spoon each of dry tapioca and sugar to each apple, put in apples, sprinkle ground cinnamon over them, fill the pan nearly full of water, and bake.—*Mrs. Mary Lee Gere.*

WHORTLEBERRY PUDDING.

One quart berries, pint molasses, cup milk, teaspoon soda, one pound and two ounces flour, one tea-spoon cloves, one of cinnamon, and one nutmeg; boil two and a half hours.—*Mrs. Emma Fay.*

GRANDMA THOMPSON'S WHITE PUDDING.

Weigh equal quantities of best beef suet and sifted flour, shave down suet and rub into fine particles with the hands, removing all tough and stringy parts, mix well with the flour, season very highly with pepper, salt to taste, stuff loosely in beef-skins (entrails cleansed like pork-skins for sausage), half a yard or less in length, secure the ends, prick every two or three inches with a darning-needle, place to boil in a kettle of cold water hung on the crane; boil three hours, place on table until cold, after which hang up in a cool place to dry; tie up in a clean cotton bag, and put away where it will be

14

both dry and cool. When wanted for use, cut off the quantity needed, boil in hot water until heated through, take out and place before the fire to dry off and "crisp." The above was considered an "extra dish" at all the "flax scutchings," "quilting frolics," and "log rollings" of a hundred years ago.

The same by measure is as follows: One pint best beef suet to two pints flour; mix thoroughly, season very highly with pepper and salt, sew up little sacks of cotton cloth half a yard long and three inches wide, fill nearly full, put to boil in hot water, boil from four to six hours; when done, take out, drain, let cool, hang in a dry, cool place, and when wanted for table, cut off as much as needed, put on hot water, boil until cooked through, take out, peel off cloth, put in a pie-pan, set in oven to dry and brown.—*Mrs. E. T. Carson, Mt. Pleasant Farm.*

SAUCES.

BUTTERLESS SAUCE.

One egg beaten separately, and white added just before serving, quarter cup sugar, and a pinch salt; flavor with vanilla.

COCOA-NUT SAUCE.

Two table-spoons butter, cup of sugar, table-spoon of flour, milk of one cocoa-nut, with a small piece grated.

CREAM SAUCE.

One tea-cup powdered white sugar, scant half tea-cup butter, half tea-cup rich cream; beat butter and sugar thoroughly, add cream, stir the whole into half tea-cup boiling water, place on stove for a few moments stirring it constantly, take off and add flavoring.

COLD CREAM SAUCE.

Beat together one cup sugar and half cup butter, and add a cup rich cream. Stir all to a cream, flavor with vanilla or lemon, and place where it will get very cold before serving.—*Mrs. A. Wilson.*

PLAIN CREAM SAUCE.

One pint cream, three ounces brown sugar, and half a small nutmeg grated.

EVERY-DAY SAUCE.

To one pint boiling water, add heaping tea-cup sugar, table-spoon butter (see general directions), pinch of salt, and table-spoon corn starch dissolved in cold water; season with nutmeg or vanilla, boil half an hour, and if good and well cooked it will be very clear. Or to a table-spoon of currant jelly, add a table-spoon of hot water; beat well and add to the above just before serving, omitting all other flavoring. Or add a tea-spoon of raspberry syrup.

LEMON SAUCE.

Two cups sugar, two eggs, juice of two lemons, and rind if you choose; beat all together, and just before serving add pint boiling water; set on stove and let boil at once. Some add one-third cup butter and table-spoon corn starch.

MAPLE SUGAR SAUCE.

Melt over a slow fire, in a small tea-cup of water, half a pint maple sugar; let it simmer, removing all scum; add four table-spoons butter mixed with a level tea-spoon flour, and one of grated nutmeg; boil for a few moments, and serve with boiled puddings. —*Mrs. Field, Brooklyn.*

ORANGE HARD SAUCE.

Select a thin orange, cut the skin into six equal parts, by cutting through the skin at the stem end and passing the knife around the orange to nearly the blossom end; loosen and turn each piece down and remove the orange. Extract juice and mix it with yellow sugar (prepared by dropping a drop or two of "gold coloring" on white sugar while stirring it) till a ball can be formed, which place inside the orange-peel and serve. The "gold coloring" may be omitted. Lemon sauce may be made in the same way.—*Mrs. A. G. Wilcox, Minneapolis, Minn.*

PINE-APPLE SAUCE.

Mix butter and sugar, flavor with pine-apple (or any other flavoring), form a pyramid, and with a tea-spoon shape it like a pine apple.

STRAWBERRY SAUCE.

Half tea-cup of butter, one and a half tea-cups of sugar, and one pint of strawberries mashed till juicy. (Canned berries may be substituted for fresh ones). Beat the butter and sugar to a cream then stir in the berries and the beaten white of an egg.

VINEGAR SAUCE.

One and a half cups sugar, one and a half table-spoons flour in a little water, two table-spoons vinegar, quarter of a grated nutmeg, and a pinch of salt; pour over this one and a half pints boiling water, and boil ten minutes; just before taking from stove add one dessert-spoon of butter.—*Mrs. G. W. Collins, Urbana.*

WHIPPED CREAM SAUCE.

Whip a pint of thick sweet cream, add the beaten whites of two eggs, sweeten to taste; place pudding in center of dish, and surround with the sauce; or pile up in center and surround with molded blanc-mange, or fruit puddings.—*Mrs. Geo. Bever, Cedar Rapids, Ia.*

PRESERVES.

Preserves, to be perfect, must be made with the greatest care. Economy of time and trouble is a waste of fruit and sugar. The best are made by putting only a small amount of fruit at a time in the syrup, after the latter has been carefully prepared and clarified, and the fruit neatly pared. It is difficult to watch a large quantity so as to insure its being done to a turn.

The old rule is "a pound of sugar to pound of fruit," but since the introduction of cans, three-quarters of a pound of sugar to a pound of fruit is sufficient, and even less is sometimes used, the necessity for an excess of sugar having passed away, as preserves may be less sweet, with no risk of fermentation, if sealed. Either tin or glass cans may be used, care being taken to make the sealing perfect.

Quinces, pears, citrons, watermelon-rinds, and many of the smaller fruits, such as cherries, currants, etc., harden when put, at first, into a syrup made of their weight of sugar. To prevent this they should be cooked till tender in water, or in a weak syrup made from a portion only of the sugar, adding the remainder afterward. In preserving fruits, such as peaches, tomatoes, plums, and strawberries, which are likely to become too soft in cooking, it is a good plan to pour the hot syrup over the fruit and let it remain over night, or to strew over it a part or all the sugar and allow it to stand a few hours; by either method the juice is extracted, and the fruit hardened. Another approved method of hardening fruit is to skim it out of syrup, after cooking a few minutes and lay it in the hot sun two or three hours, and then pour over it the boiling syrup.

Long protracted boiling destroys the pleasant natural flavor of the fruit, and darkens it.

Preserves should boil gently to avoid the danger of burning, and in order that the sugar may thoroughly penetrate the fruit. A good syrup is made in the proportion of half pint water to a pound of sugar. Put the sugar and water over the fire in a porcelain kettle, and, just before it boils, stir in the white of an egg beaten lightly with two table-spoons water; and, as it begins to boil, remove the scum with great care; boil until no more scum arises, and then add fruit. Or the white of the egg may be mixed thoroughly with the dry sugar in the kettle, and the boiling water poured over, when all impurities will immediately rise to the surface with the egg. Preserves may be made from canned fruit (and some prefer to do this rather than make in the hot season), using less sugar than the rule. When preserving canned peaches or apples, it is an improvement to add a few sliced oranges.

Marmalades, or the different butters, will be smoother and better flavored, and will require less boiling, if the fruit (peaches, quinces. oranges, and apples make the best) is well cooked and mashed before adding either sugar or cider. It is important to stir constantly.

In making either preserves or marmalades, follow the directions as regards kettle, sugar, and putting up, already given for jellies and jams, taking care not to cover or put away any of them till cold. When preserves are candied, set jar in kettle of cold water, and let boil for an hour; or put them in a crock kept for that purpose, set in oven and boil a few minutes, watching carefully to prevent burning. When specks of mold appear, take them off carefully, and scald preserves as above directed.

Dried fruits are much better and require less boiling, if clean soft water is poured over them and allowed to stand over night. In the morning boil until tender in the water, sweetening five minutes before removing from the stove.

To dry corn or fruits nicely, spread in shallow boxes or box covers, and cover with mosquito netting to prevent flies reaching them. When dry, put up in jars and cover closely, or in paper sacks. Dried peaches are better when halved and the cavities sprinkled with sugar in drying. The fruit must be good, however, as poor fruit can not be redeemed by any process. Another excellent way, is to dry them in the oven, and, when about half done, place in a crock a layer of peaches alternately with a layer of sugar. Cherries and currants are excellent dried as follows : Put in jars first a layer of fruit, then a layer of sugar, in the proportion of half a pound sugar to pound of fruit, let stand over night, place them to boil, skimming off all scum, let boil ten or fifteen minutes, skim out and spread on dishes to dry in the sun, or by the fire, turning frequently until dry. They may then be packed in jars with sugar, or put away in paper sacks, and are an excellent substitute for raisins in puddings or mince-pies.

The secret of keeping dried fruit is to *exclude the light.* Paper sacks, or a barrel or box lined with paper, are secure against moths. Reheating fruit makes it dark in color, and impairs its flavor. An excellent method is to steam the fruit as soon as dried, in a vegetable steamer (wrapping small fruits or corn in a cloth to prevent their falling through), stirring with the hand until the heat is too great to bear; remove to a pan, dry thoroughly, and put up in paper sacks or in stone crocks, tying a strong cloth tight over the top. Always fill a fruit-can, and keep for common use, to avoid opening the large jars often.

APPLE PRESERVES.

Take three quarters of a pound sugar to each pound apples; make a syrup of the sugar and water in which root ginger (bruised and tied in a bag) has been boiled until the strength is well extracted, add a little lemon-juice or sliced lemon, skim off all scum, and boil in the syrup a few apples at time, until they are transparent. When all are done and the syrup cooled, return the apples to it. Well-flavored fruit should be used. The ginger may be omitted if disliked.

CHERRY PRESERVES.

Choose sour ones—the early Richmond is good—seed nearly all, allow an amount of sugar equal to the fruit; take half the sugar, sprinkle over the fruit, let stand about an hour, pour into a preserving kettle, boil slowly ten minutes, skim out the cherries, add rest of sugar to the syrup, boil, skim and pour over the cherries; the next day drain off the syrup, boil, skim, if necessary, add the cherries, boil twenty minutes, and seal up in small jars.—*Mrs. J. M. Southard.*

CITRON PRESERVES.

Pare off rind, seed, cut in thin slices two inches long, weigh, and put in preserving kettle with water enough to cover; boil one hour, take out the melon, and to the water in kettle add so much sugar as there is melon by weight, boil until quite thick, replace melon, add two sliced lemons to each pound of fruit, boil twenty minutes, take out, boil syrup until it is very thick molasses, and pour it over the fruit.—*Mrs. J. H. Robinson, Kenton.*

FIG PRESERVES.

Gather fruit when fully ripe, but not cracked open; place in a perforated tin bucket or wire basket, and dip for a moment into a deep kettle of hot and moderately strong lye (some prefer letting them lie an hour in lime-water and afterwards drain); make the syrup in proportion of one pound sugar to one of fruit, and, when the figs are well drained, put them in syrup and boil until well cooked; remove, boil syrup down until there is just enough to cover fruit; put fruit back in syrup, let all boil, and seal up while hot in glass or porcelain jars.—*Gov. Stearns, Florida.*

PEAR PRESERVES.

Pare, cut in halves, core and weigh (if hard, boil in water until tender, and use the water for the syrup), allow three-quarters of a pound sugar for each pound fruit, boil a few moments, skim, and cool; when luke-warm add the pears, and boil gently until the syrup has penetrated them and they look clear; some of the pieces will cook before the rest, and must be removed; when done, take out, boil down the syrup a little and pour over them; a few cloves stuck here and there in the pears add a pleasant flavor. Put in small jars with glass or tin tops, and seal with putty.—*Miss Florence Williams.*

PEACH PRESERVES.

Take fine clingstone peaches, or any that do not mash readily in cooking, pare carefully and remove pits; take sugar equally in weight to fruit, (or if to be sealed, three-quarters pound sugar to the pound of fruit), and water in the proportion of a half pint to each pound of sugar. Boil pits in the water, adding more as it evaporates, to keep the proportion good, remove the pits, add the sugar, clarify, and when the scum ceases to rise, add the fruit, a small quantity at a time; cook slowly about ten minutes, skim out into a jar, add more, and so on until all are done, and then pour the boiling syrup over all. The next day drain off and boil syrup a few minutes only, and pour back, repeating daily until the fruit looks clear. Two or three times is generally sufficient. The last time put up the preserves in small jars, and secure with paper as directed for jellies. If to be sealed in cans, the first boiling is sufficient, after which put into cans and seal immediately. The latter plan is preferable, as it takes less trouble and less sugar, while the natural flavor of the fruit is better retained.

PLUM PRESERVES.

Allow equal weights sugar and plums; add sufficient water to the sugar to make a thick syrup, boil, skim, and pour over the plums, (previously washed, pricked and placed in a stone jar), and cover with a plate. The next day drain off syrup, boil, skim, and pour in over plums; repeat this for three or four days, place plums and syrup in the preserving-kettle, and boil very slowly for half an hour. Put up in stone jars, cover with papers like jellies, or seal in cans.— *Mrs. J. H. Shearer.*

QUINCE OR APPLE PRESERVES.

Take equal weights of quinces and sugar, pare, core, leave whole or cut up, as preferred, boil till tender in water enough to cover, carefully take out and put on a platter, add sugar to the water, replace fruit and boil slowly till clear, place in jars and pour syrup over them. To increase the quantity without adding sugar, take half or two-thirds in weight as many fair sweet apples as there are quinces, pare, quarter, and core; after removing quinces, put apples into the syrup, and boil until they begin to look red and clear, and are tender, place quinces and apples in jar in alternate layers, and cover with syrup. For the use of parings and cores, see "Quince Jelly." Apples alone may be preserved in the same way.

TOMATO PRESERVES.

Scald and peel carefully small perfectly-formed tomatoes, not too ripe, (yellow pear-shaped are best), prick with a needle to prevent bursting, add an equal amount of sugar by weight, let lie over night, then pour off all juice into a preserving-kettle, and boil until it is a thick syrup, clarifying with white of an egg; add tomatoes and boil carefully until they look transparent. A piece or two of root-ginger, or a slice of lemon may be added.

WATERMELON PRESERVES.

Pare off outside green rind, cut in pieces two inches long, weigh, throw into cold water, skim out, add a heaping tea-spoon each of salt and pulverized alum to two gallons of rinds, let stand until salt and alum dissolve, fill the kettle with cold water, and place on top of stove where it will slowly come to boiling point, covering a large plate so as to keep rinds under; boil until they can be easily pierced with a fork, drain them from the water, and put into a syrup previously prepared as follows: Bruise and tie in a muslin bag four ounces of ginger-root, and boil in two or three pints of water until it is strongly flavored. At the same time boil in a little water until tender, in another pan, three or four sliced lemons; make a syrup of the sugar and the water in which the lemons and the ginger-root were boiled, add the rinds and slices of lemon to this, and boil slowly half to three-quarters of an hour. Citrons may be prepared in the same way, by paring, coring and slicing, or cutting into fanciful shapes with tin-cutters made for the purpose.

APPLE BUTTER.

Boil one barrel of new cider down half, peel and core three bushels of good cooking apples; when the cider has boiled to half the quantity, add the apples, and when soft, stir constantly for from eight to ten hours. If done it will adhere to an inverted plate. Put away in stone jars (not earthen ware), covering first with writing-paper cut to fit the jar, and press down closely upon the apple butter; cover the whole with thick brown paper snugly tied down.—*Miss Sarah Thompson, Delaware.*

Egg Butter.

Boil a pint of molasses slowly about fifteen or twenty minutes, stirring to prevent burning, add three eggs well beaten, stirring them in as fast as possible, boil a few minutes longer, partially cool, and flavor to taste with lemon.—*Mrs. Colbert, Broadway.*

Lemon Butter.

Juice and grated rind of one lemon, tea-cup white sugar, yolks of two eggs, butter the size of two eggs; boil ten minutes. This may be made up in quantity, kept for a long time in bottles or jars, used as needed for filling tarts, etc.

Orange Marmalade.

Take equal weights of oranges and granulated sugar; quarter and peel the oranges, removing carefully all the thick inner skin from the peel, boil in clear water until tender, changing the water once, and renewing with hot. This takes off some of the rank, bitter taste. Prepare the pulp by dividing, removing the seeds and white stringy part and cutting fine; when the peel is done (so as to be easily pierced with a broom-straw), drain for a few moments in a colander, and cut into fine shreds with a sharp knife or pair of scissors; place the pulps to boil with a little water, and after it has boiled a few moments, add the sugar and shredded peel, and boil twenty minutes longer, stirring often and watching carefully to prevent burning. Put up in small jars with one paper pressed down on the fruit, and another tied closely over top of jar; or use jelly glasses.—*Mrs. J. H. Shearer.*

Orange Marmalade.

Twelve pounds sour oranges, twelve pounds crushed sugar; wash the oranges and pare them as you would apples; put the peel in a porcelain-lined kettle with twice its bulk or more of cold water; keep it covered, and boil until perfectly tender; if the water boils away, add more; the peel is generally very hard, and requires several hours boiling; cut the oranges in two crosswise, and squeeze out the juice and the soft pulp, have a pitcher with a strainer in the top, place in a two-quart bowl, squeeze the thin juice and seeds in the strainer, and the rest with the pulp in the bowl, drawing the skin as you squeeze it over the edge of the tin

strainer, to scrape off the pulp, then pour all the juice and pulp
on the sugar; the white skins must be covered with three quarts
of cold water, and boiled half an hour, drain the water on the
sugar, put the white skins in the colander, four or five together,
and pound off the soft part, of which there must be in all two
pounds and four ounces, put this with the sugar and juice; when
the peel is tender drain it from the water, and choose either of
these three modes: Pound it in a mortar, chop it in a bowl, or cut
it in delicate shreds with a pair of scissors. There is still another
way, which saves the necessity of handling the peel after it is
boiled; it is to grate the yellow rind from the orange, then tie it
in a muslin bag, and boil until soft, which you can tell by rubbing
a little of it between the thumb and finger; it is then ready for
the other ingredients, put the whole in a porcelain kettle, or in a
bright tin preserving-pan, and boil about an hour; when it begins
to thicken it must be tried occasionally, by letting a little cool in a
spoon laid on ice. To prevent its burning, pass the spoon often
over the bottom of the kettle; when it is thick as desired put it in
tumblers and cover with paper.—*Mrs. Elizabeth S. Miller, in "In
the Kitchen."*

PEACH MARMALADE.

Choose ripe, well-flavored fruit, and it is well to make with
preserves, reserving for marmalade those that are too soft. The
flavor is improved by first boiling the pits in the water with which
the syrup is to be made. Quarter the peaches and boil thirty
minutes before adding sugar, stirring almost constantly from the
time the peaches begin to be tender; add sugar in the proportion
of three-fourths pound sugar to one pound fruit, continue to boil
and stir for an hour longer, and put up in jars, pressing paper
over them as directed for jellies.

QUINCE MARMALADE.

Pare, quarter and core quinces, cut in little squares, measure
and allow an equal amount of sugar; place the fruit in a porcelain
kettle with just water enough to cover, boil till tender, and skim
out carefully; make a syrup of the sugar and the water in which
the quinces were boiled, let come to boiling point, skim well, and

drop the quinces gently in; boil fifteen minutes and dip out carefully into jelly bowls or molds. The syrup forms a jelly around the fruit so that it can be turned out on a dish, and is very palatable as well as ornamental. In this way quinces too defective for preserves may be used.—*Mrs. Mary A. Cooper.*

DRIED APPLE SAUCE.

Look over, wash thoroughly and soak fifteen minutes in clean warm water; drain, cover with cold, soft water, place on the stove, let boil slowly two to four hours, mash fine, sweeten, and season with cinnamon very highly. Never add sugar until about five minutes before removing from the stove, otherwise the fruit will be toughened and hardened. Follow the same direction in preparing dried peaches, only do not mash or season so highly. Cook in porcelain, and do not stir while cooking.

BOILED CIDER APPLE SAUCE.

Pare, quarter and core apples sufficient to fill a gallon porcelain kettle, put in it a half gallon boiled cider, let it boil. Wash the apples and put in kettle, place a plate over them, and boil steadily but not rapidly until they are thoroughly cooked, testing by taking one from under the edge of the plate with a fork. Do not remove the plate until done, or the apples will sink to the bottom and burn. Apples may be cooked in sweet cider in the same way.— *Mrs. W. W. W.*

MOCK HONEY.

Five pounds white sugar, a pint and a half water, one-fourth ounce alum; bring to boiling point gradually, skimming well; when cool, add a pound and a half real honey and four drops peppermint essence. This is excellent.—*Miss Hattie H. Cross.*

PRESERVED CITRON.

Boil the citron in water until it is clear and soft enough to be easily pierced with a fork; take out, put into a nice syrup of sugar and water, and boil until the sugar has penetrated it. Take out and spread on dishes to dry slowly, sprinkling several times with powdered sugar, and turning until it is dried enough. Pack in jars or boxes with sugar between the layers.

Tomato Figs.

Scald and skin pear-shaped (or any small-sized) tomatoes, and to eight pounds of them add three pounds brown sugar; cook without water until the sugar penetrates and they have a clear appearance, take out, spread on dishes, and dry in the sun, sprinkling on a little syrup while drying; pack in jars or boxes, in layers with powdered sugar between. Thus put up they will keep for any length of time, and are nearly equal to figs. Peaches may be preserved in the same way.—*Mrs. John Samuels, Covington, Ky.*

PICKLES.

In making pickles use none but the best cider vinegar, and boil in a porcelain kettle—never in metal. A small lump of alum dissolved and added when scalding pickles the first time, renders them crisp and tender, but too much is injurious. Keep in glass or stoneware; look at them frequently and remove all soft ones; if white specks appear in the vinegar, drain off and scald, adding a liberal handful of sugar to each gallon, and pour again over the pickles; bits of horse-radish and a few cloves assist in preserving the life of the vinegar. If put away in large stone jars, invert a saucer over the top of the pickles, so as to keep well under the vinegar. The nicest way to put up pickles is bottling, sealing while hot, and keeping in a cool, dark place. Many think that mustard (the large white or yellow) improves pickles, especially those chopped and bottled, and mangoes. Never put up pickles in any thing that has held any kind of grease, and never let them freeze. Use an oaken tub or cask for pickles in brine, keep them well under, and have more salt than will dissolve, so that there will always be plenty at the bottom of the cask. All pickles should be kept from the air as much as possible. In making sweet pickles, use best brown sugar, "coffee C," or good maple sugar.

PICKLED ARTICHOKES.

Rub off outer skin with a coarse towel, and lay in salt water for a day, drain and pour over them cold spiced vinegar, adding a teaspoon of horse-radish to each jar.

BEAN PICKLES.

Pick green beans when young and tender, string, and place in a kettle to boil, with salt to taste, until they can be pierced with a fork, drain well through a colander, put in a stone jar, sprinkle with ground black or cayenne pepper, and cover with strong cider vinegar; sugar may be added if desired. The best varieties for pickling are the white "German wax" and "Virginia snap."

BOTTLED PICKLES.

Wash and wipe a half bushel of medium-sized cucumbers, suitable for pickling, pack close in a stone jar, sprinkle over the top one pint of salt, pour over a sufficient quantity of boiling water to cover them, place a cloth over the jar, and let stand until cold (if prepared in the evening, let stand all night), drain off the water, and place the pickles on stove in cold vinegar, let them come to a boil, take out, place in a stone jar, and cover with either cold or hot vinegar. They will be ready for use in a few days, and are excellent. It is an improvement to add a few spices and a small quantity of sugar.

To bottle them, prepare with salt and boiling water as above, drain (when cold), and place on stove in cold vinegar (need not be very strong), to which a lump of alum, about the size of a small hickory-nut (too much is injurious), has been added. Have on stove, in another kettle, some of the very best cider vinegar, to which add half a pint of brown sugar; have bottles cleansed and placed to heat on stove in a large tin-pan of cold water; also have a tin cup or small pan of sealing wax heating; on table, have spices prepared in separate dishes, as follows: Green and red peppers sliced in rings; horse-radish roots washed, scraped, and cut in small pieces; stick cinnamon washed free from dust, and broken in pieces; black and yellow mustard seed, each prepared by sprinkling with salt, and pouring on some boiling water, which let stand fifteen minutes and then draw off; and a few cloves. When pickles come to boiling point, take out and pack in bottles, mixing with them the spices (use the cloves and horse-radish rather sparingly); put in a layer of pickles, then a layer of spices, shaking the bottles occasionally so as to pack tightly; when full cover with the boiling hot vinegar from the other kettle (using a funnel and small tin cup), going over them a second time and filling up, in order to supply shrinkage, for the pickles must be entirely covered with the vinegar. Put in the corks, which should fit very snugly, lift each bottle (wrap a towel around it to prevent burning the hands), and dip the corked end into the hot sealing-wax; proceed in this manner with each bottle, dipping each a second time into the wax so that they may be perfectly secure. If corks seem too small, throw them in boiling water; if too large, pound the sides with a hammer. The tighter they fit in the bottles, the better for the pickles. Glass cans, the tops or covers of which have become defective, can be used by supplying them with corks. Pickles thus bottled are far more wholesome than, and are .really superior to, the best brand of imported pickles, and, by having materials in readiness, prepared as directed, the process is neither difficult nor tedious. It requires two persons to successfully bottle pickles.—*Mrs. Florence W. Hush, Minneapolis.*

PICKLED CABBAGE.

Take nice heads of purple cabbage, pull off the loose leaves, slice from top of head, across the cabbage, in slices about half an inch in thickness, place in a stone jar, sprinkle well with salt, let stand twenty-four hours. Prepare vinegar as follows: To a gallon, add one ounce mace, an ounce pepper-corns (whole black pepper), and a little mustard seed. Drain cabbage, put back in jar, scald vinegar and spices, and pour over cabbage, repeating the scalding operation two or three times, and cover jar very tight. When done, the cabbage will be a handsome red color, and very ornamental to the table.—*Mrs. C. T. Carson.*

CHOW CHOW PICKLES.

Let two hundred small cucumbers stand in salt and water closely covered for three days. Boil for fifteen minutes in half a gallon best cider vinegar, one ounce white mustard seed, one of black mustard seed, one of juniper berries, one of celery seed, (tying each ounce separately in swiss bags), one handful small green peppers, two pounds sugar, a few small onions, and a small piece alum; pour the vinegar while hot over the cucumbers, let stand a day, repeating the operation three or four mornings. Mix one-fourth pound mus-

15

tard with the vinegar, pour over cucumbers, and seal up in bottles.—*Mrs. Ada Estelle Bever.*

CHOW CHOW.

One peck of green tomatoes, half peck string beans, quarter peck of small white onions, quarter pint green peppers mixed, two large heads cabbage, four table-spoons white mustard seed, two of white or black cloves, two of celery seed, two of allspice, one small box yellow mustard, pound brown sugar, ounce of turmeric; slice the tomatoes and let stand over night in brine that will bear an egg; then squeeze out brine, chop cabbage, onions and beans, chop tomatoes separately, mix with the spices, put all in porcelain kettle, cover with vinegar, and boil three hours.—*Miss Lou Browne, Washington City.*

CAULIFLOWER PICKLES.

Choose such as are fine and of full size, cut away all the leaves, and pull away the flowers by bunches; steep in brine two days, drain, put in bottles with whole black pepper, allspice, and stick cinnamon; boil vinegar, and with it mix mustard smoothly, a little at a time and just thick enough to run into the jars; pour over the cold cauliflower and seal while hot.—*Mrs. Col. W. P. Reid, Delaware.*

CUCUMBER PICKLES.

Wash cucumbers that have been in brine, put in a porcelain kettle, cut in two if large, pour boiling water over them; boil fifteen minutes, drain off water and replace with fresh boiling water, and repeat twice; drain, and pour over them boiling hot vinegar to which has been added one-third its quantity of sugar; let remain two or three days, pour off, and add equal parts vinegar and sugar, boiling hot.—*Mrs. Samuel Woods, Milford Center.*

CUCUMBER PICKLES.

Cover the bottom of cask with common salt; gather the cucumbers every other day, early in the morning or late in the evening, as it does not injure the vines so much then as in the heat of the day; cut the cucumbers with a short piece of the stem on, carefully laying them in a basket or pail so as not to bruise; pour cold water over and rinse, being careful not to rub off the little black briers, or in any way to bruise them, as that is the secret of keeping them perfectly sound and good for any length of time. Lay them in the cask three or four inches deep, cover with salt, and repeat the operation until all are in; pour in some water with the first layer—after this the salt will make sufficient brine. Now spread a cloth over them, then a board with a stone on it. When a new supply of cucumbers is to be added remove stone, board, and cloth, wash them very clean, and wipe every particle of scum from the top of the pickles and the sides of the cask; throw away any soft ones, as they will spoil the rest; now put in the fresh cucumbers, layer by layer, with salt to cover each layer. When cask is nearly full, cover with salt, tuck cloth closely around the edges, placing the board and weight on top; cover cask closely, and the pickles will be perfect for two or three years. Cucumbers must always be put in the salt as soon as picked from the vines, for if they lie a day or two they will not keep. Do not be alarmed at the heavy scum that rises on them, but be careful to wash all off the board and cloth. When wanted for pickling, take off weight and board, carefully lift cloth with scum on it, wash stone, board, and cloth clean, and wipe all scum off the cucumbers and sides of cask, take out as many as are wanted, return the cloth, board and weight, and cover closely. Place the cucumbers in a vessel large enough to hold two or three times as much water as there are pickles, cover with cold water (some use hot), change the water each day for three days, place the porcelain kettle on the fire, fill half full of vinegar (if vinegar is very strong add half water), fill nearly full of cucumbers, the largest first and then the smaller ones, put in a lump of alum the size of a hulled hickory-nut, let come to a boil, stirring with a wire spoon so as not to cut the cucumbers; after boiling one minute, take out, place in a stone jar, and continue until all are scalded, then pour over cold vinegar. In two or three days, if the pickles are too salt, turn off the vinegar and put on fresh, adding a pint of brown sugar to each two gallons pickles, a pod or two of red pepper, a very few cloves, and some pieces of horse-radish. The horse-radish prevents a white scum from rising.

CHOPPED PICKLES.

Take green tomatoes, wash clean, cut away a small piece from each end, slice and place in a large wooden bowl, chop fine, place in a crock and mix salt with them (one pint to a peck), let stand twenty-four hours, and drain thoroughly; take twice or three times as much cabbage, chop fine, mix salt in same proportions, add enough water to make moist, and let stand same time as tomatoes; drain, place again in separate jars, cover each with cold weak vinegar, after twenty-four hours drain well, pressing hard to extract all the juice; mix tomatoes and cabbage together, take a double handful at a time, squeeze as tightly as possible, and place in a dry crock; take the stone jar in which they are to be pickled, place in it a layer of tomatoes and cabbage, sprinkle with pepper, whole mustard seed, and horse-radish, then another layer of tomatoes and cabbage, next spice, and so on until jar is almost full, occasionally sprinkling with cayenne pepper; cover with strong cider vinegar, to each gallon of which a tea-cup of sugar has been added. Place a saucer, or pieces of broken china on the pickles to keep them under the vinegar. If a white scum rises, drain off vinegar, boil, skim, and pour hot over the pickles. Prepare mustard, pepper, and horse-radish, as follows: Take green garden peppers, cut in two, place in salt water over night; the next morning drain and chop quite fine; to a pint of mustard-seed add tea-spoon salt, pour in boiling water, let stand fifteen minutes and drain; slice horse-radish and chop fine. Tomatoes and onions are excellent prepared in the same way. For sliced pickles, take cucumbers and onions, or tomatoes and onions, and slice and prepare as above.—*Mrs. W. W. W.*

MANGOES.

Select green or half-grown muskmelons; remove a piece the length of the melon, an inch and a half wide in the middle and tapering to a point at each end, take out seeds with a tea-spoon, secure each piece to its own melon by a stitch made with a needle and white thread. Make a strong brine of salt and cold water, pour it over them, and after twenty-four hours take them out. For filling, use chopped tomatoes, chopped cabbage, small cucumbers, small white onions, and nasturtion seed, each prepared by remaining in salt water in separate jars twenty-four hours; add also green beans boiled in salt water until tender. For spice, use cinnamon-bark, whole cloves, sliced and chopped horse-radish, cayenne pepper, and mustard seed, the latter prepared as heretofore directed. Fill each mangoe with the cucumbers, onions, beans, and nasturtion seed, then add the chopped cabbage and spice, sprinkling on the cayenne pepper last. Sew in the piece in its proper place with a strong white thread; when all are thus prepared, place in a stone crock, cover with weak cider-vinegar, let remain over night; in the morning place the mangoes, and the vinegar in which they were soaked, in a porcelain kettle, boil half an hour, place in a jar, cover with good cider-vinegar, let stand all night; in the morning drain off vinegar and boil it, adding one pint of sugar to each gallon, and pour boiling hot over the mangoes; drain off and boil the vinegar three or four times, and they are done. This is not the usual way of preparing mangoes, but it is much the best. To pickle nasturtions, soak as collected in salt and water for twenty-four hours, drain, and put into cold vinegar; when all the seed is thus prepared, drain, and cover with fresh boiling-hot vinegar.

FRENCH PICKLES.

One peck green tomatoes sliced, six large onions sliced; mix these and throw over them one tea-cup of salt, and let them stand over night; next day drain thoroughly and boil in one quart vinegar mixed with two quarts of water, for fifteen or twenty minutes. Then take four quarts vinegar, two pounds brown sugar, half pound white mustard-seed, two table-spoons ground allspice, and the same of cinnamon, cloves, ginger, and ground mustard; throw all together and boil fifteen minutes.—*Mrs. President R. B. Hayes, Washington, D. C.*

PICKLED ONIONS.

Select small silver-skinned onions, remove with a knife all the outer-skins, so that each onion will be perfectly white and clean. Put them into brine that will float an egg for three days; bring vinegar to boiling point, add a little mace and whole red peppers, (or sprinkle with cayenne, adding bits of horse-radish and cinna-mon-bark with a few cloves), and pour it hot over the onions, well drained from brine.—*Estelle Woods Wilcox.*

PICCALILLI.

One large white cabbage, fifty small cucumbers, five quarts small string-beans, eight small carrots, one dozen sticks celery, five red peppers, three green peppers, two heads cauliflower; chop fine, soak over night in salt and water, wash well, drain thoroughly, and pour over them hot vinegar spiced with mace, cinnamon and allspice; turn off vinegar and scald until safe to leave like common pickles; or seal in can while hot.—*Mrs. W. L.*

PYFER PICKLES.

Salt pickles down dry for ten days, soak in fresh water one day; pour off water, place in porcelain kettle, cover with water and vinegar, and add a tea-spoon pulverized alum; set over night on a stove which had fire in during the day; wash and put in a jar with cloves, allspice, pepper, horse-radish and onions or garlic; boil fresh vinegar and pour over all; in two weeks they will be ready for use. These pickles are always fresh and crisp, and are made with much less trouble than in the old fashioned way by keeping in brine.—*Mrs. E. M. R.*

PICKLED PEPPERS.

Take large green ones, (the best variety is the sweet pepper), make a small incision at the side, take out all the seeds, being careful not to mangle the peppers; soak in salt water one or two days, changing water twice; stuff with chopped cabbage, or tomatoes seasoned with spice as for mangoes, (omitting the cayenne pepper), or a mixture of nasturtions, chopped onions, red cabbage, grapes, and cucumbers, seasoned with mustard-seed and a little mace. Sew up incision, place in jar, and cover with cold spiced vinegar.

PLUMS PICKLED LIKE OLIVES.

Make a pickle of vinegar, mustard seed, and a little salt; heat it boiling hot, and pour it over green plums before they begin to turn or ripen; let them remain one night, drain off the vinegar, heat it again, and pour over the plums. Plums may be gathered before the stone becomes hard, and pickled in the same way.—*Mrs. Theo. Brown.*

SPANISH PICKLES.

One dozen cucumbers, four heads of cabbages, one peck green tomatoes, one dozen onions, three ounces white mustard seed, one ounce celery seed, one ounce turmeric, one box Coleman's mustard, two and a half pounds brown sugar. Let the cucumbers stand in brine three days; slice the onions and chop cabbage and tomatoes, the day before making, and sprinkle with salt. When ready to make, squeeze brine out of cucumbers, wipe them off, peel and cut them in slices, let all simmer slowly in a kettle together, for half an hour, and then bottle.—*Mrs. J. W. Grubbs, Richmond, Indiana.*

RIPE TOMATO PICKLES.

Pare ripe, sound tomatoes (do not scald), put in a jar; scald spices (tied in a bag) in vinegar, and pour while hot over them. This recipe is best for persons who prefer raw tomatoes.—*Mrs. Lewis Brown.*

VARIETY PICKLES.

One peck each of green tomatoes and cucumbers, and one quart onions; pare, slice and salt each in separate jars, letting them stand in the salt twenty-four hours, and drain well; sprinkle with salt fresh green radish-pods and nasturtion seeds, and let stand for the same length of time; boil in salt water, two quarts of half-grown bean-pods (the "white wax" is best), until they can be pierced with a silver fork, take out and drain. Now place each in a separate jar, cover with cold, weak vinegar for twenty-four hours, drain well, pressing hard to get out all the juice, and then mix all well together. In a stone jar place first a layer of the mixture, sprinkle plentifully with mustard-seed, (prepared as directed in recipe for "Chopped Pickles)," horse-radish chopped fine, cinnamon bark, and a few cloves, then another layer of the mixture, then the spice with a small sprinkling of cayenne pepper. Cover with good cider-vinegar, let stand over night, drain off vinegar, and boil in a porcelain kettle, adding brown sugar in the proportion of one pint to a gallon of vinegar; skim well, pour hot over the pickles, continue to drain off and boil for several days. If not sweet enough, add more sugar, although these are not intended for sweet pickles. —*Mrs. W. W. Woods.*

PICKLED WALNUTS OR BUTTERNUTS.

Take well-grown nuts about the first of July, when tender enough to stick a pin through; put in water as salt as for fresh cucumber pickles, let stand three days, changing the water during that time, take out, rinse, and lay in the sun, turning frequently, until black ; bring to a boiling point some good cider vinegar, with spices, such as cinnamon, cloves, mace, race-ginger, mustard seed, pepper, and horse-radish, and, if you like, about a pint of sugar to a gallon of vinegar. Put nuts into a jar, pour over the hot vinegar, and they will be ready for use in a few days.—*Mrs. C. T. Carson.*

SWEET PICKLES.

SWEET PICKLED BEETS.

Boil them in a porcelain kettle till quite soft, when cool cut lengthwise to size of a medium cucumber ; boil equal parts vinegar and sugar with half a table-spoon .ground cloves tied in a cloth to each gallon ; pour boiling hot over the beets.—*Mrs. Samuel Woods, Milford Center.*

PICKLED CUCUMBERS.

Prepare and quarter ripe cucumbers, take out seeds, clean, lay in strong brine nine days, stirring every day, take out and put in clear water one day, lay in alum-water (a lump of alum size of a medium hulled hickory-nut to a gallon of water) over night, make syrup of a pint good cider vinegar, pound brown sugar, two table-spoons each broken cinnamon bark, mace, and pepper grains ; make syrup enough to cover the slices, lay them in, and cook till tender.— *Mrs. M. L. France.*

RIPE CUCUMBER PICKLES.

Cut large, ripe, solid cucumbers in rings, pare, divide into smaller pieces, and remove the seeds ; cook pieces *very slightly* in weak vinegar, with salt enough to season well, drain, and put in a stone jar in layers with a few slices of onions, some cayenne pepper, whole all-spice, whole cloves, bits of cinnamon bark, and celery seed (according to taste) between each layer of cucumber. Then cover with a syrup made of one pound sugar to one quart cider vinegar, boiled for about five minutes. Cover closely, and set in a cool place.—*Mrs. Lewis Brown, Cape Girardeau, Mo.*

SPICED CURRANTS.

Six pounds fruit, three of raisins, three of sugar, one pint vinegar, two table-spoons allspice, two of cinnamon, and one of cloves.—*Mrs. H. B. S.*

PICKLED GRAPES.

Fill a jar with alternate layers of sugar and bunches of nice grapes just ripe; fill one-third full of good cold vinegar, and cover tightly.—*Mrs. C. T. Carson.*

SPICED GRAPES.

Five pounds grapes, three of sugar, two tea-spoons cinnamon and allspice, half tea-spoon cloves; pulp grapes, boil skins until tender, cook pulps and strain through a sieve, add it to the skins, put in sugar, spices, and vinegar to taste; boil thoroughly and cool.—*Miss Mae Stokes, Milford Centre.*

SPICED GOOSEBERRIES.

Leave the stem and blossom on ripe gooseberries, wash clean; make a syrup of three pints sugar to one of vinegar, skim, if necessary, add berries and boil down till thick, adding more sugar if needed; when almost done, spice with cinnamon and cloves; boil as thick as apple butter.

SPICED NUTMEG MELON.

Select melons not quite ripe, open, scrape out the pulp, peel, and slice; put the fruit in a stone jar, and, for five pounds fruit, take a quart vinegar, and two and a half pounds sugar; scald vinegar and sugar together, and pour over the fruit; scald the syrup and pour over the fruit each day for eight successive days. On the ninth, add one ounce stick-cinnamon, one of whole cloves, and one of allspice. Scald fruit, vinegar, and spices together, and seal up in jars. This pickle should stand two or three months before using.—*Mrs. Gen. Noyes, Cincinnati.*

PEACH PICKLES.

Pare freestone peaches, place in a stone jar, and pour over them boiling-hot syrup made in the proportion of one quart best cider vinegar to three pints sugar; boil and skim, and pour over the fruit boiling hot, repeating each day until the fruit is the same color to the centre, and the syrup like thin molasses. A few days before they are finished, place the fruit, after draining, in the jar to the depth of three or four inches, then sprinkle over bits of cinnamon bark and a few cloves, add another layer of fruit, then spice, and so on until the jar is full; scald the syrup each morning for three or four days after putting in the spice, and pour syrup boiling-hot over fruit, and, if it is not sufficiently cooked, scald fruit with the syrup the last time. To pickle clingstones, prepare syrup as for freestones; pare fruit, put in the syrup, boil until they can be pierced through with a silver fork; skim out, place in jar, pour the boiling syrup over them, and proceed and finish as above. As clings are apt to become hard when stewed in sweet syrup, it may often be necessary to add a pint of water the first time they are cooked, watching carefully until they are tender, or to use only part of the sugar at first, adding the rest in a day or two. Use the large White Heath clingstones if they are to be had. All that is necessary to keep sweet pickles is to have syrup enough to cover, and to keep the fruit well under. Scald with boiling syrup until fruit is of same color throughout, and syrup like thin molasses; watch every week, particularly if weather is warm, and if scum rises and syrup assumes a whitish appearance, boil, skim, and pour over the fruit. If at any time syrup is lacking, prepare more as at first.—*W. W. W.*

PEAR PICKLES.

Prepare syrup as for peaches, pare and cut fruit in halves, or quarters if very large, and if small leave whole, put syrup in porcelain kettle, and when it boils put in fruit, cook until a silver fork will easily pierce them; skim out fruit first and place in jar, and last pour over syrup boiling hot; spice like peach pickles, draining them each day, boiling and skimming the syrup, and pouring it boiling hot over the fruit until fully done. By cooking pears so much longer at first they do not need to be boiled so frequently, but they must be watched carefully until finished, and if perfectly done, will keep two or more years. Apple pickles may be made in the same way, taking care to select such as will not lose shape in boiling.

EUCHERED PLUMS.

Nine pounds blue plums, six pounds sugar, two quarts vinegar, one ounce cinnamon; boil vinegar, sugar and spice together, pour over plums, draw off next morning and boil, pour back on plums, repeat the boiling five mornings, the last time boiling the fruit about twenty minutes.—*Mrs. Capt. W. B. Brown, Washington City.*

PICKLED RAISINS.

Leave two pounds raisins on stem, add one pint vinegar and half pound sugar; simmer over a slow fire half an hour.—*Mrs. H. C. H.*

STRAWBERRY PICKLES.

Place strawberries in bottom of jar, add a layer of cinnamon and cloves, then berries, and so on; pour over it a syrup made of two coffee-cups cider vinegar, and three pints sugar, boiled about five minutes; let stand twenty-four hours, pour off syrup, boil, pour over berries, and let stand as before, then boil berries and syrup slowly for twenty-five minutes; put in jars and cover. The above is for six quarts of berries. Pine-apples can be made in same way, allowing six and a half pounds of fruit to above proportions.—*Mrs. T. W. Jones, Charleston, S. C.*

SWEET PICKLE.

Take eight pounds of green tomatoes and chop fine, add four pounds brown sugar and boil down three hours, add a quart of vinegar, a tea-spoon each of mace, cinnamon and cloves, and boil about fifteen minutes; let cool and put into jars or other vessel. Try this recipe once and you will try it again.—*Mrs. W. A. Croffut, New York City.*

WATERMELON PICKLE.

Pare off very carefully the green part of the rind of a good, ripe watermelon, trim off the red core, cut in pieces one or two inches in length, place in a porcelain-lined kettle, in the proportion of one gallon rinds to two heaping tea-spoons common salt and water to nearly cover, boil until tender enough to pierce with a silver fork, pour into a colander to drain, and dry by taking a few pieces at a time in the hand, and pressing gently with a crash towel. Make syrup, and treat rinds exactly as directed for pickled peaches. You may continue adding rinds, as melons are used at table, preparing them first by cooking in salt water as above; when you have prepared as many as you want, and they are nearly pickled, drain and finish as directed in peach pickles, except when the syrup is boiled the last time, put in the melons and boil fifteen or twenty minutes; set jar near stove, skim out melons and put in jar a few at a time, heating gradually so as not to break it, then pour in syrup boiling hot. A rind nearly an inch thick, crisp and tender, is best, although any may be used. If scum rises, and the syrup assumes a whitish appearance, drain, boil and skim syrup, add melons, and boil until syrup is like thin molasses.

Clover Vinegar.

Put a large bowl of molasses in a crock, and pour over it nine bowls of boiling rain-water; let stand until milk-warm, put in two quarts of clover blossoms, and two cups of baker's yeast; let this stand two weeks, and strain through a towel. Nothing will mold in it.—*Mrs. McAlister, Goshen, Ind.*

Mint Vinegar.

Put into a wide-mouthed bottle enough fresh, clean peppermint, spearmint, or garden parsley leaves to fill it loosely; fill up with good vinegar, stop closely, leave on for two or three weeks, pour off into another bottle, and keep well corked for use. This is excellent for cold meats, soups, and bread-dressings for roasts; when mints can not be obtained, celery seed is used in the same way.—*Mrs. B. A. Fay.*

POULTRY.

Do not feed poultry the day before killing; cut off the head, hang up by the legs, as the meat will be more white and wholesome if bled freely and quickly. In winter, kill from three days to a week before cooking. Scald well by dipping in and out of a pail or tub of boiling water, being careful not to scald so much as to set the feathers and make them more difficult to pluck; place the fowl on a board with head towards you, pull the feathers away from you, which will be in the direction they naturally lie (if pulled in a contrary direction the skin is likely to be torn), be careful to remove all the pin-feathers with a knife or pair of tweezers; singe, but not smoke, over blazing paper, place on a meat-board, and with a sharp knife cut off the legs a little below the knee, to prevent the muscles from shrinking away from the joint, and remove the oil-bag above the tail; take out the crop, either by making a slit at the back of the neck or in front (the last is better), taking care that every thing pertaining to the crop or windpipe is removed, cut the neck-bone off close to the body, leaving the skin a good length if to be stuffed; cut a slit three inches long from the tail upwards, being careful to cut only through the skin, put in the finger at the breast and detach all the intestines, taking care not to burst the gall-bag (situated near the upper part of the breast-bone, and attached to the liver: if broken, no washing can remove the bitter taint left on every spot it touches); put in the hand at the incision near the tail, and draw out carefully all intestines; trim off the fat from the breast and at the lower incision; split the gizzard and take out the inside and inner lining (throw liver, heart, and gizzard into water, wash well, and lay aside to be cooked and used for the gravy);

wash the fowl thoroughly in several waters (some wipe carefully
without washing), hang up to drain, and it is ready to be stuffed,
skewered, and placed to roast.   To make it look plump, before
stuffing, flatten the breast-bone by placing several thicknesses of
cloth over it and pounding it, being careful not to break the skin,
and rub the inside well with salt and pepper.   Stuff the breast first,
but not too full or it will burst in cooking; stuff the body rather
fuller than the breast, sew up both openings with strong thread,
and sew the skin of the neck over upon the back or down upon the
breast (these threads must be carefully removed before sending to
the table).   Lay the points of the wings under the back, and fasten
in that position with a skewer run through both wings and held in
place with a twine; press the legs as closely towards the breast and
side bones as possible, and fasten with a skewer run through the
body and both thighs, push a short skewer through above the tail,
and tie the ends of the legs down with a twine close upon the
skewer (or, if skewers are not used, tie well in shape with twine);
rub over thoroughly with salt and pepper, thin lard (see p. 141),
or place in pan and lay on slices of pork, or fat taken out of the
fowl, and dredge well with flour, and place to roast in an oven rather
hot at first, and then graduate the heat to moderate until done, to
test which insert a fork between the thigh and body; if the juice is
watery and not bloody it is done.   If not served at once, the fowl
may be kept hot without drying up, by placing over a skillet full
of boiling water (set on top of stove or range), and inverting a
dripping-pan over it.   Many persons roast fowls upon a wire rack
or trivet placed inside the dripping-pan.   The pan should be three
inches deep, and measure at the bottom about sixteen by twenty
inches, with sides somewhat flaring.   In roasting a turkey, allow
fifteen minutes time for every pound.   Some steam turkey before
roasting, and a turkey-steamer may be easily improvised by placing
the dripping-pan containing the turkey, on top of two or three pieces
of wood (hickory or maple is the best) laid in the bottom of a wash-
boiler, with just enough water to cover the wood; put on the lid,
which should fit tightly on the boiler, and as the water boils away
add more.   Add the liquor in the dripping-pan to the turkey when
placed in the oven to roast (do not use the water from the boiler).

Boil the giblets until tender in a separate dish, and add them, well chopped, together with water in which they were cooked, to the gravy.

TO CUT UP A CHICKEN.

Pick, singe, and draw; lay the chicken on a board kept for the purpose, cut off the feet at first joint; cut a slit in the neck, take out the windpipe and crop, cut off the wings and legs at the joint which unites them to the body, separate the first joint of the leg from the second, cut off the oil bag, make a slit horizontally under the tail, cut the end of the entrails loose, extend the slit on each side to the joint where the legs were cut off; then, with the left hand, hold the breast of the chicken, and, with the right, bend back the rump until the joint in back separates, cut it clear and place in water. Take out the entrails, using a sharp knife to separate the eggs (if any), and all other particles to be removed, from the back, being careful in removing the heart and liver not to break the gall-bag (a small sack of a blue-green color about an inch long attached to the liver); separate the back and breast; commence at the high point of the breast and cut downwards toward the head, taking off part of the breast with the wish-bone; cut the neck from that part of the back to which the ribs are attached, turn the skin off the neck, and take out all lumps and stringy substances; very carefully remove the gall-bag from the liver, and clean the gizzard by making an incision through the thick part and first lining, peeling off the fleshy part, leaving the inside whole and ball-shaped; if the lining breaks, open the gizzard, pour out contents, peel off inner lining, and wash thoroughly. After washing in second water, the chicken is ready to be cooked. When young chickens are to be baked, with a sharp knife cut open the back at the side of the back-bone, press apart, and clean as above directed, and place in dripping pan, skin side up.

Chickens are stuffed and roasted in the same way as turkeys, and are much better for being first steamed, especially if over a year old. Roast for twenty or thirty minutes, or till nicely browned. Some prefer to broil or fry old chickens after first steaming until tender, but stewing or boiling is better.

Some, in making chicken or meat pies, line the dish with the lower crust, and place in the oven until well "set," then fill, cover, and bake; others, instead of lining the entire surface of the dish, line only the sides.

The garnishes for turkey and chicken are parsley, slices of lemon, fried sausages, or forced-meat balls.

BAKED CHICKENS.

Dress the chickens and cut them in two, soak for half an hour in cold water, wipe perfectly dry and put in a dripping-pan, bone side down, without any water; have a hot oven, and, if the chickens are young, half an hour's cooking will be sufficient. Take out, and season with butter, salt, and pepper; pack one above another as closely as possible, and place in pan over boiling water, covering them closely—this keeps them moist until served—boil the giblets in a little water, and, after the chickens are taken from the dripping-pan, put into it the water in which giblets were boiled, thicken it, and add the chopped giblets. This manner of baking chickens is fully equal to broiling them.—*Mrs. E. W. Herrick, Minneapolis, Minn.*

BAKED SPRING CHICKEN.

Cut each of four chickens into seven or nine pieces, wash thoroughly and quickly, and put in a colander to drain; put a half table-spoon each of lard and butter into a dripping-pan, lay in the pieces, and add half a pint hot water; let steam and bake half an hour, turn, taking care that they get only to a light brown, and, just before taking up, add salt and pepper to taste; when done take out in a dish and keep hot. To make the gravy, add a half pint or more of water, set the dripping-pan on the stove, and add one table-spoon flour mixed with half cup of cream or milk, stirring slowly, adding a little of the mixture at a time. Let cook thoroughly, stirring constantly to prevent burning, and to make the gravy nice and smooth; season more if necessary.—*Mrs. L. Hush.*

BAKED CHICKEN WITH PARSNIPS.

Wash, scrape, and quarter parsnips, and parboil for twenty minutes; prepare a young chicken by splitting open at the back, place in a dripping-pan, skin side up, lay parsnips around chicken, sprinkle with salt and pepper, and add a lump of butter the size of an egg, or two or three slices of sweet pickled pork; put enough water in pan to prevent burning, cook until chicken and parsnips are done to a delicate brown; serve chicken separately on a platter, pouring the gravy in the pan over the parsnips.

CHICKEN CROQUETTES.

Boil two fowls weighing ten pounds till very tender, mince fine, add one pint cream, half pound butter, salt and pepper to taste; shape oval in a jelly glass or mold. Fry in lard like doughnuts until brown.—*Mrs. E. L. Fay, New York City.*

CHICKEN OR BEEF CROQUETTES.

Take cold chicken, or roast or boiled beef or veal, mince very fine, moisten with the cold gravy if at hand, or moisten well, and add one egg, season with pepper, salt and an onion or sage; make into small cakes, cover with egg and bread-crumbs, and fry in lard and butter. One cup fresh boiled rice may be added before making into cakes.

BROILED CHICKENS OR QUAILS.

Cut chicken open on the back, lay on the meat-board and pound until it will lie flat, lay on gridiron, place over a bed of coals, broil until a nice brown, but do not burn. It will take twenty or thirty minutes to cook thoroughly, and it will cook much better to cover with a pie-tin held down with a weight so that all parts of the chicken may lie closely to the gridiron. While the chicken is broiling, put the liver, gizzard and heart in a stew-pan and boil in a pint of water until tender, chop fine and add flour, butter, pepper, salt, and stir a cup of sweet cream to the water in which they were boiled; when the chicken is done, dip it in this gravy while hot, lay it back on the gridiron a minute, put it in the gravy and let boil for a half minute, and send to the table hot. Cook quails in the same way—*Mrs. A. S. Chapman.*

CHILI COLORAD.

Take two chickens; cut up as if to stew; when pretty well done, add a little green parsley and a few onions. Take half pound large
16

pepper pods, remove the seeds, and pour on boiling water; steam for ten or fifteen minutes; pour off the water, and rub them in a sieve until all the juice is out; add the juice to the chicken; let it cook for half an hour; add a little butter, flour and salt. Place a border of rice around the dish before setting on the table. This dish may also be made of beef, pork or mutton; it is to be eaten in cold weather, and is a favorite dish with all people on the Pacific coast.—*Mrs. Gov. Bradley, Nevada.*

CHICKENS FOR LUNCH.

Split a young chicken down the back, wash and wipe dry, season with salt and pepper. Put in a dripping-pan, and place in a moderate oven; bake three-quarters of an hour. This is much better for traveling lunch than when seasoned with butter.—*Mrs. W. W. W.*

CHICKEN POT-PIE.

Cut up a chicken and put on in cold water enough to cover, and take care that it does not cook dry; while boiling cut off a slice from bread-dough, add a small lump of lard, and mix up like light biscuit, roll, cut out with cake-cutter and set by stove to rise; wash and pare potatoes of moderate size, and add them when chicken is almost done; when potatoes begin to boil, season with salt and pepper, add dumplings, and season again. See that there is water enough to keep from burning, cover very tightly, and do not take cover off until dumplings are done. They will cook in half an hour, and may be tested by lifting one edge of the lid, taking out a dumpling, and breaking it open. Dish potatoes by themselves and chickens and dumplings together. Make gravy by adding flour and a little water mixed together and stirred in slowly; add water and season with salt and pepper. Or, make dumplings with one pint sour milk, two well-beaten eggs, half tea-spoon soda mixed in the flour, salt, pepper, and flour enough to make as stiff as can be stirred with a spoon; or baking-powder and sweet milk may be used. Drop in by spoonfuls, cover tightly, and boil as above. A pot-pie may be made from a good boiling piece of beef; if too much grease arises skim off.

CHICKEN PIE.

Cut up two young chickens, place in hot water enough to cover, boil until tender; line a four or five quart pan with a rich baking-powder or soda-biscuit dough quarter of an inch thick, put in part of chicken, season with salt, pepper and butter, lay in a few thin strips or squares of dough, add the rest of chicken and season as before; some add five or six fresh eggs or a few new potatoes in their season; season liquor in which the chickens were boiled with butter, salt, and pepper, add a part of it to the pie, cover with crust a quarter of an inch thick, with a hole in the center the size of a tea-cup. Keep adding the chicken-liquor and hot water if needed, since the fault of most chicken pies is that they are too dry. There can scarcely be too much gravy. Bake one hour in a moderate oven, having the heat turned to the bottom, as great care is necessary to have the bottom crust well baked.

CHICKEN PIE WITH OYSTERS.

Boil the chicken—a year old is best—until tender, line dish with a nice crust, put in chicken, season with salt, pepper and butter, add the liquor, which should be about a pint, in which chicken was boiled, cover loosely with a crust having a slit cut each way in the middle. Drain off liquor from a quart of oysters, boil, skim, season with butter, pepper, salt and a thickening of flour and water, add oysters, boil up once and (about twenty minutes before the pie is done), lift the crust and put them in.

CHICKEN PUDDING.

Dress and cut one chicken into small pieces, put it into a sauce-pan or kettle with a little water, season with salt and pepper, let boil until it begins to grow tender, then take out and put into a three-quart pudding-dish; have ready one quart green corn grated or cut fine, to which add three eggs beaten light and one pint sweet milk; season with salt and pepper, and pour this mixture over the chicken, dredge thickly with flour, lay on bits of butter and bake until done.—*Mrs. A. Wilson, Rye, N. Y.*

DRESSING FOR CHICKEN OR BEEF.

Boil potatoes, mash as if for the table except that they should be

less moist, stuff the chicken or roast with this, and bake as ordinarily; for ducks add onions chopped fine ; if the bread-dressing is
wanted too, it may be laid in the corner of the pan.—*Mrs. Carrie
Beck.*

FRICASSEED CHICKEN.

Cut up and put on to boil in a small quantity of water, season
with salt, pepper, and an onion if liked ; stew gently until tender,
add a half pint cream or milk, and thicken with butter and flour
rubbed together, add a little chopped parsley just before serving.
Or, first fry the chicken brown in a little hot lard, take out chicken,
add a table-spoon flour, and let cook a minute, stirring constantly;
add a pint water (or stock if at hand), a little vinegar or Worcestershire sauce, season with salt and pepper; when it has boiled,
remove from fire, strain, add the beaten yolk of an egg, pour over
the chicken and serve.—*Mrs. J. H. S.*

FRIED SPRING CHICKEN.

Put skillet on the stove with about one-half table-spoon each of
lard and butter, when hot lay in chicken, sprinkle over with flour.
salt and pepper, place lid on skillet, and cook over a moderate fire ;
when a light brown, turn the chicken and sprinkle flour, salt and
pepper over the top as at first, if necessary add more lard and
butter, and cook slowly until done; make gravy just the same as
for baked chicken.   As a general rule half an hour is long enough
to fry spring chicken.   To make rich and nice gravy without cream,
take the yolk of an egg, beat up light, strain and stir slowly into
the gravy after the flour and milk have been stirred in and thoroughly cooked; as soon as it boils up the gravy is done, and should
be removed from the stove.   All gravies need to be stirred well
and thoroughly cooked over a moderate fire.—*Mrs. L. H.*

FRIED GUMBO.

Cut up two young chickens, and fry in skillet; when brown but
not scorched, put in a pot with one quart finely-chopped okra, four
large tomatoes, and two onions chopped fine ; cover with boiling
water, boil very slowly, and keep the kettle tightly closed; add boiling water as it wastes, and simmer slowly three hours; season with

salt, pepper, and a little butter and flour rubbed together; serve with boiled rice.—*Mrs. J. H. S.*

JELLIED CHICKEN.

Cook six chickens in a small quantity of water, until the meat will part from the bone easily; season to taste with salt and pepper; just as soon as cold enough to handle, remove bones and skin; place meat in a deep pan or mold, just as it comes from the bone, using gizzard, liver and heart, until the mold is nearly full. To the water left in the kettle, add three-fourths of a box of Coxe's gelatine, dissolved in a little warm water, and boil until it is reduced to a little less than a quart, pour over the chicken in the mold, leave to cool, cut with a very sharp knife and serve. The slices will not easily break up if directions are followed.—*Mrs. Prof. Roberts, Cape Girardeau, Mo.*

JELLIED CHICKEN.

Cut up two chickens, boil till tender in water to cover. Take out, remove skin and bones, season the liquor (one and a half pints), with butter, pepper and salt, and juice of lemon, add a quarter of a box dissolved gelatine, put the chicken in liquor, boil up once, and pour in mold.—*Mrs. Gov. Ferris, Washington Territory.*

JELLIED CHICKEN.

Boil one chicken till it will separate from bones, take out, cut in small pieces, mix light and dark meat—not using skin; add salt, pepper, and about half a box Coxe's gelatine to the gravy; boil and pour over chicken, entirely covering it.—*Mrs. Curtis Wilcox, New Haven, Conn.*

PICKLED CHICKEN.

Boil four chickens till tender enough for meat to fall from bones; put meat in a stone jar, and pour over it three pints of cold vinegar, and a pint and half of the water in which the chickens were boiled; add spice if preferred, and it will be ready for use in two days.—*Emma Gould Rea.*

PRESSED CHICKEN.

Take one or two chickens, boil in a small quantity of water with a little salt, and when thoroughly done, take all the meat from the bones, removing the skin, and keeping the light meat separate from the dark; chop and season to taste with salt and pepper. If a meat presser is at hand take it, or any other mold such as a crock or pan will do; put in a layer of light and a layer of dark meat till all is used, add the liquor it was boiled in, which should be about one tea-cupful, and put on a small weight; when cold cut in slices. Many chop all the meat together, add one pounded cracker to the liquor it was boiled in, and mix all thoroughly before putting in the mold; either way is nice.

STEAMED CHICKEN.

Rub the chicken on the inside with pepper and half tea-spoon of salt, place in steamer in a kettle that will keep it as near the water as possible, cover, and steam an hour and a half; when done keep hot while dressing is prepared, then cut them up, arrange on the platter, and serve with the dressing over them. The dressing is made as follows: Boil one pint of gravy from the kettle without the fat, add cayenne pepper and half a tea-spoon salt; stir six table-spoons of flour into a quarter pint of cream until smooth, and add to the gravy. Corn starch may be used instead of the flour, and some add nutmeg or celery salt.

BONED TURKEY.

With a sharp knife slit the skin down the back, and raising one side at a time with the fingers, separate the flesh from the bones with knife, until the wings and legs are reached. These unjoint from the body, and cutting through to the bone, turn back the flesh and remove the bones. When bones are removed, the flesh may be reshaped by stuffing. Some leave the bones in the legs and wings, as they are most difficult to remove. Stuff with force-meat, made of cold lamb or veal and a little pork, chopped fine and seasoned with salt, pepper, sage or savory, and the juice of one lemon; sew into shape, turn ends of wings under and press the legs close to the back, and tie all firmly so that the upper surface may be plump and smooth for the carver. Lard with two or three rows on the top, and bake until thoroughly done, basting often with salt and water, and a little butter. This is a difficult dish to attempt. Carve across in slices and serve with tomato-sauce.—*Mrs. J. Flemming, Philadelphia, Pa.*

BONED TURKEY.

Boil a turkey in as little water as possible, until the bones can be easily separated from the meat, remove all the skin and slice, mixing together the light and dark parts, and season with salt and pepper. Take the liquid in which the turkey was boiled (having kept it warm), pour it on the meat, mix well, shape it like a loaf of bread, wrap it in a cloth, or put it into an oval-shaped dish, and press with a heavy weight for a few hours. A spoonful of butter and flour, braided together, and stirred into the water before boiling is an improvement. When served, cut in thin slices, and garnish with parsley.—*Mrs. R. A. Liggett, Detroit, Mich.*

BOILED TURKEY.

Wash the turkey thoroughly and rub salt through it; fill it with a dressing of bread and butter, moistened with milk and seasoned with sage, salt and pepper, and mixed with a pint of raw oysters; tie the legs and wings close to the body, place in salted boiling water with the breast downward, skim often, boil about two hours, but not till the skin breaks; serve with oyster-sauce.—*Mrs. E. L. F., New York City.*

ESCALOPED TURKEY.

Moisten bread-crumbs with a little milk, butter a pan and put in it a layer of crumbs, then a layer of chopped (not very fine) cold turkey seasoned with salt and pepper, then a layer of crumbs, and so on until pan is full. If any dressing or gravy has been left add it. Make a thickening of one or two eggs, half a cup of milk, and quarter cup butter and bread-crumbs; season and spread it over the top; cover with a pan, bake half an hour and then let it brown.

ROAST TURKEY.

After picking and singeing the turkey, plump it by plunging quickly three times into boiling water and then three times into cold, holding it by the legs; place to drain and dress as in general directions; prepare stuffing by taking pieces of dry bread and crust (not too brown) cut off a loaf of bread fully three or four days old (but not moldy); place crust and pieces in a pan and pour on a very little boiling water, cover tightly with a cloth, let stand until soft, add a large lump of butter, pepper, salt, one or two fresh eggs, and the bread from which the crust was cut, so as not to have it too moist. Mix well with the hands and season to suit taste; rub inside of turkey with pepper and salt, stuff it as already directed on page 238, and sew up each slit with a strong thread; tie the legs down firmly, and press the wings closely to the sides, securing them with a cord tied around the body (or use skewers if at hand), steam (page 238) from one to three hours (or until easily pierced with a fork), according to the size, then place turkey in pan with water from dripping-pan in which the turkey was steamed; lard the turkey, or place on the breast the pieces of fat taken from it before it was stuffed, sprinkle with salt and pepper, dredge well with flour; if not sufficient water in the pan, keep adding boiling water and baste often, as the excellence of the turkey depends much on this. Cook until a nice brown and perfectly tender; remove to a hot platter and serve with cranberry sauce and giblet gravy. To make the gravy, after the turkey is dished place the dripping-pan on the top of range or stove, skim off most of the fat, and add water if necessary; chop the heart, gizzard and liver (previously boiled for two hours in two quarts of water), and add to the gravy with the water in which they were boiled, season with salt and pepper, add a smooth thickening of flour and water, stir constantly until thoroughly mixed with the gravy, and boil until the flour is well cooked. Some, in making stuffing, try out the fat of the turkey at a low temperature, and use instead of butter; others use the fat of sweet, pickled pork chopped fine (not tried out), and a small quantity of butter, or none at all.—*Mrs. Judge J. L. Porter.*

Roast Turkey with Oyster Dressing.

Dress and rub turkey thoroughly inside and out with salt and pepper, steam two hours or until it begins to grow tender, lifting the cover occasionally and sprinkling lightly with salt. Then take out, loosen the legs, and rub the inside again with salt and pepper, and stuff with a dressing prepared as follows: Take a loaf of stale bread, cut off crust and soften by placing in a pan, pouring on boiling water, draining off immediately and covering closely;

crumble the bread fine, add half a pound melted butter, or more
if to be very rich, and a tea-spoon each of salt and pepper or
enough to season rather highly; drain off liquor from a quart
of oysters, bring to a boil, skim and pour over the bread-crumbs,
adding the soaked crusts and one or two eggs; mix all thoroughly
with the hands, and if rather dry, moisten with a little sweet milk;
lastly add the oysters, being careful not to break them; or first put
in a spoonful of stuffing, and then three or four oysters, and so on
until the turkey is filled; stuff the breast first. Flour a cloth and
place over the openings, tying it down with a twine; spread the
turkey over with butter, salt and pepper, place in a dripping-pan
in a well-heated oven, add half a pint hot water, and roast two
hours, basting often with a little water, butter, salt and pepper,
kept in a tin for this purpose and placed on the back of the
stove. A swab made of a stick with a cloth tied on the end, is
better than a spoon to baste with. Turn until nicely browned on
all sides, and about half an hour before it is done, baste with butter
and dredge with a little flour—this will give it a frothy appearance.
When you dish the turkey if there is much fat in the pan, pour off
most of it, and add the chopped giblets previously cooked until
tender, and the water in which they were cooked now stewed down
to about one pint; place one or two heaping table-spoons flour (it is
better to have half of it browned) in a pint bowl, mix smooth with
a little cream, fill up bowl with cream or rich milk and add to the
gravy in the pan; boil several minutes, stirring constantly, and
pour into the gravy tureen; serve with currant or apple jelly. A
turkey steamed in this way does not look so well on the table, but
is very tender and palatable. It is an excellent way to cook
a large turkey.

English Roast Turkey.

Kill several days before cooking, prepare in the usual manner,
stuff with bread-crumbs (not using the crusts) rubbed fine, moistened
with butter and two eggs, seasoned with salt, pepper, parsley, sage,
thyme or sweet marjoram; sew up, skewer, and place to roast in a
rack within a dripping-pan; spread with bits of butter, turn
and baste frequently with butter, pepper, salt and water; a few
minutes before it is done glaze with the white of an egg; dish

the turkey, pour off most of the fat, add the chopped giblets and the water in which they were boiled, thicken with flour and butter rubbed together, stir in the dripping-pan, let boil thoroughly and serve in a gravy-boat. Garnish with fried oysters, and serve with celery-sauce and stewed gooseberries. Choose a turkey weighing from eight to ten pounds. If it becomes too brown, cover with buttered paper.—*Mrs. C. T. Carson.*

SALADS.

In preparing the dressing, powder the hard-boiled eggs, either in a mortar or by mashing with the back of a silver spoon (if raw eggs are used beat well and strain), add the seasoning, then the oil, a few drops at a time, and, lastly and gradually, the vinegar. Always use the freshest olive salad oil, not the common sweet oil; if it can not be obtained, melted butter is a good substitute and by some considered even more palatable, but when used it should be added last of all. In making chicken salad use the oil off the water in which the chickens were boiled. It is much nicer to cut the meat with a knife instead of chopping, always removing bits of gristle, fat and skin. The same is true of celery, (in place of which celery seed may be used with white cabbage or nice head-lettuce, well chopped). To crisp celery, lettuce, or cabbage, put in ice-water for two hours before serving. Pour the dressing over the chicken and celery, mixed and slightly salted; toss up lightly with a silver fork, turn on a platter, form into an oval mound, garnish the top with slices of cold boiled eggs, and around the bottom with sprigs of celery, and set away in a cold place until needed. Many think turkey makes a nicer salad than chicken. Always make soup of the liquor in which turkey or chicken was boiled. Cabbage salad is very palatable, but few know how to prepare it properly. The milk and vinegar should be put on to heat in separate sauce-pans; when the vinegar boils, add butter, sugar, salt and pepper, and stir in the chopped cabbage; cover, and let scald and steam—not boil—for a moment, meanwhile, remove hot milk from stove, cool a little, and stir in the well-beaten and strained yolks; return to stove, and boil a moment. Dish cabbage and pour custard over it, stir rapidly with a silver spoon until well mixed, and set immediately in a cold place.

Sidney Smith's Winter Salad.

Two large potatoes, passed through kitchen sieve,
Unwonted softness to the salad give;
Of mordant mustard add a single spoon—
Distrust the condiment which bites too soon;
But deem it not, though made of herbs, a fault
To add a double quantity of salt;
Three times the spoon with oil of Lucca crown,
And once with vinegar procured from town.
True flavor needs it, and your poet begs
The pounded yellow of two well-boiled eggs.
Let onion atoms lurk within the bowl,
And, half suspected, animate the whole;
And lastly, on the favored compound toss
A magic tea-spoon of anchovy sauce.
Then, though green turtle fail, though venison's tough,
Though ham and turkey are not boiled enough,
Serenely full, the epicure shall say,
"Fate can not harm me—I have dined to-day."

Asparagus Salad.

After having scraped and washed asparagus, boil soft in salt water, drain off water, add pepper, salt and strong cider vinegar, and then cool. Before serving, arrange asparagus so that heads will all lie in center of dish; mix the vinegar in which it was put after removing from fire with good olive oil or melted butter, and pour over the asparagus.—*Mrs. Lewis Brown.*

Bean Salad.

String young beans, cut into half-inch pieces, wash and cook soft in salt water; drain well, add finely-chopped onions, pepper, salt and vinegar; when cool, add olive oil or melted butter.—*Mrs. L. B.*

Cabbage Salad.

Two quarts finely-chopped cabbage, two level table-spoons salt, two of white sugar, one of black pepper, and a heaping one of ground mustard; rub yolks of four hard-boiled eggs until smooth, add half cup butter, slightly warmed; mix thoroughly with the caboage, and add tea-cup good vinegar; serve with whites of the eggs sliced and placed on the salad.—*Mrs. Col. Hawkins.*

CREAM SLAW.

One gallon cabbage cut very fine, pint vinegar, pint sour cream, half cup sugar, tea-spoon flour, two eggs, and a piece of butter the size of a walnut; put vinegar, sugar and butter in a sauce-pan and let boil; stir eggs, cream and flour, previously well mixed, into the vinegar, boil thoroughly and throw over the cabbage previously sprinkled with one table-spoon salt, one of black pepper and one of mustard.—*Mrs. Dr. Skinner, Somerset.*

PLAIN COLD SLAW.

Slice cabbage very fine, season with salt, pepper, and a little sugar; pour over vinegar and mix thoroughly. It is nice served in the center of a platter with fried oysters around it.

CHICKEN SALAD.

Chop fine one chicken cooked tender, one head cabbage, and five cold hard-boiled eggs; season with salt, pepper, and mustard to taste; warm one pint vinegar, add half a tea-cup butter, stir until melted, pour hot over the mixture, stir thoroughly, and set away to cool.—*Mrs. C. S. Ogden.*

CHICKEN SALAD.

Boil three chickens until tender, salting to taste; when cold cut in small pieces and add twice the quantity of celery cut up with a knife but not chopped, and four cold boiled eggs sliced and thoroughly mixed through the other ingredients. For dressing put on stove a sauce-pan with one pint vinegar and butter size of an egg; beat two or three eggs with two table-spoons mustard, one of black pepper, two of sugar, and a tea-spoon salt, and when thoroughly beaten together pour slowly into the vinegar until it thickens. Be careful not to cook too long or the egg will curdle. Remove and when cold pour over salad. This may be prepared the day before, adding the dressing just before using. Add lemon juice to improve the flavor, and garnish the top with slices of lemon.—*Mrs. C. E. Skinner, Battle Creek, Mich.*

Chicken Salad.

Boil one chicken tender; chop moderately fine the whites of twelve hard-boiled eggs and the chicken; add equal quantities of chopped celery and cabbage; mash the yolks fine, add two table-spoons butter, two of sugar, one tea-spoon mustard, pepper and salt to taste, and lastly one-half tea-cup good cider vinegar; pour over the salad and mix thoroughly. If no celery is at hand use chopped pickled cucumbers, or lettuce and celery seed. This may be mixed two or three days before using.—*Mrs. Judge Lawrence, Bellefontaine.*

Chicken Salad.

Four chickens, two bunches of celery to each chicken, one pint vinegar, two eggs, two table-spoons salad oil, two of liquid mustard, one of sugar, one of salt, one salt-spoon red pepper; make a custard of eggs and vinegar, beat oil, mustard, and red pepper together, stir into custard; add celery just before using. The above is suffi-cient for twenty persons.—*Mrs. J. W. G., Richmond, Indiana.*

Chicken Salad.

Boil a young chicken tender; when cold separate from the bones, chop fine, add one cup finely-chopped cabbage, two bunches celery, and four cold hard-boiled eggs; season with mustard, cayenne pep-per, and salt and black pepper to taste. Boil half pint cider vine-gar, stir in butter size of a walnut, one table-spoon white sugar, and as soon as melted, pour over the salad, mix thoroughly, and last stir in half a cup sweet cream; mix well and set in a cool place.—*Mrs. Dr. Stall, Union City, Ind.*

Cucumber Salad.

Peel and slice cucumbers, mix with salt and let stand half an hour; mix two table-spoons sweet oil or ham gravy with as much vinegar and a tea-spoon sugar, add the cucumbers which should be drained a little; add a tea-spoon pepper and stir well. Sliced onions are an addition if their flavor is liked.—*Mrs. H. C. Mahncke.*

Ham Salad.

Cut up small bits of boiled ham, place in salad-bowl with the hearts and inside leaves of a head of lettuce. Make dressing as follows: Mix in a sauce-pan one pint sour cream as free from milk as possible, and half pint good vinegar, pepper, salt, a small piece of butter, sugar, and a small table-spoon of mustard mixed smooth; boil, add the well-beaten yolks of two eggs, stirring carefully as for float until it thickens to the consistency of starch, then set in a cool place or on ice, and when cold pour over salad and mix well —*Mrs. S. Watson, Upper Sandusky.*

HERRING SALAD.

Soak over night three Holland herrings cut in very small pieces; cook and peel eight medium potatoes and when cold chop with two small cooked red beets, two onions, a few sour apples, some roasted veal, and three hard-boiled eggs; mix with a sauce of sweet oil, vinegar, stock, pepper and mustard to taste. A table-spoon of thick sour cream improves the sauce, which should stand over night in an earthen dish.—*Mrs. H. C. Mahncke.*

LOBSTER SALAD.

Boil the lobster, five minutes for every pound, in water to which have been added, for a five-pound one, four sprigs of parsley, two of thyme, two cloves, four onions cut in slices, salt, pepper, and a tea-spoon vinegar; leave the lobster in it till cold, then take off and drain it. Chop the lobster fine after removing it from the shell, and add two heads of minced lettuce, half a cup of melted butter, two table-spoons mustard, salt and pepper to taste. Place in a dish, and over all pour a half pint of vinegar, into which six well-beaten eggs have been stirred and heated till it is thick. This should be cold when it is put on the lobster.

POTATO SALAD.

Chop cold boiled potatoes fine with enough raw onions to season nicely; make a dressing as for lettuce salad, and pour over it.

SALMON SALAD.

Set a can of salmon in a kettle of boiling water, let boil twenty minutes, take out of the can and put in a deep dish, pour off the juice or oil, put a few cloves in and around it, sprinkle salt and pepper over, cover with cold vinegar, and let it stand a day, take it from the vinegar and lay it on a platter. Prepare a dressing as follows: Beat the yolks of two raw eggs with the yolks of two eggs boiled hard and mashed fine as possible; add gradually a table spoon mustard, three of melted butter, or the best of salad oil, a little salt and pepper (either black or cayenne), and vinegar to taste. Beat the mixture a long time (some persons like the addition of lemon juice and a little brown sugar); cover the salmon thickly with a part of the dressing, cut up very small the crisp inside leaves of lettuce, put in the remainder of the mixture, and pour over with two or three larger pieces placed around the salmon and serve.

TOMATO SALAD.

Take the skin, juice and seeds from nice, fresh tomatoes, chop what is left with celery, and add a good salad-dressing.—*Mrs. E. M. Rea, Minneapolis, Minn.*

SALAD-DRESSING.

Yolks of two hard-boiled eggs rubbed very fine and smooth, one tea-spoon English mustard, one of salt, the yolks of two raw eggs beaten into the other, dessert-spoon of fine sugar. Add very fresh sweet oil poured in by very small quantities, and beaten as long as the mixture continues to thicken, then add vinegar till as thin as desired. If not hot enough with mustard, add a little cayenne pepper.—*Mrs. Gov. Cheney, New Hampshire.*

SALAD-DRESSING.

Beat yolks of eight eggs, add to them a cup of sugar, one table-spoon each of salt, mustard and black pepper, a little cayenne, and half a cup cream, mix thoroughly; bring to a boil a pint and a half vinegar, add one cup butter, let come to a boil, pour upon the mixture, stir well, and when cold put into bottles and set in a cool place. It will keep for weeks in the hottest weather, and is excellent for cabbage or lettuce.

SALAD-DRESSING.

Peel one large potato, boil, mash until all lumps are out, and add the yolk of a raw egg, stir all well together and season with a tea-spoon of mustard and a little salt; add about half a gill of olive oil and vinegar, putting in only a drop or two at a time, and stirring constantly, as the success of the dressing depends on its smoothness.

This dressing is very nice with celery or cabbage chopped fine, and seasoned with a little salt and vinegar.—*Mrs. E. L. Fay.*

SALAD-DRESSING.

The yolks of two eggs beaten thoroughly, one level tea-spoon salt, one of pepper, two of white sugar, two tea-spoons prepared mustard, one table-spoon butter; stir in the mixture four table-spoons best vinegar, put dressing into a bowl, set it in a kettle of hot water and stir constantly till it thickens; set away, and when cool it is ready for use. This is sufficient for one quart finely chopped cabbage and should be poured over while hot, and thoroughly mixed with the cabbage, which may then be placed upon a platter, formed into an oval mound and served cold.

CREAM DRESSING FOR COLD SLAW.

Two table-spoons whipped sweet cream, two of sugar, and four of vinegar; beat well and pour over cabbage, previously cut very fine and seasoned with salt.—*Miss Laura Sharp, Kingston.*

17

SHELL-FISH.

Oysters are the best known of shell-fish, and are an important article of food from September to May. In most localities they are not more expensive than meats, and the great variety of ways in which they can be cooked, makes them a favorite with house-keepers. Oysters in the shell must be kept in a cool cellar and occasionally sprinkled with salt water. When fresh the shell is firmly closed; if opened the oyster is dead and unfit for use. The small-shelled oysters have the finest flavor. For the freshness of canned oysters it is necessary to trust to the dealer. In preparing them for cooking or for the table, be careful to remove all bits of shell; never salt oysters for soups or stews till just before removing them from the fire, or they will shrivel up and be hard. In frying, a little baking-powder put into the cracker dust will improve them. Roasting in the shell best preserves the natural flavor. Always serve immediately after cooking by any of the methods given. Lobsters and crabs should be boiled as soon as caught. The most humane way to kill them is to drop them in a kettle full of boiling water.

CLAM CHOWDER.

Chop fifty clams, peel and slice ten raw potatoes, cut into dice six onions and half pound fat salt pork, slice six tomatoes (if canned use a coffee-cup full), add a pound pilot crackers; first put pork in bottom of pot and try out, partially cook onions in pork-fat, re-move the mass from pot, and put on a plate bottom side up; make layers of the ingredients, season with pepper and salt, cover with water and boil an hour and a half, adding chopped parsley to taste.

CLAM PIE.

Take three pints of either hard or soft-shell clams (if large, chop slightly), put in a sauce-pan and bring to a boil in their own liquor, or add a little water if needed; have ready four medium-sized potatoes, boiled till done and cut into small squares; make a nice pie-paste with which line a medium-sized pudding-dish half way down the sides; turn a small tea-cup bottom up in middle of dish to keep up the top crust; put in first a layer of clams, and then a few potatoes, season with bits of butter and a little salt and pepper, and dredge with flour; add another layer of clams, and so on till dish is filled, adding juice of clams, and a little water if necessary (there should be about as much liquid as for chicken-pie). Cover with top crust, cutting several slits for steam to escape, and bake three-quarters of an hour.—*Mrs. A. Wilson, Rye, N. Y.*

CLAM STEW.

Take half peck hard-shell clams, wash shells clean, and put in a kettle with about one tea-cup water; let steam until the shells open, when take out of shell, strain juice, and return it with clams to the fire; after they come to a boil, add one pint milk, a piece of butter size of an egg, three crackers rolled fine, pepper, and salt if any is needed.—*Mrs. A. W.*

FRIED CLAMS.

Remove from shell large soft-shell clams; beat an egg well and add two table-spoons water; have the clams dried in a towel, and dip them first in the egg, then in finely-rolled cracker or bread-crumbs, and fry (longer than oysters) in sweet lard or butter. Oysters may be prepared for cooking in same way.—*Mrs. A. W.*

DEVILED CRABS.

Pick the meat from a boiled crab and cut in fine bits, add one-third as much bread-crumbs, two or three chopped hard-boiled eggs, and lemon juice; season with pepper, salt, and butter or cream. Clean the shells nicely and fill with the mixture, sprinkle over with bread-crumbs and small bits of butter, and brown in oven.

Lobsters may be prepared in same way, and served in silver scallop-shells. Or, boil one pint milk, and thicken with one table-spoon corn starch mixed in a little cold milk, season with pepper (cayenne may be used) and salt, and pour over the picked-up lobster; put in baking-dish, and cover with bread-crumbs and a few pieces of butter, and brown in oven.—*Mrs. Col. S., Norfolk, Va.*

LOBSTER SALAD.

Boil a large lobster (when done it will be of a bright red color, and should be removed, as if boiled too long it will be tough), crack the claws after first disjointing, split the body in two lengthwise, pick out the meat in bits not too fine, saving the coral separate; cut up a large head of lettuce slightly, and place on a dish over which lay the lobster, putting the coral around the outside. For dressing, take the yolks of three eggs, beat well, add four table-spoons salad-oil, dropping it in very slowly, beating all the time; then add a little salt, cayenne pepper, half tea-spoon mixed mustard, and two table-spoons vinegar. Pour this over the lobster just before sending to table.—*Mrs. A. Wilson, Rye, N. Y.*

BROILED OYSTERS.

Dry large, selected oysters in a napkin, pepper and salt, and broil on a fine folding wire-broiler, turning frequently to keep the juice from wasting. Serve immediately in a hot dish with little pieces of butter on them. Or, pepper a cup of dry bread-crumbs; dry one quart of oysters in a napkin, dip each in butter previously peppered, roll well in the crumbs, and broil over a good fire for five to seven minutes. Serve immediately in a hot dish with butter, pepper and salt.

ESCALOPED OYSTERS.

Take crushed crackers, not too fine; drain liquor from a quart of oysters and carefully remove all bits of shell, butter a deep dish or pan, cover the bottom with crackers, put in a layer of oysters seasoned with salt and pepper and bits of butter in plenty, then a layer of crackers, then oysters, and so on until dish is full, finishing with the crackers covered with bits of butter; pour over the whole the oyster-liquor added to one pint of boiling water (boiled and skimmed), place in a hot oven, bake half an hour, add another pint of hot water, or half pint water and half pint of milk, in which a small lump of butter has been melted; bake another half hour, and, to prevent browning too much, cover with a tin or sheet iron lid. All bread-crumbs, or a mixture of crackers and bread-crumbs may be used when more convenient. As the amount of liquor in oysters varies, and the proportion of crackers or bread-crumbs to the oysters also varies, the quantity of water must be increased or diminished according to judgment and taste. Some prefer to cook half the time given above.

FRIED OYSTERS.

Drain carefully, remove all bits of shell, and sprinkle with pepper and salt, and set in a cool place for ten or fifteen minutes. Then, if oysters are small, pour them into a pan of crackers rolled fine, add the liquor, mix well, and let stand five minutes, add a *little* salt and pepper, mold into small cakes with two or three oysters in each, roll in dry crackers until well encrusted, and fry in hot lard and butter, or beef-drippings. Serve hot in a covered dish. Or, if large, roll each, first in cracker dust, then in beaten egg mixed with a little milk and seasoned with pepper and salt, then again in the cracker dust, and fry in *hot* lard until a delicate brown, drain and serve on a hot platter, with cold slaw, chopped pickles, or chow-chow.

Or, dip large fine oysters singly in flour; have some butter and lard hot in a thick-bottomed frying-pan; lay the oysters in, and turn each as soon as browned; when both sides are done, take them up, and serve. Grated horse-radish or pickles should be served with them.

Or, drain thoroughly, put in a *hot* frying-pan, turn so as to brown on both sides. They cook in this way in a few moments, and the peculiar flavor of the oyster is well preserved. Serve on a hot covered dish, with butter, pepper, and salt, or add a little cream just before serving, and serve on toast; or take two parts rolled crackers and one part corn meal, mix well, roll the oysters in it, and fry in equal parts butter and lard. Season with salt and pepper.—*Mrs. W. W. Woods.*

Oyster Fritters.

Drain off liquor, boil, skim, and to a cupful add a cup of milk, two or three eggs, salt and pepper, and flour enough to make a rather thick batter. Have hot lard or beef drippings ready in a kettle, drop the batter into it with a large spoon, taking up one oyster for each spoonful. The oyster must be large and plump.

Oyster Omelet.

Add to a half cup of cream six eggs beaten very light, season with pepper and salt, and pour into a frying-pan with a table-spoon of butter; drop in a dozen large oysters cut in halves, or chopped fine with parsley, and fry until a light brown. Double it over, and serve immediately.—*Mrs. T. B. Johnson, Tuscumbia.*

Oyster Patties.

Put oysters in a sauce-pan, add a little milk and a part of the liquor from the oysters, season with pepper and salt, a bit of lemon rind, and a piece of butter rolled in flour; stir together, and let simmer for a few minutes, and put in shells which have been previously made of puff-paste baked in patty-pans. They may be served hot or cold. If hot, the shells should be warmed before adding the oysters.

Oyster Pie.

Line a deep pie-dish with puff-paste, or a crust made of a scant quart sifted flour, half tea-cup butter or lard, half pint cold water, a level tea-spoon salt, and a tea-spoon baking-powder in the flour; dredge the crust with flour, pour in the oysters, season well with bits of butter, salt, and pepper, and sprinkle flour over; pour on some of the oyster-liquor, and cover with a crust having an opening in the center to allow the steam to escape. One pint of oysters will make this pie.—*Mrs. Carrie Beck.*

Oyster Short Cake.

One quart sifted flour, two tea-spoons baking-powder, one table-spoon butter, a pinch of salt, and enough sweet milk to moisten well; roll about an inch thick, and bake on tin pie-plates quickly. While baking, take one quart of oysters and a half cup of water and put on the stove; then take half a cup milk and the same of butter, mix with a table-spoon of flour, and a little salt and pepper; add all together, and boil at once. When the cakes are done, split open and spread the oysters between the pieces and some on the top. Put the oysters that are left in a gravy dish, and replenish when needed.

OYSTER STEW.

Two quarts oysters, one of sweet milk, two table-spoons best butter, one of corn starch or two of flour; drain liquor from oysters, boil and skim; set milk in a kettle of hot water to prevent scorching; when it boils, add oysters and liquor, and allow to stew not longer than five minutes; beat corn starch and butter to a cream, stir in, and season with salt and pepper; serve hot. Some omit corn starch and flour, and thicken with rolled crackers.— *F. M. W.*

PLAIN OYSTER SOUP.

Pour one quart oysters in a colander, rinse by pouring over them one pint cold water, put this in porcelain kettle, add one pint boiling water, let boil, skim thoroughly, season with pepper and piece of butter size of large egg; then add the oysters, having removed all shells, let boil up once, season with salt, and serve.

OYSTER PICKLES.

Choose the largest, put over a gentle fire in their own liquor, add a small bit of butter, simmer for two or three minutes, and when plump and white, take out with a skimmer into a flat dish; take of their own liquor half enough to cover, add as much more of best cider vinegar and heat; put a layer of oysters in a stone jar, strew over a salt-spoon of ground mace, a few cloves, some allspice and whole pepper, then oysters and spice till all are used. Then pour over them the hot liquor and set away in a cool place. They may be used in a day or two, but will remain good for months if kept cool.— *Mrs. Louise M. Lincoln.*

RAW OYSTERS.

Select fine oysters, drain in a colander, pick out all bits of shell, sprinkle well with pepper and salt, and place on ice for half an hour before serving. They may be taken to the table on a large block of ice hollowed out with a hot flat-iron, or in a dish with pieces of ice scattered over them. ᐟ Serve with slices of lemon, or vinegar and horse-radish; or freeze oysters in the shell, open, and serve, seasoning to taste.—*Mrs. V. G. H.*

STEAMED OYSTERS.

Wash and drain one quart select oysters, put in pan and place in steamer over boiling water, cover and steam till oysters are plump with edges ruffled; place in heated dish with butter, pepper, and salt, and serve.—*Mrs. E. S. W., Washington.*

SOUPS.

To make nutritious, healthful and palatable soup, with flavors properly commingled, is an art which requires study and practice, but it is surprising from what a scant allotment of material a delicate and appetizing dish may be produced. The base of soup should always be lean uncooked meat, to which may be added chicken, turkey, beef, or mutton bones, well broken up. To four pounds of lean beef (the inferior parts are quite as good for this purpose), put five quarts of cold water (soft is best), wash the meat and put it in the water without salt; let it come slowly to boiling point, and then skim well, set it back and let it simmer gently for six or eight hours until the meat is in rags; rapid boiling hardens the fiber of the meat and the savory flavor escapes with the steam; add a little pepper and salt, strain into a stone jar, let it cool, and remove all the grease. This stock will keep for many days in cold weather, and from it can be made all the various kinds of soups by adding onion, macaroni, celery, asparagus, green pease, carrot, tomato, okra, parsley, thyme, summer savory, sage, and slices of lemon; many of these may be first dried, then pulverized and put in cans or jars for winter use. Celery and carrot seed may be used in place of the fresh vegetables. Macaroni should be first boiled in slightly salted water, cut in pieces one or two inches long, and added a short time before serving. To prepare soup for dinner, cut off a slice of the jelly, add water, heat and serve. Whatever is added to this, such as rice, tapioca, vegetables, etc., may first be cooked before being added, as much boiling injures the flavor of the stock. A rich stock can also be made from a shank or shin of beef (knuckle of veal is next best). Cut in several pieces, crack the bones, add four quarts of water, and simmer until the liquor is reduced one-half; strain, cool and skim, and if boiled properly and long enough, an excellent jelly will result. Stock made from meat without bone or gristle, will not jelly, but will taste very like good beef-tea. Never boil vegetables with it, as they will cause it to become sour.

An economical soup-stock may be made of steak or roast-beef bones, adding a little piece of fresh meat, or none at all, and allowing it to simmer at least five hours; strain, remove all fat the next day, and it will be ready for use.

To make soup from any stock, put on as much stock as needed (if in jelly, scrape the sediment from off the bottom), add seasoning, water and vegetables. The potatoes should be peeled, sliced and laid in salt and water for half an hour, the cabbage parboiled and drained, and all others either sliced or cut fine before adding them to the soup; boil until thoroughly dissolved, strain through a colander and serve at once. Always use cold water in making all soups; skim well, especially during the first hour. There is great necessity for thorough skimming, and to help the scum rise, pour in a little cold water now and then, and as the soup reaches the boiling point, skim it off. Use salt at first sparingly, and season with salt and pepper; allow one quart soup to three or four persons. Keep kettle covered closely, so that the flavor may not be lost, and simmer slowly, so that the quantity may not be much reduced by evaporation, but if it has boiled away (which may be the case when the meat is to be used for the table), pour in as much hot water as is needed, and add vegetables, noodles, or any thickening desired. Vegetables should be added just long enough before soup is done to allow them to be thoroughly cooked. Thickened soups require more seasoning than thin soups; if wanted very clear and delicate, strain through a hair sieve. For a quick soup, crush the bone and cut the meat rather fine; when done, strain and serve. Every kitchen should be provided with a soup-kettle (which has a double bottom), or a large iron pot with a tight-fitting tin cover with a hole size of a large darning-needle in it at one side of the handle. For coloring and flavoring soups, use caramel, browned flour, onions fried brown, meat with cloves in it, or browned with butter.

Poached eggs are an excellent addition to some soups. They should be added just before serving, one for each person. They may be poached in water or dropped into the boiling soup, or two or three eggs, well beaten and added just before pouring in tureen, make a nice thickening. Cayenne pepper or a bit of red pepper pod, Worcestershire, Halford, or Chili sauce, and catsups, are considered by many an improvement to soup, but must be cautiously used. Force-meat balls, made of the meat boiled for the soup (chop fine, season with salt, pepper, parsley or onion, and bind together with a raw egg mixed with a little flour; make into balls and fry or boil before adding to soup), are also used.

CLAM SOUP.*

First catch your clams—along the ebbing edges
Of saline coves you'll find the precious wedges,
With backs up, lurking in the sandy bottom;
Pull in your iron rake, and lo! you've got 'em!
Take thirty large ones, put a basin under,
And cleave, with knife, their stony jaws asunder;
Add water (three quarts) to the native liquor,
Bring to a boil (and, by the way, the quicker
It boils the better, if you'd do it cutely.)
Now add the clams, chopped up and minced minutely.
Allow a longer boil of just three minutes,
And while it bubbles, quickly stir within its
Tumultuous depths where still the mollusks mutter,
Four table-spoons of flour and four of butter,
A pint of milk, some pepper to your notion,
And clams need salting, although born in ocean.
Remove from fire; (if much boiled they will suffer—
You'll find that India-rubber isn't tougher.)
After 'tis off, add three fresh eggs, well beaten,
Stir once more, and it's ready to be eaten.
Fruit of the wave! O, dainty and delicious!
Food for the gods! Ambrosia for Apicius!
Worthy to thrill the soul of sea-born Venus,
Or titillate the palate of Silenus!

BEEF SOUP.

Take the cracked joints of beef, and after putting the meat in the

---

*Written for "Buckeye Cookery and Practical Housekeeping." by W. A. Croffut, Editor of Daily Graphic, New York.

pot and covering it well with water, let it come to a boil, when it should be well skimmed. Set the pot where the meat will simmer slowly until it is thoroughly done, keeping it closely covered all the time. The next day or when cold, remove the fat which hardens on the top of the soup. Peel, wash and slice three good-sized potatoes and put them into the soup; cut up half a head of white cabbage in shreds, and add to this a pint of Shaker corn that has been soaked over night, two onions, one head of celery, and tomatoes if desired. When these are done, and they should simmer slowly, care being taken that they do not burn, strain the soup and serve. The different varieties of beef soup are formed by this method of seasoning and the different vegetables used in preparing it, after the joints have been well boiled. Besides onions, celery, cabbages, tomatoes and potatoes, many use a few carrots, turnips, beets, and force-meat balls seasoned with spice; rice or barley will give the soup consistency, and are to be preferred to flour for the purpose. Parsley, thyme and sage are the favorite herbs for seasoning, but should be used sparingly. To make force-meat balls, add to one pound chopped beef one egg, a small lump butter, a cup or less of bread-crumbs; season with salt and pepper, and moisten with the water from stewed meat; make in balls and fry brown, or make egg-balls by boiling eggs, mashing the yolks with a silver spoon, and mixing with one raw yolk and one tea-spoon flour; season with salt and pepper, make into balls, drop in soup just before serving.— *Mrs. H. B. Sherman.*

BEEF SOUP WITH OKRA.

Fry one pound "round" steak cut in bits, two table-spoons butter, and one sliced onion, till very brown; add to three or four quarts cold water in soup-kettle, and boil slowly one hour; then add pint sliced okra, and simmer three hours or more; season with salt and pepper, strain and serve.—*Mrs. T. B. J., Tuscumbia, Ala.*

BEEF SOUP.

Take bones and trimmings from a sirloin steak, put over fire after breakfast in three quarts water, boil steadily until about an hour before dinner, when add two onions, one carrot, three common-sized potatoes, all sliced, some parsley cut fine, a red pepper, and salt to taste. This makes a delicious soup, sufficient for three persons. All soups are more palatable seasoned with onions and red pepper, using the seeds of the latter with care, as they are very strong.

GRANDMOTHER'S BEAN SOUP.

Take one pint beans, wash well, put on to cook in one quart of cold water; when water boils pour off and add quart cold water again; put in piece of pork the size of the hand, salt to taste; as water boils away add so as to keep covered with water; cook till the beans mash easily; beat two eggs well, add two table-spoons water and a pinch of salt, stir in flour till as stiff as can be stirred, then drop the batter with a spoon into the soup (having previously taken two-thirds of the beans out into a pan, laid the piece of pork on the top with a sprinkle of salt and pepper, and put all into the oven to brown); when the dumplings swell up, pepper slightly and the soup is done. If the pork taste is disliked use butter instead of pork.

BEAN SOUP.

Boil a small soup-bone in about two quarts water until the meat can be separated from the bone, remove bone, add a coffee-cup white beans soaked for two hours, boil for an hour and a half, add three potatoes, half a turnip and a parsnip, all sliced fine, boil half an hour longer, and just before serving sprinkle in a few dry bread crumbs, season with salt and pepper, and serve with raw onions sliced very fine for those who like them.—*Mrs. A. B. Morey.*

TURTLE BEAN SOUP.

Soak one pint black beans over night, then put them into three quarts water with beef bones or a small piece of lean salt pork, boil three or four hours, strain, season with salt, pepper, cloves and lemon juice. Put in a few slices of lemon, and if wished add slices of hard-boiled eggs. Serve with toasted bread cut into dice and placed in the tureen.—*Mrs. H. C. Clark, Kankakee, Ill.*

MEATLESS BEAN SOUP.

Parboil one pint beans, drain off the water, add fresh, let boil until perfectly tender, season with pepper and salt, add a piece of butter the size of a walnut, or more if preferred; when done skim out half the beans, leaving the broth with the remaining half in the kettle, now add a tea-cupful of sweet cream or good milk, a dozen or more of crackers broken up, let it come to a boil, and serve.

CARROT SOUP.

Put in soup-kettle a knuckle of veal, three or four quarts cold water, a quart finely-sliced carrots, one head celery; boil two and a half hours, add a handful rice, and boil an hour longer; season with pepper (or a bit of red pepper pod) and salt, and serve.—- *Mrs. Eliza T. Carson.*

CELERY SOUP.

Put in pan a tea-cup boiled rice, two quarts boiling milk (or part water), with five or six sticks (or a head) of celery cut fine, place in steamer over boiling water, cook one hour or till celery is tender, add butter size of an egg, season with salt and pepper, add one or two well-beaten eggs, and serve hot.—*Mrs. J. H. S.*

CLAM SOUP.

Wash clams, and place in just sufficient water for the soup, let boil, and as soon as they clear from shells, take out and place clams in a jar for pickling; throw into the broth a pint each of sweet milk and rolled crackers, add a little salt, boil five minutes, and just before taking from the fire, add one ounce butter beaten with two eggs. Serve, and let each person season to taste.—*Mrs. H. B. S., Milwaukee, Wis.*

CHICKEN SOUP.

In boiling chickens for salads, etc., the broth (water in which they are boiled) may be used for soup. When the chickens are to be served whole, stuff and tie in a cloth. To the broth add a dozen tomatoes (or a quart can), and one thinly-sliced onion; boil twenty minutes, season with salt and pepper, add two well-beaten eggs and serve.—*Mrs. Smythe, New York City.*

COD-FISH SOUP.

Boil a tea-cup cod-fish (shredded fine) in three pints water for twenty minutes, add three table-spoons butter mixed till smooth with one heaping table-spoon flour and a little hot water, boil up once, add two pints milk, let boil, add three beaten eggs, serve with bread-dice, or when served in tureen add one poached egg for each person.—*Mrs. P. C. Jones, Cleveland.*

Green Corn Soup.

One large fowl, or four pounds veal (the knuckle or neck will do), put over fire in one gallon of cold water without salt, cover tightly and simmer slowly till meat slips from the bones, not allow ing it to boil to rags, as the meat will make a nice dish for breakfast or lunch, or even for the dinner. Set aside with the meat a cup of the liquor; strain the soup to remove all bones and rags of meat; grate one dozen ears of green corn, scraping cobs to remove the heart of the kernel, add corn to soup, with salt, pepper, and a little parsley, and simmer slowly half an hour. Just before serving add a table-spoon flour beaten very thoroughly with a table-spoon butter. Serve hot. To serve the chicken or veal, put the cup of broth (which was reserved) in a clean sauce-pan, beat one egg, a table-spoon butter and a tea-spoon flour together very thoroughly, and add to the broth with salt, pepper, and a little chopped parsley. Arrange the meat on a dish, pour over the dressing while boiling hot, and serve at once.

Gumbo.

Slice a large onion and put it with a slice of bacon or fat ham into a skillet and brown it; skin and cut up two quarts tomatoes, cut thin one quart okra, put all together with a little parsley into a stew-kettle, adding about three quarts water, and cook slowly two or three hours, adding salt and pepper to taste.—*Mrs. E. A. W.*

Mock Turtle or Calf's-head Soup.

Lay one large calf's head well cleaned and washed, and four pig's feet, in bottom of a large pot, and cover with a gallon of water; boil three hours, or until flesh will slip from bones; take out head, leaving the feet to be boiled steadily while the meat is cut from the head; select with care enough of the fatty portions in the top of the head and the cheeks to fill a tea-cup, and set aside to cool; remove brains to a saucer, and also set aside; chop the rest of the meat with the tongue very fine, season with salt, pepper, powdered marjoram and thyme, a tea-spoon of cloves, one of mace, half as much allspice and a grated nutmeg. When the flesh falls from the bones of the feet, take out bones, leaving the gelatinous meat; boil all together slowly, without removing the cover, for two hours more, take the soup from the fire and set it away until the next day. An hour before dinner set the stock over the fire, and when it boils strain carefully and drop in the meat reserved, which should have been cut, when cold, into small squares. Have these all ready as well as the force-meat balls, to prepare which rub the yolks of five hard-boiled eggs to a paste in a wedgewood mortar, or in a bowl with the back of a silver spoon, adding gradually the brains to moisten them, also a little butter and salt. Mix with these, two eggs beaten very light, flour the hands and make this paste into balls about the size of a pigeon's egg; throw them into the soup five minutes before taking it from the fire; stir in a large table-spoon browned flour rubbed smooth in a little cold water, and finish the seasoning by the addition of a glass and a half of sherry or Madeira wine, and the juice of a lemon. It should not boil more than half an hour on the second day. Serve with sliced lemons.

MUTTON SOUP.

Boil a nice leg of mutton, and take the water for the soup, add two onions chopped fine, potato, half a cup of barley, and two large tomatoes; season with pepper and salt, boil one hour, stir often (as barley is apt to burn), and, before taking from the fire, add one table-spoon flour wet with cold water.—*Mrs. E. R. Fay, New York City.*

NOODLE SOUP.

Add noodles to beef or any other soup after straining; they will cook in fifteen or twenty minutes, and are prepared in the following manner: To one egg add as much sifted flour as it will absorb, with a little salt; roll out as thin as a wafer, dredge very lightly with flour, roll over and over into a large roll, slice from the ends, shake out the strips loosely and drop into the soup.

OKRA SOUP.

Take a nice joint of beef filled with marrow, one gallon water, one onion cut fine, two sprigs parsley, half a peck of okra, one quart tomatoes; boil the meat six hours, add vegetables and boil two hours more.—*Mrs. E. L. F.*

ONION SOUP.

Fry brown in butter eight sliced onions with a table-spoon flour, put in a tin pail, and stir in slowly four or five pints boiling milk (or part water), set in kettle of boiling water, season with salt and pepper, and add tea-cup grated potato; cook from five to ten minutes, add tea-cup of sweet cream, and serve immediately.—*E. W. W.*

OYSTER SOUP.

Two quarts water, table-spoon salt, two of butter, half tea-spoon pepper; heat together to boiling point, add pint oysters, six rolled crackers, half cup sweet cream. Remove as soon as at the boiling point. Serve immediately.—*Mrs. Lizzie C. Robinson.*

POT AU FEU.

Take a good-sized beef-bone with plenty of meat on it, extract the marrow and place in a pot on the back of the range, covering the beef with three or more quarts of cold water; cover tightly, and allow to simmer slowly all day long. The next day, before heating, remove the cake of grease from the top, and add a large onion (previously stuck full of whole cloves, and then roasted in the oven till of a rich-brown color), adding tomatoes or any other vegetables which one may fancy. A leek or a section of garlic adds much to the flavor. Rice may be added, or vermicelli for a change. Just before serving, burn a little brown sugar and stir through it. This gives a peculiar flavor and rich color to the soup.—*Mrs. Col. Clifford Thompson, New York City.*

PEA SOUP.

Two quarts of good stock, one quart split pease, or green pease, one tea-spoon white sugar; soak the pease, if split, over night, and then boil tender in just enough water to prevent them from scorching; when tender, pass them through a sieve, and add them to the stock; add pepper and salt to taste, let all come slowly to a boil, let the soup simmer slowly for thirty minutes, and, just before serving, stir in a table-spoon of butter in which has been stirred a tea-spoon of flour. Serve hot, with chips of fried bread.—*Mrs. V. G. Hush.*

18

Green Pea Soup.

Boil three pints shelled pease in three quarts of water; when quite soft, mash through a colander, adding a little water to free the pulp from the skins; return pulp to the water in which it was boiled, add a head of lettuce chopped, and half a pint young pease; boil half an hour, season with salt and pepper, and thicken with two table-spoons butter rubbed into a little flour. Serve with bits of toasted bread. The soup, when done, should be as thick as cream.

Potato Soup.

To one gallon of water add six large potatoes chopped fine, one tea-cup rice, a lump of butter size of an egg, one table-spoon flour. Work butter and flour together, and add one tea-cup sweet cream just before taking from the fire. Boil one hour.—*Miss Lida Canby.*

Swiss Soup.

Five or six gallons water, six potatoes and three turnips sliced; boil five or six hours until perfectly dissolved and the consistency of pea soup, filling up as it boils away; add butter size of an egg, season well with salt and a little pepper, and serve. A small piece of salt pork, a bone or bit of veal or lamb, and an onion, may be added to vary this soup.

Tomato Soup.

Skim and strain one gallon of stock made from nice fresh beef; take three quarts tomatoes, remove skin and cut out hard center, put through a fine sieve, and add to the stock; make a paste of butter and flour, and, when the stock begins to boil, stir in half a tea-cup, taking care not to have it lumpy; boil twenty minutes, seasoning with salt and pepper to taste. When out of season, canned tomatoes will answer, two quarts being sufficient.—*Mrs. Col. Reid, Delaware.*

Meatless Tomato Soup.

One quart tomatoes, one of water; stew till soft; add tea-spoon soda, allow to effervesce, and add quart of boiling milk, salt, butter, and pepper to taste, with a little rolled cracker; boil a few minutes and serve.—*Mrs. D. C. Conkey, Minneapolis, Minn.*

Turkey Soup.

Place the rack of a cold turkey and what remains of the dressing and gravy in a pot, and cover with cold water; simmer gently for three or four hours, and let it stand till the next day; take off all the fat, and skim off all the bits and bones; put the soup on to heat till it boils, then thicken slightly with flour wet up in water, and season to taste; pick off all the bits of turkey from the bones, put them in the soup, boil up and serve.—*Mrs. H. B. Sherman.*

Vegetable Soup.

After boiling a soup bone or piece of beef until done, add to the broth boiling water to make the amount of soup wanted, and when boiling again add a large handful of cabbage cut fine as for slaw, a half pint of tomatoes, canned or fresh; peel and slice and add three large or four small onions, and two or three potatoes (some use a half tea-cup of dried or half pint of green corn; if dried corn is used, it should be soaked). Let boil from half to three-quarters of an hour; if you like a little thickening, stir an egg or yolk with a large spoonful of milk and a tea-spoon of flour, put in five or ten minutes before taking off; this makes it very rich. Serve with crackers.—*Mrs. H. C. Vosbury.*

Vegetable Soup.

Three onions, three carrots, three turnips, one small cabbage, one pint of tomatoes; chop all the vegetables except the tomatoes very fine, have ready in a porcelain kettle three quarts of boiling water, put in all except the cabbage and tomatoes and simmer for half an hour, then add the chopped cabbage and tomatoes (the tomatoes previously stewed), also a bunch of sweet herbs. Let soup boil for twenty minutes, strain through a sieve, rubbing all the vegetables through. Take two table-spoons of best butter and one of flour and beat them to a cream. Now pepper and salt soup to taste, add a tea-spoon of white sugar, a half cup of sweet cream if you have it, and last stir in the butter and flour; let it boil up and it is ready for the table. Serve with fried bread-chips, or poached eggs one in each dish.—*Mrs. V. G. H.*

Veal Soup.

To about three pounds of a well-broken joint of veal, add four quarts water, and set it over to boil; prepare one-fourth pound macaroni by boiling it in a dish by itself with enough water to cover it; add a little butter when the macaroni is tender, strain the soup and season to taste with salt and pepper, then add the macaroni with the water in which it was boiled; onions or celery may be added for flavoring.—*Mrs. R. M. Nixon, New Castle, Ind.*

Bread-dice for Soups.

Take slices of stale bread, cut in small squares, throw in hot lard and fry till brown, skim out, drain, and put in the soup-tureen before serving the soup. Crackers crisped in the oven are nice to serve with oyster soup.—*Mrs. V. G. H.*

Caramel for Soups.

For caramel, put one tea-cup sugar and two tea-spoons water in a sauce-pan over the fire, stir constantly till it is a *dark* color, then add a half tea-cup water and a pinch of salt, let boil for a few moments, take off and when cold bottle.

To brown flour, put one pint in a sauce-pan on the stove, and when it begins to color stir constantly till it is a dark brown, being careful that it does not burn. When cold put away in a tin can or jar covered closely, and keep in a dry place where it is always ready for soups or gravies. As it requires more of this for thickening than of unbrowned flour, it may be well sometimes to take half of each.

A few cloves may be stuck in the meat for soup; or it may first be fried in a sauce-pan with a little butter, turning till brown on all sides; or sliced onions may be fried brown and added to soup. —*Mrs. J. H. S.*

VEGETABLES.

All vegetables are better cooked in soft water, provided it is clean and pure; if hard water is used put in a small pinch of soda. The fresher all vegetables are the more wholesome. After being well washed, they should lie in cold water half an hour before using, and some peel potatoes and let them stand in cold water over night, putting them in immediately after being peeled, as exposure to the air darkens them. Green corn and pease should be prepared and cooked at once. Put all kinds into salted water, boiling hot (excepting potatoes which may be put on in salted cold water) and cook until thoroughly done, draining well those that require it. Never split onions, turnips and carrots, but slice them in rings cut across the fiber, as they thus cook tender much quicker. Always add both salt and a little soda to the water in which greens are cooked, as soda preserves color; for the same purpose French cookery books recommend a small pinch of carbonate of ammonia. A little sugar added to turnips, beets, pease, corn, squash and pumpkin is an improvement, especially when the vegetables are poor in quality. Sweet potatoes require a longer time to cook than the common variety. In gathering asparagus, never cut it off, but snap or break it; in this way you do not get the white, woody part which no boiling can make tender. Put rice on to cook in boiling salted water, having first soaked for about an hour; or steam it, or cook in custard-kettle.

A piece of red pepper the size of finger-nail, dropped into meat or vegetables, when first beginning to cook, will aid greatly in killing the unpleasant odor. Remember this for boiled cabbage, green beans, onions, mutton and chicken. All vegetables should be thoroughly cooked, and require a longer time late in their season. Potatoes especially when old are improved by removing the skin before baking, and either Irish or sweet potatoes if frozen, must be put in to bake without thawing.

Small sized white turnips contain more nutrition than large ones but in ruta-bagas the largest are best. Potatoes vary greatly in quality; varieties which are excellent early in the season lose their good qualities, and others, which are worthless in the fall, are excellent late in the spring. Those raised on gravelly or sandy soil, not over rich, are best.

Asparagus.

Wash well, put on stove in boiling water, boil five minutes, pour off water, add more boiling hot; boil ten to fifteen minutes, then put in a lump of butter, salt and pepper (some stir in a thickening made of one tea-spoon flour mixed up with cold water), cut and toast two or three thin slices of bread, spread with butter and put in a dish, and over them turn asparagus and gravy. The water must be boiled down until just enough for the gravy, which is made as above.—*Mrs. W. W. W.*

Artichokes.

Soak in cold water, wash well, boil in plenty of water with a lump of salt for an hour and a half to two hours; trim them, drain on a sieve, and serve with melted butter; some put into small cups, one for each guest.—*Mrs. E. L. F., New York City.*

A Good Boiled Dinner.

Put meat on, after washing well, in enough boiling water to just cover the meat; as soon as it boils, set kettle on the stove where it will simmer or boil very slowly; boil until almost tender, put in vegetables in the following order: Cabbage cut in quarters, turnips of medium-size cut in halves, and potatoes whole, or if large cut in two; peel potatoes and turnips and allow to lie in cold water for half an hour before using. The meat should be well skimmed before adding vegetables; boil together until thoroughly done (adding a little salt before taking out of kettle) when there should be left only just enough water to prevent their burning; take up vegetables in separate dishes, and lastly the meat; if there is any juice in the kettle, pour it over the cabbage. Boil cabbage three-quarters of an hour, turnips and potatoes one-half hour. A soup plate or saucer turned upside down, or a few iron table-spoons are useful to place in bottom of kettle to keep meat from burning. Parsnips may be substituted in place of cabbage and turnips, cooking them three-quarters of an hour.

BEETS.

Remove leaves, wash clean, being careful not to break off the little fibers and rootlets, as the juices would thereby escape and they would lose their color; boil in plenty of water, if young, two hours, if old, four or five hours, trying with a fork to see when tender; take out, drop in a pan of cold water, and slip off the skin with the hands; slice those needed for immediate use, place in a dish, add salt, pepper, butter, and if not very sweet a tea-spoon sugar, and serve with or without vinegar; put those which remain into a stone jar whole, cover with vinegar, keep in a cool place, take out as wanted, slice and serve. A few pieces of horse-radish put into the jar will prevent a white scum on the vinegar. Or, roast in hot ashes, and when tender, peel, slice, and dress with salt, pepper, butter and vinegar.

BEET GREENS.

Wash young beets very clean, cut off tips of leaves, looking over carefully to see that no bugs or worms remain, but do not separate roots from leaves; fill dinner pot half full of salted boiling water, add beets, boil from half to three-quarters of an hour; take out and drain in colander, pressing down with a large spoon, so as to get out all the water. Dish and dress with butter, pepper, and salt if needed. Serve hot with vinegar.

BAKED BEETS.

Beets retain their sugary delicate flavor much better by baking instead of boiling; turn often in the pan while in the oven, using a knife, as a fork will cause the juice to flow; when done, remove skin, slice and season with butter, pepper and salt, or if for pickle, slice into good cold vinegar.—*Mrs. S. M. Guy.*

String Beans.

String, snap and wash two quarts beans, boil in plenty of water about fifteen minutes, drain off and put on again in about two quarts boiling water; boil an hour and a half, and add salt and pepper just before taking up, stirring in one and a half table-spoons butter rubbed into two table-spoons flour and half pint sweet cream. Or, boil a piece of salted pork one hour, then add beans and boil an hour and a half. For shelled beans boil half an hour in water enough to cover, and dress as above.

Beans for Winter.

String fresh green beans, and cut down the sides till within an inch of the end, boil in water fifteen minutes, take out and drain; when cold, pack in a stone jar, first putting two table-spoons of salt in the bottom, then a quart of beans, sprinkle with a table-spoon of salt, put in layer after layer in this way till the crock is full, pour over a pint (if not filled the first time, beans may be added until filled, putting in no more water after this pint) of cold well-water, put on a cloth with a plate and weight, set away in a cool place, and in about a week take off cloth, wash it out in a little salt water (there will be a scum upon it), put back as before, and repeat operation at the end of another week; then pack away, and when wanted for use, take out the quantity wanted and soak for half an hour, put in pot in cold water with a piece of fresh pork, cook half an hour, season with pepper and a little salt if needed; or cook without pork, and season with butter and pepper.— *Bina.*

Fried Bananas.

Peel and slice the bananas, sprinkle with salt, dip in thin batter, and fry in butter. Serve immediately.—*Aunt Eliza, Selma, Ala.*

Stewed Carrots.

Take any quantity desired, divide the carrots lengthwise, and boil until perfectly tender, which will require from one to two hours. When done, have ready a sauce-pan with one or two table-spoons butter, and small cup cream; slice the carrots very thin, and put in the sauce-pan; add salt and pepper, and let stew ten or fifteen minutes, stirring gently once or twice, and serve in a vegetable dish. Some add more milk or cream; when done, skim out carrots, and to the cream add a little flour thickening, or the beaten yolks of one or two eggs. When it boils, pour over the carrots and serve. Carrots may also be boiled with meat like turnips or parsnips, but they take longer to cook than either.—*Mrs. C. T. C.*

BOILED CORN.

Put the well-cleaned ears in salted boiling water, boil three-quarters of an hour, or boil in the husk. for the same time, remove husks and serve immediately. Well-boiled corn is a wholesome dish.—*Mrs. J. H. S.*

BINA'S STEWED CORN.

Shave corn off the ear, being careful not to cut into the cob; to three pints corn add three table-spoons butter, pepper and salt, and just enough water to cover; place in a skillet, cover and cook rather slowly with not too hot a fire, from half to three-quarters of an hour, stir with a spoon often, and if necessary add more water, for the corn must not brown; if desired, a few moments before it is done, add half cup sweet cream thickened with teaspoon flour; boil well and serve with roast beef, escaloped tomatoes and mashed potatoes. Some stew tomatoes and just before serving mix them with the corn.

DRIED CORN.

For a family of eight, wash a pint of corn through one water, and put to soak over night in clean cold water (if impossible to soak so long, place over a kettle of hot water for two or three hours); when softened, cook five to ten minutes in water in which it was soaked, adding as soon as boiling, two table-spoons butter, one of flour, and a little salt and pepper. Another good way to finish is the following: Take the yolk of one egg, one table-spoon milk, pinch of salt, thicken with flour quite stiff so as to take out with a tea-spoon, and drop in little dumplings not larger than an acorn; cover tightly and cook five or ten minutes; have enough water in kettle before adding dumplings, as cover should not be removed until dumplings are done.

DRYING CORN.

Select good ears of sweet corn, husk, take off silk carefully, but do not wash; shave with a sharp knife, not too close to the cob, into a large tin pan or wooden bowl, scrape cob to get all the milk of corn; when about three quarts are cut off, line a large dripping-pan with flour-sack paper, being careful to have sides and edges covered, pour in corn, spread, and put at once in moderate oven; stir frequently and leave in oven fifteen or twenty minutes. Set a table out in the sun, cover with a cloth, pour the corn upon it and spread out evenly and thinly. Before sunset bring the corn in and spread on a table in the house; in the morning heat again in oven and spread in sun as before. If directions are closely followed, the corn will be thoroughly dried on the evening of the second day, and when shaken will rattle; store in paper bag as soon as cooled. Prepare in small quantities, because it must not stand long after being shaven, but should at once go into oven to heat. When all is dried, put in oven for final heating; place to cool, pour into the bag, tie closely, and hang in a cool, dry, dark place.

HULLED CORN.

This old-fashioned luxury is really a delicious dish when properly prepared. Take a six-quart pail full of ashes (hard wood ashes if possible, as they are stronger); put them into an iron kettle with three gallons of water; let them boil about five minutes, then set off from the fire and turn in a pint of cold water to settle it. Turn off the lye and strain; put it into an iron kettle, and put in six quarts of shelled corn; put it over a brisk fire, and let it boil half an hour, skimming and stirring frequently, (the outside skin of the kernels will then slip off); strain off the lye, and rinse thoroughly in several clear waters. When the lye is thus weakened turn the corn into a large dish-pan, and turn in water enough to cover it; then rub thoroughly with the hands, till the black chits come off; rinse and strain off till the water looks clear; then put back into a clean kettle, with water enough to cover it, and let it boil, then turn off water, put on again and parboil three or four times (it will swell to about double the first quantity); the last time boil till quite soft; it may be necessary to add water occasionally; stir often, so as not to burn at the bottom of the kettle; when quite soft, put in two large table-spoons of salt, and stir well; to be eaten with milk, or butter and sugar. It is a healthy dish, and although there is trouble in preparing it, yet it is good enough to pay for the labor and trouble. It is good either hot or cold, and was considered by our grandparents to be one of the greatest luxuries of the table. Wheat hulled in the same way is considered a great delicacy, and a very beneficial diet for invalids, but is not so staple or nutritious as Indian corn. Smaller quantities can be prepared by using less lye and corn.—*Mrs. Carrie Beck.*

PRESERVING CORN.

Scald the corn just enough to set the milk, cut from cob, to every four pints of corn add one pint salt, mix thoroughly, pack in jars, with a cloth and a weight over corn; keep in any convenient place, and when wanted for use put in a stew-pan or kettle, cover with cold water, as soon as it comes to a boil pour off and put on cold again, and repeat until it is fresh enough for taste, then add a very little sugar, sweet cream, or butter, etc., to suit taste.—*Mrs. S. M. Guy.*

GREEN CORN PUDDING.

Draw a sharp knife through each row of corn lengthwise, then scrape out the pulp; to one pint of the corn add one quart of milk, three eggs, a little suet, sugar to taste, and a few lumps of butter; stir it occasionally until thick, and bake about two hours.—*Mrs. W. G. Hillock, New Castle, Indiana.*

BOILED CAULIFLOWER.

To each half gallon water allow heaped table-spoon salt; choose close and white cauliflower, trim off decayed outside leaves, and cut stock off flat at bottom; open flower a little in places to remove insects which generally are found about the stalk, and let cauliflowers lie with heads downward in salt and water for two hours previous to dressing them, which will effectually draw out all vermin. Then put into boiling water, adding salt in above proportion, and boil briskly over a good fire keeping the sauce-pan uncovered. The water should be well skimmed. When cauliflowers are tender, take up, drain, and if large enough, place upright in dish; serve with plain melted butter, a little of which may be poured over the flowers, or a cream dressing may be used.—*Mrs. W. P. Anderson.*

FRIED CABBAGE.

Cut the cabbage very fine, on a slaw cutter, if possible; salt and pepper, stir well, and let stand five minutes. Have an iron kettle smoking hot, drop one table-spoon lard into it, then the cabbage, stirring briskly until quite tender; send to table immediately. One half cup sweet cream, and three table-spoons vinegar—the vinegar to be added after the cream has been well stirred, and after it is taken from the stove, is an agreeable change. When properly done an invalid or babe can eat it without injury, and there is no offensive odor from cooking it.—*Mrs. J. T. Liggett, Detroit, Mich.*

DELICATE CABBAGE.

Remove all defective outside leaves, quarter and cut as for coarse slaw, cover well with cold water, and let remain several hours before cooking, then drain out and put into a pot with enough boiling water to cover; boil until thoroughly cooked (which will generally require about forty-five minutes), add salt ten or fifteen minutes before removing from the fire, and when done, take up into a colander, press out the water well, and season with butter and pepper. This is a good dish to serve with corned meats, but should not be cooked with them; if preferred, however, it may be seasoned by adding some of the liquor and fat from the boiling meat to the cabbage while cooking. Or, cut the cabbage in two, remove the hard stock, let stand in cold water two hours, tie in thin netting or piece of muslin, and boil in salted water for a longer time than when it is cut finely. Drain, remove, and serve in a dish with drawn butter or a cream dressing poured over it.—*Mrs. E. T. Carson.*

SOUTHERN CABBAGE.

Chop or slice one medium-sized cabbage fine, put it in a stew-pan with boiling water sufficient to well cover it, and boil fifteen minutes; drain off all the water, and add a dressing made as follows: Half tea-cup wine-vinegar, two-thirds as much sugar, salt, pepper, half tea-spoon mustard, and two tea-spoons of salad oil; when this is boiling hot, add one tea-cup milk (cream is better), and one egg stirred together; mix this thoroughly and immediately with the cabbage, and cook a moment. Serve hot.—*Mrs. P. T. Morey, Charleston, S. C.*

STUFFED CABBAGE.

Take a large, fresh cabbage and cut out the heart; fill the vacancy with stuffing made of cooked chicken or veal, chopped very fine and highly seasoned and rolled into balls with yolk of egg. Then tie the cabbage firmly together (some tie a cloth around it), and boil in a covered kettle two hours. This is a delicious dish and is useful in using up cold meats.—*Mrs. W. A. Croffut, New York City.*

STEWED OR FRIED CABBAGE.

Slice down a head of cabbage, put in a stew-pan already prepared with a very little water; butter, salt and pepper; cover and stew about twenty minutes, taking care not to let it burn; beat and strain three eggs, add half cup good vinegar (beat while pouring in vinegar), then turn mixture on cabbage, stirring briskly all the time; serve immediately. Sour cream may be used instead of eggs and vinegar. To fry fine, place on heated skillet with a tablespoon of butter or beef-drippings, slice, season, cover, stir frequently and fry ten to fifteen minutes, being very careful not to burn it.

SAUER KRAUT.

Slice cabbage fine on a slaw-cutter; line the bottom and sides of an oaken barrel or keg with cabbage leaves, put in a layer of the sliced cabbage about six inches in depth, sprinkle lightly with salt and pound with a wooden beetle until the cabbage is a compact mass; add another layer of cabbage, etc., repeating the operation, pounding well each layer, until the barrel is full to within six inches of the top; cover with leaves, then a cloth, next a board cut to fit loosely on the inside of barrel, kept well down with a heavy weight. If the brine has not raised within two days, add enough water, with just salt enough to taste, to cover the cabbage; examine every two days, and add water as before, until brine raises and scum forms, when lift off cloth carefully so that the scum may adhere, wash well in several cold waters, wring dry and replace, repeating this operation as the scum arises, at first every other day, and then once a week, until the acetous fermentation ceases, which will take from three to six weeks. Up to this time keep warm in the kitchen, then remove to a dry, cool cellar, unless made early in the fall, when it may be at once set in the pantry or cellar. One pint of salt to a full barrel of cabbage is a good proportion; some also sprinkle in whole black pepper. Or, to keep until summer: In April squeeze out of brine, and pack tightly with the hands in a stone jar, with the bottom lightly sprinkled with salt; make brine enough to well cover the kraut in the proportion of a table-spoon salt to a quart of water; boil, skim, cool, and pour over; cover with cloth, then a plate, weight, and another cloth tied closely down; keep in a cool place and it will be good in June. Neither pound nor salt the cabbage too much, watch closely, and keep clear from scum for good sauer kraut.—*Mrs. Mary Weaver, Darby Plains.*

DANDELIONS.

They are ripe for use before they blossom. Cut off the leaves, pick over carefully, wash in several waters, put into boiling water, boil one hour, drain well, add salted boiling water, and boil two hours; when done, turn into a colander and drain, season with but-ter, and more salt if needed, and cut with a knife; or boil with a piece of salt pork, omitting the butter in the dressing.

ENCHILADAS.

Put four pounds of corn in a vessel with four ounces lime, or in a preparation of lye; boil with water till the hull comes off, then wash the corn (usually done by Mexicans on a scalloped stone made for grinding corn as was practiced by Rebecca), bake the meal in small cakes called " tortillas," then fry in lard; take some red pep-per ground called "chili colorad," mix with it sweet oi. and vin-egar, and boil together. This makes a sauce into which dip the tortillas, then break in small pieces cheese and onions, and sprinkle on top the tortillas, and "enchiladas" is the result. Any one who has ever been in a Spanish-speaking country will recognize this as one of the national dishes, as much as the pumpkin pie is a New England speciality.—*Gov. Safford, Arizona.*

EGG-PLANT.

Peel and cut in slices the purple kind, sprinkle with salt and pepper, and let drain on a tipped plate for three-quarters of an hour; make a light batter with one egg, flour and a little water, dip the slices into it and fry in butter or lard. Eggs and cracker may be used instead of the batter. Or, peel the egg-plant, boil till done, then pour off the water, mash fine, and pepper, butter and salt to taste, put in a shallow pudding-pan, and over the top place a thick layer of crushed cracker. Bake half an hour in a moderate oven.

EGG-PLANT.

Peel and slice one or two medium-sized egg-plants, boil in a little water till tender, drain, mash fine, season with salt and pepper, and add a beaten egg and a table-spoon of flour; fry in little cakes in butter or butter and lard in equal parts. Parsnips and salsify or oyster-plant may be cooked in the same way, but the oyster plant is made in smaller cakes to imitate oysters.—*Mrs. J. H. S.*

SOUTHERN FRIED LETTUCE.

Chop lettuce and tops of two onions very fine, and add to two well-beaten eggs; put a little sweet-oil or butter in hot frying-pan, pour in the well-beaten mixture, turn after a few moments, and serve with or without vinegar.—*Miss M. E. Wilcox, Selma, Ala.*

BOILED MACARONI.

Pour one pint boiling water over five ounces macaroni, let stand half an hour, drain and put in a custard-kettle with boiling milk or milk and water to cover, cook till tender, drain, add a table-spoon butter, and a tea-cup cream, and season with salt and pepper; grate cheese over the top and serve.—*Mrs. S. R. T.*

FRIED MACARONI.

Boil till tender six ounces macaroni in water; in skillet fry till brown two or three table-spoons chopped ham (not cooked) and an onion; then add macaroni, and a tea-cup tomato-juice, season with salt, and when done, grate cheese over it, and let it brown slightly, or serve at once.—*Mrs. O. S. T., Portland, Maine.*

MACARONI.

Take about three ounces macaroni and boil till tender in a stew-pan with a little water; take a pudding dish or pan, warm a little butter in it, and put in a layer of macaroni, then a layer of cheese grated or cut in small bits, and sprinkle over with salt, pepper, and small pieces of butter, then add another layer of macaroni, and so on, finishing off with cheese; pour on rich milk or cream enough to just come to the top of the ingredients, and bake from one-half to three-quarters of an hour. Rice may be used instead of macaroni by first cooking as follows: Pick and wash a cup of rice, put in a stew-kettle with three cups boiling water, and set over the fire—the boiling water makes the kernels retain their shape better than when cold water is used. When done, put a layer of rice, cheese, etc., alternately as you would macaroni, and bake in the same way.

ITALIAN MACARONI.

Place two pounds of beef, well larded with strips of salt pork, and one or two chopped onions, in a covered kettle on the back of the stove, until it throws out its juice and is a rich brown ; add a quart of tomatoes seasoned with pepper and salt, and allow this mixture to simmer for two or three hours. Take the quantity of macaroni desired and boil in water for twenty minutes, after which put one layer of the boiled macaroni in the bottom of a pudding dish, cover with some of the above mixture, then a layer of grated cheese, and so on in layers till the dish is filled, having a layer of cheese on the top; place in the oven an hour, or until it is a rich brown. Commence early in the morning to prepare this dish.

BOILED OKRA.

Put the young and tender pods of long, white okra in salted boiling water in a porcelain or tin-lined sauce-pan (as iron discolors it), boil fifteen minutes, take off stems, and serve with butter, pepper, salt, and vinegar if preferred ; or, after boiling, slice in rings, season with butter, dip in batter and fry; season and serve.—*M. E. W., Selma.*

OKRA AND TOMATOES.

Peel and slice six or eight tomatoes, take same amount of tender sliced okra, and one or two sliced green peppers; stew in porcelain kettle fifteen or twenty minutes, season with butter, pepper, and salt, and serve.—*Mrs. E. E., Tuscumbia, Ala.*

BOILED OR FRIED ONIONS.

Wash and peel, boil ten minutes, pour off this water, again add boiling water, boil a few minutes and drain a second time; pour on boiling water, add salt and boil for one hour, drain in a colander, place in a dish to send to the table, and add butter and pepper. Or, about half an hour before they are done, turn a pint of milk into the water in which they are boiling, and, when tender, season as above. Old onions require two hours to boil. To fry onions, slice and boil ten minutes each time in three waters, drain, fry, stir often, season, and serve hot.

BOILED OR BAKED POTATOES.

Wash clean, cut off the ends, let stand in cold water a few hours, put into boiling water, the larger ones first, and then in a short time adding the rest, cover, and keep boiling constantly; after fifteen minutes throw in another handful of salt and boil another fifteen minutes; try with a fork, and if it does not quite run through the potato, they are done (this is called "leaving a bone in them"). Drain, take to door or window and shake in open air to make them mealy; return to stove and allow to stand uncovered for a moment. Or, when washed, bake in a moderate oven fifty minutes—or place in a steamer half an hour over water kept constantly boiling, serve immediately; or wash and peel medium-sized ones, and bake in pan with roast meat, basting often with the drippings.

BOILED POTATOES IN JACKETS.

Put well-washed and brushed potatoes in cold water; when water boils add a little salt, boil slowly at first, rapidly at the last (cooking from twenty-five to forty-five minutes), drain, sprinkle with

19

salt, return to top of stove, keep lid partly on kettle, and dry the potatoes well. They are more mealy if cooked in a steamer.

POTATOES AND ONIONS.

Boil potatoes in skins, peel while hot and slice; about an hour before wanted, slice onions, and let stand in salt and water; while peeling potatoes, put onions in skillet with a little ham gravy or butter and a little water, and cook slightly; take out, put in vege-table dish a layer of onions, then potatoes, then onions, etc., with potatoes last; add a cup of vinegar to skillet (with ham gravy or butter), warm and pour over.

FRICASSEED AND FRIED POTATOES.

Slice cold boiled potatoes, put into a dripping-pan, add milk, salt, pepper, and small lump of butter, allowing half a pint of milk to a dozen potatoes; place in oven for about fifteen minutes, stir occasionally with a knife to keep from burning; they should brown slightly on the top; or put in sauce-pan lump of butter, when melted, add a level table-spoon flour, cook a few minutes and add a tea-cup new milk or cream, season with salt and pepper; when it boils, add sliced potatoes, and boil till potatoes are thoroughly heated. To fry, slice and fry in butter or ham or beef-drippings, using only enough fat to prevent sticking; sprinkle with salt, cover with tin lid so that they may both fry and steam.

FRIED RAW POTATOES.

Wash, peel, and slice in cold water, drain in a colander, and drop in a skillet prepared with two table-spoons melted butter or beef-drippings, or one-half of each; keep closely covered for ten minutes, only removing to stir with a knife from the bottom to prevent burning; cook another ten minutes, stirring frequently until done and lightly browned. Sweet potatoes are nice pre-pared in the same manner.—*Mrs. M. E. Southard.*

FRIED WHOLE POTATOES.

Peel and boil in salted water, remove from the fire as soon as done so that they may remain whole; have ready one beaten egg, and some rolled crackers; first roll the potatoes in the egg, and then in the crackers, and fry in butter till a light brown, or drop in boiling lard. This is a nice way to cook old potatoes.—*Mrs. C. F.*

MASHED POTATOES.

Pare and boil till done, drain, and mash in the kettle until perfectly smooth; add milk or cream, and butter and salt; beat like cake with a large spoon, and the more they are beaten the nicer they become. Put in a dish, smooth, place a lump of butter in the center, sprinkle with pepper; or add one or two eggs, pepper, mix thoroughly, put in baking dish, dip a knife in sweet milk, smooth over, wetting every part with milk, and place in a hot oven twenty minutes.

NEW POTATOES.

Wash, scrape, boil ten minutes, turn off water, and add enough more, boiling hot, to cover, also add a little salt; cook a few moments, drain, and set again on stove, add butter, salt, and pepper, and a little thickening made of two table-spoons flour in about a pint of milk; put on the cover, and, when the milk has boiled, serve. Or, when cooked and drained, put in a skillet with hot drippings, cover, and shake till a nice brown.

POTATO CAKES.

Mix thoroughly with cold, mashed potatoes left from dinner, the well-beaten yolk of an egg; make into cakes as you would sausages, place in skillet with a table-spoon hot ham or beef drippings, cover tightly, and, in five minutes, when lower side is browned, turn, remove cover, fry until the other side is a nice brown; serve hot. Make up after dinner ready for frying for breakfast.

POTATO CAKES.

Grate eight raw Irish potatoes, add salt, two well-beaten eggs, and half cup flour; roll in cakes with a spoon, and fry in butter.— *Susie Nixon, Selma, Alabama.*

POTATOES IN JACKETS.

Bake as many potatoes as are needed; when done, take off a little piece from one end to permit them to stand, from the other end cut a large piece, remove carefully the inside, and rub through a fine sieve, or mash thoroughly; put on the fire with half an ounce of butter and one ounce of grated cheese to every four fair-sized potatoes, and add boiling milk and pepper and salt as for mashed potatoes; fill the potato shells, and sprinkle over mixed bread-crumbs and grated cheese; put in hot oven and brown. Many prefer to omit cheese and bread-crumbs, filling the shells heaping full and then browning.

POTATOES IN KENTUCKY STYLE.

The potatoes are sliced thin, as for frying, and allowed to remain in cold water half an hour. The slices are then put into a pudding dish, with salt, pepper, and some milk—about half a pint to an ordinary pudding-dish. They are then put into an oven and baked for an hour. When taken out, a lump of butter half the size of a hen's egg is cut into small bits and scattered over the top. Those who have never eaten potatoes cooked thus do not know all the capabilities of that esculent tuber. The slicing allows the interior of each potato to be examined, hence its value where potatoes are doubtful, though poor ones are not of necessity required. The soaking in cold water hardens the slices, so that they will hold their shape. The milk serves to cook them through, and to make a nice brown on the top; the quantity can only be learned by experience; if just a little is left as a rich gravy, moistening all the slices, then it is right. In a year of small and poor potatoes, this method of serving them will be very welcome to many a housekeeper.—*Mrs. C. M. Nichols. Springfield.*

POTATO SOUFFLE.

Boil four good-sized mealy potatoes, pass them through a sieve; scald in a clean sauce-pan half tea-cup of sweet milk and table-spoon of good butter, add to the potato with a little salt and pepper, and beat to a cream; add one at a time, the yolks of four eggs, beating thoroughly, drop a small pinch of salt into the whites and beat them to a stiff froth, add them to the mixture, beating as little as possible; have ready a well-buttered baking-dish, large enough to permit the soufflé to rise without running over; bake twenty minutes in a brisk oven, serve at once, and in the same dish in which it was baked. It should be eaten with meats that have gravies.

SARATOGA POTATOES.

Pare and cut into thin slices on a slaw-cutter four large potatoes (new are best), let stand in ice-cold salt water while breakfast is cooking; take a handful of the potatoes, squeeze the water from them and dry in a napkin; separate the slices and drop a handful at a time into a skillet of boiling lard, taking care that they do not strike together, stir with a fork till they are a light brown color, take out with a wire spoon, drain well and serve in an open dish. They are very nice served cold.—*Mrs. Jasper Sager.*

SWEET POTATOES.

Wash clean and bake in a hot oven one hour; or place in steamer over a kettle of boiling water from half to three-quarters of an hour; or when almost done, take off, scrape or peel them, place in a dripping-pan, and bake half an hour; or cut in slices and fry in butter or lard; or peel and slice when raw, and fry, a layer at a time, on griddle, or in a frying-pan, with a little melted lard; or drop in boiling lard in frying-pan, turning till a nice brown on both sides; or halve or quarter, and bake in pan with roast beef, basting them often with the drippings.

BAKED PARSNIPS.

Put four thin slices salt pork in a kettle with two quarts cold water, wash and scrape parsnips, and if large halve or quarter, and as soon as water boils place in kettle, boil about half an hour, remove meat, parsnips, and gravy to a dripping-pan, sprinkle with a little white sugar, and bake in oven a quarter of an hour or until they are a light brown, and the water is all fried out. Add a few potatoes if you like. Those left over, fried in a hot skillet with butter, ham fat or beef drippings, make a nice breakfast dish. It is better to dip each slice in a beaten egg before frying. Parsnips are good in March and April, and make an excellent seasoning for soups.

STEWED PARSNIPS.

Wash, scrape, and slice about half an inch thick; have a skillet prepared with a half pint hot water and a table-spoon butter, add the parsnips, season with salt and pepper, cover closely, and stew until the water is cooked away, stirring occasionally to prevent burning. When done, the parsnips will be of a creamy, light brown color.—*Mrs. D. B.*

GREEN PEASE.

Wash lightly two quarts shelled pease, put into boiling water enough to cover, boil twenty minutes, add pepper, salt, and more hot water if needed to prevent burning, and two table-spoons butter rubbed into two of flour; stir well, and boil five minutes. If pods are clean and fresh, boil first in water to give flavor, skim out and put in pease. Canned pease should be rinsed before cooking.

PEASE STEWED IN CREAM.

Put two or three pints of young green pease into a sauce-pan of boiling water; when nearly done and tender, drain in a colander quite dry; melt two ounces of butter in a clean stew-pan, thicken evenly with a little flour, shake it over the fire, but do not let it brown, mix smoothly with a gill of cream, add half a tea-spoon of white sugar, bring to a boil, pour in the pease, keep moving for two minutes until well heated, and serve hot. The sweet pods of young pease are made by the Germans into a palatable dish by simply stewing with a little butter and savory herbs.—*Mrs. W. A. Croffut, New York City.*

HOW TO BOIL RICE.

Rice should be carefully picked over, washed in warm water, rubbed between the hands, and then rinsed several times in cold water till white. Put one tea-cupful in a tin pan or porcelain kettle, add one quart boiling water and one tea-spoon salt; boil fifteen minutes, not stirring, but taking care that it does not burn; pour into a dish and send to table, placing a lump of butter in the center. Cooked thus the kernels remain whole. The Southern rice cooks much quicker, and is nicer than the Indian rice. To boil rice in milk, put a pint rice into nearly two quarts of cold milk an hour before dinner, add two tea-spoons salt, boil very slowly and stir often; cook on back part of stove or range so as to avoid burning, and take it up into a mold or bowl wet in cold water a short time before serving. Some soak rice an hour or two before cooking.

Southern Rice.

After thoroughly washing and rubbing the rice, put it in salted water enough to cover it twice over, in a custard-kettle, or tin pail set in a kettle of boiling water; cover the whole closely for fifteen or twenty minutes, until the grains of rice are full and plump but not "mushy;" drain off all the water possible, and replace rice in the kettle, allowing it to cook for a half hour longer, when it is ready to serve. The grains should be full and soft, and each one retain its form perfectly. During the last half hour it should be occasionally stirred lightly with a fork, and it is improved by standing on the back of the stove a few minutes before serving.—*Mrs. P. T. Morey, Charleston, S. C.*

Salsify or Vegetable Oysters.

Wash thoroughly, scrape off skin with a knife, cut across in rather thin slices, stew until tender in water enough to cover them, with a piece of salt codfish for seasoning. Before sending to table, remove codfish, thicken with flour and butter rubbed together, toast slices of bread, put in dish, and then add the vegetable osyter. This method gives the flavor of oysters to the vegetable, and adds much to its delicacy.—*Mrs. Gov. J. J. Bagley, Michigan.*

Salsify or Vegetable Oyster.

Parboil after scraping off the outside, cut in slices, dip it into a beaten egg and fine bread-crumbs, and fry in lard. Or slice crosswise five or six good-sized plants, cook till tender in water enough to cover, then add a pint or more of rich milk mixed with one table-spoon flour, season with butter, pepper and salt, let boil up and pour over slices of toasted bread; or add three pints milk, or half milk and water, season and serve with crackers like oyster soup.

Cymlings or Summer Squash.

These are better when young and tender, which may be known by pressing the nail through the skin; do not peel or take out seeds, but boil whole, or cut across in thick slices; boil in as little water as possible for one-half or three-quarters of an hour, drain well, mash and set on back part of stove or range to dry out for ten or fifteen minutes, stirring occasionally; then season with butter, pepper, salt and a little cream. If old, peel, cut up, take out seeds, boil and season as above.—*Mrs. Wm. Farley, Collierville, Tenn.*

WINTER SQUASH.

Cut up, take out inside, pare the pieces and stew in as little water as possible, cook an hour, mash in kettle, and if watery let stand on the fire a few moments, stirring until dry; season with butter, cream, salt and pepper; be careful that it does not burn. Winter squashes are also cooked by cutting in pieces without paring, baking, and serving like potatoes; or they may be cooked in a steamer, and served either in the shell, or scraped out, put in pan, mashed, and seasoned with butter, cream, salt and pepper, and then made hot and served.

SUCCOTASH.

Take pint of shelled lima beans (green), or string beans, cover with hot water, boil fifteen minutes; have ready corn from six good-sized ears, and add to beans; boil half an hour, add salt, pepper and two table-spoons butter. Be careful in cutting down corn not to cut too deep,—better not cut deep enough and then scrape; after corn is added watch carefully to keep from scorching. Or to cook with meat, boil one pound salt pork two hours, add corn and beans, omitting butter.

SUCCOTASH IN WINTER.

Wash one pint dried lima beans and one a half pints dried corn; put beans in kettle and cover with cold water; cover corn with cold water in a tin pan, set on top of kettle of beans so that while the latter are boiling the corn may be heating and swelling; boil beans fifteen minutes, drain off, cover with boiling water, and when tender (half an hour) add corn, cooking both together for fifteen minutes; five minutes before serving add salt, pepper and a dressing of butter and flour rubbed together, or one-half tea-cup cream or milk thickened with one table-spoon flour.

SPINACH.

Look over the spinach and wash in four waters, boil twenty minutes, drain in a colander and cut with a knife while draining;

season with pepper, salt and a little butter, boil two eggs hard and slice over the top; serve hot.—*Mrs. E. L. Fay, Washington Heights, New York City.*

BAKED TOMATOES.

Cut a thin slice from blossom side of twelve solid, smooth, ripe tomatoes, with a tea-spoon remove pulp without breaking shell; take a small, solid head of cabbage and one onion, chop fine, add bread-crumbs rubbed fine, and pulp of tomatoes, season with pepper, salt and sugar, add a tea-cup good sweet cream, mix well together, fill tomatoes, put the slice back in its place, lay them stem end down in a buttered pie-pan with just enough water to keep from burning, and bake half an hour. They make a handsome dish for a dinner table.—*Mrs. S. Watson, Upper Sandusky.*

ESCALOPED TOMATOES.

Put in a buttered baking-dish a layer of bread or cracker-crumbs seasoned with bits of butter, then a layer of sliced tomatoes seasoned with pepper, salt and sugar if desired, then a layer of crumbs, and so on till dish is full, finishing with the crumbs. Bake from three-quarters of an hour to an hour.

FRIED TOMATOES.

Peel tomatoes and cut crosswise in large slices, salt and pepper, dip each slice into wheat flour, then into beaten egg, and fry at once in hot lard; serve hot. A cup of milk is sometimes, thickened with a little flour and butter, boiled and poured over them.— *Estelle Woods Wilcox.*

MOTHER'S SLICED TOMATOES.

Prepare half an hour before dinner, scald a few at a time in boiling water, peel, slice, and sprinkle with salt and pepper, set away in a cool place, or lay a piece of ice on them. Serve as a relish for dinner in their own liquor, when vinegar and sugar may be added if desired.

STEWED TOMATOES.

Scald by pouring water over them, peel, slice and cut out all defective parts; place a lump of butter in a hot skillet, put in tomatoes, season with salt and pepper, keep up a brisk fire, and cook as rapidly as possible, stirring with a spoon or chopping up with a knife (in the latter case wipe the knife as often as used or it will blacken the tomatoes). Serve at once in a deep dish lined with toast. When iron is used, tomatoes must cook rapidly and have constant attention. If prepared in tin or porcelain they do not require the same care.—*Mrs. Judge Cole.*

TOMATO TOAST.

Run a quart of stewed ripe tomatoes through a colander, place in a porcelain stew-pan, season with butter, pepper and salt and sugar to taste; cut slices of bread thin, brown on both sides, butter and lay on a platter, and just as the bell rings for tea add a pint of good sweet cream to the stewed tomatoes, and pour them over toast.—*Mrs. S. Watson.*

TURNIPS.

Wash, peel, cut in slices, and place in kettle, and keep well covered with water; boil from half to three-quarters of an hour or until you can easily pierce them with a fork; drain well, season with salt, pepper and butter and mash fine. Do not boil too long, as they are much sweeter when cooked quickly. Turnips may be cut up and baked.

BILLS OF FARE.

These bills of fare are suggestions to assist the housekeeper in providing what is seasonable for daily fare and for extra occasions, rather than arbitrary rules. They may be varied, divided or subdivided to suit tastes, purses and events.

FOR SPRING.

SUNDAY.—*Breakfast.*—Fried brook-trout; broiled ham; eggs on toast; baked beans and Boston brown bread; rice waffles; tea, coffee, chocolate. *Dinner.*—Chicken soup; boiled mutton with caper sauce; mashed potatoes, hominy, canned tomatoes, asparagus; lettuce, radishes, pickles; orange short cake, Fannie's pudding; figs, almonds; tea, coffee. *Lunch.*—Cold chicken; cold mutton; rusk; cheese; crackers; canned peaches; preserved cherries; Queen Vic cake; iced tea.

FIRST.—*Breakfast.*—Boiled ham; raw potatoes fried; boiled eggs; buckwheat cakes with maple syrup; pickles; coffee. *Dinner.*—Beef-soup; boiled pork with potatoes and cabbage, salsify; apple sauce; catsup; pickles; bread; doughnuts; bread pudding; apples. *Supper.*—Dried beef; waffles, bread and butter; canned pears; ginger-snaps; cheese; cake; tea.

SECOND.—*Breakfast.*—Cold boiled ham, fried squirrels, ham omelet; potatoes with cream, asparagus with toast; muffins, Graham bread, corn bread; oranges; coffee, tea, chocolate. *Dinner.*—Macaroni soup; baked fish with dressing and sauce; boiled ham, roast veal; asparagus, potatoes, spinach, lettuce, radishes; lemon pie, cocoa-nut pie, queen of puddings; coffee. *Supper.*—Pickled tongue, pressed beef; waffles with maple syrup; spiced peaches, chow-chow, canned fruit, preserves; cake; coffee, tea.

THIRD.—*Breakfast.*—Fried ham; potatoes boiled in jackets; radishes; scrambled eggs; fried mush, Graham bread; coffee, tea, chocolate. *Dinner.*—Veal soup; roast lamb with mint sauce or currant jelly; potatoes; asparagus, spinach, lettuce, onions; Boston brown bread, bread; pickles; horse-radish; pie-plant pie; Roly-poly pudding; apples. *Supper.*—Cold veal, catsup, piccalilli; canned blackberries; warm biscuit with maple syrup; sugar cakes and tea.

FOR SUMMER.

SUNDAY.—*Breakfast*—Nutmeg melons; fried fish; boiled plover; saratoga potatoes; sliced tomatoes; Minnesota rolls; bread; coffee and chocolate. *Dinner.*—Green corn soup; baked chicken, cold veal loaf; mashed potatoes, summer squash, green corn pudding, baked tomatoes; corn starch pudding, blackberry pies; peaches, melons; ice-cream; centennial drops; white cake; tea and coffee. *Lunch.*—Cold chicken and veal; bread, cheese; lemon jelly; blackberries; Minnehaha cake; lemonade.

FIRST.—*Breakfast.*—Fruit; fried fish; frizzled beef; milk toast; Graham gems; boiled eggs; tea and coffee. *Dinner.*—Mutton soup; roast mutton, currant jelly; potatoes fried whole, asparagus with toast; lettuce, onions, radishes; rolls, Graham bread; pie-plant pie; sponge-cake and lemonade. *Supper.*—Cold mutton with gooseberry catsup; sweet pickles; biscuit; radishes; ginger-snaps, sponge-cake; ice-cream, strawberries; tea.

SECOND.—*Breakfast.*—Oat meal mush; veal cutlets, fried liver; fricasseed potatoes, new onions; Mennonite toast, hot pocket-books; aspara-gus, radishes; coffee and chocolate. *Dinner.*—Gumbo soup; roast lamb, mint sauce; fried chicken; pease, string beans, potatoes, cucumbers; lettuce, radishes; ripe currant pie; Bohemian cream, strawberries; lady's fingers, rolled jelly cake; coffee. *Supper.*—Cold lamb; cucumber salad; bread, strawberry short cake with sweetened cream; gooseberry fool; tea.

THIRD.—*Breakfast.*—Blackberry mush; beefsteak; snipe on toast; sliced tomatoes, stewed corn; apple sauce; warm rolls; coffee, tea, or choco-late. *Dinner.*—Okra soup; roast lamb with caper sauce, chicken pot-pie; escaloped tomatoes, boiled okra, boiled corn on the cob, summer squash, potatoes in jackets; bread; apple tarts; peach cobbler, melons; coffee and tea. *Supper.*—Cold lamb, chili sauce; lobster salad; warm French rolls; peach short-cake, delicate cake; iced-milk and iced-tea.

FOR FALL.

SUNDAY.—*Breakfast.*—Quail on toast; fricatelli; fried oysters; Saratoga potatoes; Indian griddle cakes with syrup, Boston brown bread; coffee and Vienna chocolate. *Dinner.*— Swiss soup; roast spare-rib; escaloped oysters; mashed potatoes, turnips, baked sweet potatoes, canned corn; cream slaw, celery; pickles; biscuit, rye bread; snow pudding; fruit cake; raisins and nuts; coffee and tea. *Lunch.*—Canned salmon; pickled oysters; light biscuit; cold Saratoga potatoes; chow-chow; canned plums; cake; tea and cocoa.

FIRST.—*Breakfast.*—Oatmeal mush; hash and broiled liver, fried salt-pork; corn oysters, baked potatoes; Graham bread; stewed peaches; nut-meg melons; coffee and chocolate. *Dinner.*—Potato soup; baked fish, egg sauce; mutton pie with tomatoes; broiled pheasants on toast with currant jelly; potato soufflé; stewed corn, egg plant, stuffed cabbage, boiled okra; Boston brown bread; cucumber and beet pickles; coffee jelly with whipped cream; marble cake; peach pyramid, melons and grapes; coffee and chocolate. *Supper.*—Sardines, pickled salmon; cold slaw; warm biscuit and honey; bread and cheese; potato salad; frozen peaches, melons, huckle-berries; tea.

SECOND.—*Breakfast.*—Cracked wheat; broiled prairie chicken; cod-fish balls; pork fritters; fricasseed potatoes; brown bread; rice waffles with syrup; chocolate and coffee. *Dinner.*—Raw oysters; vegetable soup with poached eggs; roast duck; chicken pie with oysters; mashed potatoes browned; turnips, cauliflower, macaroni, lima beans; Estelle pudding with cream sauce; pine-apple ice-cream and cake; melons and grapes; coffee and chocolate. *Supper.*—Cold tongue, tomato catsup; fricasseed frogs; Saratoga potatoes; chicken salad (made of cabbage); cream slaw; baked sweet apples; dry toast; fruit cake; peach short-cake and cream; tea.

THIRD.—*Breakfast.*—Graham mush; fried trout; pork steak; beef cro-quettes; boiled Irish potatoes, baked sweet potatoes; corn rolls, bread; coffee and cocoa. *Dinner.*—Oyster soup; boiled white fish, Holland sauce; boiled turkey, oyster sauce; potatoes, turnips, and egg-plant; macaroni with cheese; pickles; rye and Indian bread, biscuit, crackers; cocoa-nut pudding; apples and nuts; coffee and chocolate. *Supper.*—Raw oysters; escaloped turkey, currant jelly; baked pears; pop-overs, bread; nutmeg-melons, cake; tea.

FOR WINTER.

SUNDAY.—*Breakfast.*—Baked beans with pork, Boston brown bread; fried clams; fried potatoes, apple fritters with syrup; bread; coffee and cocoa-

Dinner.—Oyster soup; deviled crabs; roast turkey and cranberry sauce; potatoes, carrots, turnips, cabbage, boiled rice; plum cobbler; kiss pudding, Scotch fruit cake; coffee and chocolate. *Lunch.*—Raw oysters; sliced cold turkey, pickled chicken; light biscuit, rusk, crackers, cookies, cheese, almon tarts; peach preserves, cake.

FIRST.—*Breakfast.*—Oat meal mush; veal cutlets breaded, fricasseed tripe; fried raw potatoes, fried onions; buckwheat cakes with syrup, bread; tea and coffee. *Dinner.*—Raw oysters; beef soup; boiled fresh cod, egg sauce; roast chicken; mashed potatoes; stewed sweet potatoes, Italian macaroni, turnips; squash or pumpkin pie; eggless plum pudding, plum preserves; oranges, raisins, figs; coffee. *Supper.*—Oyster stew; cold chicken; blackberry jelly; watermelon preserves; bread, crackers; apple sauce; Fannie's pudding; almond cake; tea.

SECOND.—*Breakfast.*—Pork tenderloin fried, hash; fried apples, potatoes in Kentucky style; buckwheat cakes and syrup, bread; sliced oranges; coffee and chocolate. *Dinner.*—Tomato soup; baked beef with Yorkshire pudding; oyster pie; mashed potatoes, hominy, dried corn and lima beans; cream slaw, celery, bottled cucumbers; half-botch plum pudding, apple pie; apples, figs, and nuts; coffee and tea. *Supper.*—Cold beef sliced, pickled oysters; chicken salad; raspberry jam; cheese; dry toast; canned peaches; cocoa-nut cake, preserve puffs; tea.

THIRD.—*Breakfast.*—Beefsteak, turkey hash, pig's-feet souse; boiled potatoes in jackets; Graham gems, buckwheat cakes and syrup; coffee and chocolate. *Dinner.*—Bean soup; boiled salmon; stuffed baked rabbit, escaloped oysters; mashed potatoes, canned corn and tomatoes, canned pease, baked winter squash; cold slaw, variety pickles, sweet pickled peaches and pears; bread, bread with mush; rice apples, lemon butter toast; apples and oranges; coffee and tea. *Supper.*—Steamed oysters; cold tongue; warm biscuit and syrup; apple jelly; ginger snaps, Buckeye cake, orange float; tea and coffee.

ECONOMICAL BREAKFASTS.—*First.*—Ham and eggs, hash, baked potatoes, hominy, Graham gems, coffee. *Second.*—Breakfast stew or fish, fried Graham mush, tomatoes, potatoes, apple sauce, corn bread or toast, coffee.

ECONOMICAL DINNERS.—*First.*—Spare ribs, roast potatoes, cabbage, rice pudding, fruit. *Second.*—Codfish, egg sauce, Lancashire pie, parsnips, horse-radish, pickles, bread, custard pie. *Third.*—Boiled pork, beans, potatoes, greens, green currant pie. *Fourth.*—Fish, potato cakes, baked tomatoes, bread pudding, apple sauce. *Fifth.*—Boiled beef, lima beans, boiled potatoes, squash, sliced tomatoes, apple tapioca pudding. *Sixth.*—Meatless bean soup, roast beef and potatoes, macaroni with cheese, apple butter, custard pie. *Seventh.*—Meatless tomato soup, broiled chicken, fricasseed potatoes, turnips, tomato toast, fresh fruit.

LUNCHES.—*First.*—Escaloped oysters, chicken salad, ham sandwiches, deviled crabs; mixed pickles; cheese; coffee jelly with whipped cream; basket of mixed cakes; ice-cream; fruit, nuts; tea, chocolate with whipped cream. *Second.*—Chicken croquettes; cold slaw garnished with fried oysters; sardines with sliced lemons; lobster salad; cold saratoga potatoes; plums pickled like olives; pickles; jelly; orange or lemon-ice; cake; coffee, chocolate with whipped cream.

THANKSGIVING DINNERS.—Oyster soup; boiled fresh cod with egg sauce; roast turkey, cranberry sauce; roast goose, bread sauce or currant jelly; stuffed ham, apple sauce or jelly; pork and beans; mashed potatoes and turnips, delicate cabbage, canned tomatoes and corn, baked sweet potatoes, boiled onions, salsify, macaroni and cheese; brown bread and superior biscuit; lobster salad; pressed beef, cold corned beef, tongue; celery, cream slaw; watermelon, peach, pear, or apple sweet-pickles; mangoes, cucumbers, chow-chow, and tomato catsup; stewed peaches or prunes; doughnuts and ginger cakes; mince, pumpkin, and peach pies; plum and boiled Indian puddings; apple, cocoa-nut, or almond tarts; vanilla ice-cream; old-fashioned loaf cake, pound cake, black cake, white perfection cake, ribbon cake, almond layer cake; citron, peach, plum, or cherry preserves; apples, oranges, figs, grapes, raisins, and nuts; tea and coffee.

CHRISTMAS DINNERS.—Clam soup; baked fish, Holland sauce; roast turkey with oyster dressing and celery or oyster sauce, roast duck with onion sauce, broiled quail, chicken pie; plum and crab-apple jelly; baked potatoes in jackets, sweet potatoes, baked squash, turnips, southern cabbage, stewed carrots, canned corn, canned pease, tomatoes; Graham bread, rolls; salmon salad or herring salad, Chili sauce, gooseberry catsup, mangoes, pickled cabbage, bottled, French, or Spanish pickles; spiced nutmeg melon and sweet pickled grapes, and beets; Christmas plum-pudding with sauce, charlotte-russe; cocoa-nut, mince, and peach pies; citron, pound, French loaf, White Mountain, and Neapolitan cakes; lady's fingers, pepper-nuts; centennial drops, almond or hickory-nut macaroons; cocoa-nut caramels, chocolate drops; orange or pine-apple ice-cream; coffee, tea, and Vienna chocolate.

NEW YEAR'S DINNERS.—Raw oysters; mock turtle soup; boiled turkey with oyster sauce; roast haunch of venison, currant jelly; deviled crabs; potato soufflé, baked turnips, stuffed cabbage, beets, lima beans, dried corn, and canned pease; biscuit, French rolls, rye and Indian bread; chicken salad; cold sliced ham; celery, cold slaw garnished with fried oysters, pickled walnuts, variety pickles; sweet pickled cucumbers, peaches, and plums, spiced currants and gooseberries; canned pears or strawberries; English plum pudding; chess pie, potato pie, mince pie; orange soufflé, pyramid pound cake, black cake, Phil Sheridan cake; Bohemian cream; oranges, raisins, figs, nuts; tea, coffee, chocolate.

NEW YEAR'S TABLE.—When receiving calls on New Year's day, the table should be handsomely arranged and decorated, and provided with rather substantial dishes, such as would suit the tastes of gentlemen. Too great profusion, especially of cakes, confectionery, and ices, is out of taste. Selections may be made from the following: Escaloped oysters; cold tongue, turkey, chicken, and ham, pressed meats, boned turkey, jellied chicken; sandwiches or wedding sandwich rolls; pickled oysters, chicken and lobster salads, cold slaw garnished with fried oysters; bottled pickles, French or Spanish pickles; jellies; charlotte-russe, ice-creams, ices; two large handsome cakes for decoration of table, and one or two baskets of mixed cake, fruit, layer, and sponge cake predominating; fruits; nuts; coffee, chocolate with whipped cream, lemonade.

REFRESHMENTS.—For small evening parties, sociables, receptions, etc., where the refreshments are handed round, and are of a simple character, every thing should be excellent in the highest degree, delicately prepared, and attractively served. Sandwiches and coffee, chocolate, or tea, a variety of nice cake, jellies, ice-cream or ices, and fruits are appropriate. For a more pretentious occasion, a simple table prettily decorated with flowers, and set with fruit, lobster salad, chicken croquettes, pickled oysters, and one or two kinds of ice-cream and cake, and coffee and tea is quite enough.

REFRESHMENTS FOR TWENTY.—For a company of twenty allow one gallon oysters, four chickens and eight bunches of celery for chicken salad, fifty sandwiches, one gallon of ice-cream, two molds charlotte-russe, two quarts of lemon jelly, one light and one dark fruit cake, two layer cakes, and one white or sponge cake; for coffee use one and a half pints ground coffee and one gallon of water; fruit cake especially, and, indeed, all rich cake, should be cut in thin slices with a keen-edged knife; a small piece of each variety is always preferred to a plate overloaded with one or two kinds.

REFRESHMENTS FOR A HUNDRED.—For a larger company of a hundred the refreshments may be more elaborate: Two gallons of pickled oysters; two large dishes of lobster salad; two small hams boiled and sliced cold, five cold tongues sliced thin, twelve chickens jellied or pressed, each dish garnished with sprigs of parsley, slices of lemon and red beets, or curled leaves of celery, or the tender center leaves of lettuce; two gallons of bottled pickles or a gallon and a half of home-made; twelve dozen biscuit sandwiches; five quarts jelly, four gallons ice-cream; fifteen large cakes, to be made from recipes for rich fruit, delicate, layer, and sponge cakes; twelve dozen each of almond macaroons and variety puffs; four large dishes of mixed fruits; five pounds roasted coffee and five gallons water, which should be served at the beginning, and six gallons of iced lemonade to serve at the close.

REFRESHMENTS FOR ONE HUNDRED AND SEVENTY-FIVE.—Six gallons oysters; three small hams, two large turkeys, ten tongues: six chickens and twelve bunches of celery for salad; three gallons pickles; seventeen dozen buns, twelve loaves bread made in wedding sandwich rolls or in plain sandwiches; twenty-two large cakes; fifteen dozen large oranges sliced, seventeen dozen meringues, fifteen dozen pears, thirty pounds grapes; seven gallons ice-cream and four gallons lemon ice; coffee made of twelve pints ground coffee and eight gallons water; serve coffee at the beginning, and lemonade at the close.

FOR THE PICNIC.

In the "Sunny South," picnics are in order as early as April, but in the more northern latitudes should never be attempted before the latter part of May, or June, and September and October are the crowning months for them around the northern lakes, where hunting and fishing give zest to the sports. First, be up "at five o'clock in the morning," in order to have the chicken, biscuit, etc., freshly baked. Provide two baskets, one for the provisions, and the other for dishes and utensils, which should include the following: Table-cloth and an oil-cloth to put under it, napkins, towels, plates, cups, forks, a few knives and table-spoons, tea-spoons, sauce dishes, tin cups (or tumblers, if the picnickers are of the over-fastidious variety); a tin bucket, for water, in which a bottle of cream, lemons, oranges, or other fruit, may be carried to the scene of action; another with an extra-close cover, partly filled with made chocolate, which may be readily reheated by setting in an old tin pail or pan in which water is kept boiling *a la* custard-kettle; a frying-pan; a coffee-pot, with the amount of prepared coffee needed tied in a coarse, white flannel bag; a tea-pot, with tea in a neat paper package; tin boxes of salt, pepper, and sugar; a tin box for butter (if carried) placed next to block of ice, which should be well wrapped with a blanket and put in a shady corner of the picnic wagon. For extra occasions, add a freezer filled with frozen cream, with ice well packed around it, and heavily wrapped with carpeting. To pack the basket, first put in plates, cups, and sauce dishes carefully with the towels and napkins, and paper if needed; then add the rest, fitting them in tightly, and covering all with the table-cloth, and over it the oil-cloth. Tie the coffee and tea-pots, well wrapped up, and the frying-pan to the handles. Pack provision basket as full as the law allows, or as the nature of the occasion and the elasticity of the appetites demand. One piece of good advice to picnickers is to try to get under the wing of some good farm-house, where coffee may be boiled, and nice rich cream, green corn, good water, etc., may be readily foraged; and for a Fourth of July picnic, nothing will taste better than a dish of new potatoes, nicely prepared at the farm-house. But if not so fortunate, a good fire may be built, where all things may be merrily prepared. In fact, in the spring and fall, the fire is a necessity for roasting or broiling game, ham, clams, fish, corn and potatoes, etc.

A delicious way to roast potatoes, birds, or poultry, or even fish, is to encase them in a paste made of flour and water, and bake in the embers of a camp-fire; or build a fire over a flat stone, and when burnt down to coals, clear the stone, lay on the potatoes, birds, etc., wrapped in wet, heavy brown paper, cover with dry earth, sand, or ashes, and place the hot coals over these, adding more fuel. The Gypsies and Indians roast their poultry in mud molds or cases, covering feathers and all.

The following bills of fare may be picked to pieces and recombined to suit tastes and occasions:

SPRING PICNICS.—Cold roast chicken; ham broiled on coals; fish fried or broiled; sardines; tongue; hard-boiled eggs; eggs to be fried or scrambled; Boston corn bread; buttered rolls; ham sandwiches prepared with grated ham; orange marmalade; canned peaches; watermelon and beet sweet-pickles; euchered plums; variety or bottled pickles; chow-chow; quince or plum jelly; raspberry or other jams; Scotch fruit, rolled jelly, chocolate, Minnehaha, old-fashioned loaf, and marble cake; coffee, chocolate, tea; cream and sugar; salt and pepper; oranges.

SUMMER PICNICS.—Cold baked or broiled chicken; cold boiled ham; pickled salmon; cold veal loaf; Parker House rolls; light bread; box of butter; green corn boiled or roasted; new potatoes; sliced tomatoes; sliced cucumbers; French and Spanish pickles; peach and pear sweet-pickles; lemon or orange jelly; strawberries, raspberries, or blackberries; lemonade; soda-beer or raspberry vinegar; coffee and tea; ice-cream; lemon or straw-berry-ice; sponge, white, Buckeye, or lemon cake; watermelon, muskmelon, nutmeg-melon.

FALL PICNICS.—Broiled prairie chicken; fish chowder; clam chowder; clams roasted or fried; beef omelet; cold veal roast; sardines; cold roast chicken; pot of pork and beans; rusk, Minnesota rolls, Boston brown bread; potatoes, Irish or sweet, roasted in ashes; egg sandwiches (hard-boiled eggs, sliced, sprinkled with pepper and salt, and put between buttered bread); mangoes; piccalilli; Chili sauce; quince marmalade; baked apples; musk and nutmeg-melon; crab apple jelly; grape jelly; black, orange, velvet, sponge, and three-ply cake; combination pie.

FRAGMENTS.

Mother's hash doesn't taste of soap grease, rancid butter, spoiled cheese, raw flour, boarding-house skillets, hotel coffee, garden garlics, bologna sausage, or cayenne pepper, neither is it stewed and simmered and simmered and stewed, but is made so nicely, seasoned so delicately, and heated through so quickly, that the only trouble is, "there is never enough to go round." Cold meat of any kind will do, but corned beef is best; always remove all surplus fat and bits of gristle, chop fine, and to one-third of meat add two-thirds of chopped cold boiled potato, and one onion chopped very fine; place in the dripping-pan, season with salt and pepper, dredge with a little flour, and pour in at the side of the pan enough water to come up level with the hash, place in oven and do not stir; when the flour is a light brown, and has formed a sort of crust, take out, add a lump of butter, stir it through several times, and you will have a delicious hash. Or, by cooking longer, it may be made of cold raw potatoes, which peel, slice, and let lie in salt and water a half hour before chopping. If of meat and potatoes, always use the proportions given above, and, before chopping, season with pepper and salt, and a chopped onion if you like (if onions are not to be had, take them out of pickle jar), place in hot skillet with just enough water to moisten, add a little butter or some nice beef drippings, stir often until warmed through, cover and let stand on a moderately hot part of the stove fifteen minutes. When ready to dish, run the knife under and fold as you would an omelet, and serve hot with tomato catsup. In making hash, meats may be combined if there is not enough of a kind. Do not make hash or any other dish greasy. It is a mistaken idea to think that fat and butter in large quantities are necessary to good cooking. Butter and oils may be melted without changing their nature, but when cooked they become much more indigestible and injurious to weak stomachs.

AFTER THANKSGIVING DINNER

a most excellent hash may be made thus: Pick meat off turkey bones, shred it in small bits, add dressing and pieces of light biscuit cut up fine, mix together and put into dripping-pan, pour over any gravy that was left, add water to thoroughly moisten but not enough to make it sloppy, place in a hot oven for twenty minutes, and, when eaten, all will agree that the turkey is better this time than it was at first; or warm the remnants of the turkey over after the style of escaloped oysters (first a layer of bread-crumbs, then minced turkey, and so on); or add an egg or two and make nice breakfast croquettes. The common error in heating over meats of all kinds, is putting into a cold skillet, and cooking a long time. This second cooking is

21

more properly only heating, and should be quickly done. All such dishes should be served hot with some sort of tart jelly. Always save a can of currant juice (after filling jelly cups and glasses), from which to make jelly in the winter, and it will taste as fresh and delicious as when made in its season.

ALWAYS SAVE

all the currants, skimmings, pieces, etc, left after making jelly, place in a stone jar, cover with soft water previously boiled to purify it, let stand several days; in the meantime, take your apple peelings, without the cores, and put on in porcelain kettle, cover with water, boil twenty minutes, drain into a large stone jar; drain currants also into this jar, add all the rinsings from your molasses jugs, all dribs of syrup, etc., and, when jar is full, drain off all that is clear into vinegar keg (where, of course, you have some good cider vinegar to start with). If not sweet enough, add brown sugar or molasses, cover the bung-hole with a piece of coarse netting, and set in the sun or by the kitchen stove. In making vinegar always remember to give it plenty of air, and it is better to have the cask or barrel (which should be of oak) only half full, so that the air may pass over as large a surface as possible. Vinegar must also have plenty of material, such as sugar, molasses, etc., to work upon. Never use alum or cream of tartar as some advise, and never let your vinegar freeze. Paint your barrel or cask if you would have it durable. Company, sickness or other circumstances may prevent making

SWEET PICKLES

in their season, but they can be prepared very nicely at any time, by taking pear, peach, plum, or apple preserves, and pouring hot spiced vinegar over them; in a few days they will make a delightful relish. It very often happens in putting up cucumber pickles that you can only gather or buy a few at a time; these can be easily pickled in the following manner: Place in a jar, sprinkle with salt, in the proportion of a pint salt to a peck cucumbers, cover with boiling water, let stand twenty-four hours, drain, cover with fresh hot water; after another twenty-four hours, drain, place in a jar, and cover with cold, not very strong vinegar; continue to treat each mess in this manner, using the two jars, one for scalding and the other as a final receptacle for the pickles, until you have enough, when drain and cover with boiling cider vinegar, add spices, and in a few days they will be ready for use. Never throw away even

A CRUMB OF BREAD,

but save it and put with other pieces; if you have a loaf about to mold, cut in thin slices, place all together in a dripping-pan and set in oven to dry, and you will find that when pounded and rolled, it will be very nice for dressing, stuffing, puddings, griddle-cakes, etc. Keep in a covered box, or in a paper bag tied securely and hung in a dry place. It is much more economical to prepare meats with a dressing of some kind, since they " go so much further."

STUFFED BEEFSTEAK

is as nice for dinner as a much more expensive roast, and it can be pre-pared from a rather poor flank or round steak; pound well, season with salt and pepper, then spread with a nice dressing—may use some of the bread-crumbs—roll up and tie closely with twine (which always save from the grocer's parcels), put in a kettle with a quart boiling water, boil slowly one hour, take out and place in dripping-pan, adding water in which it was boiled, basting frequently until a nice brown, and making gravy of the drippings; or you may put it at once into the dripping-pan, omit the boil-ing process, skewer a couple slices salt pork on top, add a very little water, baste frequently, and, if it bakes too rapidly, cover with a dripping-pan. It is delicious sliced down cold. Or a delicious dish is

STEAK PUDDING.

Mix one quart flour, one pound suet (shredded fine), a little salt, and cold water to make stiff as for pie-crust, roll out half an inch thick ; have steak (beef or mutton) well seasoned with pepper and salt, lay them on the paste and roll it up, tie in a cloth, and boil three hours. Some add a few oysters and a sliced onion to the steak. Here is something simple and nice in the way of

YANKEE DRIED BEEF.

Slice very thin, put in frying-pan with water to cover, let come to boiling point, pour off, and add pint of milk, lump of butter, and a thickening of a little flour and milk, stir well, and, just before serving, some add an egg, stirring it in quickly ; or, chip very fine, freshen, add a lump of butter and six or eight eggs, stir well, and serve at once. Very economical prepa-rations of meat are the various

STEWS,

which, if properly prepared, are very palatable. If made from fresh meat, they should be immersed in boiling water at first, and then placed where it will simmer slowly until done; season, add thickening, and flavor with an onion, or a tea-spoon of curry powder; or prepare a poor beefsteak by first trimming off all the fat and cutting in convenient pieces, fry in butter or drippings to a nice brown on both sides, then add a little sliced onion, carrots, or turnips, seasoning, a tea-spoon chili-sauce, and one pint soup stock, or water; stew gently two or three hours, skim off any grease, and stir in a a little flour mixed with milk. To make a stew of cold meat, first make the gravy of stock, add a fried sliced onion, pepper and salt, and a tea-spoon catsup ; let it boil, and set aside to cool; when nearly cold, put in thinly-cut slices of cold meat, and a few slices cold potatoes, and let heat gradually until it comes to the boiling point serve with bread cut in dice and fried.

SCRAPPLE.

Scrape and clean well a pig's-head as directed in "Pig's-head Cheese," put on to boil in plenty of water, and cook four or five hours—until the bones will slip easily from the meat; take out, remove bones, and chop the meat fine, skim off the grease from liquor in pot, and return the chopped meat to it; season highly with salt and pepper, and a little powdered sage if liked, and add corn meal till of the consistency of soft mush; cook slowly one hour or more, pour in pans, and set in a cool place. This is nice sliced and fried for breakfast in winter, and will answer in place of meat on many occasions.

LANCASHIRE PIE.

Take cold beef, or veal, chop, and season as for hash; have ready hot mashed potatoes seasoned as if for the table, and put in a shallow baking-dish first a layer of meat, then a layer of potatoes, and so on, till dish is heaping full; smooth over top of potatoes, and make little holes in which place bits of butter; bake until a nice brown.

HOW TO MAKE NICE GRAVY

is a problem many housekeepers never solve. Remember that grease is not gravy, neither is raw flour. Almost any kind of meat-liquor or soup stock, from which all fat has been removed, may be made into nice gravy, by simply adding a little seasoning and some thickening; if browned flour is used for the latter, the gravy will require but little cooking, but, when thickened with raw flour, it must cook until thoroughly done, or the gravy will taste like so much gummy paste. It is best to brown a quart of flour at a time. Put in a skillet, set in the oven or on top of the stove, stir often until it is a light brown, put into a wide-mouthed bottle, cork, and keep for use. All gravies should be well stirred over a rather hot fire, as they must be quickly made, and must boil, not simmer.

For those who prefer corn meal, here is a rule for

CORN MEAL WAFFLES.

To the beaten yolks of three eggs, add one quart of sour milk or butter-milk, corn meal to make a batter a little thicker than for pan-cakes, one tea-spoon salt, one of soda dissolved in a little warm water, then the well-beaten whites; flour may be used instead of corn meal. This is also a good rule for pan-cakes, making the batter thinner. For dressing for waffles, put on the stove a half cup cream, a table-spoon butter, and two of sugar; when hot, put two table-spoons on each waffle when placed in the dish to serve.

The following idea for

WHITE FRUIT CAKE

May be of value to some: Make up batter for a large white or silver cake, then flour and stir into it two grated cocoa-nuts, two pounds of almonds blanched and cut up fine, and one pound of citron cut in small pieces.

When you tire of custard pies, try

APPLE-BUTTER CUSTARD PIE.

Beat together four eggs, one tea-cup apple-butter, one of sugar, one level table-spoon allspice, add one quart sweet milk and pinch of salt; bake in three pies with an under-crust;—and, by the way, never omit a pinch of salt in custard and lemon pie, and, in fact, many kinds of fruit pies, such as green-apple, currant, gooseberry and pie-plant, are improved by it.

When eggs are forty cents a dozen make an

EGGLESS SQUASH OR PUMPKIN PIE.

Stew the squash or pumpkin till very dry, and press through a colander; to each pint of this allow one table-spoon butter, beat in while warm one cup brown sugar or molasses, a little salt, one table-spoon cinnamon, one tea-spoon ginger, and one half tea-spoon soda; a little allspice may be added, but it darkens the pies; roll a few crackers very fine, and add a handful to the batter, or thicken with two table-spoons flour or one of corn starch. As the thickening property of pumpkin varies, some judgment must be used in adding milk.

BREAD-CRUMBS FOR PASTRY.

Many puddings that are commonly baked in a crust, such as cocoa-nut, potato, apple, and lemon, are equally as good and more wholesome, made by strewing grated bread-crumbs over a buttered pie-plate or pudding dish to the usual depth of crust; pour in the pudding, strew another layer of bread-crumbs over the top, and bake.

STUFFED EGGS.

Cut in two, hard-boiled eggs, remove yolks, chop, and mix with them chopped cold chicken, lamb, or veal (some add a little minced onion or parsley and a few soaked bread-crumbs), season, and add gravy or the uncooked yolk of an egg, form, fill in the cavities, level, put the two halves together, roll in beaten egg and bread-crumbs, put in wire egg-basket, and dip in boiling lard; when slightly brown, serve with celery or tomato sauce.

In putting up pickles, a nice

CUCUMBER RELISH

may be made of the large cucumbers. Pare and cut in two, take out seeds, and grate, strain out most of the water, season highly with pepper and salt, add a little sugar, and as much vinegar as you have cucumbers; put in small bottle and seal.

On baking-day, if bread is light enough at breakfast time,

BREAKFAST PUFFS

may be made by taking up a little dough, pulling out to thickness of doughnuts, cut two and one-half inches in length, drop in boiling lard, and fry like doughnuts; to be eaten with butter like biscuit.

WELSH RARE-BIT.

Cut thin slices of bread, remove the crust, and toast quickly; butter it, and cover with thin slices of rather new rich cheese, spread over a very little made-mustard, and place on a pie-tin or plate in a hot oven till the cheese is melted, when cut in square pieces of any size desired, and serve at once on a hot platter, as it is quite spoiled if allowed to get cold. The mustard may be omitted if desired; and some think it more delicate to dip the toast quickly, after buttering, into a shallow pan of boiling water; have some cheese ready melted in a cup, and pour some over each slice. The best way to serve is to have little plates made hot, place a slice on each plate, and serve one to each person.

CURD OR COTTAGE CHEESE.

Set a gallon or more of clabbered milk on the stove hearth or in the oven after cooking a meal, leaving the door open; turn it around frequently, and cut the curd in squares with a knife, stirring gently now and then till about as warm as the finger will bear, and the whey shows all around the curd; pour all into a coarse bag, and hang to drain in a cool place for three or four hours, or over night if made in the evening. When wanted, turn from the bag, chop rather coarse with a knife, and dress with salt, pepper, and sweet cream. Some mash and rub thoroughly with the cream; others dress with sugar, cream, and a little nutmeg, omitting the salt and pepper. Another way is to chop fine, add salt to taste, work in a very little cream or butter, and mold into round balls.

BONNY-CLABBER.

This dish is in perfection in the summer, when milk sours and thickens very quickly. It should be very cold when served. A nice way is to pour the milk before it has thickened into a glass dish, and when thick set on ice for an hour or two, and it is ready to serve, and is really a very pretty addition to the supper table. Serve in sauce dishes or deep dessert plates, sprinkle with sugar (maple is nice), and a little grated nutmeg if liked.

POTATO FLOUR

is an addition to many kinds of breads, cakes, and puddings, making them more light and tender. Wash, peel, and grate into an earthen pan filled with pure, soft cold water; when the water begins to clear by the settling of the pulp to the bottom, pour off the water and add more, stir pulp with hand, rub through a hair sieve, pour on more water, let stand until clear, pour off and renew again, repeating several times until the farina is perfectly white and the water clear. The air darkens it, and it must be kept in the water as much as possible during the process. Spread the prepared farina before the fire, covering with paper to keep it from dust; when dry, pulverize it, sift, bottle, and cork tightly. Potato jelly may be made by pouring *boiling* water on the flour, and it will soon change into a jelly; flavor and sweeten to taste.

"SWEETIE'S FAVORITES."

Three eggs, one tea-spoon sugar, one coffee-cup sweet milk, one of warm water, four table-spoons potato yeast, flour enough to make stiff batter; beat yolks and sugar well, stir in milk, water, and yeast, and lastly flour, stir well, and set in warm place to rise; when light, beat whites to a stiff froth, and stir into batter with a pinch of salt; bake like batter cakes. These are splendid for breakfast if set the night before.

For cake, etc., always buy

SHELLED ALMONDS,

as they are more economical. One pound of unshelled almonds only makes six and one-half ounces or one coffee-cupful when shelled, while the unshelled are generally only double the price, and sometimes not that, per pound.

THE CARE OF FAT AND DRIPPINGS

is as necessary in any family as the care of last year's garden seeds or the "Family Record." Especially when much meat is used, there is a constant accumulation of trimmings of fat, drippings from meats, etc., which should be tried out once in two or three days in summer—in winter once a week will do. Cut up in small pieces, put in skillet, cover, try out slowly, stir occasionally, and skim well; add the cakes of fat saved from the top of your meat liquor, slice a raw potato and cook in it to clarify it, strain all the clear part into a tin can or stone jar, or pour over drippings a quart of boiling water and strain through muslin or a fine sieve, let cool, take out the cake which forms on the top, scrape the refuse from the bottom, pour again into a skillet, and heat until all the water is out, then pour into a jar, and you will find it very nice to use either alone or with butter and lard in frying potatoes, doughnuts, etc. The fat of mutton should always be tried out by itself, and used for chapped hands and such purposes. The fat which is not nice enough for any of the above uses, should be tried out and placed in a jar, kettle, or soft wood cask of strong lye, to which all soap grease should be consigned. Observe never to use for this purpose lean meat or raw fat. Keep a stick with which to stir occasionally, and it will need but little boiling to make the best of soft soap.

TO STUFF A HAM,

wash and scrape the skin till very white, cut out a piece from thick part (use for frying), leaving the skin on the ham as far as possible, as it makes a casing for the stuffing; put in a boiler and steam for three hours; take

out and score in thin slices all around the skin; fill the space cut out with
a stuffing made of bread-crumbs, same as for poultry, only not quite so
rich, seasoned rather highly with pepper and sage; wrap around a strip of
cotton cloth to keep in place, and bake in the stove one and a half hours,
turning so as to brown all sides nicely. The last half hour sift lightly with
powdered sugar and cinnamon. (Some peel off the skin after steaming,
stuff, and roast as before.) What remains after once serving is delicious
sliced down cold. The first we ever ate was at a thanksgiving dinner, cooked
in a Southern kitchen, by an old-fashioned fire-place, in an iron bake-oven,
and the savory flavor lingers still in our memory. Nicely-cured boiled ham
is a never-failing source of supply, from which quite a variety of dishes may
be prepared. One of the nicest relishes for supper or lunch, or for sandwiches, is

GRATED HAM.

Cut a good-sized piece from the thickest portion of a boiled ham, trim off
the fat, grate the lean part, and put in the center of a platter; slice some
tiny slips of the fat and place around the edge, together with some tender
hearts of lettuce-heads, and serve for supper or lunch.

To economise the scraps left from boiled ham, chop fine, add some
of the fat also chopped, and put in a baking-plate, first a layer of bread-
crumbs, then a layer of mixed fat and lean, then another layer of crumbs,
and so on till all is used, putting a few bits of fat over the top; pour over it
a little water, or a dressing of some kind, and set in oven till a nice brown.
This is delicious for breakfast, or for a "picked up dinner," after having
made a soup from the bone, well cracked and simmered for three hours with
a few sliced potatoes and rice, or dried corn and beans which have first been
soaked and parboiled. In boiling hams, always select an old ham; for
broiling, one recently cured. After boiling and skinning a ham, sprinkle
well with sugar and brown in oven. To make a

SQUAB PIE,

trim a deep dish with paste as for chicken pie, put in a layer of sliced sour
apples, season with sugar and spice; add a layer of fresh, rather lean pork,
sliced thin, seasoned with salt and pepper; and thus place alternate layers
of apple and pork until the dish is nearly full; put in a little water and
cover with paste; bake slowly until *thoroughly done.* A delicious

MEAT PIE

is made as follows: Put a layer of cold roast beef or other bits of meat,
chopped very fine, in bottom of dish, and season with pepper and salt, then
a layer of powdered crackers, with bits of butter and a little milk, and thus
place alternate layers until dish is full; wet well with gravy or broth, or a
little warm water; spread over all a thick layer of crackers which have been
seasoned with salt and mixed with milk and a beaten egg or two; stick bits

of butter thickly over it, cover with a tin pan, and bake half to three-quarters of an hour; remove cover ten minutes before serving, and brown. Make moister, if of veal. Or another way of making the pie is to cover any bits or bones, rejected in chopping, with nearly a pint of cold water, and let them simmer for an hour or more; strain and add a chopped onion, three table-spoons Chili sauce, a level table-spoon of salt, and the chopped meat; let simmer a few minutes, thicken with a table-spoon of flour mixed in water, let boil once, take off and let cool; put a layer of this in a pudding-dish, then a layer of sliced hard-boiled eggs and a few slices from cold boiled potatoes, then the rest of the meat, then eggs, etc.; cover with pie-crust, make an opening in the center, and bake forty minutes.

Sausage toast is made by scalding the sausages in boiling water, frying to a light brown, chop fine, and spread on bits of toast. To make

SLAP JACKS,

take a quart buttermilk, three eggs, tea-spoon soda, half tea-spoon salt, flour to thicken; bake on griddle.

Here is a nice way to

CLARIFY MOLASSES.

Heat over the fire and pour in one pint of sweet milk to each gallon of molasses. The impurities rise in scum to the top, which must be skimmed off before the boiling breaks it. Add the milk as soon as placed over the fire, mixing it thoroughly with the molasses.

Mother has many other valuable ideas on how to stop the numberless little "leaks," which keep many a family in want, while a little care and economy in these minor details would insure a fair competency, but she thinks it better to have the ideas she has already given thoroughly digested before clogging them with others. She says a neat, clean home, a tidy table, and well cooked, palatable meals, are safeguards against the evils of the ale-house, the liquor saloon, and the gambling-table. So that we may, with our frying-pans and soup-kettles, wage a mighty war against intemperance, for seldom is a well-fed man a drunkard; and thus our attempts at palatable and economical cooking may "kill two birds with one stone."

By the way, she has just taken up a paper from which she reads this item by Prof. Blot: "Wasting is carried on so far and so extensively in American kitchens that it will soon be one of the common sciences." "Just as I told you," says mother, as she folds her hands complacently together, looks down at the bright figures of the carpet, and repeats in her slow-measured way, "After all, whether we save or spend, the life is more than meat, and the body more than raiment."

	Mode of Preparation.	Time of Cooking.	Time of Digestion.
		H. M.	H. M.
Apples, sour, hard	Raw	......	2 50
Apples, sweet and mellow	Raw	......	1 50
Beans, (pod),	Boiled	1 00	2 30
Beans with green corn	Boiled	45	3 45
Beaf	Roasted	✻ 25	3 00
Beefsteak	Broiled	15	3 00
Beefsteak	Fried	15	4 00
Beef, salted	Boiled	✻ 35	4 15
Bass, fresh	Broiled	20	3 00
Beets, young	Boiled	2 00	3 45
Beets, old	....	4 30	......
Bread, corn	Baked	45	3 15
Bread, wheat	Baked	1 00	3 30
Butter	Melted	......	3 30
Cabbage	Raw	......	2 30
Cabbage and vinegar,	Raw	......	2 00
Cabbage	Boiled	1 00	4 30
Cake, sponge	Baked	45	2 30
Carrot, orange	Boiled	1 00	3 15
Cheese, old	Raw	......	3 30
Chicken	Fricasseed	1 00	3 45
Codfish, dry and whole	Boiled	✻ 15	2 00
Custard, (one quart)	Baked	30	2 45
Duck, tame	Roasted	1 30	4 00
Duck, wild	Roasted	1 00	4 50
Dumpling, apple	Boiled	1 00	3 00
Eggs, hard	Boiled	10	3 30
Eggs, soft	Boiled	3	3 00
Eggs	Fried	5	3 30
Eggs	Raw	......	2 00
Eggs	Whipped	......	1 30
Fowls, domestic, roasted or	Boiled	1 00	4 00
Gelatine	Boiled	......	2 30
Goose, wild	Roasted	✻ 20	2 30
Lamb	Boiled	✻ 20	2 30
Meat and vegetables	Hashed	30	2 30
Milk	Raw	......	2 15
Milk	Boiled	......	2 00
Mutton	Roast	✻ 25	3 15
Mutton	Broiled	20	3 00
Oysters	Raw	......	2 55
Oysters	Roasted	......	3 15
Oysters	Stewed	5	3 30
Parsnips	Boiled	1 00	2 30
Pig's feet	Soused	......	1 00
Pork	Roast	✻ 30	5 15
Pork	Boiled	✻ 25	4 30
Pork, raw or	Fried	......	4 15
Pork	Broiled	20	3 15
Potatoes	Boiled	30	3 30
Potatoes	Baked	45	3 30
Potatoes	Roasted	45	2 30
Rice	Boiled	20	1 00
Salmon, fresh	Boiled	8	1 45
Sausage	Fried	25	4 00
Sausage	Broiled	20	3 30
Soup, vegetable	Boiled	1 00	4 00
Soup, chicken	Boiled	2 00	3 00
Soup, oyster or mutton	Boiled	†3 30	3 30
Tapioca	Boiled	1 30	2 00
Trout, salmon, fresh, boiled or	Fried	30	1 30
Turkey, boiled or	Roasted	✻ 20	2 30
Turnips	Boiled	45	3 30
Veal	Broiled	20	4 00
Venison Steak	Broiled	20	1 35

✻ Minutes to the pound.   † Mutton soup.
The time given is the general average; the time will vary slightly with the quality of the article.

1 quart sifted flour (well heaped) weighs 1 lb.
3 coffee-cups sifted flour (level) weigh 1 lb.
4 tea-cups sifted flour (level) weigh 1 lb.
1 quart unsifted flour weighs 1 lb. 1 oz.
1 quart sifted Indian meal weighs 1 lb. 4 oz.
1 pint soft butter (well packed) weighs 1 lb.
2 tea-cups soft butter (well packed) weigh 1 lb
1½ pints powdered sugar weigh 1 lb.
2 coffee-cups powdered sugar (level) weigh 1 lb.
2¾ tea-cups powdered sugar (level) weigh 1 lb.
1 pint granulated sugar (heaped) weighs 14 oz.
1½ coffee-cups granulated sugar (level) weigh 1 lb.
2 tea-cups granulated sugar (level) weigh 1 lb.
1 pint coffee "A" sugar weighs 12 oz.
1¾ coffee-cups coffee "A" sugar (level) weigh 1 lb.
2 tea-cups coffee "A" sugar (well heaped) weigh 1 lb.
1 pint best brown sugar weighs 13 oz.
1¾ coffee-cups best brown sugar (level) weigh 1 lb.
2½ tea-cups best brown sugar (level) weigh 1 lb.
2¾ coffee-cups Indian meal (level) equal 1 qt.
3½ tea-cups Indian meal (level) equal 1 qt.
1 table-spoon (well heaped) of granulated "coffee A" or best brown sugar equals 1 oz.
2 table-spoons (well rounded) of powdered sugar or flour weigh 1 oz.
1 table-spoon (well rounded) of soft butter weighs 1 oz.
Soft butter size of an egg weighs 1 oz.
7 table-spoons granulated sugar (heaping) equal 1 tea-cup.
6 table-spoons sifted flour or meal (heaping) equal 1 tea-cup.
4 table-spoons soft butter (well heaped) equal 1 tea-cup.
2 tea-spoons (heaping) of flour, sugar or meal, equal 1 heaping table-spoon.

LIQUIDS.

1 pint contains 16 fluid ounces (4 gills.)
1 ounce contains 8 fluid drachms (¼ gill.)
1 table-spoon contains about ½ fluid ounce.
1 tea-spoon contains about 1 fluid drachm.
A tea-spoonful (for brevity, tea-spoon is used for tea-spoonful in the recipes of this book) is equal in volume to 45 drops of pure water (distilled) at 60 deg. Fah. Tea-spoons vary so much in size that there is a wide margin of difference in containing capacity.
4 tea spoonfuls equal 1 table-spoon or ½ fluid ounce.
16 table-spoonfuls equal ½ pint.
1 wine-glass full (common size) equals 4 table-spoons or 2 fluid oz.
1 tea-cupful equals 8 fluid oz. or 2 gills.
4 tea-cupfuls equal 1 qt.
A common-sized tumbler holds about ½ pint.

AVOIRDUPOIS WEIGHT.

16 drams (dr.) make 1 ounce (oz.)
16 ounces make 1 pound (lb.)
25 pounds make 1 quarter (qr.)
4 quarters make 1 hundred weight (cwt.)
20 hundred weight make 1 ton (T.)

LIQUID MEASURE.

4 gills (gi.) make 1 pint (pt.)
2 pints make 1 quart (qt.)
4 quarts make 1 gallon (gal.)

COMPARATIVE VALUE OF FUEL.

Shellbark Hickory	100	Red Oak	69
Pig-nut Hickory	95	White Beech	65
White Oak	84	Black Birch	62
White Ash	77	Yellow Pine	54
Yellow Oak	60	Chestnut	52
Hard Maple	59	White Birch	48
White Elm	58	White Pine	42

The same species of wood may vary in density and value, being best if grown on dry land and exposed or in open ground. Some kinds of wood, such as hickory, owe a large share of their value to the heat of the coals left after burning.

Allowance is to be made for extraordinary dryness or moisture of the article weighed or measured, and for different sizes of cups and spoons, but the tables are as correct as can be made. In "Liquids," the old French measure was "1 tea-cup equals 4 fluid ounces or 1 gill" the tea-cup being half the size of the one in use at present.

HOUSEKEEPING.

Housekeeping, whatever may be the opinion of the butterflies of the period, is an accomplishment in comparison to which, in its bearing on woman's relation to real life and to the family, all others are trivial. It comprehends all that goes to make up a well-ordered home, where the sweetest relations of life rest on firm foundations, and the purest sentiments thrive. It is an accomplishment that may be acquired by study and experiment, but the young and inexperienced housekeeper generally reaches success only through great tribulation. It ought to be absorbed in girlhood, by easy lessons taken between algebra, music and painting. If girls were taught to take as much genuine pride in dusting a room well, hanging a curtain gracefully, or broiling a steak to a nicety, as they feel when they have mastered one of Mozart's or Beethoven's grand symphonies, there would be fewer complaining husbands and unhappy wives. The great lesson to learn is that work well-done is robbed of its curse. The woman who is satisfied only with the highest perfection in her work, drops the drudge and becomes the artist. There is no dignity in slighted work, but to the artist, no matter how humble his calling, belongs the honor which is inseparable from all man's struggles after perfection. No mother who has the happiness of her daughter at heart, will neglect to teach her first the duties of the household, and no daughter who aspires to be queen at home and in her circle of friends, can afford to remain ignorant of the smallest details that contribute to the comfort, the peace and the attractiveness of home. There is no luck in housekeeping, however it may seem. Every thing works by exact rule, and even with thorough knowledge, eternal vigilance is the price of success. There must be a place for every thing and every thing in its place, a time for every thing and every thing in its time, and "patience, patience," must be written in glowing capitals all over the walls. The reward is sure. Your husband may admire your grace and ease in society, your wit, your school-day accomplishments of music and painting, but all in perfection will not atone for an ill-ordered kitchen, sour bread, muddy coffee, tough meats, unpalatable vegetables, indigestible pastry, and the whole train of horrors that result from bad housekeeping; on the other hand, success wins gratitude and attachment in the home circle, and adds luster to the most brilliant intellectual accomplishments.

One of the first ideas the young housekeeper should divest herself of is that because she is able or expects some time to be able to keep servants, it is therefore unnecessary to understand household duties, and to bear their responsibility. "Girls" are quick to see and note the ignorance or the incapacity of the mistress of the house, and few are slow to take whatever advantage it brings them, but the capacity of a mistress at once establishes discipline. The model house should not be large, nor too fine and pretentious for daily use. The mistress of many a fine mansion is the veriest household drudge. A great house, with its necessary retinue of servants, is not in keeping with the simplicity of a republic where trained servants are not known, and is seldom pleasant for the family or attractive to friends. Furniture should be selected for comfort rather than show. Most modern chairs put their occupants to torture, and throw them into attitudes any thing but graceful. Comfortable chairs should have broad seats, and a part at least, low seats for women and children. Nothing is more out of taste and "shoddy" than to crowd rooms with furniture, no matter how rich or elegant it may be. Nor is it by any means necessary to have things in *suites;* variety is preferable, and each room, especially, should have an individuality of its own. Just now the "Eastlake" style is in high favor, and perhaps there is danger of too strong a reaction from the "modern styles," most of which, however, are a hap-hazard collection of styles, without any unity of idea in them. The "Eastlake" is, in the main, a protest against the falsehoods and shams of modern fine furniture, and so far it is a real reform. In a table, for example, we usually have a foundation of pine, put together mostly with glue; this is covered with a veneer of mahogany, walnut, or other wood, and ornamented with carvings, which may mean something or nothing, and which are glued to the work. In a few years the pine framework warps and shrinks out of shape, the veneer peels, the carving gets chipped, and the whole becomes "shabby genteel." Eastlake and his associates would have the table *honest,* and be throughout what it appears to be on the surface, hence the table is made solid; and if a costly wood can be afforded—well; if not, take a cheaper wood, but let the table be just what it pretends to be; if braces or bars are needed for strength, let them show, and indicate why they are used; and if ornament is desirable, let it be worked in the material, and not glued on. A table of this kind will *last,* and may serve for several generations. Finding that our ancestors of a few centuries ago understood the matter of furniture better than the cabinet-makers of the present, Eastlake and the others reproduced many of the styles of bygone times, and with some dealers "Eastlake" is used for antique. But the matter does not depend so much upon antiquity of style, as solidity, honesty, and appropriateness. Sets are made of plain woods, such as ash and walnut, inlaid with procelain tiles, and ornamented with old-fashioned brass rings and handles. They are valued at from thirty to two hundred and fifty dollars. Bedroom sets of French and English walnut, with inlaid woods, gilt and bronze ornaments, and variegated marbles, are sold from thirty-five to fifteen hundred dollars. Parlor sets of rich, carved woods, and satin, damask, cashmere, brocade, and tapestry coverings, etc., range in price from one hundred to twelve hundred dollars. Ebony cabinets inlaid with ivory, and richly ornamented, are worth from two to eighteen hundred dollars. Marquetry tables, work tables, library tables, Oriental chairs, lounges, easels, music-racks, etc., of rich material and design, are valued at from ten to one hundred and fifty dollars. The principal woods used are walnuts of various kinds, ash, bird's-eye maple, satinwood, and kingwood. Kingwood is almost crimson in color. Book-cases are of all prices from twenty to fourteen hundred dollars, and sideboards from seventy-five to one thousand dollars. It is a good rule in selecting furniture, not to buy any thing not actually needed, to buy the best of its kind, and to pay cash or not buy Never get any thing because some one else has it, and do not be afraid to wait for bargains. Wise young housekeepers buy furniture in single pieces or small lots, as they have means, rather than expend more than they can afford in entire sets, which are really less attractive.

Carpets should as a rule be of small pattern. The stoves—if grates or fire-places are not used—should be of the kind that may be thrown open or closed at pleasure. If a furnace is used, great care must be taken that the rooms are not kept too hot in winter, and that there is most thorough ventilation, as the health of the family depends as much on the quality of the air they breathe as the food they eat. To waste heat is not so bad as to waste health and vigor, and fuel is always cheaper, on the score of economy, than doctors' bills. In furnace-heated houses—and the furnace seems to be accepted as the best heater, though apparatus for steam and hot water seems likely to be so perfected as to supplant it by furnishing a milder and more agreeable heat, entirely free from noxious gases—there should always be grates or fire-places in living or sleeping rooms; and whenever the furnace heat is turned on, there should be a little fire, at least enough to start the column of air in the chimney and secure ventilation. Without fire, chimneys are apt to draw down a current of cold air. If there are no grates or fire-places, do not rely on airing rooms from the halls, but throw open the windows and take in the outside air. This is especially necessary when a room is used as a study, or for an invalid. The air from the halls, although cold, is not pure. House-plants will not thrive in furnace-heated, houses where gas is burned, and human beings, especially the young and delicate, need quite as pure air as plants. In a study, or other room much occupied, the windows may be dropped during meals, and the room warmed anew before it is needed again. There must also be plenty of sunlight, floods of it in every room, even if the carpets do fade; and the housekeeper must be quick to note any scent of decay from vegetables or meats in the cellar, or from slops or refuse carelessly thrown about the premises. Every room must be clean and sweet. In sickness, care in all these respects must be doubled. In damp and chill autumn and spring days, a little fire is comfortable morning and evening. The food for the family must be fresh to be wholesome, and it is economy to buy the best as there is less waste in it. No housekeeper ought to be satisfied with any but the very best cooking, without which the most wholesome food is unpalatable and distressing; and no considerations of economy should ever induce her to place on the table bread with the slightest sour tinge, cake or pudding in the least heavy or solid, or meat with the slightest taint. Their use means disease and costly doctor's bills, to say nothing of her own loss of repute as an accomplished housekeeper. If children and servants do work improperly, she should quietly insist on its being done correctly, and in self-defense they will soon do it correctly without supervision. Order and system mean the stopping of waste, the practice of economy, and additional means to expend for the table and for the luxuries and elegancies of life—things for which money is well expended. It requires good food to make good muscle and good brain, and the man or woman who habitually sits down to badly cooked or scanty dinners, fights the battle of life at a great disadvantage.

THE PARLOR.

The sweeping and dusting of a parlor seems simple enough, but is best done systematically. "Dusters," made of old prints, with which to cover books, statuettes, and such articles as are difficult to dust, and larger ones to cover beds, are indispensable in sweeping and dusting. "Carpet sweepers" are only fit for daily use, when thorough work is not required, a thorough sweeping once or twice a week sufficing even the tidiest of housekeepers. Before sweeping open the blinds and let in the light, and open the windows if it is not storming or too windy. Look on the ceiling for cobwebs, and sprinkle the carpet over with moistened bran, salt, damp coffee-grounds, or tea-leaves. Clean the corners and edges with a sharp-pointed stick and stiff whisk-broom. Brush down with the feather-duster all picture-cords, frames, and curtains, and remove all cobwebs; then clear one corner of furniture and begin sweeping toward the center with a short, light stroke, going slowly and carefully so as to raise no dust, and drawing, not pushing, the broom. The second time over, increase the length and force of the stroke, and the third, brush with long and vigorous strokes, using care as the dirt at the center of the room is approached. In this way it will take twenty minutes to sweep a large room, but it will be *clean*, and the carpet will wear, bright and fresh, much longer than if the dirt were allowed to grind out the fabric. After the sweeping remove the "dusters" carefully, carrying them out of doors to shake, and rub, not simply wipe, off the furniture and other articles with a clean, soft, cotton cloth or an old silk handkerchief, or better a soft dusting-towel with fleecy surface which is sold expressly for this purpose, folding the dust in as it soils the cloth, and when it is filled with dust, shake thoroughly out of doors. Managed in this way, curtains, furniture and carpets will never be loaded with dust, but will remain bright, clean and fresh from one year's house-cleaning to another's. If any spot of dust is too firmly fixed, wash in lukewarm soap-suds, and immediately rub dry with chamois-skin. If there is open-work carving, draw the cloth through, or dust with a paint-brush; and it will be found more convenient to blow out some of the places which are difficult to reach, for which purpose a small pair of bellows may be used. To clean and dust a piano, use half a yard best canton-flannel with a nap free from all specks and grit, brushing lightly over to remove the dust; if there are finger-marks or spots, rub up and down over them, always keeping the nap next to the instrument. Dust under the wires may be blown out with a pair of bellows. Keep the piano closed at night and in damp weather; open on bright days, and if possible let the sun shine directly upon the keys, as the light will keep them from turning yellow. Tune every spring and fall. As a last finishing touch to the rearranging of the parlor, leave late papers, magazines, a volume of poetry, or a stereoscope and views, where they will be readily picked up by callers.

THE SITTING-ROOM.

The sitting-room should be the pleasantest, because most used, of all in the house. Do not put down a Brussels carpet here, because it is too hard to sweep and holds too much dust. To prevent moths under the carpets, grind black pepper coarsely, mix with camphor-gum, and strew thickly about the edges and wherever they are to be found. To clean the oil-cloth, use warm water without soap, or what is much better, milk and water. By keeping mats at the doors it will only be necessary to sweep the sitting-room thoroughly once a week, but occasionally when very dusty it may be cleaned by setting a pail of cold water by the door, wet the broom in it, knock off the drops, sweep a yard or so, then wash the broom as before and sweep again, being careful to shake all the drops off the broom, and not to sweep far at a time. If done with care the carpet will be very nicely cleaned, and the quantity of dirt in the water will be surprising. The water must be changed several times. Snow sprinkled on and swept off before it has had time to melt, is also nice for renovating a soiled carpet. A scrap bag hung on the end of the sewing machine, for storing all bits of cloth and ravelings, and ends of thread, will save much sweeping. In summer, wire doors and mosquito-nettings in the windows will keep flies out, and at the same time admit the air. Washing windows and wiping off doors once a week after sweeping, keeps all tidy. To remove finger-marks, which are constantly appearing on doors about the knobs, use a damp cloth as soon as they are observed.

THE BED-ROOM.

The family bed-room should be on the first floor if possible, if the house is properly built and there is no dampness. Matting is better for the floor than carpet, because freer from dust, and this is the room used in case of sickness. If made properly it will wear for several years. Canton mattings are made on boats in pieces about two yards long, and afterward joined on shore into pieces of fifty yards. It is easy to see where these short pieces are joined; after cutting into lengths, first sew these places across and across on the wrong side, then sew the breadths together and tack down like a carpet. Matting should never be washed with any thing except moderately-warmed salt and water, in the proportion of a pint of salt to a half pail of soft water. Dry quickly with a soft cloth. A bed-room matting should be washed twice during the season, a room much used, oftener In this room there should be a medicine closet, high above the reach of children, where are kept camphor, hot drops, mustard, strips of old linen, etc., for sudden sickness or accident. There should also be a large closet, a part of which is especially set apart for children's use, with low hooks where they may hang their clothes, a box for stockings, a bag for shoes, and other conveniences, which will help to teach them system and order. The bedding should be the best that can be afforded. The inner husks of corn make a good under-bed. Oat-straw is also excellent. Mattresses of Spanish moss are cheaper than hair, but soon mat down. A mattress made of coarse wool is quite as nice as hair, and as serviceable. When the woven-wire bed is used, a light mattress is all that is needed; and this combination makes the healthiest and best bed, because it affords the most complete exposure of the bedding to air. The best covering is soft woolen blankets. Comforters made of cotton should be used with great caution, as they need to be frequently exposed to sun and air. The best comforter is made of delaines, which may be partly worn, with wool instead of cotton quilted in. Beds are almost always made up too early. The thrifty housekeeper likes to have rooms put to rights in the morning, but it brings up the old adage of "the white glove" which "hides a dirty hand." The bed should lie open for several hours every morning, and at least once a week all the bedding should be thoroughly aired. Air pillows in wind but not in sun.

THE GUEST-CHAMBER.

The bed of the guest-chamber should always stand so that when one opens the eyes in the morning, the light from the window will not be directly upon them, as it is trying to weak eyes, and unpleasant to strong ones. Keep the bureau where the sun's rays will never strike the mirror, and where it will not be heated by the stove, as either will granulate the amalgam. Chambers should always be provided with transoms over the doors, and windows arranged so as to lower easily from the top. A light feather-bed covered with a case like a pillow, may be either used over the mattress, or a comfort may be used over it and the feather-beds under it. Tacked on the inside of the washstand-doors, two crotcheted pockets are nice for bathing sponges, and

22

there should be plenty of towels, especially of those coarse, rough ones which make a morning bath such a luxury. A broad oil-cloth in front of the washstand is also a protection to the carpet in bathing, and is needed when there is no bath-room up stairs.

HOUSE-CLEANING.

When mother earth summons the stirring winds to help clear away the dead leaves and winter litter for the coming grass and flowers, every house-keeper has a feeling of sympathy, and begins to talk of house-cleaning. The first bright sunshine of spring reveals unsuspected dust and cobwebs, and to her imagination even the scrubbing-brushes and brooms seem anxious to begin the campaign. In northern latitudes it is best, however, not to begin too soon. Do not trust entirely to appearances, for spring is almost certain to break her promises of pleasant weather, and give us a good many days when it will be any thing but pleasant to sit shivering in a fireless room, while the children become unmanageable and husband growls. So for the sake of health, peace, and comfort do not remove the stoves before the middle of May. When you begin, do not upset all the house at once, driving your husband to distraction, and the children to the neighbors. By cleaning one or two rooms at a time. and using a little womanly tact, the whole house may be renovated with little inconvenience. Before the trouble begins see that all repairs needed about the house, from cellar to garret, are attended to. Have all tools on hand and in good order, and provide lime for white-washing, carpet-tacks, good soap, sawdust, carbolic acid, and spirits of ammonia. Fold carpets by lifting one side, carrying it over to the other and laying it down carefully, thus preventing the straw and dust from the under side from soiling the upper. Carry it out, and hang on a strong line over the grass, and beat thoroughly the wrong side first, with a carpet-whip such as are sold at all house-furnishing stores, or a broom or stick, taking care not to use any thing rough that will catch into the carpet. Wash out all grease spots with a little gall soap and clean water, after the dust is entirely beaten out. Take one or two pails of sawdust, wet thoroughly and scatter well over the floor; a very little dust will arise when you sweep it off, and it will not be necessary to clean the floor before washing wood-work and windows. If you can not get sawdust, use moist earth instead. Begin at the attic and work down to the cellar; clothes, carpeting, and "trumpery" stowed away, must be thoroughly dusted and aired in sunshine and wind. Brush down all cobwebs with a long-handled broom, and sweep down the walls carefully. Wash and polish the windows, and if the walls are hard-finish, they may be washed off lightly with soap-suds, and wiped dry. Wash wood-work and floors with hot soap-suds, and rinse with strong, hot brine, or hot water with a strong mixture of cayenne pepper in it, to drive out mice, rats, and other vermin. When the floor is dry, blow cayenne pepper into every crack and crevice, using a small pair of bellows for the purpose; and the room is ready for its customary furniture, unless the more thorough renovation of kalsomining and painting is to follow the cleaning. Before replacing, every article should be thoroughly cleaned, every button and tuft of the upholstered goods receiving its share of attention from the furniture-brush. Sofas and chairs should be turned down and whipped, then carefully brushed, and all dust wiped off with a clean cloth slightly damped. Wash wood-work and carving with a soft cloth dipped in warm soap-suds, *wiping it off quickly*, and polishing with chamois-leather, to prevent the soap from injuring the varnish. When it needs it, black walnut or mahogany furniture may be washed quickly with a soft brush and soapy water, wiped dry, and then rubbed with an oily cloth. To polish it, rub it with rotten-stone and sweet oil. Clean off the oil, and polish with chamois-skin.

Sinks, drains, and all places that become sour or impure, should be cleansed with carbolic acid and water. This is the best disinfectant known, and should be kept in every house, and used frequently in warm weather. While house-cleaning, brighten up old furniture by rubbing well with kerosene oil; should it be marred or bruised use the "Magic Furniture Polish," page 342. Take bedsteads to pieces, and saturate every crevice with strong brine; nothing is better to purify and cleanse, or to destroy bedbugs. To clean mirrors, take clean warm rain-water, and put in just enough spirits of ammonia to make it feel slippery. If very dirty, rinse, if not, wipe dry, and you will be surprised at the effect. Do not polish stoves until fall if you are going to put them away during the summer, but to keep them or any iron utensils from rusting, rub over with kerosene. When polishing, six or eight drops of turpentine added to blacking for one stove, brightens it and makes it easier to polish. To remove mortar and paint from windows, rub spots of mortar with hot, sharp vinegar; or if nearly fresh, cold vinegar will loosen them. Rub the paint spots with camphene and sand. To clean paint use whiting on a damp cloth. To remove spots from gray marble hearths rub with linseed oil.

Fall house-cleaning deserves no less attention, except that white-washing and painting can best be done in the mild days of spring, when the house may be thrown open to wind and sunshine. The best time is in the constant weather of October; and before beginning, all the dirty and heavy work for the winter, such as getting in coal and wood, should be completed, and the cellar made clean and sweet.

KALSOMINING.

If papering and painting, or kalsomining are to be done, do the last named first. Wash ceiling that has been smoked by the kerosene lamp, with a strong solution of soda. Fill all cracks in the wall with a cement made of one part water to one part silicate of potash mixed with common whiting. Put it in with a limber case-knife if you have no trowel. In an hour, after it has set, scrape off the rough places, and after kalsomining no trace of the crack will appear. For the wash, take eight pounds whiting and one-fourth pound white glue; cover glue with cold water over night, and heat gradually in the morning until dissolved. Mix whiting with hot water, add the dissolved glue and stir together, adding warm water until about the consistency of thick cream. Use a kalsomine brush, which is finer than a white-wash brush, and leaves the work smoother. Brush in, and finish as you go along. If skim-milk is used instead of water, the glue may be omitted.

PAINTING.

Any woman of a mechanical turn of mind can paint a room, buying the paint ready mixed. While painting keep the room well ventilated and eat acid fruits. When done, any spatters on the glass may be removed by the application of a mixture of equal parts of ammonia and turpentine, washed off with soap-suds. To polish the glass, wash in warm water, wipe with a soft cloth, put a little whiting on the center of the pane, and rub with chamois-skin or a soft cloth. Clean paint with whiting or warm water, with a few drops of ammonia in it. Wash grained work in cold tea.

PAPERING.

In papering a hard finished wall a thin solution of white glue should be first applied with a white-wash brush. To make the paste, sift the flour, add one ounce pulverized alum to every pound of flour, mix it smoothly with cold water, and pour over it gently but quickly boiling water, stirring meantime constantly. When it swells and turns yellow it is done, but is not to be used until cool, and may be kept for some time without spoiling. Or for paste, clear corn starch is sometimes used, made precisely as made for starching clothes. It is well to use a small quantity of carbolic acid in it, as a precaution against vermin. A thin paste of wheat, or what is better, rye flour, is, however, very good for any thing except the most delicate papers. The wall should be smooth, and if very smoky or greasy in spots, it should be washed with weak lye or soap-suds. Trim the paper close to the pattern on one side. A pair of long shears is best for the purpose—allowing the roll to lie on the floor, and rolling up again on the lap as fast as trimmed. Provide a board wider than the paper, and a little longer than a single breadth when cut. Cut all the full breadths that will be required for the room, matching as you cut, and saving remnants for door and window spaces. Begin at the right hand and work to the left. The breadths may be laid one on another on the board, the top one pasted with a good brush, the top turned down bringing the two pasted sides together, a foot or two from the other end. Carefully adjust the top to its place, gently pressing it with soft towels, first down the middle of the breadth and then to each edge. In turning a corner, paste only that part which belongs to one side, fasten it in place, and then paste and adjust the rest. In selecting paper avoid contrasts in colors and large staring patterns, as they are out of taste and tiresome to the eye. Choose rather neutral tints and colors that harmonize and blend agreeably together, and with the general tone of carpets and furniture. Even with a bare floor and plain wooden chairs, the effect of a soft-tinted paper gives a vastly different impression than if the wall is disfigured with glaring figures and contrasting colors. If ceilings are low, heighten the appearance by a figure which runs perpendicularly through the wall-paper; the effect produced is very deceptive, the ceiling appearing much higher than it really is. Wall-paper is half a yard wide, and about eight yards to the roll, so that it is easy to estimate the quantity needed. It is wise always to get one extra roll for repairs. After papering a room build no fire in it until dry.

GENERAL SUGGESTIONS.

On Monday, wash: Tuesday, iron: Wednesday, bake and scrub kitchen and pantry: Thursday, clean the silver-ware, examine the pots and kettles, and look after store-room and cellar: Friday, devote to general sweeping and dusting: Saturday, bake and scrub kitchen and pantry floors, and prepare for Sunday. When the clothes are folded off the frame after ironing, examine each piece to see that none are laid away that need a button or a stitch. Clean all the silver on the last Friday of each month, and go through each room and closet to see if things are kept in order and nothing going to waste. Have the sitting-room tidied up every night before retiring. Make the most of your brain and your eyes, and let no one dare tell you that you are devoting yourself to a low sphere of action. Keep cool and self-possessed. Work done *quietly* about the house seems easier. A slamming of oven doors, and the rattle and clatter of dishes, tire and bewilder every body about the house. Those who accomplish much in housekeeping—and the same is true of every other walk in life—are the quiet workers.

SILVER-WARE.—When set away, keeps best wrapped in blue tissue-paper.

RED ANTS.—A small bag of sulphur kept in a drawer or cupboard will drive away red ants.

ICY WINDOWS.—Windows may be kept free from ice and polished by rubbing the glass with a sponge dipped in alcohol.

TO CLEANSE A SPONGE.—By rubbing a fresh lemon thoroughly into a soured sponge and rinsing it several times in lukewarm water, it will become as sweet as when new.

TO REMOVE GREASE SPOTS FROM CARPETS.—Cover spots with flour and then pin a thick paper over; repeat the process several times, each time brushing off the old flour into a dust-pan and putting on fresh.

Rainy Days.—Make the house as bright and sunshiny as possible.

To Prevent Hinges Creaking.—Rub with a feather dipped in oil.

To Drive off Fleas.—Sprinkle about bed a few drops of oil of lavender.

Soap.—It is a great saving to have bars of soap dry. It should be bought by the quantity.

To Destroy Cockroaches, etc.—Sprinkle the floor with hellebore at night. They eat it and are poisoned.

Lost Children.—Label children's hats with the name and place of residence so that, if lost, they may be easily restored.

Parcels.—When parcels are brought to the house, fold paper and put away in drawer, and roll the string on a ball kept for the purpose.

Mending.—Never put away clean clothes without examining every piece to see if they are in any way out of order. Stockings, particularly, should be carefully darned.

Hard Whitewash.—Ten cents worth of kalsomine, five cents worth of glue dissolved in warm water, two quarts of soft-soap, and bluing. This will do for halls, closets, fences, etc.—*Miss H. D. Martin.*

Bad Smells.—Articles of clothing, or of any other character, which have become impregnated with bad-smelling substances, will be freed from them by burying for a day or two in the ground. Wrap up lightly before burying.

To Clean Hearths.—Soapstone or sandstone hearths are cleaned by washing in pure water, then sprinkling with powdered marble or soapstone, and rubbing with a piece of the stone as large as a brick, and having at least one flat surface.

Lightning Cream for Paint or Clothes.—Four ounces white castile soap, four of ammonia, two of ether, two of alcohol, one of glycerine; cut the soap fine, dissolve in one quart of soft water over the fire, and when dissolved add the other ingredients.

Care of Oil Paintings and Frames.—Wash the picture, when necessary, in sweet milk and warm water, drying carefully. Give the gilt frame when new a coat of white varnish, and all specks can then be washed off with water or suds without harm.—*Miss E. B. Price.*

Magic Furniture Polish.—Half pint alcohol, half ounce resin, half ounce gum-shellac, a few drops analine brown; let stand over night and add three-fourths pint raw linseed oil and half pint spirits turpentine; shake well before using. Apply with cotton flannel, and rub dry with another cloth.—*O. M. Scott.*

Moths.—Make a solution of one ounce of gum-camphor, one ounce of powdered red pepper, in eight ounces of alcohol; let stand for one week, and strain. Sprinkle the furs or cloth with it and wrap in cloth or strong paper. To keep them out of carpets, wash floor with turpentine or benzine before laying them.

Putting Away Clothes.—Before putting away summer or winter clothes, mend, clean, brush, shake well, fold smoothly, sprinkle gum-camphor on every fold, and on the bottom of trunks or closets (unless cedar chests are used). Fine dresses, cloaks, etc., should be wrapped in towels or sheets by themselves, and placed in the tray or a separate apartment of the trunk.

To Clean Silver-ware Easily.—Save water in which potatoes have been boiled with a little salt, let it become sour, which it will do in a few days; heat and wash the articles with a woolen cloth, rinsing in pure water, dry and polish with chamois leather. Never allow a particle of soap to touch silver or plated-ware. For wiping silver, an old linen table-cloth cut up in pieces of convenient size, hemmed, and marked " silver," is very nice.

To PREVENT PAILS FROM SHRINKING.—Saturate pails and tubs with glycerine, and they will not shrink.

To KEEP FLIES OFF GILT FRAMES.—Boil three or four onions in a pint of water and apply with a soft brush.

GILT FRAMES.—Varnish with copal varnish, and they may then be washed, at any time, with cold water without injury.

To REMOVE OLD PUTTY FROM WINDOW FRAMES.—Pass a red-hot poker slowly over it, and it will come off easily.

To SOFTEN HARD WATER.—Hard water becomes nearly soft by boiling. A piece of chalk will soften hard spring-water.

PROVIDE ON SATURDAY FOR MONDAY, so as not to take up the fire with cooking, or time in running errands on washing-day.

To SOFTEN CISTERN-WATER.—Cistern-water that has become hard from long standing, can be softened by adding a little borax.

To DESTROY THE SMELL OF FRESH PAINT.—Sprinkle hay with water in which chloride of lime has been mixed, and place on floor.

ANTS AND INSECTS.—Dissolve two pounds alum in three quarts water. Apply with a brush while hot to every crevice where vermin harbor.

To CLEAN CHROMOS.—Dampen a linen rag slightly and go over them gently. If the varnish has become defaced, cover with a thin mastic varnish.

SHEETS.—When sheets are beginning to wear in the middle, sew the selvage sides together and rip open the old seam, or tear in two and hem the sides.

To MAKE ARTIFICIAL CORAL.—Melt together four parts yellow resin and one part vermilion. Dip twigs, cinders, or stones in this, and when dry they will look like coral.

To SEW CARPET-RAGS ON A MACHINE.—Make the stitch short, run it obliquely across the rags where they are to be joined, and sew a good many before cutting the thread.

To CLEAN OIL PAINTINGS.—Clean the painting well with a sponge dipped in warm beer, and when perfectly dry, wash with a solution of the finest gum-dragon dissolved in pure water.

To CLEAR CISTERN-WATER.—Add two ounces powdered alum and two ounces borax to a twenty-barrel cistern of rain water that is blackened or oily, and in a few hours the sediment will settle, and the water be clarified and fit for washing and even for cooking purposes.

To MAKE OIL-CLOTHS MORE DURABLE.—Before or after putting down new oil-cloths, put on one or two coats of linseed oil with a brush, and when thoroughly dry, add one or two coats of varnish. This makes the cloth softer and *much more durable.—Miss Eva Evans, Delaware.*

To CLEAN OIL-CLOTHS.—Take a pail of clean, soft, lukewarm water, a nice, soft piece of flannel, wash the oil-cloth and wipe *very dry* so that no drop of water is left to soak in and rot the fabric. After washing and drying, if a cloth is wrung out of a dish of skim-milk and water, and the oil-cloth is rubbed over with this, and then again well dried, the freshness and luster of the cloth will well repay the extra labor.

HOW TO WASH CHAMOIS LEATHER.—Made a good, tepid suds with hard or soft soap, put in leather, rub it on the wash-board, put soap on skin and rub again on board, and wash in this way through one or two suds, or until perfectly clean; rinse in tepid water without bluing, squeeze dry (do not wring), hang in sun and keep snapping and pulling it till perfectly dry. The leather will be as soft as new if the snapping and pulling are done thoroughly.—*Mrs. Marshall, Minneapolis.*

COAL ASHES—Make excellent garden walks. They become very hard by use and no weeds or grass will grow through them.

TO DESTROY WEEDS IN WALKS.—Boil ten pounds stone lime, five gallons water and one pound flour of sulphur, let settle, pour off clear part, and sprinkle freely upon the weedy walks.

TO RETOUCH A GILT FRAME.—Wet the rubbed spot with isinglass dissolved in weak spirits. When about dry, lay on gold leaf, and when quite dry, polish with a very hard burnisher.

TO MEND TIN.—Scrape the tin about the hole free from grease and rust, rub on a piece of resin until a powder lies about the hole, over it lay a piece of solder, and hold on it a hot poker or soldering iron until it melts.

TO TEMPER LAMP CHIMNEYS.—Lamp chimneys and glass-ware for hot water is made less liable to break by putting in cold water, bringing slowly to boiling point, boiling for an hour, and allowing to cool before removing from water.

TO KEEP AWAY MOTHS FROM FURS.—Dust furs with powdered alum, working it well in at the roots of the hair. Do not air woolen articles and furs in the summer sunshine. They should be put aside in the early spring, and left untouched until October.

TO CLEAN FURNITURE.—Take a large cotton rag well saturated with coal oil, rub each article of furniture with it until all the mud-stains and dust have disappeared, then go over it with a dry cloth, rubbing each piece until it is perfectly dry. Clean once a week.

A CHEAP CARPET.—Make a cover for the floor of the cheapest cotton cloth. Tack it down like a carpet, paper it as you would a wall with paper resembling a carpet in figures, let it dry, varnish with two coats of varnish, and with reasonable usage it will last two years.

MENDING PLASTER OF PARIS.—Gum shellac makes an excellent strong cement for joining broken pieces together, and is more convenient than glue. The shellac should be flowed upon the surfaces to be joined, firmly pressed together, and carefully set away for about one hour.

TO MAKE RAG RUGS.—Cut rags and sew hit and miss, or fancy-striped as you choose; use wooden needles, round, smooth, and pointed at one end, of any convenient length. The knitting is done back and forth (like old fashioned suspenders), always taking off the first stitch.—*Anna F. Hisey.*

TO START A FIRE IN DAMP, STILL WEATHER.—Light a few bits of shavings or paper placed upon the top of grate; thus by the heated air's forcing itself into the chimney and establishing there an upward current, the room is kept free from the gas and smoke which is so apt to fill it, and the fire can then be lighted from below with good success.

A CHEAP FILTER.—The most impure water may be rendered pure by filtering through charcoal. Take a large flower-pot, put a piece of sponge or clean moss over the hole in the bottom, fill three-quarters full of equal parts clean sand and charcoal, the size of a pea; over this lay a linen or woolen cloth large enough to hang over the sides of the pot. Pour the water into the cloth, and it will come out pure.

TO PRESERVE BOOKS.—Bindings may be preserved from mildew by brushing them over with spirits of wine. A few drops of any perfumed oil will secure libraries from the consuming effects of mold and damp. Russia leather which is perfumed with the tar of the birch-tree, never molds or sustains injury from damp. The Romans used oil of cedar to preserve valuable manuscripts. Russia-leather covered books, placed in a stationer's window will destroy flies and other insects.

A RUSTIC FRAME.—A neat rustic 'rame for pictures may be made of cattail rods. Hide the corners where they are joined with ivy, or a vine made of leather-leaves or handsome autumn leaves and the berries of bitter-sweet.

CEMENT FOR CHINA.—To a thick solution of gum-arabic add enough plaster of paris to form a sticky paste; apply with a brush, and stick edges together.

To HANG PICTURES.—The cheapest and best material with which to hang pictures is copper wire, of a size proportioned to the weight of the picture. When hung, the wire is scarcely visible, and its strength and durability is wonderful.

CEMENT FOR ATTACHING METAL TO GLASS.—Mix two ounces of a thick solution of glue with one ounce of linseed-oil varnish, and half an ounce of pure spirits of turpentine; boil the whole together in a close vessel. After it has been applied to the glass and metal, clamp together for two or three days, till dry.

To CLEAN A PAPERED WALL.—Cut into eight pieces a large loaf of bread two days old, blow dust off wall with a bellows, rub down with a piece of the bread in half yard strokes, beginning at the top of room, until upper part is cleaned, then go round again, repeating until all has been gone over. If done carefully, so that every spot is touched, the paper will look almost like new. Dry corn meal may be used instead of bread, applying it with a cloth.

A GOOD CEMENT—For mending almost any thing, may be made by mixing litharge and glycerine to the consistency of thick cream or fresh putty. This cement is useful for mending stone jars, stopping leaks in seams of tin-pans or wash-boilers, cracks and holes in iron kettles, fastening on lamp-tops; in all cases the article mended should not be used till the cement has hardened. This cement will resist the action of water, hot or cold, acids, and almost any degree of heat.

BADLY FITTING DOORS.—When blinds and doors do not close snugly, but leave cracks through which drafts enter, the simplest remedy is this: Place a strip of putty all along the jambs, cover the edge of the blind or door with chalk, and shut it. The putty will then fill all spaces which would remain open and be pressed out where it is not needed, while the excess is easily removed with a knife. The chalk rubbed on the edges prevents adhesion, and the putty is left in place, where it soon dries and leaves a perfectly fitting jamb.

INDELIBLE INK.—Two drams lunar caustic, six ounces distilled or rain-water; dissolve, and add two drams gum-water. Wet the linen with the following preparation: Dissolve one half an ounce prepared natron, four ounces water, add half ounce gum-water, (recipe below); after smoothing it with a warm iron, write with the ink, using a gold, quill, or a new steel pen. The writing must be exposed to a hot sun for twelve hours; do not wash for one week, then be particular to get out the stain which the preparation will make. If this is followed in every particular, there need never be a failure. Gum-water for the above is composed of two drams gum-arabic to four ounces water. One tea-spoon makes two drams, two table-spoons make one ounce. If at any time the ink becomes too pale add a little of pure lunar caustic. Never write without using the preparation, as it will rot the cloth.

To PASTE PAPER ON TIN.—Make a thin paste of gum-tragacanth and water, to which add a few drops of oil of vitriol. Mix a pound each of transparent glue and very strong vinegar, one quart alcohol, a small quantity of alum, and dissolve by means of a water-bath. This is useful for uniting horn, pearl, shell, and bone.—*B. H. Gilbert.*

To REMOVE GREASE FROM WOOD BEFORE PAINTING.—Whitewash the

spots over night, and wash it off in the morning. When dry, the paint will stick. Slaked lime laid on the spots and wet a little, will do as well as whitewash.

LAMP-WICKS.—To insure a good light, wicks must be changed often, as they soon become clogged, and do not permit the free passage of the oil.

STAIR CARPETS.—Will wear much longer if extra thicknesses of paper are placed over the edge of each stair, the full width of the carpet, before fastening down.

TO CLEAN LOOKING GLASSES.—Divide a newspaper in two, fold up one half in a small square, wet it in cold water. Rub the glass first with the wet half of the paper, and dry with the other. Fly-specks and all other marks will disappear as if by magic.

TO KEEP ICE-WATER.—Make a hat-shaped cover of two thicknesses of strong brown paper with cotton-batting quilted between, large enough to drop over and completely envelop the pitcher. This prevents the warm air from coming in contact with the pitcher, and the ice will last a long time.

FINISH FOR ROOM.—A room with plain white walls is finished beautifully by placing a black walnut (or the same wood with which the room is finished) molding, around the room where the border of paper is usually placed, at the junction of wall and ceiling. The molding, finished in oil, costs from one to five cents a foot, and is easily put up. The upper edge should be rounded, and a space of a quarter inch left between it and ceiling. To hang pictures, buy an S hook, sold at all hardware stores, place one hook over the molding, hang the picture cord on the other, and slip to the right or left to the desired position. This saves the wall from injury from picture-nails.

PERPETUAL PASTE.—Dissolve a tea-spoonful of alum in a quart of water. When cold, stir in as much flour as will give it the consistency of thick cream, being particular to beat up all the lumps; stir in as much powdered rosin as will lay on a five-cent piece, and throw in half a dozen cloves to give it a pleasant odor. Have on the fire a tea-cupful of boiling water, pour the flour mixture into it, stirring well at the time. In a few minutes it will be of the consistency of mush. Pour it into an earthen vessel, let it cool, lay a cover on, and put in a cool place. When needed for use, take out a portion and soften it with warm water. Paste made in this way will last a year. It is better than gum, as it does not gloss the paper which can be written upon.

TO EXTERMINATE BEDBUGS.—Scald with hot water every crack where they find refuge. Great care must be taken not to injure fine varnished furniture. If any injury is done to varnish by the hot water, it may be restored by rubbing immediately with a rag wet in turpentine or oil. Beds should be examined for vermin in July and August, and if measures are taken to exterminate them, there will be very little trouble. Another death-dealing method is to fill crevices with salt, and wash bedstead with strong brine, or use kerosene in the same way. Paris-green and mercurial ointment are deadly poisons to the bedbug, but as they are dangerous to have in the house, the first named methods are preferable. One part quicksilver to twenty parts white of an egg, applied with a feather to every crack and crevice in bedstead and room, will kill them. Most people are unable to console themselves for sleepless nights as did the Irishman, who said: "Indade, I did quite as well as the bugs, for not one of them slept a wink all night," and the above recipes, are any of them certain to remove the pests if properly and faithfully applied.

THE CARE OF MARBLE.—Never wash the marble tops of wash-stands bureaus, etc., with soap. Use clean warm water (if very much soiled add a little ammonia) and a soft cloth, drying immediately with a soft towel. There is nothing that will *entirely* remove grease spots from marble, hence the necessity of avoiding them. To clean marble or marbleized slate mantels, use a soft sponge or chamois-skin, dampened in clean warm water *without soap*, then polish with dry chamois-skin. In dusting, use a feather-duster, and never a cloth, as it is likely to scratch the polished surface. Slate hearths are preferable to marble, as they are not so easily soiled. To wash them, use a clean cloth and warm water. Many oil them thoroughly when new with linseed oil; thus prepared they never show grease spots.—*G W. Herrick, Minneapolis, Minn.*

LAYING CARPETS.—A carpet wears better if put down well, and it is better to have it done by experienced persons when the expense can be afforded and such help can be had. Lay down coarse paper or newspapers evenly on floor first; begin at one corner, and nail down one of the sides at the *cut ends* of the breadths, continuing round the selvage side, and stretching it evenly and firmly without straining the fabric. When two sides are nailed, take next the other selvage side. The last side will require the most stretching in order to get rid of puckers.

INK STAINS—On mahogany, rosewood, or black walnut furniture may be removed by touching the stain with a feather wet in a spoonful of water in which six or eight drops of nitre have been mixed. As soon as the ink disappears rub the place *immediately* with a cloth wet in cold water, or the nitre will leave a white stain. If the ink stain then remains, make the solution of nitre stronger, and repeat. Ink stains on paper may be removed by a solution made as follows : Dissolve a half pound chloride of lime in two quarts of soft water; let stand twenty-four hours and strain through a clean cotton cloth; add to an ounce of the lime-water a tea-spoon of acetic acid, apply to the blot, and the ink will disappear. Dry with blotting paper. Bottle the remainder of the lime-water closely, and keep for future use.

MOVING.—When about to move to another house, begin packing two weeks beforehand. Carefully pack small and fragile articles in boxes and barrels. In this way china, and glassware, and fragile ornaments may be stowed away with odd articles of clothing, bedding, etc. Books should be packed in boxes, or wrapped several in a package, in several thicknesses of newspaper, and tied with strong twine. They can thus be transported with very little handling. Larger pictures should be taken down and tied in couples, face to face, with rolls of soft paper between the corners to prevent rubbing. Small pictures may be packed with clothing in bureau-drawers and trunks. Take up carpets last. When about ready to move select one room up-stairs into which remove every thing possible from the other rooms, and another below for the same purpose. If the occupant of the house into which you are to move will do the same, you can easily make some rooms there ready for occupancy. Of course each room must be swept down and scrubbed. As soon as the floors are dry, carpets may be put down in the more important rooms, and the furniture moved in. On the day the transfer is made, see that coal or fuel is provided, so that a fire may be started, and take along a basket with matches, towels, napkins, knives and forks, sugar, tea, bread, and other materials for lunching. With all the caution you can exercise, you will find Franklin's old saying true, that " three removes are as bad as a fire."

ECONOMICAL MATS.—For use in front-doors, fire-places, bureaus, stands, etc., may be made of coffee-sacking, cut to any desired size, and worked in bright worsted or Germantown wool. Any simple pattern may be used, or

348 GENERAL SUGGESTIONS.

it may be entirely filled in with a plain green. The edges of the sacking may be fringed by raveling. To give it weight, line with an old piece of carpet or heavy cloth.

To Wash Dishes for Second Course.—When spoons or dishes, used in any course at dinner, will be needed also for the next, have a pan of hot soap-suds, and a dish-cloth or mop, and a clean towel ready in some convenient place in kitchen or pantry, so that they may be quickly washed and wiped.

Labor-saving Contrivances.—Every good housewife has neatly arranged cupboard and dish-closet. Every thing has its appropriate shelf and division. But there are other things for which provision should be made. A pile of books is sometimes seen in one part of the dining-room, a few newspapers in another, and a pair of shoes in a third. The inside of a closet is sometimes a mass of confusion—"a place for every thing," and every thing thrown promiscuously into it. Half a dozen garments are hung upon one nail, to crowd each other out of shape; others are thrown upon the floor amid heaps of boots and shoes. And so on to the end of the chapter of careless and slovenly disorder. There is no excuse for such carelessness, and no satisfaction in such housekeeping, Want of time is no excuse, for such want of system and order is the cause of the most prodigal waste of time. It is only necessary to use the brain a little to save the hands. Systematic habits, doing every thing well, and the hundred little contrivances which will suggest themselves to every neat and ingenious housekeeper, will save time, and establish order and cleanliness. Have shelves in the closet, and regular rows of hooks, and plenty of them; let one side be appropriated to one kind of clothing, with a hook for each article. If necessary to preserve the order, make a neat label, and paste over each hook. Make shoe-pockets (these pockets are made of about two and a half yards of calico; one yard of which makes the back, to be tacked to the door when done. Split the remaining yard and a half in two, lengthwise, and, placing the strips about one inch apart, make, across the back, three rows of pockets, by stitching first the ends of the strips to the sides of the back, and then gather the bottom of each strip to fit the back; then separate each strip into two, three, or four pockets, according to the use for which they are designed, and fasten by stitching a narrow "piping" of calico, from top to bottom of the back, between the pockets. All the work may be done on a machine. A border of leather, stitched on the edges of the back, and a narrow strip used instead of the calico "piping," make whole thing much stronger) on the inside of the doors, and never put any thing on the closet floor, where it will be trodden upon in entering for other articles. Never stuff any thing away out of sight in haste and disorder. Hiding dirtiness does not cure it. Those who write many letters should have a case, with "pigeon-holes" labeled and arranged alphabetically—a box for three or four letters is sufficient—in which to keep them, with one compartment for unanswered letters. When the case becomes crowded, or at the end of the year, wrap in packages, and label with letter and the year. Newspapers and magazines, when preserved, should be neatly filed in order and laid away, or sent away for binding. The work-basket, which is in daily use, is often a spectacle for gods and men—the very picture of confusion and disorder. When it can be afforded, one of the new ladies' adjustable work-tables, of which several admirable styles are made and widely advertised, will be found a great convenience; especially where there are children—whose little fingers delight in tumbling the contents of the basket. If a basket is used, it should be divided into compartments. A circular basket, with divisions about the edge for smaller articles, and larger spaces in the center, is convenient, and easily kept in order. All these, and hundreds of other devices like them, are labor-savers, which relieve housekeeping of a large share of its burdens. And a calculation of the time spent every year in hunting through closets for lost over-shoes or slippers, or in cleaning up the scattered items in the sitting-room when company is coming in, and searching for missing letters among a miscellaneous pile thrown into a drawer, will give a startling result, and convey some adequate idea of the real money and time-value of that love of neatness and order which is one of the cardinal virtues in women.

HOUSEKEEPER'S ALPHABET.

APPLES—Keep in dry place, as cool as possible without freezing.
BROOMS—Hang in the cellar-way to keep soft and pliant.
CRANBERRIES—Keep under water, in cellar; change water monthly.
DISH of hot water set in oven prevents cakes, etc., from scorching.
ECONOMIZE time, health, and means, and you will never beg.
FLOUR—Keep cool, dry, and securely covered.
GLASS—Clean with a quart of water mixed with tablespoonful of ammonia.
HERBS—Gather when beginning to blossom; keep in paper sacks.
INK STAINS—Wet with spirits turpentine; after three hours, rub well.
JARS—To prevent, coax "husband" to buy "Buckeye Cookery."
KEEP an account of all supplies, with cost and date when purchased.
LOVE lightens labor.
MONEY—Count carefully when you receive change.
NUTMEGS—Prick with a pin, and if good, oil will run out.
ORANGE and Lemon Peel—Dry, pound, and keep in corked bottles.
PARSNIPS—Keep in ground until spring.
QUICKSILVER and white of an egg destroys bedbugs.
RICE—Select large, with a clear, fresh look; old rice may have insects.
SUGAR—For general family use, the granulated is best.
TEA—Equal parts of Japan and green are as good as English breakfast.
USE a cement made of ashes, salt, and water for cracks in stove.
VARIETY is the best culinary spice.
WATCH your back yard for dirt and bones.
XANTIPPE was a scold. Don't imitate her.
YOUTH is best preserved by a cheerful temper.
ZINC-LINED sinks are better than wooden ones.
& regulate the clock by your husband's watch, and in all apportionments of time remember the Giver.

THE DINING-ROOM.

It may not be amiss to give a page or two to the observances of formal dinners in "society," lest some reader—who may hope, if she becomes the rare housekeeper we expect, to be called to give such dinners as the wife of a Congressman, Governor, or even as mistress of the White House itself—should be taken unawares. In every house, great or small, the Dining Room should be as bright, cheerful and cosey as possible, and at the table The mistress should wear her brightest smile. If there are trials and troubles, do not bring them to the table. They impair digestion, and send husband and children out to business or school, glum and gloomy, instead of refreshed and strengthened. The plainest room may be made beautiful by taste, and the homeliest fare appetizing by neatness and skill. Little attentions to the decoration or pretty arrangement of the table charm the eye and whet the appetite, and make the home table powerfully attractive. The every-day observance of sensible and simple table manners ought always to be encouraged, becouse in the long run it promotes the comfort and the cultivation of the family, and takes the pain of embarrassment out of state occasions. Above all, the room, the table, and its furniture should be scrupulously neat and orderly. For formal dinners, a round table, five to seven feet in diameter, is the best fitted to display the dinner and its fine wares, but the extension table, about four feet wide and of any length desired, is generally used. At the round table, conversation is, of course, easily made general, the party being small. The table-cloth must be spotless, and an under-cover of white cloth or baize gives the linen a heavier and finer appearance. A center-piece of flowers is a pretty ornament (some even place upon the table a handsome vase filled with growing plants in bloom), but the flowers must be few and rare, and of delicate odors. Fruit in variety and tastefully arranged with green leaves, and surrounded with choice dessert dishes, is always attractive and elegant. It is also a pretty custom to place a little bouquet by the side of each lady's plate, and to fold a bunch of three or four flowers in the napkin of each gentleman, to be attached to the left lapel of the coat as soon as seats are taken at the table. Napkins, which should never be starched, are folded and laid upon the plates, with a small piece of bread or a cold roll placed on the top, or half concealed by the last fold. Beside each plate are placed as many knives, forks and spoons as will be needed in all the courses, (unless the lady prefers to have them brought with each new plate, which makes more work and confusion), and a glass, to be filled with fresh water just before dinner is announced. The plates which will be needed are counted out. Such as are to be filled with ready-prepared dessert-dishes are filled and set in a convenient place. Dishes that need to be warm, not hot, are left on the top shelf of the range or elsewhere where they will be kept warm until needed. When the soup-tureen (with the soup at the boiling point) and the soup-plates are placed before the seat of the hostess, dinner may be quietly announced. The host or hostess has, of course, previously indicated to each gentleman the lady with whose escort he is charged, the guest of honor, if a gentleman, escorting the hostess, and taking a seat at her right; if a lady, being escorted by the host to a seat at his right. Each gentleman offers the lady assigned to him his right arm, and escorts her to a seat at his left, passing her in front of him to her chair which he has gracefully drawn back. The distribution of seats will tax the tact of the hostess, as the moment of waiting to be assigned to place is extremely awkward. Of course, all should have been decided on beforehand, and the places should be designated with as little confusion as possible. The success of the dinner will depend largely upon the grouping of agreeable persons. The host leads the way to the dining-room, the hostess follows last, and all guests stand until she is seated. (In France, and at large dinner parties in this country, a card with the name of each guest is placed on the plate which is intended for him.) Once seated the rest is simple routine. Ease of manner of the host and hostess, and quiet and systematic movements in attendants, who should be well trained, alert and noiseless, but never in a hurry, are indispensable. Any betrayal of anxiety or embarrassment on the part of the former, or blundering by the latter, is a wet blanket to all enjoyment.

The attendant places each dish in succession before the host or hostess (the soup, salad and dessert only being served by the hostess), with the pile of plates. Each plate is supplied, taken by the attendant on a small salver, and set before the guest from the left. Any second dish which belongs to the course is presented at the left of the guest, who helps himself. As a rule the lady at the right of the host, or the oldest lady, should be served first. As soon as any one has finished, his plate is promptly removed, and when all are done, the next course is served in the same way. Before the dessert is brought on, all crumbs should be brushed from the cloth. The finger-bowls, which are brought in on the napkin on the dessert-plate and set off to the left of the plate, are used by dipping the fingers in lightly and drying them on the napkin. They should be half full of warm water with a bit of lemon floating in it. When all have finished dessert, the hostess gives the signal that dinner is ended by pushing back her chair, and the ladies repair to the drawing-room, the oldest leading and the youngest following last, and the gentlemen repairing to the library or smoking-room. In about half an hour, tea is served in the drawing-room with a cake-basket of crackers or little cakes, the gentlemen join the ladies, and after a little chat over their cups, all are at liberty to take leave.

It is, of course presupposed that the host carves, and carves well. If he does not he should forego the pleasure of inviting his friends to dinner, or the dinner should be from chops, ribs, or birds which do not require carving.

In making up a dinner-party, it is all-important to know who will accept, and invitations, which may be written or printed, and should be sent by messenger and never mailed to persons in the same town, should receive a prompt reply, a day's delay being the extreme limit. The simplest form of invitation and reply is best, but both must be formal, this being one of the occasions on which the wings of genius must be promptly clipped. Ten minutes beyond the appointed time, is the utmost limit of tardiness admissible in a guest, and ten minutes early are quite enough.

THE HOST AND HOSTESS.

Those who entertain should remember it is vulgar hospitality, exceedingly annoying to guests, to overload plates, or to insist on a second supply. If the guest wants more, he knows that it is a delicate compliment to a dish to pass his plate the second time. Too great a variety of dishes is also a coarse display. A few cooked to a nicety and served with grace, make the most charming dinners. A sensible bill of fare is soup, fish with one vegetable, a roast with one or two vegetables and a salad and cheese, and a dessert. Parties should be made up of congenial persons, and the table should never be crowded. Novel dishes are great strokes of policy in dinners, but no wise housewife will try experiments on new dishes on such an occasion. The carver should serve meat as he cuts it, so far as possible, and not fill the platter with hacked fragments. It is ill-bred to help too abundantly, or to flood food with gravies, which are disliked by many. Above all, the plate should be served neatly. Nothing creates such disgust as a plate bedaubed with gravy or scattered food. It may be taken for granted that every one will take a piece of breast, and after that is served, it is proper to ask, "what part do you prefer?" The wings and legs should be placed crisp side uppermost, the stuffing should not be scattered, and the brown side or edge of slice should be kept from contact with vegetables or gravy, so that its delicacy may be preserved. Water should be poured at the right hand. Every thing else is served at the left. The hostess should continue eating until all guests have finished. Individual salt-dishes are used at breakfasts, but not at dinners, a cruet with salt dish and spoon, at each end of the table, being preferred as giving the table less of a hotel air. The salt-dishes should be neatly filled. Jellies and sauces are helped on the dinner-plate and not on side dishes. If there are two dishes of dessert, the host may serve the most substantial one. Fruit is served after puddings and pies, and coffee last. In pouring coffee, the sugar and cream is placed in the cup first. If milk is used, it should be scalding hot. Some prefer to make coffee strong, then weaken it with scalding hot milk, and pour into cups in which cream and sugar have previously been placed. For tea, it is better to pour first and then add cream and sugar. In winter plates should be warmed, not made hot.

INDIVIDUAL MANNERS.

Manners, at table and elsewhere, are made for the convenience and comfort of men, and all social observances have now, or have had at some time, a good reason and sound common sense behind them. It must be remembered, however, that the source of all good manners is a nice perception of and kind consideration for not only the rights but the feelings and even the whims of others. The customs of society are adopted and observed to enable us to be more agreeable, or at least not disagreeable, to friends. And nowhere is the distinction between the gentleman and the boor more marked than at the table. Some persons are morbidly sensitive, and even slight improprieties create disgust, and every true gentleman is bound to respect their sensitiveness and avoid giving pain, whether in sympathy with the feeling or not.

As this is not an etiquette book, we can only give a few hints. Once seated at table, gloves are drawn off and laid in the lap under the napkin, which is spread lightly, not tucked in. Raw oysters are eaten with a fork; soup from the side of a spoon without noise, or tipping the plate. The mouth should not go to the food, but food to the mouth. Eat without noise and with the lips closed. Friends will not care to see how you masticate your food, unless they are of a very investigating turn of mind. Bread should be broken, not cut, and should be eaten by morsels, and not broken into soup or gravy. It is in bad taste to mix food on the plate. Fish must be eaten with the fork. Maccaroni is cut and cheese crumbled on the plate, and eaten with a fork. Pastry should be broken and eaten with a fork, never cut with a knife. Game and chicken are cut, but never eaten with the bones held in the fingers. Oranges are peeled without breaking the inner skin, being held meantime on a fork. Pears are pared while held by the stem. Cherry-stones, or other substances which are to be removed from the mouth, are passed to the napkin held to the lips, and then returned to the plate. Salt must be left on the side of the plate, and never on the table-cloth. Cut with the knife, but never put it in the mouth; the fork must convey the food, and may be held in either hand as convenient. (Of course, when the old-fashioned two-tined fork is used, it would be absurd to practice this rule.) Food that can not be held with a fork should be eaten with a spoon. Never help yourself to butter or any other food with your own knife or fork. Never pick your teeth at table, or make any sound with the mouth in eating. Bread eaten with meat should not be buttered. Bread and butter is a dish for dessert. Eat slowly for both health and manners. Do not lean your arms on the table, or sit too far back, or lounge. Pay as little attention as possible to accidents. When asked "what do you prefer?" name some part

23

at once. When done, lay your knife and fork side by side on the plate, with handles to the right. When you rise from your chair leave it where it stands. Of course, loud talking or boisterous conduct is entirely out of place at table, where each should appear at his best, practicing all he can of the amenities of life, and observing all he knows of the forms of good society.

BREAKFAST PARTIES.

Breakfast parties are becoming fashionable in cities, because less formal and expensive than dinners, and quite as agreeable to guests. The courses, which are usually fewer in number, are served precisely as described for dinners. Oat-meal porridge is a favorite and healthful first course, and oranges, melons, and all fruits are delicious breakfast dishes. The variety of omelets is also a great resource, and hundreds of other delicacies and substantials are described elsewhere. But in breakfast—and the same is true of dinners—it is better to have a few, a very few, dishes delicately and carefully cooked, than to attempt more and have them less perfect. In fact the trouble often lies in attempting too many, and the consequent hurry in the kitchen. At breakfast, the coffee is set before the mistress, with cups in their saucers in front of it, in one or two rows. The meat with plates is set before the the master. For an ordinary table one castor in the center is sufficient. Fruit is served first; then oatmeal or cracked wheat, next meat and vegetables, followed by hot cakes and coffee. Meats are covered, and cakes are brought in between two plates. Butter is put on in small pats with lumps of ice about it. Honey or maple syrup, for cakes or hot biscuits, is served in saucers. A breakfast-table may be spread attractively with a white cloth, and a scarlet and white napkin under each plate, with white table-mats with a scarlet border.

For evening parties it is often less expense and trouble to place supper in the hands of a regular confectioner, but for small card or literary parties the trouble need not be great. For regular reception evenings, ices, cakes and chocolate are enough.

In all cases where no "help" is employed it is better to have some one of the family wait upon the table, the daughters taking turns in serving, as the pleasure of a meal is greatly marred by two or three persons jumping up every now and then, for articles needed.

TABLE OUTFIT.

In the selection of table-wares, there is a wide field for the exercise of taste, and those whose purses permit, need not be at a loss to find the most elegant and artistic designs. An admirable table outfit is an elegant dessert-set, all the pieces of which, except the plates, may decorate the table during the whole dinner, and the rest of white and gilt china. Some have table-ware decorated to match the colors of the dining-room, or sets of different patterns for each course, or harlequin sets in which each piece may be of different pattern or even of different ware. Chinese and Japanese sets are also fashionable. In every case, ware should be the best of its kind, and for economy's sake should be plain, so that broken pieces may be readily and cheaply replaced. Light knives and forks, heavy tea-spoons, and thin glasses for water are most elegant. The chairs should have no arms to interfere with ladies' dresses, and to prevent noise the legs should be tipped with rubber.

CLEARING THE TABLE.

Gather up the fragments that nothing be lost or wasted. When each meal is over, if you do not have a crumb cloth under the table, which, when the chairs are removed, can be lifted carefully at the edges and the crumbs shaken into the center, it is best to take a broom and sweep the crumbs lightly under the table until the dishes and victuals are removed, then brush on a dust pan. To clear the table, bring in a dish-pan, gather up all the silver, cups and saucers, butter and sauce plates, and glassware, carry to the kitchen, place them in the sink and return with the pan. Scrape the plates. as clean as possible and put in, add platters and vegetable dishes, saving all the remnants of food that are to be kept, on smaller dishes, to be taken to the cellar or refrigerator. To wash the dishes, have clear hot water in the pan, and first wash the silver without soap or cloth, using only the hands; if any are greasy, wipe with a soft paper before putting in the water, rinse in clear hot water and wipe off immediately on a perfectly dry, soft, clean towel; in this way the silver is kept bright, and does not get scratched. Add some soap in the water, make a suds, wash the glassware, rinse and wipe dry. Next take cups and saucers and so on, leaving those most greasy till the last. Always keep a clean dish-cloth. One lady writes, "I have smelt a whole houseful of typhoid fever in one sour, dirty dish-rag." Many prefer the use of three dish-cloths, one for the nicest articles, one for the greasy dishes, and one for the pots and kettles, keeping each cloth perfectly sweet and clean, and, after using it, washing, rinsing, and hanging to dry on a small rack kept for this purpose. The towel for wiping dishes may also dry here. A dish mop or swab for washing small deep articles is convenient.

Let no one suppose that because she lives in a small house, and dines on homely fare, that the general principles here laid down do not apply to her. A small house is more easily kept clean than a palace; taste may be quite as well displayed in the arrangement of dishes on a pine table as in grouping the silver and china of the rich. Skill in cooking is as readily shown in a baked potato or a johnny-cake as in a canvass-back duck. The charm of good housekeeping lies in a nice attention to little things, not in a superabundance. A dirty kitchen and bad cooking have driven many a husband and son, and many a daughter too, from a home that should have been a refuge from temptation. "Bad dinners go hand in hand with total depravity; while a properly fed man is already half saved."

THE KITCHEN.

It is almost impossible to give any directions except in a general way regarding the kitchen, as there is an endless variety of plans and arrangement. The main point is to systematize every thing, grouping such things as belong to any particular kind of work. For instance, in baking do not go to the china closet for a bowl, across the kitchen for the flour, and to the farther end of the pantry or store-room for an egg, when they may all just as well be within easy reach of each other. Study and contrive to bring order out of the natural chaos of the kitchen, and the head will save the hands and feet much labor.

If kitchen floors are simply oiled two or three times a year, no grease spot is made when grease drops on them, for it can be easily wiped up—carpet or paint is not advisable. Neither paint nor paper the walls, but once a year apply a coat of the good old-fashioned whitewash. Do not have the wood-work painted; the native wood well oiled and varnished lightly is much the best finish. A wide, roomy dresser is a great convenience; it should have two wide closets below and three narrower ones above, with a row of drawers at top of lower closets. Here should be kept all pots and kettles, sauce-pans, waffle-irons, kitchen crockery, tins, etc., all arranged and grouped together so as to be convenient for use. If possible, have good sliding doors, and at top and bottom of same have a narrow sliding panel for a ventilator, which should be closed when sweeping. By this arrangement every article of kitchen ware can be inclosed from the dust and flies. A well-appointed sink is a necessity in every kitchen, and should be near both window and range, so as to have light, and also be convenient to the hot water. It should be provided with a "grooved" and movable dish drainer, set so as to drain into the sink. Always have bracket or wall lamps placed at each end, or at the sides, so that the room may be well lighted in the evening. The sink should be washed and *wiped dry* daily, or it will become foul, especially if the weather is warm. When possible, a long table at the end of the sink, and so close to it that water can not drip between, on which to dress vegetables, poultry, game, etc., saves time and steps; and the good light, which is a necessity in this part of the room, leaves no excuse for slighted or slovenly work. Under this table may be two drawers, with compartments in one for polishing materials, chamois leather, and articles needed for scouring tin and copper; and in the other, articles for keeping the stove or range in order. Back of the table and sink, the wall should be ceiled with wood for three feet above them, and here may be put up galvanized iron hooks and nails on which to hang basting-spoons, ladles, cooking forks and spoons, the chopping-knife, cake-turner, etc. A set of drawers close at hand for salt, pepper, and spices is also convenient. There should never be bevel, beading, or molding on kitchen window or door frames; and the kitchen door, leading to the dining room, should be faced with rubber and closed with a not too strong spring. Not less than three large windows are desirable in every kitchen, which should be cheerful, pleasant, well ventilated, convenient, and clean.

In houses of the old style there was either no pantry at all, the kitchen being furnished with a dresser and shelves, or it was merely a small closet to hold the articles in less common use. In modern houses the pantry is next in importance to the kitchen, and it should be so arranged as to accommodate all the appliances used in cookery, as well as the china, glass-ware, cutlery, and other articles for the table, unless a dresser is used as before suggested. In arranging a plan for building, the pantry should receive careful consideration, as next in importance to the kitchen; it should be sufficiently roomy, open into both the dining-room and the kitchen, and, in order to "save steps," should be as convenient to the range or cooking-stove as circumstances will allow. The window should be placed so as to give light without infringing on the shelving; the shelves should be so arranged as to not obstruct the light from it; the lower ones should be two and a half feet from the floor, and two feet or more in width, and project about three inches beyond the closets and drawers below; and the part near the window, where there is no shelving, may be used for molding and preparing pastry, and such other work as may be most conveniently done here. Other shelves, or a china closet, should be provided for the china and other table furniture in every-day use. The pantry should have an abundance of drawers and closets, of which it is hardly possible to have too many—the upper closets for the nicer china and glass, and the lower ones to hold pans and other cooking utensils in less frequent use. The drawers are for table-linen and the many uses the housekeeper will find for them. If possible, the window should be on the north side, but in any case it should have blinds for shade, and a wire gauze or other screen to keep out flies. Instead of spreading shelves with paper, a neat marbled oil-cloth is better, as it is easily cleaned.

Use a cloth to wash potatoes. It is no trouble to keep one for this purpose, and it will save hands and time. Some prefer a brush. Tie a strip of muslin on the end of a round stick, and use to grease bread and cake-pans, gem-irons, etc. Have two large pockets in your kitchen apron, and in one of them always keep a holder. A piece of clam or oyster shell is much better than a knife to scrape a kettle, should you be so unfortunate as to burn any thing on it. If you use a copper tea-kettle, keep an old dish with sour milk and a cloth in it, wash the kettle with this every morning, afterward washing off with clear water, and it will always look bright and new. Cut a very ripe tomato and rub over a kitchen table to remove grease. The juice will also remove stains from and whiten the hands. A piece of sponge fastened on the end of a stick or wire is the best thing with which to clean lamp chimneys.

If you use oil, buy the best kerosene. To test it, place a small quantity in a tea-cup, and if it does not easily ignite when brought into contact with a lighted taper or match, it is good; poor oil will ignite instantly. Keep oil in a ten-gallon can with a faucet at the lower part, so as to draw off into a smaller can or lamp-filler; set the large can in a cool dark place; keep all the articles used for cleaning, filling, and trimming lamps by themselves. For these purposes provide an old waiter (to hold the things), a lamp-filler, pair of scissors or a lamp-trimmer, box of wicks, soap, washing soda, and several soft cloths and towels, also a wire hairpin with which to keep open the vent in the burner. When lamps need an extra cleaning, add one table-spoon soda to a quart of water, being careful that none of the bronze or gilding comes in contact with the soda. When the wick becomes too short to carry up the kerosene, and if you have not time to put in a new wick, a piece of cotton rag pinned on below will prove a good feeder. If a hole is broken in a glass chimney, paste on a piece of paper and it will answer its purpose until you get a new chimney. When the burners of lamps become gummy and prevent the wicks moving freely, boil them up in suds over the fire a short time, and they will become entirely clean and work well. Lamps may become incrusted inside with settlings from the oil, and ordinary wash-ing will not remove it. Take soap-suds and fill the lamp about one-third full, then put in a little sharp sand, and shake vigorously. A few minutes will remove every particle of settlings. Always fill the lamps every day and in the day-time; never fill a lamp after dark near a lighted lamp; never light an almost empty lamp, as the empty space is nearly always filled with a very explosive gas. In putting out a lamp, turn the flame down low, and wave a fan, book, or paper across the top of the chimney. Blowing down a chimney is very dangerous when a lamp is nearly empty and turned up high. Never start a fire with the oil.

Fill new tin pans with boiling water (having a little soda in it), let stand on a warm part of the range for a while, wash in strong soap-suds, rinse, and dry well. Scouring tins very often with whiting or ashes wears them out; if properly taken care of, washed in suds and thoroughly dried, they will not need scouring.

Boil ashes or a bunch of hay or grass in a new iron pot before cooking in it; scour well with soap and sand, then fill with clean water, and boil one or two hours. Knives for the table should never be used to cook with; those for the former purpose may be a cheap plated set for every-day use, and should be kept by themselves, and never allowed to be used in the kitchen.

Never place a range or cooking stove opposite a door or window if it can be avoided, as any draft will prevent the oven from baking well.

A necessity in the kitchen, because a great protection against clothes taking fire, is a large kitchen apron made full length with bib, and sleeves if wished, the skirt to button close around the dress-skirt. A wooden mat (made by laying down six pieces of lath eleven inches long, one inch wide, and an inch apart, and nailing across these, at right angles, six other similar pieces, about the same distance apart) is a great protection to the kitchen table, which should be of ash. Hot kettles and pans from the stove may be set on this without danger, as the construction of the mat secures a circulation of air under it.

There is an old and true saying that "a woman can throw out with a spoon faster than a man can throw in with a shovel." In cooking meats, for instance, unless watched, the cook will throw out the water without letting it cool to take off the fat, or scrape the dripping-pan into the swill-pail. This grease is useful in many ways. Bits of meat are thrown out which would make good hashed meat or hash; the flour is sifted in a wasteful manner, or the bread-pan left with dough sticking to it; pie-crust is left and laid by to sour, instead of making a few tarts for tea; cake batter is thrown out because but little is left; cold puddings are considered good for nothing, when often they can be steamed for the next day, or, as in case of rice, made over in other forms; vegetables are thrown away that would warm for breakfast nicely; dish-towels are thrown down where mice can destroy them; soap is left in water to dissolve, or more used than is necessary; the scrub-brush is left in the water, pails scorched by the stove, tubs and barrels left in the sun to dry and fall apart, chamber-pails allowed to rust, tins not dried, and iron-ware rusted; nice knives are used for cooking in the kitchen, silver spoons used to scrape kettles, or forks to toast bread; cream is allowed to mold and spoil, mustard to dry in the pot, and vinegar to corrode the casters; tea, roasted coffee, pepper, and spices to stand open and lose their strength; the molasses jug loses the cork and the flies take possession; vinegar is drawn in a basin and allowed to stand until both basin and vinegar are spoiled; sugar is spilled from the barrel, coffee from the sack, and tea from the chest; different sauces are made too sweet, and both sauce and sugar are wasted; dried fruit has not been taken care of in season, and becomes wormy; the vinegar on pickles loses strength or leaks out, and the pickles become soft; potatoes in the cellar grow, and the sprouts are not removed until they become worthless; apples decay for want of looking over; pork spoils for want of salt, and beef because the brine wants scalding; hams become tainted or filled with vermin, for want of the right protection; dried beef becomes so hard it can't be cut; cheese molds and is eaten by mice or vermin; bones are burnt that will make soup; ashes are thrown out carelessly, endangering the premises, and wast-

ing them; servants leave a light and fire burning in the kitchen, when they
are out all the evening; clothes are whipped to pieces in the wind, fine
cambrics rubbed on the board, and laces torn in starching; brooms are
never hung up, and are soon spoiled; carpets are swept with stubs hardly
fit to scrub the kitchen, and good new brooms used for scrubbing; towels
are used in place of holders, and good sheets to iron on, taking a fresh one
every week; table linen is thrown carelessly down, and is eaten by mice, or
put away damp and is mildewed; or the fruit stains are forgotten, and the
stains washed in; table-cloths and napkins used as dish-wipers; mats forgotten to be put under hot dishes; tea-pots melted by the stove; water forgotten in pitchers, and allowed to freeze in winter; slops for cows and pigs
never saved; china used to feed cats and dogs on; and in many other ways
a careless or inexperienced housekeeper wastes, without heeding, the hard-
earned wages of her husband. Economy counts nowhere so well as in the
kitchen.

———

TEA.—Keep tea in a close chest or canister.

BREAD.—Keep bread or cake in a tin box or stone jar.

NUTMEGS.—Always grate nutmegs at the blossom end first.

COFFEE.—Keep coffee by itself, as its odor affects other articles.

RED ANTS.—Scatter branches of sweet-fern where they congregate.

STAIN ON SPOONS—from boiled egg is removed by rubbing with a little
salt.

CRANBERRIES.—Cranberries will keep all winter in a firkin of water in a
cellar.

TO PRESERVE MILK.—A spoonful of grated horse-radish will keep a pan
of milk sweet for days.

ORANGES.—Oranges and lemons keep best wrapped in soft paper, and,
if possible, laid in a drawer.

CORKS.—When corks are too large to go into a bottle, throw them into
hot water a few moments, and they will soften.

CHARRED CASKS.—Water and salt meat may be preserved pure a long
time if put up in casks with the inside charred.

POLISHING.—Flour of emery, which is cheap and is kept at all drug-
stores, is excellent for polishing every thing except silver. Keep it in an
old pepper box.

SILVER POLISH.—To one quart rain water add two ounces ammonia
and three ounces of precipitated chalk. Put into a bottle, keep well corked,
and shake before using.

CEMENT FOR CHINA.—The whites of two eggs, and enough quicklime to
form a thick paste. The quicklime should be finely powdered; this makes
a good cement for mending broken china, marble, or glass-ware.

TO CLEAN SILVER.—"Indexical Soap" is the best thing for the purpose
in use, not for every day, but when thorough cleaning is required. It is
well, also, to keep it in a convenient dish, and rub on with a bit of flannel
whenever a spot appears on the silver.

TO CLEAN BRASS KETTLE.—When much discolored, scour with soap and
ashes, then put in a half pint vinegar and a handful of salt, put on stove,
let come to a boil, take cloth, wash thoroughly, and rinse out with water.
If using every day, the salt and vinegar and rinsing are sufficient.

To keep Cutlery from Rust.—Wipe dry, and wrap in coarse brown paper.

Drains.—Chloride of lime dissolved in water should occasionally be poured down the drains.

To Remove a Tight Glass Stopper.—Apply a cloth wet in hot water to the neck of the bottle; or wind a cord around once, and "saw" back and forth a few times. This will heat and expand the neck of the bottle.

Rust on Steel Implements or Knives.—Cover the steel with sweet oil, rubbing it on well. Let it remain for forty-eight hours, and then, using finely powdered unslaked lime, rub the steel until all the rust has disappeared.

To Preserve Lamp Chimneys from Breaking.—Place a cloth in the bottom of a large pan, fill the pan with cold water, and place new chimney in it; cover the pan, and let its contents boil one hour; take from fire, and let chimney remain in the water until it is cold.

Cement for Knife Handles.—Set handle on end, and partly fill cavity with powdered resin, chopped hair or tow, chalk, whiting, or quicklime; heat the spike of the knife and force it in to its place. Equal parts of sulphur, resin, and brick-dust also make an excellent cement.

Water—boiled in galvanized iron becomes poisonous, and cold water passed through zinc-lined iron pipes, should never be used for cooking or drinking. Hot water for cooking, should never be taken from hot-water pipes; take from cold-water pipes, and keep a supply heated for use in kettles.

Table Cover—to be thrown over table after it is set, is best made of calico. Pink mosquito netting is handsomer, but does not keep off dust when the table is set for next meal immediately after the dishes are washed—the most convenient plan where the dining room is not used for other purposes.

Cabbage Water.—Be careful that no cabbage water is poured down the kitchen sink, as the smell of it—a singularly unpleasant one—is so strong that it will penetrate all over the house, and produce the suspicion of a bad drain. The water in which any kind of cabbage has been boiled, should be thrown away out of doors, in a distant corner of the garden, if possible.

A Good Way to Mend Glass.—Pound flint-glass as fine as it can possibly be made on a painter's stone, and mix it with the unbeaten white of an egg. Rub the mixture on the clean edges of the broken glass, place them carefully together, and, where it can be done, bind together with a string. Set aside for some days or weeks, and one can scarcely discern that there was ever a crack in the bowl or dish.

To Clean Coffee or Tea-pots.—Musty coffee-pots and tea-pots may be cleaned and sweetened by putting a good quantity of wood ashes into them and filling up with cold water. Set on the stove to heat gradually till the water boils. Let it boil a short time, then set aside to cool, when the inside should be faithfully washed and scrubbed in hot soap-suds, using a small brush that every spot may be reached; then scald two or three times, and wipe till well dried. Pots and pans or plates that have been used for baking and grown rancid, may be cleansed in the same way. Put the plates into a pan with wood ashes and cold water, and proceed as above stated. If no wood ashes can be had, take soda. Pie-plates and baking dishes cleaned after this fashion will keep sweet all the time.

To Wash Preserve Jars.—Preserve jars or bottles should be carefully washed as soon as emptied, taking care that the stoppers and covers have their share of attention. It is well to put soda or ammonia into the jars or bottles, fill up with water, and let stand an hour, putting the stoppers or covers into a bowl to soak in the same way. Then pour out and scald nicely, but not with boiling water as that cracks the polished surface inside, wipe dry, set in the sun or wind to air, and then set away carefully.

To CLEAN KNIVES.—Cut a good-sized, solid, raw potato in two; dip the flat surface in powdered brick-dust, and rub the knife-blades. Stains and rust will disappear. Or rub up and down in the ground.

PULVERIZED CHARCOAL,—should be kept in every house in a glass jar, with a wide mouth, containing a half pint. The coal should be freshly burned—the best is not from the hardest or the softest wood, but a medium—pulverized finely in a mortar while the coals are yet red. Cork tight; it is invaluable in preserving meats and poultry, and is sometimes even given as a remedy for indigestion.

To KEEP TABLE CLOTHS CLEAN—for a long time. After clearing the table, place a clean towel under any spots that may have been made during dinner, and rub the spot with a fresh clean cloth wet with clean soap-suds, then rinse with clean water, dry with a clean dry towel, fold and lay under a heavy weight. In changing table cloths during the week, contrive to bring the fresh table cloth on first at dinner. Place a large napkin over each end of table-cloth, to protect it from soiling in the process of serving the plates, removing when the crumbs are brushed.

WASHING DISHES.—In washing dishes, in addition to directions given in " Dining Room," care must be taken not to put tumblers which have had milk in them into hot water, as it drives the milk into the glass, whence it can never be removed. They should be first rinsed well in tepid water. Tumblers and goblets should be placed in hot soapy water, dipping the sides first, and turning them rapidly, thus heating the outside and inside at the same time and preventing breaking; when wiped, they should not be turned down until put away in a china closet. Yeast jars should always be washed in cold water, and afterwards thoroughly scalded.

DISH CLOTHS, WIPERS, TABLE LINENS, ETC.—Roller towels for the hands should be marked with the number of each, and also with the whole number; as 1-6, 2-6, etc., where the whole number is six. This shows at once the whole number to be accounted for, and also makes it easy to use them in rotation, so that they may be worn equally. Of dish cloths, of which there should be six—two for the best dishes. two for greasy, and two for pots and kettles, the first two may be marked, "B-1-2" and "B-2-2;" the second two, "G-1-2" and "G-2-2;" the third, "P-1-2" and "P-2-2." Wiping towels, of which there should be six, two to be used each week, washing every other day, may be marked in a similar way, which is equally good for napkins, table cloths, cloths for silver, etc.

FLAVORING EXTRACTS, FRUIT-JUICES, ETC.—The following directions for the preparation at home of extracts, etc., are contributed by a trustworthy and experienced dealer, and may be relied upon. Of flavoring extracts put up for the general market, almond and peach are seldom pure, and are sometimes even poisonous. The other kinds are less liable to be adulterated.

To prepare vanilla, take one ounce of fresh vanilla beans, cut fine, and rub thoroughly with two ounces granulated sugar, put in a pint bottle, and pour over it four ounces pure water, and ten ounces of ninety-five per cent. deodorized alcohol. Set in a warm place, and shake occasionally for fourteen days.

To prepare lemon, cut in small pieces the rinds of two lemons, put in a four-ounce bottle, and fill with deodorized strong alcohol, set in a warm place for a week ; then put two drams fresh oil of lemon, four ounces of deodorized strong alcohol, and the juice of half a lemon, in a bottle of sufficient size to hold all; then strain in the tincture of lemon peel.

To make orange extract, use the rind and oil of orange, as directed for lemon.

To make rose extract, put one ounce of red rose leaves in one pint of deodorized alcohol, let stand eight days; press out the liquid from the leaves, and add it to a half dram of otto of roses.

Oils must be fresh and pure, or the extract will have a turpentine taste; and always use *deodorized* alcohol.

For fruit juices, select clean, ripe fruit, press out juice, and strain it through flannel; to each pint of juice, add six ounces pure granulated sugar; put in a porcelain kettle, bring to boiling point, and bottle while hot, in two or four ounce bottles.

Canned-fruit juice may be used in the same way. These juices are a perfect substitute for brandy, wine, etc., in all puddings, and sauces, etc.

For gold coloring, take one ounce tumeric to two ounces alcohol.

To filter water and alcoholic solutions (not syrups), pass through filtering paper, folded in conical form, so as to set into a funnel (a half-pint glass funnel is best). The paper is kept at all drug stores.

THE NEW "PATENT PROCESS FLOUR."—In all markets the best and highest-priced flour is now known as the Minnesota "Patent Process." A few years ago the process was invented and first used in the young city of Minneapolis, which now exports nearly a million and a quarter barrels of flour yearly, and finds a market for it in every quarter of the United States and Europe. The wheat from which this flour is made, is the hard spring wheat, *raised in the extreme North*, that raised south of Minnesota and Dakota being inferior, and most of it not available for the best grades, while that raised on the line of the North Pacific, and in the rich valley of the Red River of the North, makes the very highest grades of flour. This hard wheat is first passed through rollers and mashed; then, to the stones, which are run at a low rate of speed, and so dressed that the grinding is nearly all done near the outer edge of the stone, the "runner" being set high, so as not to heat the flour, but to leave it in hard, sharp globules. From this stone it is conveyed to a series of bolts, where the bran is separated, the softer and finer particles being passed through and put up as lower grades of flour, known as "All-Wheat Flour." The coarser particles and "middlings" are separated by this process, and conveyed to the "purifiers," where they are thoroughly cleaned of all bran and impurities; after which, they go to the stones to be reground and rebolted, and thus made into the "Patent Process Flour." These middlings are mainly from the outer portion of the kernel, which lies immediately below the flinty and worthless husk (which goes off in bran), and is rich in the nutritious gluten—the nitrogenous principle of wheat which makes it rank first as a "force-producing" food. Before the introduction of this process, the stones were driven at a high rate of speed, and the wheat thoroughly ground by the first run through the mill, the flour coming out quite hot, and much of its strength lost by the heating. The comparative rate of speed may be known by the fact that only five bushels are ground per hour by the new process; while, with the old, from fifteen to eighteen would have been consumed. By the old process, the "middlings" made a second-rate dark flour; by the new, it is transformed into the best known to the trade.

That this flour is the most economical for use, there is no doubt among those who have tried it. The hard spring wheat makes a much stronger flour than any of the soft varieties of spring or winter wheat, because it contains a larger proportion of gluten and less starch; and a given quantity will make from fifteen to twenty per cent. more loaves of bread of the same size and weight than the best winter wheat flour. This fact is what has given Minnesota baker's grades their popularity. Another advantage possessed by this flour, especially for family use, is that bread from it does not become stale and dry as soon as that made from winter wheat, but retains its moisture and good table qualities much longer.

The following in regard to the New Process Flour is from George H. Christian, Esq., who has spent years in studying the best methods in use in this country and Europe, and is the largest manufacturer in the United States:

"In regard to the economy of the New Process Flour, made from Minnesota spring wheat, it is claimed, and I believe, has been established, that the best qualities will make forty or fifty pounds of bread to the barrel more than flour from the best quality of winter wheat. This is explained by its superior affinity for water, which, being held in that much greater quantity in the bread, insures its keeping moist for a long time. Perhaps it might interest the scrupulous housewife to know that the New Process Flour is cleaner, all of the shell or bran being taken away before this kind of flour is made by the mill-stones. The authorities give the chemical analysis as 20 parts gluten, 50 parts starch, 10 parts dextrine, glucose, etc., 5 parts salts, fatty material, etc., and 15 parts water, for flour made from the best Minnesota spring wheat by the new process. The above percentage of gluten is nearly double that of flour made from the soft varieties of wheat (that of Minnesota is of the hard). Gluten is the most important compound of flour, and is the substance which renders the dough firm, and gives it sufficient consistency to hold the gases, generated by fermentation, long enough to make it rise well, and ensure a light palatable bread. It is well known also that bread from spring wheat is sweeter. The percentage of gluten in New Process Flour is more than in flour made of the same wheat by the old process."

KITCHEN UTENSILS.

EGG-BEATER.—The best is the "Dover Egg-beater."

PANCAKE-LIFTER.—Made with a broad flat blade, for turning pancakes.

APPLE-CORER.—A tin-tube, tapering slightly from one end to the other, for coring apples; may be made of any desired size.

CAN-OPENER.—Several good ones are made, which are very cheap, and save time and trouble and knives in opening tin-cans.

KNIFE FOR PEELING—potatoes or fruit, which has a wire guard on the side of the blade to regulate the thickness of the paring.

LARDING-NEEDLES—for larding fowls, may be purchased at any house-furnishing store. A penknife may be used as a substitute.

WIRE BASKET FOR FRYING.—A basket of tinned wire which is lowered into hot fat with any article to be cooked by immersion in it.

POTATO CUTTER.—An instrument with an adjustable knife for slicing potatoes, for frying in hot lard. Costs half a dollar, and is a great convenience.

CREAM WHIPPER.—A small syringe with the bottom perforated with holes, through which the cream is forced back and forth until it becomes a froth. Costs twenty-five cents.

CUSTARD-KETTLE.—The best is an iron kettle with a strong handle, with a smaller kettle, also with handle, fitted inside of it, leaving space around the smaller one for water. The inside kettle is lined with block-tin The custard-kettle is invaluable in cooking articles which are easily scorched.

MOLDS FOR JELLIES, ETC.—Are made of tin in various designs.

A GRAVY-STRAINER—made of gauze wire, in the shape of a tunnel, is best.

SKEWERS.—Made of tinned wire, with a ring at one end to draw them by, are convenient and easily made.

A DUST-PAN—with handle leaning down instead of up, so that the end will rest on the floor, tipping the blade slightly so that the edge will keep close to the floor to receive the dust, saves stooping down in sweeping.

COPPER UTENSILS.—The safest utensils for cooking are iron or porcelain lined. Tin-lined vessels, when only partly filled, often become so much heated that the tin is oxydized, and mingles with the food, and is an irritant poison.

SPICE CABINET.—A little bureau, about a foot high, with each drawer labeled outside, "nutmegs," "cloves," etc., and put up near where cakes, etc., are made. It costs little, probably about two dollars, and is a great convenience.

THE BAIN MARIE—is an open vessel filled with hot, not boiling water, and set on back of stove or range. In this, tin stew-pans or cups with handles and tight covers, containing vegetables, sauces, and other articles that need to be kept warm.

FLOWER FORMS.—Forms in the shape of a circle, cross, anchor, or other fanciful device, may be made of tin, about one inch deep, in which to arrange flat bouquets in wet sand or water, for the table. Very small ones in initials may be made to designate the plate to which guests are assigned.

FISH-KETTLE.—An oblong kettle for boiling fish, which has a false bottom of perforated tin, with handles at either end. The fish is placed on this perforated tin, lowered into the kettle, boiled, and, when done, lifted out again, and gently slipped from the tin to the platter on which it is to be served.

TEA-KETTLE BOILER.—A long tapering tin dish, with a long handle, made to lower into the tea-kettle, and large enough at the top to fill the opening, and long enough to reach to the bottom. The cover of the tea-kettle may be used to put over it. It is used for cooking gruels, custards, etc., and serves as a steamer for puddings, brown bread, etc., for a small family.

JELLY-STAND.—Four upright posts about a foot high, set about a foot apart, and joined at top and bottom with rounds, as the legs of the chair are joined. This makes a frame, with which the jelly bag (the top of which should be whipped over a strong wire) may be suspended by cords running from the wire in the top of the bag to each corner post. Pour in the jelly or soup, place a dish underneath, and allow to drain.

THE FERRIS COOKER—Is a round pile of pans, placed over an iron dish of boiling water, each dish or pan ready for any food—meat, poultry, vegetables, pies, puddings, or bread—all cooking at once, and all covered closely so as to retain the steam, by a round top that shuts down over every dish and fits tightly into the reservoir of water beneath. It makes a tall pile on the stove, but takes up no more room than one kettle, and its height does not interfere with any other kettle or sauce-pan that may be on the range.

A TOASTER—is made of a sheet of tin large enough to contain six slices of bread. The edges are turned up about half an inch and bound with wire, and perforations are cut about two inches apart in the shape of a V through the bottom, and the sharp points turned up so as to penetrate and hold the bread in place. A stiff wire handle is fastened firmly to the middle of the back, so that the toaster is kept at the right angle before the fire, and, if it toasts too rapidly at top or bottom, it may easily be inverted.

POLISHER AND STAND.—A small neat stand, made of coppered iron, with a surface of emery (three extra emery pads go with each) for cleaning starch, etc., from flat-irons.

A KNIFE BOARD.—A board two feet long by one wide, with a half-inch strip fastened to the edge, and raised a little above it all round, to keep the sand from falling off. At one end fasten in some way a scouring brick (such as all grocers keep), and on the other tack a piece of buff leather, three by seven inches. A few strokes over the leather after scouring gives a high polish.

STEAMING KETTLE.—A shallow pan with a perforated bottom, lowered its full length into a deep kettle. To steam vegetables, puddings, or in fact any thing that is usually cooked by immersion in hot water, put water in the deep kettle, place article in the perforated pan, cover closely, and keep the water boiling. It is impossible for any article so cooked to become water-soaked.

THE KITCHEN GEM.—A kettle-shaped vessel made of tinned wire, to be filled with articles to be boiled, and lowered into another kettle which contains the water. It is provided with a bail by which to lift it out, and with projecting flanges which rest on the top of the outer kettle, touching neither the bottom or sides, so as to keep it suspended either in or over the water; when done, the cooked articles are lifted out in it. It is admirable for vegetables, for making soups (especially when the meat is to be served on the table), and for boiling eggs, as well as for steaming dumplings, puddings, etc.

CAKE-PAN.—The bottom and sides are not permanently attached, but when fastened together, are in the shape of an ordinary cake-pan. When the cake is done, by unfastening the hooks that join the two ends of the strips of tin that forms the sides of the pan, it opens and leaves the cake standing on the bottom of the pan, from which it is slipped on a plate without inverting, as is necessary with the old-style pan. The bottom is also provided with a movable stem, which may be taken off when using the dish for puddings, bread, etc.

BOSOM BOARD.—A board twenty inches long, and ten to twelve inches wide. The shirt is slipped over it and buttoned at the neck; at the other end of the board is a strip about an inch wide, fastened to the board by an arm at each end, running along the sides of the board. This strip is pushed down, one "flap" of the shirt drawn through between it and the end of the board, and then it is raised up so that its surface is again on a level with the board. It thus holds the shirt firmly in position while it is being ironed and polished.

OTHER CONVENIENCES.—Among these are a soup-kettle (with a double bottom); a polishing iron for shirts (or a substitute may be made by selecting your best iron, and rounding and polishing both ends); a jagging-iron, to mark and ornament paste for pies; a pair of good scales; a movable sink, set on very large strong casters, which may be run into the dining-room to recieve the dishes from the table and pushed out to the kitchen; for summer use, a gas-stove, or when gas is not used, a Houchin pocket cooking stove, on which modest meals for a small family may be cooked without building a fire in the kitchen stove. The latter is also useful for travelers, at camp meetings, and in the sick-room for making toast, and keeping articles warm; a soap-shaker, a perforated oval tin box with a long handle, which, after a cake of soap has been placed in it, is shaken in the dish-water to make a suds; and a cast-iron soap dish, which fastens on the side of the wash-tub, while washing with hard soap.

THE MANAGEMENT OF HELP.

In all families whose style of living demands help in the household duties, the management of "girls" is the great American puzzle. "Girls" come and go like the seasons, sometimes with the weeks. The one who is "such a treasure" to-day, packs her trunk and leaves her mistress in the lurch to-morrow, or, if she happens to have a conscience and works on faithfully, she becomes the mistress and runs the household in her own way, her employer living in mortal fear of offending and losing her. This state of things is due partly to the fact that all girls who go out to service, do so as a make-shift until they marry or obtain some more congenial work. Few of them have any ambition to do their work well, and few ever dream of making themselves a necessity in the family, becoming a part of it, sharing its joys and sorrows, and so establishing that honorable and close relation which exists between servants and families in Europe. Here, it is so much work for so much pay, and no bond of sympathy or attachment is allowed to spring up on either side. Another cause is the fact that too many American women who ought to know better, regard work as degrading, instead of positively elevating and ennobling when it is well and conscientiously done. Is it wonderful that "girls" catch something of this vicious sentiment, and that it poisons their minds with false views of life, until they look upon their work as brutal drudgery, and strive to do as little of it as they possibly can and collect their wages.

Perhaps the reason why girls prefer situations in stores, or shops, or even factories, to housework, is that their work there is confined to certain hours after which they are free, and it is quite possible that an arrangement which would give the domestic certain hours of the day for her own, would work a reform; or still better, certain reasonable tasks might be allotted her to do, after which she would be free.

The fixed wages which prevail in most cities and towns offer no inducement for the "girl" to try to become skillful or expert at her work. Among men the best, neatest, and most skillful workman commands the largest pay, but the "girl" who is a superior cook, or maid of all work, gets only the same wages paid to a bungler who lives next door. Such a thing as a combination among ladies who employ help, to grade wages and protect each other from the imposition of untidy, dishonest, or indolent "girls," has never been made, and perhaps, indeed, it is no more called for than a combination of "girls" to protect themselves from lazy, tyrannical, or too exacting mistresses. Certain it is that the whole system by which domestics are hired and serve is demoralized beyond any speedy reform. All that any individual can do is to remedy its evils so far as is possible in her own family. In

employing a new domestic, there should be the utmost frankness. She ought
to be fully informed as to what she is expected to do, what her wages will
be and how paid, and what privileges will be granted. If she is not pleased,
let her depart without regret. If you engage her, let her understand first
and always that you are mistress, and claim the right to have the work
done in your way, which, if you are as skillful a housewife as you ought to
be, you will be able to show her is the best way. The mistress ought always
to be able to do every thing better and quicker than any domestic ever dared
think of doing it. If she gives orders which betray her ignorance, she may
as well resign her sceptre at once in shame and humiliation. No mistress
who does not know how to do work herself can ever be just to her help, and
even when she is a thorough housekeeper, a turn in the kitchen for a day or
two will often be like a new revelation to her.

Above all, the utmost kindness should be shown, and the mistress of the
house should always be mistress of her temper. She should put herself in
the "girl's" place, and apply the golden rule in all dealings with her. Give
unqualified praise when deserved, but never scold. If any thing is done improperly, take some proper time and have it done correctly, again and again
if necessary. Give domestics all the privileges possible, and when obliged
to deprive them of any customary indulgence, make it up soon in some
other way. Never to find fault at the time an error is committed, if in the
least irritated or annoyed, is an invaluable rule in the management of domestics or children, and indeed in all the relations of life. A quiet talk
after all feeling has subsided, will do wonders towards reform, while a sharp
and bitter rebuke would only provoke to further disobedience. It is especially
important and right to respect religious and conscientious scruples, no matter
how light and misguided they may seem. To cherish what beliefs she
pleases is an inalienable right. The care for the comfort and attractiveness
of the domestic's room is also a duty which every generous mistress will
cheerfully look after. The servant who is tucked away in a gloomy attic,
unfinished, uncarpeted, and uncurtained except by cobwebs, with the hardest
bed and the meanest bed-clothing in the house, can hardly be expected to be
neat and tidy in her personal habits. But after all, it will be impossible to
secure and keep really good "girls," unless they can be won into sympathy
and attachment to the family, so that they will regard themselves as a part
of it, with a future identified with its fortunes. To do this, the mistress
must respect her maid as a sensitive woman like herself, and not class her
as a mere drudge of an inferior order of creation. She must recognize the
fact that character, and not station or wealth, make the lady, and that it is
possible for those who serve to respect themselves. She must let her domes
tics see that she does not consider their work degrading, but honorable, and
that she does not for a moment expect them to regard it in any other light.
Above all, she must never show them, by word, look, or action, that she
"looks down" on them because of their work. By the cultivation of such
amenities as these, the house may really be made a *home* for the domestic as

well as the family, and the mistress who has accomplished this may well congratulate herself on having escaped the worst and most perplexing ills of the life of the American housewife. In her efforts to bring about such a result, she may confidently count on meeting many cases of incompetence, stupidity, and even ingratitude, but the experiment itself is in the right direction, and if it fails of complete success can not be wholly without good results.

HINTS TO "HIRED HELP."

Be neat in person and dress.
Keep your hands clean and hair tidy.
Do not waste time in gadding about and gossip.
Be quiet, polite and respectful in your manners.
Tell the truth always, but especially to children.
Do not spend your money foolishly in gewgaws of dress.
Always follow your mistress' plan of work, or explain why you do not.
Keep your room neat and orderly, and make it as attractive as possible.
Do not waste any thing. To waste carelessly is almost as wrong as to steal.
Never tell tales out of the family, or repeat in one what you have seen in another.
Never break a promise to children, and do not frighten them with stories, or help them to conceal wrong-doing.
Remember that there is nothing gained by slighting work. Doing every thing as well as possible always saves labor in housekeeping.
Remember that the best and most faithful girls command the highest wages, get the easiest and best places, and never are out of employment.
In engaging a new place, have a clear understanding as to wages, work, and the evenings and time you are to have. It may save trouble afterwards.
Learn from books or from those who have had more experience, the best way of doing work, and plan to do it, with as much system and few steps as possible.
Don't change employers. There are trials in every place, and it is better to put up with them, and make them as light as possible, than to change to new ones.
If your mistress scolds and loses *her* temper, be sure and control *yours*. If you feel that you are wronged, talk quietly and kindly after the storm has blown over.
Instead of trying, as many do, to see how little you can do and get your wages, try to see how pleasant and useful you can be as a member of the family. Work for its interests and happiness, lighten its burdens, be ready to give help when it is needed, even if it is out of your own line of work, and try to win the esteem and love of all by cheerfulness, kindness, truthfulness, and the practice every day of the golden rule.
Above all, do not think your work degrading. No work is more honorable. The happiness and health of the family depends on you, and no lady or gentleman will "slight" you or "look down" on you because you work. You need not be on the lookout for slights unless you are vain, or lazy, or slovenly, or dishonest. Whoever looks down on you because you do honest work conscientiously and well, is a fool, and not worth minding.

24

HINTS ABOUT MARKETING.

Very few housekeepers understand how to select meats wisely or how to buy economically. Most trust the butcher, or buy at hap-hazard, with no clear understanding of what they want, and no consideration at all for economy; and yet a little knowledge of facts, with a moderate amount of experience and observation, will enable any one to buy both intelligently and economically. It is best, when possible, to buy for cash. Ready money always commands the best in the market, at the lowest prices. It is also better to buy of the most respectable regular dealer in the neighborhood, than of transient and irresponsible parties. Apparent "bargains" frequently turn out the worst possible investments. If a dealer imposes on you, drop him at once. In buying beef, select that which is of a clear, cherry-red color after a fresh cut has been for a few moments exposed to the air. The fat should be of a light straw color, and the meat marbled throughout with fat. If the beef is immature, the color of the lean part will be pale and dull, the bones small, and the fat very white. High-colored, coarse-grained beef, with the fat a deep yellow, should be rejected. In corn-fed beef the fat is yellowish, while that fattened on grasses is whiter. In cow-beef the fat is also whiter than in ox-beef. Inferior meat from old or ill fed animals has a coarse, skinny fat and a dark red lean. Ox-beef is the sweetest and most juicy, and the most economical. When meat pressed by the finger rises up quickly, it is prime, but if the dent disappears slowly, or remains, it is inferior in quality. Any greenish tints about either fat or lean, or slipperiness of surface, indicate that the meat has been kept so long that putrefaction has begun, and, consequently, is unfit for use, except by those persons who prefer what is known as a "high flavor." Tastes differ as to the choice cuts. The tenderloin, which is the choicest piece, and is sometimes removed by itself, lies under the short ribs and close to the backbone, and is usually cut through with the porterhouse and sirloin steaks. Of these the porterhouse is generally preferred, the part nearest the thin bone being the sweetest. If the tenderloin is wanted, it may be secured by buying an edgebone steak, the remainder of which, after the removal of the tenderloin, is equal to the sirloin. The small porterhouse steaks are the most economical, but in large steaks, the coarse and tough parts may be used for soup, or, after boiling, for hash, which, in spite of its bad repute, is really a very nice dish when well made. A round steak, when the leg is not cut down too far, is sweet and juicy, the objection being its toughness, to cancel which it may be chopped fine, seasoned, and made into breakfast croquettes. The interior portion of the round is the tenderest and best. The roasting pieces are the sirloin and the ribs, the latter being most economical at the family table, the bones forming an excellent basis for soup, and the meat, when boned and rolled up (which should be done by the butcher), and roasted, being in good form for the carver, as it enables him to distribute equally the upper part with the fatter and more skinny portions. A roast served in this way, if cooked rare, may be cooked a second or even a third time. There are roasts and other meats equally good in the fore quarter of beef, but the proportion of bone to meat is greater.

Veal should be clear and firm, and the fat white. If dark and thin, with tissues hanging loosely about the bone, it is not good. Veal will not keep so long as an older meat, especially in hot or damp weather, and when going, the fat is soft and moist, the meat flabby and spotted, and inclined to be porous like a sponge. Overgrown veal is inferior to that which is smaller but well fatted.

Mutton should be fat, and the fat clear and white. Be wary of buying mutton with yellow fat. An abundance of fat is a source of waste, but as the lean part of fat mutton is much more juicy and tender than any other, it should be chosen. After the butcher has cut off all he can be persuaded to remove, you will still have to trim it freely before broiling. The lean of mutton is quite different from that of beef. While beef is a bright carnation, mutton is a deep, dark red. The hind quarter of mutton is best for roasting. The ribs may be used for chops and are the sweeter, but the leg cutlets are the most economical, as there is much less bone, and no hard meat as on the ribs. Almost any part will do for broth. As much of the fat should be removed as practicable, then cut into small pieces and simmered slowly until the meat falls to pieces. Drain off and skim off any remaining fat, and thicken with rice or vermicelli.

Lamb is good at a year old, and more digestible than most immature meats. The meat should be light red and fat. If not too warm weather, it ought to be kept a few days before cooking. It is stringy and indigestible if cooked too soon after killing.

Great care must be taken in selecting pork. If ill-fed or diseased, no meat is more injurious to the health. The lean must be fine-grained, and both fat and lean very white. The rind should be smooth and cool to the touch. If clammy, be sure the pork is stale, and reject it. If the fat is full of small kernels, it is an indication of disease. In good bacon the rind is thin, the fat firm and the lean tender. Rusty bacon has yellow streaks in it. Hams are tried by sticking a knife into them. If when drawn out it has no bad odor, the ham is good.

Meat should always be wiped with a dry, clean towel as soon as it comes from the butcher's, and in loins the pipe which runs along the bone should be removed, as it soon taints. Never buy bruised meat.

When found necessary to keep meat longer than was expected, sprinkle pepper, either black or red, over it. It can be washed off easily wher. ready for cooking. Powdered charcoal is excellent to prevent meat from tainting. Meat which has been kept on ice must be cooked immediately, but it is much better to place meats, poultry, game, etc., by the side of, not on, ice, as it is the cold air, not the ice, which arrests decay. All meats except veal, are better when kept a few days in a cool place.

GAME AND POULTRY.

The choice of venison should be regulated by the fat, which, when the veni-son is young, should be thick, clear, and close, while the meat is a reddish brown. As it always begins to taint first near the haunches, run a knife into that part; if tainted, a rank smell and a greenish appearance will be perceptible. It may be kept a long time, however, with careful manage-ment and watching, by the following process: Wash it well in milk and water, and dry it perfectly with a cloth until there is not the least damp remaining; then dust ground pepper over every part. This is a good pre-servative against the fly. The flesh of a female deer, about four years old, is the sweetest and best of venison.

To preserve game and poultry in summer, draw as soon as possible after they are killed, wash in several waters, have in readiness a kettle of boiling water, plunge them in, drawing them up and down by the legs so that the water may pass freely through them; do this for five minutes, drain, wipe dry, and hang in a cold place; when perfectly cold rub the insides and necks with pepper; prepared in this way they will keep two days in warm weather; when used wash thoroughly: Or wash well in soda-water, rinse in clear water, place inside several pieces of charcoal, cover with a cloth, and hang in a dark, cool place. The most delicate birds can be preserved in this way. If game or poultry is at all strong, let it stand for several hours in water with either soda or charcoal; the latter will sweeten them when they are apparently spoiled. English or French cooks, however, never wash poultry or game in dressing, unless there is something to wash off. With skillful dressing, none is necessary on the score of cleanliness, and much washing tends to impair the fine flavor, especially of game. In all game and poultry the female is the choicer.

Sportsmen who wish to keep prairie chickens, pheasants, or wild fowl in very hot weather, or to ship long distances, should draw the bird as soon as killed, force down the throat two or three whole peppers, tying a string around the throat above them, sprinkle inside a little powdered charcoal, and fill the cavity of the body with very dry grass. Avoid green or wet grass which "heats," and hastens decay. If birds are to be shipped without drawing, force a piece of charcoal into the vent, and tie a string closely around the neck, so as to exclude all air, and make a loop in string to hang up by. Prepared in this way, they will bear shipment for a long distance.

A young turkey has a smooth black leg, and if male, a short spur. The eyes are bright and full, and the feet are supple, when fresh. The absence of these signs denotes age and staleness.

In young geese, the bills and feet are yellow and supple and the skin may be easily broken; the breast is plump and the fat white; an old goose has red and hairy legs and is unfit for the table.

Young ducks feel tender under the wings and the web of the foot is transparent; those with thick, hard breasts are best. Tame ducks have yellow legs, wild ducks reddish ones.

Young fowls have a tender skin, smooth legs and comb, and the best have yellow legs. In old fowls the legs are rough and hard.

In pheasants and quails yellow legs and dark bills are signs of a young bird. They are in season in autumn.

Pigeons should be fresh, fat and tender, and the feet pliant and smooth.

In prairie chickens, when fresh, the eyes are full and round, not sunken, and if young, the breast bone is soft and yields to pressure. The latter test also applies to all fowls and game birds.

Plover, woodcock, snipe, etc., may be chosen by the same rules.

FISH.

When fresh, the eyes of fish are full and bright, and the gills a fine clear red, the body stiff and the smell not unpleasant. Mackerel must be lately caught or it is very indifferent fish, and the flavor and excellence of salmon depends entirely on its freshness. Lobsters when freshly caught have some muscular action in their claws which may be excited by pressing the eyes. The heaviest lobsters are the best. The male is thought to have the highest flavor, the flesh is firmer, and the shell has a brighter red; it may be readily distinguished from the female, as the tail is narrower, and the two uppermost fins, within the tail, are stiff and hard; those of the female are soft, and the tail broader. Hen lobsters are prepared for sauces on account of their coral. The head and smallest claws are never used. If crabs are fresh, the eyes are bright, the joints of the legs are stiff and the inside has an agreeable smell. The heaviest are the best, the light ones being watery. Scallops are not much used; when fresh the shell closes tight; hard-shell clams are also closed tight when fresh. Soft-shell clams are good only in cold weather, and should be fresh. Oysters, if alive and healthy, close tight upon the knife. They are good from September to May.

In fresh-water fish the same signs of freshness are good tests. Of course it is impossible to name all the excellent varieties, as they differ with the locality. In the South is the shad, the sheep's-head, the golden mullet and the Spanish mackerel; in the North-west the luscious brook trout, and the wonderful and choice tribes that people the inland lakes. Among the best of the fresh-water fish sold generally in the markets of the interior, are the

Lake Superior trout and white fish, and coming from cold waters they keep best of all fresh-water fish; the latter is the best, most delicate, and has fewer bones, greatly resembling shad. The wall-eyed pike, bass and pickerel of the. inland lakes are also excellent fish, and are shipped, packed in ice, reaching market as fresh as when caught, and are sold at moderate prices. California salmon is also shipped in the same way, and is sold fresh in all cities, with fresh cod and other choice varieties from the Atlantic coast, but the long distance which they must be transported makes the price high. The cat-fish is the staple Mississippi river fish, and is cooked in various ways. Lake Superior trout are the best fresh fish for baking. All fish which have been packed in ice should be cooked immediately after removal, as they soon grow soft and lose their flavor. Stale fish must never be eaten. Fresh fish should be scaled and cleaned properly on a dry table and not in a pan of water. As little water should be used as is compatible with perfect cleanliness. When dressed, place near ice until needed, then remove and cook immediately. If frozen when brought from market, thaw in ice-cold water. Fresh cod, whiting, haddock, and shad are better for being salted the night before cooking them, and the muddy smell and taste of fresh-water fish is removed by soaking, after cleaning, in strong salt and water.

Eels must be dressed as soon as possible, or they lose their sweetness; cut off the head, skin them, cut them open, and scrape them free from every string. They are good except in the hottest summer months, the fat ones being best. A fine codfish is thick at the back of the neck, and is best in cold weather. In sturgeon the flesh should be white, the veins blue, the grain even and the skin tender.

The best salt mackerel for general use are "English mess," but "bloaters" are considered nicer. In selecting always choose those which are thick on the belly and fat; poor mackerel are always dry. The salt California salmon are excellent, those of a dark rich yellow being best. To freshen, place *with scale side up.* Salmon boiled and served with egg sauce or butter dressing is nice. No. 1 white fish is also a favorite salt fish, and will be found in all markets.

A good deal of sturgeon is put up and sold for smoked halibut. The skin of halibut should be white; if dark it is more likely to be sturgeon. Smoked salmon should be firm and dry. Smoked white fish and trout are very nice, the former being a favorite in whatever way dressed. Select good firm whole fish. White fish is very nice broiled. Each of the above is better than herring.

CARVING.

It is no trifling accomplishment to carve well, and both ladies and gentlemen ought to so far make carving a study that they may be able to perform the task with sufficient skill at least to prevent remark. There are no real difficulties in the way of mastering the accomplishment; knowledge simply is required. All displays of exertion are in bad taste, because they indicate a want of ability on the part of the carver, or are a strong indication of the toughness of the roast or the age of the bird. A good knife of moderate size and great sharpness is a necessity. Fowls are easily carved, and in roasts such as loins, breasts, forequarters, etc., the butcher should always have instructions to separate the joints. The platter should be placed so near to the carver that he has full control over it; if far off, nothing can prevent an ungraceful appearance. In carving a turkey, place the head to the right, cut off the wing nearest you first, then the leg and second joint; then slice the breast until a rounded, ivory-shaped piece appears; insert the knife between that and the bone and separate them; this part is the nicest bit of the breast; next comes the "merry-thought." After this, turn over the bird a little, and just below the breast you will find the "oyster," which you can separate as you did the inner breast. The side bone lies beside the rump, and the desired morsel can be taken out without separating the whole bone. Proceed in the same way upon the other side. The fork need not be removed during the whole process. An experienced carver will dissect a fowl as easily as you can break an egg or cut a potato. He retains his seat, manages his hands and elbows artistically, and is perfectly at his ease. There is no difficulty in the matter; it only requires knowledge and practice, and these should be taught in the family, each child taking his turn. Chickens and partridges are carved in the same way. The trail of a woodcock on toast is the choicest bit of the bird; also the thigh of a partridge.

A fillet of veal is cut in thin, smooth slices off the top, and portions of the stuffing and fat are served to each. In cutting a breast of veal, separate the breast and brisket, and then cut them up.

SIRLOIN OF BEEF.—In carving beef, mutton, lamb, and veal, thin, smooth and neat slices are desirable —*cut across the grain* taking care to pass the knife through to the bones of the meat. There are two modes of helping a sirloin of beef; either by carving long, thin slices from 3 to 4, and helping it with a bit of the fat underneath the ribs, or by cutting thicker slices, from 1 to 2, through the tenderloin.

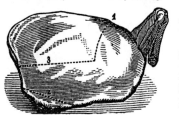

SHOULDER OF MUTTON.—A shoulder of mutton should be cut down to the bone, in the direction of the line 1, and then thin slices of lean taken from each side. The best fat is found at 2, and should be cut in thin slices in that direction. Several tempting slices can be cut on either side of the line 3, and there are nice bits on the under side near the flap.

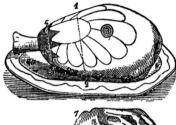

HAM.—A ham may be carved in three ways: first, by cutting long, delicate slices through the thick fat from 1 to 2, down to the bone; secondly, by running the point of the knife in the circle in the middle, and cutting thin circular slices, thus keeping the ham moist, and last, and most economically, by beginning at the knuckle. 4–5. and slicing upward.

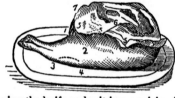

LEG OF MUTTON.—In carving a leg of mutton the best slices are obtained from the center, by cutting from 1 to 2; and some very good cuts are found on the broad end from 5 to 6. Some epicures prefer slices nearer the knuckle, but they are dry. The cramp-bone is a delicacy, and is obtained by cutting down to the bone at 4, and running the knife under it in a semicircular direction to 3. The fat so esteemed by many lies on the ridge 5. By turning over the meat some excellent slices are found, and can be cut lengthwise.

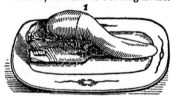

TONGUE. — A tongue should be carved as "thin as a wafer;" its delicacy depending in a great degree upon that. A well-cut tongue tempts the most fastidious; and this applies, in fact, to all kinds of roast and boiled meats. A chunk of beef we turn from with disgust—an artistic slice we enjoy. The center slices of the tongue are considered the best, and should be cut across at the line 1, and the slices taken from each side, with a portion of the fat which is at its root, if it is liked. The question should be asked.

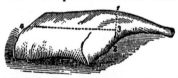

HAUNCH OF VENISON.—A haunch of venison should be cut across to the bone on the line 1–3–2, then turn the dish a little, and put the point of the knife at 3, and cut down as deep as possible in the direction of 3–4, and continue to cut slices on the right and left of the line. The fattest parts are found between 4 and 2. A loin of veal or a loin of mutton should be jointed by the butcher before it is cooked, and the carver easily cuts through the ribs. He should serve a portion of the kidney and the fat on each plate.

In serving fish, some practice is needful, for lightness of touch and dexterity of management are necessary to prevent the flakes from breaking. In serving mackerel, shad, etc., a part of the roe should be placed on each plate. The fins of the turbot are the most sought for; the fish is placed underpart uppermost on the platter, as there lies the primest part. In carving salmon, a portion of the back and belly should be served to each person. The choicest morsels are next to the head, the thin part comes next, and the tail is the least esteemed. The flavor of the fish nearest the bone is not equal to that on the upper part.

HOW TO CUT AND CURE MEATS.

It is often economical for a family to buy beef by the quarter, and smaller animals whole, especially when wanted for winter use, and every housekeeper ought to know how to cut up meats and to understand the uses and relative value of the pieces. It is not difficult to cut up beef, and is very easy to reduce any of the smaller animals to convenient proportions for domestic use, and in order to make the subject clear we present the accompanying engravings, the first of which represents the half of a beef, including, of course, the hind and fore quarters. The letters indicate the direction in which the cuts should be made, beginning in the order of the alphabet, cutting first from A to B, then C to D, etc. In the fore quarter cut from A to B, from B to C, from D to E, etc. For cutting, use a sharp, long, and pointed knife, and a saw of the best steel, sharp, and set for butcher's use. The beef should be laid on a bench or table with the inner side up. In hind quarter 1 represents the "rump," which is best corned; 2, "round," the under part of which makes steaks, the outside good corning pieces, or the whole may be used for dried beef; 3. "shank" for soups; 4, "rump steaks;" 5, "veiny piece" for dried beef or corning; 6, sirloin, the best steak; 7, flank for corning or stews; 8, porterhouse, the upper part of which is equal to sirloin. Cut in this

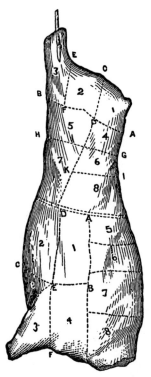

way a part of the tenderloin, the choicest bit of the beef, lies in the sirloin, and a smaller part in the upper part of the porterhouse steak. In the fore quarter 1 is the "rib piece" for boiling or corning; 2, the "plate" piece for corning; 3, the "fore shank" for soup; 5, the "rib roast," first cut; 6, "rib roast," best cut, and the best roast in the beef; 7, "chuck rib roast," commonly used for "pot roast;" 8, neck piece, for corning or pie meat; 9, best cut for corn-beef.

VEAL.

A—Loin, best end, for roasting.
B—Loin, chump end, for roasting.
C—Fillet, for baking or roasting.
D—Knuckle, for stewing.
E—Fore knuckle, for stewing.
F—Neck, best end, for roasting.
G—Neck, scrag end, for stewing.
H—Blade bone.
I—Breast, for stewing.
K—Brisket, for stewing.

PORK.

A—Back, lean part for roast.
B—Loin, for roast.
C—Bacon, to be cured.
D—Shoulder, to be cured.
E—Ham, to be cured.

MUTTON.

A—Leg, for boiling piece.
B—Loin, for roast.
C—Rump piece, for roast.
D—Chops, frying or broiling.
E—Fore shoulder, for boiling.
F—Neck, for stewing or roasting.
G—Brisket, for stewing.

How to Cut up Pork.—Split through the spine, cut off each half of head behind the ear, remove the pieces in front of the shoulder, for sausage. Take out *leaf* which lies around kidneys for lard, cut out the lean meat, ribs, etc., then the ham and shoulder, and remove the loose piece directly in front of the ham, for lard. Cut off a narrow strip of the belly, for sausage, and cut up the remainder, which is clear pork, into five or six strips of about equal width, for salting down. Smoke the jowl with hams, and use the upper part of the head for boiling, baking, or head-cheese. Scorch the feet over the fire until the hoofs remove easily, scrape clean, place in hot water a few minutes, wash and scrape thoroughly, and they are ready for cooking. All the flabby pieces should be tried up for lard. Remove all fat from intestines, saving that which does not easily come off the larger intestines for soap-grease. The liver, heart, sweetbreads, and kidneys are all used for boiling or frying, and the smaller intestines are sometimes used for sausage cases.

To Clean Beef Tripe.—Empty the paunch, rinse it thoroughly in cold water; (being careful not to let any of the contents get on the outside Make strong cleansed water or white lye, let it heat a little, too warm to hold the hands in, pour it over the tripe in a tub, let it stand two or three hours, then tack it up against a board, and with a knife scrape downwards, taking off the inner skin, or rinse it clean in cold water; sprinkle lime over, put in a tub, cover with warm water, and let it stand two or three hours, then scrape it with a knife, if the dark does not all come off easily, sprinkle more lime on, and let it lie for an hour longer, then scrape again, and rinse in cold water until clean. Place it in water enough to cover with a large handful of salt, let it remain in the salt water three days and nights, changing it each day, then take it out, cut in pieces about six inches wide and twelve long, lay in buttermilk for a few hours to whiten; then rinse it clean, in cold water, and boil until tender; it will take from four to ten hours, as it should be done so that it can be mashed with the fingers. After thus prepared it can be cooked as preferred.

CORNED BEEF.—Make a brine as follows: To one hundred pounds of beef take four gallons of water, six pounds of salt, two pounds of sugar, half pound soda, two ounces saltpeter, and six red peppers; let come to a boil, skim, and set away to cool. Pack meat in a wooden vessel or large stone jug, and when the brine is cold, pour over it, and put a weight on to keep it under the brine. This is also an excellent recipe for curing beef to dry.

SPICED CORNED BEEF.—To ten pounds beef, take two cups salt, two cups molasses, two table-spoons saltpeter, one table-spoon ground pepper, one table-spoon cloves; rub well into the beef, turn every day and rub the mixture in; will be ready for use in ten days.

PICKLED TONGUE.—For one dozen tongues make a strong brine sufficient to cover, add one tea-spoon of pulverized saltpetre and half pound sugar: keep a weight on them so that they may be covered with brine. Let them remain two weeks, then hang up to dry or smoke if you like.—*Ada Estelle Bever.*

TO CURE AND DRY BEEF TONGUES.—For one dozen tongues make a brine of a gallon and a half water (or enough to cover them well) two pints good salt, one of molasses, or one pound brown sugar, and four red peppers; bring to a boil, skin, and set to cool. Pack the tongues in a large jar, and when the brine is entirely cold, pour it over them, put on a weight, let remain ten or twelve days, take out, drain, and hang to smoke about two days, then dry moderately, and put away in a flour sack in a dry place. When wanted for use, boil six or eight hours in a pot filled with water, adding more when necessary so as to keep well covered all the time until done; when done, take out and set away to cool, but do not skin till needed for the table.—*Mrs. Jas. Henderson, Marysville.*

BRINE FOR BEEF—To one hundred pounds beef, take eight pounds salt, five of sugar or five pints molasses, (Orleans best, but any good will do), two ounces soda, one ounce saltpeter, four gallons water, or enough to cover the meat. Mix part of the salt and sugar together, rub each piece and place it in the barrel, having covered the bottom with salt. When the meat is all in, put the remainder of salt and sugar in the water. Dissolve the soda and saltpeter in hot water, add it to the brine and pour over the meat; place a board on top of meat, with a weight sufficient to keep it under the brine. Let the pieces intended for dried beef remain in the brine for three weeks, take out, place in a tub, cover with water, let stand over night, string and dry. When dried put in paper sacks, tie up tightly, and hang in a cool, dry, dark place, or put in an empty flour barrel, and cover closely. When hams and shoulders are smoked, sprinkle with ground black pepper, and put away in the same manner. Boil brine, skim well, let cool, and pour over the bony pieces left. These are good boiled and eaten either hot or cold, and they will keep good for several months. Tongue may be pickled with the beef. Brine made the same way, with the addition of two pounds more of salt, is good for hams and shoulders. Brine for pickled pork should have all the salt it will dissolve, and a peck or half bushel in bottom of barrel. If pork is salted in this manner it will never spoil, but the strength of the brine makes it necessary to salt the hams and side-meat separately. Pork when killed should be thoroughly cooled before salting, but should not remain longer than one or two days. It should never be frozen before salting, as this is as injurious as salting before it is cooled. Large quantities of pork are lost by failing to observe these rules. If pickled pork begins to sour, take it out of the brine, rinse well in clear cold water, place a layer in a barrel, on this place charcoal in lumps the size of a hen's egg or smaller, add a layer of meat and so on, until all is in the barrel, cover with a weak brine, let stand twenty-four hours; take meat out, rinse off the charcoal, put it into a new strong brine, remembering always to have plenty of salt in the barrel (more than the water will dissolve). If the same barrel is used, cleanse it by placing a small quantity of quicklime in it, slack with hot water, and add as much salt as the water will dissolve, and cover tightly to keep the steam in.—*D. Buxton.*

TO CURE HAMS.—For every ham, half a pound each of salt and brown sugar, half an ounce each of cayenne pepper, allspice, and saltpeter; mix and rub well over the hams, laying them in the barrel they are to be kept in with the skin side down; let them remain a week; make a pickle of water and salt strong enough to bear an egg, add to it half a pound of sugar, pour over the hams till they are thoroughly covered, let them remain four weeks, take out and hang up to dry for at least a week before smoking; smoke with corn-cobs or hickory chips. An old but a good way.—*Mrs. S. M. Guy.*

TO KEEP HAMS.—For one hundred pounds of meat, take eight pounds salt, two ounces saltpeter and four gallons water; put hams in this pickle in the fall, keeping them well under the brine; in April take out, drain three or four days, slice as for cooking, fry nearly as much as for table, pack in stone jars, pressing down the slices as fast as they are laid in the jar; when full put on a weight, and when entirely cold, cover with the fat fried out. Prepared in this way they retain the ham flavor without being smoked. The gravy left from frying will be found very useful in cooking.

TO SALT HAMS.—Take a barrel (oak is best), place in it a layer of meat, then a layer of salt, and so on, until barrel is full and meat well covered with salt. After five or six weeks, take out meat, and if not salt enough, repack in a less amount of salt than was at first used. Take out again, and smoke over hickory chips and chunks eight or ten days, and then hang up until used. Some put hams thus smoked and cured into paper sacks; when this is done watch closely to prevent mold. Others pack them away in oats or in ashes, or rub them with black pepper coarsely ground, putting cayenne pepper on where the bone is exposed. All these are safeguards against flies and mold.

TO SALT PORK.—Allow the meat to stand until the animal heat is entirely out of it; cut into strips crosswise; cover the bottom of a barrel with salt, and pack in the pork closely edgewise, with rind next the barrel, cover each layer with salt, and proceed in like manner until all has been put in. Make a *strong* brine sufficient to cover the pork (soft water is best, and there is no danger of getting it too salt), boil, skim, and pour into the barrel while *boiling hot.* Have a board cut out round, a little smaller than the barrel, put over the pork, and on it place a weight heavy enough to keep it always under the brine. If at any time the brine froths or looks red, it must be turned off, scalded, and returned while *hot. Never put cold brine on old pork* unless you wish to lose it. In salting down a new supply of pork, boil down the old brine, remove the scum, and then pour it over the pork as directed above.—*R. S. Wilcox, Madison.*

To CURE HAMS AND SHOULDERS.—Make a pickle of salt and water, with one ounce saltpeter and half a pint molasses or one-fourth pound brown sugar for each ham of ordinary size; pack hams as closely as possible in barrel, sprinkle on a little salt, and pour over them the pickle boiling hot. Let them remain two weeks, take out, drain a few days, and smoke according to taste. Corn-cobs or sawdust are best for this purpose.

To KEEP HAMS AFTER CURING.—Wrap in brown paper, and place in a *tight* bag so as to secure from flies; or if preferred, cut hams in slices suitable for cooking, trim off the rind, and pack as compactly as possible in a stone jar; over the top pour melted lard so as to completely exclude the air. When ham is wanted for use, scrape off the lard, remove a layer of meat, and *always be particular* to melt the lard and return it *immediately* to the jar. Prepared in either of the above ways, ham will keep through the season.

OR, TO PRESERVE SMOKED MEATS THROUGH THE SUMMER.—Pack in clean, sweet hay before flies come; cover the box or barrel tight, and keep in a dry place.

TRYING LARD.—Cut the fat in small pieces, put into kettle, and pour in enough water to cover the bottom; boil gently until the "scraps" settle or until the water has all evaporated, stirring often to prevent burning. Take off, strain into stone jars, and set in a cool place. The quality of the lard is improved by sprinkling over and slowly stirring in one table-spoon of soda to every five gallons of lard, just before removing from the fire. The *leaf* should be tried by itself for the nicest cooking. That from the smaller intestines and the flabby pieces, not fit for salting, should be tried by themselves, and the lard set away where it will freeze, and by spring the strong taste will be gone. A tea-cup of water prevents burning while trying.

To CORN BEEF.—Pack the meat in barrel with a sprinkling of salt between layers; let it lie three or four days, then turn in the pickle, made as follows: For one hundred pounds meat, take nine pounds salt, six gallons water, one quart molasses, (brown sugar may be substituted) and one-fourth pound saltpeter; boil together, skim, and turn on either hot or cold.

In packing beef, lay that which is intended for *dried* meat on top of barrel; let it remain ten or twelve days, take out, string, and hang to dry near the kitchen fire placing the pieces so that they will not overlap each other. Some prefer to smoke dried meat.

SAUSAGE.—For twelve pounds meat, take one tea-cup salt, one and a half cups pulverized sage, eight even tea-spoons black pepper, two table-spoons ginger; mix, sprinkle over meat before cutting. (Some add a small quantity of summer savory). When nicely minced, pack in jars, and treat precisely as in preceding recipe "To keep Hams." If kept in a cool place and care taken to replace the lard, there is no difficulty in keeping sausage perfectly fresh almost any length of time. Some persons partially cook meat before packing, but this is *not* necessary. Fresh meat may be kept nicely in the same way, being first seasoned with salt and pepper.

Or, one pound salt, one-half pint of sage, and three and one-half ounces pepper, scattered over forty pounds of meat before grinding.—*Charles Phellis, Jr.*

For ten pounds of meat take five table-spoons sage, four of salt, and two of pepper.—*Wm. Patrick, Midland, Mich.*

To Keep Lard from Molding.—Use a tub that has had no tainted lard or meat in it; scour it out thoroughly with two quarts of wheat bran to four of boiling water, but use no lye or soap. Try the lard until the scraps are brown, but not scorched or burned; remove from the fire, cool until it can be handled, and strain into the prepared tub; when cold, set it away in the cellar. Lard dipped off as fast as it melts will look very white, but will not keep through the summer. No salt should be added, as it induces moisture, and invites mold.

A New Way to Smoke Hams.—Smoke the barrel, in which the hams are to be pickled, by inverting it over a kettle containing a slow fire of hard wood, for eight days (keeping water on the head to prevent shrinking); in this barrel, pack the hams, and pour over them, after it has cooled, a brine made in the proportion of four gallons of water, eight pounds of salt, five pints of molasses, and four ounces saltpetre, boiled and skimmed in the usual manner. They will be cured in eight or nine days, and they may be kept in the pickle for a year without damage.

Beaf-steak for Winter Use.—Cut the steaks large, and the usual thickness; have ready a mixture made of salt, sugar, and finely powdered saltpetre, mixed in the same proportion as for corning beef; sprinkle the bottom of a large jar with salt, lay in a piece of steak, and sprinkle over it some of the mixture, as much or a little more than you would use to season in cooking, then put in another slice, sprinkle, and so on till jar is filled, with a sprinkle of the mixture on top; over all, put a plate, with a weight on it, and set in a cool, airy place, where it will not freeze. This needs no brine, as it makes a brine of its own. Twenty-five or thirty pounds may be kept perfectly sweet in this way. Take out to use as wanted, and broil or fry as usual.

To Cure Hams.—In the fall, about the first of November, people in the country generally kill a good-sized pig, to last until "butchering time." To cure the hams of such, first, rub well, especially around the bone on fleshy side, with one-half of the salt, sugar, cayenne, and saltpetre, well pulverized (same proportions as for corned beef), adding a tea-spoonful allspice to each ham; put a layer of salt in bottom of cask, and pack in hams as closely as possible; let stand three or four days, then make a brine of the other half of salt, etc., and pour over meat, putting a good weight on top; when it has lain three or four weeks it is ready for use.

HINTS ON BUTTER-MAKING.

No sloven can make good butter. The *one thing* to be kept in mind, morning, noon and night, is neatness, neatness, neatness. The milking should be done in the cleanest place that can be found, and the cows should be kept as clean as possible. Wash the teats *and udders* thoroughly with plenty of cold water, and wipe with a cloth or towel. Never wash with the hand moistened with milk from the cow. The least impurity taints the cream, and takes from the sweetness of the butter. Milk perfectly clean, (as the last quart is twice as rich in butter as the first,) and the quicker the milking is done the more milk is obtained. The milk-room should be clean and sweet, its air pure, and temperature about 62 degrees. As soon as a pail is filled, take to the milk-room and strain the milk through a fine wire-cloth strainer, kept for the purpose, and not attached to the pail (the simple strainer being more easily kept clean). Never allow milk to stand in the stable and cool, as it absorbs the foul odors of the place. The pans (flat stone crocks with flaring sides are better that tin pans. In winter hot water should be poured into them while milking is being done, and poured out just before straining the milk into them) should be set on slats, rather than shelves, as it is important to have the milk cooled from the animal heat as soon as possible. Skim each day, or at longest within twenty-four hours. Souring does not injure the quality of the cream, but the milk should not be allowed to become watery. Do not use a perforated skimmer, but remove a little of the milk with the cream, as this does not injure the quality or lessen the quantity of butter, and gives more well-flavored buttermilk, which is a favorite and wholesome drink. If there is cream enough each day, it should, of course, be churned, and this plan makes the best butter, although it takes longer to churn it. If not, the cream should be set aside in a cool place, covered, and stirred thoroughly whenever more is added. It ought not to stand more than two days, and must not be allowed to become bitter and flaky. The best plan is to churn as soon as it becomes slightly acid. Scald the churn and dash thoroughly, and put in the cream at a temperature of 58 degrees. The motion of the churn will soon bring it up to about 60 degrees. When the butter comes put a quart or two of cold, soft water (or ice is better) into the churn to harden the butter, and make it easier to gather up. After gathering it as well as possible with the dash, it should be removed to the table or bowl, and thoroughly worked with a flat wooden paddle, (never with the hand, as the insensible perspiration will more or less taint the butter,) using an abundance of cold *soft* water to wash out the buttermilk and harden the butter. By this process the buttermilk is removed quickly, and there is no need of excessive working, which injures the grain of the butter. This is especially true of that which is to be packed, as it keeps longer when well washed. If to be used immediately, the washing may be less thorough. Another and better plan is to remove the butter to a marble slab and lay on the top of it a piece of ice. As it settles down by its own weight, work it up around the edges with the paddle, and the water from the melting ice will wash out and carry off the buttermilk. Before or during the churning, the bowl (which should never be used for any thing else) in which the butter is to be salted should be filled with scalding water, which should remain for ten minutes; pour out and rub both bowl and paddle with hard coarse salt, which prevents butter from sticking. Rinse thoroughly and fill with cold or ice-water to cool. After washing butter free from milk, remove to this bowl, having first poured out the cold water, and (the butter-bowl and paddle should occasionally be scoured with sand or ashes, washed thoroughly with soap-suds, and rinsed until all smell of soap has disappeared,) work in gradually salt which has been pulverized by rolling, and freed from foreign substances. If wanted for use, one-half ounce of salt to the pound of butter is sufficient, but if wanted for packing, use three-fourths of an ounce or even an ounce of salt. Use only the best quality of dairy salt. After salting, cover with cotton cloth soaked in brine, and set away in a temperature of about 60 degrees for twelve hours. Work the second time just enough to get the remaining buttermilk out. This, however, must be done thoroughly, as otherwise the acid of the buttermilk will make the butter rancid. At the end of the second working it is ready for use, and should be kept in a clean, sweet place, as it soon absorbs bad odors and becomes tainted. The air of a cellar in which are decaying vegetables soon ruins the sweetest butter. In packing for market, (ash butter-tubs are the neatest and best packages,) soak the package for twelve hours in brine strong enough to float an egg, pack the butter in evenly and firmly, having first put in a thin layer of salt. If the tub is not filled by the first packing, set away until next churning, in a cool place, with a cotton cloth wet in brine spread over the butter, and place cover carefully on the tub. When filled, lay over the butter a cotton cloth (from which the sizing has been washed) soaked in strong brine, nail up the tub, and set away in a clean, cool place until ready to sell.

In packing for family use, work into rolls, lay in large stone crocks, cover with brine strong enough to float an egg, in which a level tea-spoon of salt-peter and a pound of white sugar to each two gallons have been added; over it place a cotton cloth and a weight to keep the butter under the brine, and tie a paper over the top of crock. Or pack in a stone jar, pressing it solid with a wooden pestle, cover with a cloth wet in brine, and sprinkle over it salt an inch thick. When ready to pack the next churning, remove the cloth with the salt carefully, rinsing off with water any that may have been scattered in uncovering it, pack butter as before, replace cloth with salt over it, and repeat until jar is filled to within two inches of the top, cover all with cloth, add salt to the top of crock, tie paper over the top and set in a cool place. In removing for use each churning comes out by itself.

THE LAUNDRY.

When removed from the person, clothing, if damp, should be dried to prevent mildew, and articles which are to be starched should be mended before placing in the clothes-basket. Monday is the washing day with all good housekeepers. The old-fashioned programme for a washing is as follows: Use good soft water if it can be had. If not, soften a barrel-full of well-water by pouring into it water in which half a peck or more of hard wood ashes have been boiled, together with the ashes themselves. When enough has been added to produce the desired effect, the water takes on a curdled appearance, and soon settles perfectly clear. If milky, more ashes and lye must be added as before, care being taken not to add more than is necessary to clear the water, or it will effect the hands unpleasantly. On the other hand, if too little is put in the clothes will turn yellow. Gather up all clothes which are ready on Saturday night, and the rest as they are taken off; separate the fine from the coarse, and the less soiled from the dirtier. Scald all table linen and articles which have coffee, fruit or other stains which would be "set" by hot suds, by pouring over them hot water from the tea-kettle and allowing them to stand until cool. Have the water in the tub as warm as the hand will bear, but not too hot. (Dirty clothes should never be put into very hot clear water, as it "sets" the dirt. Hot soap-suds, however, has the opposite effect, the water expanding the fiber of the fabric, while the alkali of the soap softens and removes the dirt.) Wash them, taking the cleanest and finest first, through two suds, then place in a boiler of cold water, with soap enough to make a good suds. (A handful of borax added to the water helps to whiten the clothes and is used by many, especially by the Germans, who are famous for their snowy linen.) Let them boil not more than five or ten minutes, as too long boiling "yellows" the clothes. Remove to a tub, pour over them cold water slightly blued, and turn all garments, pillow-slips, stockings, etc., wrong-side out. If there are more to boil, take out part of the boiling suds, add cold water, and fill not too full with clothes. Repeat until all are boiled. The removal of part of the suds, and filling up with cold water, prevents the suds from "yellowing" the clothes. Wash vigorously in this water, wringing very dry by hand, or better with the wringer, as the clear appearance of. the clothes depends largely on thorough wringing. Rinse in another tub of soft water, washing with the hands, *not* simply lifting them out of the water and then wringing, as is practiced by some, because all suds must be rinsed out to make them clear and white. Wring out again from water pretty well blued, dipping only one

25

article at a time, as the blue sometimes settles to the bottom, and thus spots the clothes. (This time well-water may be used if soft water is difficult to obtain.) Wring out again and for the last time, placing the clothes which are to be starched in one basket, and the rest, which may be hung out immediately, in another. Have the starch (see recipes) ready as hot as the hand can bear, dip the articles and parts of articles which need to be very stiff, first, "clapping" the starch well in with the hands, especially in shirt-bosoms, wristbands and collars, and then thin the starch for other articles which require less stiffening. When starched, hang out on the line to dry, first wiping the line with a cloth to remove all dirt and stains. Shake out each article until it is free from wrinkles, and fasten securely on the line (with the old-fashioned split clothes-pins), being careful to hang sheets and table-linen so that the selvage edges will be even. The line should be stretched in the airiest place in the yard, or in winter a large attic is a better place for the purpose. (Freezing injures starch, and for that reason it is better in winter to hang clothes out unstarched until dry, then taking in, starching and drying indoors.) When dry remove from line to clothes-basket, place clothes-pins as removed in a basket kept for the purpose, take down and roll up the line, remove basket, line and pins to the house, and put the two latter into their proper places. Turn all garments right side out, shake out thoroughly, sprinkle (re-starching shirt-bosoms, wristbands and collars if necessary). Shake out night dresses and under-garments so as to free them from creases, and if they are ruffled or embroidered, dip them in thin starch, pull out smoothly, fold first, and then, beginning at the top of each garment, roll up, each by itself, in a very tight roll, and place in the basket; fold sheets without sprinkling, having first snapped and stretched them, and lay on the rest; over all spread the ironing blanket, and let them stand until next morning. Next day iron, beginning with the sheets (which, as well as table linen, must be folded neatly and carefully, so that the selvage edges will exactly come together), and taking shirts next, cooling the iron when too hot on the coarse towels. In ironing shirts a "bosom-board" is almost indispensable, and an "ironing-board" is a great convenience for all articles. The former is a hard wood board an inch thick, eighteen inches long, and eight wide, covered with two thicknesses of woolen blanket stuff, overlaid with two more of cotton cloth. The cloth is wrapped over the sides and ends of the board and tacked on the back side, leaving the face plain and smooth. The ironing-board is covered in the same way, but is five feet long, two feet wide at one end, and narrowed down with a rounded taper from full width at the middle to seven inches at the other end, and the corners rounded. This board may be of any well-seasoned wood which will not warp, and should be about one inch thick; on this all the clothes are conveniently ironed. Always use cotton holders for the irons. Woolen ones are hot to the hand, and if scorched, as they often are, the smell is disagreeable.

In ironing a shirt or a dress, turn the sleeves on the wrong side, and leave them until the rest is done, and then turn and iron them. In this way the bosoms are less likely to become rumpled. Pull muslin and lace out carefully, iron it over once, and then pull into shape, pick out the embroidery and proceed with greater care than before. Embroideries should be ironed on the wrong side over flannel. Always have near a dish of clean cold water, so that any spot which has been imperfectly ironed may be easily wet, with a soft sponge or piece of linen, and ironed over again, or any surplus bit of starch removed. As fast as articles are finished, they should be hung on the clothes-dryer until thoroughly dry, especial care being taken with those which are starched stiff, as they retain the starch much better if dried very quickly.

If a machine is used in washing, it is better to soak the clothes over night in warm soft water, soaping collars and wristbands, and pieces most soiled. Have separate tubs for coarse and fine clothes. In soaking clothes for washing Monday, the water should be prepared Saturday night, and all clothes which are ready thrown in, and the rest added when changed. If washing fluids are used, the recipes which follow are the best.

Another method is to half fill tubs Saturday night with clear, soft water, warmed a little if convenient, but not hot; in one put the finer articles, such as muslins, cuffs, collars and shirts; in another put table-linen; in another bed-linen; in another the dish-cloths and wiping-towels, and in still another the coarsest and most soiled articles; cover all well with water and press down. Rub no soap in the water, as it may "set" spots or stains. Of course, articles which can not be had on Saturday night are put in the next day as they are changed. Monday morning, heat not very hot a boiler full of clean soft water, add to it water in which soap was dissolved Saturday night by pouring hot water over it, and stir it thoroughly; drain off the water in which the clothes were soaked after shaking them up and down vigorously in it, pressing them against the sides of the tub to get out all the water possible. Then pour over them the warm suds, and wash out as before described, washing each class separately. If found impracticable to make so many divisions, separate the coarse and fine, and the least soiled and the dirtiest.

In the summer clothes may be washed without any fire by soaking overnight in soapy soft water, rubbing out in the morning, soaping the dirty places, and laying them in the hot sunshine. By the time the last are spread out to bleach, the first may be taken up, washed out and rinsed. This, of course, requires a clean lawn.

In washing flannels use soft *clean, cold* water, in winter merely taking the chill off. Let the hard soap lie in the water, but do not apply it to the clothes. Wash the white pieces first, throw articles as fast as washed into blued cold water, let them stand twenty or thirty minutes, wash them

through this water after dissolving a little soap in it, wring hard, shake and
hang up. Never dry in the house. If they freeze, so much the better. In
warm weather hang in the shade out of doors. Wash colored flannels in
the same way (but not in water used for white, or they will gather the lint),
and rinse in several waters if inclined to "run." When very dirty, all flannels should soak longer, and a little borax well dissolved should be added
to the water. This process is equally good for washing silk goods and silk
embroideries. Calicoes and fancy cotton stockings may be washed in the
same way, except that no soap should be used in the rinsing. Wash gray
and brown linens in cold water, with a little black pepper in it, and they
will not fade.

WASHING FLUID.—Bring to a boil one pound of sal-soda, half pound of unslaked lime, a small lump of borax and five quarts water. Let cool, pour
off and bottle. Use one tea-cup to a boiler of clothes. This is superior.
—*Mrs. Gov. Hendricks, Ind.*

WASHING FLUID.—Dissolve five pounds sal-soda and one of borax in a
gallon of boiling water; slake one pound of lime in another gallon of
water, pour both together and allow to stand till perfectly clear, pour off
into glass jars and keep for use. Put clothes to soak over night, with soap
on the soiled parts; in the morning wring out, put into a boiler filled in
the proportion of one pint of the fluid to four pails of water, with soap also
added. Boil for ten minutes, take out, rub through one water, and rinse
through two. If a machine is used, take from the boiler to the machine,
and rinse as above.

WASHING FLUID.—The very best known, as it saves time, labor, clothes
and soap. One pound sal-soda, one-half pound stone lime, five quarts soft
water; boil a short time in copper or brass kettle, stirring occasionally, let
settle and pour off the clear fluid into a stone jug, and cork for use; soak
white clothes over night in simple water, wring out and soap wristbands,
collars and dirty stained places; have boiler half filled with water, and
when at scalding heat put in one common tea-cup of fluid, stir and put in
clothes, and boil half an hour, rub lightly through one suds only, rinsing
well in the bluing water as usual, and all is complete. Instead of soaking
clothes over night, they may soak in suds for a few hours before beginning
washing. For each additional boiler of clothes add half a cup only of the
fluid, of course, boiling in the same water through the whole washing. If
more water is needed in the boiler for the last clothes, dip it from the sudsing tub. This fluid brightens instead of fading the colors in calico, and is
good for colored flannels. It does not rot clothes, but they must not lie
long in the water; the boiling, sudsing, rinsing and bluing must follow each
other in rapid succession, until clothes are hung on the line, which should
be by ten o'clock in the morning. Some of this fluid, put in hot water, is
excellent for removing grease spots from the floor, doors and windows; also
for cleansing tin-ware, pots, and kettles.—*Mrs. Rose Sharp, Kingston, O.*

GALL SOAP.—For washing woolens, silks, or fine prints liable to fade:
One pint beef's gall, two pounds common bar soap cut fine, one quart
boiling soft water; boil slowly, stirring occasionally until well mixed; pour
into a flat vessel, and when cold cut into pieces to dry.

MOTHER'S HARD-TIMES SOAP.—Take all the bits of soap that are too
small to be longer used, shave down, and let soak in soft water enough to

cover them over night; in the morning add more soft water, and boil until thoroughly melted and of the consistency of taffy; pour into molds and you have a nice cake of soap.—*Miss Addie Munsell.*

SOAP FOR FAMILY USE.—Much of the toilet and laundry soaps in the market are adulterated with injurious, and, to some persons, poisonous substances, by which diseases of the skin are occasioned or greatly aggravated, and great suffering results, which is rarely traced to the real cause. The fat tried from animals which have died of disease, if not thoroughly saponified, is poisonous, and sometimes produces death. If in making soap the mass is heated to too high a degree, a film of soap forms around the particles of fat; if at this stage resin, sal-soda, silicate, and other adulterations are added, the fat is not saponified, but filmed, and if poisonous or diseased it so remains, and is dangerous to use. A bar of such soap has an oily feeling, and is unfit for use. If it feels sticky, it has too much resin in it. The slippery feeling which belongs to soap properly made can not be mistaken. Another test of pure soft or hard soap is its translucent or semi-transparent appearance. Soft soap that is cloudy is not thoroughly saponified, or else has been made of dirty or impure grease. It is not only safer but more economical to buy pure soap, as the adulterations increase the quantity without adding to the erasive power. Some of the brown soaps sold in the market are seventy-five per cent. resin, and the buyer gets only twenty-five per cent of what he wants for his money. Fifteen per cent. of resin improves the quality, but any excess damages it, and is worse than useless. Almost any family may make excellent soft soap with very little expense by saving grease, and using lye from pure hard wood ashes or pure potash. Never use concentrated lye. Melt the grease and boil with the lye if possible; if not, put cold lye into cask, melt the grease and pour into the lye. Twenty-five pounds of grease will make a thirty-two gallon cask of soap. Stir thoroughly occasionally for a day or two. If the lye is too weak or too strong, it will not cut the grease; if too strong, add water, if too weak, add lye. To test, take out some in a dipper and experiment with it. The lye should bear up an egg so that only a part as large as a ten cent piece is exposed. The soap when done should be almost transparent and free from any cloudy appearance. Always put lye or soap in soft wood casks. Pine is the best. It will not pay any family to make hard soap, but great care should be taken to get only that which is perfectly pure. "Dobbin's Eclectic" is the only pure brand I know of that is widely sold.—*I. F. Fletcher, Minneapolis, Minn.*

TO DRY-STARCH, FOLD AND IRON SHIRTS.—In doing up shirts, wristbands and collars should be starched first if the collars are sewed on. Dip them into the hot starch, and as soon as the hand can bear the heat (and dipping the hand in cold water often will expedite the work) rub the starch in very thoroughly, taking care that no motes or lumps of starch adhere to the linen. Then starch the shirt-bosom the same way, keeping the starch hot all the time by setting the dish in a deep pan of water. Rub it into the linen very carefully, pass the finger under the plaits and raise them up so that the starch shall penetrate all through evenly. Some rub it into the plaits with a piece of clean linen, but we think the hand does the work more thoroughly and evenly. When perfectly starched, shake out the shirt evenly, fold both sides of the bosom together and bring the shoulders and side seams together evenly; that will lay the sleeves one over the other, and after pulling the wristbands into shape smoothly they can thus be folded together and the wristbands rolled tightly and, with the sleeves, be folded and laid even on the sides of the shirt. Then turn the sides with the sleeves over on the front, and beginning at the neck roll the whole tightly together, wrap in a towel and let it remain so several hours before ironing—all night if starched and folded in the evening—and in the summer put in a cool place where the starch will not sour, and in the winter keep warm enough to prevent freezing. To do up shirt-bosoms in the most perfect way, one must have a "polishing iron"—a small iron rounded over and highly polished on the ends and sides. Spread the bosom on a hard and very smooth board, with only one thickness of cotton cloth sewed tight across it. Spread a wet cloth over and iron quickly with a hot iron, then remove the cloth and with a polishing iron, as hot as it can be used without scorching, rub the bosom quick and hard up and down, not crosswise. Use only the rounded part of the front of the iron, that puts all the friction on a small part at one time, and gives the full benefit of all the gloss in starch or linen.—*Mrs. Beecher in Christian Union.*

How to do up Shirt-bosoms.—Take two table-spoons best starch, add a very little water to it, rub and stir with a spoon into a thick paste, carefully breaking all the lumps and particles. Add a pint of boiling water, stirring at the same time; boil half an hour, stirring occasionally to keep it from burning. Add a piece of "Enamel" the size of a pea; if this is not at hand use a table-spoon gum-arabic solution (made by pouring boiling water upon gum-arabic and standing until clear and transparent), or a piece of clean mutton tallow half the size of a nutmeg and a tea-spoon of salt will do, but is not as good. Strain the starch through a strainer or a piece of thin muslin. Have the shirt turned wrong side out; dip the bosoms carefully in the starch and squeeze out, repeating the operation until the bosoms are thoroughly and evenly saturated with starch; proceed to dry. Three hours before ironing dip the bosoms in clean water; wring out and roll up tightly. First iron the back by folding it lengthwise through the center; next iron the wristbands, and both sides of the sleeves; then the collar-band; now place the bosom-board under the bosom, and with a dampened napkin rub the bosom from the top towards the bottom, smoothing and arranging each plait neatly. With smooth, moderately hot flat-iron, begin at the top and iron downwards, and continue the operation until the bosom is perfectly dry and shining. Remove the bosom-board, and iron the front of the shirt. The bosoms and cuffs of shirts, indeed, of all nice, fine work, will look clearer and better if they are first ironed under a piece of thin old muslin. It takes off the first heat of the iron, and removes any lumps of starch.

Care of Irons.—When irons become rough or smoky, lay a little fine salt on a flat surface and rub them well; it will prevent them sticking to any thing starched, and make them smooth; or scour with bath-brick before heating, and when hot rub well with salt, and then with a small piece of beeswax tied up in a rag, after which wipe clean on a dry cloth. A piece of fine sandpaper is also a good thing to have near the stove, or a hard, smooth board covered with brick dust, to rub each iron on when it is put back on the stove, so that no starch may remain to be burnt on. Put beeswax between pieces of paper or cloth and keep on the table close by the flat-iron stand. If the irons get coated with scorched starch, rub them over the paper that holds the starch and it will all come off. Rubbing the iron over the waxed paper, even if no starch adheres, adds to the glossiness of the linen that is ironed.

To take out Scorch.—If a shirt-bosom, or any other article, has been scorched in ironing, lay it where bright sunshine will fall directly on it. It will take it entirely out.

Bluing.—Take one ounce of Prussian blue, one-half ounce of oxalic acid; dissolve in one quart of perfectly soft rain water; insert a quill through the cork of bluing-bottle to prevent waste, or putting too much in clothes, and you will be pleased with the result. One or two table-spoons of it is sufficient for a tub of water, according to the size of the tub. Chinese blue is the best and costs twelve and a half cents an ounce, and the acid will cost three cents. This amount will last a medium-sized family one year.

COFFEE STARCH.—Make a paste of two table-spoons best starch and cold water; when smooth stir in a pint of perfectly clear coffee, boiling hot; boil five or ten minutes, stir with a spermaceti or wax candle, strain, and use for all dark calicoes, percales, and muslins.

FLOUR STARCH.—Have a clean pan or kettle on stove with one quart boiling water, into which stir three heaping table-spoons flour, previously mixed smooth in little cold water; stir steadily until it boils, and then often enough to keep from burning. Boil about five minutes, strain while hot through a crash towel. The above quantity is enough for one dress, and will make it nice and stiff. Flour starch is considered better for all calicoes than fine starch, since it makes them stiffer, and the stiffness is longer retained.

TO MAKE FINE STARCH.—Wet the starch smooth in a little cold water, in a large tin pan, pour on a quart boiling water to two or three table-spoons starch, stirring rapidly all the while; place on stove, stir until it boils, and then occasionally. Boil from five to fifteen minutes, or until the starch is perfectly ·clear. Some add a little salt, or butter or pure lard, or stir with a sperm candle; others add a tea-spoon kerosene to one quart starch; this prevents the stickiness sometimes so annoying in ironing. Either of the above ingredients is an improvement to flour starch. Many, just before using starch add a little bluing. Cold starch is made from starch dissolved in cold water, being careful not to have it too thick; since it rots the clothes, it is not advisable to use it—the same is true of potato starch.

ENAMEL FOR SHIRT-BOSOMS.—Melt together with a gentle heat, one ounce white wax and two ounces spermaceti; prepare in the usual way a sufficient quantity of starch for a dozen bosoms, put into it a piece of this enamel the size of a hazel-nut, and in proportion for a larger number. This will give clothes a beautiful polish.

TO WASH FLANNELS IN BOILING WATER.—Make a strong suds of boiling water and soft soap—hard soap makes flannels stiff and wiry—put them in, pressing them down under the water with a clothes stick; when cool enough rub the articles carefully between the hands, then wring—but not through the wringer—as dry as possible, shake, snap out, and pull each piece into its original size and shape, then throw immediately into another tub of boiling water, in which you have thoroughly mixed some nice bluing. Shake them up and down in this last water with a clothes stick until cool enough for the hands, then rinse well, wring, shake out and pull into shape—the snapping and pulling are as necessary as the washing—and hang in a sunny place where they will dry quickly. Many prefer to rinse ,in two waters with the bluing in the last, and this is always advisable when there are many flannels.

TO WASH FLANNELS IN TEPID WATER.—The usefulness of liquid ammonia is not as universally known among housewives as it deserves to be. If you add some of it to a soap-suds made of a mild soap, it will prevent the flannel from becoming yellow or shrinking. It is the potash and soda contained in sharp soap which tends to color animal fibers yellow; the shrinking may also be partially due to this agency, but above all to the exposure of the flannel while wet to the extremes of low or high temperatures. Dipping it in boiling water or leaving it out in the rain will also cause it to shrink and become hard. To preserve their softness flannels should be washed in tepid suds, rinsed in tepid water, and dried rapidly at a moderate heat.

How to wash Blankets.—All that is necessary is abundance of soft water, and soap without resin in it. Resin hardens the fibers of wool, and should never be used in washing any kind of flannel goods. Blankets treated as above will always come out clean and soft. A little bluing may be used in washing white blankets.—*North Star Woolen Mill, Minneapolis, Minn.*

Blankets should be shaken and snapped until almost dry; it will require two persons to handle them. Woolen shawls, and all woolen articles, especially men's wear, are much improved by being pressed with a hot iron under damp muslin.

To wash Lace Curtains.—Shake the dust well out of the lace, put in tepid water, in which a little soda has been dissolved, and wash at once carefully with the hands in several waters, or until perfectly clean; rinse in water well blued, also blue the boiled starch quite deeply and squeeze, but do not wring. Pin some sheets down to the carpet in a vacant, airy room, then pin on the curtains stretched to exactly the size they were before being wet. In a few hours they will be dry and ready to put up. The whole process of washing and pinning down should occupy as little time as possible, as lace will shrink more than any other cotton goods when long wet. Above all it should not be allowed to "soak" from the mistaken idea that it washes more easily, nor should it ever be ironed. Another way is to fasten them in a pair of frames, which every housekeeper should have, made very like the old-fashioned quilting-frames, thickly studded along the inside with the smallest size of galvanized tenter hooks, in which to fasten the lace, and having holes and wooden pins with which to vary the length and breadth to suit the different sizes of curtains. The curtains should always be measured before being wet, and stretched in the frames to that size to prevent shrinking. Five or six curtains of the same size may be put in, one above the other, and all dried at once. The frames may rest on four chairs.

To wash Lace Ruchings.—Wash with the hands in warm suds (if much soiled, soak in warm water two or three hours), rinse thoroughly and starch in thick starch, dry out doors if the day be clear; if not place between dry cloth, roll tightly and put away till dry, then with the fingers, open each row and pull out smoothly (have a cup of clean water in which to dip the fingers or dampen the lace), then pull out straight the outer edge of each with the thumb and finger and draw the binding over the point or side of a hot iron. If the ruche is single or only two rows, it can be ironed after being smoothed (the first process). Blonde or net that has become yellow can be bleached by hanging in the sun or lying out over night in the dew.

To wash Thread Lace.—Cover a bottle with white flannel, baste the lace carefully on the flannel and rub with white soap; place the bottle in a jar filled with warm suds, let remain two or three days, changing the water several times, and boil with the finest white clothes on washing day; when cooled a little, rinse several times in plenty of cold water, wrap a soft dry towel around it and place in the sun; when dry, unwind, but do not starch.

To wash a Silk Dress.—To wash a silk dress with gall soap, rip apart and shake off the dust; have ready two tubs warm soft water, make a suds of the soap in one tub, and use the other for rinsing, wash the silk, one piece at a time, in the suds, wring gently, rinse, again wring, shake out, and iron with a hot iron on what you intend to be the wrong side. Thus proceed with each piece, and when about half done throw out the suds and make suds of the rinsing water, using fresh water for rinsing.

To PREVENT BLUE FROM FADING.—To prevent blue from fading, put an ounce of sugar of lead into a pail of water, soak the material in the solution for two hours, and let dry before being washed and ironed; good for all shades of blue.

To WASH COLORED MUSLINS.—Wash in warm (not hot)suds, made with soft wate and best white soap, if it is to be had. Do not soak them, and wash only one thing at a time. Change the suds as soon as it looks dingy, and put the garments at once into fresh suds. Rinse first in clear water, then in slightly blued. Squeeze quite dry, but don't *wring* the dress. Hang in a shady place where the sunshine will not strike it, as that fades all colors.

To WASH DELICATE COLORED MUSLINS.—Boil wheat bran (about two quarts to a dress), in soft water half an hour, let it cool, strain the liquor, and use it instead of soap-suds; it removes dirt like soap, keeps the color, and the clothes only need rinsing in one water, and even starching is unnecessary. Suds and rinsing water for colored articles should be used as cold as possible. Another way is to make thick corn meal mush, well salted, and use instead of soap; rinse in one or two waters, and do not starch.—*Miss Juana James, West Killingly, Conn.*

To BLEACH MUSLIN.—For thirty yards of muslin, take one pound of chloride of lime, dissolve in two quarts rain water; let cloth soak over night in warm rain water, or long enough to be thoroughly wet; wring out cloth and put in another tub of warm rain water in which the chloride of lime solution has been poured. Let it remain for about twenty minutes, lifting up the cloth and airing every few moments, and rinse in clear rain water. This will not injure the cloth in the least, and is much less troublesome than bleaching on the grass.

Or, scald in suds and lay them on the clean grass all night, or if this can not be done, bring in and place in a tub of clean soft water. In the morning scald again and put out as before. It will take from one to two weeks to bleach white. May be bleached in winter by placing on snow. May is the best month for bleaching. To whiten yellow linens or muslins, soak over-night or longer in buttermilk, rinse thoroughly and wash the same as other clothes. This will also answer for light calicoes, percales, lawns, etc., that will not fade. Some use sour milk when not able to procure buttermilk. To whiten yellow laces, old collars, etc., put in a glass bottle or jar in a strong suds, let stand in sun for seven days, shaking occasionally.

BROWN LINEN—May be kept looking new until worn out if always washed in starch water and hay tea. Make flour starch in the ordinary way. For one dress put on the stove a common sized milk pan full of timothy hay, pour on water, cover, and boil until the water is of a dark green color, then turn into the starch, let the goods soak in it a few minutes, and wash without soap; the starch will clean the fabric, and no rinsing is necessary.

To CLEANSE ARTICLES MADE OF WHITE ZEPHYR.—Rub in flour or magnesia, changing often. Shake off flour and hang in the open air a short time.—*Mrs. A. S. C.*

HOW TO CLEAN VELVET.—Invert a hot flatiron, place over it a single thickness of wet cotton cloth, lay on this the velvet, wrong side next the wet cloth, rub gently with a dry cloth until the pile is well raised; take off the iron, lay on a table, and brush it with a soft brush or cloth.—*Miss Alice McAllister.*

To CLEAN RIBBONS.—Dissolve white soap in boiling water; when cool enough to bear the hand, pass the ribbons through it, rubbing gently, so as not to injure the texture; rinse through lukewarm water, and pin on a board to dry. If the colors are bright yellow, maroon, crimson, or scarlet, add a few drops of oil of vitriol to the rinse-water; if the color is bright scarlet, add to the rinse-water a few drops of the muriate of tin.

TO TAKE OUT PAINT.—Equal parts of ammonia and spirits of turpentine will take paint out of clothing, no matter how dry or hard it may be. Saturate the spot two or three times and then wash out in soap-suds.

TO REMOVE INK-STAIN.—Immediately saturate with milk, soak it up with a rag, apply more, rub well, and in a few minutes the ink will disappear.

TO TAKE GREASE OUT OF SILKS, WOOLENS, PAPER, FLOORS, ETC.—Grate thick over the spot French (or common will do) chalk, cover with brown paper, set on it a hot flatiron, and let it remain until cool; repeat if necessary. The iron must not be so hot as to burn paper or cloth.

SUBSTITUTE FOR WASHING-SODA.—A German scientific journal recommends laundresses to use hyposulphite of soda in place of common washing-soda. It does not attack the fabric in any way, and at the same time exerts some bleaching actions which greatly improve the appearance of linen and calicoes.

FRUIT-STAINS.—Colored cottons or woolens stained with wine or fruit should be wet in alcohol and ammonia, then sponged off gently (not rubbed) with alcohol; after that, if the material will warrant it, washed in tepid soap-suds. Silks may be wet with this preparation when injured by these stains.

TO WASH WOOLEN GOODS.—Many woolen goods, such as light-colored, heavy sacques, nubias, etc., may be washed in cold suds and rinsed in cold water. The garments should be well shaken out and pulled into shape.

In ironing woolen goods, especially pants, vests, etc., it is well to let them get dried, then spread them out on an ironing-board (not on a table), wring a cloth out of clear water and lay over the article, then iron with a hot iron till dry; wet the cloth again and spread it just above the part already ironed, but let it come a half inch or so on that which has been pressed, so that there will be no line to mark where the cloth was moved; continue this till the whole garment has been thoroughly pressed. Woolen garments thus ironed will look like new; but in doing this care must be exercised that every spot that looks at all "fulled" or shrunk should be stretched while being pressed under the wet cloth. Bring the outside to fit the linings, as when new, but if not quite able to do this rip the lining and trim off to match. All the seams, especially on pants, must be first pressed on a "press board," then fold the pants as they are found in the tailor's shop, and go over them with the wet cloth and hot iron.

TO REMOVE THE COLOR FROM BUFF CALICO.—If some kinds of buff calico be dipped in strong soda water, the color will be removed and the figures of other colors remain on a white ground. This is valuable sometimes, as buff calico spots easily. If pink calico be dipped in vinegar and water after rinsing, the color will be brighter.

TO REMOVE IRON-RUST.—While rinsing clothes, take such as have spots of rust, wring out, dip a wet finger in oxalic acid, and rub on the spot, then dip in salt and rub on, and hold on a warm flatiron, or on the tin or copper tea-kettle if it have hot water in it, and the spot will immediately disappear; rinse again, rubbing the place a little with the hands.

TO REMOVE THE STAIN OF NITRATE OF SILVER—From the flesh, or white goods of any kind, dissolve iodine in alcohol, and apply to the stain; then take a piece of cyanide potassium, size of hickory-nut, wet in water, rub on the spot, and the stain will immediately disappear; then wash the goods or hands in cold water.—*G. W. Collins, Urbana.*

ERASIVE FLUID.—For the removal of spots on furniture, cloth, silks, and other fabrics, when the color is not drawn, without injury. One ounce castile soap, four of aqua ammonia, one of glycerine, and one of spirits of wine; dissolve the soap in two quarts soft water, add the other ingredients, apply with a soft sponge, and rub out.—*A. Peabody, Cincinnati, O.*

To RESTORE VELVET.—When velvet gets crushed from pressure, hold the parts over a basin of hot water, with the lining of the dress next the water. The pile will soon rise and assume its original beauty.

To PRESS SATIN.—All satin goods should be pressed upon the right side. To press and clean black silk, shake out all the dust, clean well with a flannel cloth, rubbing it up and down over the silk; this takes out all dust that may be left; take some good lager beer and sponge the silk, both on the wrong and right side, sponging across the width of the silk, and not down the length, and with a moderately-warm iron, press what is intended for the wrong side. After sponging, it is better to wait a few minutes before pressing, as the irons will not be so apt to stick.

To TAKE OUT MILDEW.—Wet the cloth, and rub on soap and chalk, mixed together, and lay in the sun; or lay the cloth in buttermilk for a short time, take out, and place in the hot sun; or put lemon juice on, and treat in the same way.

To CLEAN ALPACA.—Put goods in a boiler half full of cold rain-water, and let boil three minutes. Have ready a pail of indigo-water (very dark with indigo), place goods in it, after wringing out of boiling water; let remain one-half an hour, then wring out, and iron while damp.

To CLEAN BLACK LACE.—Take the lace and wipe off all the dust carefully, with a cambric handkerchief. Then pin it out on a board, inserting a pin in each projecting point of the lace. Spot it all over with table-beer, and do not remove the pins until it is perfectly dry. It will look quite fresh and new.

THE CELLAR AND ICE-HOUSE.

The cellar, when properly constructed and cared for, is the most useful room in the house, and no dwelling is complete without one. It is economy of expense and ground-space to build it under ground, and this plan gives the best cellar whenever the site of the house permits thorough drainage. The base of the foundation-wall of the house should be laid a little below the floor-level of the cellar, and the first layer should be of broad flag-stones, so placed that the edges will project a few inches beyond the outer face of the wall. This effectually prevents rats from undermining the cement floor, which they often do when this precaution is neglected, digging away the dirt until the floor breaks and gives them access to a new depot of supplies. In burrowing downwards, they invariably keep close to the wall, and when they reach the projecting flagging, give it up and look for an easier job. To secure the cellar from freezing, the wall, above the level of the deepest frost, should be double or "hollow," the inner wall being of brick four inches thick, with an air-space of two inches between it and the outer wall, which should be of stone and twelve or fourteen inches thick. The brick wall should be stiffened by an occasional "binder" across to the stone. The hollow space may be filled with dry tan-bark or sawdust, or left simply filled with the confined air, "dead air" being the most perfect non-conductor of heat known. The windows, which should be opposite each other when possible, to secure a "draft" and more perfect ventilation, should be provided with double sash, one flush with the outer face of the wall, which may be removed in summer, and the other flush with the inner face, hung on strong hinges, so that it may easily be swung open upward and hooked there. In winter, this arrangement lets in light, but with its space of confined air, keeps out the frost. A frame covered with wire-netting should take the place of the outer sash in summer, to keep out every thing but the fresh air and light. The walls should be as smooth as possible on the inner side, and neatly plastered; also the ceiling overhead. The floor should be first paved with small stones, then a coat of water-lime laid on, and over this a second coat, as level as a planed floor. There should also be double doors, one flush with each face of the wall; and a wide out-door stairway, through which vegetables, coal, etc., may be carried, is indispensable. The depth should be about eight feet.

Such a cellar may always be clean, the air pure, and the temperature under complete control. It will consequently keep apples and pears two or three months longer than an ordinary cellar, prolonging the fruit season to "strawberry-time." If it extends under the whole house—the best plan when the state of the purse permits it—it may be divided into apartments, with brick walls between, one for vegetables, one for fruits, one for provisions, one for the laundry, and a fifth for coal and the furnace, if one is used. In one corner of the cellar, under the kitchen, may also be the cistern, the strong cellar wall serving for its outer wall. A pump from the kitchen would supply water there for domestic uses; and a pipe with a stop-cock, leading through the wall into the cellar, would occasionally be a convenience and save labor. It is better, however, as a rule to locate the cistern just outside the house, passing a pipe from it through the cellar wall below the deepest frost level, and thence to the kitchen. If built in the cellar, the cistern should be square, with heavy walls, plastered inside with three coats of water lime.

All the apartments of a cellar should be easily accessible from the outside door and from the kitchen stairway. In the vegetable apartment, the bins should be made of dressed lumber, and painted, and located in the center, with a walk around each, so that the contents may easily be examined and assorted. The fruit shelves, made of slats two inches wide and placed one inch apart, should be put up with equal care and neatness, and with equal regard for convenience and easy access. Their place should be the most airy part of the cellar; the proper width is about two feet, and the distance apart about one foot, with the lowest shelf one foot from the floor. Pears will ripen nicely on the lower shelves under a cover of woolen blankets. The supports should, of course, be firm and strong. The bottom shelf should be of one board, on which to scatter fine fresh lime to the depth of an inch, changing it two or three times during the winter. A shelf, suspended firmly from the ceiling, and located where it will be easy of access from the kitchen, on which to place cakes, pies, meats, and any thing that needs to be kept cool and safe from cats and mice, is an absolute necessity. Its height prevents the articles placed on it from becoming damp, and gathering mold, as they sometimes do when placed on the cellar floor. In planning shelves for cans, crocks, casks, etc., regard should be had to economy of space by making the distance between the shelves correspond to the articles to stand on them, and it is well to so place the lower shelf that the meat barrels, etc., may be placed under it. The temperature of a cellar should never be below freezing, and if it is raised above fifty by a fire, outside air should be admitted to lower it. The best time for ventilating the cellar is at noon, taking care in hot weather not to admit so much outside air as to render it warm. A simple and excellent plan for ventilation, where the location of the kitchen chimney admits it, is to pass an ordinary stove-pipe through the floor upward beside or behind the pipe of the kitchen stove, and thence by an elbow into the chimney. The draft of the chimney will carry off all the impure air that arises in the cellar, and if too great a current is created it may be brought under complete control by a valve at the floor.

The cellar must be frequently examined and kept perfectly sweet and clean. There is no reason why it should not be as neat as the living rooms, and as free from cobwebs, decayed fruit and vegetables, and all other forms of filthiness. Whitewashing walls in winter will aid in giving it tidiness.

If the cellar is constructed above ground, the entire walls should be double, with air space between, double windows and doors being even more necessary than when under-ground. Above all, the floor should be on a level with that of the kitchen, to save the woman-killing stairs. If there are stairs, let them be broad, firm, and placed in the light if possible. Of course every cellar should have thorough drainage. In laying a tile drain, if in the horse-shoe form, place the circular side down; the narrower the channel the swifter the current and more certain to carry off sediment.

THE ICE-HOUSE.

Ice is one of the greatest of summer luxuries, and indeed is almost a necessity. It is so easily put up, even in the country, and so cheaply protected, that there is no reason why any one who is able to own or rent a house may not have it in liberal supply. A cheap ice-house may be made by partitioning off a space about twelve feet square in the wood-shed, or even in the barn. The roof must be tight over it, but there is no necessity for matched or fine lumber for the walls. They should, however, be coated with coal-tar inside, as the long continued moisture puts them to a severe test and brings on decay. Ice should be taken from still places in running streams, or from clear ponds. It may be cut with half an old cross-cut saw, but there are saws and ice-plows made for the purpose to be had in almost every village. In cutting ice, as soon as it is of sufficient thickness and before much warm weather, select a still day, with the thermometer as near zero as may be. Ice handles much more comfortably and easily when it is so cold that it immediately freezes dry, thus preventing the wet clothes and mittens, which are the sole cause of any suffering in handling it; and ice put up in sharp, cold weather, before it has been subjected to any thaw, will keep much better and be much more useful in the hot days of summer than if its packing had been delayed until late winter or early spring, and then the ice put up half melted and wet. The best simple contrivance for removing blocks of ice from the water is a plank with a cleat nailed across one end, which is to be slipped under the block, which slides against the cleat and may then be easily drawn out with the plank, without lifting. Cut the ice in large blocks of equal size, pack as closely as possible in layers, leaving about a foot space between the outside and the wall, and filling all crevices between the blocks with pounded ice or sawdust. Under the first layer there should be placed sawdust a foot thick, and arrangements should be made for thorough drainage, as water in contact with the ice will melt it rapidly. As the layers are put in place, pack saw-dust closely between the mass of ice and the wall; and when all is stored, cover with a foot, at least, of sawdust. In using ice, be careful to cover all crevices with sawdust, as the ice will melt rapidly if exposed to the air. The less ventilation and the more completely an ice-house is kept closed, the better the ice will keep. The cold air which surrounds the ice, if undisturbed by currents, has little effect on it; but if there are openings, currents are formed and the warm air is brought in to replace the cold. This is especially the case if the openings are low, as the cold air, being the heavier, passes out below most readily. For this reason great care must be taken to fill in fresh saw-dust between the walls and the mass of ice as it settles down by its own weight and the melting of the ice. There is no advantage in having an ice-house wholly or partly under ground, if it is constructed as directed above. Fine chaff, or straw cut fine, may be substituted for sawdust when the latter is difficult to obtain. Of course, the building may be constructed separately, in which case the cost need not be more than twenty-five to fifty dollars.

To KEEP TURNIPS.—When buried deep in the earth they will keep solid until March or April.

To KEEP LEMONS.—Cover with cold water, changing it every week. This makes them more juicy.

WHITEWASH FOR CELLARS.—An ounce of carbolic acid to a gallon of whitewash will keep from cellars the disagreeable odor which taints milk and meat. Added to paste and mucilage, it prevents mold.

To KEEP PARSLEY FRESH AND GREEN.—Put it in a strong boiling hot pickle of salt and water, and keep for use. Hang up and dry in bunches, blossom downward, in a dry attic or store-room, for use in soups, stuffing, etc.

To KEEP CELLAR CLEAN.—Remove all vegetables as soon as they begin to decay, and ventilate well so that the walls will not become foul. Use cloride of lime as a disinfectant freely, after taking care to make it as neat and clean as possible.

THE TEMPERATURE.—Vegetables keep best at as low a temperature as possible without freezing. Apples bear a very low temperature. Sweet potatoes (which keep well packed in dry forest leaves), and squashes require a dry, warm atmosphere.

ALL KINDS OF HERBS.—Gather on a dry day, just before or while in blossom, tie in bundles, blossom downward. When perfectly dry, wrap the medicinal ones in paper, and keep from air. Pick off the leaves of those to be used in cooking, pound, sift them fine, and cork up tightly in bottles.

KEEPING CABBAGES.—When the weather becomes frosty, cut them off near the head, and carry them, with the leaves on, to a dry cellar, break off superfluous leaves, and pack into a light cask or box, stems upward, and when nearly full cover with loose leaves; secure the box with a lid against rats.

To KEEP APPLES.—Apples are usually kept on open shelves, easily accessible, so that the decaying ones may easily be removed. They are sometimes packed in layers of dry sand, care being taken not to let them touch each other, with good results. When they begin to decay, pick out those which are specked, stew them up with cider and sugar, and fill all empty self-sealing fruit-cans, and keep the sauce for use late in the season. Or pack in dry sawdust, or any grain, as oats, barley, etc., so that they will not touch each other; or if fruit is fine, wrap each apple in paper and pack in boxes.

KEEPING PEASE FOR WINTER USE.—Shell, throw into boiling water with a little salt, boil five or six minutes, drain in a colander and afterwards on a cloth until completely dried, and place in air-tight bottles. Some use wide-mouthed bottles, not quite filling them, pouring over fried mutton fat so as to cover the pease, and cork tightly, securing the cork with resin or sealing-wax. When used, boil until tender, and season with butter. Another method is to place them on a tin or earthen dish in a mild oven (after drying as above), once or twice until they harden, and then to put them in paper bags hung in the kitchen.

KEEPING CABBAGES IN THE COUNTRY.—Take up the cabbages by the roots, set closely together in rows, up to the head in soil, roots down as they grew; drive in posts at the corners of the bed, and at intermediate points if necessary, higher on one side than the other; nail strips of boards on the posts and lay upon these old boards, doors, or if nothing else is at hand, bean-poles, and corn fodder, high enough so that the roof will be clear of the cabbages, and allow the air to circulate; close up the sides with yard or garden offal of any kind, and the cabbages will keep fresh and green all winter, and be accessible at all times. Exclude moisture but never mind the frost.

TO KEEP GRAPES.—A barrel hoop suspended from the ceiling by three cords, from which grape stems are hung by means of wire hooks attached to the *small* end, sealing the other with hot sealing-wax, each stem free from contact with its neighbors, is said to be the best contrivance for keeping grapes. The imperfect grapes must be removed, and the room must be free from frost, and not dry enough to wither them or too moist. The simplest way to keep grapes is to place them in drawers holding about twenty-five pounds each, piling the boxes one over another. Or the drawers may be fitted into racks. A dry cellar, or a room not exposed to frost, is most favorable. The fruit must be mature and perfect. They do not freeze as readily as apples.

PACKING VEGETABLES.—For present use they should be laid away carefully in a bin with a close lid (hung on hinges) so that the light may be excluded. To keep them for a longer time, the best plan is to pull them on a dry day, cut off the tops and trim, and pack them in clean barrels or boxes, in layers with fine clean moss, such as is found in abundance in woods, between them. The moss keeps them clean and sufficiently moist, preventing shriveling of the roots on the one hand, and absorbing any excess of dampness on the other. When moss can not be conveniently obtained, sand is a good substitute, but is more difficult to handle, and the vegetables do not come out of it so clean and fresh. The varieties which come to maturity late in the season, are easiest to keep and retain their flavor longest.

SOMETHING ABOUT BABIES.

A child's first right is to be well born, of parents sound in body and mind, who can boast a long line of ancestors on both sides; an aristocracy, based on the cardinal virtues of purity, chastity, sobriety, and honesty.

If the thought, the money, the religious enthusiasm, now expended for the regeneration of the race, were wisely directed to the generation of our descendants, to the conditions and environments of parents and children, the whole face of society might be changed before we celebrate the next Centennial of our national life.

All religious, educational, benevolent, and industrial societies combined, working harmoniously together, can not do as much in a life-time of effort, toward the elevation of mankind, as can parents in the nine months of pre-natal life. Locke took the ground that the mind of every child born into the world is like a piece of blank paper, that you may write thei son whatever you will; but science proves that such idealists as Descartes were nearer right when they declared that each soul comes freighted with its own ideas, its individual proclivities; that the pre-natal influences do more in the formation of character than all the education that comes after.

Let the young man, indulging in all manner of excesses, remember that in considering the effect of dissipation, wine, and tobacco, on himself and his own happiness or misery, he does not begin to measure the evil of his life. As the High Priest at the family altar, his deeds of darkness will entail untold suffering on generation after generation. Let the young woman with wasp-like waist, who lives on candies, salads, hot bread, pastry, and pickles, whose listless brain and idle hands seek no profitable occupation, whose life is given to folly, remember that to her ignorance and folly may yet be traced the downfall of a nation.

One of the most difficult lessons to impress on any mind is the power and extent of individual influence; and parents above all others, resist the belief that their children are exactly what they make them; no more, no less; like producing like. If there is a class of educators who need special preparation for their high and holy calling, it is those who assume the responsibility of parents. Shall we give less thought to the creation of an immortal being than the artist devotes to his statue or landscape? We wander through the art galleries in the old world, and linger before the works of the great masters, transfixed with the grace and beauty, the glory and granduer, of the ideals that surround us; and, with equal preparation, greater than these are possible in living, breathing humanity. The same thought and devotion in real life would soon give us a generation of saints, scholars, scientists, and

26

statesmen, of glorified humanity; such as the world has not yet seen. To this hour, we have left the greatest event of life to chance, and the result is the blind, the deaf and dumb, the idiot, the lunatic, the epileptic, the criminal, the drunkard, the glutton—thousands of human beings, in our young republic, that never should have been born; a tax on society, a disgrace to their parents, and a curse to themselves.

Well, born—a child's next right is to intelligent care. If we buy a rare plant, we ask the florist innumerable questions as to its proper training; but the advent of an immortal being seems to suggest no new thought, no anxious investigation into the science of human life. Here we trust every thing to an ignorant nurse, or a neighbor who knows perchance less than we do ourselves.

Ignorance bandages the new-born child, as tight as a drum, from armpits to hips, compressing every vital organ. There is a tradition that all infants are subject to colic for the first three months of their existence; at the end of which time the bandage is removed, and the colic ceases. Reason suggests that the bandage may be the *cause* of the colic, and queries as to the origin of the custom, and its use. She is told, with all seriousness, "that the bones of a new-born child are like cartilage, that, unless they are pinned up snugly, they are in danger of falling to pieces." Reason replies: "If Infinite Wisdom has made kittens and puppies so that their component parts remain together, it is marvelous that He should have left the human being wholly at the mercy of a bandage;" and proposes, with her first-born, to dispense with swaddling bandages, leaving only a slight compress on the navel, for a few days, until perfectly healed.

Ignorance, believing that every child comes into the world in a diseased and starving condition, begins at once the preparation of a variety of nostrums, chemical and culinary, which she persistently administers to the struggling victim. Reason, knowing that after the fatigue of a long and perilous march, what the young soldier most needs is absolute rest in some warm and cozy tent, shelters him under her wing, and fights off all intruders, sure that when he needs his rations the world will hear from him. His first bath should be preceded by a generous application of pure, sweet olive oil, from head to foot, in every little corner and crevice of his outer man; and then he should be immersed in warm soap-suds, so nearly the temperature of the body as to cause no shock. Great care should be taken that neither oil nor soap touch the eyes. The room should be very warm, all drafts excluded; and on emerging from the tub, a hot soft-flannel blanket should be closely wrapped around him, in which he may rest awhile before dressing. The softest garments, simply made, and so cut as to fasten round the throat and rest on the shoulders, should constitute his wardrobe; eschew all bands, pins, ligatures, ruffles, embroidery, caps, socks, etc.

Let the child's first efforts at foraging for an existence be at his mother's breast; there he will find the medicine he needs, and just what she needs, too, to dispose of.

The child's mouth and the mother's nipples should be carefully washed before nursing; thus, much suffering, for both mother and child, will be prevented.

"Give the baby water six times a day," was one of the most important messages ever sent over the telegraph wires to a young mother.

Ignorance bathes her baby on a full stomach, because she finds it will go through the ordeal of dressing more quietly; Reason bathes hers two hours after feeding, knowing that the vital forces needed for digestion should not be drawn to the surface. Being constructed on the same general plan with its parents, the same principle that makes it dangerous for a man to go swimming immediately after eating, makes it equally so to put a baby in its tub after nursing.

Though Ignorance eats her own meals regularly and at stated times, she feeds her baby at all times and seasons. If the child has colic from over-eating, or the improper diet of its mother, she tries to allay its suffering with additional feeding and vigorous trotting; not succeeding, she ends the drama with a spoonful of Mrs. Winslow's soothing syrup; having drugged the senti-nel and silenced his guns, she imagines the citadel safe. Reason feeds her baby regularly, by the clock, once in two or three hours, and gives the stomach some chance for rest. She prevents colic by regulating her own diet and habits of life, knowing that improper articles of food, and ill-nature or outbursts of passion in the mother, have cost many a baby its life.

Ignorance, having noticed that her baby sleeps longer with its head cov-ered, uniformily excludes the air. Breathing the same air over a dozen times, it becomes stupefied with the carbonic-acid gas, is thrown into a pro-fuse perspiration, and is sure to catch cold on emerging from the fetid atmos-phere. Reason puts her child to sleep, with head uncovered, in a spacious chamber, bright with sunlight and fresh air; where, after a long nap, she will often find him (as soon as he is old enough to notice objects) looking at the shadows on the wall, or studying the anatomical wonders of his own hands and feet, the very picture of content.

Regular feeding, freedom in dress, plenty of sleep, water, sunlight, and pure air, will secure to babies that health and happiness that in nature should be their inheritance.

"Seeing that the atmosphere is forty miles deep, all round the globe," says Horace Mann, "it is a useless piece of economy to breathe it more than once. If we were obliged to trundle it in wheel-barrows, in order to fill our homes, churches, school-houses, railroad-cars, and steamboats, there might be some excuse for our seeming parsimony. But as it is we are prodigals of health, of which we have so little; and niggards of air, of which we have so much."—*Mrs. Elizabeth Cady Stanton, New York.*

HINTS FOR THE WELL.

Cleanliness is next to godliness.

Always rest before and after a hearty meal.

Do not eat too much. Do not eat late at night.

Food, especially bread, should never be eaten hot.

Children should never be dressed in tight clothes.

Never sit in a damp or chilly room without a fire.

Supper just before going to bed is highly injurious.

Never enter a room where a person is sick with an infectious disease with an empty stomach.

When sick, send for a *good* physician, and as you value your health and life, have nothing to do with quacks.

The condiments, pepper, ginger, etc., are less injurious in summer. Fat beef, bacon, and hearty food may be eaten more freely in winter.

Let the amount of the meal bear some relation to future needs as well as present appetite; but it is better to carry an extra pound in your pocket than in your stomach.

Eat something within an hour after rising, especially if obliged to labor or study; but avoid both these before breakfast if possible, and particularly exposure to malaria or contagion.

Bad cooking may spoil good food. Pork, if eaten at all, should be thoroughly cooked. Avoid frying meat; boil, roast or broil it, beginning with a high heat; for soups begin lukewarm.

A small quantity of plain, nourishing soup is a wholesome first course at dinner. Rich soups are injurious to persons of weak digestion, and a large quantity of liquid food is not beneficial to adults.

Three full meals daily are customary, but the number, the relative quantity and quality, and the intervals between them, are largely matters of opinion, habit and convenience; regularity is the important thing.

Exercise before breakfast should be very light, and it is better to take a cracker or some trifle before going out, especially in a miasmatic climate. Early breakfasts are a necessity to the young and growing.

Remember that when the stomach is sour after eating, the food is actually rotting—that is a nauseating word but it expresses the absolute facts in the case—and it means that some of the rules above given have been violated.

Eat in pure air and in pleasant company; light conversation and gentle exercise promote digestion, but hard work of any kind retards it. Avoid severe bodily or mental labor just before and for two hours after a full meal.

Most people drink too much and too fast. A small quantity of water sipped slowly satisfies thirst as well as a pailful swallowed at a draught.

Drinks at meals should be taken at the close, and not too strong or hot. Dyspeptics especially should drink sparingly. Children need more than adults, but too much is injurious.

Adults need to eat at regular intervals two or three times a day, allowing time for each meal to be fully digested before another is taken. It would spoil a loaf of bread, half baked, to poke a lump of cold dough into the middle of it.

Use good palatable food, not highly seasoned; vary in quantity and quality according to age, climate, weather, and occupation. Unbolted or partially bolted grains are good and sufficient food for men; but nature craves variety. As a rule, the flesh of meat-eating animals is not wholesome food. Hot soft bread digests slowly.

Don't eat too fast; the digestive organs are something like a stove, which if choked up and out of order, burns slowly, and if you keep piling in fuel, grows more and more choked. The wiser course is to let it burn down and put in fuel only when needed. It is a foolish notion that food always keeps up the strength. Only what we digest helps us; all beyond that is a tax upon the system, and exhausts the strength instead of increasing it.

Masticate well; five minutes more at dinner may give you better use of an hour afterward. Drink little at meals and never a full glass of very hot or very cold liquid. Never wash down a mouthful. Avoid waste of saliva.

Avoid tobacco, alcohol in all forms, and all stimulants. Every healthy man is better, stronger, has a clearer head, more endurance, and better chances for a long life, if free from the habitual use of stimulants. The boy who begins the use of tobacco or liquors early is physically ruined.

Avoid colds and break up as soon as possible when taken. As soon as conscious that the pores are closed, keep warm within doors, drink warm ginger tea, relax the bowels, and take a vapor bath. Breaking a cold up early, often saves a severe attack of congestion, pneumonia, often even a fever.

Panaceas are *prima facie* humbugs; their makers and takers, their vendors and recommenders are knaves or fools, or both. Nature cures most diseases, if let alone or aided by diet and proper care. There are no miracles in medicine; remember that to keep or to get health generally requires only a recognition of Nature's powers, with knowledge of anatomy and physiology, experience, and common sense.

Never sleep in clothing worn during the day, and let that worn at night be exposed to the air by day. Three pints of moisture, filled with the waste of the body, are given off every twenty-four hours, and mostly absorbed by clothing. Exposure to air and sunlight purifies the clothing and bedding of the poisons which nature is trying to get rid of, and which would otherwise be brought again into contact with the body.

The lungs should be trained to free, full, and vigorous action. "The breath is the life." A man will exist for days without food, but when the breath is cut off life ceases. If breathing is imperfect, all the functions of the body work at a disadvantage. It is a common fault to breathe from the surface of the lungs only, not bringing into play the abdominal muscles, and so not filling the more remote air cells of the lungs. By this defective action the system is deprived of a part of its supply of air, and by inaction the air-cells become diseased.

Evacuate the bowels daily, and above all regularly; the best time is after breakfast; partly to be rid of a physical burden during the day, but chiefly to relieve the bowels. Constipation is safer than diarrhœa. For the former, exercise, ride horseback, knead the belly, take a glass of cool water before breakfast, eat fruit and laxative food; for the latter, follow an opposite course—toast, crust, crackers and rice are the best food. Pain and uneasiness of digestive organs are signs of disturbance; keep a clear conscience; rest, sleep, eat properly; avoid strong medicines in ordinary cases.

Keep the person scrupulously clean; change the clothing worn next to the skin (which should be flannel) often. Don't economize in washing bills. A cold bath every morning for very vigorous persons, or once or twice a week and thorough rubbing with a coarse towel or flesh-brush mornings when bath is not taken, for the less robust, is necessary to keep the functions of the skin in health, and is very invigorating. After warm baths a dash of cold water will prevent chill and "taking cold." In bathing in winter, the shock from cold water is lessened by standing a minute in the cold air after the removal of clothing before applying water.

A very prolific source of disease is defective drainage. In the country, slops and waste water are thrown into the back yard to trickle back into the well and pollute it, or to form a reeking cesspool which poisons the air. In cities, the sewer-connections with houses allow the foul gases to rush back through the waste-pipes to closets or sinks and into the house. Neatness will cure the first, and a flue connecting each system of drainage-pipes with the tallest chimney in the house where a fire is used, will draw off and consume the gases in the second.

It should be remembered that the use of chloride of lime, and other fumigants, does not destroy filthiness, but only renders it less evident. Cleanliness, fresh air, and sunlight will purify. Cleanliness is a very strong word. Carpets filled with dust or grease, dirty furniture, or walls covered with old paper, defile the atmosphere as much as a refuse heap in the cellar or back yard. A dark house is generally unwholesome and dirty. The sunlight is second only in importance to fresh air. To convince one that light purifies, it is only necessary to go into a darkened room and note the corrupt smell.

Ventilation can not be accomplished by simply letting the pure air in; the bad air must be let out. Open a window at top and bottom, hold a lighted candle in the draft, and see the flame turn outward at the top and inward at the bottom, showing the purifying currents. Windows on opposite sides of the room ventilate still more perfectly. In sleeping rooms, avoid "drafts" when possible, but danger of taking cold from them may be averted by extra clothing. In living-rooms, an open fire-place or grate insures ventilation. The use of close stoves, and close rooms, are the causes of the increased prevalence and fatality, in winter, of small-pox, scarlet fever, and other contagious diseases.

Colds are often, if not generally, the result of debility, and are preceded by disordered digestion. Such cases are prevented by a removal of the cause by diet and pure air. Extreme cold or heat, and sudden exposure to cold by passing from a heated room to cold outside air, is very injurious to the old or weak. All such should avoid great extremes and sudden changes. In passing from heated assemblies to the cold air, the mouth should be kept closed, and the breathing done through the nostrils only, so that the cold air may be warmed before reaching the lungs, which have just been immersed in a hot-air bath. The injurious effect of such sudden changes is caused by driving the blood from the surface to the internal organs, producing congestions.

Bad smells mean that decay is going on somewhere. Rotten particles are floating in the air, and penetrating the nostrils and lungs. Their offensiveness means that they are poison and will produce sickness and death, or so reduce the tone of the system that ordinarily mild disorders will prove fatal. In all such cases remove the cause when possible. Many of these poisons are given off by the body, and are removed by pure air as dirt is washed away by water. Soiled or foul air can not purify any more than dirty water will clean dirty clothes. Pure air enters the lungs, becomes charged with waste particles, which are poison if taken back again. An adult spoils *one gallon of pure air every minute,* or twenty-five flour barrelfuls in a single night, in breathing alone. A lighted gas-burner consumes eleven gallons, and an ordinary stove twenty-five gallons a minute. Think of these facts before sealing up the fire-place, or nailing down the windows for winter.

A DYSPEPTIC'S FIGHT FOR LIFE.

Judge W. was a depressed, despondent, discouraged, listless, moody, nervous, wretched dyspeptic for five weary years. He tried travel, but neither the keen air of the sea-shore nor the bracing breezes of the northern prairies brought him relief. He tried all the panaceas and all the doctors at home and abroad in vain. Some told him that he had heart disease, others thought it was inflammation of the spleen, gout, Bright's disease, liver complaint, lung difficulty, or softening of the brain. Bottle after bottle of nostrums went down the unfortunate Judge's throat, and it was only when physicians and friends gave him up, and pronounced him to all intents a dead man, that he threw bottles, plasters, powders and pills to the four winds, and with the energy of despair, set about disappointing his doctors, and getting ready to live despite their ghastly predictions. Then began a fight for life against dyspepsia, a fight which many have begun, but few have won. He bathed the whole body every morning in cold water, summer and winter, not by a shower or a plunge, but by vigorously dashing the water on the body with the hands, and afterwards rubbing briskly with a coarse towel. This was continued without missing a single morning for years. In the meantime the strictest diet was instituted. By experimenting, the patient found what he could eat without harm, and ate that only in very small quantities, measuring his food on his plate before beginning his meal, and limiting himself rigidly to that quantity. His principal food for nearly three years was cracked wheat and Graham mush, and the last meal was taken at two o'clock in the afternoon—not a particle of food passed his lips from that time until the next morning, thus giving the stomach complete rest and time to begin the work of recuperation. Special attention was given to eating slowly and thoroughly masticating the food, and not to eat too much, too fast, or too often were rules strictly and rigidly observed. Bathing, diet, rest, sleep, and gentle exercise in the open air did the work. It was a dreadful conflict—days of struggle and temptation, requiring more heroism and steady tenacity of purpose than would nerve a soldier for battle, for such a battle is for the day, but this fight was renewed every morning and continued every day for months and years. But patience, courage, intelligent judgment, and a strict adherence to the above regimen won the day without a grain or a drop of medicine, and Judge W. believes that the good Lord of us all has never permitted any man to discover or invent medicine that will cure dyspepsia. Nature is the only perfect physician. Cold water, fresh air, the natural grain (wheat), sleep, rest and gentle exercise make up the grand panacea. With these alone, and the self denial and moral courage to persist in the good fight, the confirmed, nervous, miserable dyspeptic, became a well, strong, and hearty man in five days? No. In five months? No. In five years? Yes; and after the fight, when contemplating the victory won, he could say with the model philanthropist, Amos Lawrence, after his battle of fifteen long years with the same disease, "If men only knew how sweet the victory is, they would not hesitate a moment to engage in the conflict."

HINTS FOR THE SICK-ROOM.

The sick-room should be the lightest, most cheerful, and best ventilated room in the house. Patients in the sunny wards of hospitals recover soonest, and the sick, in nearly all cases, lie with their faces to the light. Every thing should be kept in perfect neatness and order. Matting is better than a carpet, though when the latter is used it may be kept clean by throwing a few damp tea-leaves over only a part of the room at a time, then quietly brushing them up with a hand broom. A table not liable to injury, a small wicker basket with compartments to hold the different bottles of medicine and a small book in which to write all the physician's directions, two baskets made on the same plan to hold glasses or cups, screens to shade the light from the eyes of the patient, a nursery-lamp with which to heat water, beef-tea, etc., a quill tied on the door-handle, with which the nurse can notify others that the patient is asleep by merely passing the feather-end through the key-hole, several "ring cushions" to give relief to patients compelled to lie continually in one position (these cushions are circular pieces of old linen sewed together and stuffed with bran; or pads may be used, made of cotton-batting basted into pieces of old muslin of any size required), and a sick couch or chair, are a few of the many conveniences which ought to be in every sick-room.

Pure air in a sick-room is of the utmost importance. In illness, the poisoned body is desperately trying to throw off, through lungs, skin, and in every possible way, the noxious materials that have done the mischief. Bad air, and dirty or saturated bed-clothes, increase the difficulty at the very time when the weakened powers need all the help they can get. Avoid air from kitchen or close closets. Outside air is the best, but, if needed, there should be a fire in the room to take off the chill. A cold is rarely taken in bed, with the bed-clothes well tucked in, but oftener in getting up out of a warm bed when the skin is relaxed. Of course any thing like a "chill" should be avoided, and it is not well to allow a draft or current of air to pass directly over the bed of the patient.

In disease less heat is produced by the body than in health. This decline occurs even in summer, and is usually most evident in the early morning, when the vital powers slacken, the food of the previous day having been exhausted. The sick should be watched between midnight and ten or eleven in the morning, and if any decline in heat is noticed, it should be supplied by jugs of hot water. A sick-room, should above all be quiet. Any rustling sound, such as that of a silk dress or shoes which creak, should be entirely avoided. If it is necessary to put coal on the fire, drop it on quietly in small paper sacks, or rolled in paper slightly dampened. Visitors should never be admitted to a sick-room. The necessary attendants are usually a sufficient annoyance to a weak patient, and many a tombstone might truthfully and appropriately be inscribed "talked to death by well-meaning friends." It is not generally the loudness of a noise that disturbs the sick, but the sound that produces expectation of something to happen. Some can not bear any noise. Any thing that suddenly awakens is injurious. Never awaken a sleeping patient unless ordered to do so by the physician. In sickness, the brain is weakened with the rest of the body, and sleep strengthens it. If rest is interrupted soon after it is begun, the brain is weakened so much the more, and the patient becomes irritable and wakeful. If sleep lasts longer, he falls asleep again more readily. Never speak within the hearing of the sick, in tones which can not be fully understood. An occasional word, or murmur of conversation, or whisper, is intolerable, and occasions needless apprehension.

Few persons have any idea of the exquisite neatness necessary in a sickroom. What a well person might endure with impunity, may prove fatal to a weak patient. Especially the bed and bedding should be scrupulously clean. In most diseases the functions of the skin are disordered, and the clothing becomes saturated with foul perspiration, so that the patient alternates between a cold damp after the bed is made, and a warm damp before, both poison to his system. Sheets which are used should be dried often from this poisonous damp, either in the sun or by the fire, and the mattress and blanket next the sheets, should also be carefully aired as often as possible. In changing very sick patients (particularly women after confinement) the sheets and wearing-clothes should be well aired by hanging by the fire for two days, or smoked by holding them over hot coals sprinkled with bran. Move the patient close to one side of the bed, turn the under sheet over close to the invalid, then smooth the mattress, removing any thing that may be on it. Make ready the clean sheet, by rolling one half into a round roll, lay this close by the invalid, spread the other half smoothly over the bed. Now assist the patient on the clean sheet, unroll, and spread over the other side of the bed. Have the upper sheet ready, which must be carefully and gently laid over the invalid, then add the other bed-clothes. (In dressing a blister where a bandage has to be placed around the body, roll one half the bandage, place it under the invalid, so that the attendant at the other side can reach it, unrolling, and placing it around the patient without disturbing him.) Light blankets are best for coverings. Never use the impervious cotton counterpanes and comforters. The clothing should be as light as possible with the requisite warmth. The bed should be low, and placed in the light, and as a rule the pillows should be low, so as to give the lungs free play. Scrofula is sometimes caused by children sleeping with their heads under the clothing, and patients sometimes acquire the same injurious habit.

Bathing should always be done under the advice of a physician, but soap and water are great restoratives. In most cases, washing and properly drying the skin gives great relief. Care should be taken, while sponging and cleansing, not to expose too great a surface at a time, so as to check perspiration. The physician will regulate the temperature. Sometimes a little vinegar, whisky, or alcohol added to the water, makes the bath more refreshing, and bay-rum for the face, neck, and hands is often acceptable. Whenever the bath is followed by a sense of oppression, it has done harm. Its effect should be comfort and relief.

Chamber utensils should be emptied and thoroughly cleansed immediately after using, and in no case allowed to remain standing in the sick-room. Slop-pails, into which nothing should be allowed to go except the waste water from the wash-stand, must be emptied and cleansed thoroughly at least twice a day.

Patients are often killed by kindness. A spoonful of improper food, or the indulgence of some whim, may prove fatal. A physician's directions should always be observed with the strictest fidelity. Medicines and things which will be wanted during the night should all be prepared before the patient grows sleepy. Every thing should be done quickly but quietly, and with precision. In talking, sit where the patient can see you without turning his head. Never ask questions when he is doing any thing, and never lean or sit upon the bed. Sick persons generally prefer to be told any thing rather than to have it read to them. A change in the ornaments of the room is a great relief, and the sick especially enjoy bright and beautiful things. Flowers which do not have a pungent odor are always a great delight.

In convalescence great care is necessary, and the physician's directions should be implicitly obeyed, especially in regard to diet; a failure in obedience often brings on a fatal relapse. A little food at a time and often repeated, is the general rule for the sick. A table-spoonful of beef-tea, every half hour, will be digested, when a cupful every three or four hours will be rejected. (In giving a drink or liquid of any kind a moustache-cup will be found a great convenience). The sick can rarely take solid food before eleven in the morning, and a spoonful of beef-tea, or whatever stimulant the physician has ordered, given every hour or two, relieves exhaustion. Brandy, whisky, or other alcoholic stimulants, however, should never be ordered in cases where there is a hereditary tendency to use them, or where they have been used as a beverage, or where the associations of the patient in the future would be likely to make an acquired taste for them a temptation. In most cases substitutes may readily be found. Untouched food should never be left at the bed-side. Every meal should be a surprise, and the patient should be left alone while eating. Food for the sick must be of the best quality, and neatly and delicately prepared. The cook should do half the patient's digesting.   Keep the cup and saucer dry, so that no drops will fall on the bed or clothing.

Beef-tea contains a certain amount of nourishment, and may be given in almost any inflammatory disease.   Eggs do not agree with all patients, but are nourishing food when admissable.   Tenderloin of beef, cut across the grain, and broiled on live coals, without smoke, and well cooked or rare as the physician may direct, is always relished, and a tender lamb-chop, broiled in the same way with the fat removed before serving, is easily digested and nutritious   Roasted potatoes, very mealy, are preferred to other vegetables. Milk is a representative diet, and when it agrees with the digestion, is probably better adapted to strengthen the body in sickness than any other one article of food, but it must be fresh and pure.   The least taint of sourness is injurious.   Butter-milk, however, when fresh, is useful in fevers, bilious diseases, and dyspepsia.   Cream is even' better than milk, and is less apt to turn acid in the stomach.   Many patients thrive on Indian-meal mush and cream, and any preparations of Indian-meal are especially good for persons who are suffering from the loss of natural warmth (see Bread-making).   Oat-meal, Graham and rye mush, and home-made brown bread are important articles of diet, greatly relished by the sick.   There are instances of persons recovering from serious illness where a table-spoonful of rye mush, and half tea-cupful buttermilk, three times a day, were all that could be taken for two or three weeks.   A patient's craving for any particular article of food should be communicated to the physician as it is often a valuable indication of the wants of the system.   These cravings should be gratified whenever possible. Watermelons act on the kidneys, and are good in many cases of fever, bowel complaint, etc.   Celery also is good in some diseases of the kidneys, and in nervousness.   Fresh, crisp, raw cabbage, sliced fine and eaten with good vinegar, is easily digested, and often highly relished by a patient suffering from a "weak stomach."   New cider is also excellent in many cases of nervous dyspepsia.   Fruits and berries, raw, ripe, and perfect, used in moderation, are admirable remedies in cases of constipation and its attendant diseases.   The grape has a wide range of curative qualities.   The seeds are excellent for costiveness, the pulp is very nutritious and soothing to irritated bowels, while the skins, if chewed, act as an astringent.   Raw beef is excellent in dysentery; it should be minced very fine, and given in doses of a spoonful at a time every four hours, the patient in the meantime eating nothing else.   Bananas, or baked apples are good in chronic diarrhœa.   A rind of bacon is good for teething children to chew.   Rice-water or rice-jelly are advisable in many cases of convalescence from acute fever, summer complaint, and like diseases.   Fresh pop-corn, nicely salted, clam-broth, the juice of a roasted oyster in the shell, soda-water, and peppermint-tea are remedies for sick stomach.   Vegetable acid drinks, herb-teas, toast-water, and all such drinks are often much relished.   A custard made from a preparation of liquid rennet, as directed on bottle, is a delicate dish. Buttered-toast, either dry or dipped, though so generally given, is rarely a suitable article for the sick, as melted oils are very difficult of digestion. In quinsy, diphtheria, inflammation of lungs, typhus and other putrid fevers, acids are of very great benefit. Take a handful of dried currants, pour over them a pint of boiling water, let them stand half a minute without stirring, then drain off the water, strain it through a cloth, and set it away to cool; when given to the patient, dilute well so that the acid taste is very slight. Acid fruits should be eaten early in the day. Above all, it should be remembered that it is not the nourishment which food contains, but *that which the stomach can assimilate*, that builds up; a sick person will thrive on what would not sustain a well man.

It is of the utmost importance that the food be delicately and carefully administered, and this should never be left to servants. It should be made as attractive as possible, served in the choicest ware, with the cleanest of napkins, and the brightest of silver. If tea is served, it should be freshly drawn, in a dainty cup, with a block of white sugar, and a few drops of sweet cream. Toast should be thin, symmetrical, well yellowed, free from crust, and just from the fire. Steak should be a cut of the best tenderloin, delicately broiled, and served with the nicest of roasted potatoes. The attention given to these simple matters is in many cases worth more than the physician's prescriptions.

The craving for tea and coffee is almost universal with the sick. A moderate quantity is a great restorative, but an excess, especially of coffee, impairs digestion. Neither should be given after five in the afternoon, as they increase excitement, and cause sleeplessness; but sleeplessness from exhaustion in the early morning is often relieved by a cup of tea or coffee. The patient's taste will decide which should be used. In cases of thirst, the physician will prescribe what other drink should be given to satisfy it. Cocoa is not often craved by the sick, and possesses no stimulating qualities. Crust-coffee is very nourishing.

The following recipe makes a delicious, refreshing, and cooling wash for the sick-room.

Take of rosemary, wormwood, lavender, rue, sage, and mint, a large handful of each. Place in a stone jar, and turn over it one gallon of strong cider vinegar, cover closely, and keep near the fire for four days, then strain, and add one ounce of pounded camphor gum. Bottle, and keep tightly corked.

There is a French legend connected with this preparation (called *vinaigre a quatre voleurs*). During the plague at Marseilles, a band of robbers plundered the dying and the dead without injury to themselves. They were imprisoned, tried, and condemned to die, but were pardoned on condition of disclosing the secret whereby they could ransack houses infected with the terrible scourge. They gave the above recipe. Another mode of using it is to wash the face and hands with it before exposing one's self to any infection. It is very aromatic and refreshing in the sick-room; so, if it can accomplish nothing more, it is of great value to nurses.

FOOD FOR THE SICK.

ARROWROOT CUSTARD.—One table-spoon of arrowroot, one pint of milk, one egg, two table-spoons sugar; mix the arrowroot with a little of the cold milk; put the rest of milk on the fire and boil, and stir in the arrowroot, and egg, and sugar well beaten together; scald and pour into cups to cool; any flavoring the invalid prefers may be added.

SAGO CUSTARD.—Soak two table-spoons sago in a tumbler of water an hour or more, then boil in same water until clear, and add a tumbler of sweet milk; when it boils add sugar to taste, then a beaten egg and flavoring.

BEEF BROTH.—Cut in small pieces one pound of good lean beef; put on in two quarts cold water and boil slowly, keeping it well covered, one and one-half hours; then add half a tea-cup tapioca which has been soaked three-quarters of an hour in water enough to cover, and boil half an hour longer. Some add with the tapioca a small bit of parsley, and a slice or two of onion. Strain before serving, seasoning slightly with pepper and salt. It is more strengthening to add, just before serving, a soft poached egg. Rice may be used instead of tapioca, straining the broth, and adding one or two table-spoons rice (soaked for a short time), and then boiling half an hour.—*Mrs. F. M. W.*

BEEF-TEA.—Cut pound best lean steak in small pieces, place in glass fruit jar (a *perfect* one), cover tightly and set in a pot of cold water; heat gradually to boil, and continue this steadily three or four hours until the meat is like white rags and the juice thoroughly extracted; season with very little salt, and strain through a wire strainer. Serve either warm or cold. To prevent jar toppling over, tie a string around the top part, and hang over a stick laid across the top of pot. When done, set kettle off stove and let cool before removing the jar and in this way prevent breakage. Or when beef-tea is wanted for immediate use, place in a common pint bowl (yellow ware) add very little water, cover with saucer, and place in a moderate oven; if in danger of burning add a little more water.

BARLEY WATER.—Add two ounces pearl barley to half pint boiling water; let simmer five minutes, drain and add two quarts boiling water; add two ounces sliced figs and two ounces stoned raisins; boil until reduced to a quart; strain for drink.

BAKED MILK.—Bake two quarts milk for eight or ten hours in a moderate oven, in a jar covered with writing-paper tied down. It will then be as thick as cream, and may be used by weak persons.

BUTTERMILK STEW.—Boil one pint buttermilk, add small lump butter and sweeten to taste. Some add a tea-spoon of ginger and honey instead of sugar.

BRAN BISCUITS.—Take cup bran (as prepared by Davis & Taylor, 24 Canal St., Boston), five cups sifted flour; scald the bran at tea-time with half pint boiling water; when cool pour it into the middle of the flour, add one half cup good yeast (or part of a yeast-cake, soaked till light), one tea-spoon salt and two table-spoons sugar; wet with new milk into soft dough, much thicker than batter. Let it stand covered closely in a warm place to rise. In the morning, spoon into hot gem or patty pans, and bake in a quick oven to a brown crust. Part of the dough may be baked in a small loaf to be eaten warm. (It can be made with water by using a little butter, but is not so good.) Any remaining may be split for dinner or toasted for tea.— *Mrs. L. S. Williston, Jamestown, N. Y.*

BROILED BEEFSTEAK.—Many times a small piece of "tenderloin" or "porterhouse" is more wholesome for an invalid than broths and teas, and with this may be served a potato, roasted in the ashes, dressed with sweet cream (or a little butter) and salt, or nicely cooked tomatoes. Have the steak from half an inch to an inch thick, broil carefully two or three minutes over hot coals, turning often with a knife and fork, so as not to pierce it. When done, put on a small dish, season slightly with salt and pepper and a *small bit* of butter, garnish with the potato and serve *hot.—Mrs. E. T. Carson.*

BROILED CHICKEN, QUAIL, SQUIRREL OR WOODCOCK.—Any of these must be tender. Take the breasts of the first two, or the thighs of the others; place on hot coals or on a broiler, turning often to prevent burning. When done, remove the burned parts, if any, season *slightly* with butter, pepper and salt, and serve at once.—*Mrs. W. W. W.*

CHICKEN BROTH.—Take the first and second joint of a chicken, boil in one quart of water till very tender and season with a very little salt and pepper.—*Miss M. R. Johnson.*

CRUST COFFEE.—Toast bread very brown, pour on boiling water, strain and add cream and sugar, and nutmeg if desired.

CREAM SOUP.—One pint boiling water, half tea-cup cream; add broken pieces of toasted bread and a little salt.—*Mrs. Mary A. Thomson.*

EGG GRUEL.—Beat the yolk of an egg with a table-spoon of sugar, beating the white separately; add a tea-cup of boiling water to the yolk, then stir in the white and add any seasoning; good for a cold.

UNCOOKED EGG.—This is quite palatable, and very strengthening, and may be prepared in a variety of ways. Break an egg into a goblet and beat thoroughly, add a tea-spoon sugar, and after beating a moment add a tea-spoon or two of brandy or port wine; beat well and add as much rich milk, or part cream and milk, as there is of the mixture. Or, omit brandy and flavor with any kind of spice; or, milk need not be added, or the egg may be beaten separately, stirring in lightly the well-whipped whites at the last.

FEVER DRINK.—Pour cold water on wheat bran, let boil half an hour, strain and add sugar and lemon-juice. Pour boiling water on flax-seed, let stand till it is ropy, pour into hot lemonade and drink.

GRAHAM GEMS FOR INVALIDS.—Mix Graham flour with half milk and half water, add a little salt, beat, making the batter thin enough to pour; have the gem-pan very hot, grease it, fill as quickly as possible and return immediately to a hot oven; bake about thirty minutes. Practice will teach just the proper consistency of the batter, and the best temperature of the oven. It will not be good unless well beaten.

JELLICE.—One-half tea-spoon of currant, lemon or cranberry jelly put into a goblet, beat well with two table-spoons water, fill up with ice-water, and you have a refreshing drink for a fever patient.

MULLED BUTTERMILK.—Put on good buttermilk and when it boils, add the well-beaten yolk of an egg. Let boil up and serve. Or stir into boiling buttermilk thickening made of cold buttermilk and flour. This is excellent for convalescing patients.

MILK PORRIDGE.—Place on stove in skillet one pint new sweet milk and a very little pinch of salt, when it boils have ready sifted flour, and sprinkle with one hand into the boiling milk, stirring all the while with a spoon. Keep adding flour until it is about the consistency of thick molasses; eat warm with a little butter and sugar. This is excellent for children suffering with summer complaint. Or, mix the flour with a little cold milk until a smooth paste, and then stir into the boiled milk. Or, break an egg into the dry flour and rub it with the hands until it is all in fine crumbs (size of a grain of wheat), then stir this mixture into the boiling milk.

OLD-TIME FOOD FOR CONVALESCENTS.—Roast good potatoes in hot ashes and coals; when done, put in a coarse cloth and squeeze with the hand, and take out the inside on a plate. Put a slice of good pickled pork on a stick three or four feet long, hold before a wood fire until it cooks slightly, then dip into a pan of water and let it drip on the potato to season it; repeat until the meat is nicely cooked on one side, then turn the other, dip in water, etc. When done place on plate beside the potato, serve with a slice of toast dressed with hot water and a little vinegar and salt, or use sweet cream instead of vinegar. A cup of sage tea, made by pouring boiling water on a few leaves of sage and allowing it to stand a few minutes, served with cream and sugar, is very nice; or crust coffee, or any herb tea is good. Food prepared in this way obviates the use of butter.—*Mrs. Mary A. Thomson.*

OAT-MEAL.—Mix a table-spoon of meal with a little cold water till perfectly smooth, pour gradually into a pint of boiling water, and boil slowly for twenty or thirty minutes, stirring almost constantly; do not let it scorch; season with a little salt, sugar, spice of any kind if desired, and brandy or wine if the nature of the case will permit.

PANADA.—Take two richest crackers, pour on boiling water, let stand a few minutes, beat up an egg, sweeten to taste, and stir all together; grate in nutmeg and add brandy or wine to suit the invalid. Or, break in a pint bowl toasted bread and pour over boiling water, adding a small lump of butter, two table-spoons wine, brandy or whisky; sweeten to taste and flavor with nutmeg or cinnamon.

RASPBERRY VINEGAR.—Pour over two quarts of raspberries in a stone jar, one quart of very best vinegar; let stand twenty-four hours, strain, and pour liquor over fresh fruit, and let stand in the same way; allow one pound sugar to a pint of juice; put into a stone jar and set in pot of boiling water one hour; skim well, put into bottles, cork and seal tight. Diluted with water this is very nice for the sick. Toasted bread may be eaten with it.

RASPBERRY RELISH.—To each pint of berry juice add one pound of sugar. Let it stand over night; next morning boil ten minutes, and bottle for use.—*Mrs. W. G. Hillock, New Castle, Ind.*

PREPARED FLOUR FOR SUMMER COMPLAINT.—Take a double handful of flour, tie up tightly in cloth and put in a kettle of boiling water, boil from three to six hours, take out, remove the cloth and you will have a hard, round ball. Keep in a dry, cool place, and when wanted for use, prepare by placing some sweet milk (new always preferred) to boil, and grating into the milk from the ball enough to make it as thick as you desire, stirring it just before removing from the stove with a stick of cinnamon; this gives it a pleasant flavor; put a little salt into the milk. Very good for children having summer complaint.—*Mrs. W. W. W.*

PARCHED RICE.—Cook in custard-kettle a half cup parched rice in one pint boiling salted water; when done serve with cream and sugar.

RICE JELLY.—Mix one heaping table-spoon of rice-flour with cold water until it is a smooth paste, add a scant pint of boiling water, sweeten with loaf-sugar; boil until quite clear. If the jelly is intended for a patient with summer complaint, stir with a stick of cinnamon; if for one with fever, flavor with lemon juice, and mold. Rice-water is made in the same manner, by using twice the quantity of boiling water.—*Estelle Woods Wilcox.*

SEA-MOSS FARINE.—Dessert-spoon of sea-moss farine, quart boiling water; steep a few minutes, sweeten and flavor with lemon (leaving out rinds). This is a very pleasant drink and is good for colds.—*Mrs. S. N. Fuller, Washington Heights, N. Y.*

SAGO JELLY-PUDDING.—Wash thoroughly one tea-cup of sago, cook it in three pints of water fifteen or twenty minutes, till perfectly clear, add a very little salt; stir in half a jelly-glass of currant, grape or other jelly and two spoonfuls sugar. Mold and serve cold with cream and sugar; or, eat warm.

CURRANT SHRUB.—Make the same as jelly, but boil only ten minutes; when cool, bottle and cork tight, (see directions for canned fruits). Raspberry, strawberry and blackberry shrubs are made in the same way; when used, put in two-thirds ice-water.

SASSAFRAS DRINK.—Take the pith of sassafras boughs, break in small pieces and let soak in cold water till the water becomes glutinous. This is good nourishment and much relished.

TO REMOVE GREASE FROM BROTHS FOR THE SICK.— After pouring in dish, pass clean white wrapping-paper quickly over the top of broth, using several pieces, till all grease is removed.—*Mrs. E. T. Carson.*

TAPIOCA JELLY.—One half pint tapioca, one quart water, juice and some of the grated rind of a lemon; soak the tapioca for three or four hours in the water, sweeten it and boil for one hour in a custard-kettle, or until quite clear, stirring it often. When almost done, stir in the lemon, and when sufficiently cooked, pour into molds. Serve with sweetened cream.—*Mrs. T. B. J.*

TAMARIND WHEY.—Mix an ounce of tamarind pulp with a pint of milk, strain and sweeten. Or, simply stir a table-spoon of tamarinds into a pint of water.

VEGETABLE SOUP.—Two tomatoes, two potatoes, two onions and one table-spoon rice; boil the whole in one quart of water for one hour, season with salt, dip dry toast in this till quite soft, and eat; this may be used when animal food is not allowed.

WINE WHEY.—One pint of boiling milk, two wine-glasses of wine, boil a moment stirring well, take out the curd, sweeten and flavor the whey.

CRACKED WHEAT PUDDING.—To one quart new or unskimmed milk add one-third cup cracked wheat, same of sugar (or a little more if preferred), a little salt and small piece of stick cinnamon. Place in moderate oven and bake two hours or longer. When about half done stir in the crust already formed, and it will form another sufficiently brown. When done the wheat will be very soft, and the pudding of a creamy consistency. It can be eaten hot or cold, and is nice for invalids. A handful of raisins added is considered an improvement by some.—*Mrs. L. S. W.*

CORN-MEAL GRUEL.—Add to three pints boiling water two table-spoons corn meal, stirred up with a little cold water; add a pinch of salt and cook twenty minutes. For very sick persons, let it settle, pour off the top, and give without other seasoning. For convalescents, toast a piece of bread nicely, and put in the gruel with one or two table-spoons sweet cream, a little sugar and ginger, or nutmeg and cinnamon. When a laxative diet is allowed this is very nourishing. Or, take a pint of meal, pour over it a quart or more of cold water, stir up, let settle a moment and pour off the water; repeat this three times, then put the washed meal into three quarts of cold water, and place where it will boil; cook three hours, and when done add a pinch of salt. This is a very delicate way of cooking, and it may be eaten with or without other seasoning. This is an old and very valuable recipe, used thirty years ago by Dr. Davenport, of Milford Center, Ohio.

27

BEEF-TEA SOUP.—To one pint of "beef essence" (made, in a bottle, as directed in recipe on a preceding page), quite hot, add a tea-cup of the best cream, well heated, into which the yolk of a fresh egg has been previously stirred; mix carefully together, and season slightly, and serve.

CINNAMON TEA.—To a half pint fresh, new milk add stick or ground cinnamon enough to flavor, and white sugar to taste; bring to boiling point, and take either warm or cold. Excellent for diarrhœa in adults or children. A few drops or a tea-spoonful of brandy may be added, if the case demands.

STEWED OYSTERS.—Remove all bits of shell from a half dozen *fresh*, select oysters, place in a colander, pour over a tea-cup of water, drain, place liquor, drained off, in a porcelain-lined sauce-pan, let come to boiling point, skim well; pour off, into another heated dish, all except the last spoonful which will contain sediment and bits of shell which may have been overlooked, wipe out sauce-pan, return liquor, add oysters, let come to the boiling point, add a small lump of good butter, a tea-spoonful of cracker dust, a very little cayenne pepper and salt, and a half tea-cup fresh, sweet cream.

MEAT FOR INVALIDS.—The following method of rendering raw meat palatable to invalids is given by good authority: To 8.7 ounces of raw meat, from the loin, add 2.6 ounces shelled sweet almonds, .17 ounces shelled bitter almonds, and 2.8 ounces white sugar—these to be beaten together in a marble mortar to a uniform pulp, and the fibres separated by a strainer. The pulp, which has a rosy hue and a very agreeable taste, does not at all remind one of meat, and may be kept fresh for a considerable time, even in summer, in a dry, cool place. Yolk of egg may be added to it. From this pulp, or directly from the above substances, an emulsion may be prepared which will be rendered still more nutritious by adding milk.

RAW BEEF.—Chop fresh, lean beef (the *best* steak or roast) very fine, sprinkle with salt and pepper, and put between thin slices of Graham or white buttered-bread. This is a very nutritious diet.—*Mrs. L. S. W.*

RAW BEEF-TEA.—Cut up lean, frest meat, soak eight or ten hours in a small quantity of cold water. This is good after severe cases of typhoid fever.

ARTICLES FOR THE SICK-ROOM.—A rubber bag, holding two quarts, to be one-half or three-quarters filled with hot water, and placed about the patient where needed—under head in neuralgia, around the side in liver-congestion, etc.; or can be filled with very cold water in cases needing such applications —is very flexible and agreeable, and can be used where a soap-stone or bottle would hurt. Price, $2.00.

A pair of very long, loose stockings, knit of Saxony wool, or any soft yarn, without heels, to draw on towards morning in fever cases, or to keep a patient warm when she is up; they might come half way between the knee and thigh. Every housekeeper should have a pair to be used in cases of sickness.

A board, three inches wide and as long as the window is wide, to be placed under the lower window-sash when raised a little, to give a gentle circulation of air between the sashes without the possibility of a draught on any one.

THE ARTS OF THE TOILET.

Beauty and health constitute a royal inheritance. The child born with such a heritage, and brought up by a mother who has the good sense to discard soothing syrups, narcotics and cordials, and carefully trains up to cleanly habits, proper exercise, plenty of air and sunshine, and wholesome food, starts in life with a capital that will in the long run tip the balance against the largest fortune in dollars. To keep health and beauty, or to restore it when lost, it is necessary to observe the laws of health, discarding quackery and panaceas of all kinds as superstitions, and inventions of the devil. Pure air and plenty of it, free sunshine and plenty of it, are better restoratives than all the patent medicines under the sun. Too often the doctor brings the medicine only to have the medicine bring the doctor again. The sunlight will give a lady's cheek a fresher tinge and a more delicate complexion than all the French powders and rouge in Paris.

THE BATH—Not only promotes cleanliness, but is a tonic. The skin does one third of the work of breathing, and if the myriad of pores are closed, the lungs are overburdened, or else the work is left undone. The tonic effect is caused by the contraction of the surface blood-vessels, driving the blood back to the larger blood-vessels and the heart, bringing on a re-action which rushes the blood back to the skin, causing a glow, freer respiration, and more vigorous action of the whole muscular system. A sponge or hand bath are the simplest forms, and should be taken in a moderately warm room. As a rule, the more rapidly a bath is taken the better, and it should always be followed by friction with the hand or with a not too rough towel.

THE FACE.—To wash properly, fill basin two-thirds full with fresh, soft water, dip face in the water and then the hands; soap the hands well and rub with a gentle friction over the face; dip the face in water the second time and rinse off thoroughly, wiping with a thick but soft towel. Pure soaps do not irritate the skin. The best are castile, curd, glycerine and other neutral soaps. Medicated or highly colored or perfumed soaps should never be used.

FOOD.—A good complexion never goes with a bad diet. Strong coffee, hot bread and butter, heated grease, highly spiced soups, meats, or game, hot drinks, alcoholic liquors, fat meats, are all damaging to its beauty. Strong tea, used daily, will after a time give the skin the color and appearance of leather. Coffee affects the skin less but the nerves more, and a healthy nervous system is necessary to beauty. Late suppers, over-eating at meals, eating between meals, the use of candies, sweetmeats, preserves, etc., produce pimples and blotches.

CORPULENCY.—An excess of fat is a disease. To reduce the excess, eat little or no butter, fat meat, gravies, sugar, vegetables, or other articles containing large amounts of starch or sugar.

LEANNESS—Is caused generally by lack of power in the digestive organs to digest and assimilate the fat-producing elements of food. First restore digestion, take plenty of sleep, drink all the water the stomach will bear in the morning on rising, take moderate exercise in the open air, eat oat-meal, cracked wheat, Graham mush, baked sweet apples, roasted and broiled beef, cultivate jolly people, and bathe daily.

DRESS.—The first object of dress is protection of the body, second to enhance and bring out its beauty. Dress which does not enhance the beauty of the wearer, or which attracts attention from the wearer to itself, is out of taste. To be in correct taste it must be "becoming," and in this sense dressing is an art worthy of the attention and study of the most intellectual and accomplished woman. The beauty of dress, to a cultivated eye, does not lie in its money-value, but in its perfection in detail and perfect adaptation to the wearer and the occasion for which it is intended. Any simpleton in petticoats, who has plenty of money, can order her clothes from Worth, in the latest Paris styles, but some quiet woman, with brains and taste, in simpler costume, will be sure to outshine her in "society." Low-necked dresses, dragging skirts, corsets and stays, paddings, heavy skirts which rest on the hips, heavy veils, high-heeled boots, and every other unphysiological abomination in dress, mars beauty and destroys health.

THE HAIR.—Combs of tortoise-shell, bone, or rubber, with not very sharp teeth, should be used. Sharp teeth injure the scalp and produce dandruff. Two brushes, one hard, to clean the hair and scalp, and the other soft, to smooth and polish, are best. Clean brushes by rubbing them with bran, or wash with one part ammonia and two of water. Combing or brushing should be done in the natural direction of the hair, and never against it. In the proper way it can not be brushed too much. To keep the scalp clean wash in tepid soft water with a little pure soap in it, rinse in pure water, dry with towels and then in the sun or by the fire. Oily hair may be washed once a week, light hair less often. Some occupations require that it should be washed much oftener. All preparations for the hair are more or less injurious. Healthy hair has enough oil of its own, and the application of foreign oil destroys its vitality. Preparations containing alcohol fade hair and make it brittle. The only time when oil is admissable is after washing. The best preparation is one part of glycerine to three of rose-water. Powders made of starch, when used, must be washed out of the hair to prevent injury. Those made of colored glass are very injurious, cutting and otherwise damaging the hair. At night, the hair should be loosened and left free. Night-caps are a relic of barbarism, Hair-dyes are very injurious, as they all contain more or less sugar of lead, nitrate of silver, and other ingredients, which affect the brain, produce paralysis, inflammation of the eyes, and impairment of sight. Gray hairs are an indication that the hair-producing organs are weakening. When found they should be cut down to the healthy part, and the head should be exposed as much as possible, except in the middle of the day, to the sun and air. When hair falls out, it indicates a disease of the scalp. To cure, dip the head twice a day in cold water and rub with a brush until a glow is produced. In case the hair is too long to wet, brush until a glow is produced, and then rub into the roots a wash made of three drachms of *pure* glycerine and four ounces of lime-water. After the use of this for two or three weeks, add half an ounce of the tincture of cantharides to the above mixture. Use this treatment once or twice a day; if tender, diminishing the application, if insensible, increasing it. If baldñess comes in spots, the skin should be brushed with a soft tooth-brush dipped in distilled vinegar, at morning and evening, and then brushed as above.

SUPERFLUOUS HAIRS—Are best left alone. Shaving only increases the strength of the hair, and all depilatories are dangerous and sometimes disfigure the face. The only sure plan is to spread on a piece of leather equal parts of galbanum and pitch plaster, lay it on the hairs as smoothly as possible, let it remain three or four minutes, then remove it with the hairs, root and branch. This is severe, but effective. Kerosene will also remove them. If sore after using, rub on sweet oil.

THE SKIN AND COMPLEXION.—Washing in cool, but not excessively cold, water, and general cleanliness, keeps the skin healthy and complexion clear.

LIPS OR HANDS CHAPPED by cold weather or wind, should be rubbed with glycerine gently when about to be exposed to the air, or rubbed with honey after washing. Never kiss the lips of persons not in health, as disease is sometimes contracted in this way, as well as by the use of towels, cups or tumblers used by unhealthy persons.

TEETH.—Cracking nuts, biting thread, eating hot food, especially bread and pastry raised with soda, very cold drinks, alternate contact with cold and hot substances, highly seasoned food, alcoholic liquors and tobacco, metal toothpicks ,and want of cleanliness, are injurious to teeth. After eating, the mouth should be rinsed with lukewarm water, and such pieces of food as are not thus washed away, removed by a quill toothpick. Tooth-brushes should be elastic and moderately hard. Those with hairs not too close together are best and most durable. A brush that is too hard may be permanently softened by dipping in hot water. Rub up and down as well as across the teeth. Teeth should be often examined by a competent dentist.

THE BREATH.—Nothing makes one so disagreeable to others as a bad breath. It is caused by bad teeth, diseased stomach, or disease of the nostrils. Neatness and care of the health will prevent and cure it.

THE EYES.—Damp, foggy weather, the reflection of the bright sunshine, intense cold, dusty wind, reading on cars in motion, reading by gas or lamplight when the light falls directly on the eyes, sitting before a glowing fire, wearing of glasses when not needed, wearing veils, and all indulgences that weaken the nervous system, injure the eyes. The most pleasing light for work is from a northern exposure. A shade that protects the eyes from the light that falls on paper, book or work is an advantage. The light should not come from different points, but that from behind the worker is best. A very weak or very bright light should be equally avoided. Diseases of the eye are often the result of general weakness, and in such cases local treatment has little effect. In fitting glasses to the eye great care should be taken to adjust the lens to the eye with accuracy. Crown glass is preferable to flint on account of its superior hardness, its entire want of color, and its non-decomposition of light. Scotch pebbles are unobjectionable except as to cost.

THE EAR.—The outer ear should be well-cleansed and the passage wiped out daily with a rag on the end of the little finger, but nothing should be inserted further. The insertion of a pin, or any hard substance, frequently ruptures the ear. When cleansing is necessary on account of accumulation of wax by cold, or other cause, it should be done by syringing with warm water, having dropped in two or three drops of glycerine the night before to soften the substance to be removed. This often cures sudden deafness. Cotton-wool stuffed into the ear is injurious and is seldom necessary. In conversing with deaf persons, it is important to remember that clearness, distinctness, and a musical tone of voice is understood much more easily than a loud tone.

THE NOSE.—Excessive wiping, snuffing, and blowing, especially in children, deforms the nose, and should be practiced only when necessary for cleanliness. A nose leaning to one side, caused by wiping in one direction, may be cured by using the handkerchief with the other hand, or by wearing occasionally an instrument surgeons employ for that purpose. Large, fleshy noses are reduced by wearing at night a contrivance which compresses the artery that supplies the nose. Red noses become so by exposure to heat or the sun, by alcoholic drinks, or by a debility of the blood-vessels of the skin. The latter cause is removed by gentle friction and cold bathing of the feet.

THE NECK.—Too tight collars and neckerchiefs are apt to produce permanent swelling of the throat.

THE HANDS.—The use of gloves, especially kids, help to preserve the softness of the hands. Cleanliness and sprinkling with orris-root counteracts excessive perspiration. Warts are removed by steeping the hands in warm water for half an hour, and then paring away the white and insensible surface. The nails should be cut frequently, always in oval shape. The nail-brush should be full and soft. It should be rubbed on a cake of soap and then used vigorously. Biting nails is a bad habit. To break it up in children, dip the ends of the fingers in a solution of aloes.

THE FEET.—The largest pores of the body are located in the bottom of the feet. For this reason the feet should be frequently and thoroughly washed, and the stockings changed often. If great cleanliness is not observed, these great pores become absorbent, and the poisons given off are taken back into the system. The nails ought to be cut squarely. Blisters may be prevented by rubbing the feet, after washing, with glycerine. Bunions are caused by wearing shoes too tight or too short. They are difficult to get rid of, but may be alleviated by wearing easy-fitting shoes, poulticing and putting a rubber ring around the spot. Corns, which are caused by a continued pressure on the foot, may be prevented by wearing woolen stockings and shoes that fit well. To cure, soak feet for half an hour, nightly, in hot water in which two table-spoons of soda have been dissolved. After each bath scrape as much away as possible. Soft corns may be removed by sprinkling a piece of cotton with prepared chalk, and placing it between the toes where the corn is. The chalk absorbs the moisture and a cure is soon effected.

FRECKLES.—Grate horse-radish fine; let it stand a few hours in buttermilk, then strain and use the wash night and morning. Or squeeze the juice of a lemon into half a goblet of water and use the same way. Most of the remedies for freckles are poisonous, and can not be used with safety. Freckles indicate a defective digestion, and consist in deposits of some carbonaceous or fatty matter beneath the skin. The diet should be of a nature that bowels and kidneys will do their duty. Daily bathing, with much friction, should not be neglected, and the Turkish bath taken occasionally, if convenient.

PIMPLES—Are caused by improper diet, and can never be cured except by correcting the habits. Cosmetics only injure.

MOLES.—To remove, moisten a stick of nitrate of silver, touch the moles, and they will turn black and sore, and soon they will dry up and fall off of themselves. If they do not entirely go, repeat. It is better, however, never to attempt their removal without consulting a physician.

MOTHER'S MARKS—Should never be interfered with except by the advice of a physician.

WARTS.—Wash with water saturated with common washing soda, and let dry without wiping; repeat frequently until they disappear. Or pass a pin through the wart and hold one end of it over the flame of a candle or lamp until the wart fires by the heat, and it will disappear.

TETTER OR RINGWORM of the face is caused by a disordered stomach, and must, be cured by proper diet.

FLESH WORMS.—Black specks on the nose disfigure the face. Remove by washing thoroughly in tepid water, rubbing with a towel, and applying with a soft flannel a lotion made of three ounces of cologne and half an ounce of liquor of potash.

STAINS ON THE HANDS—From nitrate of silver may be removed by a solution of chloride of lime. Fruit-stains are removed by washing the hands without soap, and holding them over the smoke of burning matches or sulphur.

TO REMOVE SUNBURN.—Scrape a cake of brown Windsor soap to a powder, add one ounce each of *eau de Cologne* and lemon juice, mix well and form into cakes. This removes tan, prevents hands from chapping, and makes the skin soft and white.—*Miss Mary R. Collins.*

TEETH.—Many, while attentive to their teeth, do more injury than good by too much officiousness, daily applying some dentifrice, or tooth-powder, often impure and injurious, and rubbing them so hard as not only to injure the enamel by excessive friction, but also to hurt the gums even more than by a toothpicks. Tooth-powders advertised in newspapers are to be suspected, as some of them are not free from corrosive ingredients. Charcoal (which whitens the teeth very nicely), pumice-stone, cuttle-fish, and similar substances, are unfit for use in tooth-powders, as all are to a certain extent insoluble in the mouth and are forced between the margin of the gums, forming a nucleus for a deposit. Below will be found a few good formulas for dentifrices: Three and one-half pounds of *creta preparata*, one pound each of powdered borax, powdered orris-root, and white sugar, and two ounces cardamom seeds; flavor with wintergreen, rose or jasmine. If color is desired, use one pound of rose-pink and as much less of *creta preparata*. Tooth-powders should be thoroughly triturated in a wedgewood mortar, and finely bolted.

The following is a simple and cheap preparation, and is pretty good. Take of prepared chalk and fine old Windsor soap pulverized well, in proportion of about six parts of the former to one of the latter. Soap is a very beneficial ingredient of tooth-powder.—*H. W. Morey, D. D. S.*

CUTTING TEETH.—The time the first teeth make their appearance varies, but the following dates approximate the time: Central incisors from five to eight months after birth; lateral incisors from seven to ten; first molars from twelve to sixteen; cuspids, or eye-teeth, from fourteen to twenty; second molars from twenty to thirty-six. The first teeth should be protected from decay as far as possible by careful cleaning daily; if decay makes its appearance, the cavity should be promptly filled, and the tooth saved until displaced by the permanent teeth. About the sixth year the first molars of the permanent teeth made their appearance. They are generally supposed to belong to the first or milk teeth and are frequently lost for want of care. A little more attention given to the first teeth would save parents and children sleepless nights and suffering.—*B. L. Taylor, D. D. S., Minneapolis.*

FOR COMPLEXION.—Blanch one fourth pound best Jordan almonds, slip off the skin, mash in a mortar and rub together with best white soap,. for fifteen minutes, adding gradually one quart rose-water, or clean, fresh rainwater may be used. When the mixture looks like milk, strain through fine muslin. Apply after washing, with a soft rag. To whiten the skin and remove freckles and tan, bathe three times a day in a preparation of three quarts water, one quart alcohol, two ounces cologne, and one of borax, in proportion of two tea-spoons mixture to two table-spoons soft water.

To KEEP OFF MOSQUITOS.—Rub exposed parts with kerosene. The odor is not noticed after a few minutes, and children especially are much relieved by its use.

CEMENT FOR JET.—Use shellac to join, and then smoke the joints to make them black.

To CLEAN JEWELRY.—Any gold jewelry that an immersion in water will not injure, can be beautifully cleaned by shaking it well in a bottle nearly full of warm soap-suds to which a little prepared chalk has been added, and afterwards rinsing it in clear cold water, and wiping it on a towel.

QUEEN BESS COMPLEXION WASH.—Put in a vial one drachm of benzoin gum in powder, one drachm nutmeg oil, six drops of orange-blossom tea, or apple blossoms put in half pint rain-water and boiled down to one tea-spoonful and strained, one pint of sherry wine. Bathe the face morning and night; will remove all flesh-worms and freckles, and give a beautiful complexion. Or, put one ounce of powdered gum of benzoin in pint of whiskey; to use put in water in wash bowl till it is milky.

COLOGNE WATER.—One quart alcohol, three drachms oil lavender, one drachm oil rosemary, three drachms oil bergamot, three drachms essence lemon, three drops oil cinnamon.

BOSTON BURNETT POWDER FOR THE FACE.—Five cents worth of bay rum, five cents worth of magnesia snow-flake, five cents worth of bergamot, five cents worth of oil of lemon; mix in a pint bottle and fill up with rain-water; perfectly harmless and splendid.—*Emma Collins.*

FOR CHAPPED HANDS, FACE AND LIPS.—Ten drops carbolic acid in one ounce glycerine; apply freely at night. Pure mutton tallow is also excellent.

COLD CREAM FOR CHAPPED LIPS.—One half ounce spermaceti, twenty grains white wax, two ounces pure oil of sweet almonds, one ounce pure glycerine, six drops oil of rose; melt first three ingredients together and when cooling add the glycerine and oil of rose, stirring until cold.—*Miss Alice Trimble.*

TONIC FOR THE HAIR.—Ounce best castor-oil, two ounces each of French brandy and bay rum; scent with rosemary and rose-geranium.

ACCIDENTS AND SUDDEN SICKNESS.

It is no longer considered a mark of the highest type of the feminine mind to faint away at the smallest fright, and to sink into helplessness at the first appearance of danger. Indeed, self-possession in emergencies is evidence of a clear brain, which, at the critical moment, asserts its supremacy over physical weakness, and takes command of the demoralized forces; besides, fright and confusion are a confession of ignorance as well as want of self-control. Those who know exactly what to do in emergencies rarely become panic-stricken. And it is particularly important for women, who are, doubtless, constitutionally more timid than men, to fortify themselves against danger, by learning what to do in such accidents and emergencies as are likely to occur in the life of every one. It would prove a rare case, indeed, if such knowledge did not, at least once in a life-time, enable the possessor of it to save a valuable life, perhaps one infinitely dearer to her than her own. Of course, within the limits of such an article as is permissible here, only a few hints can be given, rather to suggest further investigation than to be a complete guide.

ACCIDENTS IN GENERAL.—The first and most important thing, after sending for a surgeon, when an accident has occurred, is to keep off the crowd. No one, except one or two in charge, should be allowed nearer than ten feet; and the kindest thing a by-stander can do is to insist on such a space, and to select such persons as are willing to go for whatever is needed by the surgeon or physician, so that there may be no delay, if any thing is needed. If there has been a "shock" from a fall or blow, although there may be no fracture or external injury, the person is "faint," and should be placed flat on the back, with the head, neck, and shoulders *slightly* raised; the limbs should be straightened out, so that the heart may act as easily as possible; the cravat, collar, and clothing, if in the least tight, should be loosened. A sup of cold water will bring reaction soon if the injury is slight; a tea-spoonful of brandy, in a table-spoonful of water, every two minutes, gentle friction to the extremities, a handkerchief wet with cologne-water held to the nostrils, a fan, if weather is hot, will all aid in restoring full consciousness. If thought best to remove the patient to his residence, or to a more favorable place for treatment, place on a stretcher, settee, or shutter, slipping him on gently, taking care that the body is supported along its whole length; throw a handkerchief over the face to prevent the unpleasant sensation of the staring crowd, and let the stretcher be borne by persons of uniform gait, if possible. A policeman's services, if in a city, are invaluable in keeping off a crowd. When a surgeon arrives, his directions will suffice.

DROWNING.—Death is caused by cutting off the supply of fresh air from the lungs, so that the process of purification of the arterial blood centres. Life is rarely restored after an immersion of five or six minutes, but recovery has been recorded after twenty minutes. Efforts to restore should be continued for at least two hours, or until the arrival of a physician. What is done must be done quickly. The body should be recovered, without loss of time, from the water, and laid face downward for a moment, while the tongue is pressed back by the finger to allow the escape of water or any other substance from the mouth or throat (no water can ever by any possibility get into the lungs). This may be done while the body is being conveyed to the nearest house; on arrival, strip off clothing, place on a warm bed, with head raised very little, if any, apply friction with the dry hands to the extremities, and heated flannels to the rest of the body. Now breathing must be artificially restored. "Silvester's ready method" is most favored by physicians, and consists in pulling the tongue well forward, to favor the passage of air to the lungs, and then drawing the arms away from the sides of the body, and upward, so 'that they meet over the head, and then bringing them down until the elbows almost meet over the "pit of the stomach." These movements must be made, and persisted in, at the rate of sixteen to the minute. Another method is to place the body flat on the face, press gently on the back, turn body on its side or a little beyond, and then, turning back upon face, apply gentle pressure again, repeating at the rate of sixteen times a minute. As soon as vitality begins to return a few drops of brandy, in a little water, may be administered, and, in a few minutes, some beef-tea or light nourishment. Persons at all weakened by debility, especially by any thing that affects the nervous system, or those recovering from sickness, or in the least indisposed, should never venture into water beyond their depth, as such conditions predispose to "cramp," against which the best swimmers are helpless.

HANGING.—Death is from the same cause as in drowning. Cut down the body without allowing it to fall, place on face, press back tongue with finger to allow any accumulation to escape from the mouth, place on the back, and treat as directed for the drowned. If body is still warm after the removal of clothing, stand off six feet and dash several times with a bowl of cold water, the face, neck, and chest.

SUFFOCATION.—This often occurs from carbonic-acid gas, or "choke-damp," on entering wells or old cellars; this gas being heavier than air falls and rests at the bottom. Before entering such places, test by lowering a lighted candle; if the flame is extinguished it is unsafe to enter until the gas has been removed by throwing down a bundle of lighted shavings or blazing paper, sufficient to cause a strong upward current. When a person is overcome by this gas, he must be *immediately* rescued by another, who must be rapidly lowered and drawn out, as he must do all while holding his breath; a large sack is sometimes thrown over the person who goes to the rescue. As soon as brought out, place the person on his back, bare the neck and throat, loosen clothing, and strip as quickly as possible; if he has not fallen in the water, dash cold water freely over head, neck, and shoulders, standing off several feet and throwing it with force; artificial respiration should be used meantime, as in case of drowning, with as little cessation as possible. If the person has fallen into the water when overcome by the gas, place in a warm bed, and use the means of artificial respiration vigorously.

Suffocation from burning charcoal, from anthracite or bituminous coal, or from common burning gas, or the foul gases from drains and cess-pools, is treated as if from carbonic acid gas.

CHOKING.—A piece of food lodged in the throat may sometimes be pushed down with the finger, or removed with a hair-pin quickly straightened and hooked at the end, or by two or three vigorous blows on the back between the shoulders.

SUNSTROKE.—This is favored by intemperance, and by debility brought on by work in a heated atmosphere. Those who sleep in badly ventilated apartments are most subject to it. Most cases are preceded by pain the head, wandering thought and loss of mental control, disturbed vision, irritability, sense of pain, and weight at pit of stomach, and labored breathing. The skin is hot and dry, or covered with profuse perspiration; the face bluish; the breath rapid and short; and the action of the heart "fluttering." In many instances the patient does not move an eyelid, from the beginning of the main attack until death ensues.

Carry the person attacked at once to a cool, airy spot, in the shadow of a wall, or to a large room with a bare floor, remove clothing gently, place patient on the back, raise head two inches by a folded garment, dash entire body with water profusely, supplying basin with cold water from two buckets, one of which is filled with water and finely pulverized ice while the other is supplying the water used by the attendant. Dash on water with force, particularly on head and chest. Two persons may also rub the entire body, particularly the head, with a towel in which is wrapped pulverized ice. As soon as a *decline in heat* is noticed remove patient to a dry place, and wipe dry. If heat comes on again when consciousness is restored, renew cold applications. As soon as the heat declines, artificial respiration must be resorted to, until the natural takes its place. There being real asphyxia, as in drowning, no medicine is of use, and alcoholic stimulants should be carefully avoided. To prevent sunstroke, use no malt or alcoholic liquors, avoid overwork and exhaustion, take plenty of sleep in a well-ventilated room, bathe every night, avoid drinking large quantities of water, especially at meals, wear loose-fitting garments, protect the head with a covering that will shelter from the sun and yet permit free circulation of air over the scalp; a straw hat of loose texture, with a lining that may be wet when going out, and a broad brim to protect neck and shoulders, is best.

LIGHTNING.—If the person shows no signs of life, strip and dash the body with cold water, dry and place in bed with bottles of hot water at the pit of the stomach and extremities, keeping up artificial respiration until the natural breathing is restored; a tea-spoonful of brandy in a table-spoonful of water, may be given every few minutes. Burns from lightning should be treated like burns from any other cause.

SHOCK OR COLLAPSE from lightning, sudden and severe injuries, burns extending over a large extent of surface, or powerful emotions, produces something analogous to fainting. Place the patient flat on the back, with the head raised not more than an inch, and give a tea-spoonful of brandy in a table-spoonful of water, every minute for six or eight minutes. If the temperature of the body has been raised, and the action of the heart is restored, enough has been given. Application of heat to the stomach and extremities is useful. The nausea and vomiting that sometimes accompany it may be allayed by swallowing whole small chips of ice, split off by standing a piece with grain upright and splitting off a thin edge with the point of a pin. Ammonia applied to the nostrils is often useful, and cologne on a handkerchief is sometimes of service.

FAINTING.—Debility of the nervous system favors fainting. The head should be kept low; and if the patient faints in a chair, the simplest treatment is to grasp the back of it and depress it until the floor is reached, while another holds the knees so as to prevent slipping off the side. The patient will usually recover by the time the head has reached the floor.

SHOCK FROM COLD WATER.—Prostration from drinking or bathing in cold water while exhausted by heat or exercise should be treated as described for shock from other causes. Cold water should be taken in small quantities when the body is heated and exhausted, and a cold bath is often fatal under such circumstances.

BURNS AND SCALDS.—First put the fire out. If the clothing is on fire, throw the person on the ground and wrap in carpet, rug, or your coat, if nothing else is at hand. Begin wrapping at the neck and shoulders, and keep the flames away from the neck and face, so as to prevent breathing the hot air and consequent injury to the lungs. If prostration and shock or fainting is produced, a little brandy, repeated often until there is a revival of strength, should be given. A superficial burn covering a large surface is often more dangerous than a deeper one confined to less surface. If there is any cause for apprehension that the hot air has been inhaled, send for a physician at once. If the burn is slight in character, apply the water-dressing, by placing two or more thicknesses of old linen (from table-cloth or sheet), slightly dampened over a surface a little larger than the wound; fasten on by slips of sticking-plaster, or tie on with bandages, and keep it wet by frequent applications of water. When the pain has moderated a dressing of *pure* hog's-lard is one of the best. It may be purified, when doubtful, by boiling in water until the salt and impurities have settled, and then set away to cool until the floating lard hardens; this is gathered, placed in a bowl, set in hot water, and kept hot until all the water in the lard has passed off, when it is ready for use. A good dressing for a slight burn or scald is the white of an egg, applied with a soft rag or brush, applying fresh as the first layer dries; a lather of soap from a shaving-cup often allays pain, and keeps out the air. If so serious that a physician has been sent for, it is better not to apply any thing, as it may interfere with his examination and treatment of the case. In cases too severe for the mild treatment given above, send at once for a physician.

BURNS BY ALKALIES.—Such as lime, caustic potash, soda, ammonia, etc., are stopped in their progress by applying vinegar, lemon-juice, or other dilute acid; they must be then treated like other burns.

BURNS FROM ACIDS.—Such as oil of vitriol and aqua fortis may be checked by the free application of water or handfuls of moist earth. The first dilutes the acid, and the second contains alkali enough to neutralize the acid.

FRACTURE.—Send at once for a physician, and simply make the patient as comfortable as possible. If he is to be conveyed to some distance, the fractured part should be supported in its natural position by handkerchiefs loosely tied. Allow no more handling than is absolutely necessary.

WOUNDS.—If an artery has been severed, and the blood spurts out at each heart-beat, press on the point of division firmly with the finger, to diminish the size of the blood-vessel, until a clot is formed. If this does not produce the desired effect, find the artery which supplies the wound, and press it as firmly as possible. If this is not successful, place the patient on his back, and hold up wounded arm or leg, and compress the artery by placing a large, firm knot in a handkerchief over it, tying it about the limb, and tightening it by passing a stick through it, and twisting it until the flow is stopped. When the bleeding ceases, remove the foreign substances and the clots by a stream of water from a sponge, and bring the edges carefully together, holding them in place by strips of adhesive plaster. The best dressing is the "water dressing;" but it must be used with an adhesive plaster which is not dissolved by water. If chilliness appears from the use of water, it must be discontinued for a time. After twenty-four hours the linen dressing may be removed, and renewed if the wound is clear of discharge of blood or other material; and the same treatment must be continued, remembering that all foreign substances are injurious and should be removed. Whenever the wound does not heal properly by this process, owing to the condition of the patient, a physician should be consulted. If any part of the body has been cut off, it should be cleaned of foreign matter, and at once replaced, wrapped in cotton to retain warmth, and a gentle pressure kept on it to retain it in place. Circulation is often restored and the union made complete.

Punctured wounds need a pad at the surface to cause clotting of the blood in the wound, but are otherwise treated like cuts. If pain follows and inflammation ensues, the pad must be removed to permit the results of the inflammation to escape. Thorns or splinters, when run into the flesh, should be removed by cutting in far enough to get hold of and draw them out. Slivers under the nail, when not reached from the end, should be removed by scraping the nail thin, and cutting through it to the foreign body, and so withdrawing it; the part should then be tied with a cloth wet with water, in which a few drops of laudanum have been mixed. A puncture, by a rusty nail or some such substance, of the finger, toe, hand, or foot, frequently causes inflammation, and yet there is not room for the foreign matter left in the wound to escape through the tough skin, and lock-jaw results; in all such cases the wound should be cut open to provide a way of escape for the blood, etc., and a piece of linen wet with laudanum inserted. Wounds from bruises and lacerations especially demand careful treatment, on the same general principles given above.

STINGS OF INSECTS—Are relieved by the application of ammonia, or common table salt, well rubbed in, or a slice of an onion, to the part.

BITES OF DOGS.—The only safe remedy in case of a bite from a dog suspected of madness, is to burn out the wound thoroughly with a red-hot iron, so as to destroy the entire surface of the wound.

POISONOUS WOUNDS.—Wounds by which poison has been carried into the system require instant treatment. The wound must be burned out by a stick of lunar caustic, or by inserting a large, red-hot nail.

BITES OF SERPENTS.—When bitten by a rattlesnake, or other poisonous serpent, pinch the skin, and, if the wound can be reached, suck out all the blood possible; if the skin of the lips and mouth is sound, no harm will be done. Whisky or brandy should, however, be administered freely, to intoxication.

FOREIGN BODIES IN THE EYE.—The particle almost invariably lodges under the upper lid, adhering to it. If that lid is grasped by the thumb and finger, drawn outward and then downward, and then released, the lashes of the lower lid act as brush, and sweep off the intruder. If, however, it adheres to the eye-ball, it may be removed by rolling the upper lid over a knitting-needle, and holding it there in such a position as to expose the surface, when the particle can be removed by the corner of a handkerchief. Sometimes it may become imbedded in the membrane which covers the eye-ball, or eye-lid, and require the aid of a surgeon. Never use any of the eye-waters, lotions, or salves, advertised as popular. A particle of lime in the eye is very dangerous, and vinegar diluted with water should be applied at once; even when done immediately the eye will be seriously inflamed.

FOREIGN BODY IN NOSTRIL.—Children often push foreign bodies up the nostril. To remove it, make the child draw a full breath, and then, closing the other nostril with the finger and the mouth with the hand, expel the air from the lungs by a sharp blow on the back. If it can not be removed in this way, compress the nostril above it to prevent its going up any further, and hook it out with the bent end of a wire or bodkin. If this fails, call a surgeon.

FOREIGN BODIES IN THE EAR.—Take the head of the child between the knees, face downward, and inject a stream of warm water into the ear, holding the nozzle of the syringe outside, so as to allow the foreign body to come out with the water. Probing, with any substance whatever, is very dangerous, and may inflict permanent injury. When the above plan does not succeed, call a surgeon. Kill insects that get into the ear by pouring in sweet oil or glycerine, which drowns and brings them to the surface.

FREEZING.—Keep the frozen person, or part, away from the heat. If the person is insensible, take him to a cold room, remove clothing, rub with snow or cloths wrung out of ice-water. The cold friction should be kept up for sometime; and when the frozen parts show signs of life, the patient should be carefully dried and put into a cold bed in a cold room, and artificial respiration used until the natural is restored; and then brandy, beef-tea, and ginger-tea administered. The patient must be brought by degrees into the warmer air. Parts frozen should be treated by the same rule.

CHILBLAINS—Are the result of a chilling of the part. To cure, keep away from the fire, and at night, before going to bed, wash in cold water, or rub in snow, and apply the compound resin ointment, made by all druggists, with a little oil of turpentine added to it.

EPILEPTIC FITS.—In these there is nothing which a by-stander or friend can do, except to keep out of reach such articles as may injure the patient during the convulsive movements; to loosen the clothing about the neck and throat, and to assist to some place of safety when the semi-conscious state returns. Other convulsions are treated in the same manner.

BURNING-HOUSES.—When a house is on fire, close all the doors, and prevent currents of air. If the fire could be entirely shut in, it would smother and die out. The check will give time to get help, or, at least, to remove furniture and make all lives secure. If up-stairs when the stairway below is on fire, tear clothing to make cords to let yourself down by. If a room is full of smoke and flame, crawl on the floor, as the lower air is the colder.

PANICS.—If in a public hall in a panic, keep your seat; even in case of fire the chance of life is greater if free from the crowd.

RUNAWAYS.—In all runaways it is safer to remain in the vehicle, and to stop with it, than to jump while the horse is running. The vehicle helps to break the shock of the final stop.

BREAKING THROUGH ICE.—In assisting persons who have broken through ice, get a long pole, or stick, or board, to distribute the weight over a greater surface of ice. In attempting to get out of water upon the ice, after having fallen in, the best way is to approach it sidewise, and roll out rather than to attempt to raise the body up by the arms alone, as the weight is more widely distributed.

A LIFE-PRESERVER.—A felt or silk hat held so as to keep the crown full of air will sustain a person above water for a great length of time.

ANTIDOTES TO POISONS.

The first thing to do is to cause their rejection by vomiting, to do which place mustard mixed with salt on the tongue, or give large quantities of lukewarm water, or tickle the throat with a feather. These failing, instantly resort to active emetics, like tartar emetic, sulphate of copper, or sulphate of zinc. After vomiting has taken place with these, continue it if possible by copious draughts of warm water till the poison is entirely removed. Of course, if vomiting can not be induced, the stomach pump must be employed, especially if arsenic or narcotics have been taken. A brief table, formulated as follows, may be useful for emergencies:

POISONS.	ANTIDOTES.
ACIDS.	Alkalies—Soap and milk, chalk, soda, lime-water.
ALKALIES.	Vegetable Acids—Vinegar, oil in abundance.
ALCOHOL.	Common salt, moderately.
ARSENIC.	Send for the doctor and his stomach pump.
ANTIMONY.	Oak-bark, strong green tea.
BARYTA OR LIME.	Epsom salts, oils, and magnesia.
BISMUTH.	Whites of eggs, sweet milk.
COPPER.	Whites of eggs, or strong coffee.
GASES.	Cold douche, followed by friction.
IODINE.	Starch, wheat flour in water.
CREOSOTE.	Whites of eggs, sweet milk.
LEAD.	Lemonade, strong, epsom salts.
OPIUM AND OTHER NARCOTICS.	Emetics—Cold douche, exercise, and heat.
PHOSPHORUS.	Magnesia, in copious draughts.
ZINC.	Whites of eggs, sweet milk.
MAD-DOG BITE.	Apply fire in some form to the wound, thoroughly and immediately.
BITE OF INSECT.	Ammonia, applied freely.
BITE OF SERPENT.	Same as for mad dog, followed by whisky to intoxication.

The foregoing are the more common and more important poisons and their antidotes.—*P. L. Hatch, M. D., Minneapolis, Minn.*

MEDICAL.

DIPHTHERIA.—The first symptoms are great debility, fever, and the char-acteristic deposits. These may appear on one or both tonsils, the back of the throat, or the arches of the palate. Frequently, there is some swelling of the glands on the neck and under the jaw. Its progress is shown by an increase of the fetor of the breath; by an extension of the deposits into the cheeks, or into the larynx and bronchi; by an extension upwards through the passages into the nose or into the passage to the ear. The swelling of the glands increases with the progress of the attack.

The unfavorable symptoms that may present themselves while the de-posits are spreading, are: Decrease of, or entire suppression of urine, great restlessness and tossing about, followed by stupor, from which the patient is awakened by attacks of suffocation. The fever during this time has been increasing, the pulse becomes smaller and harder, or intermittent or slower.

The favorable indications are an arrest of the further development of the characteristic deposits and their gradually more definite boundaries, the edges standing out more prominently above the mucus membrane, the swell-ing of which diminishes, and the patches begin to break up into smaller sections, or separate and come off by the efforts of coughing or to clear out the throat.

The characteristic symptoms of this disease are the great weakness, the small, hard, and frequent pulse, and the odor from the secretions of the parts affected. The attendant symptoms are as various as the modifications of individual constitutions and temperaments.

When attacked with diphtheria the patient must be kept in bed with suf-ficient clothing over the body to give the utmost comfort, and *no more*. The mind must be kept tranquil by quiet, and the room thoroughly pure by indirect ventilation. At the same time give nourishment regularly every two hours of well prepared beef-tea. If made by putting the beef into a bottle without water, and boiling, a large spoonful will do for an adult, and less according to the age. The neglect to nourish the patient well in the early stages of the disease is the one persistent error of the profession. The rapid destruction of the blood by the disease does not, as in typhoid states, suspend the functions of nutrition by diversion of the vital forces, but cre-ates a demand for supply of blood to meet the exhaustion incident to the waste which the results will demonstrate. The appropriate medication may arrest the local manifestation of the blood-poison, but will not re-supply the loss of vitalized blood upon which, after all, the recovery depends.

The domestic treatment of this terrible disease will be confined to the earliest stage, unless it be in the milder cases, and hence only the more common symptoms will be anticipated. If possible, obtain a competent physician at once in any event, and get his decision as to the gravity of the case, for many which appear as the slightest are really the most serious, while, as is often the case, a simple, common sore throat gives friends the direst apprehension.

A case having arisen, begin at once with aconite and belladonna, alter-nately every hour. If after four hours there is no improvement, and the characteristic prostration, and the patches on the tonsils are increasing, stop the aconite, and supply its place with the proto-iodide of mercurius.

Let these two remedies be continued until there is a marked change for better or worse. If for the former, let the intervals be increased to one and a half or two hours; for the latter, and there is approaching unconsciousness, with frequent arousing to cough up or hawk up the detached fragments of the deposits, that brings up tough, ropy, yellowish mucus, give kali bichromicum alone every hour.

When the patient becomes really better, stop, and give no more medicine while the improvement goes on satisfactorily.—*P. L. Hatch, M. D., Minneapolis, Minn.*

A SKILLFUL SURGEON'S PETS.

Dr. H. H. Kimball of Minneapolis, Minn., one of the most successful surgeons of the West, contributes the three following valuable recipes:

FOR DRESSING CUTS, WOUNDS, OR SORES.—Surgeon's solution of carbolic acid and pure glycerine mixed in equal parts, and applied on soft lint or linen cloth.

FOR BURNS.—Lime-water, olive oil, and glycerine, equal parts ; applied on lint.

LINIMENT.—Three ounces each of tincture of opium, camphorated oil, and soap liniment.

FOR THE HAIR.—Wash in cold sage-tea.

FOR COLDS.—Drink hot pennyroyal-tea.

FOR WORMS.—Give rue-tea.

FOR COLIC IN CHILDREN.—Give catnip-tea.

CURE FOR WOUNDS FROM RUSTY NAILS.—Dip fat pork in turpentine and bind it on the wound.

FOR QUINSY.—Gargle with water as hot as can be borne. This gives great relief, even in severe cases.

BEEF-TEA.—To make beef-tea more palatable for some patients, freeze it. —*Mrs. L. N. Fuller.*

TO STOP BLEEDING.—Apply wet tea-leaves or scrapings of sole-leather to a fresh cut and it will stop the bleeding, or apply a paste of flour and vinegar.

TO STOP BLEEDING AT THE NOSE.—Bathe the feet in very hot water, drinking at the same time a pint of cayenne pepper-tea, or hold both arms above the head.

ALUM WHEY.—Mix half ounce powdered alum with one pint sweet milk, strain, and add sugar and nutmeg: it is good in hemorrhages, and sometimes for colic.

FOR SORE THROAT.—Take five cents' worth chlorate of potassa, dissolve, and take a tea-spoon every hour, and also gargle with it.—*Estelle Woods Wilcox.*

FOR ERYSIPELAS.—A simple poultice made from cranberries, pounded fine, and applied in a raw state, is said to be a certain cure; or slip off the outer bark of elder, break up the wood with the inner bark, and steep in buttermilk; drink, and apply to the parts affected,

TO REMOVE WARTS.—Touch the warts with caustic potassa, or liquor potassa, or acetic acid. The operation is not painful, does not discolor the skin, and removes the warts in a short time, leaving the skin perfectly smooth.

28

LINIMENT.—The common May-weed blossoms put in alcohol are much superior to arnica for the same use.

FOR SPRAINS.—The white of an egg, and salt mixed to a thick paste is one of the best remedies for sprains, or bruises, or lameness, for man or beast. Rub well the parts affected.

SPRAINS OR LAMENESS.—Two ounces camphorated spirits, two ounces sweet oil, two ounces ammonia, two ounces chloroform; shake well before using, and rub it in by a fire. It is very excellent for a family liniment.

MOTH PATCHES—May be removed from the face by the following remedy: Into a pint bottle of rum put a table-spoonful of flour of sulphur. Apply this to the patches once a day, and they will disappear in two or three weeks.

TO DROP MEDICINE.—Shake the bottle so as to moisten the cork. With the wet end of the cork moisten the edges of the mouth of the bottle, then holding the cork under the mouth, let the fluid pass over the cork in dropping.

AN APERIENT FOR CHILDREN.—Ginger-bread made from oat-meal instead of flour.

TO PREVENT CORNS.—Wear easy shoes, which fit well, neither too loose nor too tight, and bathe the feet frequently with warm water with a little salt in it.

FOR JAUNDICE.—The yolk of an egg, raw or slightly cooked, is excellent food in jaundice.

TO RELIEVE ASTHMA.—Wet blotting-paper in strong solution of saltpeter, dry it, and burn a piece three inches square on a plate in sleeping-room, and it will afford quick relief.

DANDRUFF.—One ounce flour of sulphur to one quart of water. Shake well at intervals, for a few hours, and when settled, saturate the head with the clear liquid every morning.

HEADACHE.—Elixir of guarana, prepared by Brewer & Co., Springfield, Mass. Take one tea-spoonful every half hour until four have been taken, on the first intimation that the headache is coming on.

A SELF-HOLDER FOR A SPOON.—In dropping medicine into a spoon, place the handle between the leaves of a closed book lying on the table, and then both hands may be used in dropping the mixture.

BEE STINGS.—Any absorbent will give relief from bee stings, but perhaps nothing is more effectual than lean raw meat. The sting of a bee or wasp may be almost instantly relieved by it. It is said to cure the bite of a rattlesnake, and relieve erysipelas.

TO CURE CHILBLAINS.—Soak feet for fifteen minutes in warm water, put on a pair of rubbers, without stockings, and go to bed.

SALVE FOR CUTS AND BURNS.—To one-half pound of sweet lard, add one-fourth pound of beeswax and the same of resin; beat all together till well mixed; pour in a little tin box. Apply a little to the wound on a soft cotton cloth.—*Mrs. Ford.*

WHOOPING-COUGH.—Mix one lemon sliced, half pint flaxseed, two ounces honey, and one quart water, and simmer, not boil, four hours; strain when cool, and if there is less than a pint of the mixture, add water. Dose: one table-spoon four times a day, and one also, after each severe fit of coughing. Warranted to cure in four days if given when the child first "whoops."

TO CURE A CORN.—Apply sweet oil night and morning, or wash for two or three evenings in a pretty strong solution of common soda, which softens the corn so that it falls out. Cotton wet with opodeldoc or turpentine, applied to a soft corn, will cure it.

To Prevent taking Cold.—If out in cold weather with insufficient clothing or wrappings, fold a newspaper and spread across the chest. Persons having weak lungs can in this way make for themselves a very cheap and perfect lung protector. Large papers spread between quilts at night, add much to the warmth.

For a Cold.—Cayenne pepper-tea for a cold. Put a quarter of a teaspoon of cayenne pepper in a tea-cup; pour over hot water and sweeten with sugar. Or, steep horseradish in a gill of vinegar, add a gill of honey, and take a tea-spoon every twenty minutes.

Cure for Felon.—When a felon first makes its appearance, take the inside skin of an egg-shell, and wrap it around the part affected. When the pressure becomes too painful wet it with water, and keep it on twelve hours.—*Mrs. Jane M. Woods, Milford Center, Ohio.*

To Prevent a Child Coughing at Night.—Boil the strength out of ten cents worth of "seneca snake-root" in one quart of soft water; strain through a cloth, boil down to a pint, add one cup powdered sugar made into a thick molasses. Give one tea-spoonful on going to bed.

For Stiff Joints.—Oil made by trying up common angle worms, is excellent to apply to sinews drawn up by sprains or disease.

For the Lungs.—A quart (or less if too strong) of tar, stirred six minutes in a gallon of water, and one-fourth or a tumbler taken four times a day, an hour or two after meals, is said to clear the lungs, and give greater ease in public speaking.

For Rheumatism.—To one pint alcohol, add one table-spoon pulverized potash, and a lump of gum-camphor, the size of a walnut. Use as a liniment.

Neuralgia.—One-half drachm sal-ammonia in one ounce of camphor-water. Take a tea-spoonful several times, five minutes apart, until relieved. Another simple remedy is horseradish. Grate, and mix it in vinegar, the same as for table purposes, and apply to the temple when the face or head is affected, or the wrist, when the pain is in the arm or shoulder.

For Ivy Poisoning.—A simple and effectual remedy for ivy poisoning, is said to be sweet spirits of niter. Bathe the affected parts two or three times during the day, and the next morning scarcely any trace of the poison will remain.

For Burns or Bruises.—Apply peach-tree leaves, the smooth side next the skin, and bind them on. For burns, when there is danger of mortification or even if it has already set in, bind on strips of cloth dipped in clean tar.

For Sore Mouth in Nursing Babies.—A tea-spoon each of pulverized alum and borax, half a salt-spoon of pulverized nut-galls, a table-spoon of honey; mix, and pour on it half a tea-cup boiling water; let settle, and with a clean linen rag wash the mouth four or five times a day, using a fresh piece of linen every day.

Cherokee Liniment.—One ounce gum-camphor, dissolved in alcohol, one ounce each of spirits turpentine, sweet oil, hemlock oil, origanum oil, and cedar oil, two ounces spirits hartshorn. Use externally. Shake well before using.

Bad Breath.—Bad breath from catarrh, foul stomach, or bad teeth, may be temporarily relieved by diluting a little *bromo chloralum* with eight or ten parts of water, and using it as a gargle, and swallowing a few drops just before going out. A pint of *bromo chloralum* costs fifty cents, but a small vial full will last a long time.

Wound from Rusty Nail.—Smoke this or any inflamed wound over the fume of burning woolen cloth, wool, or sugar, for fifteen minutes, and the pain will be taken out.

TAPE WORMS are said to be removed by refraining from supper and breakfast, and at eight o'clock taking one-third part of two hundred minced pumpkin seeds, the shells of which have been removed by hot water; at nine take another third, at ten the remainder, and follow it at eleven with strong dose of castor oil.

TO PREVENT WEARING THROUGH THE SKIN WHEN BED-RIDDEN.—Apply to tender parts of body with a feather, a mixture made by beating to a strong froth the white of an egg, dropping in while beating two tea-spoonsful of spirits of wine. Bottle for use.

CURE FOR STAMMERING.—If not caused by malformation of organs, reading aloud, with the teeth closed, for at least two hours a day for three or four months will work a cure.

TO PREVENT SEA SICKNESS.—Make a pad of wool or horse hair; and bind over the stomach. Brandy and water, very weak, is the best remedy to allay the heat and irritation.

TO PREVENT SKIN FROM DISCOLORING AFTER A BRUISE.—Apply immediately or as soon as possible, a little dry starch or arrow-root, moistened with cold water, or rub over with common table butter.

TO RELIEVE TOOTHACHE.—Apply powdered alum, or fill mouth with warm water, and immediately after with cold; or saturate a piece of cotton with a strong solution of ammonia, and apply to the tooth. For toothache and inflamed face caused by it, apply a poultice of pounded slippery-elm bark and cold water.

ULCER IN THE EAR. Children are often troubled with ulcers in the ears after scarlet fever and other children's diseases. Roast onions in ashes until done, wrap in a strong cloth, and squeeze out juice. To three parts juice, add one part landanum and one part sweet oil, and bottle for use. Wash ear out with warm water, shake bottle well, and drop a few drops into the ear.

EYE WASH.—Sulphate of zinc two grains, sulphate of morphine one-half grain, distilled water one ounce; mix, and bottle. Drop in the eye (a drop or two at once), then wink the eye several times, so that the wash may reach all the parts; and keep quiet, and do not use the eyes for about an hour. This wash is for blood-shot eyes, and when used it will produce quite a smarting sensation.—*Dr. D. W. Henderson.*

FOR ITCHING SORE EYES.—Scorch a handful of pure salt, burn five cents worth white vitriol (as you would alum). Boil the whites of three eggs in one pint pure rain-water, or snow-water is better. Add ingredients in proportion of two tea-spoons scorched salt to one of vitriol, until all the vitriol is used, then add one-half tea-spoon each of burnt alum and sugar of lead; strain through a cloth, squeezing it dry, let settle well, then pour off the top, and bottle for use. Use at night by pouring a little in the palm of the hand, and wet the edges of the eyelids. If the eyes are very sore, weaken what is in the hand by addding a little rain-water.—*Mrs. E. T. Carson.*

HEALING SALVE FOR WOUNDS.—Pint olive oil, half ounce common resin, half ounce beeswax; melt well together, and bring oil to boiling-heat; add gradually of pulverized red lead—three eighths of a pound; (for summer use a trifle more lead) in a short time after it is taken up by the oil, and the mixture becomes brown or a shining black, remove from the fire, and when nearly cold add two scruples pulverized camphor. It should remain on the fire until it attains a proper consistence for spreading, which may be known by dipping a splint or knife in the mixture from time to time, and allowing it to cool. When used, spread thinly on a piece of tissue-paper or old, fine linen. Excellent for frost sores or any kind that are hard to heal.—*Mrs. W. G. March.*

To Cure A Felon.—Procure five or six lemons, cut off the end of one, thrust the sore finger into the lemon, and let it stay till the lemon is warm; proceed in the some way till all the six are used. Or, put a piece of Spanish-fly plaster over the spot affected, and that will draw the trouble to the surface; or, on the first appearance, apply a poultice of the common Fleur de Lis root well mashed. It will cure in a short time.

Blackberry Cordial.—Put a half bushel of blackberries in a preserving-kettle, and cook until scalded through well; strain and press out all the juice; put juice in kettle with the following spices well broken up and put into a bag; one-quarter pound allspice, two ounces cinnamon-bark, two ounces cloves, and two nutmegs; add loaf-sugar, about one pound to every quart of juice or more if preferred, and cook slowly ten or fifteen minutes, remove from the fire, let cool a little, and add good pure brandy in the proportion of one pint to every three pints of juice. A smaller quantity may be made, using the same proportions. This is an excellent remedy for diarrhœa and other diseases of the bowels.

Cough Mixture.—Take 5 cents worth each of elecampane, spikenard, dandelion, sarsaparilla, licorice-root, Indian turnip, comfrey and hoarhound. Boil roots in two quarts soft water until it is reduced to one pint, add one pound loaf-sugar, and give one table-spoonful three times a day, before eating; or dissolve one-fourth pound gum-arabic in half pint boiling water, add a half tea-cup sugar and honey, and two table-spoons lemon juice, steep for five or ten minutes; bottle, and cork, add water, and take; or boil one ounce each of licorice-stick and anise-seed, and half ounce senna in one quart of water, ten minutes; strain, add two tea-cups molasses or honey, boil down to a pint, and then bottle.

For Constipation.—The same remedies will not affect all persons. One or two figs eaten fasting is sufficient for some, and they are especially good in the case of children, as there is no trouble in getting them to take them. A spoonful of bran in a glass of water is a simple remedy and quite effective. One or two tumblers of hot water will move almost every one, but is difficult to take. In chronic cases a faithful manipulation and moving of bowels and limbs with gentle rotary movement with the open palm, and giving all natural motions to the parts, with proper diet, will almost invariably secure the desired result. It has been known to cure a case of lifelong habit, where inherited too, and although it involves patience and perseverance it is certainly better than to suffer the ills that result from so many patent medicines and quack nostrums. "An ounce of prevention is worth a pound of cure," and *regularity of habit* in this matter is the great thing to be impressed on people generally.

Catarrh.—Wet and cold at the surface of the body is a cause of catarrh, but the most fruitful source is wet and cold feet, and yet there is nothing more easy to avoid. Warm socks, horse-hair soles, and goloshes will always keep the feet dry and warm. It does not seem to be understood that although a boot or shoe may not leak, yet if the sole is damp, it by evaporation conducts away the heat from the foot, and ought never to be worn when not exercising. The neck should be covered lightly, but too much covering predisposes to catarrhal troubles by causing congestion of the membrane affected in this disease. Bed-rooms ought to be well aired, and warmed if possible, by an open fire, in damp chilly weather.

Conklin's Salve.—One pound of resin, two ounces mutton tallow, one of beeswax, one-half gill alcoholic spirits, add a little of the gum of balsam; boil all together slowly, until it has done rising or foaming, or until it begins to appear clear. Pour the mixture into a pail of cold water, and when it gathers, take it out, roll on boards and cut it off. Care must be taken not to burn it. Moisten the hands in brandy while working.—*Mrs. H. F. Wilcox, Norwalk, Conn.*

FOR COLD IN THE HEAD.—As soon as you feel that you have a cold in the head, put a tea-spoonful of sugar in a goblet, and on it put six drops of camphor, stir it, and fill the glass half full of water; stir, till the sugar is dissolved, then take a dessert-spoonful every twenty minutes. This is a *sure* cure if taken as directed.—*Miss H. D. Martin, Washington Heights.*

OIL SILK—Placed over the chest of those suffering from pneumonia or pleurisy will give great relief and hasten recovery.

MANNA AND MILK.—Take a quart of fresh skim milk, and boil in it one ounce of manna; drinking this quantity cool, in small draughts, at intervals during the day, is good for consumptives.

SCARLET FEVER—Like small pox, spreads by infection and contagion. The first symptom is generally vomiting; fever soon sets in: the throat is slightly sore; there is headache, thirst, restlessness, and slight delirium at night. These symptoms continue about forty-eight hours, when the rash makes its appearance over the lower part of the neck and upper part of the chest. This rash is of a bright scarlet in healthy persons, having a velvety appearance, but not raised or rough. On the second day of the rash it spreads over the body, and on the third over the limbs. At this period it begins to fade on the chest and body, and the third day from its appearance on the hands and feet it disappears altogether. It returns, however, as a slight blush for several days, with more or less fever. With the subsidence of the eruption there appears over the body a dandruff-like scurf. This stage is very dangerous, from the fact that the removal of this outer coating renders the patient peculiarly liable to suppression of perspiration on the slightest exposure to cold. Judicious nursing is far more important than medicines, but no case should be without a competent physician The room should have a uniform temperature day and night of about 68° to 70°; should be well aired, without exposure to drafts. In this room the patient should remain until thoroughly well, unless it be in the summer season. The clothing should be light during the rash, and increased after it until convalescence is established. Give cold drinks very sparingly. When the skin is hot, sponge the body frequently. It is well to bind a piece of fat salt pork on the throat, or put around it a light flannel scarf, rubbing the throat daily and freely with camphorated oil. The diet should consist of light gruels and liquids until the eruption subsides, when it may be solid but still simple. After the early stages are passed, the danger will depend upon the exposure of the new tender surface to cold, and the resulting dropsy. The change of an article of clothing, lowering of temperature in the room at night, stepping into a cold room, are but few of the many ways of so chilling the skin as to suppress perspiration and induce dropsy. There are two simple methods of rendering patients less liable to dropsy after scarlet fever. First, rub them over frequently with fatty substances, as lard, or oil, or cocoa butter; second, frequent warm baths during convalescence. After the bath great care should be taken to remove the refuse water beyond the reach of exposure, or disinfect it.—*By an eminent physician.*

DIPHTHERIA SYMPTOMS.—Diphtheria appears in three varieties, which are thus briefly described: 1. Fever, severe pains in the back and limbs, and very great prostration. There may be no soreness of the throat, but small white specks will be noticed on the tonsils. 2. Large patches of false membrane both on the tonsils and back of the throat; but the glands of the neck do not become swollen. 3. True malignant diphtheria, with swelling of the glands of the neck and under the jaw; profuse and often offensive exudations in the mouth and throat; more or less discharge from the nostrils. Simple treatment will usually cause a recovery in a majority of cases under the first and second varieties Chlorate of potash put into a tumbler of water until no more will dissolve, is the best remedy for home use in the early stages of the disease. But the advice of a good physician should be sought on the appearance of the first symptoms of this dangerous disease, as prompt measures are often necessary to save life.

SURE CURE FOR CROUP.—Boil pigs feet in water, without salt, and let it stand over night; in the morning skim off the fat (which will be formed in a cake on top), put in a tin pan, boil until all water is evaporated; bottle, and keep for use. Give a tea-spoon every fifteen minutes on the appearance of the first symptoms, and apply freely to chest and throat, rubbing well. A celebrated physician says that a child can not have the croup if pigs feet oil is administered at the first symptoms. Or warm a tea-spoon with a little lard in it or goose grease; thicken with sugar, and give it to the child; it may produce vomiting, which is always desirable, thus breaking up the membrane that is forming. Apply lard or goose grease to throat and chest, with raw cotton or flannel. Care should be taken, removing only a small piece at a time of these extra wraps to prevent taking cold.

MUSTARD PLASTER.—Mix with boiling water, vinegar, or white of an egg (the latter is best when a *blister* is not wanted) to consistency the same as if for the table. Some add a little flour when not wanted so strong. Spread on half a thin muslin cloth, cover with the other half, or put on cloth, and put over it a thin piece of gauze; apply, and when removed, wash the skin with a soft sponge, and apply a little sweet cream or oil.

FOR RHEUMATISM.—(Internal remedy).—Three drams iodide of potash, dissolved in one-half pint of hot water. Take a table-spoonful three times a day, and drink lemonade at intervals between.

(External remedy). Liniment.—Two ounces tincture arnica, one ounce camphor, one ounce belladonna, one ounce cannabis indica, one-half ounce aconite (if neuralgia), one-half ounce oil hemlock, one-half ounce wormwood, one-half ounce sassafras (if there are humors), one-fourth ounce origanum, one-fourth ounce tar, (if there are sores), one-fourth ounce cajeput, one eighth ounce peppermint, one-fourth ounce chloroform, six ounces aqua ammonia. Wet a flannel with this liniment, and rub the parts affected; or place the flannel over the rheumatic part, and cover it with thick paper, and place near it a warm brick. Immediate relief will be obtained.

REMEDY FOR PILES.—Mix a tea-spoon of sulphur with a tea-cup of milk, and take twice a day, morning and night, until improvement takes place; then take occasionally.

FOR SICK HEADACHE.—Whenever the symptoms are felt coming on, drink a cupful of thoroughwort or boneset-tea.

CATARRH COLD.—Ten drops carbolic acid, and seven and a half each of iodine and chloroform; heat a few drops over a spirit lamp in a test tube, holding the mouth of the tube to the nostrils as soon as volatization is effected. Repeat every two minutes, until the patient sneezes a number of times, when the troublesome symptoms will disappear.—*Scientific American*

FLORAL.

MY MORNING GLORIES.

Doubtless we all have a great respect for our mother Eve, whom a well known author, in utter defiance of Blair or Murray, has called the "fairest of all her daughters," but it may be we have felt at times that but for her early experiments in pomology, our lives would have been very different from what they are, and that cooks and cook-books would have been unnecessary; that we should have roamed, at our own sweet will, among lovely flowers and odorous shrubs, satisfying our hunger with fruits, fresh and perfect, right from God's own hand, never suffering pain or sorrow, reposing when weary on soft couches of moss and fragrant flowers, lulled to slumber by the sweet songs of birds and the soft rustling of leaves above our heads, and awakening refreshed to new pleasures and enjoyments in this blissful Arcadian life, which would have gone on forever. And this train of thought came into my mind this morning from seeing a lovely morning-glory vine adorning the plain fence which surrounds my garden, glorifying it with its bewitching grace and brilliant color, illuminating the whole landscape, giving sweet thoughts to the working man as he goes forth to his toil, lighting up with pleasure the faces of the little children as they pass along to school, and warming and brightening wonderfully the heart of the careworn, anxious mother with recollections of her merry girlhood time, when *her* precious mother took the responsibilities of housekeeping, and she sang merrily as she trained the vines and arranged the vases and bouquets, to make the dear home bright and beautiful. And as I admire the freshness of the new-made blossoms, I wonder if Eve had any thing in Eden more lovely and delicate, and if she, surrounded by a wealth and luxuriance of flowers, with Adam to dress and train them for her, appreciated them as much, or looked upon them as lovingly as we do our floral beauties, for which we labor and toil. I can hardly believe she did, and thinking it all over, it seems to me that it is our duty and should make a large part of our enjoyment to cultivate these beautiful vines which grow so readily and reward us so well, in greater profusion so that all who pass by them on their way to daily toil, may inhale large draughts of pleasure from their coronets of many-colored blossoms, arrayed in such wondrous beauty as far surpasses Solomon in all his glory, and may be led by their silent unintrusive teachings to thank God for His beautiful gifts, and to love Him sincerely

for strewing the rough paths of life with such perfect unsullied loveliness.—
Mrs. Gen. Van Cleve, Minneapolis, Minn.

HOUSE PLANTS.—Plants that require a high or low temperature, or a very moist atmosphere, and plants that bloom only in summer are undesirable. Procure fresh sandy loam, with an equal mixture of well rotted turf, leaf mold and cow-yard manure, with a small quantity of soot. In repotting use one size larger than they were grown in; hard burned or glazed pots prevent the circulation of air. Secure drainage by broken crockery and pebbles laid in the bottom of the pot. An abundance of light is important, and when this can not be given, it is useless to attempt the culture of flowering plants. If possible they should have the morning sun, as one hour of sunshine then is worth two in the afternoon. Fresh air is also essential, but cold, chilling draughts should be avoided. Water from one to three times a week with soft luke-warm water, draining off all not absorbed by the earth. Do not permit water to stand in the saucers, as the only plant thriving under such treatment are calla lilies, and even for these it is not necessary unless while blooming. Dust is a great obstacle to the growth of plants; a good showering will generally remove it, but all the smooth-leaved plants, such as camellias, ivies, etc., should be occasionally sponged to keep the foliage clean and healthy. Plants succeed best in an even temperature ranging from sixty to seventy degrees during the day, with from ten to twelve degrees lower at night. If troubled with insects put them under a box or barrel and smoke from thirty to sixty minutes with tobacco leaves. For the red spider, the best remedy if to lay the plants on the side and sprinkle well or shower. Repeat if necessary. The soil should be frequently stirred to prevent caking. If manures are used give in a liquid form. Some of the most suitable plants for parlor culture are pelargoniums, geraniums, fuchsias, palms, begonias, monthly roses, camellias, azaleas, oranges, lemons, Chinese and English primroses, abutilons, narcissus, heliotrope, stevias, bouvardias, petunias, and the gorgeous flowering plant *poinsettia pulcherrima.* Camellias and azaleas require a cooler temperature than most plants, and the *poinsettia* a higher temperature. Do not sprinkle the foliage of the camellias while the flower-buds are swelling, as it will cause them to droop, nor sprinkle them in the sunshine. They should have a temperature of about forty degrees and more shade. By following these rules, healthy flowering plants will be the result.—*J. S. Robinson.*

THE CARE OF HOUSE PLANTS.—When plants are frosted sprinkle with fresh cold water, and place under a box or something that will exclude the light and prevent too great a change in temperature. Keep them thus for two days. After sprinkling, be careful to put them where they will not chill again. Horse-manure, two years old, is best for carnations. For begonias good drainage is indispensable. The whole family thrive in a compost of one-half loam and one-half leaf-mold with a slight portion of sand. From September to February give pelargoniums only enough water to keep them from wilting; then water freely, and when they begin to bud, apply a little liquid-manure, or add ammonia to the water twice a week. Double geraniums should be kept in small pots, as they will not bloom well until the roots become compact. They require a higher temperature than the single varieties. During warm weather, the foliage of fuchsias should be well sprinkled every evening to prevent its becoming seared too early. To obtain plants of the greatest beauty in form and color, plenty of light and space is essential. Do not allow the foliage of one plant to overshadow another. —*Mrs. Prof. F. Wood.*

HINTS ABOUT PLANTS.—Few things are necessary for the successful cultivation of house plants. A patient, untiring spirit is most important. The other requisites are plenty of sunlight, fresh air, and water when they need it. It is better to give a good supply of water when called for by drooping leaves, than to give a little at a time often. Never leave pots to set in water in saucers except for the calla lily. To repot, turn plant upside down on the left hand, rap pot sharply with stick; this will loosen it from the ball of earth; lift it off, and place the plant in a pot two sizes larger, or in the ground. Do not have the soil too rich with manure but well mixed, and composed of sod-soil, wild or leaf-mold, and well-rotted stable manure. Cut plants back pretty closely when you change them, and they will thrive better afterwards. Water well at first, then only moisten slightly until they begin to grow. A good rule for watering plants is once a week in winter if the weather is mild, or when it has moderated have a gallon watering-can filled with blood-warm water, stir in a tea-spoonful of aqua ammonia, and as you set the plants in a convenient place (I set mine on the kitchen floor), pour in pot a plentiful supply of this warm water, and after this, sprinkle well with warm water without ammonia. In summer two or three times a week is the rule. Ivies need large pots, and should be repotted every year in the summer time.

A good way to start slips is to partly break off the slip, but do not entirely sever it from the parent stock, leaving it hanging for ten or twelve days; then remove, and plant in a box of half sand or brick-dust and half leaf-mold, and it will be well rooted in a week. Do not water too freely, or the slip will rot. This is better for both slip and plant, as the slip will get nourishment from plant while healing over, and its removal will not weaken the plant so much. Hyacinths are very attractive flowers for window-gardening, and at the same time require very little care or trouble. Get the bulbs in the fall before frost from any good florist (Vick is my favorite), and keep in a cool place until December, then plant each one in a four-inch pot with soil one-fourth sand, one-fourth well-rotted manure, one-fourth garden or sod-soil, and one-fourth broken bits of moss and leaf-mold; water thoroughly at first, and set in dark closet until the first of January, then bring to light, and give plenty of water. A very good way is to set half a dozen or more pots in a large dripping-pan, pour hot (not boiling) water in the pan, and let set for one hour. After they are done blooming, let them dry out gradually. They will not bloom the second season as well as the first.—*M. E. C.*

IF HOUSE PLANTS—Are watered once a week with water in which are mixed a few drops of ammonia, they will thrive much better. Sometimes small white worms are found in the earth; lime-water will kill them. Stir up the soil before pouring it on to expose as many as possible. For running vines burn beef-bones, pulverize, and mix with the earth.

TO KEEP PLANTS WITHOUT A FIRE AT NIGHT.—Have made of wood or zinc, a tray about four inches deep, with a handle on either end, water tight —paint it outside and in, put in each corner a post as high as the tallest of your plants, and it is ready for use. Arrange your flower pots in it, and fill between them with sawdust, this absorbs the moisture falling from the plants when you water them, and retains the warmth acquired during the day, keeping the temperature of the roots even. When you retire at night spread over the posts a blanket or shawl, and there is no danger of freezing. The tray may be placed on a stand or table and easily moved about.

WINDOW GARDENING.—All the varieties of English ivy, the hoyacarnosa, the passion flower, the jasmine, the pilogyne suavis, and begonias are especially suitable for window culture. Very pretty effects may be produced at the cost of a few cents, by planting verbenas, morning-glories, cobea scandens, and the maurandias in baskets or flower-pots, which may be concealed behind statuary or bronzes. The best fertilizer for them or any other house plants is that afforded by the tea-pot: the cold tea-grounds usually thrown away, if poured as a libation to these household fairies, will produce a miracle of beauty and perfume.

SURE SHOT FOR ROSE SLUGS.—Make a tea of tobacco-stems and a soap-suds of whale-oil or carbolic soap, mix, and apply to the bush with a sprinkler, turning the bush so as to wet the under as well as the upper part of the leaves; apply before the sun is up three or four times.

ANOTHER.—About the first of June, small worms make their appearance on the rose bushes, and in a very few days eat every leaf on them; to destroy these pests take four gallons water, add one table-spoon paris green, stir thoroughly, and apply to the bushes with a garden syringe or watering-pot, early in the morning; keep the water well stirred or shaken while applying, or the last in the pot will be too strong and kill the leaves of the bushes.—*Mr. C. Phellis, Sr.*

TO PREPARE AUTUMN LEAVES AND FERNS.—Immediately after gathering, take a moderately warm iron, smear it well with white wax, rub over each surface of the leaf once, apply more wax for each leaf; this process causes leaves to roll about as when hanging on the tree. If pressed more they become brittle and remain perfectly flat. Maple and oak are among the most desirable, and may be gathered any time after the severe frosts; but the sumac and ivy must be secured as soon after the first slight frost. as they become tinted, or the leaflets will fall from the stem. Ferns may be selected any time during the season. A large book must be used in gathering them, as they will be spoiled for pressing if carried in the hand. A weight should be placed on them until they are perfectly dry; then, excepting the most delicate ones, it will be well to press them like the leaves, as they are liable to curl when placed in a warm atmosphere; these will form beautiful combinations with the sumac and ivy.

TO PREPARE SKELETON LEAVES.—When properly prepared, skeleton leaves form a companion to the scrap-book or collection of pressed ferns, fronds, etc. This is a tedious operation, and requires skill and great patience to obtain satisfactory results. Some leaves are easier to dissect and make better specimens than others, and as a rule a hard, thin leaf should be chosen; that is, when a special variety is not required. Among those which are skeletonized, most successfully, are the English ivy, box elder, willow, grape, pear, rose, etc. They should be gathered during the month of June, or as soon as the leaf is fully developed. The leaves should be immersed in a vessel of rain-water, and allowed to remain till decomposed; when this takes place, press the leaf between pieces of soft flannel, and the film will adhere to the flannel, leaving a perfect net-work; dry off gradually, and clean the specimen with a soft hair-pencil, place between folds of soft blotting-paper, and when perfectly dry, place in your collection. To bleach the leaves, dissolve one-half pound chloride of lime into three pints of rain-water, strain, and use one part of solution to one of water. For ferns, use the solution full strength. When perfectly white remove to clear water, let stand for several hours, changing water two or three times, float out on paper, and press between blotting-paper in books. In mounting, use mucilage made of five parts gum-arabic, three parts white sugar, two parts starch; add very little water, boil, and stir till thick and white.

To KILL EARTHWORMS.—Ten drops of carbolic acid in a pint of water, poured over earth in flower-pots will kill all earthworms.

CUT FLOWERS.—Large soup-plates or dishes, filled with wet sand or wet cotton, will keep cut flowers fresh for a long while, or many seeds may be started in such receptacles, and will grow luxuriantly in them.

TEMPERATURE.—The principal difficulty in keeping house-plants healthy is overheated rooms; the temperature should never go above 80° nor below 40°, in order to keep plants healthy.

To KEEP CUT ROSES FRESH.—Roses, camellias, and all hard-wooded flowers, such as are used for head-dresses, button-hole bouquets, etc., may be kept fresh, and their beauty preserved by the following plan: Cut stems off at right angles, and apply hot sealing-wax to the end of the stalk immediately; this prevents the sap flowing downwards, thereby preserving the flower.—*Gov. Kemper, Virginia,* 1788.

IVIES.—A successful cultivator of ivies feeds them with iron and cod-liver oil; the iron in form of rusty nails, mixed into the earth. Another produced a luxurious growth by watering once a week with tobacco-water; making a tea of refuse tobacco-leaves and stems, or of coarse tobacco. The water from the washing of fresh beef is also of great benefit to ivies.

To REVIVE WITHERING FLOWERS.—Take them from the vase, throw out the cold water, and replace it with hot water in which you can hardly hold your finger, put in it the flowers immediately; or burn the ends; or throw a little salt in the water. The effect is wonderful.

FLOWERS FOR TABLE.—A very beautiful way to arrange flowers is to use tin forms, filled with water or sand, made in any desired shape, such as crosses, circles, half-circles, triangles, etc. They are made easily by any tinner, and should be about one inch deep. Tiny forms of tin in the shape of the letters of the alphabet, containing the initial letter of the name of the guest, may be placed at the plate to which each is assigned. The flowers may be arranged so as to conceal the tin form if desired.

WARM WATER.—Plants will thrive much better if warm water is used upon them instead of cold. If every saucer is filled with boiling water every morning, it will add to the luxuriance of the plant, and frequently no other moisture will be needed for several days; tea-leaves can also be added in small quantities to the soil of the pots. Ivies are always beautified by such an application, and it is an excellent thing to wet a sponge in tea, and moisten the leaves with it. Wax plants are especially susceptible to the benefit of warm water application.

HANGING BASKETS.—A correspondent of the *Gardner's Monthly* tells of a new style of hanging basket made of round maple sticks, about one inch in diameter, eight inches in length at the bottom, increasing to fourteen at the top. In constructing, begin at the bottom and build up, log-cabin fashion; chink the openings with green moss, and line the whole basket with the same. They are easily kept moist, and the plants droop and twine over them very gracefully. A good way to keep the earth moist in a hanging basket without the bother of taking it down, is to fill a bottle with water and put in two pieces of yarn, leaving one end outside. Suspend the bottle just above the basket, and allow the water to drip; this well keep the earth moist enough for winter, and save a great deal of time and labor. Plant morning-glory seeds in hanging baskets in winter: they grow rapidly and are very pretty.

MISCELLANEOUS.

TO DRIVE NAILS.—Nails dipped in soap will drive easily in hard wood.

INK SPOTS ON BOOKS.—A solution of oxalic acid will remove them without injuring the print.

MICE.—Pumpkin seeds are very attractive to mice, and traps baited with them will soon destroy this little pest.

POUNDED GLASS—Mixed with dry corn meal, and placed within the reach of rats, it is said, will banish them from the premises; or sprinkle cayenne pepper in their holes.

SPOTS—In cloth or calico, produced by an acid, may be removed by touching the spot with spirits of hartshorn. Spots produced by an alkali may be removed by moistening them with vinegar or tartaric acid.

WOOD—May be fastened to stone with a cement made of four parts of pitch, four parts of pounded brick-dust or chalk, and one part of beeswax. Warm it before using, and apply a thin coating to the surface to be joined.

POSTAGE STAMPS—Will stick and not turn up at the corners, if the face is wet after applying them.

TO GET LIGHT IN A WELL OR CISTERN.—Reflect it in by a looking-glass. Any steel or metal lost in a cistern may be drawn out by lowering a strong magnet.

WHEN A CHIMNEY TAKES FIRE—Throw salt on the fire, and shut off the draught as much as possible, and it will burn out slowly.

LEAKY ROOFS.—A cement made of sand and white-lead paint will stop leaks.

TO KEEP OFF FLIES.—Paint walls or rub over picture-frames with laurel oil.

DOOR-LATCHES AND LOCKS—Will work easily and quietly if oiled occasionally.

LEAKS ABOUT CHIMNEYS—May be stopped by a cement made of coal-tar and sand, neatly applied.

DISH-WATER AND SOAP-SUDS—Poured about the roots of young fruit-trees, currant and raspberry bushes, etc., facilitate their growth.

A LAYING HEN.—When a hen's comb is red and full of blood, and shakes with every movement of the head, depend upon the unfailing indication of a laying bird.

TO MAKE HENS LAY IN WINTER.—Keep them warm; keep corn constantly by them, but do not feed it to them. Feed them with meat scraps when lard or tallow has been tried, or fresh meat. Some chop green peppers finely, or mix cayenne pepper with corn meal, to feed them. Let them have a frequent taste of green food, a little gravel and lime, or clam shells.

OUTSIDE GARMENTS.—Bonnets, cloaks, hats, shawls, scarfs, and the like, will last clean and fresh, much longer, if the dust is carefully removed from them by brushing and shaking after returning from a ride or walk.

CHEAP PAINT FOR IRON FENCING.—Tar mixed with yellow ochre makes an excellent green paint for coarse woodwork or iron fencing.

TO CATCH WILD GEESE OR DUCKS ALIVE.—Soak wheat in strong alcohol and scatter where they are in the habit of feeding, and take them while they are drunk.

A WET SILK HAT.—Shake off the water, rub the way the nap lies with a clean linen cloth or silk handkerchief, and hang some distance from the fire to dry; a few hours after, brush with a soft brush.

SETTING HENS.—Set hens in the evening; and arrange the coop, if possible, so that it will be dark and quiet for two or three weeks.

TO KEEP PEARLS BRILLIANT.—Keep in common, dry magnesia, instead of the cotton wool used in jewel cases, and they will never lose their brilliancy.

DIAMOND CEMENT.—Dissolve thirteen ounces of white glue in a tin dish containing a pint and a half soft water (set in a kettle containing boiling water); when the glue is dissolved, stir in three ounces of white lead, and boil till well mixed; remove from fire, and when cool, add half pint alcohol; bottle immediately, and keep well corked.—*W. F. Wilcox.*

COCOA BUTTER.—Apply, at night, to face and hands, and wash off in the morning. This is excellent for the skin, and keeps it soft and clear.

CHAPPED HANDS.—Grind one side of a pumice stone; wet, and, with the smooth side, rub the hands. If badly chapped, oil them at night, and dry in by the fire; or, at night, wet the hands, and rub a little honey over them, drying it in before the fire.

SQUEAKING BOOTS.—Drive a peg into the middle of the sole.

TO SCOUR TINS.—Use whiting moistened with kerosene.

TO CLEAN STEEL.—Unslaked lime cleans small articles of polished steel —like buckles, etc.

TO REMOVE FINGER-RING.—Hold hand in very cold water.

TO CLEAN BLACK KIDS.—Add a few drops of ink to a tea-spoonful of salad oil; rub on with a feather, and dry in the sun.

FOR IVY POISON.—Apply sweet oil.

MOROCCO LEATHER—May be restored with a varnish of white of an egg.

RUST IN IRON.—Kerosene oil will remove it.

SEALING WAX—Is made of two parts of beeswax and one of resin, melted together.

TO CLEAN WELLS OF FOUL AIR.—Throw down a peck of unslaked lime. The heat produced carries out the foul air with a rush.

TO HARDEN WOOD.—Cut the wood in the shape desired, and boil eight minutes in olive oil.

TO BLOW OUT A CANDLE.—If a candle is blown out by an *upward* instead of a downward current of air, the wick will not smoulder down. Hold the candler higher than the mouth in blowing it out.

COCHINEAL COLORING.—To a pound of wool take two gallons of rain water, one ounce cream tartar, one and a half ounces cochineal, two ounces solution tin, one-fourth ounce tumeric; first, put the cold water in a copper kettle, and let it boil, put in the cream tartar; in five minutes, the cochineal; in five minutes, solution tin; in five minutes, tumeric; in five minutes, yarn; boil an hour; stir all the time. Rinse in cold water.

CEMENT FOR RUBBER OR LEATHER.—Dissolve one ounce of gutta percha in one-half pound chloroform. Clean the parts to be cemented; cover each with solution, and let them dry twenty or thirty minutes; warm each part in the flame of the candle, and press very firmly together till dry.

RAZOR STRAPS—Are kept in order by applying a few drops of sweet oil. After using a strap, the razor takes a keen edge by passing it over the palm of the warm hand; dipping it in warm water also makes it cut more keenly.

UNFERMENTED WINE FOR COMMUNION.—Weigh the grapes, pick from the stems, put in a porcelain kettle, add very little water, and cook till stones and pulp separate; press and strain through a thick cloth, return juice to kettle, and add three pounds sugar to every ten pounds grapes; heat to simmering, bottle hot, and seal. This makes one gallon, and is good.

SHINGLES.—Dip well-seasoned shingles in lime, wash and dry before laying, and they will last longer and never take on moss.

To CLEAN ERMINE.—Rub with corn meal, renewing the meal as it becomes soiled.

To PRESERVE STEEL PENS.—Steel pens are destroyed by corrosion from acid in the ink. Put in the ink some nails or old steel pens, and the acid will exhaust itself on them, and the pens in use will not corrode.

To KEEP WALKS CLEAN.—Sprinkle with weak brine through a water-sprinkler, or scatter salt along the walks.

MELTED SNOW—Produces one-eighth of its bulk in water.

GLUE.—Powdered chalk added to glue strengthens it. Boil one pound glue with two quarts skimmed milk, and it will resist the action of water.

PAINT.—New woodwork requires one pound of paint to the square yard, for three coats.

To MAKE OLD VARNISH DRY.—"Sticky" varnish may be dried by applying a coat of benzine, and after two or three days apply a coat of good varnish, and let dry thoroughly before using the furniture.

WHEN TO PAINT.—Oil-paint lasts longer when put on in autumn.

WHERE TO HITCH A HORSE.—In hitching a horse to a rail fence, always tie to the inside corner; it is stronger, and the halter will not become entangled in the rail-ends.

COLOR OF PAINT FOR TOOLS.—Tools exposed to the sun should be painted with light-colored paints, as they reflect instead of absorbing the heat.

DIRTY COAT-COLLARS.—Apply benzine, and after an hour or more, when the grease has become softened, rub it, or remove with soap-suds.

To KEEP BUTTER FRESH. —Work until solid, make into rolls, take two gallons water, one pint white sugar, one level table-spoonful saltpetre—make the brine strong enough with salt to bear an egg; boil and skim. Let cool, pour over butter, and keep under brine with a weight. Butter will thus keep for a year as sweet as when churned.—*Mrs. Mary Weaver.*

To MAKE ARTIFICIAL BUTTER.—Render beef suet at a very low temperature, churn it in fresh buttermilk and yolks of eggs, and treat like butter, when removed.

TIME TO CUT TIMBER.—Hard wood for timber or fire-wood should be cut in August, September, or October. Hoop-poles should be cut before frost comes; cut at other times, there is danger of worms.

VALUABLE CEMENT.—Two parts, by weight, of common pitch and one part gutta percha, melted together in an iron vessel, makes a cement that holds together, with wonderful tenacity, wood, stone, ivory, leather, porcelain, silk, woolen or cotton. It is well adapted to aquariums.

FRUIT—Stains may be removed from the fingers in the following manner: Mix together half an ounce of cream tartar and half an ounce of powdered salt of sorrel; apply a solution of this to the fingers, and the stains will disappear. Dilute sulphuric acid may be used, but care should be taken that none of it touches any fabric, as the acid will destroy it.

To MAKE BOOTS AND SHOES DURABLE.—Apply to the soles four or five successive coats of gum-copal varnish; and to the uppers, a mixture of four parts of lard to one of resin. Apply while warm.

To PREVENT PUMPS FROM FREEZING.—Take out the lower valve in the fall, and drive a tack under it, projecting in such a way that it can not quite close. The water will then leak back into the well or cistern, while the working qualities of the pump will not be damaged.

FRICTION MATCHES—Should never be left where mice will get them, as they carry them to their nests, and sometimes ignite them. They are poison to children, and are dangerous to women, who ignite them by stepping on them, and endangering their clothing from fire.

To Thaw Out a Pump.—Pour hot water directly on the ice, through a tin tube, lowering it as fast as the ice thaws. Ice may be thawed in this way at the rate of a foot a minute; while by pouring hot water into the pump, the ice would hardly be affected, the hot water being lighter than the cold and rising to the top.

A Good Paste.—To one pint cold water add two heaping table-spoonfuls flour. Put the flour in a pan, add a little of the water, stirring until smooth; then add the rest of the water, stir thoroughly, place on the stove and stir constantly until it boils. After taking from the stove, add one-fourth tea-spoonful ground cloves to keep it sweet.

To Keep Silk.—Silk goods should not be folded in white paper, as the chloride of lime used in bleaching the paper will impair the color of the silk. Brown or blue paper is better; yellow India paper is better still. Silk intended for dress should not be kept in the house long, as lying in folds causes it to crack or split, particularly if thickened with gum. White satin dresses should be pinned up in blue paper, with coarse brown paper on the outside, sewed together on the edge.

To Remove Stains from the Hands.—Damp the hands first with water, and then rub them with tartaric acid or salts of lemon, as you would with soap, rinse them, and rub them dry. Tartaric acid or salts of lemon will quickly remove stains from linens. Put less than a half tea-spoonful of salts or acid in a table-spoonful of water, wet the stain with it, and lay it in the sun for at least an hour; wet it once or twice in the time with cold water. If it does not remove the stain, repeat and lay it again in the sun.

Hot-water Proof Cement.—If properly applied, this will be insoluble, even in boiling water. Gelatine, five parts; soluble acid chromate of lime, one part. Cover the broken edges with this, press lightly together, and expose to the sunlight; the effect of the latter is to render the compound insoluble.

Chickens.—Should not be fed for twenty-four hours after they are out of the shell; then feed moderately but often on soft cooked food. Hard boiled eggs and milk or mush and chopped feed are excellent for a day or two. Boiled potatoes and hashed meat are both good food. Always keep pure water within reach.

To "Do Up" Black Silk.—Boil an old kid glove (cut up in small shreds) in a pint of water till the water is reduced to a half pint; then sponge the silk with it; fold it down tight, and, ten minutes after, iron it on the wrong side while wet. The silk will retain its softness and luster, and, at the same time, have the "body" of new silk.

Excellent Interest Rules—For finding the interest on any principal for any number of days, the answer in each case being in cents; separate the two right hand figures to express it in dollars and cents.

Four per cent.—Multiply the principal by the number of days to run; separate the right hand figure from the product, and divide by 9.

Five per cent.—Multiply by number of days, and divide by 72.

Six per cent.—Multiply by number of days, separate right hand figure, and divide by 6.

Eight per cent.—Multiply by number of days, and divide by 45.

Nine per cent.—Multiply by number of days, separate right hand figure, and divide by 4.

Ten per cent.—Multiply by number of days, and divide by 36.

Twelve per cent.—Multiply by number of days, separate right hand figure, and divide by 3.

Fifteen per cent.—Multiply by number of days, and divide by 24.

Eighteen per cent.—Multiply by number of days, separate right hand figure, and divide by 2

To BUILD A CHIMNEY.—Fire-places for a parlor or sitting-room should be about two feet and eight or ten inches between jams, and about the same height, and eight or nine inches deep. The jams should flare about four inches, so as to leave the back two feet between jams. The back should be carried up plumb fourteen or fifteen inches, and then gradually brought forward six inches to a level with the mantel bar, and then two more courses laid plumb, all backed up solid. This offset forms a shelf which sustains the weight of the cold air, which must be set in motion before the fire begins to draw. The fire and hot air, passing through the narrow throat, forms an eddy at the shelf, and the draft is at once established as the warmer air moves upward. Two or three of these offsets do no harm if it is convenient to put them in. The flue of the chimney should gradually taper to twelve by twelve, or even ten by ten inches when the building is two stories.

To CLEAN LIGHT KIDS.—Put the glove on the hand, and rub thoroughly with white corn meal, using a piece of cotton flannel.

To REMOVE GREASE FROM SILK, COTTON, LINEN, OR WORSTED GOODS. —Rub magnesia freely on both sides of silk or worsted goods and hang away. Benzine, ether, or soap will take out spots from silk, but remember the goods must not be rubbed. Oil of turpentine or benzine will remove spots of paint, varnish, or pitch from white or colored cotton or woolen goods. After using it they should be washed in soap-suds. Spots from sperm candles, stearine, and the like, should be softened and removed by ninety-five per cent. alcohol, then sponged off with a weak alcohol and a small quantity of ammonia added to it. Holding white cotton or linen over the fumes of burning sulphur, and wetting in warm chlorine water, will take out wine or fruit stains. The sooner the remedy is applied, after any of these spots or stains are discovered, the more effectual the restoration. From white linen or cotton by soap-suds or weak lye, and from calicoes with warm soap-suds. From woolens by soap-suds or ammonia. On silks use either yolk of egg with water, magnesia, ether, benzine, ammonia, or French chalk.

LIME-WATER AND ITS USES.—Place a piece of unslaked lime (size is immaterial, as the water will take up only a certain quantity) in a perfectly clean bottle, and fill with cold water; keep corked in a cellar or a cool dark place; it is ready for use in a few minutes, and the clear lime-water may be used whenever it is needed. When the water is poured off, add more; this may be done three or four times, after which, some new lime must be used as at first. A tea-spoon in a cup of milk is a remedy for children's summer complaint; also for acidity of the stomach; when added to milk it has no unpleasant taste. When put into milk that would otherwise curdle when heated, it prevents its curdling, so that it can then be used for puddings and pies. A small quantity of it will prevent the "turning" of cream and milk. It also sweetens and purifies bottles which have contained milk. Some add a cupful to a sponge of bread to prevent it from souring.

THE LIGHTNING ROD.—When properly put up, the lightning rod is a perfect protection; but, when not scientifically constructed, is only a source of danger. The following are essentials: 1. It must extend several feet into the ground so as *always to be in contact with moist earth*, or *into a never-failing* supply of water; 2. It must be *sharp* at the top, and, if there are several points, all the better; 3. It must be half as high above the top of the building as the distance horizontally to the most remote part of the roof of the building; 4. It should be large enough to convey off every discharge .

29

without being melted or broken; 5. The best material is iron with copper below the surface of the ground, as iron rusts away rapidly in the moist earth. Copper is the best conductor, but costs more and is not as stiff to withstand the wind. One-half to five-eighths of an inch in diameter is large enough. Bright points are not essential, and glass insulators are of no use whatever, as when wet they are good conductors, and, even if they were not, a small charge even would leap across the short distance from the rod to the iron staple. The best way to fasten the joints, is to weld them, which any black-smith can do, passing the rod through opposite doors of his shop, afterwards dragging it home. If the building is so high that it can not be readily put up in one piece, the best joint is made by screwing the two ends firmly into one nut. The points are easily made by welding several smaller wires to the large one, and filing them sharp. A rod will protect a space the distance of which is four times the height of the rod. The cheapest and best support is wood. The only point to be considered is to secure the rod firmly. The round rods are the best. If there are iron water-pipes or steam-pipes in the building, they should all be connected with the lightning rod, or directly with the moist earth, eight or ten feet below the surface.

THE CISTERN.—An abundant supply of good water is a necessity for every house, and capacious cisterns are a necessity. Two essential requisites are good hydraulic lime and clean pure sand. The hydraulic cement becomes in a few months as hard as sandstone, but the sand must never exceed two parts to one of lime. The cheapest form of cistern is simply a hole dug in the ground with sides sloping like those of a narrow-bottomed tub. The water-lime mortar is applied directly to these sides, the shape of the sides sustaining the mortar until it hardens. The breadth of such a cistern, if large, makes it difficult to cover, but this may be done with plank supported by strong scantling, over which should be placed earth to the depth of the lowest frost. There must be a hole through the covering, left for cleaning, which should be curbed, and may admit the pump if the locality is right, or a pipe may go from cistern into cellar below the frost-line, and thence to the kitchen. The mortar on the walls should never be less than an inch thick, and they should have at least two coats, and three are better. As the mortar begins to dry in a very short time after mixing, it is best to mix the lime and sand dry, and apply water to small quantities at a time as needed. A more capacious cistern may be made at a greater expense by digging a hole with perpendicular walls, and laying walls of brick in the form of the upper half of a barrel, on which to lay the mortar. This form has a smaller top, and is much more easily covered than the other. The wall should be laid as well as plastered with water-lime. A filtering attachment is made by building a small receiving cistern beside the larger one, with filtering apparatus between them, or a strong wall may be built through the middle of the cistern, receiving the water in one division and filtering it through into the other.

CONTENTS OF CISTERN.—The following gives the contents of a cistern for each foot in depth. If the diameter at top and bottom differ, strike the average and use that as the basis of the estimate:

5 feet diameter	4.66 barrels.	8 feet diameter	11.93 barrels.
6 " "	6.71 "	9 " "	15.10 "
7 " "	9.13 "	10 " "	18.65 "

WEIGHT OF GRAIN.—Wheat 60 pounds in all states except Connecticut, where it is 56; corn 56, except in New York, where it is 58; oats 32; barley 48; buckwheat 46 to 50, but generally 48; clover seed 60, but 64 in Ohio and

New Jersey; timothy 44; flax seed 56; potatoes 60; beans 60, but in Ohio 56, and New York 62; dried peaches 28 to 33; dried apples 22 to 28.

MOCKING-BIRDS—Should have large cages with tight board backs, kept scrupulously clean. Cover the bottom of the tray with paper, and on it spread sand, fine gravel and bones that have been burned and powdered. Hang a small bag of sulphur in the top of the cage, and red pepper in the pod should be tied to the sides. Give meat of some sort every day; either a bit of beefsteak half an inch long and the size of the little finger (this should be cut with scissors across the grain into small pieces), or grasshoppers, angle-worms, or white garden grubs. Most birds relish apples and berries, and are healthier for eating them. They are also fond of lettuce leaves, which are good food for them. A large bathing dish should be placed in the cage in the morning, and removed after the bird has taken a good bath. Sudden changes of temperature, or hanging the cage in a draft, must be avoided. In buying a bird, question the dealer concerning the kind of food on which it has been brought up; for bird-raisers differ as to what food is best, and success or failure may depend on this knowledge, when it changes owners. Whatever food the bird has been brought up on it is best to continue, or bring about a change gradually. If sick, give a brown spider, and it will generally cure. Sometimes a warm bath will relieve. Occasionally bunches will come on the head: rub on a little camphor, taking care not to get it in the eyes. Almost all diseases come from want of cleanliness or neglect. Sore eyes come from perches that have not been kept clean. They shed their feathers in August, and will not sing, and often act stupid; but their songs will be loud enough when their feathers come again. The male bird is much the *best singer*. Some say the female sings a little, and some say only a chirp and a squawk. It is difficult to distinguish them. Bird, merchants say that the male birds have nine white feathers on the wing, and the female only eight, and this is the rule usually given. They do not mock with full power until they are a year old. Tunes are best taught them with a flute, the player sitting under the cage and out of sight.

CANARY BIRDS.—Do not keep in a room that is being painted or has odor of new paint. Do not hang over a stove or grate which contains fire. Do not set the cage in a window, and shut it down upon it; the draft is injurious. Do not wash cage bottom, but scrape clean with a knife, and then put on some fresh gravel; the moisture breeds red mites, and is injurious to the bird. Do not keep the birds you intend to breed in the spring together during the winter. Do not keep single birds in a room where others are breeding, or males and females in mating season in the same room in separate cages, as it is likely to cause mating fever. Feed canary on rape seed, but no hemp. For diarrhea put a rusty piece of iron in water dish, changing water not oftener than twice a week, and bread boiled in milk as for asthma; boil well in this case, so that when cold it will cut like cheese; give freely with plenty of vegetables.

Moulting is not a disease, yet during this season all birds are more or less sick, and some suffer severely. They require plenty of nourishing food. Worms, insects, and fruits to those which eat them; and to those which live upon dry seeds, bread dipped in milk, fruit and vegetables.—*Mrs. Mary Winget.*

The German metallic-enameled cages are the best—white and green (a combination of) or a light chocolate are the best colors; they are not painted as are the cages made here in America, but the color is burnt into the wires. Avoid wooden or brass cages, also conical "fountains" for food and drink; for the latter, square or round cups of china or glass are the best. The perches should be plain, round, unvarnished sticks, and no two of the same size. Clean the cage thoroughly every morning. Prepare fresh, clean bathing and drinking water, and if sand is used on the bottom of cage, clean it (the sand) by boiling in water. Scrape the perches well, and twice a week plunge them in boiling water to kill any red mites that may have lodged there. Give plenty of seed, also green parts of many plants, such as poppy, rape, hemp, etc.; also the seeds of weeds like the chickweed, plantain, etc., and the fresh, tender leaves of beets, cabbage and lettuce. Avoid fruits containing a large percentage of acid, but give occasionally a hard-boiled egg. Never give them sugar, but all the red pepper they will eat. It is the best thing for them. And if your bird feels hoarse at any time, put a piece of fat salt pork in the cage and see how the little fellow will enjoy it. Give him flax-seed once in a while, and if he appears dumpy occasionally give him a diet of bread and water, with red pepper sprinkled in.

For lice, cleanliness is the best preventive, but not always sure. For cure you have simply to cover your cage at night with a white cloth, rise early in the morning, remove the cloth and dip in scalding hot water. Repeat every night as long as there shall be found any vermin upon the cloth.

In raising birds, make just half the fuss directed in the bird-book over the matter, and you will have, doubtless, better success.

CHICKADEES IN WINTER.—A cup of pumpkin-seeds, set on the window-sill, will attract chickadees, and they will become quite tame, and are very amusing with their antics. They may be kept about the house from December to May by feeding and kind treatment.

TO REMOVE WHITE SPOTS ON FURNITURE, caused by a hot iron or hot water, or to restore blistered furniture.—Rub with a No. 1 sand-paper somewhat worn, or apply pulverized pumice stone mixed with a few drops of linseed oil, then with a cotton cloth rub on some shellac varnish thinned well with turpentine.—*A. Morey.*

BUCKEYE POLISH.—Take one ounce each shellac and coal oil, half an ounce each linseed oil and turpentine, bottle and keep well corked, shake well before using and apply with a sponge. Good for marred furniture.—*Charles D. Morey*

SHELLAC VARNISH.—Put shellac in a bottle, pour 90 per cent. alcohol to cover, cork tight and put in a warm room, shake occasionally, and if not all dissolved in three or four days, add more alcohol. This is good to varnish almost any thing and will dry in half an hour.—*A. Morey.*

TO KEEP PAINT-BRUSHES.—Turn a new brush bristles up, open, pour in a spoonful of good varnish, and keep in that position until dry, and the bristles will never "shed" in painting. The varnish also keeps it from shrinking and falling to pieces. As soon as a job is finished, wipe brush clean, wrap in piece of paper, and hang it in a small deep vessel containing oil, letting the brush descend into the oil up to the wrapping cord. This will keep painting and varnish brushes clean and ready for use.

FURNITURE FILLING.—Mix two gallons plaster of paris, one pint flour, one ounce each of pulverized pumice-stone and prepared chalk; add one half gallon boiled oil and one gill Japan drying.—*C. D. Morey.*

TO MAKE OLD PAINT DRY.—Old paint which is "sticky" may be made hard and dry by applying a coat of benzine, then after a day or two, if the coat of paint is good, go over it with a thin coat of laquer mixed with one third of its bulk of boiled oil. If paint is thin apply a second coat in which more laquer is used.

TO RENOVATE HAT-BANDS WHEN STAINED BY SWEAT.—Dissolve one and a half ounces white castile soap in four ounces alcohol and one ounce each of sulphuric ether and aqua ammonia, apply with a sponge or tooth-brush, rub smartly, rinse out with clear rain water. This is equally good to renovate any cloth with fast color.—*Dr. J. W. Fields.*

BLACK FOR WOOLENS.—One ounce vitriol, one ounce extract logwood to two pounds goods; color in iron. Dissolve the extract over night in warm water; pulverize the vitriol, put it into boiling water sufficient to cover the goods; wash the goods well, rinse in warm water, then simmer a few minutes in vitrol water; take out, wash thoroughly in clear water, then dip in boiling logwood dye till the color is good, stirring often and lifting up so it will get the air; dry, then wash in a suds and rinse. In renovating black alpaca that has become rusty, dissolve the logwood only, as nothing is needed to set the color. Wash the goods well in suds, rinse, dip in log-wood dye, boil a few minutes, stirring and lifting to air. When dry, wash again in suds and rinse in water in which a little gum arabic has been dis-solved, and press smoothly on the wrong side while damp. Dyed in this way the color will not rub off more than from new goods, and looks as good as new. When extract of logwood is used, it is only needful to boil enough to dissolve before putting in the goods.

COLORING.—In coloring always use plenty of water, never crowd the goods, taking care that they float in the liquid. In rinsing always use plenty of clear water, and in preparing goods for coloring, clean off all dirt and grease spots. To test color of dye, pour it from a dish held high, and look through it to the light. A pound of extract of logwood is equal to four pounds of log-wood chips. Fustic should be boiled in a sack of open texture; the other ingredients are put into the water. All black goods should be washed in soap-suds after coloring.

To color Woolen fine Claret.—Boil thirteen pounds of goods two hours with seven pounds of camwood, one-tenth pound logwood, and one-fourth pound of copperas to darken.

To color Woolen Russian-brown.—For thirteen pounds goods, boil two pounds fustic and four pounds camwood an hour, and if too light color add one-tenth pound each copperas and alum, to darken.

To color Woolen Bottle-green.—Boil ten pounds woolen with one-tenth pound chrome, one-fifth pound alum; take out, put in a vessel of clean water three pounds fustic and one and a half pounds logwood, and boil another hour.

To color Woolen Black.—For twenty-five pounds of goods, boil goods in a solution of five-eighths pounds each bichromate of potash and blue vitriol, and one-half pound argol, one hour, take out, refill kettle with clean water, and add three pounds dissolved extract of logwood; put in goods and sim-mer one hour and a half; take out, rinse, scour with soap, and dry. This makes a blue-black. To make a jet black, add three pounds fustic with the logwood.

To color Cotton Blue.—Put ten pounds cotton, two and a half pounds cop-peras, in fifteen to twenty gallons water, and boil two hours; after boiling, take out, rinse in clear water, refill kettle with water, and add one-half pound prussiate of potash. Boil goods in this half an hour, lift out goods and slowly add one-half pound oil of vitriol; return goods, and boil half an hour. Rinse in clear water and dry.

To color Cotton Green.—Add eight pounds fustic and one-half pound alum to the blue mixture of the preceding rule, put in goods and simmer until the required shade of green is obtained.

To color Cotton Chrome-yellow.—For fifteen pounds cotton goods or yarns dis-solve eight ounces of white sugar of lead in one tub, and eight ounces of chrome in another. Put goods first in with sugar of lead, wring out good well, and shake back into the liquid again, repeating the operation five times (in order to make the goods absorb as much color as possible); then put them through the chrome tub in the same way; then return again to the sugar of lead tub, treat as before, rinse off well, and dry. To make a dark shade use brown sugar of lead, repeating three times in the sugar of lead and twice in the chrome.

To color Cotton a good Black.—To a tub of cold water add for twenty pounds goods, five pounds sumac, wring and shake out goods and return to liquid a few times, let stand all night in sumac, then to another tub of water add a few pails of lime-water, put in goods, wring out, and put into another tub of cold water in which is two pounds of dissolved copperas and a pailful of old sumac liquor, wring out six times; wring out and put into the lime tub again, adding two more pails of lime water. Prepare another tub of water, and add to it six pounds of logwood and one pound of fustic previously scalded, put in the cotton, and wring out and return ten times; lift out, darken liquid with a little copperas, and return the goods. The omission of the sumac gives a purplish black, while the recipe as above gives a jet black.

To color Silk Royal-blue.—Take ten pounds of silk, make up a tub of nitrate of iron at six degrees, to which add one pint of good muriate of tin and four ounces of tartaric acid; wring out and return, repeating for about an hour; in another tub add one and a half pounds of dissolved prussiate, and one gill of oil of vitriol. Wash goods out of iron tub, and put into prussiate tub, repeat in iron twice and once in prussiate, wash out of the iron, and put in a tub in which oil of vitriol until it tastes sour has been dissolved; give six wrings to clear off any rust that may adhere to it. More prussiate will produce a darker, and less a lighter color, but the same quantity of iron and tin must be used.

To color Woolen-yarn Yellow-brown.—For ten bunches dye with two pounds of camwood, five pounds fustic, one each of logwood and copperas.

To color Woolen-yarn Scarlet.—Boil eight pounds yarn one hour with one-half pound cochineal, two pounds of young fustic, seven-tenths pound of white or brown tartar, three tenths of a quart of oxalic muriate of tin.

To color Ladies' Cloth Purple.—For twenty-five yards goods, boil two and a half hours with ten pounds of alum, two pounds of argol, and one-fourth of a quart nitrate of tin; wash well and finish with seven and a half pounds logwood and one pound of peach wood in a clean vessel. Put in cool in finishing, and heat to boiling point.—*Thomas Wharton.*

EXTRAS THROWN IN.—To purify a room of unpleasant odors, burn vinegar, resin, or sugar; to make chicken gravy richer, add eggs found in chicken, or if none, yolk of an egg; soak garden seeds in hot water a few seconds before planting; to prevent cholera in chickens, put assafoetida in water they drink, and let them pick at coal ashes; in using hard water for dish-water add a little milk; to clean paint, add to two quarts hot water two table-spoons turpentine and one of skimmed milk, and only soap enough to make suds, and it will clean and give luster; iron-rust on marble can generally be removed with lemon-juice; a thin coat of varnish applied to straw-matting makes it more durable and adds to its beauty.

NOTE.—The compilers take pleasure in acknowledging their indebtedness for many valuable points embodied in this book, to "Care of the Sick;" "Accidents and Emergencies;" "Health Hints," published by Cowan & Co., New York, "In the Kitchen," by Mrs. Elizabeth S. Miller, and to the excellent articles on Housekeeping, contributed by Mrs. H. W. Beecher, to the "Christian Union."

THE INDEX.

It will help those who consult this book to remember that the recipes of each department in Cookery, as well as the departments themselves, are arranged in the simple order of the alphabet, so far as has been possible, and that the "running heads" at the top of each page show the subject treated below. There is also a full Table of Contents at the beginning, for ready reference to departments. The following is a complete alphabetical index to all recipes given and subjects treated.

455